CONGRESS AND THE CONSTITUTION

KF
4541
.M6

CONGRESS

AND THE

CONSTITUTION

A Study of Responsibility

DONALD G. MORGAN

THE BELKNAP PRESS OF
HARVARD UNIVERSITY PRESS
CAMBRIDGE, MASSACHUSETTS 1966

151489

© *Copyright 1966, by the President and Fellows of Harvard College*
All rights reserved
Distributed in Great Britain by Oxford University Press, London
Library of Congress Catalog Card Number 66–18252
Printed in the United States of America

To the Congress of the United States

8.06

mv

9/21/67

Preface

I believe that there have been most eminent men in our State whose customary function it was to interpret the law to the people and answer questions in
regard to it, but that these men, though they have made great claims, have
spent their time on unimportant details . . . while I do not consider that those
who have applied themselves to this profession have lacked a conception of
universal law, yet they have carried their studies of this civil law, as it is
called, only far enough to accomplish their purpose of being useful to the
people.

    Cicero, *De Legibus,* I. IV. (Loeb Classical Library; trans. C. W. Keyes).

The letter killeth, but the spirit giveth life.

                      St. Paul, 2 Corinthians, 3:6.

Some years ago, in studying the Supreme Court of John Marshall, I was
struck by two characteristics of the early constitutional period, both of
which have long since lost their force. One was the solicitude with which
citizens and officials, when contemplating measures of government
action, probed constitutional issues. The other was the ambidextrous
manner in which public men demonstrated knowledge and insight in the
two fields of government and law. Aspirants to the bar learned their
law from men active in politics and accordingly learned about politics,
too. The giants of that formative period—Adams, Jefferson, Hamilton,
Madison, Marshall—combined knowledge of law with knowledge of the
theory and practice of government.

    Today government and law have become two separate, even isolated,
studies. Those who study government and its processes in college and
graduate school often do so with minimal exposure to the accumulated
body of the law; hence, constitutional rules and principles easily acquire
the appearance of mere data relative to this or that political system,
wrenched from context and essential function. Law students seek professional training in special schools with curricula which often ignore
those institutions and procedures of government which shape the law
and gain popular acceptability for it.

    The result: two distinct and often contradictory ways of looking at
political life, the one seeing it dominated by will and force, the other,
by reason and a self-executing body of law. Students of the political

process tend to see government as moved essentially, even exclusively, by blind forces converging more or less ruthlessly on decision-makers. They relegate the operation of reason to lawyers and judges in courts, though even there will and force are likely to prevail in the long run. Lawyers, trained as they are in the case method, tend to agree insofar as reason and the judiciary are identified. Is it any wonder that in their approaches to political life, whether domestic or international, the two groups generally rely on two distinct bases of order, the balance of power and the rule of law?

These divorces between government and law and between force and reason have doubtless contributed to a third, between policy and constitutionality. Conditions of our time have furnished a major impetus. Technology, industrialization and urbanization, economic distress, total war, cold war, and the arms race have all created irresistible demands for swift, effective government action expressed in policy. The men and groups who clamor for programs to satisfy needs they deem vital see constitutional restraints as of secondary importance. The complexities of constitutional interpretation, coupled with the availability of a corps of legal experts and a separate judicial branch have fostered the notion that constitutional problems like most problems today are technical, hence appropriate only for the experts. As public awareness of the origin, meaning, operation, and value of great constitutional principles diminishes, citizens confuse the maintenance and renewal of these principles with the interpretation of them and consign both to the lawyer and judge. The simple dichotomy of policy and constitutionality makes it easy to attribute the operation of reason and the achievement of genuine deliberation only to the bar and bench and to view the whole process of policy formation, from the initial murmurings of interest groups to the final enactment and execution of legislation, as one long struggle of forces, without direction, without control, without thought, and without regard to a general or public interest. Such a dichotomy tends, however, to minimize the very factor which distinguishes constitutional government from despotic government—the operation of controlling principles and values throughout the political process itself.

This denigration of constitutional principles and their consignment to a special guild and forum occurs precisely at the time of greatest peril to constitutional government. The conditions which formed the matrix of constitutional government in the West are vanishing. In Britain and even more in the United States, effectively restrained governments took form in societies characterized by geographical isolation, local and personal self-sufficiency and independence, absence of a large professional military, and a leisurely pace of life. These are gone.

The forces which have wiped them out are concentrating political power at a pace hard to exaggerate. Science and technology are molding societies in unpredictable directions and at an unparalleled speed. One result, however, is clear. Governments are demanding and exercising unprecedented power. Into the hands of rulers, even in democratic countries, are drifting the means of regimenting the lives, the liberties, even the very thoughts of their citizens. Is it wise, is it safe at such a time to view constitutions as subordinate, technical, esoteric, and traditionalistic? Should the nation consign the entire maintenance of the constitutional order to a tiny segment of citizens, a segment many of whose members devote their attention to specialized branches of the field and find private business consuming their whole time and energy? Instead, this is a time for reappraisal, innovation, and general enlightenment.

It is my purpose to explore this problem at the point where constitutional restraints have their most direct and recurrent impact—in the halls and committee rooms of Congress. The responsibility of members of Congress for considering a variety of sorts of constitutional questions raises the central issue. Can we rely on the balancing of forces to sustain limited and ordered government and the values it protects and consign constitutional inquiry wholly to an outside and somewhat ponderous judicial process? Or by contrast, must those forces be partially tamed and directed at an earlier stage in the political process, closer, that is, to the actual formation of policy?

In pursuing my objective, I have tried to employ empirical methods. Principal reliance has been on case analyses. By applying to a wide range of constitutional controversies in Congress a method as precise, uniform, and effective for its ends as possible, I have sought to achieve both accuracy and depth. In a sense, the cases chosen are atypical since I have minimized those numerous questions which members of Congress settle by applying recent and pertinent court precedents. I think the cases are typical, however, of those other sorts of questions for which such precedents are unavailable. In selecting these controversies, I have sought historical depth, variation in types of questions, political climate, and party line-up, and full utilization of the special knowledge and skills of my research assistants. These case studies I have supplemented with shorter probes of congressional practice, returns from a congressional questionnaire, numerous interviews, readings in history, theory, constitutional law, and congressional practice, and the intellectual ferment which nothing sets off so well as the questions of undergraduates.

I offer this book to the general reader and most especially to my fellow political scientists and to lawyers. Students of political behavior may enhance their awareness of ways in which the political process in this country is impregnated throughout its course with constitutional values and inhibitions. In chapter 2, I build my theoretical framework on the concept of the constitutional settlement and on a definition of constitution that goes beyond that which confines it to court-made rules. Decisions in Congress are more than results of group pressures; they are also shaped by what I call the elements of responsibility—principles and values and the three factors which effectuate responsibility: first, knowledgeable participants and expert sources, second, appropriate organs and procedures, and third, affirmative conceptions of their obligation held by members. From the evidence I conclude that the prevailing model which many political scientists and lawyers apply in their understanding of Congress and of the Constitution has shortcomings and that a somewhat different model has greater validity.

Lawyers will find here solid demonstration of the crucial part their fraternity has played in establishing and maintaining the rule of law in the United States. They may also detect factors other than legal knowledge that have served that purpose and some of the pitfalls in assuming that lawyers and judges could carry the entire burden of maintaining the Constitution.

My conclusions may appear to some biased in favor of the South and Border States and against those in the Northeast and Midwest. As a native of Illinois and longtime resident of New England, I must plead that as clearly as I can read it, the evidence leads directly to my conclusions. New England and her daughters to the west have contributed their own distinct elements to our political heritage. I venerate their ancient concern for the dignity and equal opportunity of each person, and as a town-meeting member, New England's zeal for full participation in politics. I am here concerned with another ingredient of our tradition—what I call constitutional wisdom and constitutional leadership—to which other states, notably Virginia, have given so much.

I shall acknowledge the aid of a host of persons in another place and here accept full responsibility for evidence and conclusions. I offer my conclusions not as dogma but as tentative findings, to be corroborated, corrected, or disproved by others. Here let me express my thanks for two tangible forms of support: first, to the Social Science Research Council, the American Philosophical Society, through its Penrose and Johnson Funds, and the Walter E. Meyer Research Institute of Law, Inc., for the fellowships and grants which have made this project possible; second, to officers at the Harvard Law School and at Littauer Center, home of the Harvard Department of Government, for generously furnishing study and library facilities. Here were tangible expressions of cooperation between our two disciplines, both so vital to the preservation of constitutional government in America.

Donald G. Morgan

South Hadley, Massachusetts
October 1965

Acknowledgments

Thomas Jefferson advised one of his innumerable correspondents that successful constitutions resulted from "quiet, leisure, much inquiry, and great deliberation." If this book makes some slight contribution to knowledge of constitutions it will be due in part to the quiet and leisure which foundation generosity and the cooperation of my college have facilitated and in part to the deliberations I have engaged in with scholars and officials and the exhaustive inquiry conducted by my research assistants.

In deliberation and inquiry alike I have enjoyed the help of both lawyers and political scientists. The late Professor V. O. Key, Jr., of the Government Department at Harvard heard my initial and tentative plans for the project with a sympathetic curiosity and later gave generously of time and thought in reading and making suggestions concerning chapters 1 to 5, 7 and 8, 15, and the questionnaire described in Appendix A. Professor Carl J. Friedrich read several early chapters and made valuable suggestions for pertinent reading. Professor Joseph Cooper gave advice during the formative stage based upon his own rich familiarity with congressional procedure and commented later on chapters 1 to 5, 9, and 15.

At Mount Holyoke two colleagues have offered helpful advice. Professor Emeritus Ellen D. Ellis read several chapters during the early years and advanced many questions and suggestions with her customary clarity and incisiveness. From his rich background in comparative government, Professor Gerhard Loewenberg offered many theoretical and practical suggestions concerning chapters 1 to 4, 9, and 15.

At the Harvard Law School Professor Paul A. Freund provided advice and encouragement and furnished valuable suggestions concerning the early chapters, especially 3 to 5. Professor Mark Howe offered fruitful advice on several chapters, and Professors Arthur E. Sutherland and Henry M. Hart, Jr., helped with useful suggestions during the formative stage. In addition, two practicing lawyers have examined my manuscript: Eugene C. Gerhart, Esq., of Binghamton, New York, who read chapter 1 and Judge Russell L. Davenport of Holyoke, Massachusetts, who read the entire manuscript.

ACKNOWLEDGMENTS

Most of my counselors in Washington, D.C., appear in Appendix B. But I want particularly to acknowledge the advice and encouragement of Senator Leverett Saltonstall of Massachusetts who granted me an interview in 1958 and offered valuable suggestions concerning my venture in general and my questionnaire in particular. More recently, Senator Sam J. Ervin, Jr., of North Carolina gave counsel and offered comments on chapters 1, 5, 14, and 15. As chief counsel of the Hennings Subcommittee on Constitutional Rights of the Senate, Mr. Charles H. Slayman, Jr., gave invaluable help in arranging interviews and later read portions of the manuscript.

If this book offers the fruits of "much inquiry," this results largely from the researches of a series of gifted and earnest assistants. I owe much to all of them both for their labors and for the insights their questions and observations have called forth. Five students at the Harvard Law School contributed extensively to investigation: Mr. Eugene B. Granoff conducted the basic research for chapter 8, Mr. Herbert W. Yanowitz for that part of chapter 12 pertaining to wiretapping, Mr. Eugene E. Dais for chapter 6 and for a study of the 1957 Civil Rights Act, and Mr. Albert Hand and Mr. Raymond D. Horton for chapter 14.

Graduate students in political science at Harvard were of equal importance. Mr. Donald D. Kummerfeld prepared the original analysis for chapters 9 and 12, Mr. Donald Carlisle for chapter 11, Mrs. Katharine D. Kane for chapter 13 and the Bradley Case section of chapter 2, Miss Catherine L. McArdle for chapter 10, and Mr. Randall B. Ripley for chapter 7.

For additional probes and for provocative commentary I relied on Messrs. Hand and Carlisle and for many insights and partial revision of chapters 6 through 12, on Mr. Ripley.

A number of Mount Holyoke undergraduates have lent skill and dedication to the accuracy and consistency of this manuscript. From their numbers I here mention only my assistants during recent summers, Miss Louise E. Kelleher, Miss Cornelia C. Clark, Miss Jeanne E. Krochalis, and especially Miss Merrianne Caprini. Mrs. Barbara Bender and Mr. and Mrs. Richard A. Langlois deserve recognition for their work in typing the final manuscript.

All these and others have shaped this book, by correcting the author's lapses of knowledge, inaccuracies of inference, and vagaries of expression. To all I express my deep thanks.

Contents

CONTENTS

TABLES

PART I

The Problem: Character and Dimensions

I Introduction: Crisis and Discord

CONGRESS IN DISCORD

The scene was the Senate chamber. The date, June 27, 1958. The measure under debate, a bill to admit Alaska as the forty-ninth state. In three short days the Congress would pass the bill; a belated tide of support for the bill had begun to roll in, engulfing all resistance.

A Senator rose to make a point of order. Section 10 of the bill, he asserted, was unconstitutional. This provision, to which Alaska must accede as a condition for admission, empowered the President to withdraw more than half the territory of Alaska from the normal operation of most of the laws of the state. It authorized the President to place this area under federal, in fact under presidential, control and came perilously near to violating a rule almost as old as the Constitution. Since the 1790's, Congress and more recently the Supreme Court have declared that states must enter the Union on an "equal footing" with existing states.[1]

What is the duty of a Senator at such a time? The speaker, who chaired the committee principally charged with rendering constitutional advice to the Senate, put it this way: "A Senator has an obligation under his oath of office to pass upon the constitutionality of proposed legislation."[2] Other Senators, seeking to block admission, came to his support. Senator Sam J. Ervin, Jr., of North Carolina declared that he could not reconcile his oath to support the Constitution with a vote for a bill containing "such a constitutional and legal monstrosity as this."[3] The Ohio Senator, Frank Lausche, added that he would be violating his responsibilities as a Senator if he cast a vote for a section of a bill which he believed to be unconstitutional.[4] In these and other ways, some Senators described their oath-bound obligation to pay strict heed to the constitutional question.

Senators from the Northwest spearheaded the drive to pass the bill and answered the constitutional point. Actually the question had arisen in a more general form in committee—the place where ordinarily it would receive fullest deliberation. At hearings before the Senate Committee on Interior and Insular Affairs, the Chairman of the Joint Chiefs of Staff and the General Counsel for the Defense Department had testified. At these hearings, and in the ensuing report, committee members had discussed the general issue of validity.[5]

Testimony developed a strong case for the necessity of the withdrawal provision to the defense of the nation in its struggle with Communism. The precise question of equal footing under the Constitution was never raised in committee. Significantly, this committee contained no member from any state east of the Rockies. Evidently the interests and opinions of the states opposed to the admission and, hence, the views of Senators most likely to press constitutional objections went unrepresented at this vital committee stage; only one of the fifteen members later supported the constitutional point of order, and none opposed the bill itself in the final vote.[6]

When the bill reached the floor, committee members defended it from constitutional attack. The main issue was the defense of the nation —"the razor's edge of security,"[7]—as one Senator put it. The constitutional responsibility of members was deemed secondary and, in fact, provisional. The people of Alaska, insisted Senator Frank Church of Idaho, could decide for themselves whether to accept the challenged provisions when they voted on admission; besides, citizens who later found their rights violated by a presidential withdrawal of territory under the act would be free to take their cases to the courts for a decision on constitutionality.[8]

This last suggestion received a fuller development at the hands of Senator Henry Jackson of Washington. He said that the matter was proper only for the courts, and that it was difficult to predict how the Court would decide any constitutional question. He continued:

> ... it is an inescapable fact that 50 per cent of the lawyers are wrong in every law suit.
>
> We would spend the rest of this session and all of the next arguing the legal authorities on both sides of this question. But that is not the function of this body. Our function is to make a legislative decision: Do we want statehood for Alaska, or do we not?
>
> Nothing we do here can change the Constitution, nor is it intended to do so. Nothing is more certain in our law than the fact that State laws and the laws of Congress must conform to the Constitution as interpreted by the Supreme Court of the United States.[9]

Senator Jackson went on to declare his formula for Senators who find themselves confronting constitutional questions. Although he said he had worked out his own earlier constitutional misgivings, he gave this advice to others: "Whatever doubts may exist on the subject, I believe they should be resolved in favor of constitutionality."[10] In other words, only when legislators find a bill clearly unconstitutional, should they let such considerations sidetrack them from the policy aspects of the bill.

In the final vote, the constitutional objection lost by nearly two to one, and the Alaska statehood bill became law without amendment.[11] Nevertheless, a substantial number of Senators, including backers of the bill, voiced grave doubts about the validity of section 10. Very likely, many put aside their doubts and voted for the bill for the very reasons stated by Senator Jackson. They must have told themselves that courts of law are the only proper agencies for handling what they regarded as technical, legal questions, and that Congress, lacking the time, expertise, organs, and procedures which such questions require, should devote itself to shaping policy.

But suppose the Supreme Court, in deciding cases, interprets the Constitution in a manner distasteful to Senators? Are the lawmakers bound to follow such interpretations or may they examine them for themselves and take corrective action? Within two months of the colloquy of June, the Senate had before it the Jenner-Butler bill.[12] In a long series of decisions, the Court had narrowed the scope or denied the legality of stringent measures for promoting internal security. This it had done in the interest of individual rights.

In retaliation, Senator William Jenner of Indiana drew up a bill to curtail the appellate jurisdiction of the Supreme Court over several of these subjects. The Court, he said, had attempted "to legislate its opinions into the law of the land."[13] Senator John M. Butler of Maryland defended the modified bill when it came to the floor. Some had denied that Congress possessed a power to whittle down the Court's jurisdiction, but the Senator believed such a power necessary. It constituted part of the system of checks and balances and was, he maintained, the only check which the Constitution gave Congress "as a protection against attempted usurpations by the Supreme Court of legislative prerogatives."[14]

By presupposing that Congress might judge whether Court interpretations fell within the judicial function or infringed on the powers of other departments, the Senator was, in effect, denying that constitutional questions were by nature exclusively technical and asserting a reviewing power in Congress. Senator Jacob K. Javits of New York pointed this out with arguments paralleling Senator Jackson's: "We are trying to tell the Court what is constitutional, and saying that the Court must not tell us what is constitutional . . . The very essence of constitutional government requires a final court to determine what is and what is not the paramount law of the land."[15]

The same day the Senate tabled the Jenner-Butler bill, but the incident exposes a marked division of opinion. In their drive to resist Communism, externally through the statehood bill, internally through the Jenner-Butler bill, the Senators took divergent positions on their own responsibility. One position conceived of constitutional questions as technical in nature, suited for the courts, and calling for only cursory attention in Congress. The other conceived of the Constitution itself as a subtle collection of principles and rules, rooted in part in the understandings of the people and developed in part by the representative body. The former minimized and the latter elaborated a duty and power in members of Congress to examine constitutional issues for themselves.[16]

This division of opinion was far from unique to 1958. Next year Senator Javits was backing a constitutional amendment to confirm the Supreme Court's power to review all cases involving constitutional issues in order to place the Court's defense of individual rights beyond "the reach of political pressures or adverse reactions to individual decisions . . ."[17] Four years earlier Senator Thomas C. Hennings, Jr., of Missouri had got Senate approval for a subcommittee to look into "any and all matters pertaining to constitutional rights."[18] Holding hearings, observed Senator Allen J. Ellender of Louisiana, would cure no existing evils, and anyone whose rights were infringed could always go to court.[19] Senator Hennings, however, quoted the Chief Justice of the United States, who had warned of the inroads on individual liberties caused by World War II and a decade of "chronic tension and crisis."[20] Despite skeptics, the Senate Subcommittee on Constitutional Rights was to find much to investigate.

As late as 1964 Senators were expressing a somewhat similar cleavage on a rider to counteract decisions on legislative apportionment.[21] And three decades earlier President Franklin D. Roosevelt had shown a like dualism in his efforts to carry out the program of the New Deal. In 1935, he urged a House committee to approve a badly needed soft-coal bill despite an adverse Court precedent of two months' standing. In his letter the President developed a cogent constitutional argument in support of the bill, but added words that anticipated those of Senator Jackson:

> Manifestly, no one is in a position to give assurance that the proposed act will withstand constitutional tests, for the simple fact that you can get not ten but a thousand differing legal opinions on the subject. But the situation is so urgent and the benefits of the legislation so evident that all doubts should be resolved in favor of the bill, leaving to the courts, in an orderly fashion, the ultimate question of constitutionality . . . I hope your committee will not permit doubts as to constitutionality, however reasonable, to block the suggested legislation.[22]

6

Within two years the President was expressing views of a different sort. The Court had overturned the soft-coal act and all or parts of eleven other New Deal laws. The President called for judicial reform. The Constitution, he still maintained, was "what the judges say it is," in the unguarded words of Charles Evans Hughes.[23] The recent decisions, however, went beyond the power of the Court and merely expressed the personal political and economic views of the justices. Accordingly, Congress should make it possible to rejuvenate the Court by the appointment of additional justices.[24] The major premise of the court-packing bill was that the people, through their representatives in Congress, might pass judgment on the constitutional interpretations of the Supreme Court. In his search for power adequate for the crisis the President, perhaps inadvertently, took positions on congressional responsibility which were seemingly irreconcilable.

What has prompted all this division of opinion concerning congressional responsibility? For more than three decades Americans have lived in an atmosphere of crisis. A condition of chronic emergency with the resulting clamor for strong policy direction by government has encouraged an altered view of constitutional questions. At the depth of the Depression, when in May 1933 Congress, despite constitutional objections, was completing action on the Administration's proposed Agricultural Adjustment Act, a lawyer-Representative from Colorado made this appeal to the House:

> The real issue before this Congress and before the administration, the question into which all other questions may be resolved, is not these fine-spun technical and constitutional questions that able lawyers discuss here, but that question is whether, through the orderly processes of a national election and through the ordinary procedure of legislative enactment, we can rescue this country from this terrible condition and establish a new deal.[25]

This is the key. If one substitutes for the closing four words such other phrases as "win the war," "win the Cold War," "achieve a predominance of military power," "revive economic growth," or "defeat the Communist enemy within," the same speech could have suited later occasions. Crises have multiplied and all have had one thing in common —they have called for government action, for what President Roosevelt promised in his First Inaugural, "direct, vigorous action."[26] This, in turn, has subjected to strain the system which for a century and a half had been slowly erected to limit governmental powers, namely the Constitution. Crises have fostered the notion of constitutional questions as being technical, subordinate, and referrable to the experts in the courts. When the courts, in turn, have adopted constitutional interpretations seeming

7

to impede popular policies, legislators and executives have called the courts to judgment. The result—a continuing discord in Congress over the concurrent responsibility and capabilities of judges and members of Congress.

The extent of that discord is suggested in returns from a questionnaire which the author sent the members of Congress in 1959.[27] Some 38 per cent of the members responded—a quota sufficiently large and well distributed to suggest typical attitudes toward responsibility and the support given each. Responses showed that most members encounter constitutional issues with some regularity and that those questions vary widely as to type.

One of the questions posed the central problem. It read: "Generally speaking, should Congress pass constitutional questions along to the courts rather than form its own considered judgment on them?" Some 187 members marked either "yes" or "no." Of these, 31 per cent said "yes" and 69 per cent said "no." Thus nearly one-third of those indicating an opinion chose to view the Judiciary as the principal, perhaps the sole, agency for settling constitutional issues.

Members elaborated their positions in comments. One who favored reference to the courts stated, "The Constitution should not be made a 'fetish.' It is one of the chief purposes of the courts to exercise a check on Congress. Let them do the job." Another expounded the opposing position: "On taking the oath of office the only thing a Congressman swears to uphold is the Constitution. Therefore, it must naturally follow that the concern about constitutionality is the prime task of both houses of Congress."

The exponents of the two positions spelled out their supporting grounds. Those minimizing the responsibility of Congress explained that the Court is better fitted to decide such questions because of its non-political atmosphere and procedures. It serves as a check on other branches, and in any case, the decisions of Congress are merely provisional. In addition, constitutional interpretation calls for time and expert knowledge.

Those endorsing an independent responsibility for Congress, on the contrary, rested their position on the oath of office, on the doctrine of the separation of powers which ordains three equal and coordinate branches and which enables each to block incursions on its powers by the others, and on the practical difficulties which would ensue should Congress through inattention pass numerous unconstitutional laws.

The simple two-to-one preference for congressional responsibility is clouded by another factor, namely the frequency with which members, even those acknowledging a responsibility, explicitly excepted "doubtful" questions from the sphere of congressional duty. Members phrased the obligation variously, saying that legislators ought to attend to constitutional questions where the measure in question was "patently unconstitutional," "obviously unconstitutional," "clearly unconstitutional," or "pretty clearly unconstitutional." Where doubt existed, however, the situation was different. Said certain members: "Congress should act if legislation appears to definitely be good and constitutionality only questioned"; and "If there were merely a doubt, I think most members would decide their vote on the merits of the legislation, and leave the constitutional questions to the courts."

Another question probed impressions of the motivation behind constitutional questions. Members were asked: "In your experience when constitutional questions are raised in your house, are they more likely to be *bona fide* issues or political maneuvers?" Fifty-four per cent of those recording opinions marked *"bona fide,"* 30 per cent marked "political maneuvers," and 16 per cent signified, by write-in response, that they thought "both" was the proper answer. It was noteworthy that those who had shown a preference for the courts as determiners of constitutional questions were much less inclined to see such questions in Congress as *bona fide* than those who acknowledged a responsibility in Congress.

Similar results were produced by a question concerning the effect of committee and floor discussion on the final votes on constitutional questions. Here again, a two-to-one majority said they noticed such an effect, although many sought through annotations to sharpen their responses. Once again, a member's answer here tended to correlate with his conception of the responsibility devolving on Congress, and those favoring court referral seemed skeptical of the utility of discussions in Congress.

On the whole, perhaps the most striking correlation that appeared was that between region and conception of congressional responsibility. A clear divergence appeared between members from the South and Southwest, at one extreme, and those from the Middle Atlantic states at the other. Note the following: only 3 per cent of the Southerners said constitutional questions occurred in Congress only rarely, while 23 per cent of the Middle Atlantic members recorded this impression. More significant, whereas 86 per cent of the Southerners thought Congress should consider constitutional questions independently, only 60 per cent of Midwestern and 47 per cent of Middle-Atlantic members expressed this view. These figures might tempt one to conclude that each region shapes its view of legislative responsibility according to its reaction to recent Supreme Court decisions on civil rights and related matters. Subsequent chapters will show the inadequacy of such an explanation.[28]

The returns from this questionnaire reinforce the evidence from floor debate of divergent opinions in Congress. Members disagree about the character, the degree, and the scope of their responsibility and about the manner in which it is discharged. Congress has, at the least, two minds about its own capability and its own function.

TWO THEORIES OF CONSTITUTIONAL RESPONSIBILITY

Each of two theories manifested by the actions of Congress on issues involving constitutional questions has its own distinct rationale. One can be called the "judicial monopoly" theory and the other, for want of a better term, the "tripartite" theory. Each can be expressed in a cluster of propositions.

The judicial monopoly theory embraces the following:

1. Policy and constitutionality are distinct subjects. They are so distinct that they can safely be separated and confided to distinct and independent organs of government.

2. Constitutionality is a matter for experts. Highly technical in nature, it requires decision under a highly specialized procedure by a body of specialists which is rendered structurally independent of other organs.

3. This combination of judicial process, independence, and lawyer-dominance exists only in the courts, notably the Supreme Court. Only the Judiciary is fit to consider constitutional questions.

4. Policy is what legislatures and executives exist for and is usually the product of intense pressure and struggle. It is the resultant of converging forces and reflects a precise measurement of the relative strength of those forces.

5. Congress, under presidential leadership, provides the arena for this struggle. The function of Congress is to represent, mirror, and effectuate policy forces and this is its exclusive function.

6. Accordingly, constitutional questions arising in Congress ought properly to be referred to the courts, unless the answers are clear.

7. This division of functions is salutary. It provides a single, final umpire for all constitutional controversies and a representative body for policy.

The items in this catalogue are familiar to most politically informed Americans. They are clear and plausible. Nevertheless there is an alternative cluster of ideas, and these all go to support a substantial function for Congress, and one may add the Executive, in the consideration of constitutional questions. Later chapters will show that the tripartite theory itself has from the start appeared in two somewhat distinct sub-forms, but the theory will be stated here in its more generalized form:

1. The simple distinction between policy and constitutionality is illusory. The terms are imprecise, the processes they connote difficult, perhaps impossible, to isolate and assign to distinct departments.

2. The Constitution itself makes no such distinction. It speaks of "legislative" and "judicial" power. Congress is empowered to "pass laws" and not to "make policy." Its members take an oath to support the Constitution, a duty which implies an inquiry into constitutional questions in dispute.

3. For generations the Court has given substantial weight to constitutional determinations in Congress. "It is but a decent respect due to the wisdom, the integrity, and the patriotism of the legislative body by which any law is passed," wrote Justice Bushrod Washington in 1827, "to presume in favor of its validity until its violation of the Constitution is proved beyond all reasonable doubt."[29] If judges may presume acts of Congress valid, so, some would argue, may the members of Congress.[30] Yet it is hard to defend judicial presumption unless Congress itself deals conscientiously with constitutional questions.

4. Constitutional questions are often more than technical. In this field, as elsewhere, law may in a genuine sense be the product of the community and, as with desegregation, achieve vital compliance only with the slow formation of a supporting community consensus. The isolation of the courts from political pressures may promote impartiality but may also inhibit the courts, as in the 1930's, from informing themselves on community needs and attitudes. As a representative body, Congress is better fitted than the courts to interpret community sentiment, and accordingly it should share in the handling of constitutional questions.

5. Sole reliance on court determination may present difficulties. Among such hazards are delay, failure of parties to appeal, and the public odium which courts incur when they invalidate broadly supported acts of Congress. Furthermore, the courts' own precedents may be obsolete, irrelevant, or conflicting.

6. Some constitutional issues never reach the courts. Among these are certain "political" questions such as those concerning foreign relations or congressional rules of procedure. Others may be difficult or impossible to appeal, for example the uses for which moneys may be appropriated. Still others may involve the implementation as distinguished from the interpretation of constitutional provisions, thus issues concerning the establishment of executive departments or the formulation of election laws. If one confines the term "constitutional questions" to those issues concerning the fundamental law which the courts decide finally, one runs the risk of leaving large areas of our system of constitutional limitations neglected or through inattention made the butt of partisan contest.

The tripartite theory predicates for Congress important responsibilities for considering constitutional questions and accordingly expands and

11

complicates the already mountainous workload of that body. The consequences of minimizing or denying those responsibilities, however, may be even more serious.

DISCORD IN THE JUDICIARY

Such are the ideas that support the two conceptions of responsibility. It would be a mistake, however, to assume that the discord in theory exists only in Congress. Somewhat the same discord, although with a stronger backing for judicial monopoly, exists elsewhere, notably in the Supreme Court and in the world of scholarship and legal commentary.

It is true that the Supreme Court with scarcely a dissent has for a generation been broadly construing the powers of Congress and narrowly construing property rights where these impinge on measures for social and economic reform. On many issues of civil liberties, however, the Court has often split. The so-called "activists," led by Justice Hugo L. Black, have sought boldly to assert the power of the Court to review legislative acts. The late Justice Felix Frankfurter and, more recently, Justice John Marshall Harlan have favored self-restraint as the appropriate stance of the Court in many of these areas.

While the issue dividing these groups has been the scope and extent of judicial review, behind that issue has lain another, the capability and hence the responsibility of the legislature. Justice Black, the former Senator, would on many issues abandon the presumption that statutes even of Congress are valid and call for a vigorous judicial enforcement of the Bill of Rights, partly, one may assume, because of ingrained or acquired doubts of legislative impartiality and objectivity. Justice Frankfurter, the former law professor and student of judicial institutions, doubted judicial infallibility and assumed a power and capacity in the legislature to weigh the competing interests of society, including constitutional questions.[31] It seems likely that similar considerations have led to disagreement on the scope of political questions, those assigned for final determination by the legislature and executive. One who distrusts the capacity of legislatures to weigh such questions objectively might be expected to narrow that scope, one having higher expectations of legislative capacity might broaden it.

Occasionally the language of the Court as a whole has fostered an exaltation of the Judiciary as constitutional mouthpiece. Ever since Marbury v. Madison in 1803, the Court has denied that it possesses sole surveillance of constitutional questions. Yet in their unanimous decision in the Little Rock Case in 1958, the justices described their control in sweeping terms. The Chief Justice drew from the Marbury decision the basic principle that "the federal judiciary is supreme in

12

the exposition of the law of the Constitution . . ."[32] The Court, wrote Justice Frankfurter in concurring, was "the organ of our Government for ascertaining" the Supreme Law.[33] The justices were here reviewing the law of a state. Their words, however, could easily lead the uninitiated to conclude that the Court's supremacy also extends to every decision and action of the Congress, and induce a diminution of independent congressional responsibility.

DISCORD IN SCHOLARSHIP AND LEGAL COMMENTARY

If a substantial body of congressional opinion and occasional Supreme Court dicta support judicial monopoly ideas, the total effect of recent books on the Court and on Congress is also strong backing for that position. The lawyers, political scientists, journalists, and public officials who write about these institutions create one overriding impression— the importance of the Court as expounder of the Constitution in a time of stress.

Authors of the recent flood of books about the Court have for the most part lauded that tribunal.[34] From these writings the reading public has gained awareness of the Court's importance and insight into its processes. Authors and readers alike, one may suppose, esteem the Supreme Court partly because of its recent liberal interpretations of the Constitution. Unlike the situation a generation earlier,[35] it is now not liberals but ultra-conservatives who launch full-scale attacks on the Court for gross usurpation of power and gross misconstruction of the Constitution.[36]

The modern champions of the Court do differ on some points, notably on the issue between activism and self-restraint in that area within which judicial review of the acts of Congress still thrives. Yet the dominant message of books on the Supreme Court is the crucial constitutional role of the Court. It is not merely that the Court emerges as the final interpreter of the whole Constitution; but that no other organ of government, it would appear, bears any significant share of the burden of adapting the fundamental law to the strange new world of the 1960's. If "the Court is the Constitution,"[37] then Congress is relieved from adhering to the canons of constitutional wisdom within its vast sphere of power.

Congress, too, has become the subject of scholarly effort, but its reputation has gained little in the process. In 1908, Arthur F. Bentley published his *Process of Government,* a work of inestimable importance in calling attention to the crucial role played by interest and pressure groups throughout the political system.[38] In the course of his book, however, Bentley practically denied that one could speak of any public

13

interest apart from competing group interests[39] and minimized the importance of deliberation, especially in the legislature. Logic and abstract reasoning were themselves but forms of group pressure.[40] It is not surprising, therefore, that some of Bentley's followers have seen the legislative process as a battle, and seen the organs and practices which Congress has created to ensure orderly and deliberate proceedings as mere weapons in the hands of stronger forces.[41] Such writings offer the image of a body torn and wracked by the warfare of contending factions, each promoting its own special interest, and of a body consequently incapable of directing its attention and attainments to the thoughtful consideration of questions of national purpose and public interest.

By the mid 1960's, the books on Congress were multiplying,[42] and Congress itself had, for the second time in twenty years, set up a joint committee on its own organization and procedure.[43] Under Court pressures, state legislatures were undergoing reapportionment and redistricting, and the ultimate prospect was a more representative Congress. Whether it could become more deliberative was another matter. The idea was growing that only the President and the Supreme Court could be trusted with the task of formulating and expressing the "national interest." Congress, it would appear, is incapable of weighing constitutional issues. Some assume that one must choose between the Court and Congress in this area.[44] If this be the case, many of the books leave only one option.

But is it a simple either–or choice? There may be factors that require that Congress supplement the Court in the consideration of constitutional questions. Observe that the late Professor Edward S. Corwin occasionally counseled that Congress set forth a declaration of its construction of the Constitution as a guide to the courts.[45] In his 1958 Holmes Lectures, Judge Learned Hand treated judicial review itself as a pragmatic solution to the problem of discovering a constitutional arbiter in the early government.[46] Yet courts, he said, must accord to legislators a wide latitude of discretion to appraise those "values and sacrifices" which proposed statutes involve.[47] In reply, Professor Herbert Wechsler traced the reviewing power back to the constitutional text, but went on to show that the Court should leave to Congress those constitutional issues which take the form of political questions.[48] Further, Professor Wechsler admonished the Court to rest decision on what Chief Justice Roger B. Taney called the true basis of its authority, "the force of the reasoning by which it is supported."[49] Indeed, the tendency of the recent Court occasionally to support its decisions with only perfunctory opinions fully accords with the notion that the Constitution is "what the judges say it is."

Moreover, the pressure of time, so often used to justify legislative

14

neglect of constitutional questions, has also created difficulties for the judges. Professor Henry M. Hart, Jr., has written: "To call upon judges to vote upon complex and often highly controversial issues after only a couple of hours more or less of private study of briefs and records is to invite votes which are influenced more strongly by general predilections in the area of law involved than they are by lawyerlike examination of the precise issue presented for decision."[50] The Court, he urged, should decide fewer cases and write better reasoned opinions.[51] One may remember that Congress, too, has been charged with reaching determinations by the amassing of votes pro and con rather than through reasoned deliberation.

These recent criticisms of the Court, when coupled with recent strictures against Congress, might drive one in despair to conclude that in this age of crises no organ of government can be trusted with the function of constitutional decision-making. At the least, the long-smoldering disagreement over the appropriate shares of Congress and the Judiciary in the function of exploring constitutional issues calls for study. Perhaps the crucial subject for analysis is not which organ is better suited to perform the function, but what is the nature of that function itself and what structures and processes does it require?

2 *Constitutional Settlements:*
A Framework for Analysis

THE CASE OF GENERAL BRADLEY

An occurrence before a Senate committee in 1951 will epitomize the problem under consideration and set the stage for a statement of its character and dimensions.

At 1:00 a.m. on April 11, President Truman announced that he was relieving General Douglas MacArthur of command in Korea. The General, he declared, was "unable to give his wholehearted support to the policies of the United States Government and of the United Nations in matters pertaining to his official duties."[1] The General had not only viewed the appropriate policy and strategy in the Far East in a way which differed from the President's but had corresponded about it with the minority leader in the House of Representatives, Joseph R. Martin of Massachusetts. The public was staggered by the dismissal, and the General was soon describing his policies to a joint session of Congress. The affair tested the principle of civilian control and jeopardized the future of the United Nations; to one observer it constituted "perhaps the gravest and most emotional Constitutional crisis" since the Depression.[2]

What made it doubly serious was the partisan complexion it instantly assumed. Important elements in the minority Republican party sympathized with MacArthur's aims and suspected the Administration of partisan motives. There was also some thought that Secretary of State Dean Acheson had given in to pressure from the Allies.[3] The next year would bring a presidential election and this summary removal of a popular general could help return the Republican party to the White House after an absence of eighteen years.

To get at the facts of the affair and to air Far East policy, two Senate committees, Foreign Relations and Armed Services, were soon conducting joint hearings. The members included fourteen Democrats and twelve Republicans.[4] Senator Richard B. Russell, Georgia Democrat, presided and opened the hearings May 3 with this appeal: "The guiding light here today, and in the days to follow, must be the national interest,

16

for the national interest transcends, in importance, the fortunes of any individual, or group of individuals. If we are to exercise one of the highest legislative functions, we must see that the American people are brought the truth, and the whole truth, without the color of prejudice or partisanship, and with no thought as to personalities."[5] General MacArthur was the first to testify and after him General George C. Marshall, Secretary of Defense. On May 15, General Omar N. Bradley, Chairman of the Joint Chiefs of Staff, appeared. He was describing a White House meeting of the President with his top advisers which had led to the dismissal when Senator Alexander Wiley, Wisconsin Republican, precipitated a constitutional controversy. This interchange took place:

> Senator Wiley. All right. Now, tell us what was said then.
>
> General Bradley. Senator, at that time I was in a position of a confidential adviser to the President. I do not feel at liberty to publicize what any of us said at that time.
>
> Senator Wiley. Well, that raises a question, I suppose, that the Chair will have to rule on . . . When you come before a committee, sir, to give information as to a very important matter that the public is entitled to know about, unless it goes to the question of endangering the public welfare, it seems to me that you waive the right you claim now, as to the President—
>
> General Bradley. Senator, it seems to me that in my position as an adviser, one of the military advisers to the President, and to anybody else in a position of responsibility who wants it, that if I have to publicize my recommendations and my discussions, that my value as an adviser is ruined . . . it seems to me that when any of us have to tell everything that we say in our position as an adviser, that we might just as well quit.
>
> Senator Wiley. I am not going to ask you to do that.
>
> There is one issue before the bar of public opinion, and only one in this matter, as I see it . . . and that is—whether or not this action, taken in the manner it was taken, can be justified by the facts, before the bar of public opinion.[6]

The Senator then intimated that some of the President's advisers had defended the General and asked the chairman to rule that his question was pertinent and relevant. On the ground that American law recognized "certain well-established and clearly defined confidential relations," Senator Russell ruled that the witness could decline to answer.[7] After further discussion, Senator Wiley appealed the ruling to the whole committee. Three days and 107 record pages later the committee sustained the ruling of the chair by a vote of 18 to 8. Moreover, the committee's settlement of the issue held throughout the remaining six weeks of the hearings. Just as the hearings as a whole quieted public alarm over the dismissal of a war hero by revealing the grounds for Administration policy, so the decision on executive privilege gained general acceptance in Congress and in the country.

This episode of General Bradley exhibits several noteworthy features. One was the partisan atmosphere of the discussion. Senator Wiley was holding secret meetings after hours with seven other Senate Republicans to explore the legal issue and map strategy.[8] When the committee finally voted down his demand for disclosure he accused it of conducting a "white wash" of the Administration.[9] The appearance of a "cover-up" by the Democrats might prove useful in later Republican campaigning.[10] On his part, Senator Russell, on learning of the Republican strategy meetings, objected to party "huddles," which, he warned, might disrupt the hearings.[11] Other Democrats accused Republicans of bad motives: thus Senator Brien McMahon of Connecticut told the committee that certain committee members, dissatisfied with the progress of the hearings, were introducing irrelevancies "for purposes that do not bear the light of day."[12] Ten of the Democrats, defensive about Republican charges, and the nominal Republican, Senator Wayne Morse of Oregon, wanted a quick decision on the question of privilege and speedy resumption of testimony.[13] Four Republicans favored postponing the issue.[14] Three of the remaining eleven wanted to drop the issue, and eight, four from each party, withheld comment on the constitutional question.[15] By the last hour of the second day, the committee had reached a stalemate; it was unable to ballot on the issue, postpone it, or drop it. Motions, points of order, parliamentary questions, requests for unanimous consent followed one another in bewildering succession. Politics had produced a serious constitutional issue, and politics appeared to paralyze efforts to deal with it.

Yet the question demanded a decision by the committee. Issues of executive privilege, the right of executive officials to be free in their conversations and papers from legislative scrutiny, is as old as the republic. It is a matter that the political branches have handled without court intervention. Members at first called the question here "procedural,"[16] then legal, and finally constitutional.[17] Senator Morse warned of a possible future court test,[18] but it became increasingly certain that the committee must reach its own decision.[19]

What made it possible for the committee to achieve a settlement of the issue by the close of discussion the third day? Senator John Stennis, Mississippi Democrat, turned the tide a half hour before recess the second day. The former state judge proposed that committee leaders of both parties work out a plan for an argument of the case the next day

18

with suitable limitations and apportionment of time. Others elaborated the proposal until all present were able to accept the version of Senator William Knowland, California Republican.[20]

Accordingly, the entire session the third day, from 10:20 a.m. to 1:00 p.m., was devoted to debate on the constitutional question. Many of the arguments had appeared earlier, but now they were systematized, focused, and related one to another. Senator Russell himself led off with allusions to statutes of Congress, the Constitution, Supreme Court dicta, constitutional commentaries, opinions of the Attorneys General, legislative precedents, and state cases concerning the powers of governors. Under the separation of powers, he maintained, each branch requires a degree of privacy sufficient to protect confidential relationships. Senator Wiley followed with seven legal principles to demonstrate that under present circumstances a witness could not assert the privilege, and that the information was essential to the discharge of senatorial duty and important to the people.[21] Senator Knowland, who had earlier warned that the ruling would draw an "iron curtain" on presidential consultations,[22] asserted that the country was drifting into a "twilight constitutional zone" in which the Executive was wielding the power to make war without the restraint of popular accountability.[23] Senator Morse supported the ruling by alluding to existing legislative checks on the Executive, defending the exigencies of executive power, and rebutting points of the opponents. He said that Wiley's claim that the witness could waive his right to privilege was appropriate in private law situations but not in the field of constitutional law.[24] Citing Willoughby and Wigmore, he concluded by grounding the privilege firmly on the separation of powers and the power of the President as chief executor of the laws. After further discussion, questions and responses, and individual declarations, the members voted to support the ruling.

In this way the Senators succeeded in detaching the constitutional question from the policy question thoroughly enough and long enough to enable them to consider the constitutional argument on its own merits. Thus they confronted the leading principles pertinent to this issue of executive vs. legislative power and viewed them in relationship to one another.

This confrontation was rendered possible on this occasion by three factors. First, the participants possessed the qualities requisite for the task. Two-thirds of them were lawyers, among them Senators Russell, Wiley, and Morse. The former law school dean, Senator Morse, was able to expose the weakness in the concept of witness-privilege put forward by the former trial lawyer Senator Wiley. Senator Knowland was no lawyer, yet more than any other, he detected the disturbing implications of executive privilege for democratic government in the jet age. Moreover, these men had had long experience in Congress, eleven years on the average. Many, accordingly, were able to cite analogous situations they had encountered in other committees, and Senator Tom Connally, Texas Democrat, could put the unwisdom of the Wiley claim in colloquial terms:

> How could a President do anything if all you would have to do would be to station a man out in front of the White House and take down the name of anybody that should go in and see the President and then jerk him up before a committee and say, ". . . Tell us all of the confidential conversation that transpired between you and the President of the United States."
>
> Mr. Chairman, it is unthinkable. It is absolutely destructive of our constitutional concepts.[25]

Members also exhibited that intangible quality, moderation, which deterred some of them from automatic public commitment on the constitutional issue and enabled them to consider the constitutional challenge on its own merits. The caliber of the two constituent committees was a fortunate factor in the handling of the Bradley case.

Second, the procedure for handling the question facilitated what Senator Stennis asked for, a "reasonable presentation of the question."[26] Many members helped to shape that procedure and all accepted it. It defined the constitutional question with precision; it allotted equal time to the opposed sides and gave each an interval of time, however brief, for preparation; it made it possible to carry on the deliberative process with a mild degree of seclusion from outside pressures by closing the doors on press and public; and it put the votes of members on record, while providing them a kind of reasoned justification in the form of the published transcript.[27] These features of the proceedings furnished the rudiments of a fair and objective weighing of the evidence. Whether appearance or reality, that weighing produced results.

Third, the conception of responsibility which seemed to prevail favored a probing of the constitutional question. Alone of the ten Southern Democrats to vote against the ruling was Senator J. William Fulbright of Arkansas. The Republicans, he explained, had criticized the hearings as partisan, and he had no desire to appear to the public to be hiding important facts; for this reason he preferred to shelve his personal convictions and let the matter go to the courts. Senator Morse retorted that if the Senator believed that the Constitution made the President's communications privileged, "then I think under his oath of office, it is his duty to sustain the doctrine of the separation of powers . . . and not pass the buck to the courts . . ."[28] Senator Russell showed more than a veneer of respect for the discretion of the members and the capabilities of Congress. He appealed to his colleagues to vote not by party but by conscience and intelligence.[29] He paid respect to the people, on whose decisions the government depended for existence and for whose enlightenment these very hearings were intended,[30] but he also acknowledged a significant function for Congress. The committee's decision of the question confirmed the faith of the founders in the ability of Congress to resolve critical issues "in the light of facts and reasoned judgment . . ."[31]

Although the Russell conception seemed to prevail, others gave hints of something like the judicial monopoly theory. Senator Wiley typified the view. He seemed to regard the decision not as one of constitutional principle, but as one of policy which should go to the people for final determination. He demanded whether his colleagues were "mice or men."[32] He put it this way, "I speak to you as men of the Senate who have been elected as representatives of the people in the States, not subordinates, not yes men, but men who are now defining a policy that may rise up to haunt you and those who come after."[33] The Senator from Wisconsin, whose appeal both the other Midwestern members supported, felt little constraint, in the absence of clear judicial precedents, to take the committee decision as anything but a politics-ridden decree. His words and deeds seemed to reflect doubts of the genuineness of the constitutional issue, of the motives of those who raised it, and of the very obligation of Congress to probe such issues.[34]

The combination of informed participants, effective procedure, and attitudes favoring the acceptance of responsibility made possible the discussions which quieted the constitutional controversy and enabled the committee to return to the testimony. In an atmosphere charged with political contentiousness, a group of Senators had met, grappled with, and bested a grave constitutional question.

POLITICAL DEMANDS AND CONSTITUTIONAL QUESTIONS: THE STATE OF TENSION

The dispute over General Bradley's reluctance to testify suggests the problem central to the issue of responsibility: the interconnection and tension between political demands and constitutional questions. I shall here explore that tension in general terms, and then discuss the essentials of a system for disentangling and resolving constitutional issues. My purpose is to provide a theoretical framework for the subsequent analysis. The probes of congressional experience which make up the principal content of this book will follow in somewhat greater detail and precision the pattern of the Bradley case.

The first of the two poles in tension is the political demand. Although

21

demands may relate to continuity or change in the constitutional system itself, they usually relate to public policy. "Policy" I am here defining in a somewhat restricted sense. Contrary to recent usage, my definition excludes constitutional issues, and identifies policy with the general course of government action, chiefly in relation to matters external to government. It may relate to foreign affairs, as in the Bradley case, or to domestic affairs, but in both instances policy lies close to the vital ends of government—peace, defense, order, welfare. It is the main "output" of the system and impinges primarily on individuals and groups outside government. The usual test of policy is its efficiency in promoting its objective.

Demands for policy carry an immediacy and an urgency often overwhelming. For decades the standard test of foreign policy has been how well it serves the vital interest of the nation, a standard which, because it is associated with self-preservation, seldom has an effective rival. For a generation and more the concept of policy as a promoter of national interest has come to dominate domestic affairs as well. With technological change, economic expansion, and social complexity, political demands have proliferated, and more and more matters once left to voluntary action or state and local control have moved toward the national political scene. Farm policy, urban policy, even air pollution policy, have acquired something of the same cruciality, immediacy, and involvement with the national interest that Senator Wiley appeared to see in Far Eastern policy.

Furthermore, policy must be flexible. Conditions, foreign and domestic, change rapidly, and those who formulate policy require breadth of discretion within which to adjust policy to those changes. The greater the urgency and immediacy the greater the range required.

To be effectual, policy therefore calls for broad and ample power, the control of the material and personal resources of the nation. The proponents of policy—individuals, collectivities, such as political parties and special interest groups, and governmental organs, local, state, and national—seek to employ power as the essential means for achieving the policies they champion. It is the characteristic posture of these policy forces to exalt the policy they favor as clothed with the national interest and to insist that the effectuation of the policy calls for prompt, ample, and flexible grants of power.

It is also their characteristic stance to deprecate opposition. Those individuals, collectivities, and organs which challenge the policy or seek to deny or curtail the power are branded as negative, obstructionist, self-serving, disloyal, or even treasonous. Policies may promote the general interest, but they also usually serve some special interests and burden

22

others. The conflict between the groups served and the groups burdened is inevitable and often bitter.

Like demands for policy, constitutional questions are concerned with power, but for a very different purpose. I would define a constitution as all those principles and rules according to which the power of government officials is distributed and limited. Often its operation is positive, but in established political systems, that operation is usually negative, that is, it serves to restrain power, in some instances by prohibiting the ends, more commonly by regulating the means of government action. This makes collision between the pretensions of policy and provisions of the constitution inescapable.

Often the term policy is stretched to embrace constitutional practice and principle with the effect of obscuring the purpose of the constitution, yet a vital purpose there is. Power is somewhat analogous to forms of physical energy. Like falling water, fire, or atomic energy, it has great potential utility for mankind but also danger. Indeed, it carries a special danger, its corrupting effect on those who wield it. Testimony to this effect came in 1956 from an unusual quarter. At a Party Congress, Premier Khrushchev had this to say about his predecessor, "Possessing unlimited power, he indulged in great wilfulness and choked a person morally and physically."[35] The exercise of political power carries with it a potential threat, whether willfull or unintentional, to important social and individual values, values that lie close to the heart of civilized life. That is why questions concerning the adoption and interpretation of constitutional restraints lead one ultimately to values. Just as Senator Russell sought to safeguard the confidential character of presidential consultations allegedly to safeguard the smooth operation and hence the usefulness of the Executive, so those who raise constitutional objections to wiretapping assert the importance of privacy in social life. Constitutional formulae are the tough outer rind for inner and often forgotten values. To erect standards for limitation is to defend human social values from the intrusion of governmental power. Yet in the clamor for policies to meet needs urgently felt, one fact is easily lost sight of, that these values and the restraints on power that protect them are likewise matters of urgent national interest or purpose.

Accordingly, it is important that men impart a high degree of permanence to constitutional limitations. They must be deemed fundamental. Oliver Cromwell's distinction between the fundamental and the circumstantial in the "Establishment" as Professor Herbert J. Spiro shows is important. The circumstantial, with which we may equate policy, may vary with conditions, but the fundamental, as Cromwell put it "may *not* be parted with; but will, I trust be delivered over to Posterity, as the

23

fruits of our blood and travail."[36] Policy requires flexible power, constitutions aim at stable limitations on power.

In the resulting tension between political demands and constitutional questions lies the chief difficulty faced by constitution-makers and interpreters. Madison summed up that difficulty thus: "You must first enable the government to controul the governed; and in the next place, oblige it to controul itself."[37] The constitution, writes Professor Carl J. Friedrich, is "the process by which political action is limited and at the same time given form."[38] The canals and ditches of an irrigation system prevent floods and direct the water to parched lands, the massive walls of the blast furnace hold the flame to the ore, the lead shields of the atomic power plant protect the workers and the neighboring community: the rules of the constitution confine the flow of policy decisions to their proper objectives. In order to make the constitutional walls durable, those rules are described as law. Although the term law carries the hazard that some will confine it to court-made rules and exclude others based, for example, on usage, custom, or the spirit of the constitution, the concept of the rule of law carries a meaning which every citizen or subject of government can comprehend.

What distinguishes the rules of the constitution from those of ordinary law is that their commands run to men already in power and to the forces, usually collective, that support those men. The constitution speaks not to citizens or groups of citizens, but to the government. He who invokes the law of the constitution invokes it against the wielders of power and their backers. He must find counter-forces and counter-arguments strong enough to deter them.

The initiative in raising constitutional objections falls, of course, to those political forces which resist policy and the backers of policy. Individuals, parties and pressure groups, levels and organs of government press the constitutional claim in order to defeat the policy they oppose. In a sense this is fortunate. Were no one on hand directly concerned in opposing policy, constitutional objections might die by default, whether the forum be the court or the legislature.

No less important than the initiation of the constitutional objection is the search for a rationale. In many instances unless those pressing the objection are able to articulate principles and values, they run the risk of undergoing the charge of mere obstructionism, of reaction, even of subversion. The dynamism of the struggle for policy with its mood of urgency and immediacy makes the constitutional appeal seem at the least pointless, at the worst sheer treason. The problem then is one of separation, of detachment, of the constitutional question from the policy demand in order to expose to all concerned not only the existence but also the basic justification of constitutional restraints.

24

CHARACTER OF CONSTITUTIONAL SETTLEMENTS

If political demands tend to overawe and smother constitutional questions, satisfactory settlement of constitutional questions is nonetheless necessary. American history is stained with episodes in which constitutional issues went unresolved. A few of them will appear in later chapters. Failure to achieve settlement may cause inconvenience, confusion, disorder, retaliation, violence, and even civil war. The Russell Committee talked its way to a conclusion that evidently satisfied all but the single initiator. Had it cut off discussion at the first word of protest by a party-line vote, the result might have been serious.

One important feature in lasting settlements is the articulation and explanation of constitutional rules and principles. The constitutional question is put with clarity and the appropriate principles adduced with insight. Commonly, the question is put in a legal form: "Does the official have the power?" Commonly, also, it is sufficient merely to cite pertinent court precedents to furnish the answer. To cite the precedent or, in some cases, to state the rule incorporated in the precedent is enough.

Yet sometimes it is not enough. None of those defending Senator Russell's ruling found a clear court precedent so the question became, "*should* the official have the power?" or, in this case, "enjoy the privilege?" The task then became one of searching a variety of sources for the pertinent principles and by comparison determining the most appropriate one. In the Bradley case, the successful principle was an ingredient of the separation of powers, the independence essential to the Executive. In other instances, it may be another form of divided power —the principle of federalism, the distribution of power between the federal and state governments. In still others, it may concern the rights of the individual.

Note that Senator Wiley called the committee decision one not of principle, but of policy. Judicial monopoly views lead to the conclusion that where a question lacks court precedent, the legislature is cut loose from the obligation to probe principles, and is free to deal with the question on policy terms. In that case, the issue may easily lose its fundamental character and assume one of circumstantiality.

The exposition of legal precedents and often of ultimate principles must take place in the presence of the protagonists to the dispute. Supporters and opponents of the Truman policy on the Russell Committee came to see that behind the claims of the contending policies lay another plane of reality, the pros and cons of the constitutional question. At the close of hearings, the Republican foes of Administration policy branded it a "catastrophic failure," but the justification of the Russell ruling and the committee decision had secured their acquiescence.[39] It

25

is essential that in some fashion the spokesmen or representatives of special interests contending over policy confront the constitutional rationale, in order that a satisfactory accommodation of those special interests may be achieved. Political demands need to be separated, although not isolated, from fundamental constitutional principles and values for adjustment to be attained. The weighing of demands against long-run values is the essence of constitutional deliberation.

The willingness to consider the relinquishment of policy ends or means potentially unconstitutional is the essence of moderation in the sense in which I shall use that term. Since that sort of moderation is hard to expect in those who are dedicated and publicly committed for or against a policy, another feature of settlements is the presence of others able and willing to retain a measure of impartiality. Such men run the risk of incurring the charge of "pussy-footing," or lack of courage. Yet without the participation or effective presence of men disposed to pose constitutional questions and to work for a detached confrontation with rules and principles, the policy issue is likely to carry the day. Before the committee came to its vote on the Russell ruling, the Vermont Republican, Senator Ralph Flanders, expressed what was ostensibly a genuine concern to decide the constitutional question on its own merits: "If I vote to sustain the judgment of the Chair, am I voting to break a precedent which Congress has upheld over many years, as to its right to get access to information from the executive department? I might feel one way toward this particular situation, and another way toward the breaking of a long-established precedent."[40] The statement reflects something approximating the judicial temperament, and, of course, it was a former state judge, Senator Stennis, who first proposed an orderly facing of the constitutional question.

Senator Wiley, however, threatened to appeal the committee's rejection directly to the "bar of public opinion." The precise meaning and even the existence of a "public opinion" are topics for disputation among political scientists. Nevertheless, it is evident that the settlement of constitutional questions calls for more than a certain kind of decision-making at the level of government; it calls for understanding and commitment in the public at large. Citizens, or at least their opinion-leaders, need a measure of constitutional maturity: this includes an awareness and conviction that behind the policy plane there is a constitutional plane, the ability to recognize that the raising of constitutional questions is not necessarily self-serving obstructionism, and at least a rudimentary knowledge of crucial constitutional principles and the values they serve. These are the ingredients of the constitutional consensus. To be lasting, settlements must accord with such a consensus.

26

Note the importance not only of consulting that consensus, but of continually informing and re-educating it. I suggest that an issue central to our problem is the volume and quality of publicity, whether judicial or legislative in origin.

Another way of stating the question is, what can be done to make decisions on policy legitimate? Those who would consign all constitutional settlements to the courts place most of the burden of imparting legitimacy to government action upon the Judiciary. Yet the settlement of constitutional questions calls for more than judicial review and the application of judicial precedents.

THE CHOICE OF FORUM: COURT VS. REPRESENTATIVE BODY

If these are some characteristics of lasting constitutional settlements, it is important to the analysis to ask which is the most appropriate forum, the court or the representative body? Is it true that the Judiciary alone provides a locus for settlements that is both effective in resolving issues and acceptable to the public?

The most obvious answer is to point to Great Britain. There for generations Parliament has been supreme both in matters of policy and in matters of constitutional import. The representatives of the British people can make and unmake the constitution and interpret it as they will. The paradox of a body with absolute power that consistently observes a vast complex of restraints received recent elucidation by Sir Raymond Evershed. The "standards of value and legality" have endured, he said, because of a prevailing spirit of moderation among public officeholders, forbearance and mutual respect between Parliament and the courts, universal solicitude for fair procedures, and public vigilance to safeguard traditional ways from official intrusion.[41]

M.P.'s and judges alike share in the spirit of moderation. For centuries the Parliament and the courts developed not as rivals but as allies against a common adversary, the absolute monarch. The guild of lawyers had its headquarters and training school at the Inns of Court, and the judges, increasingly independent of the king, slowly developed out of custom and what Lord Coke called the "artificial Reason and Judgment of Law,"[42] a body of common law. This corpus of rules and precedents included restraints on executive officials which constituted a leading ingredient of the constitution. Its own origins as a high court and its continuing affiliations with the legal fraternity helped Parliament retain in its proceedings something of a judicial atmosphere. Those with legal training, however, usually make up less than a quarter of the members

27

of Parliament, and one must ascribe to factors other than lawyer predominance the traditions, attitudes, and practices which make for deliberation.

Under these influences, the House of Commons developed procedures for decision-making that maximized both genuine deliberation and focused publicity. An important feature of that procedure is early reference of issues of principle, not to small standing committees, but to the entire House meeting under informal rules for discussion in the Committee of the Whole. The practice had become standard by the eighteenth century and indeed passed to many of the Middle and Southern colonies in America.[43] It assured that questions of high constitutional importance would undergo probing discussion in a body fully representative to the extent of the suffrage and election laws. Despite the mounting control of the Cabinet, the organization of the House into two disciplined parties, and recent efforts to strengthen standing committees, the practice continued in postwar Britain to facilitate constitutional settlements.[44] Settlements take place in the presence of the people's representatives and, through press coverage and printed debates, with full publicity.

Of course a kind of final appeal runs from the Commons to the people. The alertness of the British public to departures from traditional ways is familiar. The obligation of Parliament to talk out constitutional disputes, under procedures sustained by a general commitment and with full publicity, may well be both an effect and, in the long run, a formative cause of the British consensus on constitutional principles.

The system in the United States differs from the British in both origin and character. The framers created Congress at a stroke and many of them feared the prospect of legislative tyranny. They bound it down with legal limitations and erected the Executive and the Judiciary in part as counterweights to the Legislature.

The result has been recurrent friction between court and Congress with regard to constitutional issues. Under American conditions, judicial review has captured public esteem and, indeed, the courts offer distinct advantages as constitutional forums. It is not simply that the Constitution endows judges with independence of political pressures. A military commander could be set up with a like independence but with results for constitutional settlements that would be disastrous. It is also that here the legal profession enjoys a monopoly of control, unadulterated by lay participation. Here the lawyers can sustain procedural rectitude from the assaults of policy forces and inexperienced legislators, and here the body of inherited legal concepts and principles is preserved and applied with professional expertise. "Those of us who are lawyers," Senator Javits told the Senate in 1959, "do understand and recognize the effectiveness within our constitutional system of a judicial tribunal to give final interpretations of the Constitution."[45] Not only do lawyers monopolize control in running courts, but those courts have peculiar advantages in defending individuals against unconstitutional government action. Legislatures indulge to some degree in speculation and prediction in weighing proposed policies against constitutional provisions; courts apply those provisions to situations that are immediate and concrete. All this gives courts a special appeal to the bar.

Yet the very independence and professionalism of courts partially unfits them for constitutional settlements. After all, it was a representative assembly, and not a court of law, that framed the Constitution of the United States, and other assemblies that ratified it. In conventions and legislatures, moreover, lawyers have always been numerous.

The Legislature which the framers established has several advantages, actual or potential, in the handling of constitutional issues. First, Congress represents individuals, interests, parties, localities, and states. In possessing this characteristic, Congress embodies a principle of legitimacy that is fundamental. No institution, short of a convention, one may assume, is as competent as Congress to reflect the popular consensus, and, assuming adequate publicity, to inform that consensus. Second, Congress is in a position to engage in full, free discussion for the airing, confrontation, and accommodation of interests. Such discussion offers a unique means of revealing the general interest on both policy and constitutional planes, promoting understanding and moderation, and informing the public of constitutional issues and settlements. Success here depends on appropriate organs and procedures and on the kind and quality of publicity. Third, members of Congress possess extensive experience in politics, with resulting insights into governmental processes and skills in the art of compromise. Fourth, Congress has access to a number of devices for the flexible resolution of constitutional issues. It can resort to a variety of tools, old and new—for example, national commissions—unknown to the courts and inappropriate for them. Representation, free discussion, political experience, and a capacity for institutional innovation all equip Congress to share in the function of constitutional settlement.

It is my position here that the problem is not whether Congress should share in that function, but to what extent and in what manner.

ELEMENTS OF CONGRESSIONAL RESPONSIBILITY

If Congress is to share in that function, then its members bear a measure of responsibility for the task. Several elements of that responsibility will be mentioned.

First, the object of that responsibility is the mass of precedents, rules, principles, and values that comprise the Constitution. To discharge their responsibility, members need, on the one hand, to define the question pertinent to the issue of power and, on the other, to search for the appropriate precedents, rules, principles, and values.

The third day's debate on the question in the Bradley episode led to a satisfactory settlement because of the quality of the discussion. Close analysis shows that the consideration was both thorough and effective. By thorough I mean that members brought out the leading arguments pro and con and consulted the appropriate sources and authorities. Discussion of principles was far from exhaustive, but for the purpose it juxtaposed the most relevant arguments. Thoroughness is one of the tests of the quality of consideration in later case analyses.

The other test is effectiveness—whether the consideration of the constitutional question is genuinely detached from the policy question. This is a matter difficult to measure objectively. Yet criteria exist which in combination offer approximate accuracy.

One can learn something by studying the record of the discussion on its face, with whatever external evidence may be available. The Russell Committee argued their question in a manner that pertained to the subject, sustained with only occasional lapses a focus on the subject, included relevant documentary evidence, and followed something like a logical, sequential pattern. Some of the speeches reflected careful preparation, but, in addition, members exchanged views. Senator Morse rebutted points made by the other side, and several members sought to clarify the issue and the appropriate principles by questions. Statements by the uncommitted may thus be revelatory of the genuineness of the debate.

Another set of criteria makes use of changes of position and voting patterns. Some members may alter their initial stands. Others may take a stand on the constitutional question that goes counter to their commitments on the policy. Three of the Senators who had announced their opposition to the ouster of MacArthur or to the Truman policy nevertheless supported the ruling of the chair.[46] Or, votes may depart from straight party lines; thus, two of the fourteen Democrats and six of the twelve Republicans broke with predictable party positions on the Russell ruling.[47] Again, votes may reflect a measure of detachment to the extent that they depart from regional alignment. The Bradley vote followed regional more closely than party lines. For purposes of this book the country will be divided into six regions, shown in the map.[48] The Far West and New England, as Table 1 shows, maintained the greatest flexibility of position. In the chapters that follow similar criteria will be applied in an effort to determine the extent of detachment characterizing the consideration of constitutional questions.[49]

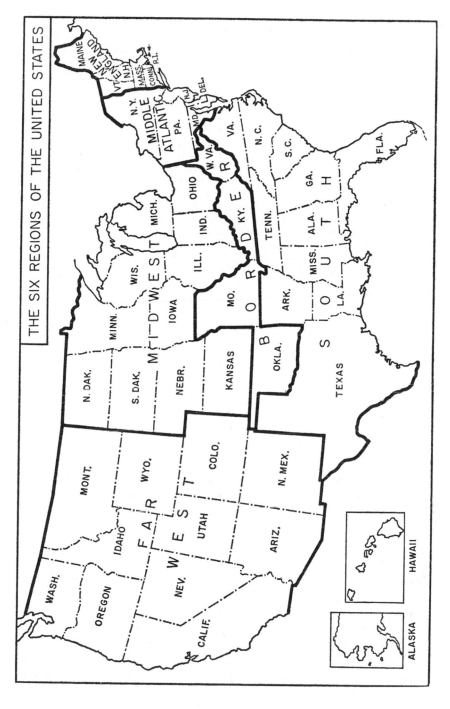

THE SIX REGIONS OF THE UNITED STATES

TABLE 1. The Vote to Support the Russell Ruling, by Regions, 1951

Region	Yea	Nay
Middle Atlantic	1	0
South	9	1
New England	6	2
Far West	2	2
Midwest	0	3
Border	0	0
Total	18	8

SOURCE: *Military Situation in the Far East*. Hearings before the Committee on Armed Services and the Committee on Foreign Relations, United States Senate, 82nd Congress, 1st sess. (1951), pt. 2, p. 872.

If legislators bear an obligation to relate questions of power back to pertinent rules, principles, and values, there is clearly no assurance that they will do so. Hence, it is important to examine a second element, the three factors which are instrumental in furthering the discharge of responsibility. All three contributed to settlement of the Bradley issue. First, the participants in the settlement affect the outcome. Must lawyers assume the leadership and dominate the proceedings? Senator Lodge's retort to a taunt that he lacked legal training, "The Constitution does not require that we have to be lawyers,"[50] states a fact and suggests that non-lawyers, at least in the legislature, may contribute too. The qualities of moderation, of constitutional wisdom as distinguished from constitutional legality, of a willingness to initiate and press for reasoned deliberation of constitutional issues, as epitomized by Senators Stennis and Flanders, all these affect the contribution of participants. One may employ the term constitutional leadership to characterize the role played by certain members of Congress, drawn more often than not from particular regions of the country.

Another factor is the mode of consideration, that is, the legislative organs in which constitutional settlements are achieved and the rules governing the process for consideration of the questions. For the legislature to claim any measure of legitimacy for its settlements of constitutional questions, it should embody the representative principle not only in its own total structure but also in the particular organs which bear the chief burden of consideration. Assuming fair apportionment, the chambers as totalities would afford the fullest representation. When conditions necessitate that settlement of constitutional questions take place in committees, or subcommittees, or even in national commissions, the degree to which those smaller units embody the representative principle furnishes a key to its capacity to embody legitimate, that is, popularly acceptable, settlements. Had the Bradley Committee contained only Democrats, or only Southerners and Easterners with, let us say, one Midwesterner to precipitate the constitutional issue, it is doubtful that the ensuing settlement would have commanded respect. As it was, the geographical balance of the committee was somewhat deficient.

In addition, the rules by which these organs control discussion help condition the outcome. In subsequent chapters the rules of procedure will receive attention, as judged by the same five criteria or standards already applied to the procedure of the Russell Committee. Advance agreement on procedure helps to exclude irrelevancies and resentments from the discussion. A clear definition of the constitutional question distinguishes it from the policy issue and promotes resort to pertinent precedents, rules, and principles. A full free discussion, with time and opportunity for diverse individuals and groups to prepare and submit opinions, helps guarantee that no significant opinion is excluded or overlooked and facilitates the process of accommodation through juxtaposing special and general interests. General Bradley's claim of executive privilege was argued out finally under procedures of adversary discussion, which under some conditions may offer a special advantage. Flexibility of rules to meet the needs of each special case is important. Yet full deliberation seems also to require an element of privacy, an opportunity for those charged with decision-making to consult and weigh alternatives free from outside pressures or observation. Finally, the prospect of a public vote puts participants on their mettle. Roll call votes on constitutional questions have the merit of compelling each participant to take a stand. At the same time, publication of supporting arguments furnishes a basis for that stand.

The final factor in the discharge of responsibility is the operative attitudes toward responsibility held by the members of the organ attempting the settlement. Unless the members possess and sustain a personal sense of obligation to detach constitutional questions from the policy framework and relate them to pertinent precedents and principles, satisfactory settlements cannot be achieved. Later chapters will relate expressions of attitude to the several theories of congressional responsibility that have emerged during history. Here it is pertinent to relate this factor of attitudes to available sanctions of responsibility.

Spokesmen of the judicial monopoly theory tend to view responsibility in legal terms. Here is the statement of a Senator during committee discussion in 1964: "Now we all take an oath to support the Constitution, and the Constitution is what is written plus what the Supreme Court says it is."[51] Such a definition binds the member of Congress to follow

33

implicitly the decisions of the Supreme Court, in effect makes the oath an oath to the Court. It has the merit of simplicity and certainty, but it contracts the Constitution to legal precedent and presupposes that the verdict of precedents is clear and emphatic. It also presupposes that the Court alone in case of neglect by members of Congress is capable of correcting all lapses and of compelling Congress to right its own wrongs.

Another sanction for responsibility is political. In Britain the electorate corrects lapses in parliamentary responsibility, and the opposition party operates as a corrective, or at least a public critic within the Parliament itself. In the United States, too, the electorate has a measure of control, but the framers also divided political power in a variety of ways to help ensure that the shirking of responsibility by one branch or organ would undergo correction by another. The three branches of government, declared the Massachusetts Constitution of 1780, are separated "to the end it may be a government of laws and not of men."[52] Federalism, the separation of powers, bicameralism, all contribute to maintaining fidelity of officeholders to established power limits. The system has the merit of any system of balanced power. The danger is that where power is distributed in a manner too exacting, officials may be tempted to disclaim obligation and pass the buck!

Accordingly, it has been necessary to bring responsibility to the individual conscience. Anglo-American constitutionalism has from the start preserved an element of moral responsibility, a duty in each power-wielder to observe constitutional rules and principles because it is right to do so. The oath of office epitomizes that obligation and places the sanction of religion behind it. Note the oath which Elizabeth II uttered in 1953 in the presence of the representatives of her people at Westminster. She knelt before the spiritual leader of the Church of England and solemnly promised to govern the people of her several realms, "according to their respective laws and customs" and to make judgments according to "law and justice, in mercy." These things, she declared, hand on Bible, "I will perform and keep. So help me, God."[53] The President of the United States solemnly swears to execute his office faithfully and to "preserve, protect and defend the Constitution," traditionally adding "so help me God." He does this with hand on Bible before the robed Chief Justice, successor to the Archbishop of Canterbury.

For many these actions appear an empty ritual of a past when religion controlled men's actions and the imprecations of the Church carried terror. At the Philadelphia Convention, James Wilson called oaths of office a "left handed security only,"[54] yet other Americans of the formative period saw them as an effort to harness the force of religious commitment to the maintenance of constitutional safeguards.[55] The device is

34

an ancient, if embryonic instrument by which man has sought to compel rulers to temper the struggle for power and the fruits of power, so that thought may be given to the consequences of the projected action for fundamental values.

Later chapters will examine to what extent the members of Congress have succeeded in probing the principles essential to lasting settlement, and the role which the three factors—participants, mode, and attitudes have played in the process.

FORMS OF CONSTITUTIONAL SETTLEMENT

Constitutional settlements take four leading forms. Two points need stressing here. I am giving the terms "constitutional questions" and "constitutional settlements" a scope wider than that familiar to most lawyers, and I am maintaining that in all of the forms which settlements take, the same elements of responsibility apply. In other words, the same need exists in all four for detaching the constitutional question from its political matrix and considering it on its own merits.

The first and most familiar of the forms is interpretation. The very term "constitutional question" immediately suggests a topic of court argument. I shall employ the term "narrow" to describe questions of that sort, questions necessitating the interpretation of the constitutional document. By the twentieth century the majority of such questions are readily disposed of simply by reference to accumulated court precedents. Yet even these narrow questions sometimes come before Congress. What is the responsibility of Congress for such questions?

A number of such questions of interpretation are ineligible for court review. These include "political questions" such as the scope of presidential powers in foreign relations or the meaning of a "Republican form of government" in Article IV of the Constitution. They also include questions that may never reach the courts because parties lack legal authority to take them there. If such questions are to be settled, Congress must settle them.

Another group of narrow questions embraces those which, while potentially subject to judicial review, have yet to undergo that review. The next few chapters will illustrate this category of questions and analyze the resulting settlements. It would be foolhardy to suppose that no new questions of interpretation remain for congressional consideration because court precedents now cover every possible contingency. This book will show to what extent the Court has relied to some degree on prior congressional deliberation of such questions and how the invitation to leave clarification to the Court may cause difficulties.

Finally, Congress encounters innumerable narrow questions already encrusted with judicial precedents. Is the existence of such precedents a sufficient reason for Congress to abandon inquiry? Does the age of a pertinent precedent affect that responsibility? Does its remoteness from the facts of the situation before Congress? And what if Congress faces a "controlling" precedent; that is, both recent and directly pertinent?

All these categories of narrow, or what some would call legal, questions raise issues of congressional responsibility.

There is, in addition, another sort of question which calls for interpretation, not so much of the words of the constitutional text, as of the spirit, and the accumulated customs, practices, standards of political morality, and tenets of democratic government that surround the words. In other words, there are innumerable actions which Congress has legal power to take which fundamental principle would nevertheless counsel against. I shall call these the "broad" questions of interpretation. Chapter 13 will show how supporters of the Jenner-Butler bill thought they had disposed of the constitutional issue when they demonstrated that under a Supreme Court precedent, Congress had power to withdraw specific areas of appellate jurisdiction from the Supreme Court. Opponents of the bill tried to show that what Congress could do, it ought not to do, since such action would undermine a principle vital to the constitutional order, the independence of the Judiciary. The settlement reached there, like the settlement reached in the congressional disposal of President Roosevelt's court-packing appeal, was in part an affirmation of that principle. The definition of broad questions is subtler than that of narrow, yet the precise character of responsibility raises issues similar to those for narrow questions.

Besides interpretation, three other forms of constitutional settlement exist, in two of which Congress takes a direct hand. Thus, in setting up executive departments, drafting election laws, and framing the organic law for a new territory, it is implementing or supplementing the provisions of the document. Its power here is often clear, yet the precise terms of such legislation may call for a search of constitutional principles not unlike that which took place at Philadelphia. Again, Congress proposes amendments to the Constitution for submission to the states. This form of settlement, as chapter 11 will show, also poses the problem of responsibility and even invites a kind of buck-passing all its own.

Finally, the most complex and worrisome form of settlement occurs at the framing of a constitution. Those who create or revise a constitution face the problem of detachment writ large. If interpretation presents constitutional questions in the usual lawyers' sense, nevertheless implementation, amendment, and framing also call for a search of principles and depend on the factors of participants, mode, and attitudes.

CONCLUSIONS: THE PHILADELPHIA CONVENTION

If one views the Supreme Court as an always-faithful reflector of the intent of the Founding Fathers, it is logical to cast the blame for unpopular or obsolescent judicial interpretations on the framers. Perhaps such a conception of the Supreme Court has influenced scholars like Charles A. Beard in launching criticisms of the Fathers.[56]

Yet interpretation, like the other three forms of constitutional settlement, has an original and creative aspect, and the Fathers ought not be blamed for the interpretative sins of their descendants.

In calling attention to facts concerning the fifty-five men who met in Philadelphia from May to September in 1787, my purpose is to show that the complex of settlements embodied in the constitutional document resulted from the presence in high degree of the same elements of responsibility already described.

Note at the outset the problem which the framers confronted. It was the problem of creating a strong central government by an affirmative transfer of power from the separate, even sovereign, states to central institutions—a government not only efficient in policy-making, but bound down by limitations sufficiently strong to preserve constitutional principles and values and to win popular acceptance. They had to contend with potent and vocal political forces working steadily to maintain the sovereign rights of the states and the local and special interests of regions and localities. George Washington, during the Convention, identified the chief obstacles to a firmer Union as "the independent sovereignty . . . so ardently contended for" by the states and the preoccupation of the states with "local views" and "separate interests."[57] The high voltage latent in these forces compelled the framers to insulate the process of framing from these forces, and to probe principles so thoroughly and so effectively that the people of the states could be persuaded of the conformity of the Constitution to the true general interests and long run purposes of the nation.

The durability of the resulting document is proof of their success. With good cause, Alexander Hamilton could praise the example of America in creating governments by "reflection and choice" rather than by "accident and force."[58] And years later, Thomas Jefferson could counsel a Greek correspondent that permanent constitutions could only result from "quiet, leisure, much inquiry, and great deliberation."[59]

A reading of James Madison's *Notes* shows clearly the success with which the Convention related questions to fundamental principles. To be sure, they drew their principles from many sources, from the common law, from natural law, from writers on political theory, from direct experience with government, yet their awareness of principles was intimate,

37

almost second-nature. Nothing was "so pernicious" observed James Wilson, "as bad first principles,"[60] and nothing, one may assume, was so necessary as good.

In fashioning the new system, the framers very probably sought to rely on all three sanctions of responsibility I have referred to: moral, political, and legal. The character of the men themselves was an important factor in the brilliant and successful exploration of principle. The thirty-four lawyers present, 62 per cent of the whole, brought knowledge of common law and procedural sophistication to the task, and imparted to the document much of its clarity, precision, and inner consistency. Yet others, like George Mason and Elbridge Gerry, and, in a different way, Washington and Benjamin Franklin, contributed to the result. Experience both in politics and in constitution-making was also significant. Of the fifty-five men, seven had signed the Declaration of Independence, twelve had helped draft state constitutions, forty-nine had held office in their states, and forty-three had served in the Continental Congress.[61] The times had brought the best men into politics, and the times had drilled them in the art and science of constitution-building. Experience coupled with wide reading had contributed to constitutional wisdom.

Here constitutional leadership reached a high point. Noteworthy was the role of Virginia. Even without the reluctant Patrick Henry, the absent Jefferson, and the young John Marshall, Virginia had ability equal to the task. Virginians had summoned the states to meet and sent their strongest available leaders, Washington, Madison, Mason, George Wythe, and Edmund Randolph; Virginians directed the Convention, devised the plan, cogently and generally worded, which became the basis for discussion, offered concessions, sought accommodation, sustained the tone of deliberation, and tolerated difference of opinion even among themselves. It is worth noting that Virginians, and men from the Border States settled by Virginians, have continued to take the lead in achieving firm settlements on constitutional issues since the Constitutional Convention.

Furthermore, the Convention furnished an instrument and rules of procedure well calculated to produce settlements. Hamilton had reported for the Annapolis Convention the year before, that what was needed was "a deliberate and candid discussion, in some mode, which will unite the Sentiments and Councils of all the States."[62]

The convention form facilitated this by partially freeing its participants from the pressures of policy-making and fence-mending so common to legislatures, and enabling them to devote themselves to the single task of constitution-building. Destined for early and permanent dissolution, the Convention had no corporate interests of its own to obscure the public interest. Furthermore, the delegates were drawn from all the participating states and from most of the economic sectors of the country. Their settlements would accordingly carry weight at home. It is true that one numerous segment of the population, small farmers, was underrepresented.

But this deficiency was counteracted by the ability and intent of these men to adapt the Constitution to the popular consensus. Thus James Wilson consulted the "*sense* of the people at large," Mason the "genius" of the people and the "mind" of the people, Hamilton the "prejudices" of the people, and Madison the "manners, habits and prejudices" of the people of the different states.[63] The body approximated a psychological, if not a mathematical representation. In addition abundant time, small numbers, and social camaraderie after hours promoted a genuine give and take.

Rules were likewise noteworthy. The Convention began its work by appointing a committee of three lawyers to draft those rules. Chairman was the teacher of Jefferson and Marshall, George Wythe of Virginia, whom Jefferson afterward lauded for his unique command of parliamentary rules.[64] The other members were Hamilton and Charles Pinckney of South Carolina; Pinckney warned that "In a Council so important, as I trust the Federal Legislature will be, too much attention cannot be paid to their proceedings."[65] To these lawyers the procedure for discussion was a condition for its success.

Three features of the procedure deserve comment. While the Virginia plan gave structure and an inner corps of leaders gave direction to the discussion, debate was full and free; complex questions were readily subdivided, and issues which had been decided or postponed were easily reconsidered. The normal mode was adversary argument, followed by a vote. During its opening weeks, the Convention employed a "Committee of the whole House to consider of the State of the American union,"[66] which, like its counterpart in Parliament, combined the flexibility of a committee with full representation.

Occasionally the Convention adopted small committees, but under two precautions. First, they tried wherever possible to have questions of important principle settled in full session before referral; thus when Gerry and Pierce Butler of South Carolina moved to leave to a committee a clause on the executive branch which left undecided whether to vest power in a single or plural executive, James Wilson objected: "Mr. Wilson hoped that so important a branch of the System would not be committed untill a general principle should be fixed by a vote of the House."[67] Second, in constituting committees the delegates considered not only competence but geographical representation.[68] Representation, wrote Charles Pinckney, should be "the sign of the reality," and Pinckney hoped Congress would never "incautiously contract a disease" which was then consuming the House of Commons.[69] The disease of malapportionment was destined to consume not so much Congress itself as its standing committees.

Finally, the rules assured privacy. Just as the streets were spread with sod to muffle the sound of carriage wheels, so the rules promoted seclusion. The Convention removed a provision for record votes on particular motions, in recognition that the body was not legislative but merely advisory and that to require members to go on record would inhibit many from changing their opinions.[70] It also prohibited members from publishing anything said in convention.[71] Despite later objections of Jefferson and others to secrecy, this rule, in combination with others, promoted a kind of scientific objectivity, a mood of experimental inquiry. Men could change their views without dramatizing their inconsistency, and immediate pressures of constituents and groups were hushed. That the discussion served to educate the delegates is verified by the testimony of Randolph, who declared that every member would acknowledge that his opinions had changed between the opening and close of the Convention.[72] It is apparent that the Convention debate taught the delegates, for example, the high importance of having the new government bear directly on individuals rather than on the states in their corporate capacities.[73] The delegates not only spoke, but listened, compared ideas, and reached new insights. Publicity came later, before and during the state ratifying conventions, where the framers defended or attacked the completed document.

The talents of the delegates and the mode for discussion, to be fully effective, required an acceptance of responsibility by those present. To be sure, there were those who counseled a cautious preoccupation with the limited concessions which might be forthcoming from states and people. Were they ambassadors from sovereign states, bound by instructions to minimum concessions, or free agents, commissioned to search principles in detachment so as to create the best, most competent system of constitutional government possible?

The familiar words which Gouverneur Morris of New York attributed to Washington probably epitomized the prevailing attitude. Washington doubted that any plan of the Convention would win adoption, and in recognition that the alternative to an orderly constitutional settlement was a violent settlement, called for acceptance of responsibility: "Perhaps another dreadful conflict is to be sustained. If to please the people, we offer what we ourselves disapprove, how can we afterwards defend our work? Let us raise a standard to which the wise and honest can repair. The event is in the hand of God."[74]

Yet already the Convention gave hints of a basic cleavage, a cleavage partially regional in origin, on the exigencies, the capability, and the responsibility of the members of representative assemblies. Little was said of the obligation of future members of Congress to pay heed to constitutional issues, but some statements presaged future discord. On June 12, Oliver Ellsworth and Roger Sherman of Connecticut moved that members of the future House of Representatives serve one-year terms. A Maryland delegate proposed three-year terms, urging that frequent elections fostered popular indifference and made the "best men" unwilling to perform so precarious a task. Madison of Virginia and Gerry of Massachusetts then took up the issue. Note the divergent conceptions of the representative:

Mr. Madison seconded the motion for three years. Instability is [one of] the great vices of our republics, to be remedied. Three years will be necessary, in a Government so extensive, for members to form any knowledge of the various interests of the States to which they do not belong, and of which they can know but little from the situation and affairs of their own. One year will be almost consumed in preparing for and traveling to & from the seat of national business.

Mr. Gerry. The people of New England will never give up the point of annual elections. They know of the transition made in England from triennial to Septennial elections, and will consider such an innovation here as the prelude to a like usurpation. He considered annual Elections as the only defence of the people against tyranny. He was as much against a triennial House as against a hereditary Executive.

Mr. M[adison] observed that if the opinions of the people were to be our guide, it would be difficult to say what course we ought to take. No member of the Convention could say what the opinions of his Constituents were at this time; much less could he say what they would think if possessed of the information & lights possessed by the members here; & still less what would be their way of thinking 6 or 12 months hence. We ought to consider what was right & necessary in itself for the attainment of a proper Government. A plan adjusted to this idea will recommend itself—The respectability of this convention will give weight to their recommendation of it. Experience will be constantly urging the adoption of it and all the most enlightened & respectable citizens will be its advocates. Should we fall short of the necessary & proper point, this influential class of citizens will be turned against the plan, and little support in opposition to them can be gained to it from the unreflecting multitude.

41

Mr. Gerry repeated his opinion that it was necessary to consider what the people would approve. This had been the policy of all Legislators.[75]

Admittedly, these comments related to both a future Congress and the Convention. Yet embodied in them is a clear divergence concerning the nature of representation itself. The Gerry conception, as applied to a future Congress, would expect of members a close conformity with contemporary constituent opinion, however ill-formed or uninformed; it would work against initiative and discretion in the legislature, where constitutional questions were concerned. Madison's view would support the need for broad discretion and for an independent scrutiny of important questions, including constitutional questions.

The Constitution was the product of solid deliberation. It was the work of men thinking, speaking, and voting not in blocs but as individuals. The document emerged from the Convention not only as the recommendation of the ten states still present, but as the project of the thirty-nine men who individually signed and of others who declined to sign or left before adjournment. The Convention was an exercise in detachment, in the creation of the conditions which enabled representative leaders, lawyers, politicians, planters, merchants, financiers, Southerners, and Easterners to put political pressures aside and conduct a search for principles of constitutional government appropriate for the purpose.

While the Bradley case was a modern counterpart in miniature of the Philadelphia Convention, Congress has on other occasions fallen short of the standards required for constitutional settlements. Congressional behavior is complex and reflects in its variety changes in society itself. Yet the same elements of responsibility that promoted settlement in 1787 and 1951 affect, by their presence or absence, the success of other settlements in Congress. The spelling out of theories concerning the responsibility appropriate for Congress had to await the lessons of practice under the new document.

PART II

The Problem in Origins

3   *Trial and Error, 1789–1801*

When President Washington and the members of the First Congress took office in the spring of 1789, they faced a formidable assignment. The Constitution remained a paper plan; only eleven states had approved it, and many of these had conditioned acceptance on the early adoption of a bill of rights. The executive agencies held over from the Confederation were rudimentary and disorganized, and the Judiciary consisted of little more than six short paragraphs in the constitutional document. The army had fewer than a thousand men. To the slowly forming Federalist party, which, except for an interval in the lower house, controlled the government until 1801, it largely fell to convert a blueprint into a habitable structure.

Action during those years took several forms. Eleven amendments were added to the document, ten of them comprising the Bill of Rights, the eleventh overruling a decision of the Supreme Court.[1] In addition, the early Congresses enacted a myriad of organic laws to implement the constitutional generalities. These laws created executive departments and courts of law and provided for elections and for meetings of Congress itself. They regulated minutely the manner in which the new governing authorities might call on armed forces to defend the country and execute its laws. To support and supplement this program, Hamilton pressed his policies on revenue, the public debt, banks, and customs duties. Lastly, the new officials, aware that they were blazing trails, set up precedents in their dealings with one another and with the public which passed into custom and gave a permanent shape to constitutional practice. The continuing process of changing, implementing, and supplementing the document had begun.

This process forced men to expound the document itself and even to augment it with new creations of constitutional import. The Eleventh Amendment, in effect, gave an interpretation of Article III which contradicted that of the Court. The Judiciary Act of 1789, which implemented that article by organizing the Supreme Court and establishing lower federal courts, necessitated frequent inquiry into the framers' intent. Where that intent was obscure and especially where gaps appeared in the blueprint, officials had to conduct the same kind of search into "first principles" which the framers had undertaken at Philadelphia.

I shall first touch on incipient theories concerning the responsibility of Congress and then examine two instances of constitutional inquiry in order to pinpoint the quality of discussion, the character of participants, the procedures, and the operative attitudes which marked the Federalist period.

THE INCIPIENT THEORIES

As they approached their task, the members of those early Congresses had at hand constituent elements of several distinct theories concerning the consideration of constitutional questions. Formulation of the theories would come later, but some of the rudiments were there, not merely of the two theories stated in chapter 1, but of three theories—that is, the judicial monopoly theory and two versions of the tripartite theory.

In fact, one finds occasional statements that might have given rise to a fourth. If later realities had conformed to the image of Congress which George Washington described in his First Inaugural, then a theory of legislative supremacy in constitutional inquiry might have taken hold. Washington trusted in "the talents, the rectitude, and the patriotism" of the legislators and observed that these qualities were the surest guarantees that "no local prejudices or attachments, no separate views nor party animosities will misdirect the comprehensive and equal eye which ought to watch over this great assemblage of communities and interests." They would also assure that the bases of national policy would be laid in "the pure and immutable principles of private morality" and that the superiority of free government would be demonstrated by "all the attributes which can win the affections of its citizens and command the respect of the world."[2]

The first President was here speaking of policy-making, but his words also had implications for constitutional settlements. Had Congress conformed to the pattern set by this Virginian and given primacy to the national interest and purpose, constitutional questions could have been confided to it with confidence. In later times many would attribute this devotion to the general interest, moral integrity, and sense of responsibility chiefly to the judges. In calling for talents, rectitude, and patriotism in legislators, he implied an exalted conception of the representative function and a high level of maturity in electors. Thomas Jefferson later acknowledged the theory of legislative supremacy in constitutional inquiry to be persuasive, though not convincing. While never effectuated

46

in the United States, the theory operates in Great Britain, and to some degree in other Commonwealth nations.

Among Americans the three other theories have competed for favor. Two comprise versions of the tripartite theory. In 1938 Edward S. Corwin identified these two conceptions as the "political" (or "departmental") and the "juristic."[3] In time Jefferson and Marshall would spell them out, but in the 1790's, the distinction remained obscure. Probably the prevailing doctrine, if any doctrine prevailed, was the tripartite theory in its first or political formulation, affirming as it did that all three departments to some extent possessed independent authority to settle constitutional questions.[4]

The theory assumes, for one thing, that conscience will often serve as a restraining force not only for judges, but for all officials. At its first session in 1789, Congress prescribed for every official, federal or state, other than the President, an oath of office that was a masterpiece of simplicity and directness: "I do solemnly swear (or affirm) that I will support the Constitution of the United States."[5] Note that this was a strictly constitutional oath; its purpose was to bind the officeholder to observe and maintain the limitations on power established by the constitutional document. But the Civil War was to bring a significant change. The stress of conflict and the widespread fear of disloyalty to the Union cause impelled Congress to add a pledge of national loyalty. At first Congress required executive personnel to swear that they would "support, protect and defend the Constitution and Government of the United States against all enemies, whether domestic or foreign. . . ."[6] Chapter 6 will detail the wartime changes in the oath, but here I shall show the outcome. As phrased in 1868 and extended in 1884 to all federal officers and employees other than the President, the present oath combines and even confuses the elements of constitutional fidelity and national loyalty and exacts repetition in its effort to ensure compliance. Today the Senators in groups of four and the Representatives en masse declare:

> I do solemnly swear (or affirm) that I will support and defend the Constitution of the United States against all enemies foreign and domestic, that I will bear true faith and allegiance to the same, that I take this obligation freely without any mental reservation or purpose of evasion, and that I will well and faithfully discharge the duties of the office upon which I am about to enter. So help me God.[7]

One may well speculate over the effect of the altered oath. Perhaps by emphasizing protection of the government and nation from enemies foreign and domestic, it has minimized preservation of constitutional limitations. Clearly the original oath, which, oddly enough, Congress still exacts of state officials,[8] was an effort to harness the force of conscience, even of religious conviction, to the maintenance of constitutional safeguards.

The tripartite theory, however, relies even more on political than on moral sanctions. Later history and the developed tenets of constitutionalism suggest that the oath of office is insufficient reliance for holding legislators to their duty. In the tenth *Federalist* paper James Madison sought protection against the instability, disorder, and injustice characteristic of pure democracies. He found it in republican or representative government, especially when applied to an extended territory such as that of the United States. Aware of contrasts between a New England town meeting and the Virginia House of Burgesses, he praised two features of the proposed republic. One has become famous—his reliance on a pluralism of contending groups as a counterweight to faction—but the other is also of interest here. He seemed to expect the representative process to "refine and enlarge the public views, by passing them through the medium of a chosen body of citizens, whose wisdom may best discern the true interest of their country, and whose patriotism and love of justice, will be least likely to sacrifice it to temporary or partial considerations."[9] Sometimes it might produce an opposite result, but the larger the republic the more it was likely that representatives would be elected whose "enlightened views and virtuous sentiments render them superior to local prejudices, and to schemes of injustice."[10] The Constitution thus offered "a Republican remedy for the diseases most incident to Republican Government."[11] Since Madison saw violation of private rights and the rights of minorities as among those diseases, he must have conceived of the republican principle as a basis for entrusting constitutional settlements to some extent to the national legislature.

Perhaps the chief doctrinal support of the political version of the tripartite theory is the principle of the separation of powers. Three independent, equal, and coordinate departments sustain constitutional limitations in the process of defending themselves from one another; each helps sustain the balance through the use of checks on the actions of the others. Power is made to check power within the government itself, and this mutual interaction helps maintain constitutional standards.

If the political version enjoyed a kind of hegemony in the early decades, it had a potential rival in the juristic version. The conception of the rule of law in combination with the influence of Coke and the common-law tradition and the tacit presuppositions of the legal profession furnished fertile soil for it. The next chapter will show how much the political and juristic versions of the tripartite theory have in common. Yet the major mark of distinction was the kind of emphasis placed on judicial review. For supporters of the juristic version, the Judiciary offers an additional and more secure safeguard for individual rights and for final interpretation of most constitutional provisions.

Occasionally in those early years one detects hints of a third theory, that of judicial monopoly. Conditions would not bring it to the fore until a century and more had passed. Yet some of the elements were there in the suspicion of legislative rectitude which Elbridge Gerry had reflected at Philadelphia and which flourished in the Northern states, and in fears of state legislative encroachments on vested rights and federal powers. Another element lay in emanations from Alexander Hamilton's famous seventy-eighth number of the *Federalist*. Hamilton intended that number as a defense of permanent tenure for judges but expressed views that seemed to repudiate the legislature as a forum for constitutional settlements. The judges, he implied, were *the* mouthpiece of the people where the interpretation of the people's document was concerned. Was the legislature the constitutional judge of its own powers? Did its constructions bind the other departments? This, said Hamilton, could not be the "natural presumption," for the document gives no basis for it. The Constitution could not have intended the representatives to substitute their will for that of their constituents. He continued, "It is far more rational to suppose that the courts were designed to be an intermediate body between the people and the legislature, in order among other things to keep the latter within the limits assigned to their authority."[12] Such language taken uncritically could induce a simple either-or choice between legislature and courts to the benefit of the latter. It could also counsel that a constitution is solely the concern of the people and the judges, with the representatives in a role subordinate in constitutional matters to both. The result could be a conception of judicial review unlimited in scope and in effect and a responsibility for constitutional inquiry that belonged to the courts alone.

A probing of the experience of the early Congresses will suggest to what extent these three theories then commanded support.

THE "DECISION OF 1789": PRESIDENTIAL REMOVAL POWER

Two occurrences on the floor of Congress during the 1790's will supply evidence. The first of these was the familiar "Decision of 1789" on the power of the President to remove major executive appointees and the second the Sedition Act of 1798.

From May 19 to July 20, 1789, the houses had before them a project to establish a department of foreign affairs or, as later termed, the State Department. This first session of the First Congress with its ample quota of Philadelphia Convention delegates created the structure of the new government, including several executive departments and most features of the Judiciary. One may suppose that its actions and utterances would disclose in pristine form the prevailing conceptions of the legislative function at the outset of the government.

Discussion on the bill hinged almost solely on the question whether to make the head of the department removable by the President alone. The Constitution in Article II gave the Senate a power to pass upon major appointments by the President but was silent on the power to remove.[13] The question arose, therefore, whether the bill, by endorsing a power to remove in the President alone, did not by inference violate Article II or other provisions of the Constitution.

In the end, Congress endorsed the provision for presidential removal and thereby gave enduring support to the energy and authority of the executive branch. This legislative decision furnished the Supreme Court of the twentieth century with a precedent of the utmost importance and persuasiveness when a parallel problem came before that tribunal.[14] How did the men of 1789 proceed in reaching their decision?

Prevailing conditions favored calm inquiry, yet the record gives hints of bitterness and dissension. A Georgia Representative asserted that the sponsors of the bill had acted "ingeniously" in their timing of its introduction.[15] A Virginian warned that this effort to enlarge federal powers by construction would excite "alarm and terror" in Virginia and Kentucky.[16]

While the bill was in the Senate, one of its most determined and voluble critics, Senator William Maclay of Pennsylvania, recorded nightly in his journal his impressions of the debate. This veteran of the Revolutionary War and resident of the farming, debt-ridden western section of his state suspected the motives of the bill's backers. His pages repeatedly complain of the tactics of the "court party," and of the ease with which the opponents of the bill succumbed to executive blandishments and recanted. Said he: "I see plainly public speaking on this subject is now useless, and we may put the question where we please. It seems as if a court party was forming; indeed, I believe it was formed long ago."[17]

Vice President John Adams appeared to him a key figure in the plot. The Senate divided evenly on the final vote with Adams breaking the tie, but before that, Adams had drummed up support for the bill: "It was all huddling away in small parties. Our Vice-President was very busy indeed; running to every one. He openly attacked Mr. Lee before me on the subject in debate, and they were very loud on the business. I began to suspect that the court party had prevailed."[18]

50

These words of resentment give early testimony to the difficulty of disentangling political motive from constitutional argument. From that day to this, one side in disputes is wont to interpret the actions and votes of its opponents as dictated solely by political expediency.

Unfortunately, this debate in the Senate, like others of that period, was held in secret and hence went unreported. The House debate, however, does appear in abbreviated form in the *Annals of Congress*.

In their search for the most satisfactory disposition of the constitutional question, the Representatives explored four alternatives. The least acceptable to the House was advanced chiefly by William L. Smith of South Carolina; it held that since the Constitution mentioned only impeachment as a means of removal, it must have intended this as the sole means. Next was the argument that the power to remove derived from the power to appoint and that the Constitution in vesting appointment in the President and Senate had also intended to vest removal in both. Elbridge Gerry of Massachusetts, where an executive council was a prominent feature of the constitution, advanced this position but without notable success. The two remaining theories in combination won the support of a majority. The "legislative-grant" theory held that in delegating to Congress the power to create offices the Constitution implied that Congress had discretion to determine the means of removal. The "constitutional-grant" theory maintained that Article II, in imposing on the President the duty of faithfully executing the laws, implied as a necessary incident of that duty the power of removal at his pleasure. Both theories had strong support, but it was the constitutional grant theory, advocated by James Madison and stressing the illimitable power of the President to remove executive officers, that won Supreme Court approval later on.[19] For this whole debate on the character and exigencies of executive authority and especially for Madison's contributions, the episode has gained renown.

It is equally revealing of our central problem. A close study of the members of Congress at this time shows that lawyers were somewhat less numerous then than later. Yet already one finds their number substantial. While of the fifty-nine members of the House, only 46 per cent were lawyers, 64 per cent of the twenty-two Senators were lawyers. Likewise, lawyers came in larger proportions from New England than from the rest of the country. If the South furnished fewer lawyers than New England, one may suppose that its non-lawyer spokesmen could boast some familiarity with the law; in New England law was becoming a specialized profession; in the South, for planters at least, it was probably, as in England, an important ingredient in the gentleman's education.[20] In the debates, lawyers held the floor—in the House they made up two-thirds of all who spoke. Yet none asserted that the task of resolving constitutional issues was lawyers' business alone.

A surprisingly large number of Representatives took part in the debate. Of the fifty-one who cast votes on the bill, more than half, or twenty-seven, spoke on it. In spite of some repetition, what they said had relevance and cogency. This was doubtless the reflection of broad experience in politics and constitution-making. It is not so much that the House contained numerous Philadelphia Convention delegates—these numbered but a handful of the members; it was more that the members as a whole lived and held leadership in an age of constitutional innovation.[21] Hence, it was possible for John Laurance of New York to declare that where the Constitution was silent, it was proper to rely on the "wisdom of the Legislature."[22]

Leadership in the case for the bill and for presidential removal fell to James Madison. With Hamilton and Jefferson yet to enter the cabinet, Washington doubtless left to the young Virginian the task of conducting the legislation through the House.[23] Virginia contributed the leading figure in the debate, and the South as a whole furnished half of the principal speakers.[24] In this crucial early debate, the constitutional question fell to men combining, under Southern leadership, experience and political insight with legal training.

Throughout the discussion the members showed their awareness of the importance of the issue and of the need of full and thorough deliberation. John Page of Virginia, Jefferson's friend and an opponent of the bill, urged his colleagues "not to cast the die, on which the fate of millions was hazarded, until they had maturely considered the subject."[25] Another Virginian, Richard Bland Lee, wanted the subject decided "on cool and dispassionate reasoning, and not in the heat of fervid declamation, or under . . . fears and apprehensions . . ."[26]

The procedures which the members adopted for the conduct of the debates were successful, for after four full days of discussion, Thomas Sumter of South Carolina, a non-lawyer and opponent of the bill, asked for more discussion of the constitutional point; he said he had gained "considerable information from the discussion which had already taken place, and . . . hoped that more light would still be thrown upon it . . ."[27] That the balloting on the issue found only limited bloc voting by state delegations suggests the effectiveness of the examination of the question.[28]

Several factors promoted an air of detachment and facilitated arrival at a reasoned consensus. With its small numbers and its closed doors, the Senate had obvious advantages in discussion. The House, too, however, was small in contrast with its modern counterpart, and time was abundant. On three separate occasions, the Representatives considered the bill at length.[29] Business was so arranged as to present a clear-cut issue and focus debate on that issue.[30] Repeated roll call votes occurred, and on some members had to voice their convictions on the constitutional issue itself.

Of special interest is the use the members made of committees. In adopting rules for its proceedings, the House had made provision for frequent use of the Committee of the Whole and had thus assured freedom and flexibility for debate.[31] When on May 19 the House took up, not the draft of a bill, but a resolution to agree on general principles concerning the structure of the executive departments, it acted in Committee of the Whole. Some members objected; James Jackson of Georgia "wished the motion had been referred to a sub-committee to digest: it seemed to him they were building the house before the plan was drawn."[32] But the leaders were adamant. It was settled practice in the House, asserted Boudinot, that a Committee of the Whole was "the proper place for determining principles before they were sent elsewhere . . ."[33] Madison wanted the principles settled here; he favored determining the "outlines of all business in a Committee of the Whole." Such a mode "would be found, on experience, to shorten their deliberations."[34]

Thus, the entire membership, acting under rules assuring free discussion, came to a preliminary decision on the constitutional question even before the bill itself was drawn. The drafting fell to a special committee headed by Abraham Baldwin of Georgia; this committee of eleven represented ten of the eleven states and included both opponents and supporters of presidential removal.[35]

Madison had wished to have the "sense of the House explicitly declared,"[36] and clearly he and other leaders wanted the House to come to some decision on the constitutional issue as well as other issues before assigning the details to a smaller committee, chosen with an eye to representation. The mode they chose for deliberation mirrored that employed at Philadelphia and served its purpose well.

If the members practiced the canons of effective deliberation, they likewise avowed a distinct role for Congress in considering constitutional questions. In their speeches they made frequent allusions to the problem of responsibility. From these we can assess the relative standing of the contending theories.

Of all those who spoke in the debate, only one clearly endorsed the judicial monopoly theory. This was the thirty-one-year-old South Carolinian, William L. Smith. Like many Southerners, Smith had studied law at the Inns of Court, but he had not returned to America until 1783.

Besides practicing law in Charleston, he had briefly held state office during the turbulent postwar years. Smith bitterly opposed presidential removal. A determined strict constructionist, he nevertheless inferred a power in the courts to hear and adjudge constitutional questions. For Congress to try to decide such questions would be an "infringement of the powers of the judiciary"; by a similar course, state legislatures had caused much "mischief"; it was the duty of legislators to make laws and of the judges to expound them. For Congress to attempt to bias the judgment of the courts would be "highly criminal."[37]

One other speaker, the non-lawyer Elbridge Gerry, verged on the judicial monopoly theory. The issue, he said, was not one of "policy" but only one of "constitutionality."[38] He wished the House to take no position on the removal power; if, when an issue arose, the President and Senate did not understand the Constitution, they should, he said, "let it go before the proper tribunal; the judges are the Constitutional umpires on such questions."[39] Gerry was even prepared to sanction advisory opinions. In doing so, he reflected a practice which had existed in his own state since 1780. The President, he showed, was empowered by the Constitution to require written opinions of heads of departments, and hence, "the President and Senate may require the opinion of judges respecting this power, if they have any doubts concerning it."[40] Without finally committing himself, the New Englander showed his confidence in the courts as constitutional expositors and his fears of usurpation if Congress were permitted to declare its construction of the Constitution.[41] Only these two—Smith dogmatically, Gerry tentatively—took the extreme position.

Most of the speakers voiced the tripartite theory in one form or the other. Many explicitly or implicitly accepted the doctrine of judicial review but qualified either its scope or its exclusiveness.[42] Several supporters of the bill found it hard to conceive how the constitutional question could be brought before the courts.[43] Judicial review was seen as no substitute for House determination of the question. Abraham Baldwin of Georgia, a Philadelphia delegate, looked ahead to the effect which House neglect of the question might have on the judges: "Let gentlemen consider themselves in the tribunal of justice, called upon to decide this question on a mandamus. What a situation! Almost too great for human nature to bear, they would feel great relief in having had the question decided by the representatives of the people."[44]

In fact, a dominant theme in the debate was that legislative consideration of such questions, instead of being a discretionary power, was a moral and constitutional duty. Most striking were the number and conviction of those asserting that the House should declare its own construction of the Constitution on the central question. Speaker after speaker openly supported such action.[45] These numbered fifteen out of the twenty-seven who spoke, and doubtless many of the remaining twelve acceded to the doctrine tacitly. Three of the six Philadelphia delegates who spoke were among the fifteen and two others took no position on House responsibility. Six of the eight who had attended state ratifying conventions were included, and all of the fifteen but Jackson were lawyers.[46]

These advocates of legislative declaration gave a variety of reasons for their position. That doubt enveloped the question furnished no ground for ignoring it or leaving it to others. Smith was alone in maintaining that the constitutional question should be "left to the decision of the Judiciary."[47] This statement by Michael Stone of Maryland was typical in its acceptance of individual responsibility in the face of doubts:

> I think it necessary, Mr. Chairman, to determine the question before us. I do not think it would do to leave it to the determination of courts of law hereafter. It should be our duty, in cases like the present, to give our opinion on the construction of the Constitution.
>
> When the question was brought forward I felt unhappy, because my mind was in doubt; but since then I have deliberately reflected upon it, and have made up an opinion perfectly satisfactory to myself.[48]

Madison thought that conditions for a legislative decision were auspicious, since the House was here unaffected by passion, factionalism, or bias and all desired to "see and be guided by the benignant ray of truth"; he took comfort in the prospect of subsequent action by the President and Senate, the departments directly affected by the bill.[49] A firm decision now, he said, would give a rule to guide officials. Failure to act would leave the matter in doubt and would necessitate either a new bill for fixed tenure or the extreme measure of impeachment.[50]

Men from all over the Union favored congressional action, from Baldwin of Georgia to the conservative Fisher Ames of Massachusetts, the one to become a Republican, the other an extreme Federalist. The strongest statement of the tripartite theory came from James Madison. In a passage of prophetic insight, Madison denied that House determination would be officious as interfering with the work of President and Senate:

> It is incontrovertibly of as much importance to this branch of the Government as to any other, that the Constitution should be preserved entire. It is our duty, so far as it depends upon us, to take care that the powers of the Constitution be preserved entire to every department

55

of Government; the breach of the Constitution in one point, will facilitate the breach in another; a breach in this point may destroy that equilibrium by which the House retains its consequence and share of power . . .[51]

Some say, he went on, that the legislature has no right to construe the Constitution; that wherever the meaning was in doubt, "you must leave it to take its course, until the Judiciary is called upon to declare its meaning." Madison countered with a strong assertion of the tripartite theory, coupling judicial review with action by the other departments and grounding his position immediately on the separation of powers and ultimately on accountability to the people.

> I acknowledge, in the ordinary course of government, that the exposition of the laws and Constitution devolves upon the Judiciary. But I beg to know, upon what principle it can be contended, that any one department draws from the Constitution greater powers than another, in marking out the limits of the powers of the several departments? The Constitution is the charter of the people to the Government; it specifies certain great powers as absolutely granted and marks out the departments to exercise them. If the Constitutional boundary of either be brought into question, I do not see that any one of these independent departments has more right than another to declare their sentiments on that point.[52]

Madison suggested the manner by which disputes among the branches might be settled. He knew of no government in which provision was made for a specific authority to decide limits of constitutional divisions of power between branches. In all systems there were "points which must be adjusted by the departments themselves, to which no one of them was competent." If this failed, there was no recourse left but "the will of the community, to be collected in some mode to be provided by the Constitution" or "dictated by the necessity of the case."[53] The phrase "necessity of the case" was to become the chief matter in dispute, and on this ground, experience would argue strongly for a primary role for the courts. Madison himself took the matter with a pinch of pragmatism, for after listening to four days of constitutional debate, he insisted that nothing had yet been said which invalidated his doctrine.[54] The question at issue in this debate pertained to the distribution of power among the three federal branches. For this field of constitutional inquiry, at least, the burden of the debate was a clear assertion of responsibility for members of Congress.

In its handling of the removal power, this first of all the Congresses professed and practiced the tripartite theory. Its members had the required qualifications—knowledge and insight, moderation, skill in deliberation, and constitutional leadership. Lawyers and non-lawyers worked together in devising a procedure which gave affected interests a full and fair hearing and strengthened the mood of detachment for the search into constitutional principles. That procedure, supported mainly by Madison and other Southern leaders, paralleled closely that of Parliament and the Philadelphia Convention. For some the temptation to do nothing and leave the question to others was strong, yet most wanted the House to face the issue. Failure to face it and to face it in the proper way could lead to serious difficulties.

THE SEDITION ACT OF 1798 AND FREE SPEECH

Sharply contrasting with this experience of 1789 was the manner in which Congress disposed of the Sedition Act of 1798 and the issues it posed of freedom of speech and of the press.

Passage of this measure was in certain respects one of the most unfortunate events in the history of Congress. A variety of circumstances combined to produce the law. The Federalist party was still in power, but the leadership of that party had declined in authority and awareness of popular sentiments. The reassuring figure of Washington had gone into retirement, and the new President, John Adams, for all his brilliance of political speculation, lacked his predecessor's firmness of execution and moderation of utterance. Although Hamilton had left the cabinet, he continued as a kind of absentee prime minister and directed the policies and performance of many of the Federalists in Congress and the Executive.[55] The courts were solidly Federalist.

The party was proud of its achievements and convinced of its right and duty to rule as an elite. It looked upon the opposition Republicans, led by Vice President Jefferson, as incompetent and even subversive. No one better personified the smug self-assurance of the "High Federalists" than the Secretary of State, Timothy Pickering of Massachusetts, to whom was entrusted the task of enforcing the Alien and Sedition Acts.[56] When the inflexible Pickering declared that the Sedition Act was aimed at the punishment of the "pests of society and disturbers of order and tranquillity,"[57] he was thinking, no doubt, of the spokesmen of the opposition party.

This was only half the picture, however. The French Revolution had gone to extremes and aroused fears of democracy. In the spring of 1798, the United States verged on war with France. The corrupt revolutionary

Directorate in Paris was causing depredations to American commerce, treating the American XYZ emissaries with contempt, and boasting of its organized support in America. The intemperate language of some Republican editors caused resentment among the Federalists and suspicion of collusion with the French. Like so many former colonies turned nation in our own time, the country faced the arduous task of maintaining defenses abroad and security at home and at the same time keeping open the channels of popular discussion and opposition. In the end, the opposition party took office without civil war or military rule, the first instance of such a change under a written national constitution.

The Fifth Congress, at its second session, had to consider a series of war and defense measures. During June and July it passed three laws bearing down on aliens; the Naturalization Act, the Alien Enemies Act, and the Alien Friends Act.[58] The Sedition Act, signed by President Adams on July 14, extended the security program to citizens, and particularly to editors and printers. The second section of this brief bill made it a crime for anyone to "write, print, utter, or publish . . . any false, scandalous and malicious writing . . . against the government of the United States, or either House of the Congress . . . or the President . . . with intent to defame the said government . . . or to bring them . . . into contempt or disrepute; or to excite against them . . . the hatred of the good people of the United States, or to stir up sedition within the United States . . ."[59] The act thus gave Pickering and the Federalist-manned courts a convenient instrument for curbing Republican newspapers and publicists.

It would be hard to exaggerate the gravity of the consequences of this act. On the eve of the presidential campaign in 1800, the Federalist Administration brought a score and more of prosecutions, singling out Republican editors and all the major Republican papers; from the Federalist courts came no fewer than seventeen indictments, resulting in ten convictions.[60] The judges, most notably Justice Samuel Chase, applied the act with obvious partisan rancor. In the end, the electorate repudiated the party and its stringent act by putting Jefferson and his Republicans into power.

The act, however, had left its mark. A generation later, Justice Joseph Story would write that the legislation remained a "theme of reproach" for politicians.[61] The Federalist party had begun its descent to oblivion, the federal courts had temporarily incurred public scorn and contempt, and the Republicans, in their desperation, had adopted measures equally ill-advised and ominous in their consequences—the Virginia and Kentucky Resolutions. In a sense, Madison's earlier warning that one breach of the Constitution would provoke another was borne out. In using the states as forums of protest, the Republicans voiced constitutional arguments which would later furnish convenient justification for state resistance and secession.

It is true, as Leonard W. Levy has emphasized, that the confrontation of 1798 had a favorable consequence. It impelled the Republican victims of the legislation to set forth and defend an interpretation of the freedom of political criticism, broader than that which had prevailed before 1798, which in turn passed into prevailing constitutional doctrine.[62] Yet this long-run benefit for the cause of civil liberty was probably outweighed by the harm to the Union.

One feature of the episode was the way partisan hostility dominated the entire process of consideration. As pressure mounted, the President made no resistance to the legislation and even stated publicly his contempt for press calumny, and the need for disciplining the press. Of all the Federalists, great and small, only one publicly registered disapproval, and this only on grounds of inexpediency. This was the future Chief Justice, John Marshall of Virginia.[63]

In Congress, the Federalists strove for a solid front in support of their program, including the sedition bill. On occasion they caucused for the purpose.[64] One gains the impression from the debates and surrounding circumstances that the Federalists had determined on a stiff sedition measure and were, at this point, merely executing the party will. As the crisis deepened, the Republicans tried to rally in like fashion against the bill.

The record of the House debate clearly reflects the ascendancy of party conflict. In the first place, the two sides seemed unable to converge on the same question; in the second place, each constantly questioned the motives of the other. Thus, Representative Robert Williams, a North Carolina Republican, while noting the "impolicy" of the proposed legislation, confined himself to the constitutional question.[65] James A. Bayard, a Delaware Federalist, observed that the validity of the act was "extremely clear," and the only question was whether the law was necessary.[66] Before the final vote, Albert Gallatin of Pennsylvania asked why such a law had become necessary after nine years without it;[67] Robert G. Harper of South Carolina told him, in effect, that a war was on.[68]

Federalist speakers laid major stress on the conditions which had elicited the bill, and on its necessity. They thought they found ample constitutional authority in the necessary and proper clause, the general welfare clause, Article III, the preamble to the Constitution, and the sovereign power of self-preservation. Harrison G. Otis of Massachusetts declared that, to the majority of the House, the power of Congress appeared "self-evident" and "perfectly plain and undeniable"; he asserted that some were trying to "deceive the people and alarm their fears" over a possible loss of a valued privilege.[69] The Federalists stood solidly on English common law, and especially Blackstone, in rejecting the notion that the First Amendment protected all press criticism from government restriction. From the standpoint of inherited legal doctrine they may well have been correct.[70]

In reply the Republicans declared that the central issue was constitutional. That issue, be it noted, was never precisely defined. The argument which they stressed here and later incorporated into the Virginia and Kentucky Resolutions was that the Constitution had never delegated the power to punish seditious libel to the central government, but had reserved that power to the states.[71] Some, however, did appeal to the First-Amendment safeguard of freedom of speech and press. Edward Livingston of New York said the bill tried to deal with error and truth by "force of arms" rather than by reason, and John Nicholas of Virginia called freedom of the press the "heart and life of a free Government."[72] These were tentative efforts to develop a new constitutional principle, a principle which many of the framers would probably not have understood or accepted—the right of the political opposition to organize, advance its views, and gain office. Gallatin, indeed, asserted that the bill could only be seen "as a weapon used by a party now in power, in order to perpetuate their authority and preserve their present places."[73] Yet the meaning of the principle and its bearing on values latent in free and representative government never came into focus. The bitterness of the party conflict and the suspicion each party held of the motives of the other prevented a genuine meeting of minds on the constitutional issue.

Another noteworthy feature of the episode was the character of the chief participants. In the Senate, James Lloyd of Maryland and in the House, Robert Goodloe Harper of South Carolina launched and directed the Federalist attack.[74] Both were lawyers, both were young (Harper only thirty-three), both were weak in political experience, and both had only recently taken up Federalism after election as Republicans. One may suppose that among the qualities that caused party managers to give them the lead were eloquence and skill in debate and the fervor of the convert. The *Dictionary of American Biography* describes Harper as "self-confident to the point of bumptiousness" and "the most insolent man in the house."[75] The ease with which this pro-French democrat in Charleston became a pro-British ultra-Federalist and social lion at Philadelphia hints at an incapacity for objectivity and moderation.

In some respects, Harper typified the participants in the House debate, especially the Federalists. Thus, all of the nine Federalists who spoke on the bill were lawyers as were nearly two-thirds of those who voted "aye" in the final roll call. On the Republican side, only five of the eight who spoke and one-third of those who cast "nay" votes were lawyers.[76] By this time the quota of lawyers in each house—71 per cent in the Senate, 50 per cent in the House—had risen to approximately the modern level. Again New England led all other regions but one; four-fifths of its Senators and five-eighths of its Representatives had had legal training.[77]

It was natural, therefore, for the young Boston lawyer, Harrison Gray Otis, to support the bill with arguments drawn from the English common law. Otis recoiled from the political speculation that marked both the American and French Revolutions; like so many others, he turned away from ideology and looked for guidance in what he called the "immemorial laws and customs of the country."[78] To him, the common law seemed the safest standard for interpreting the technical terms of the Constitution,[79] and seditious libel had long been a crime at the English common law. Federalist speakers, like some Federalist judges, found authority in Article III, even in the absence of a statute, for the courts to try such crimes as offences against the United States. Here the lawyers drew on their professional training not merely for logical thinking and fair procedure, but for substantive readings of the Constitution. But to go "over the water for precedents," asserted Nathaniel Macon, was to reason "from a people in a very different situation from that of Americans." This was to neglect the political realities and political values of the new situation.[80]

This oversight may have resulted from their youth; Federalist speakers averaged thirty-six and Republican thirty-nine years of age, and some leading debaters were much younger.[81] This was no rarity, however, for that time. Somewhat more important was lack of political experience. Harper, Otis, and Allen, who led the Federalist assault, had served briefly in state legislatures, Otis for only a year; but only Harper had served previously in Congress. Gallatin, Nicholas, Livingston, and Macon, the leading Republican speakers, all had served earlier in Congress as well as in state legislatures; Gallatin had even attended a state constitutional convention.

Coupled with inexperience was extremism. At this session the proportion of moderates in the House hit a low point,[82] and by June and July many experienced leaders who remained, especially from the Republican side, had departed in dismay to their states. In the crisis, counsels of moderation, the lessons of a brief national experience, and the attitudes and the convictions of the people were forgotten.

Harper, in fact, typified the tone of the proceedings. In the debate on the Alien bill, he strongly implied that the Republicans were resorting

61

to constitutional arguments only as a means of obstructionism and that their leaders were leagued with traitors and hence sought to cripple the government in its defense efforts. In a heated reply, Albert Gallatin, Swiss-born and educated, called for a show of facts to support such charges. Otherwise the impugning of motives could only do harm. He appealed for a return to the conditions of effective discussion. As the *Annals of Congress* reported it: "Mr. G. did not believe that insinuations of this kind, thrown out against members upon this floor, were calculated to produce the welfare of the country. If gentlemen desire unanimity in the councils of the nation, it could only be produced by an exercise of rational confidence in the motives of one another."[83] The report of Harper's reply stated "Mr. Harper did not know how it was that some gentlemen on this floor should be so extremely sore upon everything which relates to motives. He had said nothing about the motives of any gentleman in this House. The gentleman from Pennsylvania, however, knew best whether his motives are pure or not; but when a gentleman who is generally so very cool, should all at once assume such a tone of passion, as to forget all decorum of language, it should seem as if the observation had been properly applied to that gentleman."[84] In this whole affair, the leadership of lawyers failed to assure a detached inquiry; in the heat of partisan extremism, the Federalists assumed that their party's reading of the Constitution was the Constitution.

The manner in which the constitutional questions were considered departed in important respects from earlier practice. In the upper House, Senator Lloyd's bill, which was referred to committee on June 27 and which later became the basis of the House bill, was so harsh that Hamilton scrawled a cautionary note to Oliver Wolcott, Secretary of the Treasury, complaining that it was likely to provoke civil war.[85] After brief skirmishes on the second, the Federalists arranged to bring up the bill for debate on the Fourth of July. The outcome was a nearly straight party vote of 18 to 6 in favor of the bill.[86]

Some notion of the character of the Senate's deliberations on this epochal bill is given in a letter which Senator Stevens T. Mason of Virginia sent to Vice President Jefferson: "There seemed to be a particular solicitude to pass on it that day . . . The drums, Trumpets and other martial music which surrounded us, drowned the voices of those who spoke on the Question. The military parade so attracted the attention of the majority that much the greater part of them stood with their bodies out of the windows and could not be kept to order. To get rid of such a scene of uproar and confusion, an attempt was made at adjournment and then of a postponement of that question. These were both overruled and the final decision taken."[87]

This travesty on deliberation was not entirely duplicated in the House. As early as mid-May, Representative Samuel Sewall of Massachusetts, a somewhat moderate Federalist, sought and got permission for his Committee on Commerce and Defense to bring in a general alien and sedition bill, modeled, one may suppose, on recent British legislation. In June, the House debated the resulting bill, and again touched on possible sedition legislation during discussion of the Alien Friends Bill. The extremist Harper had taken command by July 5, when the Senate bill reached the House; this bill was subjected to two days of procedural wrangling and amended on the basis of Harper's own proposals, discussed in Committee of the Whole July 9, and debated and passed with amendments on July 10.[88]

Here, by later standards, were many of the ingredients of fair procedure: adequate time, referral to committees for study and recommendations, debate on general policy and details, with opportunity for a hearing of varied opinions and arguments, and a final roll call vote with four-fifths of all members participating. The House Federalists, led by their lawyer members, showed awareness of canons of fair consideration.

Furthermore, the Republicans appeared to be negligent, evasive, and obstructionist. Many Republicans, especially in the Senate, had left their posts and returned to their native states; Vice President Jefferson had at first deplored this practice, but at length had followed suit.[89] House Republicans appeared to be trying to throttle discussion when they pressed to a vote a motion to reject outright the Senate bill.[90] When referral to the Sewall Committee was proposed, it was a Republican who initiated a successful move to prevent it.[91] One might assume that the whole Republican effort, including the argument of unconstitutionality, was one massive political maneuver.

These Republican moves, however, must have been dictated by desperation. By July, the High Federalists were in the saddle, and their spokesmen, Lloyd and Harper, in command of Senate and House majorities. Repeated statements by these and other leaders strongly suggested a determination to strike at Republican leaders and journalists. Preliminary votes showed a high degree of party cohesion behind Federalist measures; and Senator Lloyd got the Senate to refer his bill with little if any prior discussion to a committee made up entirely of confirmed Federalists,[92] contrary to prevailing bipartisan practice. Jefferson's lieutenant in the Senate wrote concerning the opening day of House debate: "The sedition bill yesterday brought up personal abuse and with more violence than ever. It evident [sic] that the political de-

63

lirium which has for some time raged has not yet got to its highest pitch."[93]

Why, in the more deliberative House, however, did some Republicans object to committee consideration of the Senate bill? Perhaps they were discouraged by Chairman Sewall who answered Harper's proposal for referral by saying the committee had generally considered the subject and supported the bill because its own earlier bill was "pretty much the same as this." If the pending measure were passed, he presumed the committee would withhold its own bill.[94]

Yet the answer probably lies elsewhere. For one thing, Harper's proposal for referral to a select committee, as a substitute for the Committee of the Whole, raised an issue of procedure on which the parties, throughout this session, had taken opposite stands.

This running dispute over procedure, with members lining up by party and by region, had an ominous ring. It had shown up early in the session. It was customary after the President's message, for the House to refer particular sections of the message to select committees and to request them to report on those sections. On December 11, however, soon after Adams' message, Sewall asked leave for his Committee on Commerce and Defense not merely to report but to report by bill. The Republicans, spearheaded by Nicholas of Virginia, objected heatedly, contending that before a committee such as this proceeded to the details of a bill, the House, in Committee of the Whole, should settle the principles at stake. It had never been House practice, asserted Joseph Varnum of Massachusetts, to take up "great national questions" until it had decided them in Committee of the Whole.[95] Gallatin agreed: "He knew of no instance where a committee, appointed for general purposes, had asked this leave. They had several standing committees; but they never came forward at the beginning of a session to ask leave to report by bill . . ."[96] Evidently the weight of House practice since the beginning had been to discover the sense of the whole in open informal sessions for the guidance afforded by decision on principle.[97]

But many Federalists had acquired a distaste for the Committee of the Whole. In the First Congress, the Boston Federalist, Fisher Ames, had found it a bad way to do business. "Virginia," he had written, "is stiff and touchy against any change of the Committee of the Whole . . . They are for watching and checking power; they see evils in embryo; are terrified with possibilities, and are eager to establish rights, and to explain principles, to such a degree, that you would think them enthusiasts and triflers."[98]

Federalists now rallied to Sewall's side. Samuel Sitgreaves said select committees, by gathering and organizing the facts and laying them before the House, served as "pioneers of discussion." Such committees alone

64

fully possessed the pertinent facts and could best judge the form in which to present the subject.[99]

A new member, Thomas Pinckney of South Carolina, confessed ignorance of House practice, but thought the proposal correct. He said the House should avoid "abstract questions" for it was liable to misunderstand them and to reach wrong decisions.[100] On this procedural point, the Federalists were now reflecting a skepticism about the capacity of representative bodies to deliberate, at least in the absence of firm executive or other leadership. Yet not for some years would the effort to make standing committees the "pioneers of discussion" succeed.[101] So evenly were the parties balanced in December when the House voted on Sewall's motion for leave to bring in a bill, that only the Speaker's affirmative vote broke the tie.

In addition, it is probable that the Republicans opposed Harper's effort to refer the Senate sedition bill because of dissatisfaction with the House committee's complexion. The Senate committee was scarcely an encouraging model; the Sewall Committee was evidently little better. From 1790 on, the Speaker of the House had been empowered to appoint all select committees "unless otherwise specified." Jonathan Dayton, Speaker in 1798, had become an ardent Federalist, and showed it by placing five Federalists on this seven-man committee.[102] The American Speaker, unlike his present-day British counterpart, was distinctly partisan and was here constituting committees in a partisan fashion.[103]

Here then in embryo was a later obstacle to fair and searching congressional consideration of constitutional questions—the standing committee, empowered to discuss, draft, and report bills, and chaired and constituted in such a manner as to fail accurately to represent important shades of opinion, major interests, and regions.

If the Republicans doubted that floor discussion would be effective, the final vote bore them out. When this roll call came on July 10, the parties faced each other with virtually unbroken fronts. The forty-four favoring the sedition bill were, with one possible exception, all Federalists; the forty-one opposed, with three noteworthy exceptions, were all Republicans.[104]

The members likewise strongly diverged along regional lines; New Englanders favored the bill by 25 to 3, and the Southerners opposed it by 23 to 4. Between July 5, when discussion began after the defeat of a motion to reject, and July 10, when a vote on the bill ended discussion, only three Federalists[105] and no Republicans had shifted their positions. In a time of hysteria and partisan rancor, procedures for ease of amendment and open debate may prove insufficient to ensure genuine deliberation. The calm communication between minds that had marked the 1789 episode was gone in 1798.

Only two of the Philadelphia framers remained in the House, and when one of these, Speaker Dayton, charged the other with grossly misrepresenting the intent of the framers, this other, Abraham Baldwin of Georgia, decried the tone of the proceedings. Never, he said, had the "councils of the United States" exhibited such harshness of manner and indecorum as in this Fifth Congress. The members of the House lived in "situations so remote from each other that there is scarcely a sufficient degree of mutual dependence to secure the usual deference and civility of social life towards each other while they are together transacting public business . . ." He said that he had tried to "cultivate that respect and decorum in his deportment to each individual who has been thought by his country worthy of a seat . . . which he thought indispensably necessary to secure proper respect and decorum to the House itself."[106]

In this new and unique federal system, with its tenuous links of union, it was important that the representatives of parties and of regions agree on sound procedures and proprieties. Discord or departures could jeopardize the Union itself. Already in 1798 there were signs of trouble: party and regional discord over the capabilities of the representative body as a whole and crisis-induced departure from committees truly representative in complexion.

If, under the impetus of extremism and procedural vagaries, the adversaries in the debate never found common ground on the constitutional question, they nonetheless spoke out on the nature of such questions and the responsibility for considering them. Federalists showed less concern with the problem than Republicans. Fearing foreign attack and domestic subversion, they repeatedly cited the emergency, the sovereign character of the government, and its right to self-preservation. As shown, they found legal precedents in the common law, with its leanings toward prerogative powers. They deemed it unthinkable that the Constitution placed shackles on the government at such a time. It was they who, to support the law, drew on what might then have been called technical legal arguments.

By contrast, the Republicans looked for principles more appropriate for the American scene and the new political system—principles yet to be rooted in what we now call constitutional law. Fearing centralized government and a precedent which might permanently jeopardize free expression and responsible popular government, they sought restraining standards in the Tenth and First Amendments. Taken together, their speeches comprise a kind of dialogue on the need for constitutional limitations and the problem of enforcing such limitations.

Their mood was earnest and urgent. To them the maintenance of constitutional restraints had a high priority. Livingston thought a breach in the Constitution was more serious than "war, pestilence and every other calamity . . ." "Time," he continued, "may remove these, but of an unforgiving, dreary despotism, who can see the end?"[107]

One Southerner intimated that he might have withheld his vote to ratify the Constitution had such a law as the one under consideration been in prospect,[108] and another observed portentously that if the government could pass this bill it could as validly emancipate the slaves.[109] If this law should pass, cried Macon, it was doubtful that any future bill could be successfully opposed on the score of unconstitutionality.[110]

In their desperate search for sanctions, the Republicans invoked moral and even religious obligations. Livingston referred to the influence of "every sanction, human and divine."[111] Several cited the constitutional oath as a restraining force;[112] however, that the oath alone was an insufficient means of control is the burden of this comment by Senator Mason in a letter to Jefferson; evidently speaking of Senator Martin's part in the July Fourth debate, he asserted: "Our friend M—— in character with himself made a speech of ¾ of an hour to prove the [Sedition] Bill unconstitutional, which after he had repeatedly asserted and almost sworn to, he voted for the passage of the Bill to evince his determination to support Government, and was afterwards silly enough to declare publicly that the Bill was unconstitutional but that it was a lesser evil to violate the constitution than to suffer printers to abuse the Govt."[113]

It is no surprise that the House Republicans placed greater stress on political than on moral restraints. When Edward Livingston advanced the revolutionary notion that individuals have a right to disregard laws which "manifestly infringe the Constitution,"[114] he touched off a searching discussion. The Federalist, John Allen of Connecticut, found proof in this comment that the insurrectionary movement had penetrated Congress itself; the Republicans consequently sought to tone down the comment. Livingston himself shifted his ground slightly by asserting that the legislators were the servants of the people and that the "people of the United States" were final judges of constitutional validity.[115] Congress itself could avert revolution by refraining from adoption of "unconstitutional and arbitrary laws."[116] Macon presaged the Republicans' resort to the state governments as forums for denouncing the Sedition Act in declaring that "This Government depends upon the State Legislatures for existence."[117]

Several times, members from both sides spoke of judicial review. None of these even hinted that the existence of the judicial check constituted any sort of justification for minimizing congressional responsibility, but all visualized it as an additional precaution for the protection of individuals. Thus Allen told Livingston that it was for the courts, and not for individuals, to decide whether particular laws of Congress were constitutional.[118] The Republican Gallatin asserted that, notwithstanding the ultimate control of the people, "appeal must be made to another tribunal, to the Judiciary in the first instance, on the subject of a supposed unconstitutional law."[119] Just before the vote, Macon concluded that if the majority were determined to pass the law, all he could do was "hope that the Judges would exercise the power placed in them of determining the law an unconstitutional law, if, upon scrutiny, they find it to be so."[120]

If no speaker denied such a power in the Judiciary, none minimized a parallel responsibility in Congress. In fact, the whole discussion evidently proceeded on the assumption that Congress can and should attend to constitutional questions. The character and content of the debate reflects conviction on this point. Macon's comment that several laws had previously been adopted which violated the spirit, but none which directly violated the letter of the Constitution,[121] suggests a belief in such a responsibility, neglected yet real.

In other words, the legislators of 1798 like those of 1789 evidently saw need for constitutional inquiry by both Congress and the courts. Missing from the discussion were allusions familiar to later generations, allusions to the question as strictly legal, to the all-embracing final and exclusive control of the Supreme Court, and, of course, to rules of constitutional law. Citations to American court precedents were almost non-existent,[122] for the growth of a body of constitutional law, incorporating as it would elements of the common law and principles of popular constitutional government, lay with the future.

Just as 1789 had thrust on Congress a narrow constitutional question under the Executive Article, so 1798 thrust on it a similar, if more serious, question under the First Amendment. Its failure to achieve the kind of constitutional settlement the crisis required resulted ultimately from public alarms, and immediately from the heat of the party struggle. Federalists in Congress, in the Executive, and even in the Judiciary had welded themselves into a bloc behind a party policy. By sounding the alarm and mobilizing their numbers in Congress, they deterred individual members from thinking and voting as free agents. While accepting congressional responsibility, they seemed deaf to the opposition's assertions that a constitutional question existed. Extremist leadership and a crisis mood caused them to view procedural safeguards as mere hurdles in the path to a predetermined party goal.

At the next session Jefferson would deplore a new tactic of the Federalists. In January 1799, they received Republican arguments against sedition legislation at first in total silence and later with noisy commotion.[123] Yet even in 1798 communication was absent figuratively. It was this absence of true interchange that led the Federalists to fall back on ancient English legal precedents and to ignore at their own ultimate cost both the emerging principles of the constitutional order and the "sense of the people."

CONCLUSIONS

With the election of 1800 and the ascendancy of the Republicans, the years of Federalist rule and constitutional implementation abruptly ended. It had been a period of experimentation, a period which, as the decline of the electoral college shows, had subjected the work of the framers to testing. Who should resolve constitutional issues and by what processes—these questions underwent the same empirical scrutiny as did the structure of government itself.

Prevailing thinking dispersed the consideration of constitutional issues rather widely; during this brief decade, no fewer than four possible forums for that consideration, the executive branch excepted, were discussed. The early adoption of eleven constitutional amendments, ten correcting the framers and one the Court, shows that as an ultimate, although cumbersome appeal this mode had promise.

Two additional forums, Congress and the courts, served actively during the period. The tripartite theory enjoyed broad support and as yet no sharp distinction was drawn between the political and juristic versions. This theory credited all branches of the central government with a share in the function of constitutional inquiry and settlement and brought the electorate into the process as a kind of corrective for certain errors. In these formative years Congress carried the major share of that function.

To judge from the foregoing episodes the Senate did poorly, but this impression may be the result of secrecy and the attendant paucity of records. In the House, especially in the Committee of the Whole, constitutional questions evidently received effective deliberation under most conditions.

The coincidence of crisis, inexperienced and immoderate newcomers, and latent disagreement over the capabilities of the legislature caused a breakdown of procedures and produced a threat to the new system of government. Rudiments of later House practice were already present in 1798.

In the end the voters, by replacing the Federalists with Republicans and repudiating the Alien and Sedition Acts, restored order and sanity. This was possible, however, only because top leaders sustained a course of moderation and forbearance. Adams had pressed for peace with France and downgraded extremists in his own party, Jefferson had cautioned his followers to call off their military preparations in Virginia,[124] and Marshall, now in Congress, had caused a sufficient break in Federalist unity to thwart passage of a law which might have produced a Federalist administration in 1801 in the event of a Republican victory at the polls.[125] Its performance in 1798 may well have undermined the reputation of Congress to such an extent that many, especially Republicans, looked to other forums for constitutional settlements.

The courts, of course, remained a third possibility. Slow in starting, and occasionally misjudging the temper of the American public, as in the Chisholm case, they nevertheless had deep roots in popular thinking. Potentially they had promise, yet the partisan behavior of Federalist judges in applying the Sedition Act must have caused dismay, particularly among Republicans. But for Chief Justice Marshall that behavior might have prevented the realization of that promise.

Jefferson and his followers took sanctuary in a fourth alternative, the state veto. They elaborated it in the Virginia and Kentucky Resolutions by stressing the states as parties to the constitutional compact and hence ultimate judges of federal powers. Republican electoral success in 1800 removed the necessity for the state veto and hence veiled its anarchistic tendency. What were needed, as Jefferson was aware, were forums national in operation but less ponderous than the amendment process. Some, however, were soon responding to this need by assigning the whole task of constitutional interpretation to the federal Judiciary. The Federalist New Hampshire Legislature in 1799 replied to the Virginia doctrine by resolving that the duty of deciding the constitutionality of federal laws was "properly and exclusively confided to the judicial department."[126] The precipitancy of the Federalist majority in Congress in 1798 had driven the opposition to seek defense in the state veto; now New England Federalists were attacking that veto in language which, taken literally, asserted the judicial monopoly theory.

Clearly the 1790's furnished an experiment on which leaders would soon build the principal theories of responsibility.

4   *The Emerging Theories*

The opening years of the new century were crucial. Experience had demonstrated the need of spelling out in theory and implementing in practice the shares of Congress and the courts in the consideration of constitutional issues. Both branches had incurred popular odium because of the Alien and Sedition Acts. Congress had performed better than the courts, however, since the House, at least, had afforded the Republican minority some opportunity to be heard, whereas the federal courts had presented an apparently solid wall of partisan resistance to Republican appeals to the Constitution. Both branches were in need of renewal and procedural reform.

The task of enunciating theories and instituting reform fell largely to two Virginians, Thomas Jefferson and John Marshall. During his eight years in office, Jefferson used his influence as President and party leader to carry into effect his matured ideas about responsibility, ideas that he would long continue to hold. With him, accordingly, will always be associated the political version of the tripartite theory. Almost simultaneously, John Marshall assumed leadership of the Supreme Court, and, during his thirty-four years in that post, he worked steadily to articulate the juristic version of that theory and to give the Judiciary a prominent, though not exclusive, share in the task of constitutional deliberation. Party allegiance, personal dislike and mistrust, and, to a degree, political conviction embittered the struggle between the two men. This invites the assumption that their positions were totally antithetical. An analysis of their utterances and acts will help to show those points on which they diverged and those on which they agreed. A study of Marshall's two young associates, William Johnson and Joseph Story, will give further evidence of the points in dispute and likewise suggest some of the roots of the third theory, that of judicial monopoly.

It is easy now to forget that all these men faced a common task—the perfecting of a viable central government for dispersed political communities. Local and sectional interests constantly tended to produce basic conflicts, whether between seaboard East and frontier West, or commercial and financial North and plantation South. Such interests sought expression through the separate states and through assertion of state sovereignty. The task of statesmen was so to create and manage central institutions as to evoke popular support for the federal government and hence to counteract centrifugal tendencies. The individual states were too inclined to see a menace to their immediate interests in federal policies or to overlook the long-run effects of their own policies on the Union; accordingly, they assailed federal measures as unconstitutional and asserted a right to resist.

The situation cried out for institutions and procedures which would maintain an impartial surveillance over federal powers while effectively confining state governments within a sphere of power narrow enough to prevent conflicts with federal interests or with those of other states. It was primarily federalism, and not the separation of powers or the rights of individuals, which increasingly occasioned the bitterest constitutional controversies. Jefferson and Marshall, each in his respective office, met the challenge.

JEFFERSON AND THE POLITICAL VERSION

When Jefferson became President in 1801, he embarked on what he often later referred to as a revolution in the principles of the government. In this enterprise he had the support of his Republican party, rooted in Virginia, successful in the recent elections, and now in command of the legislative and executive branches. Only the courts lay outside its control, and President Adams had made sure that for the time being those who manned the bench for life terms were safe Federalists. But that party was soon to decline, and within a decade Republicans would predominate on the Supreme Court.

The year he took office President Jefferson wrote out his conception of official responsibility for constitutional issues. In claiming a power as President to pardon Sedition Act violators on the ground that that act was unconstitutional, he set forth the doctrine that each branch of the government within its own assigned functions and where it acts without appeal could apply its own judgment in deciding constitutional questions. Thus the three branches were equal and independent in constitutional decision-making within their respective spheres, as thus defined.[1]

The principles which Jefferson and many of his party sought to apply in assuring a proper handling of constitutional issues by Congress were, first and foremost, republicanism, second, the separation of powers, and third, deliberation fortified by the rule of law. On taking his oath, the new President stated his principles in detail. This First Inaugural, accordingly, contains a classic statement of the Jeffersonian view of the guide lines for the new government. The will of the majority should prevail, he declared, but to be "rightful," that will must be "reasonable."[2]

The formulation which Jefferson then gave to his guiding concepts is noteworthy on several counts. First, they were stated as principles, and not, in the language of some present-day writers, as policies. Those pertaining to foreign affairs, the economy, and defense would, in the course of time, become outmoded, at least in part. Others were, in import, essentially constitutional. Thus he expressed his first principle as "equal and exact justice to all men, of whatever state or persuasion, religious or political." Jefferson then gave his prescription for managing the federal system: "the support of the State governments in all their rights, as the most competent administrations for our domestic concerns and the surest bulwarks against anti-republican tendencies; the preservation of the General Government in its whole constitutional vigor, as the sheet anchor of our peace at home and safety abroad."

This exaltation of states' rights and this confinement of federal powers to matters of diplomacy, defense, and domestic order would gradually lose its force. Nevertheless, it represented an effort to reason out in principle a basis for the federal division of power. It likewise embodied the lasting values of local and regional autonomy.

Other principles concerned the working of democratic government, for example, "a jealous care of the right of election by the people—a mild and safe corrective of abuses which are lopped by the sword of revolution where peaceable remedies are unprovided; absolute acquiescence in the decisions of the majority, the vital principle of republics, from which is no appeal but to force, the vital principle and immediate parent of despotism; . . . the supremacy of the civil over the military authority; . . ." Finally, Jefferson spelled out principles which served to underpin the democratic structure: "diffusion of information and arraignment of all abuses at the bar of the public reason; freedom of religion; freedom of the press, and freedom of person under the protection of the habeas corpus, and trial by juries impartially selected."[3] Here was tacit recognition that the nation would continue to confront broad constitutional questions as well as narrow, and that settlement of these questions would require not merely a balancing of policies but a return to first principles.

Again, note that Jefferson addressed his remarks to his fellow-citizens. Aware that sole reliance on the Judiciary for the maintenance of constitutional limitations was illusory, he offered these as enduring standards by which the electorate might judge the conduct of legislators and, in fact, of all officials:

These principles form the bright constellation which has gone before us and guided our steps through an age of revolution and reformation. The wisdom of our sages and blood of our heroes have been devoted to their attainment. They should be the creed of our political faith, the text of civic instruction, the touchstone by which to try the services of those we trust; and should we wander from them in moments of error or of alarm, let us hasten to retrace our steps and to regain the road which alone leads to peace, liberty, and safety.[4]

The moral tone of the speech was obvious. Free republican government was as much the product of deliberate effort as of fortunate circumstance. To survive, it required the continuing application of industry and intelligence in the education of citizens and in the conduct of government. It called for something besides judicial power and judicial zeal. Jefferson's expression, "the bar of the public reason," revealed his assumption that in the last analysis the electorate was capable of a measure of impartial judgment.

To the new Congress, Jefferson was soon expressing his confidence that it was potentially a deliberative body, and was exhorting it to realize this potentiality. In his first Annual Message, he declared that as President his function was to inform the legislators and carry their judgment into effect. Congress embodied the "collected wisdom" of the Union. "The prudence and temperance of your discussions," he told the legislators, "will promote within your own walls that conciliation which so much befriends rational conclusion, and by its example will encourage among our constituents that progress of opinion which is tending to unite them in object and in will."[5]

The people were the safest depository of power, and hence their representatives must be held strictly accountable to them. Likewise officials were obligated to deliberate with restraint and moderation, first, to reach reasoned decisions expressing common interests of the whole people, and second, to educate the electorate. By their own conduct, officials could strengthen and sustain those conditions which assured a citizenry both loyal and informed.

It is not surprising, therefore, that throughout his career, Jefferson propounded a theory attributing a substantial share in the settlement of constitutional issues to the elected legislature. He spoke on the point in a series of letters spread over two decades.[6] Thus, as early as 1804 he denied the view which Abigail Adams of Massachusetts pressed upon him, namely, that the constitutionality of laws was for the Supreme Court alone to decide.[7]

Two letters written during his retirement elaborated his position. In 1815, he flatly opposed the proposition of a Georgia correspondent that the judges possessed "exclusive authority to decide on the constitutionality of a law."[8] Nothing in the Constitution, said Jefferson, warranted such a view. In his mind only two doctrines possessed merit. One of these favored legislative supremacy. This had distinct advantages in that it ascribed final control to the public at elections; the voters, by repudiating their representatives at the polls, could offer judges and executive officials support for opinions contradicting those of the legislature. Such a doctrine might well have conformed to pure republican theory. It prevails, with some qualifications, in present-day Britain.

Yet Jefferson out of respect for the separation of powers preferred another doctrine, attributing a share in the resolution of constitutional questions to each branch:

> Questions of property, of character and of crime being ascribed to the judges, through a definite course of legal proceeding, laws involving such questions belong, of course, to them; and as they decide on them ultimately and without appeal, they of course decide *for themselves.* The constitutional validity of the law or laws again prescribing executive action, and to be administered by that branch ultimately and without appeal, the executive must decide for *themselves* also, whether, under the Constitution, they are valid or not. So also as to laws governing the proceedings of the legislature, that body must judge *for itself* the constitutionality of the law, and equally without appeal or control from its co-ordinate branches. And, in general, that branch which is to act ultimately, and without appeal, on any law, is the rightful expositor of the validity of the law, uncontrolled by the opinions of the other co-ordinate authorities.[9]

This version of the tripartite theory appeared to distinguish between types of questions by their nature and accordingly to imply a distinction between what were later to be called political and justiciable questions.

One weakness in this position lay in its very vagueness. Who should control the availability of appeal? On this point, Marshall would seize in his assertion of broad judicial review. Moreover, in time legislators and executives would often come to regard themselves as "controlled by the opinion" of the Judiciary. Yet a zone of independent determination would remain to both political branches, and insofar as each branch continued to make determinations of what Jefferson called not policies, but "laws," just that far would legislatures exercise a legitimate share in constitutional inquiry.

Jefferson himself mentioned another objection in this same letter. It was true that contradictory decisions by different branches would be inevitable. Yet he was prepared to rely in most cases on the prudence of

75

officials and the authority of public opinion for accommodation. From British and American experience Jefferson concluded that divergences in decision need not produce inconvenience.[10]

He elaborated these views five years later. A lawyer from Pittsfield, Massachusetts, William C. Jarvis, sent him a copy of his recent book, *The Republican*.[11] In setting forth the "principles" as well as the "policy" of "free states," this New Englander had dealt cursorily with the legislature, but had exalted the judiciary. In America, in contrast to Britain, he said, the separation of powers provided scant protection against arbitrary governmental action since here the executive and the upper and lower houses were derived from the same source, the people. Written fundamental laws were a more effective restraint than separation of powers, and from all this it was an easy step to insist on the judiciary as the leading defender of the constitution.[12] In two chapters on the judiciary, he placed the highest value on judges who were learned, upright, and independent. Judicial ignorance, corruption, or dependence were the greatest of calamities. The injured and the oppressed would gain protection from these "consecrated men around the alters [sic] of justice . . ."[13]

In a long letter Jefferson acknowledged Jarvis' book with thanks and with general approval. But he singled out one "error" into which the author, like many others, had fallen. "You seem," he said, "to consider the judges as the ultimate arbiters of all constitutional questions; a very dangerous doctrine indeed, and one which would place us under the despotism of an oligarchy."[14] The rest of the letter was a repudiation of the judicial monopoly theory. Once again, Jefferson relied in part on the separation of powers. The Constitution had made all the departments "co-equal and co-sovereign." Jefferson said that if the Legislature failed to provide a census, to pay the judges and other officials, to set up a militia, or to regulate naturalization or even to convene, or if the President failed to appoint new judges and other officials, or to issue commissions, no court could compel performance of these constitutional duties: "They [the judges] can issue their mandamus or distringas to no executive or legislative officer to enforce the fulfillment of their official duties, any more than the President or legislature may issue orders to the judges or their officers."[15]

The judges, he conceded, acted more frequently on constitutional questions than did the other branches, since the judicial department embraced the "laws of *meum* and *tuum* and of criminal action, forming the great mass of the system of law . . ."[16] Judicial review was thus a safeguard to individual rights. To push it beyond its proper function would to Jefferson be a threat to responsible government. "When the legislative or executive functionaries act unconstitutionally, they are responsible to the people in their elective capacity. The exemption of the judges from that is quite dangerous enough." Judges were no more honest than other men. They had the "same passions for party, for power, and the privilege of their corps." Their aim was to inflate their jurisdiction, and life tenure removed them from popular control. The Constitution had wisely provided no single arbiter of constitutional issues, knowing that "to whatever hands confided, with the corruptions of time and party, its members would become despots."

In closing, Jefferson returned to the people, whose intelligent awareness and support of constitutional principles was basic to the preservation of a free constitution.

I know no safe depository of the ultimate powers of the society but the people themselves; and if we think them not enlightened enough to exercise their control with a wholesome discretion, the remedy is not to take it from them, but to inform their discretion by education. This is the true corrective of abuses of constitutional power.[17]

In the end, then, Jefferson regarded judicial monopolism as a threat to free popular government. The branches were separated and made independent of one another in exercising their distinct authority as a means of defending popular rule, as a necessary condition, in Jefferson's words, for "continuance of our government on its pure principles."[18] If, in the short run, this view invited discord and presumed too much on the moderation of legislators and the constitutional acumen of the people at large, in the long run it highlighted the need of constitutional circumspection elsewhere than in the Judiciary and the bar and the truth that constitutional readings, to endure, must conform to popular understandings, values, and expectations. If the elected representatives reached determinations of such questions, the people in turn would participate in resolving such issues finally at elections, and thus come to understand them and accept the constitutional order itself. Primarily, it was republicanism that drove Jefferson to support a role for Congress in the handling of constitutional questions.

This same emphasis on popular participation or representation Jefferson also applied to the other branches. In choosing subordinates in the executive branch, President Jefferson sought to give representation to the two parties in "due proportion,"[19] a practice which may well have sprung, in part at least, from his republicanism. So too with the Judiciary; when the Jeffersonians came to reorganize the federal courts as left by the Federalists, they re-established circuit duty for Supreme Court justices and required that insofar as feasible each newly appointed member of the Supreme Court should come from and reside in the circuit in which he was to hold court.[20] A grand jury in Savannah in 1804 testified to the value of this provision. When Jefferson's first appointee, Justice William Johnson, a native of Charleston, South Carolina, took his oath in Circuit Court in Savannah, and thus became qualified to serve in the Sixth Circuit comprising South Carolina and Georgia, the jury professed its pleasure. They welcomed to the bench a "gentleman who from having been born and bred up in the midst of those people to whom he is to administer the law, is acquainted with their wants, their habits, & their opinions."[21] Whatever one may think of circuit duty for Supreme Court justices in other respects, it is likely that the resumption of the practice, coupled with the requirement of local residence for appointees, and its continuation throughout most of the century had important effects. It helped assure that Supreme Court decisions on constitutional questions would reflect popular needs and predilections and command popular support. Jefferson's great concern to fortify trial by jury in federal courts was another expression of the principle of representation and participation.[22] Juries helped to guarantee that the application of the law to particular cases conformed to the prevailing attitudes, values, and traditions of local communities.

If Jefferson's republicanism drove him to emphasize the power and responsibility of the elected legislature, another principle prompted him to promote within that branch conditions favoring genuine deliberation. Congress was capable of achieving the "sense of the whole" on important matters, and the principle that would ensure such a result was the rule of law, applied this time within the legislature itself.

Jefferson's labors in behalf of better congressional procedure resulted in his famous *Manual of Parliamentary Practice,* first printed in 1800. As Vice President, he had slowly compiled this document. He wanted, he said, to dispel prevailing ignorance on the subject and bring "reason into the national councils." For guidance he went, not to theoretical speculations on the way a legislative body ought to conduct its affairs, but to the experience of the British Parliament; the rules of Parliament, he told his old teacher, George Wythe, were the "best known to us for managing the debates, and obtaining the sense of a deliberative body."[23] Those rules had slowly advanced toward uniformity and accuracy and had, by this time, "obtained a degree of aptitude to their object beyond which little is to be desired or expected." To Judge Edmund Pendleton of Virginia he wrote in a similar vein, seeking his help in fixing the minutiae of procedure on the assumption that British practices were "the same we used to follow in Virginia."[24] So unoriginal did he deem the *Manual* that he once opposed its inclusion in his public papers.[25]

Jefferson himself set forth the purpose his rules would serve. While presiding over the Senate, he had, he said, felt keenly the need of recurring to "some known system of rules." Such rules would prevent his indulging in "caprice or passion" and free him from the imputation of such action. By publishing the rules, he was giving the Senate in writing the "standard" by which he would judge and could be judged. Rules, when codified and printed, would help ensure not only "accuracy in business, economy in time, order [and] uniformity," but also "impartiality."[26] Jefferson seems to have conceived of legislative procedure less as a guarantee of majority will and more as a safeguard to the rights and interests of minorities, for he wrote: "So far the maxim is certainly true, and is founded in good sense, that as it is always in the power of the majority, by their numbers, to stop any improper measures proposed on the part of their opponents, the only weapons by which the minority can defend themselves against similar attempts from those in power, are the forms and rules of proceedings which have been adopted as they were found necessary from time to time, and become the law of the house; . . ."[27]

Jefferson thus deemed the rules of legislative procedure to be ingredients of the rule of law. If supporters of judicial review took the precedents, if not the powers, of British courts as models, this backer of legislative authority sought faithfully to reproduce the practices of Parliament.

His *Manual* came out, not only in a multitude of printings in English, but in three languages on the Continent.[28] Europeans, however, mainly received instruction in parliamentary law from Jeremy Bentham. Bentham's influence on continental parliaments was often unfortunate, a result, presumably, of his aim and method. Unlike Jefferson, Bentham thought rules of procedure should merely facilitate the expression of the will of the majority; his method was that of theory free from a close adherence to practice.[29]

One who reads the *Manual* today is struck by the minor role allotted to standing committees and the importance attached to the Committee of the Whole. The House of Commons for centuries has relied on this device for early discussion of important matters, including constitutional questions.[30] So it was with Jefferson, who sought to embody in Congress the practice he had known in Virginia and which had facilitated the work of the Philadelphia Convention and the First Congress. Before select committees corrected the details of bills, those bills should come before the entire membership for decision on principle; matters suitable for the Committee of the Whole included "[t]he speech, messages, and other matters of great concernment . . . resolutions, . . . [and p]ropositions for any charge on the people." "The sense of the whole," wrote

Jefferson, "is better taken in committee [of the Whole], because in all committees every one speaks as often as he pleases."[31] The statements presupposed that the whole was capable of making sense, that on important matters, such as constitutional issues, all have a right to be heard at an early formative stage, and that in general committee the members could engage in the free and informal colloquy conducive to exploration and clarification of consensus.

Moreover, the views which Jefferson incorporated in the *Manual* conformed closely with the aims of his party. In a recent study of committees in Congress, Dr. Joseph Cooper has distilled from early congressional proceedings the procedural tenets which the Republicans sought to embody in practice.[32] First, Jefferson's followers disliked entrusting the bulk of investigation essential for legislation to the Executive. In general, they accepted information gathered by departments but rejected or downgraded executive opinions, plans, and especially bills. Once in power, however, they instituted informal contacts between small committees and department heads and even referred to the Executive certain substantive problems. Yet often they objected to formal congressional dependence on executive reporting.

Here, of course, was the chief point at which American practice was diverging from British. Parliament had developed as a counter-weight to an all-powerful monarchy, and by leaving much of the spade work on legislation to the responsible Executive, it could effectively and informedly devote its energies to deliberating questions of principle. In the process it assured a place for itself as a leading forum of deliberation in British government.

In the United States, Congress appeared on the scene before the regular executive departments. Under Hamilton, the Federalists had emphasized executive investigation and initiation in lawmaking. The Republicans, fearing executive influence and prerogative, opposed that emphasis in theory, if not always in practice. They tried to combine in one legislative body the functions of both preliminary investigation and deliberation on principle.

The second of the Republicans' procedural tenets called for initial reference of important matters to Committee of the Whole. Accordingly the whole house would settle important questions of general or abstract principle and furnish guide lines for smaller committees charged with drafting bills. Not only did the full house thus take up resolutions initially and bills at second reading, but it also controlled the introduction of bills, since both individual members and committees must "obtain leave" to bring in bills. This helped assure a corporate chamber control of legislative work.

80

Third, the Republicans tried to hold smaller committees to limited tasks. Normally these were temporary select committees chosen for the specific purposes of systematizing the decisions of the full body and drafting bills. With mounting frequency, however, such committees also played a role prior to Committee of the Whole by gathering facts and arranging details suitable for principled decisions there. These tasks then gradually fell to permanent standing committees. There were five by 1801 and nine by 1809, but usually these still worked under strict control of the house.

At the outset, these committees imparted continuity and specialized knowledge to legislative work; they served as agents of the house itself, often included members from every state, practiced majority rule internally, and worked under chairmen who were moderators rather than aggressive and independent leaders. In a sense, therefore, smaller committees were both servants and miniature copies of the house.

If some of these aims were destined for early frustration, their import was clear: the assurance of conditions of general and reasoned discussion, fortified by specific rules.

In addition to all this, Jefferson supported full publicity for debates, especially in the lower house. In this way the legislature would educate the public. Publication of speeches and balloting would also furnish evidence of the discharge by each member of his individual responsibility. A public informed about the grounds for action, whether legislative or judicial, was to Jefferson the best guarantee of responsibility and stability in the federal government.

Jefferson achieved only partial success in his campaign to make Congress truly deliberative. When in 1826 one of his followers reported that the *Manual* was "giving the law to deliberative assemblies throughout the Union,"[33] he overstated the issue. In Congress, the *Manual* was being ignored in many points at an early date. The Senate used it only as a sort of guide to Senate presidents, and the House, in 1837, adopted the provisions of the *Manual* only to control in cases "to which they are applicable."[34] In both houses, the zone of *Manual* applicability was to diminish steadily with the passage of time.

Jefferson's difficulties were immense. He had but eight short years in office in which to establish reforms. As President he stood at arm's length from Congress and had to work through party lieutenants there. Not all parts of the country shared the Virginian conception of the legislature and the importance of procedures for high-level deliberation. Most members of Congress received their basic training in state legislatures and in many of these the Committee of the Whole was either

81

unknown or subjected to early replacement by standing committees. Graduates of these local assemblies would carry to Congress their notions of a disintegrated and nondeliberative legislature.[35]

In addition, Congress found it increasingly difficult to curb the pretensions of violent personalities and local interests. Impetuous men like the Virginian John Randolph of Roanoke scorned procedural restraints and created a rancorous atmosphere.[36] As Chairman of the House Ways and Means Committee, Randolph once provoked a protest with a modern ring. A New Jersey Representative charged that he had held up business by his absence, kept the appropriation estimates in his pocket or on his desk for months, and reported bills and forced them through the House near the close of sessions when many had departed and others were preparing to depart and when there was no time for "that full investigation and cool deliberation necessary to decide with propriety on important subjects by which laws may be passed injurious to the interests of the United States and derogatory of the House . . ."[37]

Similarly, state and local interest seemed to monopolize the public attention. Feeble media of communication hindered the discovery and publicizing of national interests. Extreme state consciousness hence made Congress seem more like an aggregation of ambassadors than a deliberative legislature. The representative principle narrowly conceived was already assuming dominance over the deliberative.

Jefferson's efforts for a deliberative Congress, however unsuccessful in the long run, were consistent with his view of congressional responsibility. His insistence on a genuinely independent congressional share of constitutional decision-making would not only help thwart shifts of responsibility to the courts, but also promote accommodation of interests at a stage prior to the judicial, ensure that the courts would have the advantage of earlier spadework in Congress, and, above all, impart to constitutional settlements the legitimacy that comes with representation and public enlightenment.

JOHN MARSHALL AND THE JURISTIC VERSION

John Marshall shared with his fellow Virginian many tenets of the tripartite theory. Where his juristic version differed from the political was principally in the importance, scope, and conclusiveness it assigned to judicial review.

Marshall's experience was the reverse of Jefferson's. Appointed in 1801 to a post many deemed a sinecure, he headed a branch of government which had just reached its nadir in public esteem. His own party was cool to him because of his moderation during the last agitated years of Federalist rule. His prospects in 1801 were dim indeed.

82

Yet Marshall had several advantages. In addition to his prerogatives as chief of all the judges were his broad political experience and his capacity for leadership and for winning the loyalty of his associates. He started off with a Court unanimously Federalist, hence united before the common adversary. This enabled him to root so deeply his principles and his practices for court business that later Republican appointees could change them only with difficulty.

Furthermore, the new appointees came on gradually. Most of them were young—Johnson and Story but thirty-two—and still somewhat impressionable; several were able and legally erudite. Moreover, for a dozen crucial years after 1811, the Marshall Court combined geographical representation with a complete continuity of membership. The six associate justices came from every quarter of the Union and, excepting the six or eight weeks in Washington, lived and worked in their home regions.[38] The Court's fixed composition gave it a striking advantage over Congress which, as the next chapter will disclose, was now shifting in membership at an extraordinary rate. All of this enabled Marshall to put the imprint of his mind and purposes on the doctrines and practices of the Court.

If Jefferson's first principle was republicanism, Marshall's was the rule of law, with the corollary that the independent courts were its safest executors. The new Chief Justice had to wait two years to give his own "first inaugural." Later on, advocates of judicial monopoly would cite Marbury v. Madison as the manifesto of that theory.[39] Nevertheless, for all his hostility to Jefferson and his personification of the power and majesty of the Supreme Court, Marshall's own writings favored a form of judicial review qualified both in character and scope. On close analysis, his ideas appear in fact more like corollaries than antitheses of Jefferson's.

That Marbury v. Madison should, for some, stand as authority for judicial monopoly is surprising. Of course, it was a party dictate, being occasioned by Federalist court-packing, initiated by a Federalist appointee, and argued by a single Federalist attorney before a unanimously Federalist bench. Because of the ultimate finding of no-jurisdiction many of Marshall's pronouncements verged on obiter dicta. To later generations, the case would be known only by its closing pages, expounding the power of judicial review in sweeping terms. Marshall, it is clear, took this occasion to spell out an unassailable argument for the principle of the rule of law and for the Court as the leading expositor of the Constitution.

Note the manner in which he developed his argument. First, William Marbury was entitled to the commission which President Adams had signed but which President Jefferson, fresh to office, had withheld, for it was of "the very essence of civil liberty" that every individual should have a right to "claim the protection of the laws whenever he receives an injury."[40] By making it the duty of the Secretary of State to deliver the commission, the laws set "a precise course" which had to be strictly followed.[41]

Second, the laws afforded Marbury a remedy: "every right, when withheld, must have a remedy." "The government of the United States has been emphatically termed a government of laws, and not of men. It will certainly cease to deserve this high appellation if the laws furnish no remedy for the violation of a vested legal right."[42] Furthermore, "the question, whether a right has vested or not, is, in its nature, judicial, and must be tried by the judicial authority."[43]

Third, although Marbury ought to receive his writ of mandamus, the Court could not oblige him because the Judiciary Act, in authorizing such writs to issue, violated Article III of the Constitution. The Court had to deem that act invalid. A constitution is a body of "fundamental and paramount law" since it stems from the people's right to create a government and since it is put in writing for greater definitiveness and permanence. Thus, declared Marshall without qualification, it is "emphatically the province and duty of the judicial department to say what the law is."[44]

Note that Marshall rested judicial review not on the principle of checks and balances, but on other doctrines—"civil liberty," the rule of law, and the Constitution as a written popular enactment. This was no rejection of the principles of representation and electoral responsibility but rather an assertion that for full security, the rights of individuals required the added safeguard of enforcement by an independent judiciary. Earlier in his opinion, Marshall made it abundantly clear that like Jefferson, he conceived of some questions, doubtless including constitutional questions, as finally determinable by the political branches. "By the constitution of the United States," he wrote, "the president is invested with certain important political powers, in the exercise of which he is to use his own discretion, and is accountable only to his country in his political character, and to his own conscience."[45] Subjects thus entrusted to the President and by him to department heads, Marshall called political since "They respect the nation, not individual rights, and being intrusted to the executive, the decision of the executive is conclusive."[46]

Here one finds important similarities to Jefferson. Marshall, too, confined court determination of constitutional questions to cases pertaining to individual rights. Courts, furthermore, had no right to examine "political questions," which the political branches decided finally, and for which moral and political sanctions alone operated to compel obedience to constitutional provisions. It seems likely that Marshall would have conceded the President, as did Jefferson, Monroe, and Jackson, a duty and right to apply his own constitutional interpretation in wielding, for example, the pardoning power or the veto power.[47] Legal sanctions were unavailable for control of the political branches in such areas.

Marshall, of course, might have treated judicial review in the Marbury case as an ingredient of the check-and-balance system, as a means, that is, of defending the constitutionally ordained boundaries of the Court's power and jurisdiction. Instead, he put this rhetorical question concerning the judges: "If they can open it [the Constitution] at all, what part of it are they forbidden to read or to obey?"[48] The question might, admittedly, have implied judicial review of all constitutional controversies, but in context such review is confined by Marshall to matters affecting individual rights. What he probably intended, and in this he supplied the element missing from Jefferson's formula, was that the Supreme Court possessed final legal power to determine which questions were political and which reviewable by courts; in other words, to determine jurisdiction over the several categories of constitutional questions. If for Marshall the courts had any monopoly it was over this sort of jurisdiction. This monopoly, because of its effect on the equality and independence of the other branches, Jefferson would probably have rejected.

Clearly, Marshall attributed to others besides the judges a responsibility for considering constitutional questions. Marshall's comments in the great case of McCulloch v. Maryland, upholding the national bank, strongly implied a parallel responsibility in Congress. A generation after the First Congress had incorporated the bank initially, Marshall observed that the question of constitutional power, "if not put at rest by the practice of the government, ought to receive a considerable impression from that practice." He attributed much importance to an "exposition of the constitution, deliberately established by legislative acts . . ."[49] Thus the judges must presume that Congress had discharged its duty of weighing constitutional issues even in cases clearly subject to judicial review.

Furthermore, in the case of Cohens v. Virginia, Marshall acknowledged that some constitutional questions lay outside the sphere of court review. Twice he intimated that maintenance of the Constitution called for more than judicial vigilance;[50] further, he baldly asserted that the judicial power did not extend "to every violation of the constitution which may possibly take place, but to 'a case in law or equity,' in which a right, under such law, is asserted in a court of justice."[51]

Marshall agreed with Jefferson that Congress had a distinct sphere within which it reached final decisions on constitutional questions and within which only moral and political sanctions operated. Even for

85

questions reviewable by courts Congress had a parallel responsibility. Both leaders saw judicial review as intended primarily to safeguard individual rights in cases presented in proper form.

Marshall differed from Jefferson, of course, on the extent of judicial review of state laws and decisions. Presumably he differed also in the power he seemed to claim for the Supreme Court to assign particular questions for decision to particular departments. Difficult to assay is the extent to which they differed on the binding effect of court precedents on the other branches. Jefferson would probably have attributed finality to adjudications in particular cases as between the parties, but would probably have denied that precedents bound Congress in matters which were only analogous to those involved in such cases. The courts, however, had the advantage in that most legislation was potentially matter for litigation between parties. In this assurance, Marshall doubtless expected his opinions to bind the other branches not by broad legal compulsion but by their logic and persuasiveness. He would probably have acceded to President Jackson's assertion that the justices should not control Congress in its legislative functions but should have only that influence which "the force of their reasoning may deserve."[52] President Lincoln made similar statements later[53] and Marshall's awareness that the Court must persuade rather than command Congress in areas peripheral to cases lay behind the eloquence of his opinions. It was Marshall's interpretations of the Constitution more than his claim of the power to interpret that principally roused Jefferson's ire.

In the course of time, the limits to judicial review which Marshall acknowledged and his intimations of a parallel responsibility in Congress would be blurred and by some forgotten. Only later would the justices begin repeatedly to challenge congressional legislation and, under new influences, gradually assert a broad and comprehensive power.

Behind all that Marshall said doubtless lay misgivings about the moderation and impartiality to be expected from legislators, federal or state. Note, however, that, except in the Marbury decision, he wielded judicial review solely against state as distinguished from federal legislation. As the states came before the Court one by one to defend their laws against charges of unconstitutionality, the Marshall Court applied itself to the question of validity. In many of these controversies the states were in collision with direct prohibitions of the Constitution, and these controversies Congress was foreclosed from considering. Under the circumstances, it is not surprising that we find Marshall insisting in McCulloch that these conflicts of power must be resolved peaceably "or remain a source of hostile legislation, perhaps of hostility of a still more serious nature . . ." Hence, he concluded that a peaceful settlement lay with "this tribunal alone."[54] Marshall's purpose in enunciating principle was to create rules of law wise enough, and a tribunal to enforce them strong enough, to impart harmony and durability to the federal system.

To make the Court acceptable to the states under such conditions called for high statesmanship. It was not enough to establish doctrine favoring the rule of law for the adjustment of federal-state and interstate conflicts. The problem was also to shape the procedures of the Court for the handling of constitutional questions in such a way that, notwithstanding short-run defeats by particular states, all would deem the umpirage of the Court essential and salutary. Marshall, in short, faced somewhat the same problem in molding the deliberative process in the Court that Jefferson faced in Congress. Apart from establishing doctrine, his main achievement, and that of his Court, lay in crystallizing that process.

Several features of the procedures are noteworthy. In its early years, the Marshall Court had the advantage of abundant time. The workload was such that the judges could reflect and confer and write opinions with a limited regard for deadlines. "The mode of arguing causes" wrote Story in 1812, "is excessively prolix and tedious; but generally the subject is exhausted, and it is not very difficult to perceive at the close . . . where the press of the argument and of the law lies."[55] Somewhat this same condition prevailed, however, in the early Congresses.

Ample time contributed to a second feature—a full and fair public hearing for arguments bearing on the constitutional question. Questions were formulated with precision, and counsel presented their arguments orally, sometimes for days at a time. Under Marshall's lead, and in accord with the traditions of the bench, the judges strove to maintain an atmosphere of dignity, decorum, and objective inquiry. Fairness was enhanced by the right granted parties to request a re-hearing. Difficult or highly controversial questions could be held in abeyance until argument shed further light, until wavering judges came to a decision, or until the public achieved an informed understanding of the issues.

Third, the justices lived and worked under conditions which enhanced deliberation. The Marshall Court combined the continuity and privacy of the permanent standing committee with some of the representativeness and informality of the Committee of the Whole. This Court was peculiarly fitted to discover a sense of the whole, for the accent was on close give and take in intimate group consultations. Not only did the judges pursue private studies and meet for a regular "consultation day" at the Capitol,[56] but in addition they gathered informally in their common boardinghouse to explore issues. To judge from Story's comment, the social intimacy of the Philadelphia Convention was recreated at Washington. "My brethren are very interesting men, with whom I live in the most frank and unaffected intimacy . . . We moot every question as we proceed, and my familiar conferences at our lodgings often come to a very quick, and I trust, a very accurate opinion, in a few hours."[57]

Thus, full public hearing of opposing argument was succeeded by individual study and reflection and private group consultation. The decision was corporate, for, with occasional lapses, Marshall had his Court work as a unit. Neither then nor since has the tribunal followed the example of Congress by relinquishing its responsibilities to smaller committees. Decorum permitted oratory but usually frowned on unduly emotional or irrational appeals. The result was to combine fairness and thoroughness in the canvassing of arguments with detachment from immediate pressures in the weighing of them.

Fourth, and finally, the Marshall Court supported its decisions with clear reasons. Marshall himself gave a majority of the Court's opinions in constitutional cases, and these, because of their logic and their deft use of principles, carried an intellectual persuasiveness that made the decisions appear inescapable. Marshall shared with Jefferson and his whole generation an insight into constitutional principles, and his clarity and versatility in applying them gave his opinions immortality.

One weakness from which the Court suffered was a dearth of publicity for its decisions and especially its opinions. Only a very few of the great cases, such as Marbury, McCulloch, and Gibbons received full nationwide coverage in the press.[58] This imposed an added burden on bench and bar. Both responded. On the one hand, the judges maintained abundant local contacts and through circuit duty articulated principles and rules to local juries and courtrooms. On the other hand, the legal fraternity furnished an indispensable supplement by communicating and interpreting court decisions to citizens, organized interests, and local officials. What the press failed to do, the bar supplied, and, in doing so, it gave impetus to its own importance and influence.

It was characteristic that Marshall and Jefferson should disagree on the proper mode for delivering the Court's opinions. Marshall strove not only for group consultations but for a single eloquent group voice, even though individual justices might at times have to swallow personal convictions in acceding to the announced opinion of the Court. The Court, he must have thought, would most effectively enhance its own authority and educate the public by maintaining a single coherent body of doctrine. To Jefferson, such a course was a repudiation of the representative principle. Even on the bench, the official bore a responsibility individually to account for his acts; hence, Jefferson's insistent campaign for separate opinions by all the judges. Unanimous opinions, he wrote in 1822, "having been done in the dark . . . can be proved on no one." The adoption of separate opinions would show "whether every judge has taken the trouble of understanding the case, of investigating it minutely, and of forming an opinion for himself, instead of pinning it on another's sleeve. It would certainly be right to abandon this practice in order to give to our citizens one and all, that confidence in their judges which must be so desirable to the judges themselves, and so important to the cement of the union."[59] This is further evidence that Jefferson's "public" was capable of reason, of discriminating between sound and unsound arguments concerning constitutional readings.

These two Virginians and students of George Wythe worked simultaneously for better procedure. Both were intent on imparting effectiveness and authority to the new federal organs. The effect of the *Manual* on Congress, as shown, was limited and in part temporary.

Marshall's influence was more enduring. Yet in the Court, too, time would bring changes. Many forces, including a crushing load of constitutional and other cases, would necessitate departures from the exploratory procedures of the early Court. Pressure of time would confine argument largely to written briefs, with only an hour more or less for oral presentation; the complexity and manysidedness of issues would suggest greater representation for outside parties through the appearance of *amici curiae*. The genial and leisurely sessions at quarters would drop out, leaving only individual investigation, the formal conference, and such informal consultations at chambers as the schedule would permit. Majority opinions would sometimes appear perfunctory, the result in part, perhaps, of more formalized court deliberation.

In his own day, however, Marshall enjoyed a striking success. His doctrines and his efforts to make the Court a fair and objective forum caused it to rise in public esteem. By 1819, Niles could describe it as a "tribunal so far removed from the people, that some seem to regard it with a species of that awful reverence in which the inhabitants of Asia look up to their princes."[60] By 1828, he was asserting that nowhere could the "supreme power" be vested more safely than "in the Supreme Court, as at present filled."[61]

The instrument which Marshall improved and polished served mainly to confine state powers rather than congressional. Only later would it be turned on Congress. If Jefferson stressed the republican principle and Marshall the rule of law as judicially expounded, this should not blind us to their points of agreement. For both, the rule of law was important and each, in his respective office, worked to strengthen the processes of deliberation. In a sense the difference was less of kind than of emphasis.

JOHNSON, STORY, AND THE JUDICIAL MONOPOLY THEORY

One may gain further light on the principles and practices associated with Jefferson and Marshall and on factors contributing to the judicial monopoly theory by examining the work of Marshall's two young associates, William Johnson of South Carolina and Joseph Story of Massachusetts. The two judges came to the Court within a decade of each other and boasted careers which were singularly parallel. Both came of humble but respectable families and received university education, the one at Princeton, the other at Harvard. Both read law with prominent Federalist leaders, the one with Charles Cotesworth Pinckney, the other with Samuel Sewall of Sedition Act fame. Both espoused the party of Jefferson, served in the state legislature, and rose to the rank of Speaker. Both came to the Supreme Court at the age of thirty-two.

Yet there were notable differences: Johnson had four years on the state bench, Story one session in Congress. Johnson was bold, eloquent, cantankerous, impatient, and fiercely independent; Story, methodical, bookish, and amiable. Most notable was the contrast in regional associations. In South Carolina, the planter aristocracy had created a system in which the legislature had great power and prestige, and filled it with men most of whom stood agreed on standards for public service and constitutional principle. The Jeffersonian conception of republican government and legislative concern for procedural rectitude could fit harmoniously into such a system.

In Massachusetts, ideas and institutions prepared men to distrust legislatures and revere the courts of law. The town meeting, which met annually in every locality to settle the affairs of the community, was apt to foster, by its occasional factionalism, disorder, and precipitancy, a restricted conception of the capability of public deliberative assemblies. The leading political theorist of New England, John Adams, sought above all to balance governmental powers by dispersing them. Adams and the other drafters of the Massachusetts Constitution of 1780 had created a legislature in which the members of both houses sat for one-year terms. Simultaneously, they made it possible for the governor and council, and each branch of the legislature to seek constitutional advice from the state supreme court, whose members were to be as "free, impartial, and independent as the lot of humanity will admit." The habit of resorting to advisory opinions might easily enhance doubts about legislative responsibility for constitutional questions. The system would spread with variations to the states of New Hampshire, Maine, Rhode Island, Florida, Colorado, South Dakota, and Delaware,[62] several of which would later send to Congress men committed to judicial monopoly.

Justice Johnson, who from 1804 on served three decades beside Marshall, sought in his writings and actions to harmonize Marshall's views with those of Jefferson. On one occasion, in fact, he even told Jefferson who had written him harshly criticizing Marshall's Court and its Federalist doctrines that the "pure men" of both the two early parties "never were in principle very far removed."[63] To Johnson, also, the great problem of constitutional elaboration was to reconcile the discordant impulses of the separate states and win support for the federal authorities. He repeatedly deplored the "sensitive irritability" of sovereign states, where their wills or interests collided.[64] Although impetuous and undiplomatic, Johnson was intellectually capable of seeing the need of wise principles and moderation in the adjustment of the respective powers of states and nation.

He, too, supported judicial review of acts of Congress. In Marshallian terms, he told a Savannah grand jury which had attacked one of his decisions invalidating an order of the Jefferson Administration that he had only interposed "the authority of the laws in the protection of individual rights, of your rights and the rights of succeeding generations."[65]

At the same time, Johnson assigned Congress a prominent role in the handling of constitutional questions. Like Jefferson, he deemed the legislature capable of genuine deliberation. Thus, in rendering the Court's opinion in the first case upholding a power in Congress to punish for contempt, he described that body as "a deliberative assembly, clothed with the majesty of the people, and charged with the care of all that is dear to them; composed of the most distinguished citizens, selected and drawn together from every quarter of a great nation; whose deliberations are required by public opinion to be conducted under the eye of the public, and whose decisions must be clothed with all that sanctity which unlimited confidence in their wisdom and purity can inspire . . ."[66] Not only did he go as far as any in upholding broad substantive powers in Congress, but he also frequently urged Congress to take a hand in regulating state powers. For example, to avoid doubts concerning the effect of a federal law on the concurrent powers of states, he called for congressional clarification. Instead of relying solely on judicial interpretation of the intent of Congress, a practice which has often occasioned congressional resentment in our own times, he would have Congress include in its statutes specific and precise declarations concerning the extent of federal preemption.[67]

As Nullification gained strength in his own state, Johnson spoke out in vindication of Congress as well as the Court. When a former governor of South Carolina, John Taylor, told him the country needed some other tribunal than the Court for curbing the usurpations of the federal government,[68] Johnson replied that the states already had such a body in the Senate. "They are all there," he contended, "equally represented and every law which passes that body involves a decision on its constitutionality—a decision made by a body sworn to decide impartially, and in which the smallest state has as much weight as the greatest."[69] The argument gave little satisfaction to the planters of the state who deemed the federal protective tariff a threat to their vital economic interests, yet it reflected Jeffersonian confidence in the principle of electoral representation and in a modicum of moral responsibility in national lawmakers.

On another occasion, Johnson rebutted the extremist pro-state views of Robert J. Turnbull by coupling a defense of a judicial umpire with a plea for confidence in the national representatives. Thus he wrote of the Court:

> Once admit that the decisions of that tribunal which the Constitution has established to pronounce on the validity of Congressional enactments, is not to be regarded *as final*—is not to bind, definitively, the will of States, as well as of individuals, (and I understand you as going the full length of this,) and no barrier is left against mutual encroachments, mutual dissentions, and civil war. The very cement of the Union is gone.[70]

Simultaneously, he asserted that the constitutional interpretations of successive administrations were entitled to great weight; no commentary had authority equal to the "settled practice of the Government."[71] But ultimate reliance had to be placed not on the judiciary, but on the character of the people and of their officials. Security against usurpation lay in "the virtue and intelligence of the people at large—the political, and *moral* responsibility of the depositories of power—and the perfect sameness of interest that subsists between them."[72]

The efficacy of such a political and moral responsibility depended finally on the electorate. A people who had grown ignorant and vicious had no business with free institutions. When that happened, destruction was bound to come: "The forms of our political institutions may remain for a season; but the spirit will have fled."[73]

Finally, Johnson sought to implement these views by bringing the work of the Court not merely to the bar, but to the public in general. Aware of the Court's political role, he sought by Jeffersonian means to promote confidence in the Court. Thus on one occasion he urged President Monroe to have the McCulloch opinion printed and distributed throughout the nation as a means of fostering public awareness of the principles it inculcated.[74] On another, he told Jefferson he had backed an effort in Congress to repeal the Court's appellate jurisdiction over state courts in order to secure a vote of confidence for the Court.[75]

Most notable was his assault on unanimous court opinions. When Jefferson repeatedly urged upon him the wisdom of separate opinions as a means of enforcing the judges' accountability to the public and fostering public confidence,[76] Johnson complied. While asserting the need of privacy for court consultations and circumspection concerning its inner workings, he agreed on the wisdom of separate opinions. Long before this, he explained, he had got the Court to adopt the practice it still employs for rendering opinions. He now renewed his individual utterances and, in 1824, he introduced a separate opinion in Gibbons *v.* Ogden, by affirming, that "in questions of great importance and great delicacy, I feel my duty to the public best discharged by an effort to maintain my opinions in my own way."[77]

Here was an expression of the Jeffersonian call for diffusion of information and the testing of officials at the "bar of the public reason." If that insistence asked too much of the public where constitutional adjudications were concerned, the practice of dissenting opinions has furnished the legal profession with materials for judging, criticizing, and publicizing the reasons for decisions. Through the medium of the bar, judges would bring their arguments to the public and win the public confidence they required.[78]

Johnson blended Jefferson's reliance on an enlightened and alert public and responsibility in elected representatives with Marshall's esteem for the independent Judiciary and judicial review.

Justice Story, however, put almost the whole of his emphasis on the judicial function. Story came to the Court in 1811 and remained thirty-four years, all but the last ten during Marshall's tenure. Like Jefferson, Marshall, and Johnson, he devoted his energies to the perfecting of the federal system. For most of his public career, Story opposed the views of Jefferson, with whose theories he had little sympathy. In introducing his famous *Commentaries on the Constitution,* published in 1833, he declared that on matters connected with government he had always sought to avoid "metaphysical refinements."[79] "A constitution of government," he said, "is addressed to the common-sense of the people, and never was designed for trials of logical skill or visionary speculation."[80]

Story's distaste for high-level political speculation caused him to put his trust in law and legal theory. Like his fellow New Englanders, Fisher Ames and Harrison G. Otis, he distrusted general political principles, and in doing so turned his back even on Marshall. His writings convey the notion that a constitution consists essentially of court precedents and rules of law with only a vague reference to the principles and values that lie behind these. Thus he asserted: "A constitution is in fact a fundamental law or basis of government, and falls strictly within the definition of law as given by Mr. Justice Blackstone. It is a rule of action prescribed by the supreme power in a state, regulating the rights and duties of the whole community . . . It is a rule prescribed; that is, it is laid down, promulgated, and established."[81] By minimizing general principles as an ingredient in constitutions, Story opened the way for others to maintain

93

that all official actions of legislators affecting the powers and limits of officials, not being strict law as courts propound it, were wholly matters of policy.

In his *Commentaries,* Story took up the problem of responsibility in a chapter entitled "Who is Final Judge or Interpreter of Constitutional Controversies." He there devoted one brief initial section to showing that all officials of government were in conscience bound to observe the limits of their constitutional powers. Thus, "if a proposition be before Congress, every member of the legislative body is bound to examine and decide for himself whether the bill or resolution is within the constitutional reach of the legislative powers confided to Congress. And in many cases the decisions of the executive and legislative departments, thus made, become final and conclusive, being from their very nature and character incapable of revision."[82] This acknowledgment of the oath-bound obligation of officials to consider power-limits and of the finality of many of their decisions was tripartite. Yet Story followed it with comments on political questions so brief and general as to obscure his meaning. His emphasis throughout the chapter was not on the *equality* of the three branches, but on the *supremacy* of the Judiciary. A half page separated the above quotation from another stressing the constitutionally-established "final and common arbiter . . . to whose decisions all others are subordinate . . ."[83]

Further on, Story revealed the basis of his misgivings about settlements of constitutional questions elsewhere than in the Supreme Court. In a footnote, he quoted an assertion by John C. Calhoun of South Carolina to the effect that, notwithstanding the Supreme Court, not a single constitutional question of a political character since the beginning had been "settled in the public opinion, *except that of the unconstitutionality of the Alien and Sedition Laws . . .*"[84] Story then used language strongly implying that the Court alone was capable of resolving such issues:

> If public opinion is to decide constitutional questions, instead of the public functionaries of the government, in their deliberate discussions and judgments (a course quite novel in the annals of jurisprudence), it would be desirable to have some mode of ascertaining it in a satisfactory and conclusive form; and some uniform test of it, independent of mere private conjectures. No such mode has, as yet, been provided in the Constitution. And perhaps it will be found, upon due inquiry, that different opinions prevail at the same time, on the same subject, in the north, the south, the east, and the west. If the judgments of the Supreme Court (as it is more than hinted) have not, even upon the most deliberate *juridical* arguments, been satisfactory, can it be expected that *popular* arguments will be more so? . . . In

truth, it is obvious that, so long as statesmen deny that any decision of the Supreme Court is conclusive upon the interpretation of the Constitution, it is wholly impossible that any constitutional question should ever, in their view, be settled. It may always be controverted; and, if so, it will always be controverted by some persons.[85]

Here was no express repudiation of Congress as a forum for constitutional controversies. Yet Story's language supporting Court determination of such controversies seemed to imply such a denial. It was the immediate thrust of his argument that danger to the nation lay in recognizing a right in the separate states to decide the meaning of the federal Constitution, and that the only safe recourse was to accept Supreme Court review and determination. Said Story: "Will the case be better, when twenty-four different States are to settle such questions as they may please, from day to day or year to year,—holding one opinion at one time and another at another?"[86] Elsewhere Story cited with approval a statement by his friend and fellow-commentator, Chancellor James Kent of New York, declaring that judicial review was essential to the existence of the union of the states under a single national government.[87] It was mainly to prove the need of a judicial umpire over the federal system that Story developed his case in twenty-two closely-reasoned sections of the *Commentaries*. What he stressed was the finality and universal conclusiveness of Supreme Court decisions on constitutional questions as these decisions affected the states; what he neglected to explore in depth was the precise extent of the scope and character of the responsibility of the other branches of the federal government for constitutional questions. He exalted the Court out of fear of excesses by the states. It would be easy for later men in their zeal to push policies through Congress to invoke Story as authority for exclusive judicial surveillance of all constitutional questions whatsoever.

Story's view that the only satisfactory constitutional settlements were judicial settlements sprang from his esteem for courts as the source of law. "Ours is emphatically a government of laws and not of men," he wrote, "and judicial decisions of the highest tribunal, by the known course of the common law, are considered as establishing the true construction of the laws which are brought into controversy before it." Courts not only decided cases, but in doing so stated "principles" to bind future cases of like nature;[88] for Story, the Constitution consisted of these court-declared rules. If some had sufficient generality to be principles, they derived their authority not from any intrinsic truth or reasonableness, but from their source—the Judiciary.

The passion of Story's life was the study of the common law. If Johnson tried to bring constitutional expositions to the public at large, Story put his greatest efforts into educating the bar. His *Commentaries on the Constitution* formed but one of a series including treatises on bailments, conflict of laws, equity, agency, partnership, bills of exchange, and promissory notes. These writings, and Story's work after 1829 as Dane Professor of Law at Harvard, had incalculable value in instructing the legal profession.[89] His writings on constitutional law helped assure that the thought and experience of the first half century of national life, as expressed especially in the opinions of John Marshall, would reach the growing legal profession in clear, documented, and systematic form.

Yet his teaching and writing had additional effects. In his misgivings about popular and legislative wisdom and circumspection, in his distaste for abstract political theory, in his zeal for the courts as sole guardians of the rule of law, and in his devotion to judge-made law, including common law, as the safest reservoir of tested rules and principles, Story provided some of the ingredients of the judicial monopoly theory. One can safely assume that no reputable commentators of Story's time or, for that matter, later, articulated a full-blown judicial monopoly theory. Both prevailing theory and actual practice contradicted such a conception. Nevertheless, in their enthusiasm for courts, for court-made law, and for the bar as its priesthood and in their effort to defend the Supreme Court as the only safe umpire of the novel and precarious federal system, Story and doubtless others used language which later times could read as upholding not only final but exclusive judicial surveillance of constitutional issues. The forum they advocated for *many* issues could one day be recommended for *all* issues.

CONCLUSIONS

If the three leading theories of congressional responsibility came to reveal distinct differences, one from another, the men who voiced them had much in common. All agreed on a duty in members of Congress to scrutinize the Constitution for clear evidence of granted power. This duty was kept vital by both moral and political sanctions, by conscience, and by the corrective action of other branches and the electorate. All four of these men acknowledged a zone of independent constitutional inquiry in Congress—Story the least explicitly—an area of political questions where legislative determinations, constitutional in nature, were necessarily final, controlled, that is, only by the ballot and in some instances by the veto. Judge Learned Hand has likened this tripartite obligation of the separate departments to the posture of Leibnizian monads "looking up to the Heaven of the Electorate, but without any mutual dependence,"[90] but probably a closer analogy and more direct influence was the Protestant notion of private judgment applied to the reading of the Constitution. Yet all four of these writers affirmed a distinct, even broad, area for judicial review, seeing in the independent Judiciary a haven for individuals from the depredations of political forces.

They differed mainly in concepts and principles and in what these implied. Jefferson's faith in the electorate as both informed and educable, his view of republican government as both representative and deliberative, and his concern for a genuine equality among organs of government led him to assert an independent power and moral duty in Congress to reach constitutional settlements of certain questions. The presence of other and somewhat contradictory theories, a gradual breakdown in procedures for deliberation, and political events of the century would work against his theory, especially after the Civil War. Yet the tripartite theory in its political version offered much of value. It combatted the concentration of power and prestige in a small, quasi-permanent, hence nonaccountable, organ, it retained a portion of constitutional discussion and accommodation within the political process with consequent relief for the Court, moderation of political forces, and constant re-education of legislators, and it brought popular understandings of the Constitution to bear on decision-makers and in turn supplied a means of nurturing those understandings. Paradoxically it was the leading apologist of American independence that came closest to insisting on a role for Congress in constitutional affairs comparable to that of Parliament. To assign Congress a share in the handling of constitutional issues is to take advantage of its national representative character and to foster that degree of public concern and maturity about constitutional principles which characterizes Great Britain.

Marshall doubted the wisdom and circumspection of legislators, especially of state legislators, and revered the independent Judiciary as chief formulator of the rule of law. He evidently never denied or depreciated congressional responsibility, and although acknowledging a zone of unreviewable congressional determinations, he put his chief trust in judicial review, at the outset as a shield for individual rights, increasingly as a sanctuary, a kind of hurricane's eye where federal-state disputes, especially sectional in origin, could come to settlement safely and effectively. Marshall built up the Supreme Court in both effective power and public reputation and in doing so, provided a source from which even Congress in later times could take guidance in its constitutional perplexities. With Congress declining both in public image and in procedural correctness, the courts would later fill a gap in the maintenance of constitutional principles.

Conceivably Marshall foresaw some of these changes. The juristic version in practice kept for the Court the decision on what questions

97

were political and what reviewable, and on what cases conformed to jurisdictional proprieties. In language, if not in principle, Marshall's opinions read like pronunciamentos to all officials of government. All this gave the court room for maneuver and the appearance of circumspection, while enhancing the impression of universal court domination in the constitutional sphere. It was not only the force of Marshall's reasoning that made his decisions persuasive with later Congresses; it was also the moderate stance his Court took toward Congress in practice.

Johnson, the South Carolinian, elucidated consistencies between Jefferson and Marshall. While supporting judicial review, he reminded the judges of their long-run dependence on popular comprehension of their decisions as a condition to popular acceptance. The South was long to retain strong infusions of Jefferson's ideas, and the Border States, those of Jefferson and Marshall.

Story accepted some of the tenets of the Jeffersonian view, at least nominally, but his heart was with Marshall and with the Court as protector of the federal peace. That revival of state pretensions, especially after 1815, which drove Jefferson to denounce the Court, and Marshall and Johnson to emphasize its settlements as alternatives to disunion and war, led Story to employ language that suggested not only the finality of its decision but its exclusive control of constitutional settlements. In 1799 New England states had replied to assertions of a state veto by proclaiming such a control; in 1830 Daniel Webster took the same route in Congress in answering Hayne.[91] It was natural for Story, given the New Englander's doubts of legislative judgment and impartiality and special esteem for the bench, to talk of the Supreme Court as a grand umpire of all constitutional disputes in the Union. Marshall enhanced the role of the Court; Story helped prepare the bar to support that role and present their cases before it. The habit of viewing the Constitution as just another branch of court-made law, the practice of going to lawbooks for advice on every sort of constitutional problem, the continuing decline of legislative deliberation, the emergence of a victorious North steeped in the commentaries of Story and James Kent would help make bench and bar a kind of constitutional elite. The Constitution would thus come to appear less like public business and more like lawyer's business.

Jefferson's conception of congressional responsibility would prevail, with lapses, until the Civil War, even though his procedural standards were losing their force. Congress would continue to resolve basic constitutional issues, including many affecting the federal system. After the war, Marshall's theory would come to the fore. Much later, judicial monopoly would gain recruits.

Such were the theories which a half century of constitutional innovation and discussion had shaped. It is time to examine them in congressional practice.

PART III

Congressional Practice
in the Nineteenth Century

5

The Jeffersonian System: The Anderson Contempt Motion in the House, 1818

In January 1818, the House of Representatives spent more than a week determining that Colonel John Anderson had committed a contempt of Congress and that the House had power to act. Its decision, affirmed three years later by a unanimous Supreme Court,[1] was the fruit of full and extensive debate. The affair indicates in some measure how Congress, during the half century between the end of Jefferson's Administration and the outbreak of the Civil War, dealt with constitutional questions.

It was in the committee rooms and on the floor of Congress that the theories already described were directly applied. To survey the century in detail would be to map the ocean bottom. I shall accordingly take a limited number of soundings so spaced and so controlled as to furnish some measure of perspective and insight. I shall subject to close analysis three episodes from the years 1818, 1862, and 1890, and supplement these by more limited probes, examining in each of the three instances the policy-matrix, the constitutional question, and the operation of the several elements of responsibility. These explorations will suggest the changes wrought by the passage of time and also furnish a background against which to examine the work of the twentieth-century Congress.

The first weeks of 1818, when the Anderson affair broke on the House, were an auspicious moment for detached consideration. The Federalist party was about to expire. The War of 1812 was well over, and an era of good feeling had set in. The party of Jefferson had long enjoyed national rule; in this very debate a new member from New Hampshire, Arthur Livermore, in challenging a congressional precedent from the time of Federalist rule, condemned that party's forces in the earlier House as a "high-handed party majority, full of British notions" and praised the views of its opponents, "the whole body of the Republican members, with the great Jefferson at their head."[2] That minority had now become an overwhelming majority and party lines were melting fast.

The leading national news magazine, in reporting the opening of the

Fifteenth Congress, extolled the prevailing "peace and plenty" and went on: "Party, too, has lost its fervor—never since the political divisions of the people first began were there so few points to elicit passion as at the present calm and happy period."[3] Regional differences seemed more latent than obvious. In addition, the pace of work was leisurely. At this four-and-one-half-month session, the 182 Representatives delved unhurriedly into such subjects as United States relations with Spain and her American colonies and most extensively into the power of the federal government to construct internal improvements. Not for two years would the Missouri Compromise debate shatter the calm by disclosing fundamental sectional differences. Not for a year would the Supreme Court begin to assert its full authority in a series of great nationalizing decisions, notably McCulloch *v.* Maryland.[4] The floor of the House was to be the setting for the 1818 debate—the last place where Americans of the mid-twentieth century would expect to find calm and objective inquiry into constitutional questions.

Colonel John Anderson, a veteran of hostilities in the Michigan Territory precipitated the affair under study. On January 6, he appeared at the lodgings of Representative Lewis Williams of North Carolina to deliver a letter. This purported to promise a "gift" of five hundred dollars for the trouble which Anderson's claims against the government were causing Williams, then serving as chairman of the Committee on Claims. The House had already passed one of Anderson's claims concerned with property destroyed during the war and, as it turned out, still had before it others to the extent of nine thousand dollars in Anderson's name and twenty-one thousand dollars in the names of his clients.

Notwithstanding Anderson's repeated requests for the return of his letter and pleas for forgiveness, Williams denounced this "attack upon the integrity of Congress generally, and upon mine personally . . ."[5] and determined on action. Next day, Williams presented the letter to the House and related the episode. After discussion, the House unanimously adopted a resolution calling on the Speaker, Henry Clay, to issue a general warrant for Anderson's arrest and ordering his detention pending a decision on further action. A committee on privileges was appointed to recommend proper steps, and after debating its recommendations and alternative proposals for a week, the House brought Anderson before its bar on the charge of contempt of Congress and had him reprimanded by the Speaker. The House had affirmed its constitutional power to take such action against a nonmember.

This legislative settlement of the question proved lasting. After his release Anderson sued Thomas Dunn, Sergeant-at-Arms, for assault and battery and false imprisonment and carried his case to the Supreme

Court. Justice Johnson spoke for a unanimous Court in upholding the power of Congress.

Furthermore, the power was never again seriously questioned either within or without the House. In 1857 Congress passed a contempt statute providing for judicial prosecution of contempts of Congress. Yet this act, rushed to passage to deal with a pending controversy, had as its purpose not so much formalizing and defining the power as adding to the punishments already available.[6] In fact, discretionary contempt proceedings, such as that in the Anderson case, rather than statutory, remained the normal recourse until the twentieth century, disappearing only after World War II.[7] Anderson v. Dunn has furnished the modern Court with a foundation stone on which to rest the power of Congress to investigate.[8] Yet the contempt power, like so many others, had its first full exploration and endorsement not in the Court, but in Congress.

THE CONSTITUTIONAL QUESTION

The central question in the debate was whether the House possessed power to punish a nonmember for contempt for conduct beyond its immediate presence. Such questions were no strangers to legislative halls. In England the common law, under the head "Lex et Consuetudo Parliamenti," acknowledged a power in both houses of Parliament to punish for contempt.[9] In the colonies, the assemblies made use of a similar power, both to protect their proceedings and to obtain testimony.[10] Since the states adopted the common law on becoming independent and since the contempt power was a part of that law, it was natural for the new state legislatures to employ the power notwithstanding the silence of most state constitutions.[11] Even the Continental Congress called one Isaac Melchior to its bar "to answer for his conduct."[12]

The Constitution, in Article I, section 6, guarantees members only the freedom from arrest while sitting or while coming to or going from Congress and immunity from suit for statements made on the floor. It makes no mention of contempt powers. Nevertheless, the House of Representatives as early as 1795 had one Robert Randall and others arrested and brought before its bar on charges of attempts to bribe its members. After a hearing Randall was found guilty and remanded to the custody of the Sergeant-at-Arms. He was released eight days later on payment of fees.[13] The Federalist-controlled Senate in 1800 tried the Republican editor William Duane for publishing defamations of Congress, and sentenced him to thirty days' captivity.[14] In these and other instances, the houses came to decision only after extensive constitutional debate.

Basically, the question before the House in 1818 was whether the

Constitution, in granting legislative power to Congress, implied as a necessary incident the power to protect its processes from pollution through the medium of the contempt power. Since the question grew out of constitutional verbiage it was narrow, and since no court precedents existed, Congress was deciding it initially. The issue raised a peculiar challenge to congressional objectivity since it juxtaposed the majority against a single individual, unaided by any organized group, official or unofficial. In debate those who denied the contempt power took the strict-constructionist line in the interest of individual liberty, state reserved powers, and an exclusive judicial cognizance of contempts. Supporters of the power relied on broad construction, congressional precedents, and practical necessities. Although speakers touched on the issue of federal power vs. state power and on the issue of individual rights, their primary concern was the separation of powers. To what extent did the Constitution entrust to the legislature a power ordinarily associated with courts? To what extent did representative government necessitate a legislature strong enough to police its proceedings in this way? For support of the auxiliary powers of legislatures should one look to the common law or to the principles of republicanism?

Such were some of the questions of interpretation raised in debate, and of course, the prospect of court review was a real one. A private citizen had undergone arrest and imprisonment pending trial, and an appeal to the Judiciary was wholly possible. Members would show to what extent they thought this likelihood absolved them from probing the question on their own and applying their own judgment concerning both the legality and the wisdom of a contempt power in Congress.

COURSE OF THE DISCUSSION

Despite its occasional omissions and obvious casualness, the record of the Anderson debate shows the members of the House eager to do justice both to the accused and to the constitutional powers of the House. For seven full days members on both sides sought to expound all relevant arguments and a few not so relevant, and to shape the question into a form on which the House could declare itself with precision. Because it contrasts radically with later episodes the debate will receive a full, point-by-point treatment.

From the start of debate on Wednesday, January 7, the existence of a constitutional question was manifest to the members. As soon as Representative Williams had placed Anderson's letter before the House[15] and supporting evidence had established the offense, John Forsyth, Republican of Georgia, moved that the Speaker be directed to issue a warrant to the Sergeant-at-Arms for the arrest of Anderson and for his detention pending further decision by the House. Two New England Republicans, Nathaniel Terry of Connecticut and Livermore of New Hampshire, questioned the validity of such a warrant because of its generality and the absence of testimony taken under oath.[16] Although overruled by the Speaker, both objectors had alerted the House to the menace to civil liberties implicit in contempt proceedings. The House, however, adopted the warrant motion unanimously.

On the second day, discussion centered on a motion to submit the matter to a select committee on privileges for recommendation of appropriate procedures. Philemon Beecher of Ohio was a nominal Federalist, a label which many still bore although actual Republicans. Beecher began the attack on the proceedings by insisting that the Constitution gave sole authority to try for bribery to the courts. Although the House had inherent power to preserve decorum, that power could only reach acts committed in its presence. The constitutional enumeration of the privileges of members, he contended, was exhaustive, and the House had no such power by the common law. Livermore advanced additional strict-constructionist arguments. Parliament, he said, was no model since Parliament was omnipotent, and no federal statute declared bribery an offense.

In rebuttal, Henry Tucker, Virginia Republican, asserted that even in the absence of a statute on contempts, Congress could punish bribery of its members under its implied powers. The former Federalist, Joseph Hopkinson of Pennsylvania, cited earlier congressional precedents and asserted that Congress required the same contempt powers as the courts to preserve the purity of the legal process. A constricted reading of the Constitution would deny Congress the necessary means of self-protection. Livermore then retracted some of his earlier points but persisted in denying that Parliamentary powers were applicable in Congress. Without a contempt statute, no law existed on which to try Anderson. This neophyte member of the House put his position in this way, as summarized by the reporter: "Suppose he were to rise and say, that, as he was coming here, the Governor or Chief Justice of New Hampshire had offered him a bribe; would this House send out its warrant and bring him here? Would this be Constitutional? He hoped not. If the procedure would not be warrantable as to such men, neither would it to the meanest man in the State, for no man there was a slave . . ."[17]

This odd mixture of strict construction, state rights, and individual liberties arguments was soon subjected to dissection. Representative John Sergeant, Pennsylvania Federalist, reminded the House that Parliament, i.e. Commons and Lords together, was supreme, but when the two houses exercised their contempt powers separately, that power was no part of their supreme legislative power, but merely a privilege analo-

105

gous to that of other limited bodies. Records the *Annals of Congress:* "If the doctrine of the gentlemen from Ohio and New Hampshire prevail, . . . we shall be assailable at our door, on the staircase, everywhere until we come into this House, and this House is organized. Was this possible?"[18]

When a Virginia Republican and non-lawyer, William Ball, declared it were better to undergo a thousand insults than trample on the liberty of the citizen and that the Constitution gave express protection against contempt actions such as this, Representative Thomas Hubbard, New York Republican, replied that the Fourth Amendment provision for warrants supported by oath applied only to judicial action. Beecher summed up the opposition argument at this point: The House lacked the power inherently since the Constitution prohibits punishment except for a breach of the law. Congress acts without safeguards such as grand jury and trial by jury. "If for what is said or done out of doors, citizens may be required to answer at our bar, every man in the nation is liable to be arraigned at our will and pleasure, although in conscientiously opposing and reprobating our measures he has exercised no more than his Constitutional right."[19]

The House had made its preliminary search of governing principles. In spite of one or two mild references to partisanship of an earlier time, the discussion was searching and well informed. The motion for appointment of a committee was agreed to, and the following were named to bring in a report: four Republicans, Forsyth, Tucker, Richard M. Johnson of Kentucky, and John Taylor of New York and three Federalists, Hopkinson, Sergeant, and Timothy Pitkin of Connecticut. All were lawyers. Together they represented every major region, and all but Johnson were to vote for the contempt power on the final count.[20]

The committee met and reported back within the hour. Forsyth, as its spokesman, read a resolution which at one and the same time assumed the contested power and protected the rights of the accused:

> *Resolved,* That John Anderson be brought to the bar of the House, and interrogated by the Speaker, on written interrogatories, touching the charge of writing and delivering a letter to a member of the House, offering him a bribe, which, with his answers thereto, shall be entered on the minutes of the House. And that every question proposed by a member be reduced to writing, and a motion made that the same be put by the Speaker, and the question and answer shall be entered on the minutes of the House. That, after such interrogatories are answered, if the House deem it necessary to make further inquiry on the subject, the same be conducted by a committee to be appointed for that purpose.[21]

106

The committee had embodied the approved principles in a report and applied them in a form appropriate for the special case. In its closing minutes the House turned down Beecher's motion to refer the report to the Committee of the Whole. Such a motion would have conformed strictly to earlier Jeffersonian law-making procedure. Probably the unusual character of the proceedings, more judicial than legislative, and the uncomplicated nature of the issue made the Committee of the Whole inappropriate. The House approved the report without a division and, after brief discussion of the rights of the accused to counsel, to witnesses, and to copies of incriminating evidence, adjourned.

The next day, Friday, January 9, brought a serious challenge to the agreed action and a proposal which provided the focus of debate for nearly a week. A new member, the twenty-nine-year-old Republican, John Spencer of New York, led off with a lengthy speech and a set of resolutions. Spencer set forth most of the arguments against the pending action: the absence of express constitutional power, the threat which the action posed to specific guarantees of Amendments IV, V, and VI, the need to confine the contempt power to the premises, the delegation of power to pass necessary and proper laws only to Congress as a whole, the necessity of a statute in order to make a crime punishable, the inapplicability of the common law to federal processes, and the danger that with parliamentary precedents would come parliamentary tyranny. Spencer accordingly proposed that the House, "entertaining great doubts of its . . . power," should resolve that first, the pending proceedings cease and the prisoner be discharged; second, that the Attorney General be instructed to bring proceedings against Anderson under federal and District of Columbia laws; and third, that the Committee on the Judiciary be directed to look into the wisdom of providing by law for the punishment "of any contempt of the Senate or House of Representatives of the United States, and of any breach of the privileges of either House."[22]

Spencer said he chose this opportunity to seek a wise settlement of the central issue, since this was a "season of profound political tranquillity, when there were no party passions to stimulate our animosities or influence our decisions . . ."[23] He had warned that all legislative precedents should be distrusted. To this Forsyth, the Georgian, replied that the Randall precedent of 1795–1796 had good standing, since the House had there supported punishment by a four to one vote. To confine the power to the precincts would prove impractical, and accordingly the House must have those powers necessary for carrying out its trust.[24] None would deny an authority in the House to punish someone who caused a disturbance in the galleries; such a power was necessary notwithstanding the silence of the Constitution. Forsyth continued:

But does it stop here? Are we permitted to remove the nuisance only beyond the walls of this room[?] Extends it no farther? Cannot our deliberations be interrupted at the door, and on the staircase? The same reasoning will apply to all portions of the House and to the street. Does it stop here? Will you permit the beating of drums and the firing of cannon under your windows, in the street, in front of this hall? Can we not remove such nuisances, and prevent their recurrence, by the punishment of those who caused them, for their contempt to this body? . . . We have, therefore, by admission, the power within and without these walls. Where is the limit? . . . It . . . [is] limited only by the jurisdiction of the United States, because to the extent of the jurisdiction [is] the necessity of the legitimate exercise of the power.[25]

The Republican, Philip Barbour, who would one day sit on the Supreme Court, came to Spencer's defense, with an attack on inherent power. Yet Barbour's fellow-Virginian, Henry Tucker, insisted that some implied powers were indispensable and that the Constitution had provided for such contingencies through the necessary and proper clause. While the Constitution enumerated specific privileges of members, it also gave the House legislative power and thereby the means needed for effectuating that power. To insist that contempt could be punished only under a contempt statute would give the Executive a control in such affairs, and the Executive was the most likely source of corruption.[26]

Another Virginia Republican, Charles Mercer, added that a contempt statute would be objectionable, in that by enumerating offenses it would imply that the House could deal with no other contempts. If the House lacked the power, no statute could confer it. The Randall precedent of 1795 had peculiar authority since the heavy majority which had supported power had included as many Republicans as Federalists. Finally, he urged that no oath was needed for the warrant, since none was needed where a judge was personally cognizant of the offense as the House was, through one of its members, in this case.

The next day was Saturday, but the House continued its debate, with several additional members stating their considered views. A move to end discussion was voted down, and a Republican member from the newly-admitted state of Mississippi, former district judge George Poindexter, denied the existence of a federal common law and strictly read the Constitution with respect to contempt powers.

John Holmes, Massachusetts Republican, countered that every legislative body possessed inherent powers. The enumeration of express constitutional privileges of members was far from exhaustive. The framers, he insisted, had wished to give these privileges clear and explicit protection, since they operated beyond the time and place of sessions. To him the precedents established by Congress, far from being dangerous, were "buoys and beacons to point out to the political mariner the course he is to steer his ship, to avoid the rocks, shoals, and quicksands which lay in his way." In a peroration Holmes rested his argument finally on natural rights:

> If our own decisions smell too strong of party, cast them aside. If foreign rules have become too musty, or savor of royalty, reject them. If State or Provincial practices are too local, we will not trust them. And, as God Almighty has implanted in the hearts of man the principle of self-defence and self-protection, so let this political body, representing eight millions of people, establish the precedent that it has the power to repel and punish aggression, and announce to our constituents and the world, that no one can, with impunity, insult us *with a bribe.*[27]

When the Federalist Henry Storrs of New York spoke, he went no further than Holmes in upholding national powers. Both state and federal governments were sovereign in their respective spheres, and the national authorities in addition had general power in the District of Columbia.

Among other speakers was a non-lawyer, the Federalist James Pindall of Virginia. His balanced summation of the argument to this point was noteworthy. He found common law inapplicable and resorted instead to writers on "natural law or ethics." To admit that the House could punish disturbance in the gallery gave the case away, for "You punish disorder in your presence, or in your gallery, because it impedes, molests, or disturbs you in the performance of your Constitutional duties; you are entitled to punish every obstruction to the due performance of those Constitutional duties, whether the obstruction or insult proceeds from the turbulent shouting of the thoughtless, or assaults of blows or bribes by the strong or designing."[28]

Members returned to the subject on Monday, and several new voices were heard. A Kentuckian and Republican, Tunstall Quarles, recapitulated arguments against the power and warned that the courts of the District might intervene through habeas corpus and seriously embarrass the House. Republicans from Delaware, Virginia, and North Carolina all supported the power: Louis McLane thought court process in such affairs inappropriate and insisted on implied and incidental powers even in a constitutional government; Alexander Smyth declared that Congress had all the powers essential to its proper working—constitutions cannot meet every contingency but must leave much to implication; Thomas

Settle of North Carolina used the occasion for his maiden speech in Congress and argued that "whenever a right is granted or duty enjoined, everything necessary to the fair and perfect enjoyment of the right, or to the faithful and honest performance of the duty, is necessarily contained in the grant or injunction, if there be no exceptions clearly and expressly made."[29]

Barbour again rose to rebut point by point his opponents' arguments. The House had no privileges aside from those of its members. Privilege against arrest obtained only while the House was sitting, hence the argument that the privilege clause was not exclusive but only mentioned personal privileges or those operating during adjournment, was invalid. There were no inherent powers, only constitutional powers. In his long speech, he pressed his strict-constructionist case in precise detail.

For three more days the debate went on. On Tuesday, James Tallmadge, New York Republican, initiated a trend toward citation of court cases to show that the contempt power was associated with the right of self-preservation and that jury trials were not required. He quoted Chief Justice Thomas McKean of Pennsylvania as follows: "If we have not a power to punish for a contempt of our authority, we shall soon become so truly contemptible that no contempt can be committed against us."[30] Hopkinson added that the common law, far from being inapplicable, had been used in conjunction with the Constitution with judicial approbation. Two Federalists, Clifton Clagett of New Hampshire and Ezekiel Whitman of Massachusetts, and Forsyth continued on Wednesday to defend the power. Attachment rather than a warrant was described as the proper mode of proceeding. The common law had come increasingly to the fore, particularly in speeches of New Englanders. Beecher of Ohio gave the major summation for the defense the same day, recounting his arguments and rebutting those of the proponents of contempt.

The climax came on Thursday, the fifteenth. For several days motions and counter-motions had come before the House. Their aim, in the words of Charles Rich, Vermont Republican and member of the Committee on Claims, was to discover the "sense of the House" on "some proposition distinct from the case of John Anderson . . ." He wanted the law settled in relation to the principle, "so far as it could be done, by a solemn decision of the House."[31] The House now took several roll calls, notably one on a proposal of Thomas Culbreth, Maryland Republican, to deny the contempt power. The House defeated his motion by 119 to 47.[32] The House then promptly voted to bring Anderson before its bar and interrogate him. The rest of that day and part of the next testimony was taken, including that of fourteen character witnesses. In consequence of these proceedings, the House decided without a record vote to order

110

Anderson reprimanded and discharged. Compliance with this order by the Speaker terminated the Anderson affair.

In the matter of Colonel Anderson the House demonstrated its capacity under some circumstances to consider constitutional questions thoroughly and effectively. The brashness of Anderson's original letter had swept the members into a unanimous vote for arrest. Gradually the principle at stake then became effectively disentangled from the circumstances of the incident, and members came to a reasoned judgment on the issue of power. The final five-to-two margin shows that many had second thoughts but also that most found the arguments for power conclusive.

The search for appropriate grounds for decision was exhaustive to the point of repetitiveness. Members displayed a wealth of knowledge of governmental theory and practice; more than a few revealed that they had done extensive homework in statute books, law reports, and commentaries. Opportunity for repeated rebuttal made it possible for members to uncover weaknesses in their opponents' reasoning and sharpen both the issue and the pertinent principles.

A rather remarkable degree of detachment resulted. Arguments were kept pertinent, the give and take followed a sequential and even logical line of development. At the same time, there was almost total absence of the charges and counter-charges and the impugning of motives which had inflamed the Sedition Act debates.

If one takes the vote of 119 to 47 as an index of the extent of the final divergence, one discovers only limited bloc-voting whether by party or by region. The ninety-six known Republicans voted better than two-to-one in support of the contempt power, and it is less surprising that all but Beecher of the twenty-seven reputed Federalists remaining in the House voted for the power.[33] Yet party affiliations, as mentioned before, were so indistinct as to make these figures inconclusive.

Not one of the original thirteen states yielded a majority against the power, but the Representatives from the five western states opposed it by 14 to 9.[34] Perhaps it was sympathy for the border Indian fighter, Anderson, and a frontier suspicion of the federal authorities that caused the men from these newer states to take this stand.

Note, however, that when the House came two months later to vote on the power to construct internal improvements, the line-up changed substantially. Table 2 shows in numbers and percentages how the four existing regions voted on the two issues. The Anderson case involved mainly the capacity of the legislature to act effectively and roused no sharp sectional or interest-group policy preferences. Internal improve-

111

TABLE 2. House Voting on Contempt Power and Power to Construct Internal Improvements, by Number and Per Cent, 1818

Region	For contempt power		For power over internal improvements	
	Number	Per cent	Number	Per cent
New England	30– 9	77–23	9–29	24–76
Middle Atlantic	48–12	80–20	49–12	80–20
South	32–12	73–27	15–28	35–65
West[a]	9–14	39–61	16– 6	73–27
Total	119–47	72–28	89–75	54–46

SOURCE: 31 *Annals of Congress*, p. 776; 32 *Annals of Congress*, p. 1385.
[a] Includes the five states in note 34, with the addition of one Representative from Indiana, voting "yea" on the second roll call.

ments involved implied powers of the federal government as a whole and affected distinct economic interests. The issue was somewhat analogous to that which Marshall faced in the Bank case a year later. And here, after extensive debate, the regions most likely to benefit immediately from improvements—the Middle Atlantic States and the West—supported the power by heavy margins. The South strongly opposed the power and New England completely reversed its earlier position. The narrow margin of success of the supporters of improvements—54 to 46 per cent—shows how closely the House was divided on this controversial issue.[35]

The Anderson episode showed dramatically that the Representatives of 1818 were capable, under auspicious conditions, of reaching a settlement on a constitutional question that was informed, objective, and lasting.

PARTICIPANTS

All of the three factors of responsibility—participants, mode, and attitudes—operated effectively in 1818. As in the 1790's a large quota of members voiced their opinions on the constitutional question. The reporter mentions thirty-three speakers out of the 182 enrolled. The remarks of twenty-nine were reported in detail; eight of these, or more than a quarter, were Virginians.[36]

Once again, lawyers predominated. The proportion of lawyers in the House had now risen to 64 per cent and the proportion among those .who spoke was even higher. Thus, all but two of the twenty-nine speakers and all seven of the principal speakers were lawyers.[37]

No one, however, hinted that only the lawyer-members were uniquely endowed with the pertinent knowledge and insight. The nearest thing to a suggestion of a special role for lawyers was almost a denial of it. When Spencer asserted that in several constitutionally-important respects civil actions were similar to criminal trials, Forsyth, the Georgian, retorted, "Every gentleman, whether of the profession of the law or not, will know the distinction . . ."[38]

The number of lawyers still diverged along regional lines. New England and the West evidently had a strong preference for lawyer-representatives, for the quotas from those regions, respectively, were 78 per cent and 76 per cent. By contrast, the South elected hardly more than half their members from the profession,[39] though these showed a flair for constitutional and political theory.

A surprising fact about this House was the striking proportion of new members. Louis McLane of Delaware, at thirty-one just starting his federal career, took note of a trend to whittle down powers which the federal government had exercised since its inception—a trend to make Congress "a naked trunk, without a limb by which its functions could be exerted." Said he: "It seems that we live in an age when Constitutional scruples, and doubts of the powers of Congress, have become fashionable, and it is not unworthy of remark that these doubts multiply as we recede from the times in which this instrument was formed, and lose sight of those men who assisted in its formation, when, and by whom, it is fair to infer its spirit and meaning were at least as well understood as they can be at the present day . . ."[40]

The young nation's problem of conveying the constitutional wisdom of the past to each succeeding Congress reached an acute stage during these years. At the very time that the Supreme Court was enjoying a stability of membership unique for any period, the House was consistently receiving more than a majority of new members at each succeeding election. Table 3 gives turnover percentages for the two houses for a number of years and shows an unusually high rate from 1815 to 1821. Turnover in both houses reached a peak in 1817: 38 per cent for the Senate, even though only one-third of the Senators were elected each biennium, and 70 per cent for the House. By contrast, the House turnover in 1955 was 13 per cent and in 1965 16 per cent; the Senate turnover in the same years was 9 per cent and 3 per cent. The heaviest turnover in 1817 was among Representatives from Ohio and Tennessee (83 per cent) and from New England (75 per cent); even the South replaced more than three-fifths of its members.[41]

Moreover, more than half of those who spoke (fifteen of twenty-nine) were newcomers. Youth still predominated, for three members were under thirty and more than half under forty; only five superannuates

113

TABLE 3. House and Senate Percentage Turnover in Various Congresses, 1791–1837

Congresses	Year	House[a]	Senate[b]
1st–2nd	1791[c]	48[d]	23[d]
4th–5th	1797	50	15
9th–10th	1807	37	35
13th–14th	1815[c]	59	37
14th–15th	1817[c]	70	38
15th–16th	1819[c]	52	35
16th–17th	1821[c]	54	26
19th–20th	1827	40	19
24th–25th	1837	47	21

SOURCE: Figures compiled from *Biographical Directory of Congress*, 1961 ed.

[a] The size of the House ranged from 67 in the 1st Congress to 273 in the 25th.

[b] The size of the Senate ranged from 30 in the 1st Congress to 52 in the 25th.

[c] Indicates one or two new states were added.

[d] Percentages include members who returned to Congress after one or more terms of absence; the range of such repeaters being from 0 in 1791 to 23 in 1819; the figure in 1817 was 20.

were over fifty! While these men could boast experience in state and local office,[42] the House faced a serious dearth of leaders with the talents and experience that term implies. It was chiefly men with previous congressional experience who assumed leading roles in the debate.[43]

In various ways the electorate was complicating the work of Congress. Divergences of opinion were intensifying along regional lines with implications for effective responsibility. On the surface the newer men from New England and the West were differing from Southerners on the hold of legislative precedents.[44] More fundamentally, the men from the Middle Atlantic and Southern states tended to rely on lessons of political experience and on principles of political theory. On the contrary, New Englanders, and Ohioans as well, predominantly lawyers and inexperienced in Congress, looked for guidance to the common law, the product of courts. Poindexter, the Mississippian, reaffirmed the Republican doctrine of 1800 in totally denying the "existence of the common law in the United States as a nation."[45] The Massachusetts Federalist, Ezekiel Whitman, however, venerated that body of precedents and rules: "It is nothing more nor less than common sense. It is that wisdom which is sanctioned by the experience of ages; which has been agreed to in all times, and in all places, as constituting the perfection of reason."[46]

In short, New England voters, distrustful both of legislatures and of the sort of political speculation to which legislators might resort, gave their votes to lawyers and the common law. This very Anderson affair elicited a similar divergence of position between Justice Johnson of Charleston and Justice Story of Boston. In his opinion for the Court in Anderson v. Dunn, Johnson used language maintaining that the chief restraints on Congress were morality, political accountability, and a body of known and time-tested rules of law with which legislators presumably were acquainted. When Story later took up the decision in his *Commentaries,* he reproduced Johnson's opinion in full but showed that his own preference among the possible controls of Congress was the common law. That body of law was, he said, "known and acted upon and revered by the people." It furnished, he continued, "principles equally for civil and criminal justice, for public privileges and private rights."[47]

Southern planters and Northern lawyers, though agreed on the immediate issue, were resting the power on grounds which frequently diverged from each other.

MODE

In dealing with the Anderson affair, the members employed procedures not unlike those favored by Jefferson and his party. Members were clearly aware of the problem of procedure, perhaps because the House was both prosecuting and judging an individual who had freely confessed his deed and continued cooperative throughout. Excepting the possibility of court review, all that stood between the accused and the power of the majority were the rules governing the House proceedings. Yet most of the talk dealt with the basic constitutional question, and for this the procedure afforded full and free discussion.

As outlined above, the discussion went through the three stages characteristic of the earlier House. After ordering the arrest, the House took up the question of constitutional power and sought to reach a preliminary decision on principles. Next came the brief, almost perfunctory, committee stage; a broadly representative select committee embodied the agreed principle in the form of a draft resolution. The House then resumed debate and, spendthrift of time, analyzed the main question from all angles and with full participation. Technically, it had ruled out Committee of the Whole, yet the abundance of available time actually permitted as full, if not as flexible, participation as if that device had been formally in effect.

Nevertheless, fundamental changes in procedure were taking place during the decades after Jefferson's retirement. Most striking of these changes as they affected the legislative process was the rise of the standing committee. By the opening of this session in December 1817, the

115

reporter for the *Annals of Congress* was able to list nineteen such committees.[48] Among them was one destined to become the chief forum for the House in the consideration of constitutional questions—the Committee on the Judiciary, established in 1813.[49] After President James Monroe delivered his annual message, the House appointed nine select committees to deal with specific subjects of his message[50] and significantly, gave them authority to report by "bill or otherwise."[51] Many of these latter were in effect standing committees. The House now had twenty-eight separate subdivisions to handle aspects of its work.

In spite of its adherence to Jeffersonian procedures in the Anderson affair, the House, on other issues, was actually in full flight from those procedures. The Committee of the Whole was losing its place as the general forum for initial discussion of important matters.

Standing committees were assuming a leading role in three respects. First, they were becoming the chief means for inquiry into facts and for the formulation of principles for the devising of plans, and even for the drafting of bills. No longer did the House grant committees formal "leave to bring in" each new bill.

Second, the Committee of the Whole was losing its preferred position as the initial forum for discussion of principles; instead, it was often merely reviewing proposals which smaller committees had already set in formal mold and in which those committees had accordingly embodied their own predetermined principles.

Third, the standing committees were achieving independence of the House; this resulted not only from their multiplicity, but from such practices as selection on the basis of experience and interest-representation, continuity of membership within the limits of House turnover, advancement by seniority, and enhancement of the prerogatives of chairmen.[52] The effect, while salutary in some respects, was to magnify the influence of local, state, and sectional interests and hinder the achievement of consensus. The handling of the issue of internal improvements at this very session exemplified some of these trends.[53] By 1825, the standing committee would become predominant as the "pioneer of discussion" in the legislative process, at least as it affected policy determination.[54]

These basic changes resulted from more than a need to divide the increased load of legislative work. In part, they resulted from an inattention to sound procedures, induced by the passing of the Founding Fathers and rapid turnover in membership. In part, they must have resulted from a revival of state consciousness and the influence of sectional interests. The centrifugal drift of power from the whole House to its component units paralleled a like tendency in the nation.

Finally, the decline in the quality of executive and party leadership took its toll. Formally under Hamilton and informally under Jefferson, the Executive had conducted much of the work of fact-gathering and policy-formulation now being assumed by standing committees.[55] Hence, it had been possible for the Congress to focus its energies and talents on matters of basic principle and to assign only perfunctory tasks to smaller committees. The Executive had likewise maintained close links with party leaders in Congress and achieved legislative cohesiveness behind Administration programs through party discipline.

When Madison succeeded Jefferson in 1809, however, all this changed. Madison was as inept in executive office as he had been brilliant in constitutional debate, and Congress broke away from the Executive. To assume the work formerly done for Congress by the Executive, committees mushroomed.[56] The need for some measure of party cohesiveness was met by a shift of power from the President to such party men in Congress as Henry Clay. Accordingly the speakership and standing committees became organs of legislative rather than presidential party leadership.[57]

Without the firm executive hand which had accompanied the growth of parliamentary procedure in England, and which to a lesser degree had helped to inaugurate parallel practice in Congress, the House now began parcelling out the major share of policy formation among its subdivisions. In the course of time, it would tend to assign to these semi-independent and often interest-dominated committees a like influence over constitutional issues.

In handling the Anderson affair, however, the House clung essentially to the mode so well adapted to achieving the sense of the whole on constitutional issues. Members had ample notice, the question was defined with increasing sharpness, full expression was given all points of view, the House weighed the arguments, this time before the public eye, it took a roll call vote on the precise question, and it furnished the public a lengthy if somewhat incomplete record of its discussion.

ATTITUDES

If the makeup and the procedures of the House were changing in 1818, the attitudes of members toward responsibility were remaining constant. None talked of the legal sanction for responsibility, many talked of the moral sanction and of what each member's responsibility entailed. Not a few insisted that each was bound, before voting on constitutional questions, to inform his own judgment as fully as possible. In offering his resolutions to head off the assertion of a contempt power, Spencer declared that he had engaged in the "most diligent research" on the subject.[58] On this "great constitutional question," Barbour said he had bestowed the "most mature deliberation" he had been able to

117

give the subject.[59] Louis McLane stated what was evidently the attitude of many. He could not, he said, "permit himself to pass upon the important subject before the House, without submitting the reasons upon which the conviction in his mind had been formed."[60]

Many members evidently felt it an individual and personal obligation to apply their own best reasoning to the question. One searches the record in vain for qualifications on this obligation, whether such qualifications relate to the type of question or the degree of responsibility. None suggested that one who merely doubted validity would be warranted in ignoring the question of validity.

The result of the researches and the expositions of its members was the emergence of what was repeatedly called the "sense of the House." A statement by Spencer on launching his challenge to the validity of the proceedings epitomized the aim of many members; it incidentally hinted that a judicial appeal was not an impossibility. Here is how the reporter summarized his statement:

> Mr. Spencer, of New York, observed, that in submitting the resolutions which had been read, his object was to procure a decision of the House on the abstract question of its right to proceed in the case of Colonel Anderson. He had offered them in this stage of the proceedings, because no opportunity had yet been given to take the sense of the House, and with a view also of preventing the influence of those feelings, which the demerits of the case might excite, in producing a decision that calm and deliberate reason might not sanction. It was more consistent, also, with the dignity of the House, that we should retrace its proceedings, if they were wrong, from our own impulse, rather than be compelled to do so on the motion of the accused or his counsel.[61]

"Calm and deliberate reason," operating under fair procedures after full and free discussion,[62] and after a committee had formulated and sharpened the issue,[63] would produce a decision of value and authority.[64]

In word and deed, the members appeared to be guided by the Jeffersonian version of the tripartite theory. While court review remained a possibility, the House spoke and acted as if its decision were final, as if, that is, it would form a part of congressionally established constitutional custom or law[65] and set the course for subsequent Congresses. The House reflected a glowing confidence in its own capacity for handling questions such as this. The press seemed to share that confidence. While virtually ignoring the Court, *Niles Register* was giving the debates in Congress such wide circulation that the electorate must have deepened its constitutional understanding and insight.[66] Congress was not only informing itself, but instructing the consensus.

118

CONCLUSIONS

The Anderson affair expressed the Jeffersonian conception of responsibility and demonstrated some of its advantages. The House talked its way to a constitutional settlement of the contempt-power issue that not only furnished a guidepost to the Court, but, more important, instructed its own fluctuating and somewhat inexperienced membership and educated the public in constitutional principles. Lasting settlement resulted not merely from favorable circumstances but also from the acumen of experienced lawyer-members, especially Virginians, from procedures furthering general discussion, and from acceptance of responsibility to conduct an impartial and deliberative search of principles.

Yet one must put this incident in perspective. For one thing, the question under discussion was of a sort for which detached congressional consideration is easier to achieve than for others. Like the issue of executive privilege in the Bradley case, and even that of presidential removal in 1789, it pertained to the operations of federal organs and to their interrelationships under the separation of powers. It related only loosely to the federal division of powers—that is, to the capacity of the federal government to act at all and to the powers reserved to the states. The Sedition Act had implications for federalism, and during the half-century from Jefferson's retirement to Fort Sumter issues of federalism posed the gravest challenges to the Constitution. The member-states, equipped to act through their own governmental organs and hence able to give full expression to local and sectional interests sometimes in defiance of the national interest, repeatedly threatened to resist constitutional readings by the federal authorities, whether legislative or judicial. Analysis of some of these disputes puts the Anderson affair in perspective and qualifies its significance. I shall draw not only on the handling of the matter of internal improvements, but also on the discussions of the Missouri Compromise of 1820, the Tariffs of 1828 and 1832, the Reapportionment Act of 1842, and the Fugitive Slave Act, which formed an ingredient of the Great Compromise of 1850.

When officials applied Jefferson's formulation to some of these episodes, the results were bizarre. Thus, this very 1818 session witnessed the President, the Senate, and the House all adopting independent and somewhat conflicting interpretations of the power over internal improvements.[67] President James Monroe later on vetoed legislation on the subject as contrary to federal powers as he construed them,[68] but in 1842, President John Tyler swallowed his own grave doubts of constitutionality and signed the Reapportionment Act of that year, yielding his opinion to that of Congress. Both houses had concluded that Congress could validly require the states to elect Representatives from single-member districts

119

instead of on the general ticket. The next year, when four of the six states which had employed the general ticket persisted in that method, a House which the Democrats had wrested from the Whigs decided to seat their Representatives anyway.[69] On issues like this the plan for separate constitutional settlement by each branch invited confusion and stalemate.

In spite of recurrent crises the three factors of responsibility continued to operate with some success in Congress. Notwithstanding the steady parade of young recruits and the rapid turnover, Congress continued, under the leadership of its experienced members, most of them lawyers and many Southern, to debate constitutional questions with focus, learning, and insight. Lawyers led, but without treating constitutional wisdom as the special province of their profession and with the evident intention of informing and maturing public understanding of the Constitution.

Procedures were undergoing change, especially on matters of policy. Even in constitutional disputes, the permanent standing committee was beginning to supplement the Committee of the Whole. Part of the probing discussion which led to the Missouri Compromise took place in House Committee of the Whole but part also in the Senate Judiciary Committee, and of course the ill-fated Tariff of 1828, which launched the Nullification movement in South Carolina, had much of its initial drafting and discussion in the House Committee on Manufactures, stacked much of the time since its formation in 1819 with protectionists.[70] Nevertheless Congress in the Great Compromise of 1850 resorted essentially to the Jeffersonian mode. It was a Senator from the Border State of Kentucky, Henry Clay, who initiated the eight resolutions embodying the proposals. It was not to a standing committee, but to the Committee of the Whole that the Senate immediately referred the proposed resolutions for debate and decision on principle. The resolutions then went to a select committee representing equally the North and the South with a chairman acceptable to both for conversion into specific bills. Debate and passage followed, and civil war was averted for another decade. This mode, combining the advantages of small committees with the consensus-revealing and educative functions of general discussion, was probably the prevailing pattern for constitutional discussions throughout this whole period.

Finally the conception which governed most members during the years from the Philadelphia Convention to the Civil War was tripartite, for most of the period in its Jeffersonian version. Congress took a leading part in settlement of constitutional questions, narrow and broad, interpretative and implementational. Rare indeed were expressions of the idea later ascribed to men of this period by sponsors of the judicial monopoly theory, that only the Supreme Court could legitimize federal action. More likely, those men increasingly felt the pressure of another sort of review. South Carolina achieved a reduction in tariff duties by threatening to nullify the tariff in 1832–1833; four states, as just mentioned, successfully defied the Reapportionment Act of 1842; and the 1850 compromise was achieved in the shadow of an impending Southern secession convention. Perhaps it was state review, the threat of state non-compliance or resistance, that habituated members of Congress to the somewhat tentative and provisional character of many of their own constitutional settlements and prepared them for the later expansion of judicial review.

The single lesson of seven decades of federal-state discord would, for some, be the importance of judicial review as the sole alternative to anarchy or war. Yet Congress settled many of the gravest disputes of that age, and in the end the Supreme Court proved as ineffectual as Congress in averting civil war.

6   Stress of War:
The Oath of Office Act of 1862

The Civil War was in full progress. A Congress shrunken by the exodus of Southerners wrestled with bills to bring victory for the North. This chapter will examine its handling of one of these, a change in the oath of office, and more succinctly two others, the National Currency Act of 1863 and the National Bank Act of 1864. It will show what was happening to conceptions of responsibility and the manner of its discharge in a Congress almost entirely Northern and in a time of crisis. It will show how far that temporary crisis was a sort of rehearsal for our own age of chronic crisis.

As is usually the case, war and nationalism subjected the constitutional system to strain. How did Congress meet the challenge in 1862? Did its handling of such questions during the war contribute to the increased activity of the Supreme Court in invalidating its laws after the war, or was that increase simply an expression, as some have contended, of the power urges of the justices?

The year 1862 found the North in trouble. Stonewall Jackson's successes in the Shenandoah Valley during March and June created grave misgivings about a Northern victory. Preserving the nation called for far-reaching measures. The urgent need of those measures bore heavily on the nation's legislators.

Besides taking steps to ensure military victory, Congress faced the problem of Southern sympathizers in the North. Public hysteria reinforced a genuine danger of subversion in pressing for action. President Lincoln himself declared "sympathizers pervaded all departments of the government and nearly all communities . . ."[1] Furthermore, the situation afforded the new and victorious Republican party an unparalleled opportunity to consolidate its control of Congress.

Congress acted with dispatch. Soon after convening in July 1861, the House approved a resolution of Representative John Potter, Wisconsin Republican, for creation of a select committee to determine the extent of disloyalty among government employees.[2] Potter led the committee with radical enthusiasm and made discoveries that in numbers exceeded

122

even his own expectations.[3] The danger was clearly present and the problem for Congress was to fashion weapons to fight it. At first, as shown earlier, the Congress extended the traditional oath to support the Constitution to include defense of the nation against foreign and domestic enemies.[4]

An oath that looked only to the future, however, had severe limitations. It permitted one to repent for past deeds and hence the departed Southern members of Congress to return and thus weaken Radical Republican control. Furthermore, to identify the disloyal remained difficult, since past acts were irrelevant in proving intentions. What was needed was an oath of past loyalty, a swearing under penalty of perjury that no acts had been committed amounting to disloyalty. Such an oath was enacted into law in April 1862, but its coverage was confined to former slaveowners in the District of Columbia who requested compensation for their freed slaves. Two months later it was extended to jurors in federal courts.[5]

On March 24, 1862, Representative James Wilson, Iowa Republican, introduced a bill in the House requiring an oath of past loyalty of all persons employed in any way by the United States government. The House Judiciary Committee considered the bill and reported it favorably. The House passed it immediately. The bill then went to the Senate Judiciary Committee, which hastily approved it. On three separate days from June 13 to 23, the Senate debated the bill and then passed it after excepting the President, Vice President, and members of Congress from its provisions. The House refused to concur in these amendments and a compromise was finally adopted in conference which excepted only the President. Both houses accepted the conference report, and President Lincoln signed the bill into law on July 2, 1862.

It was not until the bill had cleared the House and also the Senate Judiciary Committee that open constitutional objection was made to it. The bill required that one swear, in part, "I have never voluntarily borne arms against the United States . . . [and] I have neither sought nor accepted nor attempted to exercise the functions of any office whatever under any authority or pretended authority in hostility to the United States . . ."[6] Thus the bill added materially to the terms of the oath prescribed by the Constitution. Accordingly it gave rise to the three days of Senate debate. Otherwise, the Congress brushed aside most constitutional objections and failed to raise others.

In the end Congress decided to exclude the President, but to include Senators and Representatives in the coverage of the oath. This decision of Congress to place its members under legal compulsion to swear to their past loyalty had an uneven course and an inconclusive end. Within eight months of passage, Solomon Foot, Vermont Republican, and presi-

123

dent protempore of the Senate, neglected to administer the amended oath at the swearing-in ceremony.[7] When Senator Lyman Trumbull, Illinois Republican and an Administration spokesman, objected, it came to light that indeed no Senator had yet taken it. Next day, the Radical Republican from Massachusetts, Senator Charles Sumner, introduced a resolution that all Senators be immediately enjoined to take the oath, but a vote was forestalled when all the Senators voluntarily took the oath anyway.[8]

At the beginning of the next Congress in December 1863, however, Senator James Bayard, Delaware Democrat, who had been absent when the other Senators took the oath, refused to take it voluntarily. This led Sumner to revive his resolution. Bayard insisted, despite Congress's previous decision on the point, that Congress lacked the power to compel him to take any oath other than the one prescribed in the Constitution.[9] The debate raged on for an entire month, exploring matters that had been wholly overlooked in the passage of the Oath of Office Act and raising both narrow and broad constitutional questions. The resolution passed by a party vote.[10] After taking the oath, Bayard resigned his seat rather than remain in the Senate and participate in what he considered a violation of the Constitution.

In *Ex parte* Garland[11] the Supreme Court, by a five to four vote, decided that the past loyalty oath as applied to federal attorneys was void as a bill of attainder, an ex post facto law, and a legislative usurpation of the judicial power to admit and expel attorneys from practice before courts. Although this judicial condemnation of the past loyalty oath was forceful, its reach was uncertain. Was the Oath of Office Act as a whole void, or only its application to a specific profession? The question baffled everyone, even the Attorney General, who, when asked his opinion, replied, "We must again wait the verdicts of the courts."[12]

Final decision on retention of the past loyalty oath, however, lay with Congress. The weapon proved highly effective for consolidating and perpetuating Republican control of Congress.[13] Nonetheless the Republicans began to feel its bite, when some on election to Congress were effectively challenged under it.[14] Although there was no reasonable doubt as to their loyalty at any time, the mere fact that they had held office in a rebel state disqualified them. Moreover, the past loyalty oath conflicted with the political disqualification-and-redemption device of section 3 of the Fourteenth Amendment. Although Congress might vote by a two-thirds majority under that provision to remove the disability to hold government office, the past loyalty oath still remained a bar. To prevent the weapon from working on themselves and to remove the conflict with the Fourteenth Amendment, the Republicans, on July 11, 1868, modified the provisions by exempting those freed from political disabilities under the Fourteenth Amendment from the oath of past loyalty.[15]

Gradually the power of the Radical Republicans declined and with it, the chief force behind the oath. After 1870 they lost their two-thirds control of Congress and thereby the power to decide which new members of Congress must take the 1862 past loyalty oath and which only the 1868 pledge of future loyalty. In 1871 Congress passed a measure extending to ex-Confederates generally an exemption from the earlier oath,[16] but President Grant pointed out the unfairness of this obvious political expedient.[17] Only the Juror's Loyalty Oath of 1862 now remained as an effective bar to those unable to swear to past loyalty. At last, on May 13, 1884, Congress closed two decades of protest and struggle by dropping the past loyalty oath in all its manifestations. The oath of future loyalty, merged with that to uphold the Constitution, remained the test for federal officers and employees.[18]

CONSTITUTIONAL QUESTIONS

Clearly, the oath of past loyalty raised serious constitutional questions, both narrow and broad. Yet none in Congress had questioned the validity of the two preliminary bills with their narrow coverage. One, the juror's loyalty oath bill, had passed the Senate by a margin of 30 to 5. Although that margin fails to reflect the doubts which existed concerning the wisdom of the measure, the precedent was so firmly fixed that no significant debate took place concerning the policy of the oath of office bill.

It was the broadened coverage of this later bill that provoked the constitutional objection. The bill reached not only federal employees, but also the constitutional offices of Senator, Representative, Vice President, and President. Application of the oath to officers of their own rank made a majority of Senators doubtful of the competence of Congress to pass the bill. The qualifications for these constitutional offices were prescribed in the Constitution, but were these qualifications exhaustive? Were they a maximum or a minimum? In short, did Congress have the power to increase the qualifications for members of Congress and for President and Vice President by requiring an oath of past loyalty defined in terms of action which Congress willed to be evidence of disloyalty?

The question had both a narrow and a broad aspect. The former concerned the limitations which the terms of the Constitution placed on Congress. Although the Senate debate dealt with this subject, it covered only one part of it—the question already mentioned, namely, whether

125

the constitutionally prescribed qualifications were a maximum or a minimum. The Senate failed to consider whether other constitutional limitations might apply, for example, the bill of attainder and ex post facto clauses.

Nor did the Senate consider broad aspects of the issue. A "legal" determination that the constitutional qualifications were only a minimum, and that other constitutional provisions were inapplicable, would still leave other issues of constitutional import. Although Congress might possess the necessary legal power, there might be important reasons for refraining from exercising such power to the fullest in all circumstances. The wisdom of exercising powers that affect the constitutional structure of the government requires consideration on its own merits in each particular case.

On this broad question, and, since the courts would probably have deemed the oath as applied to members of Congress political, likewise on the narrow question, the decision of Congress was essentially final.

COURSE OF THE DISCUSSION

In the House. In its journey through Congress, the oath of office bill cleared both of the Judiciary Committees and House floor debate before publicly encountering constitutional objection. The action of the House Judiciary Committee on the bill went unrecorded.[19] Representative Wilson, thirty-three and a newcomer to the House, intimated that some discussion had taken place there since the bill which he reported favorably from the committee was a substitute for the bill which he had originally introduced. Besides enumerating four requirements concerning past behavior,[20] the bill also increased the penalty for perjury. Furthermore, false swearing to past acts incurred permanent disability from holding any federal office. The four requirements of past behavior and the increased penalty underwent no essential change during passage. As originally framed, the oath applied to "every person elected or appointed to any office of honor or profit under the Government of the United States, either in the civil, military, or naval departments . . ."[21]

In the House, none voiced a constitutional objection. Moreover, only three Representatives felt obliged to make public their dissent from the past loyalty oath provision. Only one of these, Representative John Phelps, Missouri Democrat, with sixteen years of House service, spelled out his reasons. Wilson had stated that the purpose of the bill was "to keep out of office under the Government of the United States men who have taken up arms against the United States, and who have endeavored to destroy the Government under which we live."[22] Phelps had two ob-

126

jections to the manner in which the bill implemented this purpose. First, an oath of past loyalty made no allowance for repentance and, second, the oath applied whether or not the person had actually renounced his loyalty. He pointed out that in Arkansas, for example, loyal citizens holding state offices had to remain in their positions since even in the rebel states law and order must be preserved.[23]

Wilson replied with heat. Those in official positions who had contributed to overturning the federal authority, he argued, did not deserve a chance to repent. In answer to Phelps's second argument Wilson said, "No man is compelled to act as sheriff, to go out and arrest the loyal men who have refused to engage in this rebellion."[24] After completing his argument, Wilson demanded an immediate vote on the bill to see "whether the House is disposed to enact any measure which shall deal with these rebels as they should be dealt with . . ."[25] The House responded by passing the bill 78 to 47.

In the Senate. The same sense of unreflective urgency characterized Senate consideration in its earlier stages. The Senate Judiciary Committee, which had opposed on nonconstitutional grounds the past loyalty oath for jurors, reported the House bill to the Senate without amendment.[26] In doing so it went along with its chairman, Senator Lyman Trumbull, Illinois Republican, who was floor manager of the bill. This former state judge, a Senator of eight years standing, moved that the Senate suspend current business and consider the bill. He expected the matter to require only a few minutes. The Senate quickly agreed, Trumbull spoke briefly, and the bill was ordered to a third reading. After the reading, the "yeas" and "nays" were ordered, and the Senate was ostensibly ready to ballot.

At this moment Senator Willard Saulsbury, Democrat of Delaware, rose and made the first constitutional protest against the bill. Saulsbury had entered the Senate three years earlier after having served five years as state attorney general. Said he:

> I shall make no objection to the passage of this bill; but I wish simply to suggest . . . that for many officers, the Constitution prescribes the oath, and says what the oath shall be. Is it competent for the Congress of the United States to pass an act requiring an additional oath, and saying that an officer who takes the oath prescribed by the Constitution shall not exercise the functions of the office unless he takes such additional oath? . . . I have no objection to Congress passing such an act; but to my mind the question is at least doubtful as to the power of Congress to say that a person who

127

takes the oath prescribed as a qualification for his office shall not exercise its functions unless he takes an additional oath prescribed by Congress.[27]

Trumbull saw fit to answer Saulsbury and thus the constitutional debate began.

Saulsbury, in arguing that Congress lacked the power to prescribe any oath as prerequisite to the office of President, Vice President, Senator, or Representative, had concluded that the constitutional oath was the maximum qualification for those positions. In rebuttal, Trumbull at first maintained that the constitutional prescription of an oath was only a minimum qualification and that Congress could increase the requirement beyond that minimum. The presidential oath, however, was prescribed in detail by Article II, section 1 whereas Article VI prescribed the oath for members of Congress only in general terms. This difference was persuasive to Trumbull. He soon conceded that Congress had no power at all over the presidential oath but insisted that it had power over the oath for members of Congress. On the second day of debate, June 21, Trumbull offered an amendment embodying this distinction and exempting the President from the coverage of the bill. Both Senate and House later went along with Trumbull's amendment.

Debate then centered on the question of prescribing a past loyalty oath for members of Congress. Senator Saulsbury, in arguing against such an oath, treated the difference between the general prescription of Article VI and the detailed prescription of Article II as irrelevant. Congress could adjust the wording of the oath, but must confine itself to an oath to support the Constitution.[28]

Senator Garret Davis, an old-line Whig and later Democrat from Kentucky, offered an amendment on the second day of debate to exclude all constitutional offices from the scope of the bill. Davis at sixty had just come to the Senate, but this farmer-lawyer had long before served eight years in the House. Even on the first day of debate Davis had argued for the position he was later to put in the form of an amendment.

He supported his position by referring to an analogous issue which had arisen in Kentucky. The Kentucky constitution prescribed the qualifications for elective offices, and the legislature stipulated an additional qualification—a denial under oath of ever having dueled. When certain state officials later refused on constitutional grounds to take this oath, the legislature itself adjudged the statute unconstitutional. Davis advanced a second reason to support his amendment. If Congress could increase the qualifications for office by means of the oath, then it necessarily followed that it could also decrease the qualifications below the constitutional requirement. Since none would admit that Congress could

128

decrease constitutional qualifications, neither, he reasoned, could it increase them.

Trumbull answered only Davis' first argument. He said that Davis' analogy to the Kentucky case was not really an analogy at all. Unlike Congress, state legislatures had the power to require two oaths of their members, one to support the federal and one to support their state constitution. It would be absurd to believe that the Article VI oath prevented the states from requiring a state oath that was truly subordinate to the constitutional oath. Therefore, since the Article VI oath could not be a maximum qualification for state legislators, neither could it for members of Congress since the same language applied to both groups.

The next speaker was John Carlile of Virginia, a Unionist who had just come to Congress from the Virginia Secession Convention after four years in the state legislature. Carlile thought Trumbull's rebuttal erroneous. Unlike Congress, the states derived power to require the additional oath to support the state constitution from their own constitution, not from Article VI. Congress derived its power to prescribe oaths for its members from Article VI. Thus that article withheld power to increase the oath requirement from state legislatures and Congress alike. State legislatures could add to oaths if their state constitutions authorized it. But, since the federal Constitution gave Congress no such explicit power, Congress was disabled from adding to the oaths required of its members.

Trumbull replied to Carlile:

The Constitution of the United States says that the Senator of the United States and the Senator of the State of Kentucky shall take an oath to support this Constitution. Then will you read it by saying the Senator of the United States shall take an oath to support this Constitution, and he shall take nothing else, and the Senator of the State of Kentucky shall take an oath to support this Constitution and he shall take something else? If this Constitution is an inhibition upon requiring any addition to the oath of a United States officer, it is also an inhibition to requiring any additional oath from a State officer, because the language is applicable to both, and precisely the same in both cases.[29]

Trumbull also applied himself to Davis' analogy. He argued that all the Kentucky legislature had done was arbitrarily to refuse to apply the statute, not to hold it unconstitutional. Trumbull cited a New York case in which the legislature had passed a statute disqualifying any person convicted of certain crimes from holding state office. The state courts held the statute constitutional, but the legislature later refused to apply it by virtue of its inherent arbitrary power.

Saulsbury on his part cited an Alabama precedent. The Alabama constitution prescribed the qualifications for attorneys, thus making them constitutional officers, and when the state legislature imposed an additional dueling oath on attorneys, the state courts held it unconstitutional. Trumbull merely replied that if such a decision existed, it was "unsound law."[30]

On the second day of debate, after both Trumbull and Davis had formally introduced their amendments, the debate became more focused on the central question, whether Congress could constitutionally add requirements to the oaths for Senators and Representatives. A few new arguments appeared. Davis suggested that lack of power to impose the past loyalty oath on its members did not disable Congress from achieving its purpose—keeping the disloyal out of Congress. After all, Congress had power to pass on the qualifications of each person presenting himself for membership, and at such time Congress could determine disloyalty and refuse membership by virtue of its powers in such cases.

Saulsbury made the only reference in the debate to the broad constitutional question.

> There are so many of these things presented here in the form of oaths and test oaths, and I have objected to them so frequently that it may seem rather ungracious and unbecoming to interpose these objections; but really the public good certainly cannot require such legislation as this, and you will find if you adopt it, embarrassment constantly meeting you in the future. All this system of test oaths will at a future day be regarded, I apprehend, as having arisen from an imperfect consideration of the circumstances in which we are placed, and as not dictated by sound policy or sound reason.[31]

Trumbull resorted to another analogy to advance his point. He cited a statute passed by Congress in 1790 which disqualified judges convicted of bribery from ever holding any federal office. This, he maintained, showed that Congress possessed power to increase the qualifications for constitutional offices since judges were included in the Article VI oath. Davis retorted to this analogy and to the New York case which Trumbull had earlier cited by saying that both merely showed that disqualification from holding governmental office could be a part of the punishment for criminal activity.

On the last day of the debate, Trumbull had to face a fourth adversary, this time a fellow Republican, James Doolittle of Wisconsin. Davis and Carlile continued their vocal opposition to the bill and their support of

Davis' amendment. The target of discussion was the 1790 bribery statute. Carlile thought the analogy defective because the power to exclude from office persons convicted of crimes was not evidence of power to increase the qualifications for constitutional offices. Doolittle, a former state judge, agreed, inasmuch as disqualification for court conviction for a crime differed sharply from disqualification for false swearing to an additional oath.

On this note the constitutional debate ended. The Senate adopted Davis' amendment to exclude all constitutional offices by a vote of 20 to 18. After a brief effort by John Henderson, Missouri Democrat, to clarify the language, the Senate passed the entire bill as amended, 33 to 5.

In Conference Committee and Final Passage. The House then refused to debate constitutional issues. It summarily rejected Davis' amendment and adopted Trumbull's compromise measure instead. The bill then went to a conference committee appointed to iron out differences between House and Senate versions. There is no evidence that this committee seriously considered the constitutional question, and Davis, one of its members, refused to sign the report.

In the final Senate consideration, Davis objected to compromising constitutional principle. No one else at this final stage in either house expressed interest in the issue of validity. The House passed the final version by voice vote, and the Senate by 27 to 8. Thus, the three separate days of somewhat brief floor debate were all that Congress was able or willing to devote to the issue.

Discussion Evaluated. Obviously the handling of the constitutional questions concerning this oath lacked both thoroughness and effective detachment. The five Senators who debated the only serious challenge to the bill—the narrow question under Articles II and VI—canvassed most of the pertinent arguments. No one, however, brought up the other arguments developed later by the Court. Not till Senator Bayard directly attacked the oath a year and a half later did the Senate discuss those objections. None seriously considered the broad question of the wisdom of oaths of this sort in general. What debate there was reflected a new tendency to rely on court precedents as a substitute for the probing of underlying principles.

Within these limits, the Senate debate was pertinent and focused, and digressions were few. Moreover, even though the debate occurred at intervals between June 13 and 23, the thread of the argument was never lost. The five debaters continued throughout to exchange informed opinions.

131

In addition the arguments against the bill succeeded in changing minds at least temporarily. The 20 to 18 vote in favor of the Davis amendment shows that a considerable number voted against both party and regional associations. In the votes on passage of the Senate bill and on the conference report most of the doubters, however, came back into line.

Table 4 shows the effect of region and party on the voting. Thirty-one of the forty-eight Senators were Republicans, all from Northern states committed to the war. Three Democrats came from the North, four from the West, and the remaining six, along with four Unionists, from the Border States, interpreted here to include Maryland and Delaware. Note that, on the Davis amendment narrowing the coverage of the oath, the second vote here shown, every Democrat and Unionist rallied to the amendment, and that even seven Republicans broke ranks to join them. Excepting nonvoters, Republicans were unanimously in favor of some oath whether it be the earlier oath of jurors or the two versions of the oath under discussion. Other Senators tended to oppose any oath, although nonvoting was popular, probably due to fear of criticism or reprisal.

TABLE 4. Senate Voting on Versions of the Past-Loyalty Oath by Party Groupings, 1862

Grouping	Number	For jurors' oath June 9	For Davis amendment June 23	For Senate bill June 23	For conference bill June 30
Republicans	31	26–0	7–18	28–0	26–0
Democrats, Northern and Western[a]	7	2–0	4–0	2–0	1–2
Border[b] Democrats	6	1–3	5–0	2–3	0–5
Border[b] Unionists[c]	4	1–2	4–0	1–2	0–1
Total	48	30–5	20–18	33–5	27–8

SOURCE: *Cong. Globe,* 37th Cong., 2nd sess. (1862), pt. 3, pp. 2620, 2872, 2873; pt. 4, p. 3014.
[a] Includes California and Oregon.
[b] Border States here were Maryland, Delaware, Kentucky, and Missouri.
[c] One Unionist came from a portion of Virginia soon to join the Union as West Virginia.

Despite this reversion to party and regional preferences the debate was not without lasting effect. After all, Trumbull, leader of the pro-oath forces, was willing to engage in constitutional discussion and to accede to the argument that application to the President was unconstitutional.

However brief and narrowly focused, the Senate debate was productive concerning the single constitutional issue raised.

PARTICIPANTS

The two most obvious characteristics of the Congress that discussed the oath bill were the absence of Southern members and the new primacy of the legal profession. The first of these had an incalculable effect on the discussion, but the second, too, was noteworthy. The discussion of this bill, in contrast to earlier episodes, lay exclusively with lawyers. Although the quota of lawyers in the House had dropped to 54 per cent, only lawyers voiced their opinions. In accordance with practice before and since, every one of the nine members of the House Judiciary Committee had had legal training,[32] as had all three of the floor speakers with anything to say. In the Senate, lawyer-members had risen to 85 per cent and from these were drawn all seven members of the Judiciary Committee[33] and all six debaters. Only lawyers, finally, served on the conference committee.[34] Although no one acclaimed it, the bar had taken over.

Did these men provide the caliber of constitutional wisdom and leadership the situation demanded? For one thing, the number of participants was small; only three spoke briefly in the House, and five at any length in the Senate. These five Senators had had no more congressional experience than the average. In party conviction they were atypical: two were Democrats, one a Unionist, and two were Republicans who would become Democrats after the war and one of these (Doolittle) had earlier been a Democrat. The sole defender of the bill, Trumbull, had been brought up in Connecticut and had practiced law briefly in Georgia and accordingly had gained experience denied to many of the Republicans. The prominence given legal precedents in the Senate discussion testifies to the new dispensation in Congress and to the orientation of the speakers. Yet it also contributed to the neglect of the broad question.

Under the circumstances, one is struck by the moderation of these men, especially the two protagonists. Just as Trumbull had acceded to the exclusion of the President, Davis, once the Senate had adopted his amendment, was willing to vote for the oath as a constitutionally acceptable compromise.

The mood of urgency and the pressure of more important war bills must have dampened efforts to raise and protract constitutional arguments. Significantly, virtually all the constitutional objections came from the Border State men, just as the discussion itself revealed regional divergences concerning congressional responsibility.

But the character of the discussion also resulted in part from the

133

exodus of the Southerners. The Southern Senators who had left before the outbreak of war contrasted in depth of experience with their Northern colleagues. Of the twenty-two who had departed, twenty were lawyers, six had been judges, their average previous service in Congress was ten and a half years, and all could claim long careers in public office in their home states. By contrast the forty-eight Senators remaining in 1862 had, for example, served an average of less than six years in Congress. The change must also have affected the kind of arguments used, since Southerners might well have pressed the appeal to constitutional principle independent of court precedents.

The exodus of Southerners also vitally affected the leadership of the Border State men. Before the war, men like Clay of Kentucky had often served as mediators and moderators who brought both sides to put aside sectional demands and accept constitutional compromises. Now the Border State men had lost their strategic position and had become a feeble last-ditch opposition to the dominant Republican majority from the North. In the Senate and in its Judiciary Committee, they had lost their power,[35] yet but for them, none in this debate would have detected and articulated the serious constitutional objections to the legislation at hand.

MODE

The mode these men employed reflected basic changes from the early period, most of all in ruling out initial consideration before the entire chamber. Each house followed what was evidently becoming standard practice—initial reference to a standing committee. The number of such committees had risen to thirty-seven in the House and twenty-two in the Senate. Committees reported out the bills, floor debate followed, and, where necessary, a joint conference committee harmonized differences.

Except for the Senate floor debate the whole process was short, hurried, even perfunctory. The complexion of the two Judiciary Committees may have affected the inadequate treatment they gave the constitutional issue, for despite their legal knowledge, the members, though including Border State men, seemed relatively inexperienced politically.[36] For whatever reason, it seems likely that neither committee explored constitutional questions. Thus, Charles Wickliffe, Kentucky Unionist, voiced doubts about the House Judiciary Committee's handling of the bill in an exchange with Representative Wilson:

> Mr. Wickliffe. Will the gentleman allow me to inquire whether this bill has been before the Committee on the Judiciary, and if so, whether a majority of that committee have recommended its passage?

134

Mr. Wilson. Yes, sir; it has been before the Committee on the Judiciary, and I have been authorized by that committee to report it to the House. I am not in the habit of reporting measures without authority.

Mr. Wickliffe. I asked the question because I have inquired of some of the members of the committee in reference to the bill, and they did not seem to know anything about it.[37]

Here, in embryo, was the persistent problem of securing from small committees representative and genuine attention to constitutional issues. Next year the House refused to submit the Greenback Act to its Judiciary Committee, evidently on the assumption that prior action by another committee, despite its emphasis on policy considerations, was sufficient.[38] How could specialized standing committees assure full probing of constitutional issues without mandatory reference to Judiciary?

After only six days, the Senate Judiciary Committee reported the oath of office bill without amendment. One may doubt that serious thought was given there to the bill as a whole and to possible constitutional objections. Chairman Trumbull in bringing the bill to the floor seemed confident of easy passage and oblivious of possible invalidity. Said he, when the California Democrat James McDougall objected to raising any issue that would lead to discussion, "I think this will not lead to any discussion. It is a bill which has passed the House of Representatives, and is reported from the Committee on the Judiciary. I think there will be no objection to it."[39]

Why was no evident protest made prior to the Senate floor? The sense of urgency, the momentum built up by the Republican majority, and the press of such war measures as taxes, military appropriations, confiscation of rebel property, construction of a transcontinental railroad —all intensified the difficulty of weighing the issue. Furthermore, the houses were discussing charges of disloyalty against nine of their members. Under the circumstances, it is not surprising that men hesitated to challenge the oath.

In spite of all this, the Senate debate itself accorded with canons of fairness. Not one Senator objected to the procedure employed. Senator Saulsbury's initial objection to the bill was so mildly worded that Trumbull's willingness to engage in debate over three separate days appears magnanimous.

On the second day he had to get the Senate to rescind its decision to order a third reading, for the "yeas" and "nays" had already been ordered. Simultaneously, Trumbull urged despatch; said he, on June 21, "I ask the Senate to take up House bill No. 371, which I think may be

135

disposed of in a few minutes."[40] When the Senate was about to consider the conference committee's report on June 30, Davis asked for postponement; Trumbull replied, "I hope it will not be postponed. The Senator from Kentucky has made two or three speeches upon this question . . . We may as well settle the matter now."[41] Thus, the readiness of Trumbull three times to hear and answer objections was probably more than most other Republicans would have shown under the circumstances. The Senate debate had clear focus, being of the adversary variety; in addition, by taking roll call votes on important questions, the Senate publicly registered the position of each of its members present.

Yet the prior committee stage meant that members in general had scant notice of constitutional issues except as earlier bills might have presented them, until the floor debate. When Trumbull reported the bill from committee and asked for passage the same day, and this late in the session, few had been alerted to basic issues. Evidently it was Saulsbury's suggestion that triggered any such thoughts in the minds of the other Senators. Under these conditions, the Senate had to meet the issue in debate, belatedly and unprepared.

ATTITUDES

Like procedure, conceptions of responsibility were showing signs of change. As shown, Senator Davis, the Kentuckian, in citing a precedent from his own state legislature, had revealed his esteem for legislative pronouncements on constitutional issues. In reply, Trumbull of Illinois shifted the discussion to judicial decisions and treated an action of the New York legislature as arbitrary and unworthy of consideration. From that time on, court precedents monopolized the constitutional debate.

The two adversaries, in fact, elucidated their positions on the first day. Their speeches show the hold which the political version of the tripartite theory still had on Border State men and how the juristic version was being expounded in the Midwest:

Mr. Davis. I know that it is becoming odious, and it is becoming stale, and almost disgusting, to make constitutional objections to a proposed law here. But, sir, I can as well conceive of repudiating the Bible in making a Christian sermon as I can of passing a law without testing that law by the Constitution. I think that the man would be just as orthodox as a preacher who should get up and attempt to preach a Christian sermon regardless of the law of God, as revealed in His word, and in violation of it, as it would be for the Congress of the United States to attempt to pass a law without measuring that law by the Constitution; and however stale and offensive it may be to gentlemen, and however distasteful to myself, whenever a bill is presented that is in my opinion justly obnoxious to constitutional objections, I shall feel bound to make them . . .

Mr. Trumbull. I quite agree with the Senator from Kentucky that no law should be passed which is unconstitutional; and I do not think there is any force in the suggestion that objections taken to laws on account of their want of constitutionality should not be made because of their staleness; but I think the Senator from Kentucky has fallen into an error in his argument . . . I think we had better pass this bill; and wherever the judicial tribunals of the country can reach I think it will be held to be constitutional and valid upon the principle decided in the State of New York, to which I have referred.[42]

Even though minorities might raise constitutional objections to frustrate policies they opposed, both these Senators agreed that the charge of staleness was no answer to such objections. Davis went no further than asserting this and insisting on voting according to his own judgment in articulating his view of the duty of members in the face of such challenges. That Congress had the duty to refrain from passing unconstitutional laws, as Davis' rhetoric emphasized, was clear. What was not clear was how its members should discharge their responsibility.

The Kentuckian deemed Congress not only responsible for searching the constitutional text on its own, but capable of doing so. Trumbull, on the other hand, both expressly and by the character of his argument, seemed to be saying that Congress, when faced with penumbral problems of interpretation, should canvass court precedents and try to predict what the courts would decide in a comparable situation. This was not to leave the problem to the courts, but rather to explore court readings and thus determine whether, if faced with the same question, the courts would hold the act constitutional. Congress, in other words, should defer to the courts, only after it had canvassed all precedents on the point in question. Trumbull, it is true, talked less of precedents than of principle, but he seemed to be looking for his principles in precedents. In time some members of Congress would begin to rely on precedents without probing the principles they embodied.

From these comments and from the course and manner of the discussion as a whole, members revealed the existence of two prevailing conceptions. All agreed that both Congress and courts must weigh constitutional questions. Some still expected an independent legislative search of principles, but Trumbull and doubtless others were moved by the spirit of Marshall. Members should explore in lawyer-like fashion the relative factors and then decide what reasons would most likely lead

137

the future judge to what decision on the constitutional question. On that basis they would reach their own decision.

The consideration by Congress of two other wartime acts reflected many of the same characteristics—the new preoccupation with court precedents and court-made rules of law, the agonizing tension between war necessities and constitutional continuity, and the priority given to policy questions.[43]

CONCLUSIONS

War and a near monopoly of Congress by the North produced notable changes in both the conceptions and the discharge of responsibility. Members continued to assert an individual obligation to make certain that acts were valid, but the chief standards they would apply in that effort would be court-made standards. Instead of providing for early consideration of constitutional questions by the whole, members now gave priority to policy and assigned investigation, discussion, and bill-drafting to committees containing only a fraction of the full membership. The trend toward treating constitutionality as just another subject for experts had begun.

When debate finally took place, few felt impelled to raise or discuss constitutional questions—three out of one hundred ninety-four in the House, and there only peripherally, and five out of forty-eight in the Senate. The Senate, furthermore, now seemed more able than the House to weigh constitutional issues. Northern lawyers were confining themselves to narrow constitutional questions, and thereby conveying the impression that the broad questions, those of constitutional wisdom, custom, propriety, were matters of policy, on the same plane of value and weight as other matters of policy. And so the Marshallian or juristic version of the tripartite theory came into its own as the chief rival of the Jeffersonian version. This version gave high priority to court precedents since it rested on doubts of the capacity of legislatures to deal conscientiously with constitutional questions. By effectuating those doubts it had an inherent tendency, in the absence of positive congressional safeguards, to deplete that capacity still further.

In the crisis, with Northern Republicans throwing their massed weight behind wartime policies, the problem of achieving deliberation and a lasting settlement for constitutional questions was awesome. Few had the hardihood to raise those questions and to insist on due consideration. Only when Senator Bayard had to take the oath himself did any member of either house argue the point with any degree of thoroughness. Most Republicans seemed content to leave the raising and the arguing of constitutional issues to others.

138

This oath-of-office episode was merely an eddy in the great flood of wartime bills, yet most of these same features characterized the handling of two other war measures. In considering the power of Congress to create a paper currency in the 1863 National Currency Act and its power to permit states to tax national bank stocks held by individuals and corporations in the 1864 National Bank Act, Congress performed much as in 1862.[44]

Although the oath as prescribed for legislators raised an issue which, like that in the Bradley case, was unlikely to reach the courts, the apparent finality of congressional decision seemed without effect in enhancing awareness of responsibility. Complications led Congress years later to repeal it, but meantime the Supreme Court in the Garland case set aside a somewhat similar oath for lawyers.

The judicial fate of the past loyalty oath is a noteworthy comment on the performance of Congress during these years. That Congress was giving much the same half-hearted and inattentive scrutiny to other constitutional questions probably is suggested by a sharp increase in judicial invalidations after the war. Congressional neglect doubtless had more to do with that increase than any judicial cravings for a renaissance of court power after the fiasco in the Dred Scott case.[45] Furthermore, wartime stresses probably had no more to do with the congressional behavior than did the absence of Southerners with their constitutional and procedural sagacity. Whereas three pieces of legislation passed prior to the Civil War met with Supreme Court invalidation, some twenty-two passed between 1862 and 1876 met the same ultimate fate. Those were the years when Congress operated without full and genuine representation from the South. After the return of the Southern contingent, it was not until 1888 that Congress passed another act destined for Court annulment.[46] The Constitution, it would appear, was safest in the hands of a Congress fully representative of the nation.

7 The Marshallian System: The Sherman Act of 1890

The nation was industrializing and business was in control. A Congress once more containing Southern members labored with economic problems. It fixed tariffs, granted subsidies, determined financial policy, and even ventured into the controversial field of regulation. One such venture was the Sherman Antitrust Act of 1890 which produced novel constitutional questions, notably concerning the commerce power. How did Congress view and how did it discharge its responsibility for weighing such questions? Brief probes of the treatment of the income tax of 1894 and the Webb-Kenyon Act of 1913 will lend perspective to this analysis of the Sherman Act. Did the 1890 discussions offer guidance or confusion to the Court when it later came to spell out the extent of the commerce power in the antitrust cases? The Court has drawn much fire for its constitutional readings in the Sugar Trust case,[1] but perhaps Congress should receive part of the blame or credit.

Appomattox had put an end to the issues of slavery and Union. After Reconstruction, industrialism became the dominant phenomenon of American life. It also furnished the leading political issue of the time. The new captains of industry sought to eliminate competition and accordingly to assure themselves exorbitant profits. Corporations found a variety of devices for fixing prices and dividing markets, among them the gentleman's agreement and the pool. These, however, being informal, were apt to collapse when one of the parties discovered that by ignoring the agreement or pool it could expand profits. The trust, on the other hand, gave members greater security. The corporations would transfer their stock to a board of trustees and receive trust certificates in return. They then received dividends on these certificates according to the value of the stock transferred. This form of agreement proliferated during the 1880's.[2] Its outstanding weakness lay in its being a matter of public record. It was highly visible, and hence this form of combination became the target of much of the antagonism against business.[3]

Many events of the 1880's reflected the growing public concern over the trusts. In 1884 the Anti-Monopoly party nominated a professional

140

radical, Benjamin F. Butler, for the Presidency and gathered 175,000 votes. In 1888 the state of New York authorized an investigation of the trust question which resulted in a successful suit against a part of the Sugar Trust. The same year the United States Senate set up its select Committee on the Transportation and Sale of Meat Products. This committee, reporting in 1890, denounced trust activities in this field. The lower house authorized its Committee on Manufactures to study the trust problem, and this committee reported both in 1888 and in 1889. No fewer than twelve separate antitrust bills were introduced in the First Session of the Fiftieth Congress.[4]

At first neither major political party showed much willingness to advocate restriction of business. The business-government relationship was initially characterized by bribery and by special privileges for specific firms.[5] But gradually honest men came to power within the parties and began to construct an ideology which favored business but opposed bribery and corruption. Blaine's "Half breeds" professed such an ideology and in time they replaced the "Stalwarts" as the controlling faction of the Republican party.

One of the leading "Half breeds" was Senator John Sherman of Ohio, sixty-six, a veteran of thirty years' congressional experience. He believed in laissez faire, sound money, and high tariff and despised the governmental dishonesty which was enriching certain corporations. At the same time he was aware that the public was demanding government action. He was a master of political compromise who had shown his skill in the controversy over the Silver Purchase Act.

Sherman favored antitrust legislation because of his own "Half breed" principles, and the pressure of political reality forced the Republicans to agree with him. In the last quarter of the century the Republicans faced a revitalized Democratic party. Between 1876 and 1892 the Democrats won a majority of the popular vote in four out of five presidential elections and the Republicans won the fifth by only 7,000 votes. In eight of the ten Congresses from 1874 to 1894 the House was controlled by the Democrats, although in seven the Senate was in Republican hands. Only between 1889 and 1891 did the Republicans control both houses and the Presidency.[6]

By 1888 both major party platforms were opposing the trusts.[7] The Democrats linked their opposition to an attack on high tariffs. The Republicans, looking for an issue which would win back the White House, came out for direct legislation against trusts. Thus they could also continue to favor high tariffs. After the election of 1888, the victorious Benjamin Harrison and the Republican majority in Congress had to deal with their own campaign promises.

The Senate of the Fiftieth Congress (1887–1889) had debated antitrust bills, but gone no further.[8] Soon after his election, President Harrison called for trust regulation.[9] On December 4, 1889, Sherman introduced another bill which the Senate Finance Committee reported favorably in January 1890. Floor debate followed in late February when a constitutional objection sent the bill back to the Finance Committee. Debate resumed on that committee's substitute bill in late March and included constitutional discussion of high quality. As a result, the Senate sent the bill and all amendments to its Judiciary Committee, with instructions to report back within twenty days. The committee reported a version which the Senate passed almost unanimously.

The House Judiciary Committee approved the Senate bill and the House added only a single amendment. This amendment occasioned seven weeks of haggling in conference but finally both houses passed the Senate version in mid-June. On July 2, 1890, President Harrison redeemed the campaign promises of the G.O.P. by signing the Sherman Antitrust Act into law. It was on the Senate floor and in the Senate Judiciary Committee that Congress probed most deeply its own power to pass such legislation.

Not until 1914 did Congress again enact further antitrust legislation. It confided the task of spelling out the reach of the commerce power in specific instances initially to the Executive, but mainly to the courts. During the Harrison, Cleveland, and McKinley Administrations, forty suits were brought under the act. The results were negligible, but no challenge to the constitutionality of the act itself was successful.[10] The only important trusts successfully broken were the cast-iron pipe combine[11] and the Joint Traffic Association, a railroad combination built around the Pennsylvania Railroad.[12] In enforcing the act, the Attorneys General exercised considerable discretion; in choosing and in preparing suits for prosecution, they laid the ground work for court decisions.

In the long run, however, it was the courts that bore the chief burden of defining regulatory power. A long series of decisions limited the scope of the act. Most notable among the earlier cases was United States v. E. C. Knight Company, the famous Sugar Trust case. Here Chief Justice Fuller drew a rigid distinction between manufacturing and commerce.[13] "Commerce succeeds to manufacture, and is not a part of it." Behind this distinction lay the doctrine of dual federalism which had gained currency at the time of Chief Justice Taney, and which, incidentally, was to hold good until the late 1930's. Fuller endorsed the doctrine: "It is vital that the independence of the commercial power and of the police power, and the delimitation between them, however sometimes perplexing, should always be recognized and observed . . ."[14]

Many historians have attributed both these distinctions to the Fuller

142

Court itself, but Court-centered analysis ignores the vital role which Congress played. We shall see that the Senators who passed the law covered much of the same ground long before the Sugar Trust case. Here as elsewhere the judges depended in part on the prior constitutional inquiries of the Legislature.

CONSTITUTIONAL QUESTIONS

The chief constitutional question lay in the field of federalism. This question—the only one to be treated in this chapter—concerned the scope of the federal power to regulate interstate commerce. This was one of the earliest times since the Civil War that Congress probed that power. Sherman's original bill as well as the Finance Committee's substitute sought to regulate conspiracies which reduced competition in the production, manufacture, and sale of domestic products and raw materials if such articles were in competition with imports upon which a tariff was levied. Sherman's bill also extended such regulation to products which found their way into interstate commerce. The Finance Committee's substitute, with Sherman's blessing, went even further by proscribing agreements concerning any product of one state which was in competition with a like product of another state. This proposal, therefore, would have set up national regulation of manufacturing, agriculture, and mining, matters which had heretofore been regulated locally under the state police power. Thus the crucial constitutional question became: May Congress regulate local affairs solely by virtue of the commerce power? To what phases in the cycle of production, sale, and transportation does the commerce power of Congress extend?

A less weighty constitutional question arose when the Finance Committee sought to bolster its constitutional case by limiting the prohibitions of its bill to contracts entered into between citizens of different states, or between citizens of a state and of a foreign nation. The issue here was whether the diversity-of-citizenship clause of Article III of the Constitution authorized congressional regulation of this kind. A final question, briefly touched upon, related to the ex post facto clause of the Constitution.

The central constitutional question was of the narrow variety since it referred to a specific constitutional clause. Even at that time, this subject lay within the customary province of the courts. Only occasionally did the debate go beyond this to broader aspects of the constitutional system. As we shall see, Congress realized that its determination would not be final. It was clear to all that the act, in whatever form passed, would soon get into the courts and undoubtedly become the subject of

143

Supreme Court decisions. We shall see how far the members used the prospect of judicial review as an alibi for ignoring the constitutional question.

COURSE OF THE DISCUSSION

Pre-1890 Debate in the Senate. Even before the leading debate of 1890, constitutional issues had made their appearance when, in 1888, Sherman had introduced his first bill.[15] This bill would have regulated agreements concerning production, sale, and transportation of articles in competition with imported goods upon which Congress had legislated a tariff or which were intended for shipment in interstate commerce. This latter provision regarding interstate commerce was later amended to apply only to goods "that in due course of trade shall be transported from one State . . . to another."[16]

In the debate over this bill members expressed varying conceptions of the commerce power. Senator James Jones, Arkansas Democrat, a Confederate veteran who had served ten years in Congress, feared the prospect of centralized power. He declared that if the framers of the Constitution had foreseen the tremendous growth of a "vast and intricate system of 'commerce among the states' " they might not have given Congress such general power as that contained in the commerce clause. He warned of the dangers implicit in the exercise of this great power. Nevertheless, he put forth a broad conception of the power itself and called it a "power of control, unlimited save by the discretion of Congress . . ." Jones also supported passage of the bill, although warning: "If we exercise all the power that we may under this clause, we practically assume control of everything."[17]

Senator Sherman's view of the commerce power was more moderate than that of Jones. He claimed that his bill went "as far as the Constitution permits Congress to go, because it only deals with two classes of matters: contracts which affect the importation of goods into the United States, which is foreign commerce, and contracts which affect the transportation and passage of goods from one State to another. The Congress of the United States can go no farther than that. It is not claimed by anybody it can."[18]

Others in this early debate stated more restrictive views of the power. For example, Senator John Reagan, Democrat of Texas, with eight previous years in the Senate, wanted the bill amended so as to deal only with conspiracies of an interstate character occurring in the transportation field itself.[19] Senator James George, Democrat of Mississippi, who was to play a vital part in the later debate, gave his own narrow definition of the commerce power. This former Confederate general, court reporter,

144

and state supreme court judge asserted "that the power of Congress exists only over the subject so far as it comes from transportation, while the transportation is being carried on; that the power of Congress does not begin as to the subject until transportation begins, and it ends when transportation is completed."[20] George was revered by his fellow-Senators for his constitutional wisdom.[21] In addition to this general statement about the commerce power, George made a more specific constitutional attack. First, he argued that the bill was an ex post facto law. An agreement might be lawful when it was made and then a future act of transporting the goods interstate, an act beyond the control of the actual parties to the agreement, might make the original agreement unlawful. Second, George seized upon the seeds of dual federalism in the Taney Court's decisions and caused them to grow until they limited the power of Congress to regulate manufacturing trusts.[22] In an exchange with Senator James Eustis, Democrat of Louisiana, George made crystal clear his radical adherence to the doctrine of dual federalism.

Mr. George. I ask the Senator from Louisiana, would it be lawful or constitutional for the State of Louisiana, or any other State, to pass a law punishing persons entering into these combinations and trusts within their respective limits, whether or not the subjects about which the trusts were made should afterwards become subjects of foreign or of interstate commerce?

Mr. Eustis. I think the States have the power.

Mr. George. You think they have, and I agree with you. If they have Congress has not, because there is a dividing line plainly marked by the decisions of the Supreme Court of the United States, upon one side of which rests the police power of the State, and on the other the commercial power of Congress.[23]

Thus did Senator George instruct his colleagues long before the 1890 debate had begun.

1890 Debate in the Senate. First Phase. When in 1890 debate got under way on the Finance Committee's bill, the general definition of the commerce power was again at issue.[24] This time the proponents of a narrow definition were even more assertive having developed further distinctions and doctrines to support their case. Senator George, asserting that he was not merely following standard Southern arguments but that he was looking at the decisions of the Supreme Court,[25] relied on the original-package rule of Brown v. Maryland[26] to show that since most imported goods were not sold in the original package their sale became

145

subject only to local control. Therefore, there was no valid reason for granting Congress the power to control contracts affecting competition with these imports. George also sought to draw a hard line between manufacturing and transportation. He contended that the courts had earlier distinguished between them and would continue to do so.[27]

Senator George Vest, Kentucky-born Missouri Democrat with three years in the Confederate Congress and ten years in the Senate, reasserted the view that commerce was merely transportation. Congress only had power "to regulate commerce in articles, whether manufactured in the State or not, after they have gone into commerce and are *in transitu* from one State to another."[28] A Connecticut Republican, Orville Platt, suggested a distinction between harmful combinations and reasonable combinations by means of which businessmen might protect themselves from operating at a loss and condemned the bill for not drawing this distinction.[29]

Most important, Northern Republicans anxious to make the antitrust bill less rigorous, now began to adopt George's earlier arguments about dual federalism. Frank Hiscock, Republican of New York, asserted that the matters with which the state's police power dealt were beyond federal control or regulation.[30]

Only a few Senators offered any kind of broad definition of commerce and the commerce power. John Marshall's broad reading in the Gibbons *v.* Ogden decision was virtually forgotten. Senator Sherman, who sat in the Senate during Reconstruction, pictured himself as the defender of a broad concept—"as broad as the earth."[31] He asked for "power to deal with so great a wrong"[32] and found that power in the commerce clause. Commerce for him meant

> the exchange of all commodities between different places or communities. It includes all trade and traffic, all modes of transportation by land or by sea, all kinds of navigation, every species of ship or sail, every mode of transit, from the dog-cart to the Pullman car, every kind of motive power, from the mule or horse to the most recent application of steam or electricity applied on every road, from the trail over the mountain or the plain to the perfected railway or the steel bridges over great rivers or arms of the sea. The power of Congress extends to all this commerce, except only that limited within the bounds of a State.[33]

From this starting point he argued that combinations *in production* so affected the course of this commerce that Congress might also "prohibit contracts and arrangements that are hostile to such commerce."[34]

A Democrat from Alabama, James Pugh, who had served in the

146

national and Confederate Congresses, was another who argued for a broad commerce power. The bill, he said, declared certain agreements void as being against public policy and then provided means of enforcing that policy. Congress possessed the needed power because of the commerce and necessary-and-proper clauses. Congress might, therefore, "define what acts are detrimental to our commercial policy and . . . prohibit them."[35] Despite these expressions of a broad commerce power, George and others had raised serious doubts about the scope of the power and thus prompted their colleagues to refer the matter to the Judiciary Committee.

1890 Debate in the Senate. Second Phase. Thus, on March 25 George moved to send the bill and all amendments to the Judiciary Committee, of which he was a member. A vote was taken after considerable debate and the motion was defeated 15 to 28. Two days later Senator Edward Walthall, Democrat from Mississippi, made the same motion, and this time it passed 31 to 28.

During the debate on this motion, Senators expressed a wide range of opinion as to the proper role and competence of the Judiciary Committee. One view was that the Judiciary Committee was the proper place to send constitutional questions and that the committee's decision on those questions should be accepted unhesitatingly by the whole Senate and probably by both houses. In making the initial motion for referral Senator George said, "I think I discharge a proper duty to the people of the United States when I ask the Senate to refer all these various propositions to that committee which by the rules of the Senate has charge of these great questions."[36] Senator Hiscock asserted that the only reason for committing the bill to the Judiciary Committee would be to get the opinion of its members on the constitutional questions involved. Platt attacked the Finance Committee members as being either apathetic toward the bill or actually opposed to it[37] and suggested that the Judiciary Committee was the only "committee that would give it careful and honest consideration . . ."[38]

Another group of Senators although deeming the Judiciary Committee especially competent in the handling of constitutional questions thought that in this particular instance it would be better for the Senate as a whole to consider the bill. Senator Reagan said that "If we can have the judgment of that committee, with its reputation for legal and constitutional ability . . . I should be willing to accept it."[39] He feared, however, that the committee would never produce a bill against the trusts but would only let the subject die. Senator James Wilson, Republican of Iowa, spoke in the same vein, asking quick Senate action instead of referral. Senator Pugh made the most perceptive statement

147

in this debate. "The difficulty in that committee is with the variety of opinion that it has both as to constitutional power and as to the provisions of a bill to reach this evil. My opinion is that the variety of that opinion will prevent any concurrence in favor of a bill that has any vitality in it . . ."[40]

A third point of view was developed by Senator Zebulon Vance, North Carolina Democrat. "Mr. President, I never have a bill in which I feel any interest referred to this grand mausoleum of Senatorial literature, the Judiciary Committee, without feeling that I have attended a funeral . . . Mr. President, the country has found out that when we desire the death of a bill and are not particularly anxious to put ourselves on record as having directly struck the blow which caused the demise, we refer it to the Judiciary Committee, where it sleeps the last sleep known to the literature of this Senate."[41] Sherman agreed with Vance that the motion to commit the bill to the Judiciary Committee had a political inspiration. He asked for "a better nursing mother than that to send the bill to."[42] The Senate, however, overrode these objections and committed the bill.

1890 Debate in the Senate. Third Phase. Chairman George Edmunds, Republican of Vermont, completing his twenty-fourth year in the Senate, and the other members of the Judiciary Committee[43] worked on the bill for only five days and produced a new version.[44] The change they wrought is epitomized in the change of title from the original Sherman bill to the Judiciary Committee's bill, which, incidentally, became the final act. The original bill bore the title "A Bill to declare unlawful trusts and combinations in restraint of trade and production,"[45] whereas the committee bill was called "A Bill to protect trade and commerce against unlawful restraints and monopolies." The committee and evidently the Senate were no longer interested in regulating production as a part of commerce.[46]

When on April 8 the Senate held its final debate, some members of the committee declared that this was the strongest possible bill allowable under the Constitution. Senator Edmunds explained that the committee felt that it "would frame a bill that should be clearly within our constitutional power, that we should make its definitions out of terms that were well-known to the law already, and would leave it to the courts in the first instance to say how far they could carry it or its definitions as applicable to each particular case as it might arise."[47] Senator George made the most honest statement concerning the results of the committee's labors. "The bill has been very ingeniously and properly drawn to cover every case which comes within what is called the commercial power of Congress. There is a great deal of this matter outside of that. The bill being of that character, it necessarily will be a disappointing measure to the people of this country."[48] These constitutional pronouncements, made by members of the Judiciary Committee, went unchallenged by any Senator and the bill passed with only one dissenting vote.

1890 Debate in the House. The House debated the Sherman Act for one day only, ignoring the constitutional questions. The House deferred to the wisdom of the Senate, the Senate Judiciary Committee, and its own Judiciary Committee, which had merely endorsed Senate action. Some Representatives were especially impressed by the apparent excellence of the consideration afforded by the Senate Judiciary Committee. Representative John Heard, Missouri Democrat, spoke of that committee as "composed of some of the ablest lawyers in the country . . ."[49] Representative John Rogers, Arkansas Democrat, used the same phrase to describe the participants in the Senate floor debate.[50] The House thus took the word of the Senate and passed the bill. Was this confidence in the Senate justified?

Discussion Evaluated. The debate in the Senate was in several respects remarkable. Thanks to ample time and the high caliber of most of the speakers, the Senate heard the leading arguments on both sides. Furthermore, the debaters presented these arguments in sequence. The comments of most were pertinent and focused on the issues at hand. The only serious confusion developed when the Senate, in Committee of the Whole, tried to perfect the bill word-by-word.

The members answered directly the arguments presented by their opponents. The prepared speeches were carefully thought out and wide-ranging in their coverage of relevant and important arguments and the questioning which followed them enriched the knowledge of those present.

Whether this high-level Senate debate actually produced changes in voting is hard to determine, since no vote bore directly on the constitutional question. The most pertinent roll call votes were on the motions to refer the bills to the Judiciary Committee. If one compares the March 25 vote of 15 to 28 with the March 27 vote of 31 to 28 for referral, one finds each party split on both votes, with Democrats moving heavily toward referral on the second vote.[51]

The key to the Senate shift in stand appears in the voting by region. Table 5 presents the manner in which the six regions cast votes on the two roll calls. Here the Midwest appears almost adamant in its opposition to the referral. The margin against referral actually increased. Since all but three Midwest Senators were Republicans, one may conclude

149

TABLE 5. Regional Voting on Motions to Refer Sherman Bill to Senate Judiciary Committee, 1890

Region	Number	For referral March 25		For referral March 27	
		Yea	Nay	Yea	Nay
Midwest	22	1	12	3	15
New England	12	2	6	3	7
Border	6	2	1	3	1
Middle Atlantic	10	4	2	4	0
Far West	10	2	2	5	2
South	22	4	5	13	3
Total	82	15	28	31	28

SOURCE: 21 *Cong. Rec.*, pt. 3, pp. 2611, 2731.

that these men feared committee burial of the bill with damage to party success in the fall elections. At the other extreme the South shifted from a margin of one vote against referral to ten for referral. The change presumably reflected confidence, inspired perhaps by leaders like George, that the committee would either moderate the terms of the bill to conform to Southern constitutional doctrines, or by inaction improve Democratic election prospects.[52] Some may have favored referral out of concern that no bill would emerge from the tedious and detailed discussion in Committee of the Whole.

Thus the Senate engaged in thorough and effective constitutional debate. Later times would denounce the motives of the men of the 1890's in most of their actions. Doubtless many, especially members of the Judiciary Committee, tailored their constitutional readings to fit their own economic or political interests, for at least two leading participants later found lucrative careers in advising trusts under the act.[53] Constitutional settlements do not exist in a political vacuum, and the accommodation of special interests is a common ingredient of such settlements. That some may have had immediate interests at stake derogates not at all from the achievement of a settlement or from the acceptance of responsibility which most members manifested.

PARTICIPANTS

One who studies the Congress of 1890 at work on the Sherman Act finds the lawyers not only in full charge of constitutional inquiries but confident of their special contribution. It was not that lawyers were numerous—the 82 per cent quota in the Senate was actually a slight reduction from the 85 per cent of 1862; it was rather that the bar was becoming professionalized and the public willing to consign constitutional issues to the profession. The American Bar Association was now twelve years old, and the law schools which had been springing up in recent decades were sending more and more graduates to Congress; the eighteen Senators whom the *Biographical Directory of Congress* lists as having attended law school falls far short of the actual quota.[54] All ten of the leading participants in the Senate debate were lawyers,[55] as were the nine members of the Judiciary Committee. Even the eleven-man Finance Committee, whose bill and whose jurisdiction were rejected by the Senate, contained seven lawyers.[56] In voting, however, the lawyers showed no consistent preference, either for or against referral to the Judiciary Committee. Singularly, the only warrantable conclusion concerning voting by lawyers is that they voted more frequently than non-lawyers.

Most notable was the attitude toward their special role which the lawyers were now expressing. In 1818, Forsyth had told the House that "Every gentleman, whether of the profession of law or not" would be aware of legal distinctions. Now the lawyers seemed to assume that only lawyers were qualified to discuss constitutional questions. They viewed the Constitution as a giant statute. Men who took sharply contrasting positions in the debate were unanimous in praising the intelligence and special expertise of lawyers. These men were themselves lawyers. Thus we find that Senators who differed on points under discussion were unanimous in their praise of the bar. Vest predicted the Court's interpretation of the bill under debate "as a lawyer";[57] Sherman praised his colleagues, George and Vest, as "eminent and distinguished lawyers."[58] Hiscock described the members of the Judiciary Committee as "very able lawyers."[59] Platt assumed throughout that only the able lawyers could straighten out constitutional snarls in the debate. William Washburn, Minnesota Republican, recognized the eminence of the lawyers conducting the Senate debate, but also noted that they were disagreeing with one another.[60] The Senate was a lawyers' world, and the trust bill, especially in its constitutional aspects, was their special preserve.

Lawyers held the floor, and yet these same men contributed more than law knowledge alone. The wisdom which they applied in hammering out the Sherman Act was also the product of long experience in government. All ten major speakers could boast long careers in public office, careers which averaged seven years in state office and sixteen in Congress, including eleven in the Senate.[61] Many of them made prolonged and informed contributions to the debate. Most relied on themselves as specialists in the meaning of the commerce clause, and likewise of the Constitution as a whole. Many followed the example of George in citing court decisions in order to bolster their own expositions with outside authority.

It was lawyers, but lawyers from the South and the Border States, who pressed constitutional doubts and sought effective and acceptable compromise of constitutional issues. It was an ex-Confederate, George of Mississippi, who voiced doubts of the validity of the bill and offered the rationale which produced a settlement, and another, Vest of Missouri, who gave him support. Once Northern Republicans had joined the chorus of protests against the original bill, Sherman and the original proponents of strong measures were willing to compromise. The final bill was drafted in the main by Northerners—from Vermont, Massachusetts, New York, and Kansas—a Mississippian being the only exception. In the end, great reliance was placed on what was becoming the Senate's leading reservoir of constitutional advice, the Judiciary Committee, and there the South and Border States held four of the nine positions. As in 1787, constitutional accommodations were brought about by men with constitutional wisdom as well as legal learning.

MODE

The procedure which the Senate used in 1890 was a mixture of the usual and the novel. As in 1862 the first stage was consideration not by the whole Senate, but by a standing committee, this time the Finance Committee. By now Congress had spawned standing committees to the number of one hundred: forty-six in the Senate and fifty-four in the House. The Senate next discussed the bill in Committee of the Whole for six days.

What was novel was that at the end of these six days the Senate referred the bill to another standing committee, not because of a quarrel over jurisdiction but because constitutional issues had arisen and the Senate seemed to assume that the Judiciary Committee was the proper forum for the settlement of such issues. A few years later, in his work on committees of Congress, Lauros McConachie described the House Judiciary Committee in terms which were doubtless equally true of its Senate counterpart. Since its founding the House Committee, he wrote, had held a favored place among committees. He went on:

> The nature of the subjects with which it has been charged has constantly drawn to it the best legal talent in a body so largely composed of lawyers as is the House, has given to its membership a long list of the brightest names in the annals of American statesmanship. Owing also to the nonpartisan character of its duties, it has held among its fellows, whether viewed in the committee room or upon the floor, the palm for examples of united action by great parties in the framing of laws.

152

McConachie emphasized the continuity in its labors, the ready cooperation between new and old chairmen, and especially the character of its
business, which included not only judicial and related affairs but "important constitutional questions . . .; questions of political science
generally, as woman's suffrage and citizenship, and many subjects presumably committed to it solely because of the high ability of its membership as compared with the committees that might naturally be
supposed to have charge of them." This committee, he concluded, had no
superior and few equals in the House.[62]

In referring the commerce clause issue to the Judiciary Committee
and then accepting its advice with scant discussion, the Senate was ex-
hibiting the important place in the handling of many constitutional
issues which that committee had now attained. Note, however, that
committee action followed lengthy floor discussion, and, as would
occasionally be true later, the committee had orders to report within a
given period.

Furthermore, the Senate consulted its constitutional advisers on the
committee only after debating the motion to refer and subjecting it
twice to roll call votes. The members of the Senate had been alerted by
the pre-1890 debate to the immanence of constitutional questions in
antitrust bills. Moreover, the six days of Senate debate went unmanaged
in any formally organized way; the tradition of unlimited debate provided a fair hearing of all arguments, time allotments were fair to both
sides, and the Committee of the Whole proceedings were flexible enough
to allow spontaneous debate or at least impromptu questioning after
prepared speeches. Time was probably adequate, except that the Senate
devoted only part of a day to the final report of the Judiciary Committee.

Deliberation, doubtless fair to both sides, took place in the private
sessions of the Finance Committee and later, of the Judiciary Committee. We know that advocates of a stronger bill on the Judiciary Committee, notably Senator Pugh, made no objection to the final result.
Furthermore, in the final April 8 debate, members of the committee who
spoke suggested that all the major questions raised on the floor had been
debated in the committee itself.[63]

Even more evidently than in any of our earlier controversies Congress
took no final vote on the chief constitutional question. Thus it obscured
the responsibility of members; one might maintain that the 31 to 28 vote
to refer to committee was somewhat tantamount to a vote on the substantive issue, since all were aware that if the committee got control of the bill
it would adopt a narrow reading of the commerce power. Nevertheless,
a vote to shift responsibility for intensive consideration is hardly the
same as a vote directly on the question.

The procedure of the Senate for handling constitutional questions was

153

beginning to obscure the responsibility of members for constitutional issues and to highlight policy questions. The Senate was beginning to route constitutional questions to others, in this case, its own committees.

Four years later, under the pressure of business panic, a mounting deficit, and party and sectional conflict, Congress considered the constitutionality of an income tax. Once again, lawyers almost monopolized the discussion, standing committees made the preliminary policy decisions, the Senate furnished the only focused and searching constitutional inquiry, and the members of the Senate Judiciary Committee led in constitutional exposition, not in committee this time, but on the floor.[64] The Senate, with advice from its committee of lawyers, had become the chief legislative forum for constitutional issues.

ATTITUDES

Moreover, in 1890 the judicial monopoly theory was beginning to be voiced along with the two versions of the tripartite theory. The expanding Midwest was evidently now home territory for the newer theory. The Indiana Democrat, David Turpie, Ohio-educated and for many years a judge and lawyer, declared that the first legislation enacted in any field was imperfect, but that he preferred imperfect laws to no laws on the subject. The only way to get control of the trusts would be by "commencing and prosecuting these different projects to the form of law, entering this domain, and asking the opinions of the Federal tribunals as to our own jurisdictional power . . ."[65] Senator Washburn, a Maine-born railroad president and power magnate from Minnesota, was even more explicit. His statement included many of the points in the full-blown judicial monopoly theory:

> I do not see how we are ever going to know whether this bill is constitutional or not until it has been referred to the Supreme Court. The most eminent lawyers in this Chamber differ in opinion, and it seems to me that we shall never reach any definite result until some law goes to the Supreme Court.
>
> So far as I am concerned I know the sentiment of the country with regard to the question of monopolies and trusts, and I believe the people expect the Congress of the United States to make an attempt to secure some valid and satisfactory legislation. While the bill of the Senator from Ohio may not be perfect, while it may not reach every point, and may finally be declared unconstitutional, yet it is a move in the right direction . . . I believe . . . that when all other means fail to defeat a bill the constitutionality of it is usually invoked for that purpose.[66]

154

Washburn's preoccupation with urgently needed policies and his impatience and skepticism concerning fine-drawn constitutional arguments in Congress led him to view the Court as the only suitable judge of constitutional questions. Since his time, increasing numbers have followed his example.

The dominant theme of articulated attitudes was the tripartite theory in its Marshallian formulation. By now the power, influence, and reputation of the Supreme Court were such that even Southerners and Border State men went chiefly to its decisions for guidance in selecting pertinent principles. George, the Mississippian, was among leading Southerners to take this route, and the Missourian Vest held a similar view. He believed that Congress had a grave responsibility for determining the constitutionality of proposed legislation but also suggested that Congress should predict, or let its leading lawyers predict, the response of the Supreme Court to the law and then make that prediction the guide for its action.[67]

Others underlined the congressional obligation in terms strong enough to be Jeffersonian. Note Senator Platt's reply to Senator Washburn:

Mr. Washburn. I should like to ask the Senator also if any special harm would come to the country or anybody else by the passage of the bill if it should be afterwards held to be unconstitutional by the Supreme Court of the United States. Would any damage be done to anybody?

Mr. Platt. . . . Whenever Congress passes a bill which the concurrent sentiment of Congress believes to be unconstitutional it does a greater damage to the people of this country than is well to be calculated.[68]

For those holding a form of the tripartite theory the question arose as to how congressional responsibility should be exercised. One opinion was the old view that the oath taken by each member of Congress bound him to investigate thoroughly and decide individually questions pertaining to the constitutionality of a bill. Senator Vest stated this view with vigor:

But, sir, even in the face of the popular indignation which may be visited upon any one who criticises any measure that looks to the destruction of this evil, I can not violate my oath to support the Constitution and all the habitudes of thought which have come to me as a lawyer educated and trained in my profession.

. . . what we want is one thing, what we can do is another; and for Congress to pass a law which will be thrown out of the Supreme Court under the terrible criticism that any such law must invoke is simply to subject ourselves to ridicule and to say to our constituents that we are powerless to enact laws which will give them relief.[69]

Others maintained that for Congress this responsibility was a corporate matter. Those who entrusted the task to a committee of experienced lawyers were expressing Marshall's presuppositions. Senator George, for example, spoke of the "grave and solemn duty which we owe to the people of the United States to do something, and something effectual" and constitutionally valid—a duty members could perform only by giving all the bills to the Judiciary Committee.[70] Senator Hiscock expressed a similar judgment.[71] For Senator Reagan, however, the proper corporation was the entire Senate, not one of its committees.

By ascribing final responsibility to congressional organs, these men, including the Southerners George and Reagan, were lifting the burden of inquiry from the individual member, and hence opening the way for concentration of the creative function of constitutional inquiry in the hands of a few "expert" members. Four years later members voiced variants of the same three positions in connection with the income tax, for which the Supreme Court had recently furnished a favorable precedent.[72] By the 1890's the prevailing idea of responsibility was Marshall's.

CONCLUSIONS

The Sherman Act Congress was a very different body from that which had handled the Anderson contempt motion. The manner in which Congress came to a decision in 1890 sheds light on changes which the nineteenth century had brought to the consideration of constitutional questions. It likewise was a bridge to practices of the modern Congress. Although as yet only a handful of members was articulating the judicial monopoly theory, some of the conditions of constitutional discussion which have helped shape that theory were by now firmly established.

In the passage of the Sherman Act the lawyers were in complete control. This was the culmination of a trend from earlier in the century, for the lawyers had usually held the lead in debates and the proportion of lawyers, especially in the Senate, had stood at a high level. To be a non-lawyer in 1890, however broad one's political experience, was to be silenced on constitutional questions under debate. By the turn of the century, men combining legal knowledge and long experience dominated constitutional discussion in both houses.

Procedure now combined floor debate with prior committee action and, in some cases, Judiciary Committee review. In 1890, over objections, the Senate wedged the Judiciary Committee into the proceedings after it had discussed the constitutional questions for more than a year. Mounting pressures of business and of politics doubtless influenced such a resort. At the same time, in spite of the press of business and of pending adjournment preliminary to elections, meaningful constitutional debate took place on the floors of both houses with the Senate employing the Committee of the Whole.

By the end of the century, then, Congress was assigning much of its responsibility for considering constitutional questions to its Committees on the Judiciary. Yet these committees were both broadly representative and highly respected. Members still opposed leaving final decision to committees; floor debates in Committee of the Whole still attracted numerous and able speakers and maintained a high standard. Congress could still conduct public deliberation, relying on the expert advice of its own members.

Yet conditions were changing. The pressure of policy, the assignment of many bills initially to committees concerned with specialized policy, the tendency of House debate to be both constricted and policy-centered, and the monopoly of discussion wielded by lawyers, all contributed to the appeal of the incipient judicial monopoly theory. In 1890 even Southern Senators were looking, in Marshallian fashion, to the Court for guidance. Fewer members were expounding the Jeffersonian appeal for independent search of principles by Congress. More and more were asserting that doubts concerning constitutionality must be substantial to justify opposition to a measure, especially a politically attractive measure, on constitutional grounds. Finally, a few Midwesterners, legally trained but limited in congressional experience, were almost relinquishing judgment in their deference to the courts. In short, the century had eroded the Jeffersonian theory and exalted the Marshallian, increasingly tinged with judicial monopolism.

The Sherman Act discussions, however, served a valuable purpose. They furnished an intellectual and doctrinal bridge from the tentative dual federalism of the Taney Court to the full-blown dual federalism of the Fuller Court. They also elaborated for the Court other doctrines, such as the distinctions between manufacturing and commerce,[73] and between good and bad trusts. This contribution, often ignored by many historians, gave comfort to business interests in their effort to narrow the scope of the commerce power, whether in Congress or in the courts. By the mid-1930's the inadequacies of the 1890 doctrine had become manifest and the contribution of the 1890 Congress had come to appear negative. Yet those men were construing the Constitution for their own times. But for that congressional inquiry, the courts would have had to come to a decision without the benefit of prior deliberation. Congress had expressed and reconciled Southern opposition to centralization and Northern opposition to business regulation.

At the end of the century, therefore, Congress could still reach important constitutional determinations. Moreover, the conditions of 1890 remained in 1913, to judge from the handling of the Webb-Kenyon Act. This was another regulation of interstate commerce, this time affecting intoxicating liquor. President William Howard Taft, on the advice of his Attorney General, vetoed the bill on constitutional grounds, and Congress passed it over his veto.[74] Once again, lawyers, with weighty experience in public office, virtually monopolized discussion.[75] Again, the profession received the plaudits of the houses for its constitutional insight.[76] Here, both houses debated constitutional questions in Committee of the Whole, having referred them to the Judiciary Committees even though the bills dealt with commercial policy. Both Judiciary Committees coupled broad representativeness with high prestige.

By 1913 attitudes had edged somewhat further from the Jeffersonian mold, but judicial monopoly remained exceptional. President Taft, in vetoing the bill, repudiated judicial monopolism. He insisted on clearing up constitutional doubts before endorsement of a bill, relied heavily on his constitutional oath, and declared: "The custom of legislators and executives having any legislative function to remit to the courts entire and ultimate responsibility as to the constitutionality of the measures which they take part in passing is an abuse which tends to put the court constantly in opposition to the legislature and executive, and, indeed, to the popular supporters of unconstitutional laws." If, however, the legislators and the Executive did their duty, Taft insisted, this onus of popular disapproval would be lifted from the courts, or at least, substantially lessened.[77]

Two Midwestern Representatives dissented from this view. Each was a lawyer with four years House experience, and each insisted on the righteousness of the pending bill. The Iowa Republican, Nathan A. Kendall, objected to presidential vetoes based on the "pretext" of unconstitutionality and asserted: "If this measure is of uncertain validity, there is a suitable tribunal organized and maintained to determine the fact—a tribunal before whose arbitrament every patriotic citizen of the Republic submits with absolute unreserve. If it offends against the organic law of the land, let the Supreme Court so declare.[78]" The Wisconsin Republican, Irvine Lenroot, would leave final decision on legal questions to the Court, "which now is the final authority, and the only place where they can be definitely settled."[79] Such views, however, were rare. While many were now declaring that doubts of constitutionality must be substantial to oblige a member to oppose a bill otherwise acceptable, many also insisted on their personal duty to consider constitutional issues seriously.[80] Thus, Representative Richard Bartholdt, Missouri Republican, complained that the prohibition lobbyists swarming the capitol had not "sworn by a solemn oath to support the Constitution. I have."[81] A Kentucky Democrat, Representative Augustus Stanley, had this to say of the suggestion that the bill be referred to the courts:

> And yet we are advised to close our eyes to its glaring defects, to shirk our high obligation, and let the Supreme Court pass upon this measure; that this is no concern of ours.
>
> Mr. Clayton. Who said such a thing?
>
> Mr. Stanley. The gentleman from Alabama is too good a lawyer to voice such a sentiment, but we have heard it intimated in this House, and the sneering intimation is more contemptible than the bold assertion.[82]

The conservative Republican, Senator Elihu Root of New York, saw here a threat to the government of laws and predicted that the courts would either have to say the bill was unconstitutional or stultify themselves. He continued:

> and when they say that they will concentrate upon themselves a measure of unpopularity, of public censure, and of public impatience with the judicial establishment which we will have shifted from our shoulders when we vote for the bill believing it to be unconstitutional. I think I shall be the better satisfied to take that burden on my own shoulders, and therefore I shall vote against the bill, because I think it is not permitted by the Constitution.[83]

Actually the Supreme Court later upheld the act. In doing so it implicitly acknowledged the value of the deliberations of both the other branches, but followed the lead of Congress.[84] Congress, in turn, in probing constitutional principles, had discovered a promising suggestion in an earlier Court opinion and based its decision to divest liquor of its interstate character partly on it. In 1913, Congress had the Court guidance it had partially lacked in 1890, so that the final constitutional settlement resulted from creative dialogue between Court and Congress.[85] In both years, however, Congress accepted and discharged its own responsibility.

By the beginning of the twentieth century, therefore, the handling of constitutional questions in Congress had become stabilized on the Marshallian model. Judicial monopolism remained the exception. The crises of ensuing decades would give it plausibility and persuasiveness.

159

PART IV

Practice in the Modern Congress

8 *Federalism in Crisis: The Bituminous Coal Conservation Act of 1935*

By the summer of 1935, when Congress passed the Guffey-Snyder "soft-coal" Act, its members were deep in measures to cure economic depression through long range reform. The National Labor Relations and Social Security Acts headed the list. Yet legislation to revive and regulate coal mining was important, too. During the seven months of intense struggle over its passage the most fearfully contested question was constitutional. The key issue was analogous to that in the Sherman Act debate—the power of the federal government to regulate conditions of production, in this case of mining, under its commerce power. Close analysis of the handling of the Guffey-Snyder Act, supplemented by brief references to the McNary-Haugen farm bills of 1927 and 1928, will show the effects of lapse of time on the handling of constitutional questions. It will also disclose the character and extent of congressional concern with the federal division of power and furnish a fitting introduction to the general workings of the modern Congress.

The striking fact about Congress since 1929 has been its absorption in action programs. Confronted by economic distress, military weakness, total war, and Cold War, the American people have demanded strong, effective government. Legislation has accordingly grown more abundant and more complex and has assigned more and more power to administrative agencies. The same progress in science and technology which brought industrialism and the problem of trusts has gone on producing effects at an accelerating pace. The resulting crises, economic, military, diplomatic, and cultural, have produced mounting demands for new policies, more power in Washington, and more discretion in administrators.

The chapters to follow will show how Congress has related those demands to the constitutional order. The issues will involve federalism, the separation of powers, the amending process, the rights of the individual, and the relations of Congress with the Supreme Court. This series of studies will show Congress at work on broad categories of questions at regular intervals and under diverse political, economic, social, and international conditions. The aim will not only be to weigh congressional support for the two tripartite theories and their rapidly burgeoning rival, judicial monopolism, but to examine how accurately each theory accords with the actual experience and exigencies of Congress.

A striking feature of the passage of the Guffey-Snyder Act was the relation between Congress and the two other branches of the government. In May 1935, the Supreme Court held the National Recovery Administration unconstitutional in the Schechter case and confined the regulatory power of Congress over intrastate conditions to those which directly affect interstate commerce.[1] The concern which the decision produced in Congress over validity of the coal bill prompted President Franklin D. Roosevelt to intervene with his famous letter to the chairman of the House subcommittee then considering the bill. Part of the letter gave a cogent argument for constitutionality under the commerce clause, contending that the bill sought to regulate conditions of production which "directly affect commerce among the States." But the President closed with advice very different from President Taft's at the time of the Webb-Kenyon Act: "I hope your committee will not permit doubts as to constitutionality, however reasonable, to block the suggested legislation."[2] In stressing the primacy of policy, the legalistic nature of the constitutional question, and the credentials of the Supreme Court as constitutional expositor, he came close to voicing the judicial monopoly theory: "The situation is so urgent and the benefits of the legislation so evident that all doubts should be resolved in favor of the bill, leaving to the courts, in an orderly fashion, the ultimate question of constitutionality. A decision by the Supreme Court relative to this measure would be helpful as indicating, with increasing clarity, the constitutional limits within which this Government must operate." Such a decision was forthcoming within eleven months. In one of its last actions against New Deal legislation, the Supreme Court, on May 18, 1936, handed down Carter v. Carter Coal Company,[3] holding six to three that the Guffey-Snyder Act was unconstitutional. In the mounting conflict between the President and the Court what was the true responsibility of a member of Congress?

The Guffey-Snyder bill was long in the making. Throughout the 1920's the soft-coal industry had been blighted. Overproduction and an extremely low margin of profit maintained only by near starvation wages had characterized the entire industry.[4] The industry had lost money even in the prosperous years of 1928 and 1929.[5] Widespread unemployment among the miners coupled with the worst possible wage standards were creating a "schism, drenched in blood and history, between the mine-owners and labor."[6]

The 1929 business Depression made miserable conditions intolerable. Coal production by 1932 had dropped to less than half of capacity,[7] and there was actual starvation in some major coal mining areas. There were "heads of families who had been on relief for three to five years; children who did not know what it was to sit down at table and eat a proper meal; rickety shacks black with coal dust."[8]

Demands for central planning to eliminate destructive competition in this industry came mainly from the labor unions, particularly from John L. Lewis' United Mine Workers.[9] Between 1913 and 1935 there were nineteen separate investigations of the industry conducted either by Congress or by commissions reporting to Congress.[10] Bills to regulate the industry were introduced in 1921, 1922, 1926, and 1932, but none was successful. In 1933, Congress passed the National Industrial Recovery Act and under its authority, the President signed the Bituminous Coal Code after bringing pressure to bear on recalcitrant producers. The National Recovery Administration code helped producers and workers, and especially the United Mine Workers, which, thanks to section 7a of the act, increased its membership from a 1933 low of 100,000 to 400,000.[11]

By the fall of 1934, however, the NRA coal code was widely ignored. Accordingly, Henry Warrum, general counsel for the United Mine Workers, working with representatives of producers' associations, drafted a bill patterned after suggestions made in the recent report of the Natural Resources Board. Senator Joseph F. Guffey, Pennsylvania Democrat, introduced this bill into Congress. Drafters of the bill provided controls of prices and labor sufficient to avoid the chaos of pure competition; by avoiding direct control of production they won over most producers. Opposition came chiefly from Southern producers and elsewhere from the largest producers. Others who violently opposed the bill were such conservative groups as the American Liberty League and likewise Republicans and Southern Democrats in Congress.[12] Lewis and his mine workers, however, threatened a nationwide strike, and under Roosevelt's leadership the New Deal Democrats in Congress drove for passage.

A brief narrative of the course of the bill in Congress will clarify the twentieth-century legislative process. After Guffey introduced his bill on January 24, 1935, a subcommittee of the Senate Committee on Interstate Commerce held hearings on it in February and March, and the committee subsequently reported it favorably to the Senate. Its report failed, however, to comment on the constitutional issues.[13] The Schechter decision of May 27, however, made constitutionality of prime concern. Accordingly, when a subcommittee of the House Ways and Means Committee opened hearings on the companion bill of Representative J. Buell Snyder, Pennsylvania Democrat, it gave prominence to constitutional questions. After nearly a fortnight, the hearings closed on

June 28, and a week later, the President sent his famous letter to the subcommittee chairman, Representative Samuel B. Hill, Washington Democrat. Not until August 14 did the parent committee report, and then on a new bill from Snyder.[14] Two days later, the House Rules Committee granted a special rule to facilitate prompt debate. After eight hours of debate, the House passed the bill on August 19 by 194 to 168. Three days later, the Senate took up and hastily passed this House bill with amendments by a vote of 45 to 37. A joint conference committee eliminated differences, and its report won acceptance in both houses, August 23. The President signed it into law on August 30.

A word of explanation of the principal features of the act will provide a background for subsequent analysis. Congress made only one change from Guffey's original bill; the House subcommittee deleted a section creating a national soft-coal reserve and appropriating $300,000,000 for the purchase of marginal-production mines to be added to that reserve. In section 1, the act declared that the mining and distribution of soft coal were affected with a public interest and directly affected interstate commerce, the intent being to explain and justify the regulation of prices, production, wages, hours, and conditions of employment. In section 2 it set up a five-man Bituminous Coal Commission in the Department of the Interior; the President was to appoint its members with senatorial approval. In section 3 it imposed a 15 per cent excise tax on coal sold at the mine, or, in the case of "captive" coal,[15] on the fair market value at the mine. The act sought to induce producers to accept the codes provided for in section 4, by permitting a 90 per cent drawback on the tax they would otherwise pay.

Section 4 was the heart of the bill. In part 1, it created boards to be elected by producers in twenty-three districts representing the various coal-producing areas of the country. It also permitted producers to set up marketing agencies. Part 2 of the section authorized the district boards, acting on their own initiative or at the direction of the commission, to fix maximum and minimum prices for coal and set forth elaborate standards to govern the determination of such prices and guaranteed producers an appeal to the commission.

The labor provisions appeared in part 3; it guaranteed collective bargaining and provided a Bituminous Coal Labor Board to enforce that right. If an organization representing half the workers signed agreements with producers of two-thirds of the tonnage in any district, then the agreed-on wages and hours would bind all code members in that district. Similarly, agreements reached nationally would bind code members throughout the country.

The remaining sections, 5 to 23, dealt mainly with procedures for the issuance and enforcement of commission orders. One section prohibited the government from purchasing coal from a noncode producer.

Judicial review was assured, and section 15 added a separability clause, stating that if any one section of the act were judicially declared invalid, the rest should remain in force.[16] The act was intricate, having been worked out initially by unions and producers with executive encouragement. In its final form it bore clear evidence of its drafters' misgivings concerning validity.

The relation between the treatment of the bill in Congress and later events is somewhat obscure. Clearly, the President's advice to leave validity to the courts was of doubtful value, since the Court promptly ruled the act invalid. The President's response to this and like decisions was to seek to change the Court's interpretation by securing from Congress the authority to pack the Court. The same session of Congress which rejected that proposal passed another soft-coal act, omitting or modifying provisions to which the Court had objected and leaving the rest unchanged.[17]

In 1940 the Supreme Court upheld this second act.[18] Changes in Court membership were of course crucial in producing this result. Yet the congressional inquiries into constitutionality in 1935 and again in 1937 may have had their effects. There is evidence, especially in Mr. Justice Douglas' opinion upholding the second act, that the congressional amassing of facts concerning the coal industry and deliberations on constitutionality may have influenced the decision of the Court itself.[19] Presidential threats may have influenced the justices, but it is also conceivable that here, as elsewhere, the prior labors of Congress in exploring the constitutional issue and alerting affected interests and the general public to existing conditions and alternative solutions may have contributed importantly to the outcome.

The 1935 deliberations of Congress had a more immediate and more evident influence on the lower federal courts. No sooner had the President signed the Guffey-Snyder Act than test cases were brought in the Supreme Court of the District of Columbia and in the Federal District Court for Western Kentucky. Although Congress had already gathered much factual material, both courts collected further evidence on whether the soft-coal industry was a part of interstate commerce. The District of Columbia Court, moved by judicial monopoly concepts, ignored congressional findings. But the court in Kentucky, more amenable to tripartite ideas, attached considerable weight to the legislative findings. In these various and even contradictory ways, the work of Congress contributed to the work of the courts.[20]

CONSTITUTIONAL QUESTIONS

The leading question posed by the Guffey-Snyder bill concerned the relative powers of the federal and state governments. Did Congress have power, under the commerce or other clauses, to regulate prices and wages in the soft-coal industry, or was this a matter reserved to the states? In addition, the bill raised the question of whether its terms unconstitutionally delegated legislative power by permitting a quota of workers and of producers in effect to determine minimum wages.

The first and more important of these questions presented two facets. On the one hand, it necessitated a search of rules and principles to determine which were appropriate for the facts of this situation. On the other hand, it necessitated findings of fact to determine whether in actual practice, under contemporary conditions, conditions of production in the soft-coal industry had a direct and substantial effect on interstate commerce. The inquiry thus became both a matter of law and a matter of fact, and each raised the issue of congressional responsibility.

The issue of federal power grew out of the constitutional text and was hence narrow in nature. Later Court decisions would expand federal regulatory powers and partially convert this question from narrow to broad. Congress and the public would then face the broad problem posed by Senator Jones in 1888 during the early antitrust debates, namely, assuming clear legal power to regulate, should Congress proliferate measures of economic regulation in view of their long-run impact on the free and regionally-autonomous constitutional order?

But in 1935 it was the narrow question that drew the principal attention. The Schechter case of May struck down the NRA, first, as a regulation of local conditions having no direct or substantial effect on interstate commerce, and second, as an unconstitutional delegation of legislative power to the President through failure to prescribe standards controlling administrative discretion. This on top of a host of existing precedents and the prospect of early court review put the issue of legal power ahead of all others.

COURSE OF THE DISCUSSION

Senate Hearings. The bill which entered the Senate in January 1935 had already undergone scrutiny by executive officials and officers of economic interest groups. Nevertheless, the Senate subcommittee under Chairman Matthew Neely of West Virginia, who had served eighteen years in Congress, held extensive hearings.[21] The printed record runs to more than six hundred pages. Most of the testimony concerned the policy and details of the bill. For example, it explored the effectiveness of the then-operative NRA coal code. It also dealt specifically with the interlocking nature of production and distribution of coal, its part in interstate commerce, and the effect of intrastate transactions in coal upon those which were interstate.

Many of the eighty witnesses were lawyers, most of them representing coal producers. Several of these filed short briefs on the issues. The proponents of the bill argued that it could be sustained as an exercise of the power to regulate interstate commerce, or as an exercise of the power to tax and spend for the general welfare, or as an exercise of some vague power to regulate what were called federal public utilities. The opponents of the bill contended that there was no general power in the federal government to regulate public utilities and that coal mining was not commerce. The opponents also attacked the allotment quotas provision, later struck out, as a deprivation of property without due process of law in contravention of the Fifth Amendment.

The committee's report[22] reflected the general lack of concern with constitutional issues which had been manifested in the hearings. Not once did the committee find it necessary to state clearly the constitutional authority on which the bill might be upheld; and nowhere did it even suggest that some thought the bill unconstitutional. The report merely assumed validity.

Despite lack of clear definition of the constitutional issues the report did make findings which could later be used to support constitutionality under several clauses.

The production of bituminous coal constitutes one of this country's greatest basic industries. Upon its service the successful operation of our transportation facilities and the prosperity of a majority of all our other important industries depend. The relationship of the coal industry to the health, comfort, and happiness of the people is immediate and inescapable.[23]

. . .

Experience, costly and sad, conclusively demonstrates the fact that the industry is beyond all hope of stabilization, excepting through governmental control—control based on a rational correlation of production and consumption, and upon adequate protection for the consuming public. Proper conservation of a great national resource, satisfactory public service in the production, distribution and sale of an indispensable commodity, and the establishment and preservation of adequate scales of wages and standards of living among those engaged in the industry all demand Federal control.[24]

In addition, the committee found that domestic coal[25] and captive coal must come within the regulatory scheme, for otherwise it would not be possible to regulate the industry.

House Hearings. The House hearings opened three weeks after the NRA decision. Chairman Samuel B. Hill, Washington Democrat, conducted them. This sixty-year-old veteran of twelve years in the House was a native of Arkansas and had studied law at the University of Arkansas before moving to Washington. He had served four years as county prosecutor and seven as county judge. The six other members of the subcommittee all came from states east of the Mississippi and outside the South.[26] Attendance was good and these and other Representatives took an active part.

With but a single clerk to assist him, Hill conducted the hearings with skill and fairness. Most of the forty witnesses represented special interest groups of one sort or another.[27] They included, for example, James A. Emery of Washington, D.C., general counsel of the National Association of Manufacturers; H. L. Findlay of Cleveland, Ohio, of the National Conference of Bituminous Coal Producers; Jonas Waffle of Terre Haute, Indiana, of the Coal Trade Association of Indiana; John L. Lewis; and William Keck of Gillespie, Illinois, president of the Progressive Miners of America. Representatives, economists, and private citizens appeared, and again the testimony filled more than six hundred pages of printed record.

The issues treated differed from those at the Senate hearings. This change was attributable to the Schechter decision, which had forced the constitutional issues inherent in the bill into the foreground. When NRA fell, the Bituminous Coal Code also fell. Thus opponents of the Guffey-Snyder bill could no longer claim that NRA already provided a regulatory system for the soft-coal industry. Rather than merely suggest modifications in the bill or take the impolitic position of opposing all regulation for the coal industry, they adopted constitutional arguments as their mainstay. The Schechter decision not only reduced the alternatives open to the opponents, but it also provided them with a strong constitutional precedent.

Furthermore, the Court had held that the commerce clause gave Congress no authority to regulate the wages and hours of employees of the plaintiff, a New York poultry slaughterer who bought and sold most of his goods locally. Speaking for the Court, Chief Justice Hughes declared such activities had no direct and substantial effect on interstate commerce. If such regulation were permitted, nothing would be safe from regulation and the federal-state balance would be disrupted.

In the House hearings, Warrum asserted that the bill had been redrafted to conform to the Schechter holding on delegation. The redrafted bill made the standards for fixing maximum and minimum prices more definite and defined unfair competitive practices with greater

170

precision. Nevertheless, opponents charged that the delegation was still unconstitutional, although they failed to distinguish sharply between delegation of power to the commission to fix prices and delegation of power to half the miners and two-thirds of the producers to fix wages and hours.

But the issue most in dispute at these hearings was the power to control the price of coal and the wages and hours of miners. The committee's subsequent report[28] gave a clear statement of the argument on both sides. The majority and the minority of the committee agreed that by Court precedents production of coal was not in itself interstate commerce.[29] Chief point in dispute was whether coal production directly affected interstate commerce, although neither side distinguished the effect of prices from that of wages and hours. The majority report contended that Schechter was not controlling, since coal had vastly greater importance than live poultry, and since the Court itself had observed that lines could be drawn with precision only in individual cases, as these came before the Court.

The majority advanced the theory that

When Congress finds and declares that an industry is subject to its power because the conduct of that industry is such that interstate commerce is restrained by it, if the subject is something of a national concern, and if its findings cannot be said to be unreasonable and arbitrary, the Supreme Court has upheld affirmative regulation by Congress.

That the findings set forth in the bill are not unreasonable and unwarranted is also clear from the long course of legislative inquiry into the soft-coal industry by Congress.[30]

The majority further found that "the condition of this industry imperatively demands the exercise of the power of Congress to remedy evils which seriously endanger the industry itself and the health and well-being of many people in many parts of the country," and that "a problem so Nation-wide in its scope and so manifold in its aspects cannot be dealt with adequately by the States." It maintained that 85 to 90 per cent of all coal went into interstate commerce. Captive coal and domestic coal competed with interstate coal and so must also be regulated.[31]

The majority then noted that the Supreme Court had upheld the power of Congress to regulate futures on grain exchanges[32] and stockyard prices.[33] Furthermore, the Court had sustained Sherman Act prosecutions against striking miners on the ground that, though production was a local activity, the strikers nevertheless restrained interstate commerce.[34] Finally, if the states could regulate an industry affected with a public

171

interest, the federal government should be able to declare an industry affected with a national public interest and impose similar regulation.

The main minority report, by six Republicans, relied heavily on the Schechter case. The stockyard and grain cases were distinguished on the ground that in those cases Congress was regulating the *flow* of interstate commerce, whereas here Congress was seeking to regulate an area in which commerce had not yet begun. The minority found the Sherman Act cases against strikers inapplicable because they turned on a specific finding of intent to obstruct interstate commerce.

Representative David J. Lewis, Maryland Democrat, wrote a separate report. Lewis, who was largely self-taught and who had held federal office for eighteen years, used a broad construction of the general welfare clause as constitutional basis for the proposed legislation. The minority, however, maintained that the Court had repudiated this argument and cited Bailey *v.* Drexel Furniture Co. and Hill *v.* Wallace to prove its point.[35]

Thus, the House hearings, sandwiched in between the Schechter case and the Roosevelt letter, conducted the participating Representatives through an intensive examination, pro and con, of court precedents and court-made rules of construction. Nevertheless one may question whether all of the majority members who favored passage had resolved doubts of constitutionality. The President had put the bill on his list of "must" legislation, and followed this with a forthright letter; the power and prestige of the White House were behind the measure. The minority reported that only political pressure had induced some members to vote to allow the bill to go to the floor.

Floor Debate. The eight hours of debate in the House provided better consideration of the constitutional issues than the sporadic debate in the Senate. The Representatives debated the constitutional issues generally along the lines laid down by the majority and minority reports. Fred M. Vinson, Kentucky Democrat and later Chief Justice of the United States, and Samuel Hill, the subcommittee chairman, led the forces supporting the bill. Allen T. Treadway, Republican of Massachusetts, and Jere Cooper, Democrat of Tennessee, led the opposition. Treadway, at sixty-eight, owned a hotel business and had served in Congress twenty-two years and Cooper, at forty-two, had served six years in Congress. The speeches of these leaders set out detailed arguments chiefly on constitutional rather than policy matters. In addition, members frequently broke in with questions on technical points in dispute and speakers yielded in order to clarify such points. Ostensibly this was an effort by both sides to win over the wavering.

172

The Senate debate did little more than indicate that the constitutional issues were in doubt. Senators talked of those issues only in the most general terms. They described the bill as invalid because it was "un-american" or "against the immutable laws of economics," or "socialistic." That they avoided precise and focused constitutional debate resulted in part no doubt from the pressure to adjourn and the unwillingness of members of both sides, four days before closing a session crowded with urgent bills, to preserve an open mind. By 45 to 37, the Senate passed the bill, an outcome which many may have foreseen. In that case, few could have expected an appeal to reason to change the result. This Senate stage and likewise the ensuing conference-committee and final-passage stages were largely perfunctory.

Discussion Evaluated. Senate debate was neither thorough nor effective, but the House record was better. The debaters in the House focused their remarks on the commerce power, the taxing power, the public interest doctrine, and the delegation of legislative power to private persons. Some of the discussion was superficial and most of it was without clear, logical sequence. Yet the speakers touched on all the cases later cited in the three Carter opinions. In the House hearings some of the members were precise in considering whether prices and wages in the coal industry directly affected interstate commerce. Certain questions, however, received careful attention only in the courts.[36]

In the hearings, the House achieved a good measure of detachment. The House subcommittee truly deliberated the constitutional issues, as did the whole House in the eight hours of debate. Representatives here exchanged views and questioned one another on these views. This debate was of high enough quality to produce at least the germ of a rationale for a broad interpretation of the commerce power. That is, Congress was here acting independently and in advance of the courts in making constitutional determinations.

Study of the House roll call on passage suggests that the constitutional discussion in the House may have influenced some Democrats to vote contrary to their normal party and regional commitments. In the final 194 to 168 vote, most Northern and Western Democrats favored passage, but thirty of them, including a staunch New Dealer, Representative John W. McCormack of Massachusetts, voted against the bill.[37] Of course factors other than constitutional scruples affected regional balloting, among them the pressures of mining interests.[38]

On this constitutional controversy, the House did better than the Senate. No doubt this resulted in part from the timing of the Schechter decision in relation to the two series of hearings. In any case, Congress here demonstrated that it was still capable in 1935 of exploring with considerable thoroughness and at least a modicum of detachment a serious constitutional issue.

PARTICIPANTS

In view of the character of the question and the great importance attached to court precedents, it is not surprising that leadership in debate fell to lawyers. The percentage of lawyers in the Senate had fallen to 71 from the 82 of 1890, and throughout the several stages of Senate discussion, lawyers maintained about this same proportion.[39] In the House, although lawyers numbered 59 per cent of the membership, those sharing in the committee work were a smaller proportion—48 per cent of the Ways and Means Committee, and 43 per cent of the subcommittee. Nevertheless, the most active members of the parent committee and subcommittee were lawyers; of the leading participants in the floor debate, they made up 88 per cent.[40] The technical nature of the problem gave lawyers such an advantage that even the two non-lawyers who took an active part in House debate repeatedly deferred to lawyers on their side of the question as having more precise knowledge than they.

The role which lawyers had achieved in constitutional debates elicited several responses from the members. Republican Representatives Tread-way and Harold Knutson of Minnesota, a Norwegian-born printer, both non-lawyers, were most vocal in opposing the bill as unconstitutional, but their reliance on lawyers was evident. When Representative Vinson pressed Knutson about lack of legal knowledge, the latter conceded, "Well, I have such distinguished company as Judge Cooper, of Tennessee . . . The gentleman realizes, of course, that there must be laymen to support lawyers."[41] Another response was that of Carl E. Mapes, Michigan Republican, who as a lawyer asserted that the legal profession as a whole opposed the bill as unconstitutional.[42] Representative Vinson exemplified a third response, that of the lawyer's disdain for the non-lawyer, who voiced views on constitutionality:

> Mr. Knutson. Assuming this measure is constitutional—and I think the best lawyers in the House do not so assume—
> Mr. Vinson. I grant you Judge Treadway and Judge Knutson, who are not lawyers, hold this bill to be unconstitutional.[43]

Yet there remained another response: that of lawyers who recognized that lawyers in both houses were disagreeing violently over constitutional issues. Charles A. Wolverton, New Jersey Republican, stated this view in the House. His remedy was to go ahead and enact the bill since

174

even lawyers—the unquestioned experts on all matters of constitutionality—could not agree.[44] Senator Millard E. Tydings, Maryland Democrat, voiced the same view: "I do not like constitutional argument on the floor of the Senate. I think men ought to resolve those things in their own minds, because lawyers may differ . . ."[45]

The prevailing assumption was that while others might speak, lawyers alone had something to say. No one questioned that assumption.

The final House debate gave a substantial number of members an opportunity to express legal judgments, and likewise the wisdom resulting from considerable experience.[46] No longer was it true, however, that Congress looked solely to its own members for legal knowledge, constitutional wisdom, or even evidence of public or interest-group opinion. By now, Congress was reaching outside for help, and using as a principal means, the device of open hearings. For advice of lawyers and other experts, and likewise for evidence of prevailing needs and desires of affected groups, both chambers employed public hearings by subcommittees. Both thus gained valuable factual information and soundings of opinion currents. Success depended on judicious leadership and a representative committee makeup.[47] Later chapters will show that in other constitutional controversies hearings have served other, and sometimes undesirable, purposes.

At the House hearings, Representative Treadway kept pressing Warrum for "impartial legal advice" and suggested the committee tap another source—the Attorney General, Homer Cummings.[48] The effort was illusory. An Arkansas Democrat, Claude A. Fuller, described the troubles of the committee in seeking Cumming's advice:

> For over a week we tried every process except sending the Sergeant at Arms to get him before the subcommittee of the Ways and Means Committee to ask him a few questions on the constitutionality of this measure.
>
> . . . When we did get him before the subcommittee he said he came directly from the White House, and he made the same argument as the White House—"Vote it out, irrespective of its constitutionality." Did he tell us he would defend it and declare for its constitutionality? Oh, no! A few moments later, for fear he had not been strong enough, our great President sent a letter to my good friend . . . [Chairman Hill], and he said, "Not to permit doubts as to the constitutionality, however reasonable, to deter you from bringing this bill out," an acknowledgment on its face that this bill is unconstitutional.[49]

Granted, the Attorney General aided by the Justice Department was a potentially valuable source of advice at least on narrow questions. Yet that official serves principally as legal adviser to the Executive and must conform to policy directives of the President. This puts him at arm's length from Congress and makes congressional dependence on his advice constitutionally dubious.

Although Vinson of Kentucky and Cooper of Tennessee led among the protagonists in debate, one cannot ascribe the harmonious outcome of the constitutional conflict primarily to Border State and Southern leadership. Here was a case in which a new political coalition—the New Deal—reinforced here by the pressures of the mining industry, carried the day. Traditional lines of cleavage melted in the heat of economic distress. The economic facts accumulated in hearings, and the doubts surrounding the constitutional question furnished the basis for the vote to pass the act. So great was the backing for the bill, that the leaders eschewed compromise, and pushed the bill to passage as reported by the Ways and Means Committee.

MODE

By 1935, most bills followed a standard procedure. Standing committees, often preceded by their subcommittees, would take them up first. Then would follow floor debate, strictly limited in the House and sometimes in the Senate. The Committee of the Whole, once so common to both houses, and in the early years the forum for first consideration of matters of principle, was now confined essentially to the House and there employed only after the all-important standing-committee stage. Note that Congress had, for the time being, stabilized its standing committees at thirty-three in the Senate and forty-seven in the House, but was now increasing the number of its subcommittees. It was now common to hold hearings, which would later appear in print.

The Guffey-Snyder bill followed just such a course of procedure. No one in the House challenged that procedure and only one incident of such a challenge occurred in the Senate. This was an unsuccessful effort by the chairman of the Senate Committee on Mines and Mining to have the bill referred to his committee, with its heavy representation of mining states.[50]

This incident suggests a query: why was not the bill referred, as in 1890, to the Judiciary Committees? Perhaps those committees had grown increasingly conservative in complexion. A more likely explanation is the increasing concern with the policy of bills and the plausibility of referring bills to committees which specialized in the subject matter of the policy in question. Note that here it was the Senate Mines Committee and not Judiciary that tried to gain jurisdiction. The effect of referral to policy-oriented committees is gravely to jeopardize genuine constitutional examination of bills, first, because policy factors are uppermost in the committee's interest and competence, second, because policy committees tend often to overrepresent areas supporting such policy, and third, because committees thus constituted give ear primarily to interest groups most vitally concerned with that policy. With committees dominating congressional discussion, the effect of all this is to amplify special interests and policy demands and to minimize the general interest including constitutional considerations.

Table 6 shows how seats were distributed according to regions on

TABLE 6. Regional Distribution of Seats in Certain Standing Committees, Spring 1935

| Region | House Committees | | Senate Committees | | |
	Ways and Means	Judiciary	Commerce	Mines	Judiciary
Border	3	4	3	1	2
Midwest	7	6	5	2	6
Far West	2	2	2	5	5
South	4	5	2	1	1
Middle Atlantic	7	6	4	2	1
New England	2	2	4	0	1
Vacancies	0	0	0	2	2
Total	25	25	20	13	18

SOURCE: *Congressional Directory,* 74th Cong., 1st sess. (April 1935), pp. 178–179, 199, 204.

the committees concerned or potentially concerned with the Guffey-Snyder bill. The order of regions here follows roughly that of coal output. In the twenty-five-man House committees, the Middle Atlantic and Midwestern States lead in representation, the South and Border States follow, while the Far West and New England hold only two seats each. In Senate Commerce, New England, with its manufacturing industry, claims one-fifth of the seats, on a par with the Middle Atlantic States, just behind the Midwest, while the Far West and South each holds only one-tenth of the seats. In Judiciary, the Midwest retains its lead, with one-third of the eighteen seats, while the Far West rises to six seats. The South, Middle Atlantic region and New England must each content itself with a single seat. The mining West nearly dominates the Mines Committee, with five of eleven occupied seats, two seats remaining vacant. The Border and Southern States, though producers of soft coal, hold one seat each, and New England is unrepresented.

In 1935 the mal-representation, insofar as coal was concerned, was tolerable.[51] This was probably a matter of chance, for on other issues, and at other times, the distribution was far worse. An example appears in the handling of the McNary-Haugen farm bill, which for five years, from 1924 to 1928, congressional spokesmen of the languishing farm industry pressed toward passage. In 1927 and again in 1928 the Farm Bloc was successful, only to encounter a veto which President Coolidge based chiefly on constitutional grounds. In both years, the bill issued from Senate and House Agriculture Committees, having heavy majorities from farming states and solid backing from the big farm organizations. Under such auspices, the constitutional questions never received a thorough and effective consideration.[52]

Yet in 1935 Congress, on balance, provided procedure marked by fairness to interested parties in and out of Congress. Members were clearly put on notice by occasional remarks on the floor, the Schechter decision, and the President's letter. After the eight hours of debate on two successive days, as ordered by the Rules Committee, the House, by unanimous consent, postponed the final vote from Saturday to Monday when most members could be present.

Again, in both houses, the subcommittees conducted proceedings so as to assure a fair presentation of constitutional issues. Hearings were public and advance notice was evidently afforded, to judge by the great variety of witnesses. Committee members willingly inserted witnesses' briefs in the record and treated witnesses courteously and without badgering. Members' questions, if at times irrelevant, reflected a genuine desire to elicit information and develop arguments. Chairman Hill reflected his status as a lawyer and his seven years' experience as judge in his judicial conduct of this inquiry.

Deliberation must have been genuine, especially in the House Committee. Floor debate was, of course, held in public, but the deliberative quality of this, too, in the House at least, was substantial. In view of the published hearings and reports, the eight hours of House debate were probably adequate, thanks to careful management of the time by the two opposed sides. Senate debate was unmanaged and largely wasted. Neither house took a roll call on the constitutional question, but both held roll calls on passage of the bill.

Even under heavy Administration pressure, Congress explored, under new procedures and old, important constitutional questions.

ATTITUDES

Notwithstanding this effort to achieve detachment Congress was now reflecting the pressures brought about by continued economic crisis in its attitude toward its own responsibility for constitutional questions.

178

Crises and distress gave plausibility to ideas of judicial monopoly, which now had a platoon of advocates. The complexity of the legislation and the technicality in which the constitutional question had become couched enhanced the appeal of those ideas. And now the theory appeared to carry the seal of the President.

Opponents still stressed tripartite views, especially in Marshall's formulation. Senator Tydings of Maryland asserted: "We are here to pass a bill which, beyond any reasonable peradventure of a doubt, will stand the test of the courts, so that we will not abuse the exercise of power which each and every one of us is sworn not to abuse."[53] Senator William H. King, Democrat of Utah, quoted at length from the constitutional commentator, Thomas M. Cooley: "Legislators have their authority measured by the Constitution: they are chosen to do what it permits and nothing more, and they take a solemn oath to obey and support it. When they disregard its provisions, they usurp authority, abuse their trust, and violate the promise they have confirmed by an oath. To pass an act when they are in doubt whether it does not violate the Constitution is to treat as of no force the most imperative obligations any person can assume."[54]

In the House, Representative Daniel A. Reed, New York Republican, invoked President Taft's veto message of 1913 warning that judicial monopolism tended to exacerbate relations between the Court and the political branches and to engender public opposition to the Court.[55] Representative Treadway also quoted Taft in rebutting President Roosevelt's "now famous letter," and observed that no legislation, "however meritorious, urgent, or politically expedient," should win official approval when that legislation is "recognized as unconstitutional by the great majority of able lawyers who have expressed themselves upon it."[56]

These comments, all from experienced legislators, combined Jeffersonian with Marshallian concepts. The minority report of the House Committee called it improper for the President and legislators to thrust on the Court the entire burden of considering constitutionality. To do that would create "an unjust and unwarranted antagonism to the Constitution and the Supreme Court to the point where the people will countenance the necessary changes in the fundamental law."[57]

Yet the more frequent opinion was that constitutional questions should be left almost entirely to the courts, especially the Supreme Court. These opinions now came not only from Midwesterners, but also from members from Eastern and Border States and from relative newcomers from the Far West and even Texas. For the most part they were Democrats with limited congressional experience.[58] Senator Guffey himself maintained through the medium of newspaper editorials inserted in the *Record* that this was an uncharted constitutional area and so the legislation

179

should be enacted, leaving questions of constitutionality to the courts.[59] Vinson cited the ultimate upholding of the Webb-Kenyon Act and suggested this was reason enough to leave constitutional determinations to the Court.[60]

Characteristic of the attitudes of Representatives favoring the bill was a comment of Mell G. Underwood, Democrat from Ohio, who declined to debate constitutionality because he was "attempting to make this effort to assist the laboring people of the country" and was "willing to leave that question to the proper tribunal, the Supreme Court of the United States."[61] Adolph J. Sabath, veteran member from Illinois, thought that a member should vote for a measure of doubtful constitutionality and then "let the courts finally decide the matter."[62] Walter M. Pierce of Oregon was willing to "Let this measure go to the Supreme Court, if necessary. We should know what authority we, the Congress, have."[63]

The most extreme suggestion was that the Court was absolutely the only organ of government that could speak on constitutionality. Representative Wolverton, New Jersey Republican, verged on this: "The binding answer can be made only by the . . . Supreme Court of the United States."[64] Maury Maverick, a newcomer from Texas, put it: "Some say the bill is constitutional. Others say it is not constitutional. Well, well, it has not been passed on yet, you know. It has not gone to the Supreme Court, and I cannot tell you in advance whether it is constitutional or not . . ."[65]

The strong possibility of a judicial veto drove some to desperate expedients. One Democrat from Ohio, Representative Robert T. Secrest, favored passage even though the bill was unconstitutional; it would be in operation for a year and a half before the courts would strike it down.[66] He was wrong by seven months.

Thus did the President's advice raise echoes in the halls of Congress. Judicial monopolism in various degrees and guises had come to the fore as a rival to the more traditional theories. But the President's role in propagating that theory should not be overstated. For one thing, his July letter dealt mainly with a reasoned constitutional defense of the bill, and this example might well serve to impel responsible members of Congress to dig beneath court precedents for the principles most appropriate for the case in 1935. For another, the earlier debates on the McNary-Haugen bills show that by the late 1920's judicial monopoly ideas had already gained wide currency in Congress. Midwest Republicans in numbers echoed the sentiments of a Kansas Representative who in 1928 praised the Supreme Court as "unbiased, unprejudiced, fair," and asserted: "This is the body where the question of constitutionality should be settled and determined, and no other body, when there is any question of constitutionality, should pass upon the question, as a reason for a veto . . ."[67] Even those who sincerely believed the bill unconstitutional, asserted a Minnesota Republican, "should support the bill and allow the court to pronounce the decision they regard as inevitable."[68] Even the Georgia Representative Malcolm C. Tarver deferred to the "eminent lawyers" in the Senate who had voted for the bill and to the two committees, which had reported it; he was willing under these conditions to let bills go to the courts for decision if their effects would be beneficial.[69] Faced with distress in his home state, this Southerner had moved toward a diminution of the member's responsibility, although qualifying his stand by the evidence of prior congressional determinations. One may well suppose that other Southerners moderated their extreme Jeffersonianism in later debates on measures to relieve distress, such as the Agricultural Adjustment Act of 1933 and the Guffey-Snyder bill.

Those views provoked replies from opponents of the farm bill, notably from the law dean and commentator, Henry St. George Tucker of Virginia, who deplored a growing tendency to defer to the courts and showed how the traditional judicial presumption of validity rested on acceptance of responsibility by legislators.[70] President Roosevelt's doctrine thus was far from new. What was new was presidential expression of it. Such auspices gave the advice a kind of legislative immortality.

CONCLUSIONS

It seems probable that the year 1935 or more properly the mid-30's represented a turning point in the congressional handling of constitutional questions. There is evidence that at this period constitutional questions and constitutional debates began to occupy less and less of the interest and time of the national legislators.[71] Clearly, the House could take credit for serious and sustained attention to the questions posed by this bill. Debate was brief as compared with earlier episodes and, coming late in the session, could hardly command the full attention and deliberate consideration of all members. Yet the preparatory work of the subcommittee and committee and the balancing of the arguments pro and con in the majority and minority reports meant that debate could be informed. The managed adversary procedure combined with flexible questioning counteracted the element of timing. The brief Senate discussion of course had all of the marks of unplanned and last-minute debate.

Conditions would be different in later Congresses and several factors help explain that change. The effect of the undiminished volume and urgency of congressional work is obvious. Another factor is procedural change. Both houses here had recourse to subcommittees and to public hearings. Subcommittees removed the detailed inquiry into constitutional questions even further from the whole house than had standing committees themselves and likewise increased the possibility that the important early and searching investigation and deliberation would rest with a minute fraction of members grossly unrepresentative of the whole and led by biased or injudicious chairmen. The recourse to hearings, when conducted by men of a different character from Representative Hill, furnished a tool which ambition, arrogance, or special pleading could warp to their own purposes and which instead of casting light on constitutional issues could becloud them. Hearings could likewise give a false image of the state of public or interest-group opinion. If some committees and subcommittees gave undue representation to special interests, then hearings before committees so constituted, could, unless managed with scrupulous fairness by chairmen, exaggerate the claims of those groups and neglect those of other groups and of the public as a whole. All of this could cripple the Congress in its treatment of basic questions.

Another factor, already present in the case of Guffey-Snyder, was legalism. It is not that lawyers held the floor most of the time. Rather it was the prevailing assumption that constitutionality is solely a matter of legality and that when one has examined, compared, and applied court precedents and predicted court behavior, one has discharged one's full responsibility. Even on legal aspects, members, and especially non-lawyers, here showed a desperate desire to obtain impartial legal advice, a desire not met here either by the Judiciary Committees, which were ignored, or by the Attorney General, or by counsel for interest groups. Congress already had other agencies of its own available for consultation, but here failed to use them. After another decade it would furnish its committees with expert staffs including counsel. The preoccupation with legality meant that broad questions were virtually ignored, and even more important, that members could be persuaded that the whole problem was technical, suitable for experts rather than for Congress.

It is not surprising that under the dual pressure of the President's letter, and an impending decision by the Court, many members found comfort in the judicial monopoly theory. In this situation, proponents had a choice; they could either leave full responsibility for constitutionality to the Court and run the risk of another Schechter decision, or they could painstakingly construct a constitutional rationale for the bill, even modifying it, if necessary, to gain Court approval. Many probably chose the first course. Opponents likewise had a choice; they could either let the bill go to the Court, in the assurance that the Court would strike it down, or they could assume the role of constitutional interpreters themselves, and attack the bill accordingly. Most opponents of the bill chose to argue the case. If the predicaments of advocates and opponents now seem academic, one should remember that at the time the pertinent judicial precedents were mixed. Advocates could take heart in Nebbia, in at least one of the Gold Clause cases, and in the Minnesota Moratorium case and opponents in the Hot Oil, Railroad Retirement, and Schechter cases.[72] Some advocates were willing to take the President's advice to leave the matter to the Court, and others to explore his argument for validity. Opponents, less disposed toward judicial monopolism, still had doubts about the chameleon-like Justice Roberts and the wily Chief Justice.

The decision of Congress on the Guffey-Snyder bill met with early repudiation in the Carter case. But just as its explorations of the constitutional issues here helped prepare the ground politically and doctrinally for a subsequent alteration in Court rulings on the immediate questions, just so other inquiries by Congress into other questions must have furnished guide lines for the other judicial reversals which began in 1937. By its decisions on the commerce, tax, and defense powers, the Court enlarged the scope of the substantive powers delegated to the federal government.[73] In other words, the Roosevelt Court nearly eliminated clauses granting federal powers as legal barriers to congressional action and thereby most narrow questions pertaining to the scope of federal in relation to state power. In this area, Congress has achieved something like supremacy. Seldom need it inquire, can we legally tax, appropriate, regulate commerce, or provide for the national defense in such and such a manner? Exceptions would occur as chapter 14 will show, and specific constitutional prohibitions still put legal shackles on the federal government, but by and large the disputes over the bounds of federal power which had agitated Congress for a century and a half came to an end by World War II.

Broad questions remain: Where should Congress draw the line in adopting federal measures for welfare, education, regulation, and defense before the free and democratic constitutional order gives way to collectivist totalitarianism? and, second, what powers should the states retain in relation to each new federal program?[74]

In these broad areas of constitutional limitation there is growing need for the community to determine and apply principles in an objective and deliberative manner. Under the impact of judicial monopolism, however, these issues of federal power, no longer questions of narrow legality, may be forgotten in the struggle over policy.

9

Separation of Powers in the Administrative State: The Reorganization Act of 1939

On January 12, 1937, President Franklin D. Roosevelt sent Congress the report of the President's Committee on Administrative Management and asked for sweeping authority to reorganize the executive branch.[1] With federal governmental activities expanding under the New Deal, the number and variety of administrative agencies kept pace, and the President insisted on the need of efficiency in the running of these agencies. The powers he requested, however, raised important constitutional questions in Congress involving concentration of power in the President and diminution of legislative controls. Like the issue in the Bradley case, these concerned the separation of powers.

Roosevelt's January request for power to reorganize came at a time of great political conflict. Within three weeks the President was asking the power to appoint six new Supreme Court justices. The political storm which raged over this proposal to reorganize the Court inevitably engulfed its predecessor. The rise of dictators in Europe stimulated fears of similar events in the United States and intensified the political tension. The Court bill failed, but after more than two years and three sessions, Congress achieved a settlement of the problem of executive reorganization. The result was the establishment of what has been termed the "legislative veto."

Three times before 1937 Congress had given the President power to reorganize and redistribute executive agencies. In the Overman Act of 1918,[2] Congress gave President Wilson the power to redistribute agencies connected with the prosecution of the war with no restrictions upon this power except that he was to report his actions to Congress.[3] In the Economy Act of 1932,[4] Congress authorized the President to regroup and consolidate agencies, but added a provision that such executive orders must lie for sixty days in Congress, during which time either house might, by resolution, disapprove such orders in whole or in part.[5] President Hoover submitted eleven reorganization plans under the provisions of this act but the Democratic-controlled House vetoed all of them.

184

Evidently no member of either house had made constitutional objections to these earlier acts. Early in 1933, however, President Hoover's Attorney General, William Mitchell, questioned the constitutional validity of congressional disapproval of executive orders. "The attempt to give to either House of Congress, by action which is not legislation, power to disapprove administrative acts, raises a grave question as to the validity of the entire provision in the Act . . ."[6] Thus when Congress passed the Economy Act of March 3, 1933,[7] it adopted an amendment offered by Senator James F. Byrnes, South Carolina Democrat, which deleted the power of either house to disapprove executive orders and simply provided that such orders should lie before Congress for sixty days while in session. Presumably a joint resolution signed by the President or passed over his veto would have been necessary to disapprove such orders.[8]

Before 1937, then, Congress had considered only one constitutional question in relation to acts granting the President reorganization authority: that is, the method and degree of control to be retained by Congress. Congress had yet to consider seriously whether the delegation of the reorganizing authority itself involved an unconstitutional delegation of legislative power. The necessities of war and depression had hindered such consideration. By 1937, however, depression had waned and fears about Roosevelt's urge for dictatorial powers had grown. Members of Congress were now to charge a violation of separation of powers. Roosevelt himself was cognizant of these fears and sought to allay them in his message asking reorganization authority. "In placing this program before you [he said] I realize that it will be said that I am recommending the increase of the power of the Presidency. This is not true. The Presidency as established in the Constitution of the United States has all of the powers that are required . . . What I am placing before you is not the request for more power, but for the tools of management and the authority to distribute the work so that the President can effectively discharge those powers which the Constitution now places upon him."[9] But the court-packing fight was creating anxiety in Congress and so the reorganization bill became just another political battlefield.

During the last part of January 1937, each house established a Select Committee on Government Organization and provided that the two committees should meet together as a joint committee to consider the President's message. This joint committee held hearings in February, March, and April on legislation granting the President broad authority to reorganize the executive branch and making no provision for congressional control. Constitutional questions arose here and were debated continually for the next two years. The House Committee reported the

185

bill favorably, adding only a provision that such orders would have to lie before Congress for sixty days; Congress could defeat them only through regular legislation. The House passed this bill in August 1937. The Senate debated a somewhat similar bill during March 1938, and likewise passed it. But in April 1938, the House ordered this Senate version sent back to the Select Committee. Before voting to recommit, the House added an amendment providing for congressional negation of executive orders by concurrent resolution, thus enabling the two houses to veto proposals by simple majorities without presidential signature. In March 1939, both houses passed a much weaker version of the bill, including a provision for congressional veto of executive reorganization plans, and the President signed it on April 3.

Congress thus reached a settlement of the constitutional questions. Later Congresses followed the 1939 precedent concerning delegation and congressional control of presidential action. The delegation of reorganization authority to the President was renewed in the Reorganization Acts of 1945 and 1949[10] and subsequently at two-year intervals. Furthermore, after 1939, Congress incorporated the legislative veto in numerous acts. The Neutrality Acts of 1939, the Alien Registration Act of 1940, the Lend-Lease Act of 1941, the First and Second War Powers Acts, and the Emergency Price Control Act of 1942[11] all contained provisions for review or termination by concurrent resolution. Although subsequent uses of this device provoked constitutional debate,[12] the 1939 settlement, later reinforced by a 1949 memorandum of the Attorney General supporting constitutionality of the legislative veto,[13] proved persuasive, and the only serious constitutional question that remained concerned use of the veto by congressional committees.[14]

Congress in practice has followed its own earlier precedents respecting delegation of power and the legislative veto, and the courts have left them undisturbed. No challenge has reached the courts testing their validity, and none is likely. In spite of repeated agitation of constitutional questions by a few, the legislative settlement of 1939 has held fast.

CONSTITUTIONAL QUESTIONS

Two leading constitutional questions arose during the 1937–1939 congressional action on reorganization bills, and each had both narrow and broad aspects.[15] The first question involved the delegation of legislative power to the Executive. Broadly speaking, this question involved consideration of the relation between the separation of powers and democratic, constitutionally limited government. In a narrow sense, the question was whether Congress could delegate power to the Executive to reorganize and redistribute executive agencies. Here there were specific precedents, both congressional and judicial.

The second question centered on the problem of congressional review of executive action. From a broad standpoint, may Congress review or veto executive action taken in pursuance of delegated power? There were few precedents, and the actual words of the Constitution were not at issue. Narrowly stated, may Congress utilize the concurrent resolution as a condition on executive exercise of delegated power? Here a section of the Constitution was involved. Article I, section 7 states that "Every bill which shall have passed the House of Representatives and the Senate shall, before it becomes a law be presented to the President . . ." But Congress had *always* used concurrent resolutions for housekeeping purposes and had never submitted them to the President for his signature.[16]

Congress discussed both the broad and narrow aspects of these questions but the discussion of the broad questions was less perceptive than it might have been. This was partly because constant talk of legality and use of legal phraseology in the debate led many members astray. Many lawyers failed to see the broad questions because of their preoccupation with the narrow, and non-lawyers tended to follow their lead. Furthermore, members might have handled the broad question more fruitfully had they avoided legalism and drawn on the experience of Great Britain. In its review of "statutory instruments" of general application, Parliament had a device somewhat analogous to the legislative veto. Since the nineteenth century, Parliament had controlled a wide variety of ministerial rules and orders with increasing frequency.[17] Yet no one in Congress seemed aware of the analogous problem and of the solution of another constitutional democracy.

Furthermore, Congress was here not merely interpreting the document, it was also implementing it. Like Parliament, it was actually creating for the burgeoning administrative state new devices for the control of power.

In seeking answers to these questions of the separation of powers, Congress seemed riveted to a legalistic approach. Perhaps this was because many throughout the discussion assumed that the act would later undergo court test. Three recent Supreme Court decisions had overturned congressional statutes on the ground that they had invalidly delegated legislative power,[18] and these caused some to think review probable. Furthermore, the reorganization authority granted the President in the Economy Act of 1933 had received a test in two recent lower-court decisions.[19] Yet Congress failed to probe its assumption about judicial review. For example, how would a litigant gain standing

187

to sue in a case under the proposed act? At all three sessions predictions of court action went unchallenged, despite the transformations which the Court underwent after 1937. Only in later Congresses did members become aware that judicial review of such questions was highly unlikely.[20]

COURSE OF THE DISCUSSION

1937 Committee Consideration. The first congressional body to consider the President's requests based on the recommendations of his Committee on Administrative Management, the Brownlow Committee, was the Joint Committee on Government Organization.[21] This eighteen-man committee took testimony from only seven persons, five connected with the Brownlow Committee and two from the Brookings Institution.[22] The constitutional questions took shape slowly in these initial hearings.

The tentative legislation proposed by the President's Committee contained no provision for congressional review of executive reorganization orders. Luther Gulick, a member of the Brownlow Committee, insisted that Congress had the power to review such orders through the process of appropriation.[23] But, after some discussion, the committee members agreed that this was a weak form of control. Said Senator Byrnes, "As a practical matter you cannot afford not to provide appropriations for the Interstate Commerce Commission as a division of the Department of Commerce, you would have to do it. The only way you can remedy it is by repealing it. The President could veto it, and then, if you wanted it to go on you would have to have a two-thirds vote. I do not think there is any way around it."[24] Byrnes, who had studied law privately, practiced in his home state, and served twenty years in Congress, was to have a prominent place in the ensuing discussions of the bill.

Later in the hearings Representative Charles Gifford, Massachusetts Republican, raised the question of the delegation of power and tied it to the question of congressional review. C. M. Hester, a consultant to the Brownlow Committee, replied to Gifford's inquiry. "You raised the question, Mr. Gifford, about ratification of executive orders by Congress. May I suggest that we have given that question very careful consideration and we have been unable to find any authority establishing the proposition that Congress, by silence, can legislate?"[25] Thus the leading positions on the question of congressional review were suggested in this committee. Administration supporters argued that no technique of congressional ratification was valid aside from regular legislation. The opponents argued that some form of congressional ratification was necessary in order to sustain the constitutionality of such a broad grant of power to the President.

188

The Senate Select Committee held separate hearings in August 1937.[26] The major part of the constitutional discussion in this committee concerned the preaudit function. The delegation and congressional-veto issues did, however, appear briefly at one point. Commenting on the absence of some device for congressional review, Senator Harry F. Byrd, Virginia Democrat, and Professor Charles E. Merriam, of the Brownlow Committee, had the following exchange, suggesting the outlines of the broad constitutional questions.

> Byrd. The bill gives vast power to the President to operate practically as he sees fit and then if Congress wants to recover this power they have to pass a law and the President can veto it and it takes a two-thirds vote of Congress to recover the power given to the President under this bill . . .
>
> Merriam. We did not invent, Senator Byrd, the two-thirds vote. That was established by the gentlemen who met one hundred and fifty years ago. You do not desire to change the veto power as laid down in the Constitution, do you?
>
> Byrd. I did not ask you that. I asked you whether in the interest of democracy, that you ought to transfer to the President the control of the business affairs of the government and then permit Congress to recover it only by a two-thirds vote?
>
> Merriam. Our intentions are to leave the executive power exactly where it is, but to transfer to the executive what belongs to him under the Constitution.[27]

Once again, a Virginian had detected an issue of general principle.

1937 Floor Debate. The bill which reached the House floor provided the President with a general authority to reorganize executive agencies, with specific exceptions, and included a provision that all reorganization orders must lie before Congress for sixty days before taking effect. Congressional correction could be only by formal legislation. It was on this bill that the three hours of House floor debate occurred in August 1937. The majority of the committee, which had written the bill, argued that the measure was necessary in order to promote efficient and effective government. In addition, an attempt was made to meet the anticipated constitutional objections through assertions that the bill delegated less power to the President than had either of the Economy Acts, that the sixty-day provision was an adequate safeguard of congressional power, and that a legislative veto by concurrent resolution, as contended by Attorney General Mitchell in 1933, would be unconstitutional.

Those opposing the bill talked generally about the concentration of power and its dangers. Representative Gifford quoted with approval the following: "The greatest menace to the legislative branch of our Government, and one threatening its very existence, lies in the delegation of power to the Executive—the abject surrender of many of the express constitutional rights and prerogatives of the legislative. To a certain extent, this may be permissible in a great national emergency, but no effort seems to be made to return them to the Congress . . . Congress seems to have forgotten that these powers are not its own to give away. Congress is the trustee of the people."[28]

Neither side developed an informed and sustained constitutional argument and the bill passed after the allotted three hours by a roll call vote of 283 to 76. But even this brief clash offered hints of the course of future debates.

The Senate engaged in little debate in 1937. But in November 1937, Senator Byrnes made a speech on the bill during a special session. Byrnes stated two key arguments for the bill. First, when questioned about the provision for congressional review, he declared, "there is no doubt it would require action by the Congress after veto, because if a proposed delegation of power is valid, then when the power is exercised and the order becomes law we cannot revoke it except by law, and that means that the President would have to sign whatever measure we passed."[29] Second, he supported the constitutionality of the delegation of power by referring to the recent Shipping Board cases in which the courts held that Congress could delegate power under certain standards and limitations.

1938 Floor Debate. On February 28, 1938, the Senate began discussion of a consolidated reorganization bill which provided for abolishing the Comptroller General's office, setting up a single civil service administrator responsible to the President, creating a department of welfare, and creating an executive staff organization for the President in addition to granting general reorganization authority to the President. Thus the month-long debate dealt largely with issues peripheral to the central constitutional issues, but these were also debated, generally along the lines laid down in 1937.

Senator Byrnes spoke on the constitutional questions early in the discussion. Quoting from a series of relevant Supreme Court decisions,[30] he summarized constitutional principles governing delegations of legislative power:

Congress cannot delegate to an agent its power to make law. However, it may authorize an agent to regulate a subject matter which Congress itself might regulate by statute, if in so doing sufficient restriction is imposed upon the power of the agent to prevent him from substituting

190

his will for that of Congress as to what the law shall be. Hence, if Congress in a statute clearly states the subject with which its agent is authorized to deal, and prescribes the policy of Congress with respect to such subject, so as to furnish an adequate standard to guide its agent in carrying out the delegated power, the statute will not be considered as delegating legislative power.[31]

Byrnes then cited the Shipping Board cases as instances in which reorganization authority in the 1932 Act was held to be constitutional. He concluded, "It is submitted that the reorganization bill contains no delegation of legislative power for the subject matter with which the President is authorized to deal, is definitely stated and an adequate policy or standard is prescribed to guide him in the exercise of his power."[32]

Opponents of the bill virtually ignored Byrnes' legal arguments. Their appeal was based upon the broad ground that the bill was repugnant to the traditional system of separated powers. That the debate was no real interchange is well illustrated by the following comments of Byrnes and Senator Burton Wheeler, Montana Democrat.

Mr. Byrnes. I do not desire to interrogate the Senator on the question of policy; but with reference to the legal question suggested I desire to ask him whether he is familiar with the case of Isbrandtsen-Moller Co. against the United States?

Mr. Wheeler. No; I have not read it.

Wheeler went on to say that the cases were not analogous and that he had intended to express only a "curbstone opinion." He said he wanted the question to go to the Supreme Court. He avoided legal questions altogether and talked about the "moral duty" of Congress "not to give any such power to anybody."[33]

Only Senator Josiah Bailey, North Carolina Democrat, answered Byrnes's argument about delegation. The courts, he agreed, had insisted that Congress lay down definite standards in delegating powers to the Executive. But "Mr. President, no rule is established. There is simply the mere statement of objectives, and those objectives are in the indefinite terms of simplicity and efficiency."[34]

Senators were more eager to answer Byrnes directly on the question of congressional review of executive action under delegated powers. Alva Adams, Colorado Democrat, put it this way: "I am quite willing to concede that if the power is conclusively delegated, and the delegation has been complete, it can be withdrawn only by an appropriate legislative act passed by both Houses and approved by the President; but my inquiry is whether the Congress cannot make its delegation of authority conditional upon the approval of one or both Houses." The Nebraska Democrat, Edward Burke, concurred with Adams. ". . . it is entirely within the power of Congress to grant authority to the President never to be fully exercised by him until certain things are done; one of them, that he should make an investigation and make certain findings; another one, that one or both Houses of Congress should give their approval to it. All of those conditions, it seems to me, limit the full grant of authority so that there can be no merit in the contention that this action would be outside the power of Congress."[35] The Senate gave scant attention to the use of the concurrent resolution as a congressional device for review and control. Senator Charles McNary, Oregon Republican, tried to refute the argument that concurrent resolutions used in this way would be unconstitutional by pointing out that the Senate utilizes resolutions for the purpose of control all the time in confirming appointments. Byrnes replied that confirmation was specifically provided for in the Constitution.[36]

The Senate passed the bill, 49 to 42, on March 28, 1938, and the House took it up immediately after. Political controversy surrounding the bill was intensifying. On the eve of the debate, Roosevelt incensed Congress with a press release in which he prescribed for Congress its constitutional duty and congratulated the majority of the Senate for not being "purchased," thus questioning the integrity of the Senators who had voted against the bill. FDR continued to insist that a concurrent resolution as a means of control would be unconstitutional.[37]

In the heat the debate melted into generalized assertions. The proponents of the bill insisted, without analysis, that their proposals were constitutional and that the legislative veto was clearly unconstitutional. The opponents also shunned close analysis. Public criticism of the "Dictator Bill" was running high partly in response to an alarmist radio broadcast by Father Charles E. Coughlin,[38] and accordingly the bill's foes in the House condemned it for its general tendency to concentrate power in the Executive.

Toward the end of the debate it became evident to the supporters of the bill that without a provision for congressional veto, the bill would never pass the House. Therefore, in behalf of the committee majority, Representative Frank Kniffin, lawyer and Ohio Democrat with seven years of previous House experience, offered an amendment incorporating a provision for negating proposed orders by concurrent resolution. This amendment put the supporters of the bill in an embarrassing position since they had previously claimed that a concurrent resolution used in this way would be unconstitutional. Kniffin, however, attempted to justify this reversal by distinguishing between the use of a concurrent resolution to make or repeal a law, which could not be done, and his proposed use of it as an integral part of a law which is "in the making."[39] In addition, Kniffin pointed out that the veto provision included the stipulation that Congress could negate by concurrent resolution only those reorganization orders "not in the public interest." He felt that the inclusion of such a standard made the legislative veto constitutionally valid. He cited Humphrey's Executor *v.* United States and Morgan *v.* United States[40] to bolster his argument and concluded

> The President . . . and likewise the majority of the two Houses of Congress under the proposed amendment, will be exercising quasi-legislative powers which are not of an executive nature in the constitutional sense. Both the President and the majority of the two Houses will be filling in the details in the statute within the limits of the policies prescribed by Congress. Under the amendment, the majority will be acting as an agent of Congress in passing upon Executive orders.[41]

Kniffin's argument was carefully documented, and the opponents of the bill failed to analyze it. Instead they ignored it and derided the seeming change in position by supporters of the bill. Gifford pointed out that FDR and Representative Lindsay Warren of North Carolina had assured them that a concurrent resolution would be unconstitutional.

> Since then it appears that diligent search has been made of the scriptures of legal phraseology to find some way to preserve the concurrent resolution process and try to convince us that by the few added words it would be regarded as constitutional . . . This surrender of power is the heart of this bill . . . I urge you to think carefully and not be led astray by the citation of legal cases to bolster up this contemplated action.[42]

The Kniffin amendment passed, but the House proceeded to kill the bill, recommitting it by 204 to 196. Thus the House acted in accord with public criticism of the bill. Ralph Church, Illinois Republican, summed up the attitude of the majority. Quoting from Montesquieu, Rousseau, and Daniel Webster on the separation of powers as fundamental to liberty, he said: "During the last 5 years Congress has conferred on the President power and more power. We are now asked to give him still more power so that he may do practically anything he sees fit with the various agencies and bureaus of this Government . . ." That, said Church, would be to violate basic principle: "The strength of this Government has been the system of checks and balances which the founders took care to establish in order that arbitrary power may not

193

be exercised by any Executive, any Congress, or any judiciary . . . It is for us to preserve that system. And it is in large part because this bill represents a departure from that system that I find it impossible to approve it."[43]

1939 House Committee Action. Between the Seventy-Fifth and Seventy-Sixth Congresses the House Select Committee held important executive sessions and drastically revised the reorganization bill. The committee eliminated altogether the sections abolishing the Comptroller General's Office, setting up a department of welfare, and establishing a single civil service administrator. It curtailed the grant of reorganization power to make it apply with numerous exceptions only to reduction of agencies. It added a provision similar to the Kniffin amendment, for veto by concurrent resolution. Finally, it called for "reorganization plans" instead of "executive orders," a change which heightened the appearance of congressional control.

The way in which the new bill was produced was summed up by John Cochran, Missouri Democrat and Chairman of the Select Committee. He gave chief credit to Representative Warren.

Immediately after the election last fall I returned to Washington to render what assistance I might be able in the preparation of another reorganization bill. I found that Mr. Warren had already been working on the measure for 2 months. In the end we had the assistance of two outstanding members of the Legislative Reference Service and of the Parliamentarian of the House.

Further I want to say that up to the hour that the bill was introduced no official nor employee of the executive branch of the Government had ever been consulted nor will you find in the bill one paragraph that was submitted or suggested by an official or employee of the executive branch of the Government.[44]

These initiatives by the Missourian and North Carolinian were to prove successful.

1939 Floor Debate. When debate was resumed early in March 1939, the supporters of the new bill were prepared to defend it with legal arguments. Representative E. E. Cox, Georgia Democrat, made the major presentation in behalf of the committee majority—an elaborate defense of the constitutionality of the bill. Cox, a former state judge and veteran of fourteen years in the House, had opposed the bill in its 1938 form. He now denied that Congress was delegating any legislative power to the Executive. "In performing under the act the President exercises

194

no legislative or executive power, but only as the ministerial agent of the Congress acts in accordance with directions that are given."[45]

Cox cited numerous precedents for his position, relying heavily upon a decision handed down the preceding month, Currin *v.* Wallace.[46] In this case the Supreme Court had upheld the constitutionality of a delegation of power to the Secretary of Agriculture to designate markets for tobacco inspection and certification when such action had been approved by a two-thirds vote of tobacco farmers. The Court had drawn broad boundaries within which power could be delegated constitutionally.

Cox conceded that the legislative veto by concurrent resolution was something new but thought it valid. The only concurrent resolution which would be unconstitutional would be one purporting to make or repeal a law, but the legislative veto attempted neither.

Opponents of the bill continued to talk about the broad principles of the separation of powers. Yet their main argument was a specific attack on the constitutionality of the concurrent resolution, a position formerly advanced by the other side. This group favored instead affirmative congressional approval of reorganization plans by joint resolution, which would necessitate presidential signature. Cox took the lead in refuting this position.

When Representative Hatton Sumners, Texas Democrat, offered an amendment providing for veto by either house alone, several of those supporting the bill attacked it as unconstitutional. Cox, however, insisted on consistency and, though opposing the amendment, admitted its constitutionality. The House defeated the amendment 209 to 193. Final House passage of the bill came on March 8, 1939, by a vote of 246 to 153.

The Senate took up the bill a week later. Both sides used arguments similar to those in the House. Senator Byrnes and Senator Alben Barkley, Kentucky Democrat, spoke for the committee majority and repeated the arguments of Representative Cox to justify delegation of reorganization authority. They, too, added Currin *v.* Wallace to their list of precedents. In addition, Senator Sherman Minton, Indiana Democrat, pointed out that in 1934 Congress had delegated to the Supreme Court power to make rules of procedure which would take effect unless Congress acted to annul them. Minton contended: "There was far more delegation of authority to the Supreme Court than there is to the President under this proposed act."[47] Two other Democratic Senators, Walter George of Georgia and Robert Wagner of New York, sought to bolster the case for constitutionality with instances of delegation of power by Congress to commissions.

For the opposition, Senators Wheeler and Adams continued to attack the delegation of reorganization authority on the broad ground that it violated the separation of powers, but they also attempted to meet the more narrow arguments for constitutionality. For example, Wheeler pointed out that delegating power to the Supreme Court in procedural matters was far different from the matter under discussion.

Shortly before debate ended, Senator William King, Utah Democrat, summed up the constitutional arguments against the bill. King, now seventy-five, had had two years on his state bench and twenty-two years in Congress. He examined each of the legal precedents advanced in favor of the bill to show its inapplicability to the present proposal and concluded that the bill was unconstitutional on four grounds.

First. Because the bill purports to confer upon the President the power to legislate . . .

Second. Because the bill purports to confer upon the President the power to change and modify the terms of statutes enacted by the Congress since the foundation of the Federal Government . . .

Third. Because the Supreme Court of the United States has held that delegations of legislative power may not be made to the President except to the extent of filling in details in accordance with a standard set up in the statute and within well-marked channels for the exercise of his discretion.

Fourth. Because any attempt of an Executive to change and modify statutes of the United States affecting the rights, privileges, and immunities of any individual or business concern would constitute a violation of the due-process clause of the Constitution . . .[48]

Finally, King attacked the constitutionality of the concurrent-resolution veto device as a clear violation of Article I, section 7 of the Constitution and an abrogation of 125 years of precedent.

The Senate thereupon voted 46 to 44 to kill the Wheeler amendment for confirmation of reorganization plans by joint resolution. The Senate passed the bill, 63 to 23, and only minor points of difference were left to be worked out in the conference committee. The two-and-a-quarter-year-long debate had ended.

Discussion Evaluated. The inattention of many members to the constitutional questions raised by the proposals helped prolong the discussion. In the end, with the exception of the relevant British experience, all the major issues and pertinent arguments found a place in the long congressional discussion. The duration of the consideration lessened its coherence,[49] and the valuable contributions of Senators Byrnes and

196

King and Representatives Kniffin and Cox failed to command the thoughtful attention of later speakers. Hence, the diffuseness of the debate.

Ironically, the same outside pressures—White House demands and public alarms—that brought politics so forcibly into the discussions, made some sort of detached consideration essential. After studying the slowly deepening understanding of the questions which three successive sessions made possible, one must judge the effectiveness of the discussion as a whole to have been substantial. Points which none had thought to advance in 1937 received wide discussion by 1939, and this greater understanding probably affected some of the final votes, notwithstanding the pull of party loyalty.[50] A solid core of forty-seven Representatives voted for the bill in 1937, after perfunctory constitutional discussion; against it in 1938, after a concentrated constitutional assault; and for it again in 1939, after modifications and a concentrated constitutional defense. Some sixteen Senators voted against it in 1938 but for the modified bill in 1939. Nearly all of these Representatives and Senators were committed to supporting the President's program.[51]

So conceivably constitutional considerations determined the outcome of the struggle. Ostensibly, those who took constitutionality most seriously and with the most detachment held the deciding votes in several of the roll calls. All of this, however, cost heavily in time and effort.

PARTICIPANTS

In a Senate containing 70 per cent lawyers and in a House containing 56 per cent, leadership in discussion, as usual, fell largely to the members of that profession.[52] The attitude which members voiced toward the bar conformed to the customary pattern; in thanking Representative Cox, Cochran praised his reputation as the ablest constitutional lawyer in the House. Later, he recommended the Kniffin amendment as bearing the endorsement of "outstanding lawyers." Although a member of the bar himself, the Iowa Democrat, Senator Guy Gillette deprecated his own knowledge and declared, "I have listened with advantage to the discussion by very learned and erudite lawyers who are Members of this body and who have approached the problem before us from many angles. I do not practice law, I am a farmer . . ."[53] For knowledge of the narrow legal questions, Congress relied heavily on the expertise of a few of its lawyer members. Yet those few non-lawyers who spoke frequently seemed aware that the question was more than merely legal and, accordingly, helped put the question in perspective.

By the testimony of Representative Cochran, however, members were also now looking to outside sources and sources other than the Attorney

General. At the outset, they made use of consultations with the experts on public administration whom the President's Committee on Administrative Management had brought together. For additional advice, and especially after congressional politics made consorting with the Executive unfashionable, the House Committee called on the House Parliamentarian and the Legislative Reference Service of the Library of Congress. Officially, the Parliamentarians only render advice to presiding officers. One must conjecture that here the consultations were strictly informal and that normally members could not count on tapping the judgment and experience of these officers.

The use made of the Legislative Reference Service was significant. Since 1915 this agency had been furnishing members and committees of Congress with expert analysis on a wide variety of topics. It had grown steadily and in 1946 would gain recognition in a statute. At this time, in 1938, it was on the way to becoming the leading research arm of Congress.[54] From its professional research aides, members could obtain facts and information free of executive or interest-group coloration. By 1958, members and committees of Congress would be directing almost 68,000 inquiries to the L.R.S., of which several hundred would involve, directly or incidentally, constitutional questions. Again, lawyers would predominate, for the bulk of these constitutional inquiries would go, not to the American Government Division, but to the American Law Division, to be investigated by lawyers.[55]

For aid of a strictly legal sort, each house of Congress since 1918 had made use of an Office of the Legislative Counsel. With the British Parliamentary Counsel to the Treasury as a partial model, Congress provided its members and committees with technical aid in drafting bills. The Office was divided into independent House and Senate branches. The Speaker and the President pro tempore appointed the respective directors who chose their associates fresh from the law schools; conditions were provided to assure a highly competent, nonpolitical, experienced body of advisers. In 1958 these men were still furnishing a variety of legal advice and opinion on topics which included narrow constitutional questions and drafting a substantial part of the public bills in each house.[56]

Increasingly, members and committees have drawn on these centers of professional aid for research and assistance in handling constitutional questions. The natural reluctance of both, however, to "take a stand on policy" may leave members without direction in resolving those issues not classifiable as narrowly legal.

Yet in the end the houses here relied mainly on their own experienced leaders.[57] Practical judgment thus supplemented legal acumen and the advice of outside experts in the forging of the legislative veto.

198

That device was the product of compromise, worked out on the initiative of many, chiefly from the South and border regions. Southerners like Byrnes, Cox, and Warren had the aid of the Missourian Cochran and the Ohioan Kniffin in winning majority acceptance.

MODE

The most striking feature of the consideration of the Reorganization Act and the constitutional questions it raised was the use of select committees, meeting jointly for investigation and separately to draft legislation for introduction.[58] Those supporting establishment of such committees argued that no standing committee had jurisdiction over such bills.[59] They also stressed the importance of experience and expertise, and Speaker William Bankhead of Alabama and Vice President John N. Garner of Texas evidently took this into account in making the appointments. The makeup of both committees gave heavy weight to long service as well as to the Southern and Border states.

The committees held two sets of hearings in 1937 and altogether issued four reports.[60] Yet nowhere in these publications do we find thorough weighing of constitutional issues. This was to be regretted. In compiling its proposals, the Brownlow Committee had put the emphasis on the demands of administrative efficiency, a matter which by 1937 had become urgent. Yet there was need, as events showed, for an equally searching study of adjustments and even improvisations in the constitutional system to meet these demands without surrendering legislative oversight.

Select committees, which had figured so prominently in the early Congresses and which the Jeffersonians had used for fact-gathering and preliminary systematizing, might have prepared the ground for an informed and focused constitutional debate. Potentially the members of select committees can be chosen because of their genuine concern for constitutional issues and in such a way as to represent diverse views and regions. Had these committees been so chosen the major constitutional questions might have been pressed to discussion and preliminary formulation.

On the whole, the procedure used reflected standards of fairness. Each house took a vote on establishing its select committee. Each agreed by unanimous consent to the restrictions on debate. Although these moves enhanced the general acceptance of the procedure, the resulting debates might have been more fruitful had there been advance notice of the constitutional questions.

That Congress devoted about forty days of debate to this legislation suggests that the members had ample time. Yet time allotments at specific phases could prove insufficient, witness the three-hour limit the House set for its own floor consideration in 1937. Subsequent debates might have proved more productive had the committees held additional hearings in 1938 and 1939, since by then the constitutional issues had changed and grown more complex.[61]

Floor time was equally divided with set speeches the rule. Final roll call votes were had on crucial amendments and on passing one version or another of the bill itself. Yet neither house held a vote on the constitutional question, with the possible exception of the Senate vote on the Wheeler amendment. Thus, if deliberation and ultimate resolution of issues came only laboriously and late, this was not the result of serious unfairness, but rather of the pressures for action and the pervasive indifference to constitutional issues.

ATTITUDES

Again, as in the debates on the Guffey-Snyder bill, members voiced conflicting conceptions of the responsibility of Congress. Again, doubt enveloped the constitutional issues, and members echoed earlier responses.

Several followed Jefferson in stressing the moral obligation of members to adhere faithfully to the Constitution. One of these was a non-lawyer businessman from New Hampshire with ten years in state office and six in the House, the Republican Charles W. Tobey: "There is something immensely more important than our respective party politics or your or my political future, and that is the responsibility imposed upon us as Members of the Congress to preserve the entity of the allocation of powers granted us under the Constitution . . . So shall we make effective our oath to preserve, protect, and defend the Constitution of the United States."[62] The same year, the North Carolinian, Senator Josiah W. Bailey, gave a similar reason for opposing the bill: "Assume that an unconstitutional act will never be tested; that, however, does not give me the right to pass it. I must stop on the threshold and consider my oath. I have a power. I am oath bound to maintain that power."[63]

Senator Prentiss M. Brown, Michigan Democrat, with five years' congressional experience, took a position closer to Marshall's. To him, the Supreme Court was the best guide, especially since some of the justices had accepted congressional doubts as a basis for leaving constitutional issues to the Court.

Let me say that I frankly believe this is a close question. I think there is some doubt about the constitutionality of the pending

200

measure; but, in my view of my duties as a Senator and of the expressions which the Supreme Court heretofore has made, I do not believe that doubt ought to prevent me from voting for a bill which I believe to be constitutional . . . The Court said very recently, I think, in the case of Evans against Gore, . . . that Senators were acting entirely within their rights in voting for a bill about the constitutionality of which they had some doubts so that the question of the power might be presented to the courts of the United States for adjudication.[64]

In 1938 Senator Alfred E. Reames, sixty-eight, Oregon Democrat, was holding a brief interim appointment, his only experience in Congress. In supporting the bill, he relied solely on court precedents: "We could not give away legislative powers if we desired . . . In 1935, in the Panama Oil case, the Supreme Court of the United States decided that the Congress could not delegate any essential legislative powers. And in the N.R.A. case, which followed the Panama oil case in the next year, the Supreme Court reiterated the same doctrine and held that no such power could be delegated."[65]

This statement by a newcomer to Congress came as near as any to a judicial monopoly position. Most members kept silent on the scope and degree of responsibility, for the great public concern about the reorganization bill of 1938 may have made it inexpedient for those supporting the bill to minimize publicly their constitutional obligation. Many may have deemed Court precedents, especially those of recent origin, as tending to support the bill. Thus preoccupied, members in general could all too easily ignore the improbability of judicial review and the significance of broad questions.

CONCLUSIONS

This problem of the legislative veto of executive action under broad delegations of power brought Congress face to face with a fundamental issue of the separation of powers. Modern urban and industrial society had necessitated a multiplicity of government programs which in turn had required grants of broad discretion to those administering them. For efficiency the President needed wide powers to reorganize the sprawling alphabetical agencies of the New Deal. Yet for popular control, Congress needed some device for ascertaining that the Executive was exercising his discretion in conformity with the legislative will. Here was an issue calling not so much for interpretation of the constitutional text, as for implementation of its general spirit. A narrow scrutiny of constitutional

201

verbiage and relevant Court decisions would create such legislative myopia that the dimensions and character of the problem would go unrecognized.

Here the broad questions were debated in generalities and emotion; and only the narrow, with a modicum of thoroughness. In a sense Congress and Court were working simultaneously on issues of delegation of power and providing reasoned discussions for each other. In the end the Court would leave to Congress within broad limits final control over this field, as well as over aspects of the federal system. Hence, Congress in 1939 was actually reaching final determinations, changeable only by later Congresses. Yet none in either house avowed this fact, probably because of the hold of the judicial monopoly theory. Here again that theory proved its shortcomings. If one avers that only the Court can decide constitutional questions and yet, in a given area the Court never acts, then such questions must go forever unanswered. Within wide areas of federalism and of the separation of powers, Congress has almost the power of a Parliament, but many of its members dodge the responsibility that goes with such power.

The experience Congress underwent in this episode shows clearly the problem of procedure. For one thing, under modern conditions, members can no longer rely on their own information and experience, or even that of their colleagues. Committees called on the President's experts on management, the Legislative Reference Service, the House Parliamentarian, and even the Attorney General, in their search for knowledge. From some of these they got help, but had full expert knowledge of the whole problem, including the relevant British experience, been at the disposal of Congress from the start, much valuable time might have been saved.

Again, the choice of select committees for investigation of the subject had rich possibilities. The committees were strong, and, to a degree, representative, and the device for joint hearings was ingenious. Yet party loyalty was compelling—committee reports always went strictly according to party line-up. Furthermore, instead of brief early hearings followed by bill drafting, the committees might well have revived hearings when constitutional objections became acute and drawn on experts in constitutional law and comparative government from many quarters. Such inquiries could have provided the basis for committee reports that would light up the pros and cons of the constitutional issues. The progress from presidential committee to joint committee to select committees to the floor meant that when the legislative proposals reached the Congress they were finished products, available for purchase with only minor adjustments in price or accessories, with all decisions on style and form completed. If such select committees are to have a place in weighing constitutional issues, to a degree beyond the Jeffersonian function of gathering facts and arranging elements into a system before debate, then one may suggest the wisdom of assuring broadly representative and experienced committees as well as extensive public hearings in order to furnish an early voicing of divergent points of view. If ensuing debate is to provide some measure of deliberation, issues should be defined with precision in advance and debate timed to avoid the pre-election steam roller.

Notwithstanding the constitutional settlement concerning the legislative veto which President and Congress finally achieved in 1939, the issue of constitutionality has continued alive. Congress later applied the veto to many sorts of executive activity and in many forms—by committee, by one house, and by both houses, through affirmation and negation. The device has great potentialities and is a credit to congressional inventiveness. There is need, however, for definitive study of the most suitable forms of the device and of procedures for greater regularity in its use.

The British Parliament through its select committees on Statutory Instruments and through general laws—the Statutory Instruments Acts of 1945 and 1946—has long since set up machinery for processing and controlling executive rules and orders.[66] In the United States, there is need for similar reforms. That the power of Congress to enter this field continued after a generation to meet constitutional challenge from a few of its own members as well as from the Justice Department,[67] one may credit, in good measure, to the judicial monopoly theory. Those who view the courts as solely capable of settling constitutional disputes can never find reassurance in legislative settlements, however reasonable, practicable, and deliberate.

I O
Separation of Powers in the Cold War: The Middle East Resolution of 1957

Just as President Roosevelt had gone to the Seventy-Fifth Congress, President Dwight D. Eisenhower, in January 1957, went to the Eighty-Fifth to request affirmation of broad power to act. Again the presidential bid touched off an important constitutional debate. As with the Reorganization Act debate, this dealt with the legitimate and appropriate distribution of powers between President and Congress under the separation of powers. But this time, as in the General Bradley controversy,[1] the policies at stake affected foreign relations. The forces which now pressed for swift and effective government action were the international Communist movement and demands for Western security through a build-up of military and economic strength. In the face of these forces, and amid the tensions created by a presidential campaign fought partly over the policies of Secretary of State John Foster Dulles, would the legislators find it possible to take up the constitutional issues? Would the unlikelihood of court review heighten their awareness of a final responsibility in this field? Was there any place for such discussions in a Cold War between powers possessing nuclear arms?

At the mid-century stage of international relations an important key to national success was flexibility. A nation, that is, must be willing and able to vary the instruments it uses in pursuing its national goals. This meant concentrating great powers in the Executive, and in the Western democracies such a concentration has met serious obstacles. Governments which are accountable to their electorates for their foreign policy have a restricted range of alternative instruments and choices. In the United States the separation of powers compounds the problem, for the Executive and Legislative, each with its assigned powers affecting foreign affairs and nearly free of judicial scrutiny, tend to cooperate only with difficulty and only under strong pressure. Article II of the Constitution makes the President the Commander in Chief; Article I, section 8, authorizes Congress to provide armed forces and declare war. The problem in the 1950's had become, how far can the Commander in Chief go in

204

using the armed forces provided by acts of Congress without himself declaring war?

President Eisenhower's 1957 request was one of a long series extending back to the aftermath of World War II. Chief executives had repeatedly asked Congress for grants of authority which would enable them to wage the Cold War with flexibility and dispatch. In approving the Truman Doctrine of 1947, the North Atlantic Treaty Organization agreements of 1949, the Southeast Asia Treaty Organization agreements of 1954, and the Formosa Resolution of 1955, Congress had endorsed broad presidential power to employ the armed forces whenever in his opinion the interests of the nation were threatened.

Throughout 1956 a situation was developing in another area of the world which appeared to call for another grant of authority. Several countries of the Middle East appeared to be slipping into the Communist bloc, particularly Syria and Egypt. In November, Britain, France, and Israel launched their abortive Suez invasions. Critics at home and abroad charged that the President was providing no leadership in the Middle East.

To meet this charge, President Eisenhower, on January 5, 1957, asked Congress to pass a resolution authorizing him to give military and economic assistance to the nations of that area and to employ the armed forces of the United States whenever he deemed that the territorial integrity or political independence of any of those nations was threatened with "overt armed aggression from any nation controlled by international Communism."[2] The President was in a difficult position politically. He had won his own election handily, but the Democrats, who had captured control of Congress midway in the President's first term, retained their majorities. Accordingly, before delivering his address to a joint session, the President had conferred with leaders of both parties from both houses. The House Committee on Foreign Affairs proceeded to hold eight days of public hearings and several closed sessions and then to report favorably a resolution embodying the President's request. The House debated it briefly and passed it by the end of the month.

The same Senate committees which had held the MacArthur Hearings in 1951—Foreign Relations and Armed Services—held fourteen days of joint hearings. After extensive closed meetings, they reported in mid-February a modified version of the resolution. Constitutional questions had been touched on all along, but the twelve days of Senate floor debate gave them their fullest airing. The Senate passed the resolution on March 5, the House endorsed the Senate version, and the President signed it on March 9. Roosevelt had got his request after two years; Eisenhower, after two months.

As finally passed, the Middle East Resolution authorized the President to cooperate militarily and economically with those Middle Eastern nations desiring to maintain their independence. It set aside two hundred million dollars already appropriated to pay for military and economic aid, such aid to go only for the purpose of self-defense. No funds could be used until fifteen days following presidential notification to appropriate committees. The resolution advised the President to support the United Nations Emergency Force in the area. It required him to report semiannually on progress, and it could expire on either presidential or congressional initiative.

The crucial provision, for present purposes, stated that "if the President determines the necessity thereof, the United States *is prepared to* use armed forces to assist any nation or group of nations requesting assistance against armed aggression from any country controlled by international communism."[3] This contrasted with the wording of the original resolution, as passed by the House, which stated that Congress *authorized* the President to employ United States armed forces when he deemed such use necessary to protect the independence of any Middle Eastern nation against overt armed aggression.

In selecting the final wording, Congress was deliberately vague. The act reflected on its face some of the constitutional objections, yet this vagueness makes it hard to say what was settled by the discussion. In a sense the Middle East Resolution was only a response to an external threat and another application of the principle of flexibility already embodied in the Truman Doctrine, the NATO agreements, and the Formosa Resolution. Earlier debates had already prepared the public for affirmations of presidential power, and the 1957 debates were only a supplement.

With court review infeasible, the subsequent use of the resolution depended on the Executive and succeeding Congresses. In the one instance where the Executive might logically have used the resolution— the Lebanon crisis in 1958—neither the President nor the Secretary of State justified the dispatch of United States forces clearly on the basis of the Middle East Resolution. Secretary Dulles mentioned it in news conferences, but without grounding current actions on it. Some attacked the movement of Marines into Lebanon on constitutional grounds,[4] but since the President had failed to cite the resolution Congress made no effort to clarify its meaning. To judge from the *Congressional Record,* no one mentioned the resolution during the Middle East trouble of the ensuing year.

And so the constitutional settlement reached in 1957 had uncertain consequences. The settlement itself was, in a sense, unsatisfactory.

Throughout the 1957 debate members repeatedly raised and discussed crucial questions of power but the results were inconclusive.

CONSTITUTIONAL QUESTIONS

The military provisions of the resolution gave rise to a number of questions, both narrow and broad.[5] The narrow questions were: 1. Did the President already possess power to employ the armed forces anywhere in the world without congressional authorization, by virtue of his powers as Commander in Chief; or, alternatively, did the power given Congress to declare war rule out such action by the President? and 2. Did the grant of authority contained in the resolution unconstitutionally delegate legislative power to the President? Obviously decision on the second question partially depended on the decision reached on the first.

The broad questions were of equal importance: How far should Congress go in altering the traditional distribution of powers to meet the exigencies of foreign relations? Are there any restraints, such as some form of legislative veto, which Congress could safely impose on executive action in the interest of constitutional democracy? In fashioning those restraints in this highly sensitive area of power, Congress once again would be adapting the ancient document to the modern age through creative implementation.

Moreover, all these questions lay finally with Congress. Whether concerned with constitutional verbiage or not, they involved the conduct of foreign relations and the inception of war and were hence "political" questions, assigned, that is, to the political branches for final decision.[6] Although few participants in the debate seemed aware of it, no court existed to review that decision. Congress could decide the questions or evade them.

COURSE OF THE DISCUSSION

House Committee Action. In its hearings[7] the House Committee on Foreign Affairs[8] began groping toward a definition of the constitutional issues implicit in the original resolution. The raising of constitutional questions came chiefly from within the committee. Few of the twenty witnesses mentioned constitutional considerations. The major proponents of the Administration's proposal, Secretary of State Dulles, Admiral Arthur Radford, Chairman of the Joint Chiefs of Staff, and General Alfred Gruenther, former Commander at Supreme Headquarters Allied Powers Europe, placed major stress on the critical nature of the Soviet threat to the Middle East and the resulting need for rapid congressional

207

action. As Secretary Dulles put it: "Until the Congress has actually spoken, there is doubt in the Middle East and there may be doubt in the Soviet Union. If those doubts persist, then the danger persists and grows . . . Only if Congress quickly dispels doubts . . . will it have done the maximum it can do to preserve peace and freedom."[9]

Most of the representatives of private organizations, including, for example, the American Zionist Committee and the Jewish War Veterans, spoke only for their special interests. Three persons with no particular group affiliations, brought up constitutional issues. These were Dean Acheson, former Secretary of State, and two Democratic Representatives, James Roosevelt of California and Abraham J. Multer of New York.

The committee members were more interested than the witnesses in the constitutional aspects of the resolution. But this interest was usually expressed in a confused way and as a minor point. Yet, even if haphazardly, the hearings hit on all the major, pertinent constitutional questions.

Interest was greatest in the narrow questions, particularly the division of power between the executive and legislative branches in the control of American armed forces. A few members expressed the opinion that the President as Commander in Chief already possessed the necessary authority to use the armed forces of the country anywhere in the world without either prior or subsequent reference to Congress. Representative Multer felt that "There cannot be any doubt but that the authority which the President now seeks he has always had. He has merely failed to exercise it."[10] Representatives Robert C. Byrd, West Virginia Democrat, A. S. J. Carnahan, Missouri Democrat, John M. Vorys, Ohio Republican, and D. S. Saund, California Democrat, all expressed the same view.

Other Representatives, however, felt that the resolution entailed a grant of new authority to the President which unconstitutionally delegated congressional prerogatives. Representative L. H. Fountain, North Carolina Democrat, called the resolution an authorization for the President to "take the country to war."[11] Representative Roosevelt referred to it as an "undated congressional declaration of war"[12] which the President could use at his discretion. When Secretary Dulles referred to the precedents for the Administration's request, Representative James G. Fulton, Pennsylvania Republican, commented: "Are we, area by area, as soon as something alarming turns up, then turning the area over lock, stock, and barrel to the President to do it? Is Congress by this series of resolutions adopting the policy of giving up its powers in any area where there is trouble?"[13]

A different version of this argument was stated by Roosevelt. He spoke of an undated declaration of war which would be an unconstitutional impairment of Congress's power to declare war. But he also felt that the precedent of the Executive's asking for this kind of power was unfortunate. "In time . . . it would be felt that the President could never exercise the power without a resolution by the Congress for him to do so."[14]

Some of the committee members, however, were unsure about the narrow constitutional issues and so asked witnesses questions designed to clear up the confusion in their own minds. Representative Albert P. Morano, Connecticut Republican, tried to make Secretary Dulles distinguish between the new authority which the President was asking and the authority which he merely wanted reaffirmed. Dulles was little help, declaring that "I think it would be a mistake to get into a Constitutional dispute in this respect," and that he could answer the question only upon "the advice of the legal people."[15] Morano later asked Dulles if he "as a great constitutional lawyer," had "ever given consideration to amending the Constitution in order to meet this problem in a more permanent way than just by attacking it piecemeal every time an emergency arises?" Dulles said he saw no necessity for such an amendment.[16]

Less comment was made on the broad constitutional questions although the majority of the members seemed to agree that for two reasons Congress must approve the resolution: first, the Communist threat to the Middle East made constitutional considerations of secondary importance; and second, the prior announcement of the proposed resolution by the Administration made it psychologically impossible for Congress to deny the President's request. A few members, however, were unconvinced of the necessity to approve the President's request. They doubted that the Administration's claim that this was a great emergency demanding immediate attention was well substantiated.

Most of the committee members thought Congress should impose stronger controls on the President's exercise of this power than he had suggested. The first proposal was to give Congress, as well as the President, the power to terminate the resolution. Representatives Fountain, Carnahan, Fulton, and Frank Coffin, Maine Democrat, felt that Congress should follow its own precedent in the Marshall Plan and give itself termination powers. Representative Multer was more specific, arguing for automatic termination in two years. Most members, however, would omit a termination date and preferred congressional termination by concurrent resolution. The second proposal was to make it mandatory that the President report to Congress. The consensus seemed to favor requiring semiannual reports.

Despite the apparent interest of many members in constitutional questions, when the committee issued its report on the resolution, it evaded the constitutional problem altogether.

209

This resolution does not detract from or enlarge the constitutional power and authority of the President of the United States as Commander in Chief, and the language used in the resolution does not do so.

Likewise, the resolution does not delegate or diminish in any way the power and authority of the Congress of the United States to declare war, and the language used in the resolution does not do so.

The committee does not in any way seek to interpret the Constitution of the United States with regard to the power of the executive and legislative branches of our Government.

We emphasize that the resolution is a declaration of the solidarity of the people of the United States expressed through their President and the Congress on our policy of cooperation with the nations of the Middle East.[17]

House Floor Debate. The five-hour floor debate of January 29 and 30 followed the lines pursued in the committee consideration. In dealing with the narrow questions, something under half the speakers said they felt the Commander in Chief already had the constitutional power to employ American troops at will anywhere in the world. Several Representatives stated this as a simple, unsupported belief. Arthur Winstead, Mississippi Democrat, thought: "Should . . . a Communist penetration occur, the President could, under existing constitutional authority, immediately order our troops into action."[18] Will Neal, West Virginia Republican, spoke in a similar vein. "I expect to vote to sustain his request in view of the fact that he already has that authority under our Constitution . . ."[19] Others analyzed the situation. Representatives Stewart L. Udall, Arizona Democrat, and John D. Dingell, Michigan Democrat, both stated that passage of the resolution would constitute a precedent for limitations of the constitutional powers of the President in this field. Dingell put his fears this way: ". . . we in Congress grandly settle upon the President powers which he already possesses. We establish a precedent which will delight the backers of constitutional amendments limiting the power of the President to make treaties and to conduct foreign affairs."[20]

Those who took the opposing side on this narrow question—that is, who deemed this resolution an unconstitutional delegation of legislative power—relied mainly on flat statement and even emotionalism. Usher L. Burdick, North Dakota Republican, repeated the argument that the resolution was a blank check to the President to declare war when he saw fit. James C. Davis, Georgia Democrat, went even further: "Little by little Congress has voted away its powers and responsibilities . . .

210

has frittered away the constitutional rights of the people . . . With the passage of time, our Congress may become as much a rubberstamp as Hitler's Reichstag. In my judgment a vote for this resolution is another step in that direction."[21]

On the floor members gave more attention to the broad questions than they had in committee. Some felt that the President's judgment of the need for this resolution was beyond challenge; self-defense requirements as defined by Secretary Dulles were more important than constitutionality. Several said a vote against the resolution was a vote for the Kremlin and against democracy and the President. Democratic Victor L. Anfuso of New York summed up the attitudes of many members when he said "I feel that it is my duty, not as a Congressman, but as a citizen to take the word of the Chief Executive and trust him with the powers he asks."[22] A few felt otherwise. Representative Chet Holifield, Democrat of California, called this resolution a "fine maneuver . . . wafted into the Halls of Congress on the big wind of a phony crisis . . ."[23] Bruce Alger, Texas Republican, regarded as fallacious the Administration's contention that defeat of the resolution would indicate national disunity. To him government by discussion should be at its height in time of crisis.

There was also debate on the broad question of limiting the President. Even before the resolution came to the floor some Representatives, led by Porter Hardy, Jr., Virginia Democrat, and George Meader, Michigan Republican, argued for restraints. Representative Hugh Scott, Pennsylvania Republican, spoke for others, "If the President's right to act on the economic and military front is confused, restricted . . . or . . . hampered by this body . . . the President's influence in the use of those powers will be similarly weakened and limited in his relations with that part of the world and with Communist Russia."[24]

The majority of the members went along with Hardy, Meader, and the committee majority by adopting the committee's amendments providing for semiannual reports to Congress and congressional termination by concurrent resolution.

Senate Committee Action. As in the House Committee, most of the witnesses appearing during the hearings[25] held by the Senate Committees on Foreign Relations and Armed Services[26] were either oblivious or indifferent to constitutional questions. Government officials spoke only about the crisis in the Middle East. Representatives of special groups again made their special pleas. Even those private individuals who had asked to testify had slight interest in constitutionality. The outstanding exception to the general rule was Senator Joseph O'Mahoney, Wyoming

Democrat, who testified for three hours on the constitutional questions. But the concern of committee members made up for the indifference of most of the witnesses.

On the narrow constitutional question, most of the members thought the President already had the powers requested. Senator H. Alexander Smith of New Jersey, led the Republican members in stating this position. A number of Democrats agreed. Senator Hubert H. Humphrey of Minnesota said, "I must confess that insofar as the military authority is concerned, I still am sufficiently old-fashioned in terms of my constitutional law interpretation to believe that the President is the Commander in Chief of the Armed Forces . . . and I am not about ready to help rewrite the Constitution here at this table."[27]

Certain Democrats thought the resolution would, in the long run, limit presidential power. Senators John Stennis of Mississippi and Mike Mansfield of Montana were among them. Senator J. William Fulbright of Arkansas was worried about the application of the legal principle that "the inclusion of one is the exclusion of another" to this situation. In questioning Dulles he said,

> You do not undertake in this resolution to state specifically all the broad power which the President as Commander in Chief has under the constitution to resist anything which he would deem to be a threat to our vital interests.
>
> Now you pick out this one particular set of circumstances . . . and you say, "We will use our forces."
>
> Is it not quite logical to conclude . . . that having picked that out, you are now saying "We won't use it under any other circumstances"?[28]

Those who regarded the resolution as an unconstitutional delegation of legislative power were few but vocal. Senator Francis Case, South Dakota Republican, asserted that the danger of presidential declaration of war in this fashion was great. Senator Estes Kefauver, Tennessee Democrat, stated bluntly, ". . . under the Constitution, I was elected a Senator on the basis of deciding, of having the prerogative of declaring, when the United States should be at war."[29]

Senator O'Mahoney, however, supported this position with solid argumentation. New England born, educated at Columbia University and Georgetown Law School, lawyer and newspaper man, O'Mahoney at seventy-three had served twenty years in Congress and eighteen on the Senate Judiciary Committee. The following comments give the essence of his position.

212

This is a history-making session of Congress. If the resolution before us is passed . . . the constitutional powers of the President will expand and the constitutional powers of Congress will contract.

In the name of defending free government for the world, we stand in grave danger of sacrificing it at home, for this resolution . . . breaks down the system of checks and balances which the framers of the Constitution believed to be the bulwark of government by the people . . .

We have been delegating away the powers of Congress at so rapid a rate during the last half century that Congress is now on the descent into complete oblivion.[30]

On the broad question of whether the necessities of foreign affairs overrode constitutional objections, most of the members seemed to agree with Dulles who said that "we are dealing here with an area of constitutional doubt which has existed for 150 years . . . The point of the resolution is this . . . that there are times and occasions when, irrespective of constitutional doubts, . . . it is vital that the President and the Congress should speak clearly with one voice."[31]

Several opposed this position, especially Senators Fulbright and O'Mahoney. These Senators questioned the magnitude of a crisis which they thought the President had partially invented. They also regarded the preservation of the traditional form of government as more important than some of the practical considerations being urged by the Administration. Senator Fulbright summed up this position in these words: "After all, we have not yet come to the point of view that the end justifies the means; in other words, it makes no difference what the means are that are employed, just because we are against the Russians taking over this area."[32]

The members of the committee were in agreement about the necessity of limiting the President's discretion in the use of this authority. There was little dissent when the committee adopted the House amendments providing for semiannual reports and for congressional termination of the resolution. The committee considered requests for even more stringent limitations but turned them down. Senator Wayne Morse, Oregon Democrat, asked for an amendment requiring the President to notify Congress before using the armed forces and to submit his subsequent actions for congressional approval. Senator O'Mahoney proposed three amendments: first, the President was to employ the armed forces only in accord with the provisions of the Constitution; second, he was to use troops only after an explanatory report had been made to the House Committee on Foreign Affairs and the Senate Committees on Foreign

213

Relations and Armed Services; and third, if he should send United States forces to the Middle East under the terms of the resolution, he was to maintain hour-by-hour contact with Congress, meeting in special session if necessary.

In reporting the resolution, the Senate Committee followed the lead of the House Committee in expressing the desire to avoid constitutional questions, and the Senate Committee was more ingenious in wording the resolution so as to make this evasion clear. Senators Mansfield and Humphrey proposed that the resolution should read that "if the President determines the necessity thereof, the United States is prepared to use armed forces . . ." This differs from a flat grant of authority, which is what the President wanted and what the House had approved. The Humphrey-Mansfield amendment was adopted by the committee. In its report to the Senate the committee praised its own cleverness:

> This language has the virtue of remaining silent on the question of the relationship between the Congress and the President with respect to the use of the Armed Forces for the objectives stated in the resolution.
>
> At the same time this formulation makes clear the importance which the United States attaches to the Middle East and the determination of the United States to use armed force to resist Communist aggression in the area should any nation request such assistance.
>
> The joint committee rejects the idea that, because the agreed language does not deal with the question of the scope of the President's authority, the language therefore may indicate a weakening of the United States determination.
>
> On this latter point, let there be no doubt. Although the joint committee was sharply divided as to the proper constitutional processes for the United States to follow in regard to the President's request, it was not divided at all as to the substantive policy involved.[33]

The new phrasing of the resolution was evidently a compromise to sidestep serious constitutional objections which had divided the committee.

Senate Floor Debate. As so often is true, the constitutional arguments adduced in the Senate floor debate followed those discussed in committee. On the narrow question of congressional power in relation to presidential power, most of the Senators supported, expressly or tacitly, the view of Senator Mansfield that the President already had the power to use American forces in the Middle East. These Senators stated no new arguments.

214

Senators Morse, O'Mahoney, and Sam J. Ervin, Jr., North Carolina Democrat, led the attack on this position. To them, Congress was unconstitutionally giving away its own powers. Senator Ervin spelled out the power which he thought the President possessed: the President could use forces only in self-defense, but the offensive use of troops required congressional approval.[34]

On the question of weighing the exigencies of foreign relations against constitutional provisions, most Senators again tended to accept the Administration's assessment of the factual situation. Senator Theodore F. Green, Rhode Island Democrat and Chairman of the Foreign Relations Committee and of the combined committee, argued that Communist reactions to the President's proposal made congressional approval even more imperative.[35] Senator Alexander Wiley, Wisconsin Republican and ranking minority member of the Foreign Relations Committee, cited Supreme Court decisions and Story's *Commentaries* to prove that enumerated powers of Congress were secondary to the requirements of "the law of 'self-preservation.' "[36]

Those who regarded constitutionality as the primary issue excepting Morse, O'Mahoney, and Ervin, failed to document their case. Speakers like Senator Allen Ellender, Louisiana Democrat, made little attempt to refute specific arguments, declaring instead that the resolution in its present form would accomplish no good.[37]

On the question of congressional restraints on presidential exercise of this authority, most Senators agreed to the House requirements of semi-annual reports and termination by concurrent resolution. The Senate in addition unanimously accepted Senator O'Mahoney's amendment requiring that actions of the President be consonant with the United States Constitution. The Senate rejected, however, amendments which imposed severe restrictions. Thus, when Senator Carl T. Curtis, Nebraska Republican, proposed a definite termination date, March 15, 1961, it was rejected by 58 to 30. Senator Morse proposed his scheme for requiring presidential notification of Congress before use of troops and congressional approval of action after it, but the Senate also defeated this, 64 to 28.

A great deal of floor discussion centered on the Humphrey-Mansfield amendment adopted in committee to sidestep the constitutional question. Some Senators resented this evasion. Senator William E. Jenner, Indiana Republican, contended that Congress had been avoiding direct confrontation of the constitutional issues since 1945 and questioned whether Congress had "the moral right to sidestep it a moment longer."[38] Senator Ralph E. Flanders, Vermont Republican, was so convinced that the Humphrey-Mansfield wording was a "diluting" of congressional re-

215

sponsibility that he formally introduced an amendment to restore the original wording of the section.[39]

But most Senators agreed with Senator Green when he praised the Humphrey-Mansfield wording; it had "the 'virtue' of avoiding a constitutional debate which might have the effect of getting an important foreign policy statement lost in a lengthy discussion of constitutional interpretation."[40] The Senate passed the resolution, as rephrased by the committee, 72 to 19.

Reconsideration in the House and Final Passage. The House agreed to the Senate's amendments, 350 to 60, after a single hour of debate. Here there was little effort to discuss constitutional issues in any detail. Most speakers confined themselves to simple expressions of opinion. Thus, Congress ended nearly two months of discussion by avoiding most of the narrow constitutional issues raised by the President's Middle East proposal. Congress had added some restraints and had given away less "authority" than requested by the President. But it had also complied with the President's demand for a demonstration of American unity before the world. In so doing, it had purposely avoided settling the most important constitutional questions.

Discussion Evaluated. In spite of the long days of hearings, executive sessions, and debates, at no time did members develop consistently and in ordered fashion the full catalogue of pertinent constitutional arguments. Unquestionably public and Administration pressures were partly responsible. Yet occasionally strong and relevant arguments were advanced, especially by members opposed to the resolution as it stood. Most Senators and Representatives preferred set speeches on policy to genuine debate on serious constitutional objections. Hence, the constitutional argument, instead of proceeding with logical progression, remained static and even retrogressed.

One may conjecture that universal public agreement on any measures for defense against Communism made it difficult for those dissenting on constitutional grounds to engage the attention of supporters long enough to permit point-by-point rebuttals. Here there was little of the public protest and resistance that had forced Congress to face the constitutional issues in the Reorganization Act fight.

A few sharp cleavages appeared along party lines. These tended to occur in the Senate rather than in the House and to represent Republican support for Administration prerogatives and Democratic attempts to limit them.[41]

Public and Administration pressures were too strong for most to resist—only nineteen Senators and sixty Representatives held out against the final version. The matter required most members to take a public stand early, even if, frequently, from inertia.

Those opposed had to be prompt in saying so and in explaining their reasons. Thus, Senator Dennis Chavez, New Mexico Democrat, was partially correct in asserting that all the Senators had made up their minds and were beyond the persuasion of debate.[42] Yet a few were undecided until the last minute, if voting reflected their true feelings. One may cite thirteen liberal Democrats who voted for Senator Morse's motion to give Congress power to approve presidential decisions under the resolution and impose requirements for strict reporting; logically all thirteen might have voted against the final resolution on constitutional grounds, yet only four did so. Here is another instance of how constitutional appeals were nearly overwhelmed by urgent policy considerations and pressures supporting them.

The final wording and the addition of minor controls shows that to a limited extent objectors on constitutional grounds managed to reach the minds of their colleagues and to influence the outcome.

PARTICIPANTS

Preoccupation with urgent policy may have heightened the loquacity of non-lawyers in the 1957 debates. The makeup of the houses may have been a minor factor, for since 1938 lawyers in the Senate were down from 70 to 61 per cent and in the House from 56 to 54 per cent.[43] Members expressed varied attitudes toward the role of lawyers. Many in both houses voiced the usual reliance on them as special custodians of constitutional wisdom. In the House Committee hearings, several addressed John Foster Dulles as a "great constitutional lawyer." Mrs. Marguerite Church relied on Dean Acheson's advice expressly because he was a lawyer. In the Senate, several asked Senator O'Mahoney to divulge his unique constitutional sagacity as a lawyer.[44]

On this occasion, however, non-lawyers demonstrated a considerable degree of self-reliance. Neither Senate nor House Committee made any noticeable effort to seek out the opinions of outside constitutional lawyers. Non-lawyers spoke often in debate, and some, like Senator Humphrey, referred with confidence to their own interpretations of the Constitution.

A few members even voiced resentment over the pretended superiority of lawyers. Representative Frances Bolton, Ohio Republican, put it this way:

. . . with a lawyer son I have a more than usually keen appreciation of the need lawyers have of splitting hairs, of toying with semantics,

217

of arguing every conceivable aspect of a case. Splendid as this is, one cannot but marvel at their ingenuity and their capacity to complicate what seems so simple.

I have studied and restudied the language of this resolution. Grateful as I am to those who argue that Congress would abrogate its constitutional prerogatives, rights, and responsibilities if it agrees to House Joint Resolution 117, I am just not interested in trying to find out how many angels can dance on the point of a pin.[45]

Senator Prescott Bush, Connecticut Republican, was even more vehement. "I have listened attentively while other Senators who are lawyers have discussed constitutional questions, and have congratulated each other on the wisdom of their remarks. I must respectfully disagree with those who find in the resolution any abdication by the Congress of its power to declare war. I am not a lawyer, but laymen can read . . ."[46]

In 1957, large numbers spoke in both houses but often emotionally and without information. For expert advice on policy, the hearings elicited extensive testimony, especially from present and former executive officials. Furthermore, the reforms provided in the Legislative Reorganization Act of 1946 had authorized most standing committees to appoint professional nonpolitical staff experts to assist them. Thus, the three committees concerned with the Middle East Resolution could boast a total of thirteen permanent or consultant experts of their own. By 1957, then, chairmen were far better able to conduct extensive hearings than was Representative Hill who, in 1935, had had the aid of a single clerk.

Even though committees were now better staffed, and many members, especially Senators, had lawyers on their office staffs, some were reaching outside the government for advice on the constitutional questions.[47] Senator John F. Kennedy placed in the *Record* a statement by a constitutional lawyer, Professor Arthur E. Sutherland of the Harvard Law School, and another member cited a political scientist, Professor James Hart of the University of Virginia.[48] The aid of authorities like these can be valuable, yet the practice of drawing on them on the spur of the moment reflects an uncertainty among members of their own constitutional knowledge and perhaps also a failure by Congress to provide itself with such knowledge on a regular, organized basis.

In the end, leadership in pressing serious constitutional objections and informing Congress on what was at stake fell to three lawyers who were also rich in pertinent experience, Senators O'Mahoney, Morse, and Ervin. Senator Morse held law degrees from Minnesota and Columbia, had been dean of the University of Oregon Law School thirteen years, and had served in the Senate twelve years; Senator Ervin had attended the Harvard Law School and served fourteen years on the North Carolina bench and five years in Congress; Senator O'Mahoney, as already shown, had spent two decades in Congress. As a group these three thus combined the benefits of law teaching, judicial experience, and service in Congress. Against the tide of public alarm over national security, they reminded their fellow-legislators that legalism was not the issue, and that the Cold War was inexorably placing in jeopardy constitutional traditions of 170 years' standing.

MODE

The consideration of the Middle East Resolution followed a procedure which, while regular, reflected the urge for speed. This urge was stronger in the House than in the Senate, particularly in floor debate. House Committee consideration was ample, although it began only two days after the President requested the resolution and before the committee was formally constituted with all members present.[49] House floor debate, however, was kept to only five hours. When the House reconsidered the resolution, after the Senate had amended it, it had only an hour for debate.

The Senate took up the resolution in a more relaxed fashion, although here, too, strong forces pressed for speed. The Senate committees held fourteen days of public hearings, which helped prepare the ground for fruitful floor debate.

Theoretically, time for Senate floor debate was unrestricted. There were twelve days of speeches on the resolution, although the Senate leaders tried repeatedly to speed proceedings. Senator Lyndon B. Johnson, majority leader, announced his intention to seek an eight-hour unanimous consent agreement. But Senators Morse and O'Mahoney both announced they would object and so Johnson dropped this request. Yet he resorted to other tactics designed to push the measure through. Thus, he secured frequent quorum calls which went unrescinded and which were not answerable by senatorial aides; he insisted on daily floor sessions of ten hours and denied permission for standing committees to meet during Senate sessions. Despite these measures, Senators Morse, O'Mahoney, and Ervin extended debate several additional days, against the wishes of both Johnson and the Administration.

Normally a matter which came up as early in a new Congress as this did might have received a good measure of deliberation. Yet post-election stresses and intense public concern operated adversely, and accordingly the committee stage assumed key importance. The Legislative Reorganization Act of 1946 had cut down the number of standing committees to fifteen in the Senate and nineteen in the House. Subcommittees, however, remained as numerous as ever—131 in 1950, divided almost equally between the houses.[50]

The two committees met with full membership present—thirty on the combined Senate units, thirty-two on the House unit—and took extensive testimony. The House Committee somewhat shortchanged the West in its representation, with only two members, both Californians, from beyond the Mississippi, but the Senate units partially made up for this distortion. In general, Senate handling showed greater depth and perceptiveness than House, a fact probably attributable to the high standing of the Senate bodies and to the Senate's special role in foreign relations.[51]

The episode exemplifies the crucial role of hearings, executive sessions, and reports. Here the committees decided to evade the constitutional issue. The desire to present a united front in support of committee reports is strong, but the houses depend for enlightenment on having the alternative arguments laid out clearly before them. These committee reports might well have included point-by-point statements of majority and minority positions.

Otherwise there was much in the procedure to commend. For one thing, House members achieved a prior agreement on procedure both in committee and on the floor. The Senate, too, maintained a consensus on the process used, although on one occasion in committee Senator Morse charged unfairness, asserting the need for ample time for questioning.[52] Several complained of the tactics of majority leader Johnson on the floor. Before the floor debate, Senators had notice that a constitutional issue would be at stake. Johnson and the minority leader, Senator William F. Knowland of California, informed the members of the imminence of the debate, and Senators Mansfield, Morse, Fulbright, and O'Mahoney all spoke in advance of the debate to put members on notice and define the constitutional issues. Time was allotted fairly and adequately both in committee and on the floor.

If deliberation took place, one may suppose it reached its peak in closed sessions where pressures could be muted. In the House hearings, Representative Fountain told Acheson: "You have at least slowed up the mental and emotional processes which have been operating in the last few days—that we should very rapidly dispose of this Resolution by passing it as is. There are quite a few who contend we should pass it simply because the President as Commander in Chief has recommended it and because he thinks it is advisable."[53] The closed sessions that followed hearings gave committee members the vital opportunity to weigh the alternatives in insulation from the pull of the immediate. Chairman Green declared that he had never heard such intense and pointed constitutional discussions as those which occurred when his combined Senate committees met to ponder the resolution.[54] Only once was forceful objection made to the secrecy of the sessions.[55]

If the result of these sessions was a generalized evasion of the constitutional issue, and if few if any clear-cut votes were taken on such issues, at least there were final roll calls both on amendments in the Senate and on passage in both houses. Under the circumstances, some deliberation occurred and interested parties gained full opportunity to present their views.

ATTITUDES

Throughout the floor debates many Senators and Representatives expressed doubts about the constitutionality of the resolution, but then indicated they felt the events in the Middle East required passage. Several others attacked their colleagues for considering only policy to the exclusion of constitutionality.[56]

A few heirs of Jefferson and Marshall still spoke in 1957. In the House there were only two expressions of the necessity for individual responsibility for constitutional questions.[57] Senators were more vocal about their personal oath to uphold the Constitution. Senator Ervin, speaking to Dulles in the hearings, said, "Mr. Secretary, I have trouble with a constitutional question. Andrew Jackson said his oath to support the Constitution obligated him to support the Constitution as Andy Jackson interpreted it. I have the same feeling . . ."[58]

Others maintained that Congress was responsible as a body for considering constitutional questions. Senator Green, although worried that "the fog of constitutional discussion might blur the new vistas" opened by the resolution, also believed that "It is the duty of the President to submit his foreign policy proposals to the Congress. But it is likewise the duty of the Congress to measure those proposals independently, not only with respect to policy, but also with respect to the constitutional implications of those proposals."[59]

Senators Morse and O'Mahoney were the most active in pointing up the need for congressional consideration of constitutionality, particularly in an area where the courts would not act. Senator O'Mahoney said he was unaware of any method by which a private citizen could test the operations of this resolution in the courts. It was up to Congress to make sure that the resolution was constitutional and O'Mahoney condemned "the lighthearted way in which some Members have spoken about the presumption that the laws passed by Congress are constitutional."[60] Senator Morse attacked the supporters of the resolution for the same reason. "To say to me, as some of them have in private conversation,

'But, Wayne, you can't get it before the Court'; doesn't in any way change the fact that it constitutes unconstitutional delegation of power. And I don't propose to vote for it even though we may not be able to get it tested before the Supreme Court, because we, as well as the Court, have the duty to protect the Constitution."[61]

The judicial monopolists expressed themselves too, despite the certainty that no court would act on this resolution. A statement by Representative Dante B. Fascell, Florida Democrat, shows the contortions in which a judicial monopolist must engage when dealing with a subject over which there will be no judicial review.

> We all know that the Supreme Court of the United States is the sole and final judge of constitutional issues. It seems obvious, furthermore, that there is little likelihood that the United States Supreme Court will ever have an opportunity to pass judgment on the question.
>
> Nevertheless, to resolve the fears and questions of many serious and well-intentioned colleagues who are gravely concerned about constitutional questions the committee spelled out in its report . . . very clearly and specifically that the resolution does not have constitutional implications and the committee intended that it should not so have. This declaration, disavowing any constitutional infringement or interpretation, could not be ignored by the judiciary, if called upon.[62]

Evidently officials of government are excused from considering the constitutional effects of their actions by simply denying such effects; furthermore such denials will bind a mythical court. A Midwesterner, Senator John W. Bricker of Ohio, saw things more clearly, for to him the doctrine of political questions regrettably left no official body to which a citizen could go "for recourse to determine whether the political bodies . . . are acting within the terms of the Constitution."[63] Such are the quandaries to which the judicial monopoly theory drives its advocates.

Senators Morse and O'Mahoney demonstrated the shortcomings of that theory, at least as applied to such areas as this, during a remarkable dialogue in the Senate hearings. Simultaneously they highlighted the crucial importance of congressional heed to political questions and to broad constitutional questions:

> Senator Morse. Our problem of course is to get the constitutional issue before the Supreme Court, and you as a lawyer know the procedural difficulty of that . . . I want the record to show that in my judgment if we could get it before the Supreme Court, this resolution, if passed, would be declared an attempt to grant a power to the President, that no Congress has the constitutional authority to grant and, therefore, the resolution is unconstitutional.

Senator O'Mahoney. May I interrupt it at that point Senator Morse?
Senator Morse. Yes.
Senator O'Mahoney. I do so because although I have myself used the words "unconstitutional" and "constitutional," I fear that when members of the general public hear those words used, they inevitably think of a lawyer's argument, a technical argument.
I would rather . . . have it understood that the Constitution is the rampart of our individual freedom, that what we are talking about is the basic liberty of the people of America to govern themselves, and that that cannot be done except under the constitution of divided powers, unless we want to change the Constitution.
It can be changed by an amendment in the formal manner or it can be changed just as certainly by a policy of drift, by which when confronted with an obvious violation of the Constitution, Congress is willing to see its powers slip away.
Senator Morse. It is that latter point I want to stress. It can be done by unconstitutional practice——
Senator O'Mahoney. Right.
Senator Morse. If such practice is permitted to continue.
It is the way you can destroy any law or any constitution. We politicians are prone to talk about a government by law and not by men. Well, let me stress . . . that here in my judgment is a good exhibit of building up a practice of government by men, not by law . . .[64]

Here is clear testimony from two of the Senate's leading constitutional lawyers of the enduring validity of tripartite ideas and the importance of congressional alertness to every departure from established constitutional practice and principle.

CONCLUSIONS

The experience of Congress with the Middle East Resolution reinforces most of the earlier conclusions concerning the Reorganization Act controversy. The discussions of presidential authority to use military forces abroad show that the Cold War was intensifying the drive toward the concentration of power in the Executive. Hence, external factors were producing the same ominous constitutional effects that internal pressures for economic growth and stability had been producing since the 1930's. Such conditions made it urgent that the public be kept aware of transformations in the structure of constitutional power and that officials and citizens alike give sustained thought to those measures which will effectively counteract the worst effects of concentrated power.

223

Yet in the area of the separation of powers, as in the area of federalism, the theory of judicial monopolism often obscures the true dimensions of the problem and hampers constructive action. With little or no likelihood of Court scrutiny, the temptation is great either to ignore constitutional challenges or brush them off as subordinate and technical in nature. Once again, within much of this area of power, Congress has final authority, even as Parliament, and yet legalism and assumptions about judicial review destroy full awareness by members of Congress of the responsibility that goes with power.

One of the lessons of these episodes is the need of making expert knowledge and experience readily available to members of Congress. In the Middle East discussions the number of members who presented serious, sustained, and documented constitutional arguments had shrunk almost to zero. This time, as in the Bradley affair, most Southern members seemed unperturbed over the intensification of presidential prerogative, perhaps because they deemed it essential to the conduct of foreign relations in the 1950's.

By good fortune the two Senate Committees which took up the resolution included Senators Morse and Ervin; these received reinforcement from Senator O'Mahoney of the Judiciary Committee who came in voluntarily to add his voice. Otherwise, neither hearings nor debate elicited from the Executive, members of Congress, or unofficial witnesses a thorough and informed discussion of the constitutional questions. The action of two Senators in seeking and placing in the *Record* the opinions of Professors Sutherland and Hart, the one a constitutional lawyer, the other a political scientist, suggests that Congress may in time need to equip itself formally and permanently with available centers for the advice of authorities such as these.

This episode shows the unwisdom of leaving the raising and discussing of constitutional issues to chance—the accidental presence on committees of members alert and knowledgeable concerning such issues. It likewise shows that expertise must go beyond legal knowledge and embrace such fields as American history, constitutional theory, and comparative government.

This episode also suggests that the Senate normally conducts better constitutional inquiries than the House. Admittedly, the subject was foreign relations, a field in which the upper house has special prerogatives and hence greater interest and knowledge. Yet Senate procedures were more conducive than those of the House to constitutional inquiry. The pair of Senate committees—Foreign Relations and Armed Services —that had conducted the MacArthur hearings so effectively brought to the present problem not only experience in foreign affairs but also concern with constitutional issues and a readiness to meet constitutional objections constructively. Those committees, while about equal in total membership to the House Committee, nevertheless were both more thorough in their probe and more representative in their composition than the latter.

In both houses, committees gathered and digested information in such a way as to make subsequent debate pertinent and fruitful. Senate debate was of a higher order than House debate. Senators seemed to keep their minds more open or at least more alert than did Representatives. The lower house passed the original wording—"authorize"—and later the revised wording—"is prepared to"—by almost identical roll call votes. The constitutional subtleties of the change in phrasing made slight difference to most Representatives, yet the change was crucial to Senate acceptance. Finally, here was fresh evidence of the leisurely pace and the tradition of free and unlimited debate which prevail in the Senate. Other things being equal, Senators are better equipped and organized than Representatives to perform as a Committee of the Whole in the Jeffersonian sense.

Invocation of the judicial monopoly theory was more than irrelevant; it was dangerous. It was not merely that courts were unavailable as devices for screening out unconstitutional provisions; had the appeals to ignore the political questions and the problem of implementing formal constitutional assignments of power succeeded, the outcome might have been serious. The resolution might have contained no restraints whatever on the powers granted, and the public at large might have remained in the dark concerning this fresh enhancement of presidential authority. Here, as in the Bradley and the Reorganization Act controversies, some members pressed for discussion of the constitutional questions. If that discussion was less searching and conclusive and the members insisting on discussion less numerous than before, this probably resulted from the intensification of the Cold War and the growing acclimatization of Americans to crisis and presidential hegemony. Nevertheless, it was still possible in 1957 for Congress to devise restraints on the power granted and to inform the public of constitutional issues and the measures for dealing with them.

At least if the public has accepted the growth of executive power, it has done so with positive understanding rather than the ignorance induced by fiat.

It is difficult to suppose that in the nuclear age the drift toward executive dictatorship will halt until the nations devise some universal system for settling disputes and restraining national power. Meanwhile Congress bears a heavy obligation to work out creative constitutional settlements in this delicate area of the separation of powers.

225

11

Amendment by Default: The Twenty-Second Amendment in Congress, 1947

In 1947, midway between the Reorganization and Middle East controversies, the Republican Eightieth Congress drafted and sent to the states what became the Twenty-Second Amendment, fixing the maximum tenure of any person in the Presidency. The two foregoing chapters showed Congress implementing constitutional restraints, through the legislative veto and provisions for accountability and for termination of powers. Here Congress will share in formally amending the document of 1787. Legalistic thinking and the same conception of the Constitution as solely the work of the people and the Court, which had helped inspire judicial monopolism, were at work throughout this episode and here too fostered a weakening of responsibility.

One would, however, expect little dispute about the responsibility of Congress for the proposal of amendments. Some might doubt the capacity, even the obligation, of Congress to interpret the document, to "decide" constitutional questions of a narrow legal sort, but how can one deny the obligation which Article V places on Congress when it prepares amendments for proposal to the states:

> The Congress whenever two-thirds of both houses shall deem it necessary shall propose amendments to this Constitution, or on the application of the legislatures of two-thirds of the several states, shall call a convention for proposing amendments which in either case shall be valid for all intents and purposes as part of this Constitution when ratified by the legislatures of three-fourths of the several states or by conventions in three-fourths thereof, as the one or the other mode of ratification may be proposed by the Congress.

When the Philadelphia framers drew up this provision they were giving Congress a task not unlike their own. The drafting of an amendment differs from the drafting of a constitutional document in scope and degree, not in kind. It necessitates the same search of constitutional principles and the values they support, the same achievement of a

226

reasoned agreement on a declaration of limited power for submission to a quota of ratifying states that marked the work of the founders. Constitutional questions accordingly occur in this form of constitutional settlement just as in interpretation, implementation, or framing of the document.[1] Members of Congress who minimize responsibility for amendments run the same risk of inattention and neglect that appears in those other forms of settlement. If changes in the fundamental law are to be the result of consensus—genuine expressions of the sense of the whole—assuming that Congress rather than a national convention proposes such changes, then that consensus can take shape only in Congress. The Executive is formally excluded from the process, and ratifying states have only an "all or nothing" choice. The following pages will show to what extent Congress in 1947 accepted its responsibility, furnished procedures commensurate with the character of the task, and used its lawyer-members to assure such procedures and bring constitutional wisdom to bear.

The maximum tenure of American Presidents had, by 1947, long been a matter of debate and controversy. The framers wrestled with it before they hit on four-year terms with no limit as to re-eligibility. But not everyone later accepted this solution. Presidents began early to create a no-third-term tradition, and in 1829 and 1833, President Jackson sent messages to Congress advocating a constitutional amendment to provide for a single six-year term. Over the years, Senators and Representatives introduced into Congress more than two hundred projects to limit a President's tenure by constitutional amendment.

Until the election of President Franklin D. Roosevelt for a third term, no man had broken the unwritten convention against serving more than two four-year terms. Roosevelt, of course, went on to win, although not to serve out, a fourth term. Many thought this break with tradition had set a dangerous precedent, fearing that ambitious men could now perpetuate themselves in the office by a shrewd manipulation of its great resources. Agitation to enact the discarded custom into a constitutional amendment mounted.

In 1947 the Republican party, deprived of the Presidency for fourteen years, and of control in Congress for sixteen years, made the cause of limitation by amendment its own cause. In 1940 and 1944 it had written into its platform a plank calling for amendment to restrict presidential tenure. The 1944 plank stated, "We favor an amendment to the Constitution providing that no person shall be President of the United States for more than two terms of four years each." When in the elections of November 1946, the party at last won control of Congress, it was in a favorable position to launch action. The proposed amendment headed the Republican list of "must" legislation.[2]

227

Thus, the shadow of FDR fell across the consideration of the Twenty-Second Amendment in Congress; seldom was the discussion free of it. Both proponents and opponents referred repeatedly to Roosevelt's record as President, and hence much of the debate concerned, not constitutional principles, but the personality and record of one man.

Congressional action on the amendment began before 1947. In 1940 and again in 1945 subcommittees of the Senate Judiciary Committee held hearings on proposals to limit presidential tenure, without producing a recommendation.

After their success in the 1946 off-year election, the Republicans took advantage of their majorities in Congress. On January 3, 1947, Representatives Everett Dirksen of Illinois and Earl Michener of Michigan introduced proposed amendments, the former's calling for a single six-year term, the latter's for a maximum of two four-year terms. From that date until final House action on March 21, the Twenty-Second Amendment moved inexorably forward. As we shall see, the central issue— the desirability of setting a maximum limit to presidential tenure— often gave place to peripheral issues.

The work of preparing constitutional amendments for floor action belongs, under the Legislative Reorganization Act, to the Judiciary Committees. In the House, accordingly, a Judiciary subcommittee, after brief hearings, reported Michener's resolution on February 5. Next day the House adopted a Rules Committee recommendation for two hours of debate, considered both plans and a proposal for convention rather than state ratification, and finally passed the Michener two-term proposal by a roll call vote of 285 to 121. Next day the Senate referred the bill to its Judiciary Committee, which reported February 21. The Senate sporadically debated the amendment on four days from March 5 to 12. It killed its own committee's proposal for convention ratification, discussed the effect of the amendment on a Vice President who succeeded to the Presidency, defeated Senator Magnuson's substitute to preclude the eligibility of anyone for election to the Presidency more than twice in succession, and accepted by voice vote a compromise proposal engineered by Senator Robert A. Taft, Ohio Republican. The Senate turned down other amendments and passed the Taft compromise by 59 to 23. The House Judiciary Committee then approved the Senate changes, and the House adopted them, giving the amendment the final seal of congressional approval on a division, i.e. no roll call, vote of 81 to 29.[3]

In its final form, the Twenty-Second Amendment which, incidentally, exempted President Truman from its operation, read in part:

No person shall be elected to the office of the President more than twice, and no person who has held the office of President, or acted as President, for more than two years of a term to which some other person was elected President shall be elected to the office of the President more than once.

Ratification by the states took almost four years. Theories which supporters voiced in the 1947 debates concerning the ratification process call for some mention of what actually happened. Congress had pre-scribed ratification by legislatures rather than conventions and allowed seven years for completion. Maine was the first state to ratify. The action came on March 31, 1947, a week after final congressional approval. The *New York Times* reported the action of the Maine legislature this way: "The Maine House voted 82 to 7 for ratification, after brief debate. All the dissenters were Democrats. The Senate voted for the proposal without discussion."[4]

By the end of May, eighteen state legislatures had ratified the amend-ment, all of them Republican-controlled except one listed as "non-partisan." But between that date and January 1951, only six more states had approved the amendment. On January 26, 1951, the Republican National Committee met and evidently decided to press for ratification of the amendment within thirty days.[5] Within those thirty days eleven more state legislatures took the requested action. On February 26, 1951, ratification by the thirty-sixth state, Nevada, put the amendment into the Constitution. A circus atmosphere reportedly surrounded the ratifica-tion by Nevada. The Nevada Senate, conscious that Utah intended to ratify the amendment on the morning of February 26, and desiring that Nevada be the thirty-sixth state, waited, after having adjourned, for news of Utah's action. After learning that Utah had acted favorably, the Nevada Senate went back into session and passed the amendment 16 to 1.[6]

One who attempts to appraise the Twenty-Second Amendment should remember how difficult it would be to change it. The same ponderous process is required for repeal as is required for adoption of amendments. Yet dissatisfaction with this amendment soon appeared both within and without Congress. Two Presidents have expressed reservations about it. President Eisenhower called it "not wholly wise" and said he felt that "the United States ought to be able to choose for its President, anybody that it wants, regardless of the number of terms he has served."[7] The *New York Times* further reported that he was "understood to believe that the amendment was in large degree an act of retroactive vindictive-ness against the late Franklin D. Roosevelt rather than the result of judicious thinking about the institutions of the Republic."[8] President Truman in 1959, spoke more strongly. What the "Roosevelt haters" actually accomplished, he said, "was to make a 'lame duck' out of every second-term President for all time in the future."[9] Truman also declared that it was one of the few amendments which "have not been thoroughly considered when the public interest is at stake."[10]

In addition, certain political scientists and historians later favored repeal of the amendment. Early in 1957, Representative Stewart Udall, Arizona Democrat, polled thirty-six scholars selected by the respective professional associations. Of twenty-nine replying, only five supported the amendment and twenty-one urged repeal.[11]

In Congress itself agitation for repeal mounted. In the first session of the Eighty-Sixth Congress, 1959, six resolutions calling for repeal were introduced. In 1957 Richard Strout of the *Christian Science Monitor* wrote, ". . . signs are gathering that the real meaning of the enactment was not fully understood either by the public, or by the Congress which launched it . . ."[12] In short, dissatisfaction with the Twenty-Second Amendment has continued. The steady intensification of the power and prestige of the President makes it vital that known and definite restraints exist, including perhaps a limit to the total tenure of any incumbent. One can question, however, whether the terms of the amendment meet the needs of our time, whether they take account of the problem of a second-term President who seeks to maintain control of subordinates aware of the limit which the calendar places on his official life, whether it takes account of the full dimensions of the office in the twentieth century. That doubts have been expressed by Presidents of both parties and by others suggests that important questions went undiscussed during the framing.

CONSTITUTIONAL QUESTIONS

Obviously, all the questions which Congress had to decide in adopting a presidential-tenure amendment were, in a genuine sense, constitutional. The task hence was not how to interpret existing words, but whether to add new words limiting power. Most basic and most general of the questions was whether or not to limit total tenure. In case of an affirmative decision, then subordinate questions followed: first, what should be the precise character of the limitation; second, by what method should the amendment be ratified? Debate tended to occupy itself with the subordinate questions.

That the courts would ever review these decisions of Congress was extremely unlikely. Yet the various states, in ratifying, would exercise a kind of post-congressional decision and accordingly would make it possible for those accustomed to shifting the burden of constitutional inquiry to the courts to follow the same route, in this instance to the states. Congress lacked the final say, and this was an open invitation to a shift of responsibility.

COURSE OF THE DISCUSSION

Pre-1947 Consideration. As we have seen, the Republican effort to limit presidential tenure began prior to 1947. Doubtless with the aid of conservative Democrats, it produced two sets of hearings; neither was fully satisfactory. From September 4 until October 30, 1940, a sub-committee of the Senate Judiciary Committee[13] held hearings on two joint resolutions to amend the Constitution in regard to presidential tenure.[14] More than forty testified, and all favored some kind of limitation. The witnesses ranged all the way from historian James Truslow Adams and Dean Young Smith of the Columbia University Law School to the Reverend Norman Vincent Peale. Yet, timing of these hearings was unfortunate, coming as they did in the middle of Roosevelt's campaign for a third term. Partisan exchanges punctuated the hearings and the result was political heat rather than constitutional light.

Members of the Seventy-Ninth Congress (1945–1946) introduced several new proposals. Another subcommittee of the Senate Judiciary Committee[15] held hearings on these in 1945.[16] The committee met for only an hour. The sole committee member present was the chairman, Senator Carl Hatch, New Mexico Democrat. Three other Senators testified and a fourth sent in his statement.[17] All four favored some sort of limitation, their testimony filling eighteen pages of printed record. Indifference to the problem in 1945 was monumental.

> Senator Hatch. So far as I know, there have been no requests to be heard—have there?
> The Clerk. None at all.
> Senator Hatch. Neither for nor against?
> The Clerk. That is right.
> . . .
> Senator Hatch. It is strange that nobody wants to be heard on this . . . There ought to be somebody for or against.[18]

In the House, 1947. Soon after the opening of the Eightieth Congress, work on a new amendment began in earnest. On February 3 Subcommittee Number 4 of the House Committee on the Judiciary[19] considered a two-term proposal of committee chairman Michener and reported it favorably to the parent committee the same day. On February 4 the full committee voted to report the bill and did so the following day. Since the subcommittee hearings were never printed, it is hard to know what arguments it considered.[20] On its part, the full committee issued a majority report and three minority reports, totaling nine pages.[21]

The majority report said little. Its main point was that since the two-term tradition had been violated and since there had been continuing discussion of this issue for many years, the people ought to be given an opportunity of registering their opinion on the matter. "This resolution has but one purpose. That purpose is to submit to the people, by and through their State legislatures, this very important problem of the Presidential tenure of office, and to let the people decide whether or not this limitation should be written into the Constitution."[22]

Two of the minority reports, one signed by Representative Emanuel Celler, New York Democrat, and the other signed by Democratic Representatives Sam Hobbs of Alabama and Ed Gossett of Texas, argued for a single six-year term. These men thought their proposal would lift the President out of politics and enhance his statesmanship. The two-term limitation, they maintained, would not accomplish this.

The third minority report, signed by six Democrats,[23] held that there should be no written constitutional limitation on tenure. Quadrennial elections provided a sufficient restraint. The proposed amendment would imply that the people could not be trusted; indeed, they insisted, Congress was here attempting to place the people in a "strait jacket." These Democrats asked, "What have the American people done to justify this restriction being placed upon the democratic process? Apparently the offense is the decision of the voters to elect Franklin D. Roosevelt for a third term."[24]

When the measure reached the House floor, the members debated both the desirability and the proper form of a limitation. The proponents argued that the amendment would merely write into the document the Washington-Jefferson tradition of a two-term limit. Since that custom no longer stood, it was necessary to put it in writing. Without such limitation, a President might become a dictator. The amendment, indeed, was needed to preserve representative government and a system of separated powers.[25]

In answering the argument that the amendment would render the government partially impotent in an emergency, the proponents pointed out that an ambitious President could create false emergencies to perpetuate his own power. Furthermore, there was no indispensable man, regardless of the emergency. Eliminating the possibility of a third term would tend to develop new leaders. Finally, as if to clinch their case, the supporters of limitation urged that submission of the amendment to the people for approval would confirm democratic principles.

In reply, opponents of the resolution divided on the necessity of a written limitation. One group, led by Representatives Celler and Hobbs, defended such a limitation but advocated a six-year term, with no re-eligibility. They asserted again, as they had in their minority reports, that this plan would remove the office from politics. Celler contended that the six-year limit "would make for more statesmanship, more courage in the Presidency because votes would not be in the balance."[26]

The other opponents comprised most of the House Democrats. They opposed any written limitation and pressed two main arguments. First, a written limitation would hamper the country in an emergency. Second, it would constitute a curb on democracy.

Another question which the Representatives discussed was the appropriate method of ratification. Representative William Colmer, Mississippi Democrat, argued for state conventions as the more popular method. He pointed out that state legislatures were elected on other issues and hence had no popular mandate concerning the amendment. Although no one clearly met Colmer's argument, his motion lost.

As the resolution finally passed the House, by a seven to three margin, it provided that "Any person who has served as President of the United States during all, or portions, of any two terms, shall thereafter be ineligible to hold the office of President . . ."[27] In March the House returned to the amendment as modified by the Senate. It adopted the Senate version by 81 to 29 almost without debate.

In the Senate, 1947. On reaching the Senate on February 7, the bill went immediately to the Judiciary Committee.[28] Under its chairman, Senator Alexander Wiley, Wisconsin Republican, that committee held no hearings; the only discussion given the bill took place in executive session. The committee issued only one report, and that was three pages long.[29]

The committee amended the House version in two respects. The final House proposal had made ineligible any person who had served any part of two terms. The Senate Committee version read: "A person who has held the office of President . . . on three hundred and sixty-five calendar days or more in each of two terms shall not be eligible to hold the office of President, or to act as President, for any part of another term; . . ."[30] This Senate Committee's version also provided for ratification by conventions instead of by state legislatures.

Like its House counterpart, this committee seemed convinced that Congress was only a middleman in passing such questions on to the people for final decision. Hence the task of Congress had nothing creative about it. "The committee believes that the wide interest manifested in the general subject over a course of many years and heightened by more recent events in the history of this country entitle the people to an opportunity to vote on this particular subject."[31]

On the floor, the Senators repeated many of the arguments used by

233

the Representatives. Yet they also considered several new points. Senator Wiley led the forces favoring amendment by arguing that it was necessary in order to prevent dictatorship.

On the other side, Senator Lister Hill, Alabama Democrat, argued at length that a rigid prohibition would tie the hands of the people.[32] Another Democrat, Senator Scott Lucas of Illinois, agreed, calling the measure purely political.

> Mr. Lucas. I should like to know where all the excitement with respect to the . . . amendment arises . . . This is a political issue, and that is all there is to it . . .
>
> Mr. Hill. Of course, as the Senator from Illinois suggests, if this were not a political matter it would not be rushed on to the floor of the Senate without hearings.[33]

One of the most perceptive arguments against the amendment was made by Senator Harley Kilgore, West Virginia Democrat. He thought it unwise to "bind the hands of our children," and argued that the amendment would seriously impair executive effectiveness since a second-term President would be politically impotent. The Border State Senator drew on his own investigations:

> . . . I have had the opportunity in the past 8 years to study the record of governors in States in which there are limitations as to terms, and I have discovered that invariably . . . incumbents have had trouble, because everybody realized they could not run again. There was no method by which they could complete their programs; but, so long as there is a possibility that they may run again, they can go ahead successfully.
>
> . . . The President is expected to be a leader and to carry the responsibility for all actions done under his administration . . . He is expected to be the leader, and he is charged with the responsibility of carrying out his program. If he cannot run again, he loses all opportunity of getting his program through . . .[34]

In spite of its merits, Senator Kilgore's argument went unanswered.

Senator Theodore Green, Democrat of Rhode Island, made another important point by tying the issue of tenure to such others as presidential disability and succession and the role of the electoral college. These matters long continued to agitate the public; they vitally affected the character of the modern Presidency. The Senate Rules Committee was at that very time considering a proposal by Senators Green and H. Alexander Smith, New Jersey Republican, which would have created a joint committee "to study and report on all phases of this question." Senator Green urged that all of these matters be considered together, not in piecemeal fashion. He then moved to postpone discussion for two weeks. This would have let the Rules Committee complete and publish its findings and made possible a more judicious inquiry into the whole subject by a joint committee.[35] The only response was defeat by voice vote.

Occasionally the Senate debate got sidetracked from the main issue. The committee proposal for convention ratification stirred controversy. Senator Chapman Revercomb, West Virginia Republican, argued that a state legislature could resolve itself into a convention, thus defeating the intention of the Senate to provide for convention ratification.[36] Debate here showed that many Senators were unaware of the intricacies of the amending process. Senator Alben Barkley, Kentucky Democrat, argued against convention ratification because of the chance of hand-picked politically-controlled conventions in most of the states.

The main argument for conventions was stated by Republicans John Sherman Cooper of Kentucky and Forrest Donnell of Missouri. They maintained that since a convention would be elected on this specific issue alone, it would reflect the views of the people more clearly than would the legislatures. The Senate went along with the opponents of conventions, however, and rejected the proposal for conventions by a vote of 63 to 20.

Another sidetrack was the extensive debate concerning the problem of a Vice President who had succeeded to the Presidency. Senator Warren Magnuson, Washington Democrat, introduced a substitute amendment to take care of this problem. "No person shall be elected to the office of the President more than twice."[37] He defended his proposal as being more fair than the pending measure to a Vice President who had succeeded.

This provoked a lengthy interchange on the relative merits and dangers of allowing a person to serve as President for as many as eleven years. Senator Taft thought it much too long. Senator Hatch was perturbed by this discussion. "What a mighty debate this has been! What a wonderful thought was conveyed to the country when the Senate . . . argued over the difference between 8, 9 and 11½ years!"[38] Senator Lucas then asked Hatch whether time had not proved the Founding Fathers correct in omitting a limitation on tenure and whether they alone had been "fair and impartial" in their treatment of the question.[39] Senator Hatch agreed: "They knew so much more than we that I am frankly ashamed of our poor, pitiful effort as demonstrated here today, when we argue over the difference between 8 and 11 years."[40]

235

Senator Magnuson, at the suggestion of Senator Spessard Holland, Florida Democrat, changed the character of his proposal. His amendment now read: "No person shall be eligible to be elected to the office of President for more than two successive terms."[41] Senator Holland defended this revised wording: "With our knowledge of the fact that this is becoming a young man's world and the actual fact that young men of proved ability and high qualities of leadership are offering and are available for the Presidency, I do not think we should adopt a course which would preclude recalling, after a vacation, such a young man who has ripened and matured by the experience of 8 years in the White House, if there were great need for him."[42]

Senator Revercomb retorted that this proposal failed to "serve the purpose of any amendment whatever on this subject."[43] The Senate defeated Magnuson's proposal 50 to 34. In fact, it never gave serious consideration to what was essentially a new proposal.

The Senate finally adopted the Taft compromise,[44] 59 to 23, which accordingly became the text of the Constitution. By permitting a Vice President to run for President twice if he has succeeded to that office no earlier than the mid-point of a prior term, in other words fixing a ten-year maximum tenure, a mathematical bargain between contending extremes was struck. It was not without ingenuity, but the discussion which led to it had given more attention to the minutiae of the problem than to the fundamentals.

Discussion Evaluated. Clearly, the discussion which the Twenty-Second Amendment received in Congress was neither searching nor detached from politics, especially party politics. The brief and sometimes barren floor debates were uninformed by prior hearings and committee reports of a sort calculated to yield insight and judgment. There was oratory but little serious discussion and meeting of minds. On the central question, few, if any, seemed to abandon preconceived notions; virtually all members apparently had made up their minds before the debate.

This lack of detachment from existing commitments showed in the voting. Table 7 gives the party lineup on four leading votes, two in committee and two on the floor. What is most striking is the solid unanimity maintained by the Republicans. Not a single dissenting vote disturbed the solid front of the G.O.P. Those Democrats, including Representative John F. Kennedy of Massachusetts, who combined with Republicans to provide the required two-thirds came chiefly from the South. Among them were many determined opponents of Roosevelt on personal or policy grounds.[45]

On subordinate issues, such as the merits of convention as against legislative ratification, debate did influence votes. Oddly, Republicans,

TABLE 7.   Party Voting on Proposed Twenty-Second Amendment, 1947

Vote	Republicans		Democrats		Total	
	Yea	Nay	Yea	Nay	Yea	Nay
House Committee, motion to report	15	0	5	6	20	6
House floor, for passage	238	0	47	120	285	121[a]
Senate Committee, motion to report	7	0	2	1	9	1
Senate floor, for final passage	46	0	13	23	59	23

SOURCE: *New York Times,* Feb. 5, 1947, p. 1; 93 *Cong. Rec.,* pt. 1, p. 872; *New York Times,* Feb. 18, 1947, p. 2; 93 *Cong. Rec.,* pt. 2, p. 1978.
[a] One American-Laborite voted against the resolution.

who acclaimed the people as the true decision-makers in amending the Constitution, showed less support for popular conventions than Democrats.[46] On the main issue debate had no appreciable effect.

PARTICIPANTS

Again, lawyers dominated the discussion. This time none commented either favorably or adversely on the qualifications of lawyers for the task. In view of the limited amount of floor discussion, the extent of participation was great. In the Senate, twenty-six members spoke, in the House, forty-six, with lawyers predominating in both cases.[47]

Yet despite all this, the speeches were often ill-informed. One looks in vain for more than a few contributions worthy of being described as wise. Members seemed unable to bring their experience to bear on the issue, and except for one narrow legal argument introduced by Senator Donnell concerning the power of a state legislature to make itself a convention, the issues were of a character not especially appropriate for lawyers, or at least for lawyers alone. Apparently neither house consulted outside experts at any stage. Committees or subcommittees might with profit have invited the testimony of historians, political scientists, men with experience in the executive branch, and others having special insight into the problem, but the only witnesses to appear at the brief House hearings were members of the House itself. Nor were there signs of genuine constitutional leadership. Senators Magnuson, Kilgore, and Green all tried to capture the attention of the Senate for proposals or arguments of merit, but failed. Conceivably their failure resulted in part

237

from the prevailing conception of congressional responsibility. As will soon appear, the committee chairmen as well as others seemed to regard the task of amending the Constitution as belonging to the people alone.

MODE

Not only the leaders but also the procedure contributed to thwarting searching deliberation on the question of tenure. The Republican majority demanded speed and got it. In 1947 the House subcommittee considered the amendment for one day only; next day the parent committee voted to report it favorably, and two days later the House held its two hours of debate and approved the amendment.[48] The Senate committee kept the resolution two weeks but held no hearings. On the Senate floor, the majority leadership again stressed speed. After three days of sporadic debate, Senator Taft felt that the matter was not progressing satisfactorily and accordingly called a recess from March 10 until March 12. The problem of a Vice President who succeeded to the Presidency had caused much disagreement and Taft referred to this in explaining the need for a recess.

> My only point is that it seems to me that if there is complete disagreement on the particular issue now before us, it will prevent the passage of the joint resolution, which I should like to see passed. It seemed to me that a recess might give an opportunity to reach some compromise with those who think the pending committee amendment cuts the tenure too short, and I thought we might do better by taking a recess than by going ahead to a vote tonight. However, I have no objection to a vote on the pending amendment, if the Senate wishes to take it. We can work the compromise out afterward.[49]

The Senate agreed to recess, and during the interval Taft engineered a compromise proposal.[50]

Once Taft got his compromise out on the floor, he would no longer brook delay. When Senator Green proposed his two-week postponement for possible joint committee study of interrelated problems of the Presidency, Taft replied, "I only wish to point out that we have considered this measure for 3 or 4 days. Senators have made up their minds, and I see no reason why we should not vote on the joint resolution tonight."[51] Again the Senate followed Taft's lead.

House consideration of the Senate version was marked by apathy, for only a quarter of the members took the trouble to vote on final passage, with little discussion and no roll call.

238

In proposing this amendment neither house used procedures which met prevailing conceptions of fairness. For the most part those procedures represented the will of the new Republican majority imposed on the Democratic minority. Democratic protests were strong but fruitless. Note this comment by the ranking member of the House Rules Committee, Representative Adolph Sabath, Illinois Democrat, objecting to that committee's proposal for regulating the imminent House debate:

Why should the Members of this House and the people of America be deprived of the right to know the facts attending the passage of this resolution and of being informed by extended debate? Why should not the people know what this proposed constitutional amendment means? If I am not mistaken, this is the first time that any resolution amending the Constitution . . . has been brought before the House under a rule which permits only two short hours for general debate. . . . Such haste seems indecent . . . this joint resolution was reported . . . only day before yesterday. They did not give that committee even time to introduce the amended resolution, nor to print the hearings for the benefit of the House membership. They were obliged to come in with a resolution which will have to be amended in accordance with the majority vote of the Judiciary Committee. I hope that in the future the Republican majority will not act so hastily and so harshly . . .[52]

Chief notification of the coming debate was the pledge contained in the 1944 Republican platform, coupled with Speaker Martin's statement that this amendment had top priority in the Republican legislative program. None of the issues was defined, however, until action began in committee and on the floor.

Neither house at any stage assigned time commensurate with the importance due a constitutional amendment. Judiciary Committee Chairman Michener tried to justify the one-day House hearings. "In view of the discussions over the past 150 years, there should be no necessity for prolonged hearings at this time."[53] But one day of hearings, followed by two hours of floor consideration, including only ten minutes on the crucial Colmer amendment providing for convention ratification, was hardly enough. It was argued, of course, that the 1940 and 1945 Senate Hearings, together with the general public discussion of the question since 1787, were sufficient to inform Congress in 1947. But the 1940 hearings were one-sided—all witnesses favoring limitation—and were conducted in the midst of the third-term campaign. The 1945 hearings were almost valueless. Furthermore, intermittent and generalized discussion throughout the nation's history differs from organized debate, in the light of contemporay conditions, on a precise question with a view to the drafting of a constitutional amendment.

The Senate did little better than the House. The Judiciary Committee held no hearings at all. And, although floor debate occurred on four days, these days were scattered and the actual duration totaled only a few hours.

Neither house made consistent use of adversary proceedings.[54] True deliberation was lacking at every stage. On the House floor Sam Rayburn, Texas Democrat and minority leader, did his best to get that body to "wait a little while and cool off a bit."[55] But the two-thirds majority plunged ahead, ignoring such counsel.

In the Senate, Senator Kilgore's reasoned argument based on observations of state governors with limited tenure, Senator Magnuson's perfected amendment allowing more than two nonconsecutive terms, and, above all, Senator Green's proposal to consider all of the related questions together—all these should have received extended deliberation. Instead, they went unheard.

Scattered through the debates were several roll call votes forcing members to take public stands. All concerned constitutional issues, although the importance of those issues seemed to escape many members. The House took only one recorded vote, that on initial passage. The Senate went further and took three of significance—deciding the method of ratification, rejecting the Magnuson amendment, and passing the final version. Since the House rushed the Senate version through without a roll call, only the Senators are on record for or against the Twenty-Second Amendment in its permanent form.

Perhaps dissident Democrats should have protested more forcefully against this precipitancy even to the point of a filibuster. Their mildness may have resulted from doubts about the possibility of success or from public indifference. In any event, the whole process demonstrates how a likeminded and disciplined party, with strong recruits from the opposition, can obtain action without thought even on a matter so fundamental as this.

ATTITUDES

It seems likely that a prominent factor in causing Congress to minimize the need of thoughtful consideration was the conception which many of its members held concerning their responsibility for considering constitutional amendments. Clearly the houses were here reaching decisions on important constitutional questions, this time with no prospect of review by the President nor, presumably, by the courts. A choice between a tripartite theory and judicial monopoly was nonexistent. Yet a somewhat analogous choice was at hand. The action of Congress was still provisional, not final. Ratification must come from the states, through legislatures or conventions, and accordingly, members of Congress could adopt either what we might call a "bipartite" theory, locating important responsibility in both Congress and the states, or a "popular monopoly" theory assigning final, hence sole, responsibility to the people acting through their state bodies. Those who chose popular monopoly would be substituting the people for the courts and in this way evading their own responsibility. Habituation to the notion that the courts are sole agents of the people in constitutional interpretation could easily induce the parallel notion that where courts are excluded from action, deliberation and decision rests with the people alone without prior legislative preparation, consideration, or leadership.

Throughout the entire discussion of the Twenty-Second Amendment, members repeatedly deferred to the people. Among these members were prominent leaders who, significantly, were also wont on issues of interpretation to espouse judicial monopolism. In the 1945 hearings, Senators Wayne Morse, E. H. Moore, Oklahoma Republican, Hatch, and W. Lee O'Daniel, Texas Democrat, all verged on this position:

Senator Morse. . . . I think it is very desirable to have the matter passed upon by the people of this country . . .[56]
Senator O'Daniel. Wherein is there any danger involved in a democratic form of government in submitting to the people or their representatives, any matter regarding a change in their Constitution?
Senator Hatch. I do not see any particular danger in submitting an amendment to the people, Senator—any amendment.
. . .
Senator Moore. . . . if it is fundamental in our form of government, the people ought to have the chance on it, or the final say.[57]

In 1947 similar views punctuated the discussions. A Florida Democrat, Senator Spessard Holland, declared, "What I should like to do would be to give to the American people a clear opportunity to decide for themselves . . ."[58] But Republicans, especially Midwestern Republicans in posts of leadership, were even more positive. Particularly significant were the views of the two committee chairmen. As we have seen, the House Committee, under Chairman Michener of Michigan, had reported that the only purpose of the amendment was to let the people decide the central issue. The Senate Committee was equally loath to pin any measurable responsibility on Congress. Its chairman, Senator Wiley of Wisconsin, gave the most extreme expression of the "leave-it-to-the-people" theory. He announced himself this way:

I wish to say again, in order that much of what has been said here this afternoon will not be misunderstood by the occupants of the galleries, that no Senator, no matter how he votes today, thereby commits himself as to his position before his constituency. He is today only voting whether he is willing to submit the constitutional amendment to the representatives of the people in the legislatures of the Nation . . .
. . . are we willing to permit the legislatures of the States to decide this matter? Are we willing to let government officials who are closer to the people than we are vote on the constitutional amendment?

The impression I have gained from much that has been said on the floor of the Senate is that we, the Congress of the United States, were deciding whether there was to be an amendment to the Constitution. Congress could decide nothing of the kind. If we submit the question to the people, or to their representatives in the legislatures of the States, they will make the decision.[59]

The idea that a Senator could take one position on the amendment in Congress and another in his own state was actually defended by Senator Hatch. He declared his intention to return to New Mexico and tell those charged with ratification to "Turn down this amendment . . .," insisting in the same breath, "I still intend to vote to submit the proposed constitutional amendment to the people of my State and to the people of the Nation so that they may determine whether they wish to adopt an amendment . . ."[60] Such sentiments make strange reading when juxtaposed with those of George Washington during the framing of the Constitution: "If to please the people we offer them what we ourselves disapprove, how can we afterwards defend our work? Let us raise a standard to which the wise and honest can repair."

This deference to the people took other forms during the 1947 discussions. Some agreed that the people should decide the issue, but contended that they had already done so. For example, Representative John Dingell, Michigan Democrat, thought the people had voted against a written limitation on tenure in the elections of 1940 and 1944,[61] while Senator Wiley, on the contrary, insisted that the people had voted for such a limitation by electing the Republican Eightieth Congress in 1946.[62] Still others accepted popular primacy, but denied that the state legislatures comprised "the people"; to Democratic Representatives John Murdock of Arizona, Francis Walter of Pennsylvania, and John Lyle of Texas, only state conventions could adequately express the will of the people on the issue.[63]

Finally, a handful of Senators and Representatives saw the congressional role in the amending process in proper perspective. Some of these indicated in general terms that the question required careful congressional consideration. Sam Hobbs, Alabama Democrat, put it this way: "I do not think our job as Congressmen is to submit everything that is proposed. I think our job as Congressmen is to decide honestly . . . what should be proposed, and not 'pass the buck' on to the States just because we want to be good fellows."[64]

Other members in both houses insisted that congressional endorsement of a proposed amendment carried great weight with the state legislatures. John Folger, North Carolina Democrat, stated: "Mr. Chairman, I cannot agree with the proposition that we are withholding from the people of the United States the opportunity or privilege of speaking upon this matter. But it is natural to assume that the representatives in the State legislatures may conclude that we are in favor of it . . . We set in motion a dangerous proposal."[65] Representative Sabath shared this view. "I venture to say that in many of the States it will be felt that in view that Congress has acted that the legislatures should not deny favorable action on the amendment."[66] Senator Lister Hill, Alabama Democrat, tried to persuade his colleagues to the same position. "If this amendment is submitted . . . it will go to the people with a certain recommendation from the Congress; it carries a congressional imprint which gives it a certain urge, as it were, for approval by the people."[67]

These protests, in House and Senate, were a valuable corrective to the invitation to avoid deliberation and leave the matter to the people. It has already been shown, in the opening of this chapter, how some of the states ratified the Twenty-Second Amendment either without discussion or in a holiday mood. Furthermore, from the beginning through 1964, Congress proposed some thirty amendments to the Constitution, of which the states ratified twenty-four, or 80 per cent. The state legislatures, it seems likely, presume that in adopting proposals for amendment, Congress weighs their merits and expresses a reasoned preference.

CONCLUSIONS

Party pressure was the leading feature of the consideration of the Twenty-Second Amendment in Congress. As on other occasions, the infraction by one party of prevailing constitutional mores, in this case the breaking of the no-third-term custom, provoked a precipitate response from the other. The Republicans, by enshrining the ban on a third term in party platforms, by placing it at the head of their legislative program, and presumably by making it a test of party loyalty, fostered an atmosphere and frame of mind which stifled mature and patient deliberation on the merits and demerits of the proposal. Yet Democrats, especially from the South, lent their support to these efforts, and those who opposed

243

them neglected to make full use of available channels for discussion and protest.

Under these conditions, procedures and attitudes which together might have produced a focused discussion prior to floor debate collapsed. Committee inquiries before 1947 were of slight value, and those in 1947 were little better. Neither 1947 committee published hearings or anything like an adequate report. Partisanship at the floor stage was inevitable, but a searching and reasoned consideration before that stage would have informed and moderated floor discussion. Except in the one-sided 1940 hearings, no effort was made at any stage to bring in outside experts and thereby deepen the members' understanding of the problem.

Most striking of all was the attitude which appeared to govern those who favored amendment. Members on both sides of the aisle saw the task of devising changes in the fundamental laws as in no sense creative but merely that of a clearinghouse. The proposal of a constitutional amendment is doubly serious; it is well nigh irrevocable—witness the struggle to repeal the Eighteenth—and once proposed, its prospects of ratification are bright. This puts to question the wisdom of those in Congress who in 1947 advised their associates to leave the matter to the people. The similarity of this doctrine to the judicial monopoly theory is noteworthy; both tend to produce confusion and discord, and even to endanger the Constitution.

The 1947 episode suggests the possibility of constitutional change by default. No one there gave the matter the full discussion it demanded. Congress heard weighty arguments against the proposed changes without listening to them; it overrode a suggestion to review all the pressing problems of the modern Presidency, including those of disability and the electoral college, matters which, except for a proposed amendment on disability, remained unchanged in 1965. If amendments continue to roll out in the same unthinking manner, the Constitution may become, like some state constitutions, a patchwork of trivial and minute modifications. The Constitution may lose its generality, lucidity, and flexibility and take on what Marshall warned against—the "prolixity of a legal code."[68]

Perhaps the Twenty-Second Amendment was wise, perhaps it was necessary. If so, such wisdom and necessity were more the products of pressure and party contention than the discoveries of deliberate inquiry. This amendment was unique in that the principle it embodied had long been embedded in custom and had behind it generations of reflection and discussion. Congress was putting what had been unwritten law into written law. Yet times had changed since the origins of the custom and the exigencies of the Presidency in the twentieth century might at the least have called for fresh study.

244

Two later incidents will place the above conclusions in perspective. In 1960 Congress proposed the Twenty-Third Amendment, in effect giving the District of Columbia three electoral votes in presidential elections. Here ratification came in a matter of months and almost without public awareness of what was taking place.[69] Congress again had difficulty achieving a focused and thorough probe of the problem and appeared to deem the amending process of slight consequence. What came out as the Twenty-Third Amendment actually began as something totally different,[70] and during the spasmodic and desultory discussion, only one member of either house seemed to perceive the importance of what was happening.[71]

Again, in 1963 as many as a dozen states voted to secure the proposal of a series of "states' rights" amendments of far-reaching implications. This time the Judiciary put the public on notice through Chief Justice Earl Warren. Appealing to lawyers to serve as "watchmen of the Constitution" and calling for a "great national debate" in cases such as this, he warned of misuse of the amending process. Such misuse by a public that was uninformed could, he said, "soon destroy the foundations of the Constitution."[72]

Unless the Congress assumes once again the responsibility imposed on it by Article V of the Constitution, the American people may be saddled with bad amendments. To paraphrase John Marshall: We must never forget that it is a constitution we are amending.[73]

I 2   *Individual Rights and National Insecurity: The Communist Control Act of 1954*

In 1954 Congress rushed to passage its third major anti-subversion law since 1940. This Communist Control Act, unlike that other response to the Communist menace—the Middle East Resolution—proceeded from a Congress that made no pretense of deliberation. As in 1798 and 1862, public alarm coincided with an imminent election. Communist subversion had preceded Communist victories abroad, and some Americans feared a like series of events at home. Here was an invitation to politicians of one party to denounce those of the other as traitors, and for the latter to react with a public display of loyalty. The result was an extreme instance of the breakdown of constitutional responsibility, aided and abetted by ideas of judicial monopoly.

Here was an issue juxtaposing the claims of effective government and of the individual. In forming general policy, Congress inevitably bears down on the legitimate interests or rights of unorganized individuals, interest-groups, and parties. Is the delineation of those rights and the adaptation of their meaning to a complex and closely meshed society the task only of the courts?

At first glance, one might conclude that questions of individual rights at least are suitable only for the Judiciary. Not only John Marshall, but Thomas Jefferson, too, saw the constitutional task of the courts as primarily that of safeguarding individuals from unconstitutional acts of government. Since 1937 the Supreme Court has exercised a mounting influence in the definition of civil rights and liberties. Chief target of its pronouncements has been the states, yet in twelve cases between 1940 and 1965 it has held legislation of Congress to violate rights of the individual.[1] The list on the opposite page shows by five-year periods how those decisions have increased in numbers. Thus half the decisions voiding acts of Congress as violative of individual rights occurred between 1961 and 1965. Critics oriented to judicial monopolism have dissected such decisions in search of the policy preferences of the judges;[2] few have studied the constitutional performance of Congress in passing those offensive acts.

246

Period	Decisions
1941–1945	1
1946–1950	1
1951–1955	2
1956–1960	2
1961–1965	6
Total	12

The fact is that ever since Congress framed the Bill of Rights, it has inevitably met a substantial number of legislative proposals affecting those rights. Its conception of its own responsibility and its machinery for discharging that responsibility can influence not only the burden borne by the justices, but also the vitality of the rights themselves.

This is true not only of rights of free expression, the subject matter of the Communist Control Act, but also of the rights to fair procedure, a matter now so common a concern of the Judiciary. For evidence of this and for perspective on the 1954 controversy, it is pertinent here to touch briefly on an earlier episode in Congress, the handling in 1941 of a House bill to authorize limited wiretapping. This was but one of seventy-one wiretapping bills which came before Congress between 1918 and 1959.[3]

Here science and technology bore directly on the Constitution. Inventors have multiplied and perfected electronic devices for official and private eavesdropping, of which wiretapping is but a particular form. As new modes of communication proliferated they thrust up challenges to privacy, both as an individual right and as a social value, that traditional legal concepts could hardly meet. Should law guarantee the privacy of telephone conversations or, alternatively, authorize certain kinds of official and private wiretapping?

When law enforcement officials, in their zeal to catch criminals, intercepted conversations and used the results as evidence in prosecutions, the question arose whether such action violated the Fourth and Fifth Amendments by effecting unreasonable search and seizure and compulsory self-incrimination.[4] The Supreme Court met the main issue in Olmstead v. United States, a Prohibition case, and by a five to four vote resolved it in favor of government law enforcement.[5] The split on the Court presaged like divisions in Congress. Chief Justice Taft put law enforcement first and read the Fourth Amendment literally as proscribing only actual physical intrusion upon one's "person, the house, his papers or his effects."[6] Justice Brandeis, dissenting, warned that, since the framing of that amendment, "subtler and more far reaching means of invading privacy" had become available and that devices might be perfected for secretly discovering and privately disclosing confidences

247

and even thoughts. Officials should observe the same rules as citizens if society was to preserve "decency, security, and liberty."[7]

Nevertheless Congress sought curbs on wiretapping by legislation and, almost fortuitously, succeeded in the Federal Communications Act of 1934.[8] This act, outlawing interception by wiretapping and disclosure of the results, was liberally interpreted in favor of privacy in the Court's two Nardone decisions.[9]

In 1941 fears about law enforcement and wartime dangers of espionage and sabotage prompted the introduction in the House of two bills to permit officials to tap wires and use the resulting evidence in certain felony prosecutions. A House Judiciary subcommittee held seven days of hearings. The full committee then cut them short and, after holding closed hearings of its own, reported a bill to the House. The House debated the bill for two hours and killed the attempt by 154 to 147. Here, as repeatedly both before and after, Congress decided not to disturb the Act of 1934 as the Court had interpreted it.[10]

Two features of the 1941 episode deserve emphasis. First, the existence of a Court precedent complicated the assessment of responsibility. Insofar as the bill challenged the Fourth and Fifth Amendments, it presented a narrow legal question. The Olmstead decision, however close, could furnish many with a ground for treating the whole constitutional issue as foreclosed. That view would leave only a policy question for Congress to decide.

How one viewed responsibility would of course determine his attitude toward the questions. Those favoring court monopoly would expect a literal adherence to Olmstead. Those adhering to Marshall's view, while following Olmstead insofar as it applied, would pursue a lawyer-like study of the arguments pro and con in Olmstead and later cases and, due to uncertainties, insist on congressional inquiry. Jeffersonians would ask, notwithstanding judicial precedents and reasoning, that Congress canvass the whole matter on its own in the process of legislating. At the hearings, two Midwesterners, Representative Earl Michener, Michigan Republican, and James Barnes, Illinois Democrat, revealed some of the perplexities facing exponents of judicial monopoly in such a controversy. When Osmond K. Fraenkel, the civil liberties lawyer, criticized the majority opinion in Olmstead and observed that Congress should take the reasoning of the dissenters there into account, Michener reminded him that, right or wrong, the Olmstead decision was the law of the land. The following interchange ensued:

Mr. Fraenkel. The law of the land at the moment; yes.
Mr. Michener. And you can't argue or do yourself any good by arguing

248

that we reverse it because this committee is going to accept the law as laid down by the Constitution and the Supreme Court.

Mr. Fraenkel. Of course.

Mr. Michener. And the only question we have before us is whether or not, we should give the [Justice] department that which it asks for in this bill.

Mr. Fraenkel. Well, of course, no committee of Congress nor perhaps any House of Congress can overrule the Supreme Court, but I have never accepted the doctrine nor do I think that.

Mr. Michener. Wait a minute. We are not interested in whether you have accepted the doctrine or whether you agree with the Supreme Court.

Mr. Fraenkel. I appreciate that. I don't believe that the doctrine is sound that because the Supreme Court has held a particular law constitutional that Congress may not for its determination, whether under the changed conditions that law still is constitutional, bearing in mind, of course, what you yourself indicated a short time ago, that the Supreme Court has recently changed its view very much. [sic]

Mr. Michener. Not much since the *Olmstead case*.

Mr. Fraenkel. Oh, yes; the dissenters in that case were Holmes, Brandeis, and Stone, whose dissents in many other cases are now the accepted view of the Supreme Court. . . .

Mr. Barnes. Leaving the constitutional question out, I think what we are primarily interested in is whether it is advisable or necessary.

Mr. Michener. That is right.[11]

Barnes and Michener evidently thought Olmstead left Congress only with the policy question, whether wiretapping was desirable and necessary. Fraenkel wanted a Marshallian scrutiny of the entire court record to establish what was suitable in 1941, and another hearing witness took a similar line.[12] A Kentucky Republican, John Robsion, wanted Congress to take an even broader look at the question. Wiretapping, as practiced in Russia and Germany, was an important tool for maintaining totalitarianism, and, earlier, invasions of privacy by the British had helped bring on the American Revolution.[13] In short, the bill raised important and complex questions, narrow and broad, for Congress to resolve, and the thoroughness of inquiry might well depend on the prevailing view of congressional duty.

A second feature of this episode is significant; the subcommittee's hearings on the bill demonstrated advantages and hazards associated with hearings in cases of individual rights. Among the twenty-seven witnesses who spoke, principally against the bill, were several from special interest groups on whom the bill would impinge with a particular severity. J. G. Luhrsen, for the Railway Labor Executives Association, showed how wiretapping would jeopardize safe transportation: "While tapping in on any wire we would have to use the wires for movements of trains, and a very, very important thing today for national defense is the expeditious and safe movement of trains for commodities . . . for defense and . . . for moving troops or whatever . . ." T. Edwin Quisenberry described the importance of the telephone in the conduct of business: "It is utterly impossible for me . . . to keep alive the exchange of views where I act as an intermediary, without the use of free, uninterrupted, and private conversation." Labor, too, had a spokesman in Bjorne Halling, of the CIO Maritime Committee; said he, "We have had instances, in the case of unions, before where wires have been tapped, and we know that in numerous instances the people that have been engaged in wire tapping have later obtained positions with the employers of labor, and that the information they may have gathered through the wire tapping has been used for the benefit of the employers . . . We believe that if wire tapping is engaged in . . . that you create an atmosphere of distrust on a national scale, both between labor and employers and between individuals."[14]

Hearings, properly conducted, afford such groups, as well as the executive branch, an invaluable channel for claiming rights. Here they helped Congress not only measure the political backing, but also foresee the constitutional effects of the proposed bill.

Yet two features of the committee stage marred the 1941 proceedings. The hearings began in a leisurely fashion, only to be abruptly terminated by the full committee with no chance for the subcommittee to digest the results and file a report. After its closed hearings with Attorney General Robert H. Jackson and Chairman James Fly of the Federal Communications Commission, the full committee filed a one-and-a-quarter-page majority report. Neither the committee majority nor the one-third minority gave the House the benefit of reasoned constitutional argument on the bill.

As electronics advanced and experience accumulated, Congress increasingly faced the need of securing expert advice on this intricate and many-sided subject. Yet not for a decade and a half did it provide itself with the instrument for securing that advice. Nevertheless in 1941 Congress took a serious, if hasty, look at the Bill of Rights.

In 1954, when the Communist Control Act posed a serious challenge to freedom of expression, the look was little more than a passing glance. This was the period when McCarthyism was at its height. Communist successes in Korea and Indo-China had alarmed the electorate and prepared it for political extremism. In February, Senator McCarthy had denounced the Democrats as the "party of communism, betrayal and treason," and referred to its tenure as "twenty years of treason."[15] The Republicans had come to power in January 1953 after promising to clean out the Communists infesting the government. In the second session of this Republican-controlled Congress a House committee was studying no fewer than twenty-two bills to outlaw the Communist party.

Yet none of these bills came to the floor. The committee killed them largely because of the opposition of J. Edgar Hoover and Attorney General Herbert Brownell. Hoover maintained that outlawing the party would drive it underground and make his work of detection more difficult.[16] Brownell contended that such a law would void the registration provisions of the McCarran Internal Security Act of 1950, since the operation of the two acts in combination would violate the self-incrimination guarantee of the Fifth Amendment.[17] It seemed likely that the new bill would hinder rather than supplement the execution of the McCarran Act and its predecessor, the Smith Act of 1940.

Thus, at the beginning of August, with adjournment only three weeks away, and election three months away, there seemed small chance that Congress would discuss, much less pass, legislation of this sort. Yet public excitement and their own election misgivings were too great for a group of liberal democrats in the Senate, led by Senator Hubert H. Humphrey of Minnesota. On the twelfth, Humphrey moved an amendment to a pending bill for the purpose of outlawing the Communist party and making membership a criminal offense. In the ensuing debate, he spelled out his motives in this way:

> I am tired of reading headlines about being "soft" toward communism. I am tired of reading headlines about being a leftist, and about others being leftists. I am tired of having people play the Communist issue as though it were a great overture which has lasted for years. I want to come to grips with the Communist issue.[18]

Observers immediately recognized the amendment as a political maneuver,[19] and the Eisenhower Administration declared against it. In an election year, however, few members of Congress could afford to risk opposing it. Once the measure had reached the floor, congressional passage was almost inevitable.

Although it took but nine days, August 11–19, for Congress to put the act together, the process was so complex as to require detailed clarification here. It demonstrates how difficult it is under such conditions for Congress to deliberate in a spirit of moderation. To begin with, a subcommittee of the House Judiciary Committee had held extensive hearings on a host of bills proposing outlawry. It had taken testimony on

251

ten separate days during the spring, and, significantly, the parent committee had reported no bill to the House.

On July 6, Senator John M. Butler, Maryland Republican, introduced a bill to deal with Communist-infiltrated labor unions. This was an original bill from the Judiciary Committee and would amend the Subversive Activities Control Act, a part of the Internal Security Act of 1950.[20] Its aim was to identify such unions, which could then be denied the services of the National Labor Relations Board and incur the penalties of the 1950 Act. The new category, "Communist-infiltrated," augmented the already existing categories of the 1950 Act, "Communist action," and "Communist front." Although a Senate Judiciary subcommittee had held two days of hearings on Communist-dominated unions in January and February, no hearings were held directly on Butler's bill or for that matter on a similar bill which the House Unamerican Activities Committee reported August 9.

After debating the Butler bill August 11, the Senate returned to the matter on the twelfth, devoting its opening hour to an amendment proposed by Senator Warren G. Magnuson, Washington Democrat. This was a promising but belated proposal to create a presidential commission to study security practices and conditions in business and government and to recommend legislation and administrative procedures in the light of the existing external and internal danger to national security. At the least, this would have provided a more auspicious forum for exploring crucial constitutional questions as raised by security affairs, and, if passed, might have averted the more extreme proposals to come. It lost, however, by a vote of 31 to 57. The Senate passed, by 87 to 1, an amendment establishing a presumption of innocence for labor organizations whose policies had been anti-Communist.

At this point, Humphrey introduced his amendment. The Senate adopted, with one dissenting vote, an amendment by Senator Price Daniel, Texas Democrat, to combine the Butler and Humphrey proposals in one bill, and by voice vote an amendment by Senator John Sherman Cooper, Kentucky Republican, to stipulate action for Communist purposes as an identifying criterion for Communists, whom the Humphrey bill made subject to criminal penalties. The Humphrey-Butler bill went through by 85 to 0.

Before the House took up the bill, its Republican leaders met over the weekend with Administration officials in an effort to moderate the terms of this bill. The resulting measure omitted the criminal provisions of the Humphrey amendment and instead denied the party any rights, privileges, or immunities previously granted by federal, state, or local laws. On the sixteenth, the House debated this bill for forty minutes and passed it by 305 to 2. On the same day and the next, the Senate took up

252

the House bill, adding certain amendments clarifying the labor provisions and adopting another Humphrey amendment by the close vote of 41 to 39. This again made willful membership in the party a felony, but added fourteen criteria for determining membership. The Senate then adopted the House amendments as amended with but one "nay" vote.

On the seventeenth, the bill was returned to the House, and that body instructed its conferees to accept the Senate position that individual membership should be a felony. Yet despite agreement by both houses that membership should be pronounced criminal, the Conference Committee, meeting on August 18, omitted this provision, preferring instead to subject members, as determined by the fourteen criteria, to the penalties of the 1950 Act. On the nineteenth, one day before final adjournment, Congress passed the conference report, in the Senate by 79 to 0, and in the House by 265 to 2. President Eisenhower signed it into law on August 24.

This act, which omitted a provision for termination, had three principal parts. First, it declared the Communist party no party at all, but an instrumentality of a conspiracy to overthrow the government, the "agency of a hostile foreign power," and a "clear present and continuing danger" to national security.[21] Hence, the party was deprived of legal standing under all statutes, excepting only the Internal Security Act. Second, it declared that members, as determined according to listed criteria, were subject to the penalties of that act. Finally, it made it illegal for a member of a Communist organization to hold office or employment with any labor organization or represent any employer in proceedings under the National Labor Relations Act, denied standing before the National Labor Relations Board of "Communist-infiltrated" organizations, and authorized the Subversive Activities Control Board to determine what organizations were Communist-infiltrated.

Writing in the *New York Times* immediately after passage, Arthur Krock asserted, "In its final form the anti-Communist measure . . . is mainly a philippic."[22] The act would remain primarily a philippic. The Justice Department by 1965 had evidently undertaken prosecutions only under the provision concerning Communist-infiltrated organizations.[23] Only in the states did overt enforcement of other provisions produce litigation. State courts evidently treated the act as the product of genuine deliberation.[24]

Party officers carried one of the state cases to the Supreme Court, which in 1961 gave its decision in Communist Party *v.* Catherwood.[25] The difficulties which faced the Court had been predicted during the passage of the bill by Senator Wayne Morse of Oregon: "When I think of the legislative record that has been made on the conference report today I am glad that I am not a member of a court which will have to determine what was the legislative intent of the bill."[26] New York state had held that under the 1954 Act the party had lost its legal right to register and secure benefits provided under the state unemployment insurance act. The effect was to raise the unemployment tax from about 1 per cent to about 3 per cent under federal statute. The state court construed the act, in depriving the party of legal "rights, privileges, and immunities attendant upon legal bodies created under the jurisdiction of the laws of the United States or any political subdivision . . ." as extending to privileges under the unemployment insurance system. The party petitioned for Supreme Court review, contending, among other things, that the 1954 provision violated the due process, bill of attainder, and ex post facto clauses.

Speaking for a unanimous Court, Justice Harlan explained that the Court avoided constitutional questions where possible and went on to construe the act in limited terms: "Apart from unrevealing random remarks during the course of debate in the two Houses, there is no legislative history which in any way serves to give content to the vague terminology of §3 of the Communist Control Act. The statute contains no definition, and neither committee reports nor authoritative spokesmen attempt to give any definition, of the clause . . ."[27] From a scrutiny of federal tax policy and legislation the Court concluded that Congress had not intended this act to effect the exclusion of the party from the state unemployment system.

Despite the effort to outlaw it, the party continued to exist. J. Edgar Hoover's remarks about a 1959 party convention gave evidence of this.[28]

In short, the Communist Control Act, in several of its provisions, remained a dead letter. Why? First, it failed to provide the government with any new and effective tools for combatting subversion. Administrations preferred to rely on the Smith and Internal Security Acts. Second, public anxiety over internal Communism moderated. Third, the Administration could hardly take the act seriously in view of the conditions of its passage. This reluctance to press enforcement helps explain why so few tests of the act have reached the Supreme Court.

Finally, the manner in which Congress considered the bill suggests that it never intended the act to be enforced, but rather meant to register a formal pronouncement against internal Communism. Senator Thomas C. Hennings, Jr., Missouri Democrat, called it no more than a "denunciation or disapproval of communism and its adherents."[29]

CONSTITUTIONAL QUESTIONS

In spite of the near unanimity of support, the 1954 Act presented serious constitutional questions, narrow and broad. The three constitutional clauses cited by the party in the Catherwood case were only briefly referred to. Congress gave somewhat more attention to issues under the First Amendment: thus, did the bill penalize individuals for membership in a political party? Did it proscribe a political party? Did it punish individuals for their political thoughts and beliefs?

And, more broadly, how far may Congress go in guarding against internal subversion without violating individual liberties essential to constitutional democracy? Narrowly interpreted, the First Amendment might permit legislation which nevertheless contravened the spirit of American democracy. These were grave and complex issues that for years had arisen over programs for loyalty and security and deserved the best thought and insight the country could muster for their resolution.

That such a result was not forthcoming here was partly due to the expectation of judicial review. Participants expected their work to go to the courts and, accordingly, added a separability clause so as to protect parts of the bill not directly affected by an adverse decision. Some members went so far as to suggest that even though Congress might have drafted the bill in slipshod fashion, the Court would remedy defects. Representative Jacob K. Javits, New York Republican, declared, "It has already been pointed out that the bill is loosely drawn and has many defects and raises many serious legal questions, and so it does. But method and implementation can be worked out in the courts."[30] Not only were the courts to fill their normal role, they were also to become a bill-drafting agency.

COURSE OF THE DISCUSSION

House Hearings. In the peremptory floor debate in 1954 Congress might have drawn, as the House did in 1941, on prior hearings. No committee of either house held hearings directly on the bill in its final form, but Subcommittee Number 1 of the House Judiciary Committee held hearings on related bills in the spring of 1954, reporting none of them. A wide range of witnesses appeared;[31] their testimony developed systematically many of the constitutional issues raised in the August debates. Yet despite their high quality, these hearings went almost unheeded in the floor discussion.

Nevertheless, these hearings had importance, since several of the participants later spoke in the debates. Furthermore, two contrasting statements on the constitutionality of outlawing the Communist party— by Attorney General Herbert Brownell, Jr., and Justice Michael Musmanno of the Pensylvania Supreme Court— were inserted in the *Record* in August.

One view on the constitutionality of outlawing the party expressed in the hearings was that it could not be done directly. For example, Representative Francis E. Walter, Pennsylvania Democrat, declared that it was "utterly impossible to outlaw the Communist Party as such"[32] and, therefore, introduced a bill making membership in any organization "advocating the establishment of totalitarian dictatorship" a criminal offense.[33]

Others insisted that the Communist party was no party at all but rather a conspiracy using the name of party. Thus membership in such a conspiracy could be punished as a felony. Representative Martin Dies, Texas Democrat, stated this view in the hearings and later introduced a bill to implement it. In a revealing aside, Dies indicated that he was less interested in truly enforceable legislation than in having Congress make a "declaration to the world that the Communist conspiracy is a criminal, treasonable movement."[34]

The author of the Dies bill, Justice Musmanno, argued for its constitutionality using both specific judicial precedent and vague, but grandly-worded statements. For Court guidance he drew on a 1951 statement by Chief Justice Vinson in Dennis v. United States: "We reject any principle of governmental helplessness in the face of preparation for revolution, which principle, carried to its logical conclusion, must lead to anarchy. No one could conceive that it is not within the power of Congress to prohibit acts intended to overthrow the Government by force and violence."[35]

Other witnesses, however, argued that the proposed legislation was unconstitutional. Norman Thomas, representing the American Civil Liberties Union, said that the party was both a true party and a conspiracy. As long as it had a party character, the Constitution protected it from congressional interference. Spokesmen of the National Lawyers Guild contended that the proposed bills violated First Amendment guarantees of free speech and assembly, constituted bills of attainder, and denied due process of law to the Communist party by depriving it of property without a trial.

Attorney General Brownell made the most influential statement in opposition to the bills. His principal attack took the ground that the bills would nullify the registration provisions of the Internal Security Act and hence undermine the entire anti-Communist program of the government. But he also questioned the constitutionality of the whole enterprise. Reminding the subcommittee of the decision in Wieman v. Updegraff,[36] he concluded that "If the legislation were so drawn that mere membership were declared to be illegal, on the background of a legislative finding which was to be conclusive and not reviewable by the courts, we have doubts that the court would sustain it."[37]

During testimony, members of the subcommittee[38] formulated their

256

own opinions. DeWitt S. Hyde, Maryland Republican, asked rhetorically: "Do we not possibly under those circumstances run into the danger of making a criminal of someone who may have no connection with, and no thought of a conspiracy or attempt to overthrow this Government, but who may have political ideas or theories which they want to advance which are repugnant to our way of free government but which, nevertheless, we must permit to exist in the market place of thought, so to speak?"[39] Perhaps it was views like this which led the Judiciary Committee to withhold recommendations for legislation.

Senate Debate. When the Senate first took up and debated the Humphrey amendment, on August 12, only one Senator raised a serious constitutional objection, an objection which the Senate met by adopting his amendment. Senator Humphrey and his twenty co-sponsors[40] seemed indifferent to constitutional issues. As Senator Humphrey put it: "The purpose of this amendment is to 'come clean.' I, for one, am growing sick and tired of having bill after bill brought to the Congress that does not reflect a willingness and the courage to go to the center of the problem."[41] Senator Herbert H. Lehman of New York stressed that "This substitute is an honest and undisguised frontal attack on the very heart of the problem. It avoids all pussyfooting. It is frank and undisguised in its nature."[42]

Senator Butler immediately observed that "The Senator from Minnesota must know that there is much doubt about the constitutionality of the amendment in the nature of a substitute which he has offered."[43] But Butler's concern was temporary, and as soon as the Senate combined his and Humphrey's bills into one, he dropped his rather general constitutional objections.

Butler's objection was immediately answered by Senator Price Daniel, Texas Democrat. He added a separability clause to his amendment combining the two bills and told Butler that this clause "would take care of that fear."[44]

Several members now voiced general statements defending the constitutionality of the bill. Senator Mike Mansfield, Montana Democrat, insisted that "Outlawing the Communist Party would not be a violation of the fundamental right of people in the United States to organize and function through a political party as the Communist Party is not a legitimate political organization . . ."[45] Senator Daniel, who had served several terms as Attorney General of Texas, and Senator Morse declared that the bill was constitutional but failed to document their positions. Senator George A. Smathers, Florida Democrat, added additional proof in pointing out that the Communist party had been outlawed in the United States from 1919 to 1924, that it was currently outlawed in from thirteen to fifteen states, and that no court had held these laws unconstitutional. Furthermore, "they must be constitutional if they help the American people defend themselves."[46]

The one serious constitutional objection to the Humphrey substitute was articulated by John Sherman Cooper, Kentucky Republican:

> I believe I am correct in saying that heretofore the Congress and the courts have proceeded upon the theory that what a man says—within certain limitations of public policy determined by the courts—his right of free speech and of free expression is a right protected by the first amendment to the Constitution.
>
> One does not speak, does not express himself without thought, without thinking. The courts have certainly held that what a man thinks is protected; is not a subject of limitation, of penalty, or conviction by a court . . . Thinking, adherence to belief, has never been a crime unless translated into action.[47]

Cooper, therefore, introduced an amendment embodying the concept that only action is punishable, and the Senate adopted it by voice vote. In Senator Humphrey's opinion, the overt act of joining the Communist party was in itself punishable action, but he agreed to accept Cooper's amendment as a further clarification of the legislative intent.

The Senate took up the bill on two further occasions, once on August 16 and 17, when it insisted on retaining the criminal penalties for membership, and again on August 19, when it accepted unanimously the conference report eliminating those penalties. The only Senator to raise constitutional objections on either occasion was the Tennesseean, Estes Kefauver, who had missed the debate on August 12. Kefauver's objections forced Senators Humphrey, Morse, and Hennings to offer a more reasoned constitutional defense.

Kefauver's first objection was that the bill outlawed the Communist party, and he disliked "the precedent of outlawing a particular group. Perhaps next year Congress will not like some other group . . . In the history of our Nation, has any group ever been outlawed or condemned as illegal by legislative enactment?"[48] In discussing the final conference report, Kefauver indicated that he thought this outlawry section "might very well be interpreted to mean that if the Department of Justice wished to prosecute the Farmer-Labor Party, the Republican Party, the Democratic Party, or the Farmers' Union it could do so under this language."[49]

His second main objection took the First Amendment. "Under the Senate bill, I felt that we would be abandoning sound ideas of freedom of speech, freedom of thought, and freedom of the press, which we have cherished in this Nation for so long, and would be following, because of a wave of hysteria, a procedure to prosecute, to outlaw, and to punish persons for their opinions and beliefs, whether they had done anything to carry them out or not."[50]

These attacks stung Humphrey into a constitutional defense of the criminal provisions of his amendment. First, he quoted Justice Jackson's separate opinion in the 1950 Douds case to support his contention that Congress could hold each member of the Communist party responsible for the goals and means of the party. "There is certainly sufficient evidence that all members owe allegiance to every detail of the Communist Party program and have assumed a duty actively to help execute it, so that Congress could, on familiar conspiracy principles, charge each member with responsibility for the goals and means of the Party."[51] Second, he contended that the conspiratorial nature of the goals and means of the party had been established. Third, the Dennis case made it clear that Congress had the power to prohibit acts intended to overthrow the government by force and violence. Therefore, Congress had the power to punish individuals for the act of joining the Communist party.

Senator Hennings added a different twist to the argument for constitutionality. The bill, by making membership a crime, would take Communists out of the hands of the Subversive Activities Control Board and place them in a court of law where they would have the benefit of a jury trial and other procedural safeguards. "Everyone—Communist or non-Communist, Fascist or non-Fascist—is entitled to his day in court."[52]

Senator Morse summed up the arguments for the constitutionality of the bill and coupled his summation with an attack on the "sophomoric nonsense" uttered by Senator Kefauver. Morse asserted that the Supreme Court would never declare the Communist party to be a political party. "I think I can hear the court say, 'It does not make any difference what label the conspirators pin on their conspiracy. We will pierce the label and look at the nature of the acts which create the conspiracy.' What is one of those acts? The joining of the party by the individual."[53] With regard to the First Amendment, Senator Morse said that "It is not a question of what a man thinks, Mr. President. It is a question of implementing his thoughts. If a man thinks that the United States Government ought to be destroyed by the tactics of the Communists . . . and he executes that thought by joining a conspiracy to accomplish that purpose, that is the time to get him."[54]

Under conditions of stress, the Senate seemed incapable in all three of its debates of dealing seriously and thoroughly with the constitutional questions.

House Debate. Attention to such questions was even more scant in the House. Most Representatives seemed to feel that the bill which the Administration had approved in the weekend consultations and which the House took up on August 16 was a necessary and proper measure against the Communists. As Chauncey W. Reed, Illinois Republican, put it: "Let us take the final step, the one necessary step to squelch once and for all the international menace of godless communism. Let us deny to the Communist Party and its subsidiary organizations the legal protection afforded by the very laws they seek to destroy."[55] Once again the feeling was expressed that this bill amounted to nothing more than an assertion of opposition to Communism and the Communists. Representative Barratt O'Hara, Illinois Democrat, stated this view: "As I see it, and as the issue is here presented on voting for this bill, imperfectly drawn though it be and of uncertain legal validity, we are putting the Congress of the United States definitely on record against communism both openly organized and subversively operated . . . The issue then is one of confession of faith."[56]

Only three Representatives expressed the belief that the bill was unconstitutional. The New Yorker Emanuel Celler, ranking Democrat on the Judiciary Committee, warned against outlawing a political party and presented a striking conception of his own responsibility: "If we can outlaw the Communist Party, there is no reason why, if the Republicans are in control, they could not outlaw the Democratic Party. And, vice versa . . . I don't like that part of the bill which outlaws the party. It is palpably unconstitutional . . . Much as I dislike some portions of the bill, however, I favor other portions. On balance the evil is outweighted by the good. I shall vote for the bill."[57]

Usher L. Burdick, North Dakota Republican, opposed the bill as an infringement of free speech. His claim was that the bill penalized what men thought, although he never explained exactly how the bill accomplished this forbidden purpose.[58]

Abraham J. Multer, New York Democrat, hurled a series of charges against the bill in explaining his opposition. "The bill to outlaw the Communist Party violates every principle of good government. Aside from being a bill of attainder and an ex post facto law, it denies not only free speech but free thought; it denies the right of assembly and the right of petition for redress of wrongs. It is a completely totalitarian technique."[59] But these charges, too, went unexplained.

Only one Representative offered reasoned constitutional arguments in support of the bill. Thomas J. Dodd, Connecticut Democrat, cited the many penalties and restrictions which Congress had already imposed upon members of the Communist party, and he noted that in the Douds case the Supreme Court had admitted that membership in the party was sufficient cause to deny privileges and rights under the National Labor Relations Act. If the Communist party was a legal political institution "standing on all fours with our traditional political parties," then "none of the above steps should have been taken against the members of the Communist Party."[60]

Once again, the legislators had approached without penetrating basic constitutional questions.

Discussion Evaluated. By neglecting the earlier House hearings and succumbing to the steamroller, both houses failed genuinely to weigh the constitutional arguments. No one tried to probe them in depth. Members repeated words like "First Amendment," "bill of attainder," "free speech," "national self-protection," "conspiracy," with no thorough grasp of what they were saying. Debate was sporadic and documentation slight. Senator Kefauver, it is true, prodded Senator Humphrey into elaborating a constitutional basis for the bill, but in the House a similar exchange of views never took place, despite the impassioned outbursts of Representatives Burdick and Multer.

By every test, the debate never achieved genuine detachment. The voting gives a clear clue to this. No Senators voted against the bill in its final form. In the House, Burdick and Multer convinced no one, for all other votes supported the bill. As Representative Charles A. Halleck, Indiana Republican and House majority leader, stated, "I say, let us pass this overwhelmingly so that the people of the world and of the country shall know what we think about the Communist Party."[61] The entire Congress responded and buried the constitutional questions without even a decent funeral. All but five of the thirteen roll calls in the two houses produced unanimity or near-unanimity; the five were on issues other than passage and exhibited genuine division—whether along lines of policy orientation or of party allegiance.[62] Seldom, if at all, therefore, did the members divide according to constitutional conviction.

PARTICIPANTS

As usual, lawyers predominated. Although their quota in the Senate here sank to 58 per cent and in the House stood at 57 per cent, their monopoly of discussion was almost total.[63] Members who spoke on the point were unanimous in praise of lawyers. Representative Thomas A. Jenkins, Ohio Republican, had no doubt that lawyers should decide constitutional questions and then enlighten the House as a whole: "I wish to say that now it seems that practically all of the leading lawyers on the Committee on the Judiciary have agreed on what should be done with reference to curtailing the activities of the Communists, I wish to approve their action and shall vote with them."[64] Senator William F. Knowland, California Republican, apologized for debating constitutionality as a non-lawyer.[65] On the other hand, for what it is worth, none of the first four listed sponsors of the Humphrey bill was a lawyer; and three, Senators Humphrey, Paul Douglas, Illinois Democrat, and Mansfield were social scientists.

For such an important bill, the number of participants who seriously attended to the constitutional arguments was minute. Senators Cooper and Humphrey and Representative Dodd at times rose to a high level of performance. But most had failed to consult any expert sources. Many of the debaters possessed a passing familiarity with Dennis and Douds, but precise constitutional knowledge went little further. Unfortunately those opposing the bill showed more courage than wisdom. Had they relied more fully on the hearings testimony of the American Civil Liberties Union and others, they would have been more convincing. Actually, the House had printed copies of the extensive hearings testimony on both sides of the question, but most members had forgotten that such hearings had even taken place.

In short, the lawyers, while holding the floor, neglected two of their most useful functions—insisting on fair procedure and constantly injecting precise legal rules and reasoning, as well as constitutional principles, into the debates.

One should also mention, however, the constitutional leadership of several members. Once again, the Border States produced an effort to moderate the severity of the bill. This effort was led by the Kentuckian John Sherman Cooper, fifty-three, who had studied at Yale and the Harvard Law School, joined a law firm, and served two years in the Kentucky House, eight years on the state bench, and four years in the Senate, as well as rendering military and diplomatic service.

The constitutional defense of the bill during its final phases in the Senate resulted from the solitary pressure of Senator Estes Kefauver of Tennessee. Kefauver, fifty-one, had studied law at Yale, served briefly in state office, and spent fifteen years in Congress, ten in the House and five in the Senate, serving on judiciary committees in both houses.

In the House, where effective protest encounters greater obstacles, two members spoke out. Representative Multer, fifty-three, had studied at City College and Brooklyn Law School in New York City, served as legal counsel to city and state officials, and spent eight years in the House. His Republican co-protestant, Representative Burdick, seventy-five, had studied law at the University of Minnesota, taught school, farmed and held state offices in North Dakota, and served in the House sixteen years. All these men had resisted the tide in behalf of principle.

MODE

The procedure used in passing the Communist Control Act was a caricature of normal Senate and House procedure. No committee held hearings directly on the question at issue. The House Judiciary Sub-committee hearings from the spring before were on the same topic but the committee made no report. Even Senator Butler's bill lacked direct prior scrutiny of hearings.

Once the issue reached the floor, procedure broke down. In the Senate, the drive for adjournment overcame the tradition of unlimited debate. Instead the Senate on August 12 debated only a few hours before rushing the bill through by a unanimous vote. When the bill returned to the Senate on August 16, a unanimous consent agreement limited general debate to three hours, with an added half hour for each amendment. But debate was postponed to the next day and then only two hours were actually used.

House discussion was even less adequate. The initial debate on August 16 was limited to forty minutes, through a suspension of the rules. Amendments were ruled out. This enabled the House to pass the bill 305 to 2 at the end of the allotted time. When the House voted 208 to 100 to concur in the Senate amendments, only fifteen minutes of debate, none of it constitutional, preceded this vote. The House approved the conference report without further debate.

The Senate at least agreed on its procedure by unanimous consent. The House neglected even this elementary canon of fairness. Representative Dodd complained, "There has been ample time in the past several months for this House to consider this grave problem with adequate provision for debate and deliberation . . . Yet once again, we are to be allowed only 40 minutes to discuss legislation which involves serious constitutional questions. This is bad legislative procedure."[66]

Furthermore, neither house received advance notice of constitutional issues. Senator Humphrey's original amendment was a surprise to most of his colleagues. Three days later the House took up the measure, but again with no advance notice. The wording of the measure which reached the floor was decided in weekend conferences, and the rank and file of members heard it for the first time on Monday morning, August 16. Indeed, one-third of the Representatives purportedly had gone home to plan their fall campaigns, since the leaders had assured them that no important business remained.[67]

Less than an hour in the House and five hours in the Senate can hardly be called adequate, especially in the absence of committee preparations. What time there was was divided fairly; but a fair division means little if the participants are either unwilling or unprepared to say anything significant.

Most important, the conditions surrounding the introduction and passage of the act made deliberation impossible. Representative Multer pointed out some of these shortcomings in the form of questions, which called for affirmative answers. "Mr. Speaker, do I understand that there

263

is no printed or typewritten copy of the bill for the membership other than the one at the desk in the exact form it was read? . . . Mr. Speaker, do I understand that we have neither hearings on this bill nor a printed report on the bill?"[68]

Senator Kefauver likewise complained of a lack of printed material, this time containing the exact wording of a series of amendments by Senator Butler. "I am sure that it will be impossible to legislate intelligently on this measure at this time, when we do not have available to us copies of the House version of the bill or copies of the amendments proposed by the Senator from Maryland to the amendments of the House."[69] Later in the House debate, Representative Multer again voiced his complaint. "I doubt whether as many as three Members of this House have had an opportunity to read the mimeographed copy of what we are told is the bill except for 'minor changes.' "[70] Even majority leader Halleck reflected on the House procedure in defending it. "We did the best we could to get the information here for you with these mimeographed copies."[71]

The lack of committee hearings on this proposal was also a serious breach of fair procedure. Members depend on such hearings and the reports from the committees conducting the hearings to give them a basis for forming their own judgment. Despite Representative Halleck's vague claim that "It has all been before committees,"[72] none of it, in this specific wording, had been before a committee. As Representative Celler of the House Judiciary Committee put it: "The Judiciary Committee never saw the instant bill. It was cooked up over the weekend . . . The Committee on the Judiciary tabled similar bills some time ago and reported a bill providing for a commission to make adequate study of this very difficult and cumbersome problem. Now, we are, in a way, buying a pig in a poke. What does this bill really entail? Nobody really knows."[73]

Finally, the public vote to pass the bill was little more than generalized endorsement of anti-Communism. No constitutional question was ever clearly defined, and few of the members in either house could have taken constitutional matters into account in casting final votes.

ATTITUDES

If the heat of the contest consumed procedural barriers, it also melted down traditional concepts of responsibility. A few members of Congress, mainly the Border State Senator Cooper and the Tennessee Senator Kefauver, professed a weighty personal responsibility for constitutional questions.[74] A few thought that constitutional issues might have some importance but not enough to occasion a negative vote.[75] Most appeared to regard constitutional questions as of minor significance in Congress,[76] and, as already shown, Representative Celler expounded a quantitative conception of a member's responsibility.

How could the members justify this attitude? Evidently by assuming that if Congress made constitutional errors, the Supreme Court stood ready to correct them. Thus, no member of either house was moved to assert a full tripartite theory of responsibility. Instead, those who expressed themselves endorsed judicial monopoly. Congress could act as it pleased with regard to constitutional questions because only the Court could deal with them. Representative Javits went so far as to expect the courts to tighten up the language of the bill. Senators Mansfield and Knowland and Representative John D. Dingell, Michigan Republican, all non-lawyers, expressed more conventional judicial monopoly ideas. Mansfield declared: "It is my opinion that, so far as the constitutionality of any law is concerned, it is a question for the Supreme Court of the United States to decide."[77] Knowland admitted that there was a difference of opinion among "the legal lights" as to the constitutionality of the bill: "No one will know the answer to that question until the Supreme Court of the United States speaks the final word . . . No one can look into a crystal ball and know what the ultimate decision in that regard may be."[78] Dingell would resolve any fears about the constitutionality of the bill "by placing my trust in court decisions which would rectify any error which the Congress might make."[79]

The reiteration and acceptance of such ideas probably intensified congressional neglect of constitutional questions. Since 1798, Americans had been aware that hysteria, born of crisis, could drive Congress to precipitate action. Yet in debating the Sedition Act and the Oath of Office Acts, members had made genuine efforts to plumb constitutionality. The 1798 debates gave the electorate some basis for judging the constitutional positions of the rival parties and for rejecting in 1800 Federalists in favor of Jeffersonians. In 1954 the illusion of early Court review and decision gave a pretext for many to sidestep responsibility with the effect of leaving the public in the dark both on the existence of a constitutional issue and on the merits of the opposing arguments and political forces. Judicial monopoly fostered doubtful legislation and public ignorance.

CONCLUSIONS

The Communist Control Act of 1954 was the fruit of alarm and partisan strife. The members of Congress were borne along by a tidal wave of public apprehension about external and internal Communism. This time, unlike 1798 and 1862, the whole nation felt the current, for public opinion polls, according to a floor statement of Representative

265

Dies, showed that 98 per cent of those interviewed favored outlawing the party.[80] Representatives Burdick and Multer castigated Congress for giving in to the prevailing public mood. Said Burdick: "Just what the purpose of this bill is, with this amendment in it, is not clear, unless it is a political sop to show the people that we have buckled up our armor and gone out barehanded and dispatched the Communists' dragon. It may win votes, but, in the long run, it will reflect upon our good sense."[81] Multer agreed, calling the House action "born of fear that you cannot prove you are a 100 percent American."[82]

With an election just ahead, the public mood prompted the parties to jockey for advantage. The Democrats openly displayed their fears that the Republicans would make gains in the November balloting by virtue of the Communist-in-government issue; hence, their effort to prove to the electorate that they, the Democrats, were more militantly anti-Communist than their opponents. A remark of Senator Morse near the end of the debates caught this attitude with great accuracy: "We shall have a very interesting campaign this fall, let me assure my colleagues, any time the Republican smear artists wish to raise the Communist issue. The record is perfectly clear as to who is responsible for the fact that the Humphrey amendment is not going on the statute books as it passed the Senate of the United States."[83] Conceivably the temptation to irresponsible action gained strength from the party disunity of an off-year election. The desire of the whole party to win the Presidency constitutes a counter-force to extremist and particularist tendencies and furnishes the national ticket with leverage for disciplining renegades. These conditions were absent in 1954 and, as the next chapter will show, would be absent again in 1958.

This was ill-considered legislation. By dodging constitutional inquiry Congress transferred that task to the Executive, which was to leave most of the act unenforced, and to the Supreme Court. Notwithstanding the scant guidance which Congress gave the justices, they did not reach the constitutional questions, preferring to construe the act in narrow terms. Perhaps constitutionality will never come to judgment. In effect this act was an anti-Communist sense resolution, doing for internal Communism in 1954 what the Middle East Resolution did for external Communism in 1957. The difference was that here, where the rights of American citizens were in question, Congress gave far less attention to constitutional questions than in the handling of the Middle East Resolution.

This brief study of the wiretapping bill of 1941 and the more extensive study of the Communist Control Act of 1954 suggest several conclusions concerning the responsibility of Congress for dealing with individual rights. In 1941 the House succeeded in going behind policy demands and exploring constitutional rules and principles in the light of prevailing

266

conditions and the exigencies of government. Wiretapping called for fuller expert knowledge than Congress then could muster, yet evidence was sufficient to head off passage. In 1954 Congress succumbed to public alarm and pressures, ignored its own earlier hearings, and rushed into action.

Attitudes, participants, and procedures all contributed to the results. Whatever its professions, Congress in 1941 was acting in a tripartite manner; in 1954 reiteration of court monopoly made it possible for members to shift their burden to others. Lawyers predominated in both episodes, in shaping procedure and discussing legal aspects of constitutional issues, yet legalism threatened neglect of broad constitutional questions in 1941 and promoted it in 1954. Finally, both incidents suggest the great value of committee hearings, executive sessions, and reports in matters affecting individual rights. Hearings, carefully planned and fairly conducted, offer a promising way of eliciting opinions and arguments from those whom decisions by Congress will affect directly and provide a forum more secluded and more leisurely in pace than the floor for members of Congress themselves to set out their arguments. Executive sessions give subcommittee and committee a time and place for private conferences, and committee reports, if reasoned out pro and con, can guide and set the tone for floor debate. In 1941 the committee work conditioned the result; in 1954 neglect of committee evidence added to the fiat character of the final decision.

Events of 1955 reflect the misgivings which many members must have shared concerning that decision. An election which gave Democrats control in Congress and the censure of Senator McCarthy prepared the stage. For one thing, Congress at long last approved the creation of a twelve-man Commission on Government Security—the President, Vice President, and Speaker each appointing four members—to study the loyalty-security program. For another, the Senate voted at this session to set up the Subcommittee on Constitutional Rights. This subcommittee consisted initially of three members of the parent Judiciary Committee, Senators Hennings, O'Mahoney, and Langer. In opening eleven days of hearings in November, Chairman Hennings cited a speech by Chief Justice Earl Warren warning that the liberties of Americans were threatened with extinction, not by external enemies, but by domestic conditions—by "relaxations in the operation of the Bill of Rights."[84] The subcommittee, Hennings declared, would proceed "without fear or favor" to examine practices in the government loyalty-security programs which seemed to violate First Amendment rights.[85] Congress had rediscovered its responsibility, thanks in part to a judicial reminder, and was employing two new instruments for exploring issues like those neglected in passage of the Communist Control Act.

267

In 1958 this same Senate subcommittee turned its attention to wire-tapping. To expect the Court to bear the whole burden of adapting a bill of rights drafted for an agricultural society to an electronic society is illusory. The pace of change and degree of social complexity is such that only legislation, supplemented indeed by executive inquiry and regulation, can deal with important elements of the problem. Under Senator Hennings, the subcommittee met the need by launching an exhaustive study of "Wiretapping, Eavesdropping and the Bill of Rights." The published hearings furnished more than two thousand pages of expert testimony, official documents, and reports and background data, domestic and foreign, on the scientific, administrative, legal, and constitutional aspects of the problem. Hennings' successor as chairman, Senator Sam J. Ervin, Jr., of North Carolina, conducted further hearings in 1961 and in 1962 authored a "Summary-Report," providing in everyday language an informed account of the main aspects of the problem.[86] Although the Senate Judiciary Committee as a whole exhibited certain deficiencies, soon to be detailed, this subcommittee, reinforced by a professional staff, provided a constitutional forum at once broadly representative, expert, and concerned with constitutional issues.

In short, individual rights, like federalism, separation of powers, and constitutional amendment, face Congress with difficult, controversial, and important constitutional questions. That issues of individual rights are peculiarly susceptible to judicial review through the direct appeal of persons affected by legislation, by no means exonerates Congress from responsibility. The twelve recent decisions of the Supreme Court annulling acts of Congress as violative of rights demonstrate the concern of the courts with the problem. Yet the increasing incidence of those decisions suggests that Congress is neglecting to provide the attitudes, leadership, and procedures for assuring protection to rights.[87] Sole reliance by Congress on the judicial screen may ultimately undermine liberty.

Furthermore, scholars may reinforce the deleterious effects of judicial monopoly views of members of Congress if they focus analysis solely on judicial behavior and ignore the congressional behavior that produces unconstitutional laws. Careful legislative histories of acts held invalid by the Court would show at what points elements making for responsibility broke down and give direction to legislative improvements.[88] "Legislatures," said Justice Holmes, "are ultimate guardians of the liberties and welfare of the people in quite as great a degree as the courts."[89]

13 Congress in Dilemma: The Jenner-Butler Bill in the Senate, 1957–1958

After twenty years, Congress was again locked in combat over the decisions of the Supreme Court. In its hectic closing days, the same Senate which the previous year had resolved the Middle East issue was agonizing over a series of bills to discipline the high court. One of these was the Jenner-Butler bill, which had as one of its aims a withdrawal of part of the Court's jurisdiction. The decisions in question all pertained to individual rights. For two decades opinion had settled down to the view—shared at the outset by both Jefferson and Marshall—that this was the leading constitutional province of the Judiciary. In 1937 the Senate Judiciary Committee had opposed Roosevelt's "court-packing" plan in the name of an independent judiciary which it called "the only certain shield of individual rights."[1] Yet now in 1957, that same committee had launched a major attack on the Supreme Court for the manner in which it had fulfilled that function.

This episode reveals the influence of the three theories of responsibility. It puts to question the assumption that Congress can consign completely and permanently whole areas of constitutional inquiry to the Court, including the area of individual rights, and it shows how men who had counseled their colleagues to leave such issues to the courts now gave them a different sort of advice. It reveals the enduring truth contained both in the Jeffersonian and in the Marshallian conceptions and the continuing tension between them. It discloses once again the inadequacies of existing organs and procedural rules for achieving effective deliberation. Finally it accentuates the need for both accessible expert opinion and a modicum of public comprehension of what is at stake in such controversies.

Behind the bill lay widespread fears about Communism and its threat to internal security. All branches of the national government, including Congress, and many state governments as well, had for years wrestled with the problem. But the major task of reconciling measures to promote internal security with the constitutionally guaranteed rights of the individual had fallen to the Supreme Court.

In discharging this task, the Court had delivered a series of decisions offensive to individuals and groups alarmed over the Communist problem. Six of these decisions incurred the sharpest attacks. Thus, in Cole v. Young in 1956, the Court construed an act of Congress as extending the federal program for security risks only to "sensitive" jobs and not to all federal programs.[2] In Pennsylvania v. Nelson, it ruled that provisions of a state sedition act penalizing subversion of the federal government were invalid because the Smith Act of 1940, as construed by the Court, was meant to pre-empt this field of legislation for the federal government.[3] In Slochower v. Board of Education, it held invalid the dismissal of a professor at a municipal university for refusing under the Fifth Amendment to answer questions asked by a congressional committee investigating subversive activities.[4]

Three more rulings came in 1957. In Konigsberg v. State Bar of California and a companion case, the Court held that one seeking admission to a state bar could not be excluded for refusing to answer questions concerning past or present Communist party membership.[5] In Watkins v. United States, the Court overturned the contempt conviction of a witness before the House Unamerican Activities Committee on the ground that the committee had failed to show the pertinence of its questions to a stated legislative purpose.[6] Finally, in Yates v. United States, it read the Smith Act restrictively; it held that the act in prohibiting advocacy of overthrow of government reached only to incitement to action and not to abstract doctrine, and in prohibiting organization of a subversive group, fell short of penalizing continued organizational activity.[7] Although none of these decisions directly invalidated a law of Congress, they nevertheless helped to sustain the public alarm that had earlier fostered the activities of Senator McCarthy and the passage of the Communist Control Act. They now gave rise to charges of judicial usurpation.

In Congress, conservative Republicans were loudest in voicing these misgivings. Yet the congressional response to the internal security decisions drew additional support as well as inspiration from Southern Democrats. In 1954 and 1955, the Supreme Court had construed the Fourteenth Amendment as outlawing racial segregation in public schools and set in motion measures for implementation.[8] These decisions and subsequent events had nurtured a growing hostility to the Court in the South. Accordingly, Southern Senators who might otherwise have defended the Court lent their votes if not always their voices to the cause of the Jenner-Butler bill.

Criticism of the Court thus came from both sides of the aisle. The leaders of neither party openly defended the Court from attack. Neither the Democratic majority leader in the Senate nor the Republican President publicly took a firm position on the bill. Instead, each worked behind the scenes to moderate the zeal of the critics or avert a fight on the floor.[9]

As a result, the Eighty-Fifth Congress produced a rash of bills aimed in one way or another at curbing the Supreme Court or modifying the effect of its decisions. One of the most far-reaching was H.R. 3 which appeared in several sessions. In 1958, the House passed it by a better than three-to-two margin, and it came within a hair of passing the Senate. Provoked chiefly by the Nelson decision, this bill would have limited the discretion of the Court in construing statutes of Congress as pre-empting fields of legislation for the federal government and withdrawing them from state control.[10]

Senator William E. Jenner, Indiana Republican, preferred to get at the Court by withdrawals of its appellate jurisdiction. On July 26, 1957, during the Senate civil rights debate, he introduced his bill, declaring: "By a process of attrition and accession, the extreme liberal wing of the Court has become a majority; and we witness today the spectacle of a Court constantly changing the law, and even changing the meaning of the Constitution, in an apparent determination to make the law of the land what the Court thinks it should be."

He closed by listing five areas in which the Court had transgressed, and declared, "You have full, unchallengeable power to pass laws immediately which would deprive the Supreme Court" of jurisdiction over all these matters.[11] Senator Jenner's original bill would have made it impossible for parties to appeal to the Supreme Court from state or lower federal courts in cases concerning any of those five areas. For example, the bill defined his fifth area, the only one to remain in the bill when it reached the floor, as "any law, rule, or regulation of any State, or of any board of bar examiners, or similar body, or of any action or proceeding taken pursuant to any such law, rule, or regulation pertaining to the admission of persons to the practice of law within such State."[12] Once adopted, this might effectually have reversed the Konigsberg decision for many jurisdictions, just as his other four areas would have reversed Watkins, Cole, Nelson, and Slochower.

The Internal Security Subcommittee of the Senate Judiciary Committee held a one-day hearing on August 7, with Senator James O. Eastland, Mississippi Democrat, in the chair. The only witnesses present were Senator Jenner, ranking Republican on the subcommittee, and its research director, Benjamin Mandel. No other Senators appeared. Next day, the subcommittee approved the bill as introduced.

The following February, at the request of Senator Thomas C. Hennings, Jr., Missouri Democrat, the parent committee ordered further hearings. These subcommittee hearings lasted nine days, concluding on March 5. On March 10, the full committee met to consider the bill, and five days later, Senator John M. Butler, Maryland Republican, offered a substitute bill by way of amendment; this retained the state bar section of the Jenner bill, dropped the provision concerning educators (Slochower), and replaced the remaining sections with new legislation setting forth the intent of Congress and thereby correcting the Court's reading of that intent. An additional section amended the Smith Act to correct the decision in Yates *v.* United States. In late April, the committee accepted these proposals with certain changes and omissions, on the thirtieth, voted 10 to 5 to report the bill as amended, and on May 15 published its majority and minority reports.

The bill had four sections, only the first of which, concerning bar admission, would have removed Supreme Court jurisdiction. The other three sections dealt with contempt of congressional committees (Watkins), federal pre-emption (Nelson), and redefinition of the Smith Act (Yates).[13]

The bill finally reached the floor of the Senate on August 19, when Senator Jenner offered it as an amendment to a minor bill.[14] Next day, the Senate debated the issue on a motion to table by Senator Hennings and adopted this motion by a roll call vote of 49 to 41. Although the Senate went on to debate other anti-Court measures in these closing days of the session, this vote effectively killed the Jenner-Butler bill.[15]

Events in the next Congress were in part at least a reflection of the character and kind of discussion held on the Jenner-Butler bill. Bills to correct decisions of the Court continued to appear in both houses, suggesting that the Senate's discussion had done little to clarify the basic issue, the adjustment of the claims of internal security and individual rights. The Senate's handling of the question whether Congress possesses power to withdraw jurisdiction may have had some effect, for only in the House did similar bills make an appearance.[16]

Another consequence of the 1958 handling of the constitutional question was the Javits proposal to amend the Constitution. It is likely that the publicity given the Jenner-Butler bill and the somewhat one-sided manner in which the central issue was discussed led opponents to seek counter-publicity in 1959. In February, Senator Jacob K. Javits, New York Republican, with several co-sponsors, reintroduced a proposal to place the appellate jurisdiction of the Court over constitutional issues beyond legislative interference, and in May, a Judiciary Committee subcommittee held a one-day hearing on the bill.[17] This effort, with its judicial monopoly overtones, never left committee.

In the Supreme Court, the reiterated protests in Congress were soon having a modest effect. Decisions of the next term represented tangible modifications of the direction of earlier Cold War cases.[18]

CONSTITUTIONAL QUESTIONS

The original Jenner bill and section 1 of the Jenner-Butler bill raised two main constitutional questions, one narrow, the other broad. In the first place, the withdrawal of jurisdiction prompted the question, does the constitutional document prohibit Congress from taking such action? Article III, section 2 of the Constitution, after defining the judicial power and the original jurisdiction of the Supreme Court, describes appellate jurisdiction in these terms: "In all the other cases before mentioned, the Supreme Court shall have appellate jurisdiction, both as to law and fact, with such exceptions, and under such regulations as the Congress shall make." Supporters of the bill argued that the language of the article was clear and expressly confirmed a power in Congress to regulate the Court's appellate jurisdiction. The opponents argued that this provision, in combination with others, operated to forestall Congress from withdrawing jurisdiction over the prescribed categories of cases.

Since the proponents of the bill had the support of a Supreme Court precedent, the McCardle case of 1868,[19] to support their position on the narrow question, the other side felt constrained to raise a second, broad question. There was irony in this, for many of these opponents normally espoused the judicial monopoly theory, deeming narrow legal questions alone to be constitutional questions, and the Supreme Court to be sole judge of such questions. But now they raised a fundamental issue for Congress itself: Does the withdrawal of appellate jurisdiction conflict with basic constitutional principles, with the spirit of the Constitution, and with canons of constitutional wisdom? This was the question which they came increasingly to pose for their fellow-Senators.

Other questions of course were involved in the Butler amendments; sections 3 and 4, by clarifying the intent of Congress, raised directly no issue of congressional power. They had constitutional implications, however, for by forcing on the courts statutory meanings which the courts had avoided as potentially unconstitutional, they might well have presented the Court with constitutional questions. Section 2 was more serious; in stating that congressional declarations on the pertinence of questions put to witnesses should control the Court in contempt prosecutions, it posed a challenge to judicial power itself. These issues, however, will be peripheral to the central problem of this chapter—issues associated with section 1.

Senators who had earlier treated constitutional questions as strictly subordinate and suitable for summary reference to the Court now counseled an intense inquiry by Congress. Admittedly, the question might have come before the courts in due time, yet the McCardle precedent made it likely that the Court would sustain the legislation. Accordingly, had Congress acted on judicial monopoly terms, the result might have been a lessening of the Court's capacity to exercise the reviewing function. True, a presidential veto was possible, but the Administration left Congress in the dark on its future actions. Thus the only prudent course for members of Congress was to assume their decisions to be final.

Moreover, a close examination of the constitutional questions was here unavoidable. As in the Bradley case and a host of others, political motives blended with constitutional conviction in prompting the participants in this affair. Those who wished to curb the Court must have had the imminent elections in mind and the support a public attack on the Court might win from constituents worried about subversion. Their tactics in introducing the bill near the close of one session, conducting the sort of hearings soon to be described, and finally forcing the bill out on the floor in the last days of another session strongly suggest such ambitions. On the other hand, the opponents were also aware of personal and party fortunes and, although some of them evidently wished to avoid a floor fight on the central issue, they found an ultimate confrontation politically unavoidable. Like considerations governed party leaders, especially majority leader Johnson, whose skill in first delaying and then controlling debate on the Court issue was crucial in defeating the assaults on the Court.[20]

Motives being what they were, a confrontation with the constitutional questions was unavoidable. And just as political motive and strategy affected the course of the discussion, the conceptions the Senators held of the role of Congress in constitutional controversies and their expressions of those conceptions had similar effects. The melee showed the influence, as well as the inadequacy, of judicial monopolism and put the two traditional versions of the tripartite theory in clear juxtaposition.

COURSE OF THE DISCUSSION

The discussion on the Jenner-Butler bill had the appearance of a tug-of-war between two determined factions, each acting from a priori conceptions of the course of Court decisions. The one opposed those decisions, the other supported them. Ostensibly the group led by Senators Jenner and Butler was endeavoring to mobilize public pressure against the Court and, to this end, was using all available congressional powers and machinery. The other, led by Senator Hennings, was organizing counter-pressures in support of the Court and in so doing was resting its case on the function of the Court as an institution. Thus we find Senator Morse proclaiming that the Judiciary was "that branch of our Government which is responsible for protecting the constitutional rights of free men and free women . . ."[21] The foes of the Court's decisions demanded sanctions; the friends pleaded the necessity of the Court rather than the correctness of its judgments.

Subcommittee Hearings: First Phase. The initial hearing of the Sub-committee on Internal Security afforded little opportunity for discussion. For twenty-five minutes Chairman Eastland, with two committee counsel, Robert Morris and J. G. Sourwine, heard two witnesses. One was Senator Jenner, who read into the record his July Senate speech and a series of rec-ommendations by the American Bar Association for legislation counter-acting recent decisions of the Court. The other was Benjamin Mandel, subcommittee research director, who placed in the record articles from the Communist *Daily Worker,* generally approving the decisions of the Court.[22] There were no opposition witnesses. As a result, the record had little to suggest that the Jenner bill was open to attack on constitutional grounds.

Subcommittee Hearings: Second Phase. The resumption of the hearings in February was tacit recognition of the inadequacy of the August sitting. For this resumption and for leadership in mobilizing resistance to the bill, Senator Hennings of Missouri was chiefly responsible. At his request and by a margin of only one vote, the full Judiciary Committee on February 3, 1958, ordered further hearings by the subcommittee.[23]

For nine days, between February 19 and March 5, the subcommittee held open hearings. Of the eight members, the four Southern Democrats, Senators Eastland, Olin D. Johnston of South Carolina, John L. McClel-lan of Arkansas, and Sam J. Ervin, Jr., of North Carolina, never put in an appearance. Each of the four Republican members, Senators Jenner, Butler, Arthur V. Watkins of Utah, and Roman L. Hruska of Nebraska was present at at least one session. With no more than one Senator present most of the time, and with counsel Sourwine conducting most of the questioning, the subcommittee gradually built up a voluminous record.

Part of the evidence took the form of oral statements and interroga-tions, and part of letters and other communications. In all, fifty-two witnesses appeared, forty-one for the bill and eleven against it. In addi-tion, thirty-six letters or statements solicited by the committee were published in the record, two-thirds of them favoring the bill. At mid-point, counsel Sourwine announced that the committee had received one hundred and three other communications, some of which went into the record, others into an extensive appendix; all but one of these, he asserted, favored the bill. It remained for Senator Hennings, appearing on March 4, to redress the balance. He placed in the record virtually all of the seventy-three replies received from a recent form letter. He had sent this letter to law school deans, law professors, and leading lawyers throughout the country and asked for their opinions pro or con concerning the bill. Sixty-nine of the seventy-three replies expressed opposition to the bill.

The record discloses two sorts of evidence, the first, emotional and general; the second, legal, constitutional, and specific. The testimony of three-fifths of the witnesses and the bulk of the communications avoided constitutional argument and instead voiced a deep, emotional concern over Communism. Counsel usually permitted these witnesses to testify without interruption. They spoke for such groups as the States Rights party of Louisiana, the Defenders of the American Constitution, Inc., and the Ladies of the Grand Army of the Republic. Besides attacking the Court, many reflected fear of internationalism and world government, hostility to the desegregation cases, and extreme anxiety concerning possible subversion. One ex-Communist warned of humanism and "Protagorean Paganism."[24] Another witness, after a formal statement, responded as follows to questioning:

> Mr. Sourwine. Do you have any knowledge, sir, of any facts which would lead a reasonable person to believe any member of the United States Supreme Court is under Communist discipline?
> Mr. Green. I do.
> Mr. Sourwine. You do have knowledge of such facts?
> Mr. Green. Yes.
> Mr. Sourwine. I can assure you will [sic] be subpoenaed to appear before this committee to testify.
> Mr. Green. But those facts are not [sic] facts which are accepted general knowledge. They are facts that anybody can go to the public library and form their own conclusions . . .[25]

Another witness said, ". . . the long series of decisions of our present Supreme Court has freed these traitors [the Communists] to continue their dastardly work of destruction, and how appalling it is to compare these findings with the stated objectives, the program of the Communists, and to realize how perfectly they fit into the current Communist line."[26]

The remaining twenty-one witnesses and some of the letters, especially those submitted by Senator Hennings, were more temperate and discussed the issues raised directly by the bill. A majority of these witnesses could be described as genuinely expert. Their testimony, when added to that of letters, developed the arguments cogently.[27] The witnesses, especially those opposing the bill, were subjected at times to close questioning. On two occasions, in addition, the committee inserted reports it had obtained from the Legislative Reference Service.[28] On another, it printed a letter from Attorney General William P. Rogers, who spelled out his own views in opposition to the bill.[29] In closing the hearings, Senator Jenner read his rebuttal to the arguments against the bill, and took occasion to rebuke Rogers for not appearing in person and for submitting only a brief letter worded like a voluntary opinion and not a documented report.[30]

The argument spelled out by the experts touched on both the constitutional questions. On the narrow question, supporters of the bill insisted that Article III in effect defined the ultimate potential limits of appellate jurisdiction, but left particular authorizations of that jurisdiction almost entirely to Congress through the medium of judiciary acts. Court decisions were educed to support this position. The opponents read that article as to some extent a direct grant of power to the courts, implying thereby that in regulating that jurisdiction, Congress is obliged to preserve most of it intact. Justice Story had developed this view in his zeal for uninhibited judicial power. It held that Congress was forbidden to deprive the Court of appellate jurisdiction to any substantial degree, since the power originates in the Constitution. Professor Harrup Freeman of the Cornell Law School wrote that the Constitution did not intend to confer a power (appellate jurisdiction) in one sentence and remove it in the next, and that "exceptions and regulations" are radically different from removals of jurisdiction.[31] Others insisted that the due process clause of the Fifth Amendment operates to limit Congress since, as Senator Hennings argued, due process requires that the Constitution mean the same to every American, and that if legal uniformity were destroyed as a result of nonappeal to the Court from state and lower federal courts, justice would depend on the accident of geography and due process would be violated.[32]

In spite of the ingenuity shown by the opposition in handling the narrow question, many fell back on the broad question, insisting that the proposed action of Congress would violate the spirit of the Constitution or clash with its basic principles. A letter from Dean Erwin N. Griswold of the Harvard Law School put the matter clearly:

> S. 2646 is probably constitutional. But not everything that is constitutional is wise or desirable. It seems to me, though, that S. 2646 is contrary to the spirit of the Constitution, and that its enactment would not be a wise exercise of the powers given to the Congress by the Constitution. It is of the essence of the Constitution that we have an independent judiciary. We will not have an independent judiciary if the Congress takes jurisdiction away from the Supreme Court whenever the Court decides a case that the Congress does not like.[33]

Other lawyers sought other answers to the broad question. Dean Jefferson B. Fordham of the University of Pennsylvania Law School asserted that removal of jurisdiction to interpret the Bill of Rights would restrict the application of those guarantees in a manner "out of harmony with the constitutional scheme."[34] Still others feared the bill would cripple the Court as final arbiter of federal-state relations. It would also destroy the balance among the three independent departments established by the Constitution.

Yet Senator Jenner, too, could rest his case on the separation of powers: "My bill only proposes to implement one of the basic check and balance provisions of the Constitution; and I fail to see how the use of a constitutional provision can be deemed to be contrary to the spirit of the Constitution."[35]

This, of course, was to exalt the letter above the spirit, and the terms in which some of the opponents of the bill cast their argument actually supported Senator Jenner's contention. As the Attorney General expressed it, the Jenner bill ignored "general considerations of policy relating to the judiciary."[36] Congress obviously had the contested power, wrote a Midwestern law professor, and hence no "legal" issue was involved, but merely questions relating to "considerations of public policy."[37] This labeling of the broad constitutional question as one of policy accorded with recent usage, but had ominous implications. Those who used such terminology may have intended no denigration of the issue before Congress, but that could prove the long term result. If the Court alone can be trusted with fundamentals of the Constitution, if the Constitution is what the judges alone say it is, then to Congress belong only the circumstantials of day-to-day policy, a fluid quantity which shifts with the ebb and flow of rival pressures and social conditions. Jefferson and Marshall would both have labeled this a matter of constitutional principle, but judicial monopolism had obscured the true character of the issue.

At the hearings, the supporters of the bill on the whole assumed that the Court had done wrong and devoted their argument to showing that Congress could and should discipline it; the opponents maintained not that the Court had done right, but that the Court was essential as an institution and that Congress should refrain from measures weakening it.

In the Judiciary Committee. After the close of hearings, the bill returned to the Judiciary Committee, where it received its most searching consideration. Between March 10, when the committee first took up the bill and April 30 when it voted 10 to 5 to report an amended version favorably, it discussed the bill at least five times.[38] The fifteen members included the eight subcommittee members already mentioned, four additional Democrats, Senators Estes Kefauver of Tennessee, Hennings, Joseph C. O'Mahoney of Wyoming, and John A. Carroll of Colorado, and three additional Republicans, Senators Alexander Wiley of Wisconsin, William Langer of North Dakota, and Everett M. Dirksen of Illinois.

That the committee was heavily preoccupied with the bill is suggested by occasional public statements by members. As early as March 24, Senator O'Mahoney indicated opposition to the Jenner bill and proposed in its place that judicial nominees, before confirmation, take a special pledge during examination before the Judiciary Committee. Thus nominees would promise to refrain from decisions changing the meaning of the Constitution or statutes and would affirm their understanding that the Constitution gave all legislative power to Congress.[39] Said the Senator, the Senate should unhesitatingly use its exclusive power of confirmation to "support and defend the Constitution against invasion of the legislative power."[40] Senators Butler and Hennings, now the leading protagonists, engaged in sporadic debate on the merits of the pending bill.[41]

At this crucial period of committee discussion, the Administration remained relatively noncommittal. Although on April 1 the Attorney General declared that he still opposed the bill even with Senator Butler's amendments,[42] the President told a news conference three weeks later that the subject should receive "a lot of studying."[43]

Finally, on May 15, the committee published its report endorsing the bill. In the hearings, Senator Butler had opposed the method, as distinguished from the aims, of the original Jenner bill. Accordingly, the Jenner-Butler bill as amended and reported kept only one section withdrawing jurisdiction; the three remaining sections essentially followed Senator Butler's amendments and for the most part sought to counteract the effect of Court decisions by clarifying the intent of Congress.

In his report for the majority, Senator Butler defended the procedure employed by the committee and stated the arguments for the bill. The power of Congress to withdraw jurisdiction, he asserted, formed part of the system of checks and balances and was "the only check provided by the Constitution to the Congress as a protection against attempted usurpation by the Court of legislative prerogatives, or improper invasion of the rights reserved to the states and to the people, which the Congress, as the representative of the states and of the people, is in duty bound to protect."[44] This use of the power to withdraw, he insisted, was merely minimal, justified by the nature of bar admission, a matter peculiarly subject to state control.

Four of the five minority Senators signed a minority report; they were Senators Hennings, Kefauver, and Carroll, Democrats, and Wiley, Republican. Senator Langer, the fifth, submitted an individual state-

279

ment.[45] The report attacked the bill as unconstitutional, undesirable, prepared under inadequate procedure, and ambiguous. It asserted that three of the four sections raised grave constitutional questions and that the three revised sections had not been subjected to hearings. Section 1 violated the due process clause because of unreasonable classification and lack of uniformity. Under the head "policy objections," the report maintained that the section was an attempt to coerce the Court into changing its opinions; it stemmed from a "kill the umpire philosophy," threatened a dangerous precedent, and struck directly at the separation of powers.[46] The bill as a whole would hinder rather than help the government in controlling subversion. It would strike at democratic traditions and would complicate the country's "difficult position as leader of the free world."[47]

The minority sought to make up for the lack of hearings on the amended bill by attaching an appendix to the report. Senator Hennings inserted a legal analysis, twenty-nine pages of letters from lawyers, law school deans, and bar associations and sixteen pages of hostile editorials; Senator Wiley submitted analyses from the Department of Justice and the Legislative Reference Service and resolutions by the American Bar Association opposing the Jenner bill. Such was the material which accompanied the committee's report, which, by ten to five, favored the Jenner-Butler bill.

Floor Debate. Not until August 20 was the Jenner-Butler bill subjected to floor debate. Pressures had built up on both sides. On July 17, Senator Jenner had complained on the floor that for two months the bill had been pigeonholed, and intimated that the Democratic majority, fearing a split within its own ranks should the bill come up, had deliberately held it back. He cited fresh instances of Supreme Court decisions opening "new opportunities" for Communists, and held the Democratic Policy Committee responsible for inaction in the Senate.[48] By early August the rival forces, Southern Democrats leagued with conservative Republicans against a combination of liberal Democrats and liberal Republicans, were girding for action.

In spite of the end-of-session rush, majority leader Johnson worked out an agreement for limited discussion. On August 19, Senator Jenner presented the committee's bill as an amendment to a pending measure. It was agreed by all concerned that on the following day the bill would receive two or three hours of discussion, followed by a roll call vote not on the bill but on Senator Hennings' motion to table, in effect kill, it.[49]

Although a dozen Senators spoke in the debate, only five played significant roles. These included Senators Jenner and Butler, for the bill, and Senators Javits, Wiley, and Hennings against it. The proponents, citing legal precedents and commentators, spelled out their hostility to the line of Court decisions and the need for legislative correction. The opponents defended the Court as an institution and reiterated a warning that if the motion should lose, lengthy, even exhaustive, discussion of the bill would ensue. What they were asking, in effect, was a vote of confidence in the Court, not a discussion of the controversial decisions.

The proponents made much of the narrow questions of constitutionality. Senator Jenner pointed out that only one of his five original sections withdrawing jurisdiction remained. The testimony, he insisted, supported the validity of this section, since admission to the state bar was traditionally and by earlier Court precedents a matter for state action alone; by forestalling Supreme Court review, the section only confirmed a traditional rule.[50]

In the major speech of the day, Senator Butler analyzed the bill in detail and showed that each of his three amendments was designed not to overrule the Court but to correct its reading of congressional intent.

On their part, the opponents of the bill played down the narrow issues. Senator Javits argued briefly that sections 2 and 4 would invite a finding by the Court of unconstitutionality since the Court itself had deliberately avoided the constitutional issue through its restrictive reading of congressional intent.[51] Senator Hennings, in concluding for the opponents, found constitutional issues in each of the three amendments.[52]

The narrow question left relatively little ground for the opponents of the bill, especially for those who were wont to put aside questions merely doubtful. Accordingly they raised the broad question pertaining to the role of the Supreme Court in the American system of government and the power of Congress to tamper with its jurisdiction or decisions.

On this fundamental issue, the debaters drew arguments directly from the several theories of congressional responsibility. Senator Jenner relied somewhat uncertainly on the representative character of the Congress: A "runaway, wild Court," he cried, was "tearing down the Constitution," and hence, Congress should "protect itself and the country against [its] usurpation."[53] More moderately, Senator Butler warned that the people were "greatly troubled and widely dissatisfied" with recent decisions and wanted Congress to act.[54] The people's representatives could not ignore the people's concern.

Yet Senator Butler put even greater reliance on the doctrine of the separation of powers. In terms later echoed by Democratic Senators John Stennis of Mississippi and Johnston of South Carolina,[55] he reasserted the traditional Southern view in terms reminiscent of Jefferson:

281

This [the clause empowering Congress to regulate appellate juris-diction] is not a provision which got into the Constitution by chance. Nothing got into the Constitution by chance. This is one of the specific check-and-balance provisions of the Constitution . . . In fact, it is the only check which the Constitution gives to the Congress as a protection against attempted usurpation of the legislative prerogatives by the Supreme Court. It is also the only check the Congress has against improper invasion by the Court of the rights reserved to the States and to the people under the 9th and 10th Amendments of the Constitution.

. . .

In order to defend properly the "separation of powers" implicit in our form of government, it is necessary to understand it. The separation of powers doctrine was not created and is not maintained for the sole benefit of any 1 or any 2 branches of the Government. It was created and is maintained for the sake of preserving the Government as a whole, by protecting the people against the oligarchy which would surely result if any one branch of government obtained complete ascendancy. Thus the separation of powers system requires checks and balances, and such checks and balances have been pro-vided in the Constitution, so that each branch of government has a constitutional power to curb either of the other two branches.[56]

In opposing judicial oligarchy and asserting that Congress might within its acknowledged constitutional powers apply its own constitutional readings, the Maryland Senator was talking Jeffersonian language. For that matter, Senator Jenner's use of the power over jurisdiction to counteract decisions of the Court which Congress deemed to exceed judicial power was likewise Jeffersonian.

In their replies, the opponents turned to arguments far more akin to the views of John Marshall than to the judicial monopoly theory. They reiterated the utility and importance of judicial review of acts of Con-gress. They insisted, in the words of Senator Javits, "The very essence of constitutional government requires a final court to determine what is and what is not the paramount law of the land."[57] These Senators, too, found the separation of powers and checks and balances at stake.

Men who had once advised their colleagues to leave constitutional questions to the Court, now insisted on a high obligation in Congress. The Wisconsin Republican, Senator Wiley, disdained "legal" arguments and put his whole stress on the need of sustaining the Court, its prestige, power, and authority. He had deep feelings and powerful convictions on the subject and to remain silent would be "an act of omission that does violence to my conscience and, I believe, my oath as a Senator of the

United States." "The most sacred aspects of the inner structure of the Constitution" were involved.[58]

He objected to the venom, the bitterness, and the rancor which characterized the attacks on the Court, and asserted that "if what the sponsors of this proposal now so ardently fight for were indeed in line with the thinking of the Founding Fathers, if it had accordingly been acted upon as decisively in the past, as it is now being acted upon by this proposed legislation, then—I ask—what role would have been left for the Court to play in American Government?"[59] To him, the maintenance of judicial review was essential to the "wisdom, and the prudence, the caution and the judgment of our legislative conduct."[60]

These Senators faced a logical difficulty. Senator Javits had warned, in relation to the narrow question, that the Court might throw out the Jenner-Butler bill. But on the broad question, that result was unlikely. Accordingly, he had to fall back, in the end, on an appeal to "self-discipline,"[61] the restraint which the members should observe in wielding their acknowledged power. For the Congress to bring pressure on the Court was, in Senator Wiley's words, a "mortal error," and accordingly, Congress should be guided in this whole affair by a "moral sense."[62] The Senators from New York and Wisconsin were reflecting Marshall's esteem for the independent judiciary and for an unrestricted power in the courts to decide not only constitutional questions but also what questions are suitable for final judicial determination. But their appeal was not to constitutional text but to the consciences of the legislators, not to legal, but to moral sanctions.

Additional evidence of the contending theories and some of their implications appears in this spontaneous colloquy between Senators Butler and Javits. Senator Butler began by asserting that the Court, in the Watkins case, had overstepped its proper bounds. Referring to judicial control of legislative access to information, which section 2 of the bill challenged, he continued:

> I say that that is a breach of the separation of powers. It puts the Supreme Court in the legislative chamber where it does not belong and I, for one, am perfectly willing to send legislation to that Court today, if I can do it, and let them declare it unconstitutional; and then the people will rise up and demand that Congress be given back its inherent power to legislate.
> Mr. Javits. That is exactly my point. I say this is nothing but an exacerbation of a dissatisfaction that already exists, and the proposed bill will only make it worse.
> Mr. Butler. I respectfully disagree with the Senator. I am the last Member of this body who would do anything to hurt the Supreme

Court as an institution. I believe we have a right to counsel the Court. When the Court thinks we have done something that is unconstitutional, they do not have any qualms in telling us about it. They are a coordinate branch of the Government. If the Government is to work well, we must work in coordination. The three branches of the Government must be able to communicate with one another. This is our method of communication. This bill would tell the Court, "In our opinion you have usurped our power. We resent it. We want you to take a second look at what you are doing."

Mr. Javits. At the same time, Mr. President, if I may sum up my deep-seated opposition to this particular bill, it is that if we approve it in either 2 stages or 1 stage, we say, "We deprive you of certain powers which you have had and exercised for over a century." This is where I think this is court-raiding, and therefore, to be equated with the court-packing bill of 1937.

Mr. Butler. When we come to talk about powers which have been exercised since the foundation of this Government, I say they have been exercised under the grant of Congress; and what powers Congress gives, those powers can be taken away.

Mr. Javits. Out of respect for the principle of the separation of powers, I do not think we should take it away, and that is why I say this is the fundamental difference.[63]

The vote of 49 to 41 which closed the debate also shelved the bill.[64] Since the motion was not for passage but for tabling, that vote failed accurately to reflect the support given the rival theories. The debate itself is noteworthy, however, in revealing, after the lapse of a century and a half, the vitality of the two traditional conceptions: Jefferson's with its stress on ultimate popular control over the course of constitutional readings, legislative enlightenment of consensus, and dialogue among the three branches in search of sound constitutional readings, and Marshall's, with its stress on the sacredness of judicial decision in the immediate area of decision, credentials of courts as objective forums, and esteem for courts as special sanctuaries for harried individuals. The Constitution continues both a people's charter and a lawyer's document.

Discussion Evaluated. The inadequacies of consideration here are obvious. Only with constant pressure from Senator Hennings did the record of the hearings develop the subject with completeness, especially concerning the Butler amendments. Debate came too late in the session to probe the issue of jurisdiction with either thoroughness or detachment. In view of this, its quality is surprising.

As for the principles advanced by the protagonists, two things can be said. First, the Jeffersonian theory gave those wishing to admonish the Court for decisions they thought erroneous an arguable basis for action in the constitutional document. Article III and the McCardle precedent furnished authority. As is well known, even John Marshall, in a moment of stress, had conceded that Congress should possess an official means of overruling decisions it was convinced were wrong. The judicial monopoly theory, however, leaves Congress no effective means of protesting court decisions short of a constitutional amendment or court-packing.

Second, the discussion and the final vote showed a marked cleavage along regional lines. Party, it is true, had some influence; the behind-the-scenes activities of party leaders doubtless affected this result. Thus, Democrats divided, thirty-one for tabling, and seventeen against; the Republicans, eighteen for tabling and twenty-four against. More significant, however, was geography. Half the members of the subcommittee, including its chairman, were Southerners, and these men must have furnished much of the impetus as well as the rationale for the bill. In debate, Senators Jenner and Butler got reinforcement from Senators Eastland, Thurmond, Stennis, and Johnston. In the end, if we exclude Senators from Tennessee and Texas who supported tabling and those from Florida, who were absent, every Senator from every state of the old Confederacy voted against tabling. Table 8 presents the vote to table

TABLE 8. Regional Distribution of Senate Votes to
Table Jenner-Butler Bill, August 20, 1958

Region	Yea–Nay
South	4–16
Midwest	10–11
Middle Atlantic	5– 4
Far West	15– 7
New England	7– 3
Border	8– 0
Total	49–41

SOURCE: 104 *Cong. Rec.*, pt. 14, p. 18687 (1958).

arranged according to regions. The North and West divided less sharply than the South, with the Midwest and Middle Atlantic regions each almost evenly balanced, and with New England and the Far West giving the motion greatest support. Most strikingly, every Senator from every Border State voted to table, preferring, one may conjecture, to support the independence of the Court until evidence of judicial error convinced them of the need for drastic action.[65] Evidently the Southerners had won recruits to their anti-Court views from Northern Republicans but had failed to dent the solid pro-Court stand of their neighbors in the border area.

PARTICIPANTS

On this major constitutional issue lawyers completely monopolized the discussion. At no time, in committee or on the floor, did any member not a lawyer speak on the bill. And this, even though at this session fewer than three-fifths of the Senators had had legal training.[66] Significantly, in spite of a lowering of the quota of lawyers in the Senate as a whole, two areas were now sending them to Congress in very high proportions —the South and New York City. Was it the issue of civil rights that caused voters there to prefer lawyers?[67]

The predominance of lawyers appeared in other ways. When Senator Javits reintroduced a resolution the next February for a constitutional amendment confirming the final authority of the Court in "all cases involving constitutional issues," he made a special claim for the profession. Lawyers, he said, understood the function served by a supreme court in furnishing final interpretations of the Constitution.[68] The Senator also showed tendencies toward judicial monopolism, since he said he hoped to place decisions well beyond the influence of "political pressures or adverse reactions."[69] Although it never left the Judiciary Committee, this proposal may have had many supporters. Nevertheless, the lawyers registered a smaller margin of difference in the final vote—29 for tabling to 26 against—than did the non-lawyers—20 to 15.

The Senators encountered serious difficulties in supplementing their own views on the constitutional and related questions with the testimony and advice of experts. Although the bill's supporters leaned heavily on witnesses with a general anti-Court position rather than on specialists, both sides made use of experts. Since the subcommittee's chief counsel conducted the hearings, and also largely drafted its annual report[70] with a view primarily to exposing the Communist threat, those opposed to the bill evidently had to look elsewhere for aid.

Thus it was that Senator Wiley secured two reports from the Legislative Reference Service. As earlier, the Department of Justice was still reluctant to advise in full measure, its subordination to the Eisenhower policy and presumably its tenuous relations with the committee chairman being what they were. These and other complications probably impelled opponents to go outside the government for recommendations. Paradoxically, both sides drew on the American Bar Association—Senator

286

Jenner on a report of one of its committees critical of Court decisions and Senator Wiley on resolutions of its House of Delegates opposing the method, though not the objectives, of the Jenner-Butler bill. Witnesses from interest groups such as the American Civil Liberties Union, the National Lawyers Guild, and the AFL-CIO testified at the hearings, but most of the views of outside experts appeared in the form of written communications printed in the hearings record or quoted in debates. Law teachers and practitioners flooded the subcommittee with letters against the bill, and both sides invoked opinions of two distinguished authorities, Judge Learned Hand and Professor Edward S. Corwin. Valuable as much of this was it suggested the continuing need of a regular reservoir of the best professional advice close to members of Congress supplemented by regular channels for tapping the opinions of legal and other authorities throughout the country on specific issues.

Once again, it was men from the Border States and their vicinity who assumed the role of moderators and mediators. It was the Maryland Senator, Butler, who tempered the Indiana Senator's zeal and by amendment and floor leadership directed the pro-bill forces along more reasonable channels. It was the Missourian, Hennings, who demanded fair procedures and championed the Court in traditional terms. Neither went so far in his assertions as other more extreme advocates, for example, Senator Jenner or Senator Javits. It was notably Senators Butler and Hennings who tried repeatedly to keep discussion on a plane of reason and compromise. The constitutional leadership of the border areas still operated in 1958.

MODE

As shown, men who had at times supported judicial monopoly now discovered the shortcomings of that position. At moments of great stress, the people thrust on Congress the task of scrutinizing the general direction of Court decisions. At such times, questions which are broadly constitutional, even though labeled "policy," cry out for thorough consideration in Congress. Such questions go to the fundamentals of the constitutional system and to deliberate carefully on them is, as these Senators asserted, a matter of high moral responsibility.

On the other hand, those who now advanced Jefferson's formulation of the tripartite theory, insisting on independent legislative concern with constitutional issues, here neglected the one great condition that theory prescribes: namely, that the members seek objectively and impartially to arrive at Jefferson's "sense of the whole." While denouncing the Court for its misdeeds and asserting a right in Congress to judge the Court,

287

some Senators displayed in their own conduct the very reasons why legislative inquiry into constitutional issues had, for many, long since fallen into disrepute.

Recognition of the procedural lacunae was late and grudging. Not for six months after introduction of the bill did the subcommittee acknowledge a constitutional question and take steps to probe it. The subcommittee hearing in August, with only the promoter of the bill and his research aide testifying, produced evidence calculated to bring the Court into opprobrium. Next day the eight-man subcommittee, only two members having had any part in the hearings, recommended the bill favorably to the full committee. No whisper of opposition was heard, no tangible hint of a constitutional issue. The obvious aim was to build up a record that might serve to drum up public alarm concerning the Court and public support for reform.

These inequities and deficiencies led Senator Hennings to ask the full Judiciary Committee to hold further hearings. He read a memorandum decrying the "limited, one-sided information" on which the committee was expected to base a decision. He demanded further hearings, with opportunity for witnesses on both sides to appear, and with an adequate interval after the hearings for the members to read and consider the testimony. "Only then," he insisted, "can we properly carry out our duty." Members, he urged, should set aside emotions and consider the bill with "deliberateness."[71]

The committee complied by a margin of one vote. It now provided for hearings publicized in advance and open to all interested parties. Senators could have particular witnesses specially invited; and witnesses must put in a prompt appearance to allow time for deliberation prior to committee action by March 10.[72]

Accordingly, the second phase of hearings represented an improvement in fairness to parties and thoroughness of investigation. That Senator Jenner chaired several of the sessions, that counsel Sourwine tended to press witnesses against the bill rather more severely than those supporting it, that at most of the sittings only one subcommittee member was present, and that none but conservative Republican members attended at any time, undermined the tone of impartiality and lessened the likelihood of objective probing of testimony. But for the further efforts of a nonmember, Senator Hennings, the hearings under these conditions might well have conveyed an overwhelming case for legislation against the Court. With Senator Butler now in the chair, Senator Hennings read into the record his replies from legal authorities and practitioners, and so helped redress the balance.[73]

The result was a document of qualified value. The 1,072 pages, including three appendices, however diverse in quality and objectivity, gave

288

the judicious reader a basis for valid judgments on the constitutional question of jurisdiction. For the uninformed, however, lengthy emotional attacks on the Court might overweigh the calm and technical arguments defending it. Especially was this true of "Appendix 4," which may have received wide circulation. This twelve-page document accused the Court of being "an instrument of Global Conquest," omitted supporting evidence, and identified its authors only as "The SPX Research Associates."[74]

Thus the original Jenner bill at last received a hearing from both expert and lay witnesses and the accumulated evidence provided the full committee with a basis for judgment. It was in the committee deliberations more than anywhere else, that the bill received its most detached examination. That the committee scrapped four of the five original sections and accepted three of Senator Butler's amendments, testifies to the attention the bill received. The evidence which Senator Hennings had amassed bore fruit.

The three new sections of the amended bill, however, presented new problems. As early as April 6, Senator Hennings pressed publicly for hearings on the Butler amendments, matters undiscussed at the earlier hearings. Nevertheless, ten days later Senator Butler told the Senate no further hearings were needed. He said such hearings might make the legislative process "interminable," and would prevent committees from arranging compromises between conflicting views. In his view, hearings served chiefly to ascertain facts, not to conduct a "trial by compurgation, whereby Members of the legislative body may count those special interest groups which are in favor of the bill and those which are opposed, as aid to making up the collective legislative mind."[75] These ideas, belying as they did the initial intentions of the subcommittee, evidently persuaded the committee, for no further hearings were held. Accordingly, Senator Hennings raised this objection to the amended bill: "Hearings would have afforded the opportunity to benefit from public opinion on the policy questions and to tighten the language . . ."[76] Even though the committee afforded time for its minority to collect and prepare opposition arguments in the form of appendices, and even though the majority and minority statements went to the Senate in clear, concise, and well written form, this omission of hearings weakened the committee majority's case from the standpoints both of fairness and of thoroughness. That the bill went to the floor with a ten-to-five committee backing, notwithstanding that three of the ten, Senators Dirksen, Watkins, and O'Mahoney later voted to table, gave it an unwarranted prestige. Yet the initial flaw in committee action was the character of the hearings. Congress had an opportunity to clarify issues and inform the public on a chronic controversy, and hence to mitigate what Senator Wiley called the "blind rage" of those convinced that the Court was the tool of Moscow. But the opportunity was lost, and the early hearings did little but enable the fearful to let off steam and distort the public understanding of the problem.

All these deficiencies made hollow the claims of those who on the floor voiced the doctrine of congressional responsibility. They furnished the opposition with telling arguments and gave credibility to the efforts of the leadership at first to avoid, and later to limit, floor discussion. The debate itself was of good quality. It was fair to the two opposed sides, provided a reasoned interchange of views, and combined temperate language with citation and documentation. Yet the strict limit on time, and the device of a tabling motion, meant that the protagonists were not converging on the same precise issues and that while one was seemingly building a case for the election to come, the other was avoiding the issue and using the veiled threat of a filibuster as an argument with members anxious to adjourn.[77] The closing four days of a Congress are no time for fair, thorough, and above all detached discussion of constitutional issues, especially when committee work has been deficient. In election years, as already shown, the end-of-session rush often produces measures highly dubious constitutionally—witness the Communist Control Act and likewise the Disclaimer Affidavit which slipped into the National Defense Education Act a week before the Jenner-Butler debate. This time the effort failed.

Central to the problem of procedure is the structure, political complexion, and leadership of the Judiciary Committee. One could contend that constitutional questions being what they are, usually calling for an inquiry prior to floor consideration that combines expertness with achievement of some kind of "sense of the whole," that committee should be constituted with a view not merely to legal knowledge but to fidelity of representation. If the Senate needs a Judiciary Committee to begin the search for sound principle, accommodation, and compromise, then the committee as constituted and led in 1958 fell short of the requirements. The same can be said of its Subcommittee on Internal Security. For generations committees and subcommittees have embodied party membership in proportion to chamber strength. Ideological or policy orientation is less tangible, but geography is measurable, and hence, like party, might serve as a criterion for committee appointments. Table 9 presents the regional distribution of the membership of the subcommittee and full committee and relates this to the complexion of the chamber as a whole and the contemporary Supreme Court. Note the heavy weight of the South on the subcommittee (four of eight) and the full committee (five of fifteen). Two regions were voiceless on the subcommittee and one on the full committee. The Supreme Court paradoxically provided every region with at least one spokesman and none with more than two.

290

TABLE 9. Regional Distribution of Seats in the Senate Judiciary Subcommittee and Committee, the Senate, and the Supreme Court, 1958

| Region | Senate Judiciary Committee | | Senate | Supreme Court |
	Subcommittee (Internal Security)	Full Committee		
South	4	5	22	2
Midwest	2	5	22	1
Far West	1	3	22	1
Middle Atlantic	1	1[a]	10	2
Border	0	1	8	1
New England	0	0	12	2[b]
Total	8	15	96	9

[a] Senator Butler of Maryland.
[b] Justices Frankfurter and Douglas. The retirement of Justice Frankfurter in August 1962 left New England with Justice Douglas as its representative.

Yet the subcommittee, in attacking the Court, claimed to be speaking for and in the name of the American people as represented in the upper chamber of Congress!

The makeup of the subcommittee and committee conditioned the whole affair in the Senate as did their leadership. Senator Eastland and, in this case, his chief collaborator, Senator Jenner, enjoyed important prerogatives even though they ranked among the most conservative members of the Senate. One may question the wisdom of entrusting Senate deliberations on constitutional questions to the guidance of such men.

CONCLUSIONS

Congress, in short, faces a dilemma. If it dispatches constitutional issues to the courts through the front door, it finds them reappearing at the back. As long as it remains a representative body and one of the three coordinate branches, it is bound at times and on particular issues to confront grave, often novel, and sometimes highly controversial constitutional questions. On the other hand, if Congress accepts as part of its task the consideration of constitutional questions, whether narrow or broad, it finds itself ill-equipped with internal machinery, procedural rules, and expert sources of advice for discharging that task. What it has to do it seemingly cannot do. The dilemma which Congress faced in 1958 was serious. In their hunger for expertise, as the next chapter will show, members would resort to an expedient which would make it more serious.

14

Enter the Executive:
The Public Accommodations Title
of the 1964 Civil Rights Act

In 1964 twenty years of gathering social and political upheaval reached a climax with passage of a far-reaching civil rights act. A decade earlier, public alarm had hurried Congress into the Communist Control Act and thereby jeopardized rights of free expression. Now a public opinion better informed and more articulate mounted a sustained and systematic pressure for action. The resulting legislation was both comprehensive and deliberate.

This time the rights at stake were those of the American Negro to equality. Demands from constituents, from organized groups, and from national party leaders called for legislative protection. This chapter will deal with constitutional questions raised by Title II of the act. Eighty-nine years earlier Congress had made a parallel effort, only to meet with Supreme Court rebuff.[1] Now at last it returned to the problem by declaring that all persons without regard to race, color, religion, or national origin "shall be entitled to equal enjoyment of the goods, services, facilities, privileges, advantages and accommodations of any place of public accommodation as defined in this chapter."[2] The tidal wave of pressure which drove Congress to stipulate these rights and to provide means for enforcement carried with it the usual menace—the possibility, even the likelihood, that important constitutional questions would go unheeded. Indeed, political forces, majority and minority, exploited legislative organs and procedures with such skill and determination that the weighing of principles which constitutional issues necessitate seemed beyond attainment. In the end, Congress arrived at a deliberated settlement, but by a process in some respects both novel and disturbing.

For a full decade after the Civil War, Congress had concerned itself with civil rights. Not only did it frame and send the states three far-reaching constitutional amendments to protect Negro rights, but it took seriously the section included in each which gave it power to enforce the article "by appropriate legislation."[3] The resulting Civil Rights Acts were evidence that Congress could implement the constitutional text. After 1875, however, legislation ceased, and the Supreme Court took over. The effect of the ensuing decisions when coupled with congressional inertia reinforced by the Southern filibuster was to slow down the movement for Negro rights. In time the Supreme Court began to change its direction. In a series of decisions in the second quarter of the twentieth century the Court began effectuating that clause of the Fourteenth Amendment which forbids a state to "deny to any person within its jurisdiction the equal protection of the laws." These decisions promoted equal rights by setting aside state discrimination respecting, for example, professional education, white primaries and other curbs on voting, and racially-restrictive land covenants.[4]

World War II brought a renewal of political action. Court decisions, wartime idealism, and the mounting electoral strength of Negroes made equal rights a key issue, and by 1944 both major parties were including civil rights planks in their platforms. Leaders of both parties began to see civil rights legislation as a means to electoral success.[5] Accordingly both parties responded favorably in 1957 when President Eisenhower called for action.[6] In the Civil Rights Act of that year Congress at last succeeded in blocking out one area of rights for protection—the right to vote—and furnished tools of enforcement with which to make a beginning at compliance. In the process the Senate achieved a hard-fought constitutional settlement in the form of a requirement for jury trials for persons charged with criminal contempt under the act.[7] In 1960, Congress strengthened the enforcement of voting rights in a second Civil Rights Act,[8] and both parties, now eager to woo the Negro vote, included strong civil rights planks in their platforms.[9] Yet President John F. Kennedy, with the narrowest of election margins, moved cautiously his first two years and registered only minor gains.[10]

The major thrust for more thoroughgoing legislation in 1963 had its origins in the demonstrations which Negroes began conducting throughout the South and East in the spring of that year and in the violence which they encountered. In January the President had touched only briefly on civil rights in his annual message. On February 28, he had sent a message requesting further protection for voting rights, assistance for school desegregation, and a four-year extension of the Civil Rights Commission, which had been established by the Civil Rights Act of 1957. But the message and the accompanying bills were silent on the matter of public accommodations in privately-owned establishments not directly connected with interstate facilities. Beginning in April, however, and lasting through the summer, officials, often with mob support, applied tear gas, clubs, fire hoses, police dogs, and guns to civil rights workers and demonstrators. In Birmingham, Alabama, Cambridge, Maryland, Jackson, Mississippi, and Savannah, Georgia, demonstrators met stiff resistance, as the nation watched on television.[11] The President

293

responded on June 19 with his second civil rights message of the year. This time the proposals were comprehensive and included a ban on discriminatory treatment of patrons in privately-owned public accommodations—the target of most of the demonstrations and sit-ins. The Civil Rights Act held the spotlight in Congress until passage over a year later. The urgency of the mass march and official brutality gave impetus to the political process.

Political forces behind the bill included three elements—Administration, parties, and pressure groups. First, President Kennedy, and after his assassination November 22, President Johnson, applied executive resources and influences to the task. Most noteworthy was the unflagging work of Attorney General Robert F. Kennedy and officials from the Justice Department. The Attorney General starred as a committee witness, and his aides served repeatedly both in party consultations and as advisers to members of Congress.

Second, the act swept forward on a wave of bipartisan collaboration. Senate and House leaders of both parties cemented coalitions early and, despite recurrent jockeying for advantage in the coming elections, held their members in line until passage of the bill. Already in June 1963, the majority and minority leaders, Senators Mike Mansfield, Montana Democrat, and Everett M. Dirksen, Illinois Republican, were meeting with Administration officials at the White House and Senator Dirksen's office to map strategy. To manage the bill on the floor, the leaders chose Senators Hubert H. Humphrey of Minnesota, for the Democrats, and Thomas Kuchel of California, for the Republicans; their tactics included issuing a bipartisan daily newsletter. In May 1964, further leadership conferences produced a compromise bill that captured sufficient votes to end the filibuster and win passage.

In the House, floor management fell to Chairman Celler and his ranking Republican associate on the Judiciary Committee, Representative William McCulloch of Ohio. These two maintained close liaison with the House leaders, Speaker McCormack and Representative Charles Halleck of Indiana, and figured prominently in conferences with the Administration in October 1963. Their discussions forged the successful House bill. This party teamwork was indispensable to success.

Opponents of the bill, relying always on the Senate filibuster to block legislation which many deemed unconstitutional, developed their own defensive operations. The Georgia Democrat, Senator Richard B. Russell, led the Senate forces, assigning fifteen hard-core opponents to three teams of five each. In the House, Representative William M. Colmer of Mississippi shared honors with Louisiana Representative Edwin E. Willis of the Judiciary Committee, both Democrats. The conflict thus became less one of party than of region.

Third, organized groups worked for passage to an almost unprecedented extent. After House debate, the *Congressional Quarterly* stated in February 1964 that Washington had witnessed "some of the most intensive and effective behind-the-scenes lobbying in modern legislative history."[12] From hotel headquarters near the Capitol, the Leadership Conference on Civil Rights spoke for some seventy-nine Negro, labor, church, and other groups. Not since the agitation for Prohibition, Senator Russell cried, had the capital seen such a "gigantic and well-organized lobby."[13] Opponents rallied to the Coordinating Committee for Fundamental American Freedoms, reputedly financed in part by the Mississippi State Sovereignty Commission. The civil rights groups resorted to novel tactics, including the posting of watchers in the galleries and the institution of a "buddy" system to check voting on the House floor.[14]

Executive, party coalition, and pressure groups combined their efforts with a remarkable stamina and intensity, a fact which complicated the task of probing constitutional questions. After the President's June message with its supporting bills, three committees were soon holding hearings simultaneously—the House and Senate Judiciary Committees and the Senate Commerce Committee. All the hearings touched on the principal constitutional question affecting Title II. The Administration had rested its bill chiefly on the power of Congress to regulate commerce, but liberals in both houses sought to extend the coverage of Title II by basing it on a broad interpretation of the Fourteenth Amendment. The limits and relative advantages of the two powers remained a key subject of discussion. The liberals prevailed on New York Representative Emanuel Celler's Subcommittee No. 5, but the full House Judiciary Committee after feverish consultations accepted a more moderate bill, based on both powers. It was this House bill, after nine days of Rules Committee hearings and ten days of floor debate preceding House passage, that the Senate took up in February 1964.

The Senate discussed the bill for eighty-one days, bypassing the Judiciary Committee, contending with a record Southern filibuster, and finally achieving passage through the imposition of cloture with its restraints on debate. Senate passage by 73 to 27 came on June 19, and the House adopted the Senate version by 289 to 126 on July 2. The constitutional questions central to Title II appeared at every stage but were effectively resolved before the bill reached the Senate. Accordingly, it was to the Senate that several issues concerned with enforcement provisions largely fell.

The Civil Rights Act of 1964 extends protection for Negro rights along a broad front. Title II, which took effect immediately, guarantees the right to equal treatment in public accommodations, extending coverage both to accommodations associated with interstate commerce and to those in which, under the Fourteenth Amendment, state action is a factor. Further, it defines enforcement procedures, including the prior applicability of state laws, the circumstances in which the Attorney General may intervene in suits brought by individuals, and the use to be made of the Community Relations Service, set up by Title X. Other titles deal with voting rights (I), public facilities (III), school desegregation (IV), fair employment practices (VII), and still others with various means of enforcement.[15]

The constitutional settlement which Congress fashioned in relation to Title II gave signs of early acceptance. In Congress itself, demands for further legislation moved to other areas of Negro rights. President Johnson announced plans for strict enforcement, and by the following June, the Department of Justice had brought seventeen suits in seven Southern states to desegregate public accommodations.[16] In the courts, Mr. Justice Hugo L. Black, as early as August 1964, was expediting an appeal to the Supreme Court, with a tribute to "one of the most thorough debates in the history of Congress."[17] In December, the Court unanimously upheld Title II in two cases, one involving an Atlanta motel, and the other, a Birmingham restaurant.[18] Despite divergent stands taken by three concurring justices, all of the opinions relied heavily on the evidence which the committee hearings had elicited concerning the character and effect of discrimination. Wrote Mr. Justice Clark for the majority, "While the Act as adopted carries no congressional findings, the record of its passage is replete with evidence of the burdens which discrimination by race or color places upon interstate commerce."[19]

Public compliance with Title II was prompt and relatively widespread.[20] Southern businessmen in many cities urged obedience to the law.[21] Even more than Court endorsement, this public response to the law argues strongly for the effectiveness of congressional deliberations. One Southern official contrasted the Court's holding in the school desegregation cases which, he said, had settled "the law of the case," to the action of Congress in the Civil Rights Act, "the law of the land."[22] The national representative body had imparted an authority and acceptability to civil rights settlements lacking in the pioneering decisions of the Supreme Court.

CONSTITUTIONAL QUESTIONS

Two sorts of constitutional questions arose during the long discussion of Title II. The first, and the focus of analysis here, was substantive: Did Congress possess power to outlaw discrimination in privately-owned places of public accommodation? The second was procedural and will receive only brief comment: Through what means and under what limitations should that power be exercised?

As we have seen, advocates of the bill asserted two distinct grounds for Title II: first, the power of Congress under section 5 of the Fourteenth Amendment to enforce by appropriate legislation the right to the equal protection of the laws and, second, the power of Congress to regulate interstate commerce. Still other grounds were occasionally suggested,[23] but these two provisions drew the principal attention.

Advocates of both grounds could invoke important Supreme Court precedents, and the existence of those precedents acted powerfully on the discussions. These issues were accordingly narrowly legal, and, whichever ground Congress chose, the legislation was clearly destined for early judicial review. A simple relegation of the whole problem to the courts was of doubtful wisdom in such a situation.

The chief precedent under the Fourteenth Amendment was the eighty-year-old holding in the Civil Rights Cases.[24] Voting eight to one, the Court had there held unconstitutional sections 1 and 2 of the Civil Rights Act of 1875, which had declared that no person could deny any citizen on grounds of race or color "the full and equal enjoyment of the accommodations, advantages, facilities and privileges of inns, public conveyances on land or water, theatres and other places of public amusement."[25] The Court had found private discrimination beyond the reach of congressional power. "No state shall make or enforce any law . . . ," proclaims the Fourteenth Amendment, and Mr. Justice Bradley asserted in his opinion for the majority, "It is State action of a particular character that is prohibited. Individual invasion of individual rights is not the subject-matter of the amendment."[26] A central issue in 1963–1964 accordingly became: What constitutes "State action"?

After 1883, the Court had gradually expanded the concept of state action. In the early 1960's the Court extended it to outlaw discrimination where the law requiring segregation was merely a local ordinance,[27] where no state or local enactment existed but where a private restaurant operator leased his premises from the state,[28] and most significantly, in Lombard v. Louisiana, where city officials and the chief of police, notwithstanding the absence of statutory provisions, had issued public statements condemning sit-in demonstrations in segregated accommodations.[29] If all these measures comprised state action in support of discrimination, and if, under Shelley v. Kraemer, judicial enforcement of restrictive land covenants also comprised state action,[30] then one might plausibly construe the amendment as encompassing state enforcement of discrimination based solely on custom or usage and lacking any prior state authorization.

297

Those favoring broad coverage could find additional comfort in the concurring opinion of Mr. Justice Douglas in the Lombard case. There he suggested that "State licensing and surveillance of a business serving the public also brings its service into the public domain," making it "an instrumentality of the State."[31] Liberals, accordingly, could appeal both to custom or usage and to the existence of state licenses to justify a finding of state action and thereby bring innumerable private acts of discrimination in public accommodations within the power of Congress under the Fourteenth Amendment.

The volume and cloudiness of Supreme Court precedents invited case-centered disputation. In relation to the commerce power, precedents were somewhat clearer. Congress and the Court once excluded important intrastate activities from the reach of the power,[32] and the Court, notwithstanding pressures from President and Congress, adhered to its restrictive readings as late as 1936.[33] In 1937, however, the Court began to approve congressional regulations of local activities on a showing of a tangible, if somewhat indirect, effect on interstate commerce.[34] Could Congress prohibit a local motel owner from refusing to serve a traveling Negro businessman on the ground that his refusal had a substantial effect on the flow of interstate commerce or had a demonstrable connection with commerce? Could Congress prohibit discrimination by a local restaurant owner who received a substantial part of his food through interstate channels?

The closest precedent was the 1942 decision in Wickard v. Filburn.[35] There the Court held that a national system of production quotas could validly be extended to a quantity of wheat which a farmer had raised in excess of his quota and evidently intended to consume on the farm and sell locally. It was the cumulative economic effect of many such instances that brought the matter within the commerce power. Could discrimination be embraced within the same doctrine? In addition, and equally important in congressional deliberations, could such an effect be demonstrated as a matter of fact? Title II would challenge congressional machinery in relation to both doctrine and fact. Except for frequent assertions that Title II violated the rights of private property under the Fifth Amendment, these issues of the commerce power and the Fourteenth Amendment dominated discussion.

Increasingly, however, debate turned from these narrow constitutional questions to broad questions and to questions associated with implementation of constitutional provisions. Opponents sought to condition enforcement of the stipulated rights in a variety of ways, notably by renewing the 1957 demand for jury trials in cases of criminal contempt. The discussion of this and other matters involved constitutional principles and values. Limitations of space will, however, make it necessary to subordinate them to the leading motif of this chapter, the questions of substantive power.

COURSE OF THE DISCUSSION

House Judiciary Subcommittee Hearings. When on June 19 President Kennedy first proposed public accommodations legislation, a House sub-committee was already at work. Judiciary Committee Chairman Celler of New York had convened his Subcommittee No. 5 for hearings on May 8. This group numbered seven Democrats, all of them, be it noted, supporters of the bill, and four Republicans. Although more representa-tive geographically than in 1957–1958, it still gave undue weight to the Northeast; only two members came from the South and only one of the remaining nine from west of the Mississippi.[36]

A wide spectrum of witnesses appeared at the twenty-two-day hear-ings. In all, 101 testified and their testimony, when added to ninety-four additional statements and communications, filled two volumes. Twenty-six Representatives testified and forty-three others submitted statements. Two Senators, sixteen officials from the executive branch, and a handful of state and local officials, chiefly Southern, testified. Negro civil rights groups furnished nine witnesses, labor unions six, and the churches twelve; twenty-one spoke for a miscellany of other groups including the American Civil Liberties Union and the Americans for Democratic Action, and five private individuals appeared.

Much of the testimony dealt generally with the problem of discrimina-tion and the character of the movement for reform. For example, Timothy Jenkins, speaking for the Student Non-Violent Coordinating Committee, described the aims of his organization. In seeking equal rights for Southern Negroes, its members had received abuse ranging from "constant villification in public, to attempted murder in private." The federal government, he insisted, had only "weakly asserted its existing powers to act in our defense."[37] To a South Carolina Repre-sentative, Albert W. Watson, however, the racial problem was a Southern problem: "Legislation by an only slightly familiar Federal Government can only inflame an already very difficult situation."[38] Much of the evidence spoke the language of broad policy and moral principle and reflected this regional cleavage.

Yet some of it dealt with constitutional doctrine. Even before the President's strong June message, the committee had touched on the cen-tral constitutional questions.[39] When the Executive Director of the American Civil Liberties Union, John DeJ. Pemberton, appeared on May 28, members quizzed him concerning the power of Congress under the Fourteenth Amendment. He in turn urged that Congress rely on the relatively certain commerce power, expressing doubt that the Court would overrule the Civil Rights Cases.[40] But the subcommittee majority seemed persuaded that the Fourteenth Amendment would provide a broader coverage since many establishments might seem insufficiently engaged in interstate commerce to provide a nexus with the commerce power. Committee member Byron G. Rogers, Colorado Democrat, and Chairman Celler conjectured that facilities which lay outside the commerce power but which were licensed by the state could be reached under the amendment on the theory that state licensing constituted state action. Pemberton conceded that Shelley v. Kraemer by analogy might lend support to this position, but repeated that he preferred the narrower coverage of the commerce clause.[41]

This interchange and others like it suggest two features of the hearings: first, there was a startling lack of controversy over the scope of the commerce power; in thirty pages of testimony Pemberton was never once called upon to explore the doctrine and coverage of that power—and this in spite of his repeated assertion that he would base the legislation upon it rather than the Fourteenth Amendment. Second, and related to this, the impetus toward the Fourteenth Amendment came from the subcommittee itself, some members of which harbored preconceptions about its scope.[42]

Attorney General Kennedy appeared on June 26 and tried repeatedly to correct those preconceptions. In his effort to get the liberal members to forsake a position which many supporters of the bill considered unwise and extreme, he faced heavy odds. He preferred the Administration bill, Title II of which would have outlawed discrimination, first, in hotels and motels "furnishing lodging to transient guests" and second, in establishments offering goods, services, or food for sale where these are provided "to a substantial degree to interstate travelers" or where a "substantial portion" of the things offered for sale has moved in interstate commerce. With one qualification,[43] sole reliance of the bill was on the commerce power.

In his opening statement, the Attorney General made explicit the position of the Administration concerning the Fourteenth-Amendment stand of the subcommittee. He conceded that the vitality of the Civil Rights Cases was questionable in view of the widened concept of state action. Yet the early precedent had never been overruled, and, he said, "In these circumstances it seems to us to be the proper course for Title II to rely primarily upon the commerce clause."[44]

Kennedy took this stand for both political and constitutional reasons, reasons which he carefully distinguished. Much of his testimony dealt with the extent of coverage desired under the commerce power. It would be difficult, he maintained, to get Title II through Congress without complicating the task by challenging a Supreme Court precedent directly pertinent to the Fourteenth-Amendment basis. The modern Court might conceivably overrule the Civil Rights Cases, but as long as those decisions remained the law of the land, they controlled.[45]

A strong counter-argument came from the young Republican, a Yale Law School graduate, serving his fifth year in the House, Representative John V. Lindsay, soon to be mayor of New York City. Sitting in at the chairman's invitation for another New York Republican, William E. Miller, Lindsay asserted that use of the Fourteenth Amendment would support a broad and extensive ban on discrimination, while a more cautious reliance on commerce might result in "not doing as much good as you would like."[46] He approved of Mr. Justice Douglas' concurrence in Lombard to the effect that state licensing was equivalent to state action, and went even further. He maintained that state action was present when police removed trespassing demonstrators from a restaurant solely at the owner's request.[47]

At the opposite extreme stood the witnesses who offered testimony opposed to all legislation. Such legislation, they insisted, would violate property rights under the Fifth Amendment, but they offered little constitutional doctrine to support their contention. One even denied that the commerce power would reach public accommodations, but as he was unaware of Wickard v. Filburn, his argument made little headway.[48]

After nearly four months devoted to the 172 bills before it, the hearings closed on August 2. Beginning on the fourteenth, the subcommittee met in executive session no fewer than seventeen days. Later a Republican member, Representative George Meader of Michigan, intimated that the subcommittee had initially agreed on moderation, avoiding controversial clauses which "could be sloughed off as trading material during the legislative process."[49] The group, he complained, had adopted a partisan tone and broadened the bill in a summary fashion.[50] The outcome was a subcommittee report spelling out Title II in the language of those who favored a broad Fourteenth-Amendment phraseology. Section 201(C)(4) of the subcommittee bill greatly extended the coverage of the Administration bill by prohibiting discrimination where the business operated under state or local "authorization, permission, or license," or where the practices of the business were "compelled, encouraged, or sanctioned by the State, directly or indirectly."[51]

Against the testimony of a number of authoritative witnesses, especially the Attorney General, the subcommittee majority had decided to press ahead with a far-reaching bill. Its action represented either extreme dogmatism on a debatable issue of constitutional interpretation; or, and

301

more likely, an intention, notwithstanding constitutional hazards, to gain the partisan political advantage of a strong bill with a view to later concession and compromise.[52]

In the House Judiciary Committee. From October 8 to 29 the full Judiciary Committee wrestled with the strong subcommittee bill. Of the thirty-five members, three-fifths were Democrats. Here the South's nine seats and the Far West's five helped balance off the Northeast and Midwest, with their combined nineteen seats. The Border States had two seats.[53]

On the tenth, the committee was still in executive session considering the subcommittee bill when a decision was suddenly made to call the Attorney General for testimony. For two days, the fifteenth and sixteenth, Kennedy spoke in closed session. The Administration, as the published testimony later disclosed, strongly opposed Title II of the subcommittee bill. Said the Attorney General:

> . . . invoking the Fourteenth Amendment generally is no substitute for specifying the establishments which Congress, enacting national law to solve a national problem, intends to cover.
>
> Surely the first step in federal legislation is to determine which public establishments present the significant kinds of problems with which federal power should be concerned. Once the decision is made all relevant sources of constitutional authority should be drawn upon to support the legislation.[54]

Next day he reiterated his belief that the proper scope of the Fourteenth Amendment should be sought in existing Supreme Court decisions. Beyond these, presumably, the Administration was not prepared to go. Said he, "Where the state action is limited to just a licensing, for instance, I don't think that that is sufficient. And, therefore, I think— my judgment is that it would probably be unconstitutional."[55]

The committee resumed executive sessions, but after the twenty-second the chairman repeatedly recessed until the twenty-eighth. The intransigeance of the Southern opponents of any legislation and of the liberals who favored the subcommittee bill was such that only the intervention of the White House itself and resumption of bipartisan conferences could produce a feasible bill. Numerous secret conferences between Justice Department officials and such committee members as Celler, McCulloch, and Lindsay devised a bill differing at many points from the subcommittee version.[56] This new, fifty-six-page bill changed the Fourteenth-Amendment provision of the subcommittee bill by stipulating that discrimination was supported by state action when "carried on under color of any law, statute, ordinance, regulation, custom, or usage" or when "required, fostered, or encouraged by action of a State or a political subdivision thereof."[57]

This new compromise or "midnight" bill was delivered to the members of the committee at 10:30 the evening of the twenty-eighth and twelve hours later, on the twenty-ninth, Chairman Celler took it up in full executive session. The committee first voted 15 to 19 against reporting the subcommittee bill, with seven Southerners supporting legislation which they hoped would be too strong to win passage, but which some of them must have deemed unconstitutional. Two Southerners opposed it, Democratic Representatives Edwin E. Willis of Louisiana and Jack B. Brooks of Texas, as also did Lindsay. The chairman then rushed the compromise bill to a vote, and the committee fell in line by a vote of 23 to 11. Publication of a descriptive committee report followed on November 20 and of the hearings, February 2. White House and Justice Department intervention had produced a bill more clearly in line with Supreme Court precedents.

House Rules Committee. On January 9, 1964, the House Rules Committee opened nine days of hearings on the new bill. One-third of its fifteen members were Southerners, including its veteran chairman, Judge Howard W. Smith of Virginia; yet all regions were represented, and the Democrats held two-thirds of the seats. The bipartisan consultations of October and the consideration that this bill had been close to the heart of the assassinated President, even more than a threat by proponents of the bill to discharge it from committee consideration, made favorable committee action likely. Recently enlarged and liberalized, the committee now provided sufficient votes, among its five Republicans and five nonsouthern Democrats, to constitute a large majority.[58] Thirty-nine witnesses, mostly Southerners, testified, but three held the spotlight: Representatives Celler and McCulloch, ranking majority and minority members of the Judiciary Committee, and Willis, chief spokesman of the opposition to legislation.

Early in the hearings, Judge Smith challenged the constitutionality of the "custom and usage" provisions of the bill. Chairman Celler replied that the Lombard case had established that "State action may, under some circumstances, be involved where the State lends its aid to the enforcement of discriminatory practices carried on by private persons."[59] Reiterating the strong subcommittee position, Celler construed the pertinent cases as meaning that "custom and usage as a result of many years may have the effect of a law or an order or an ordinance."[60] "State action falling short of a requirement," he insisted, "may constitute a sufficient degree of State 'participation and involvement' to warrant a holding of State action in violation of the 14th amendment."[61] Whether

303

the Attorney General had favored so broad an interpretation is open to doubt.

Representative Willis developed the constitutional argument against the Title. Citing the Attorney General's rebuttal to the extension of the Fourteenth Amendment, he went on to attack "custom and usage" as vague to the point of being unconstitutional. Celler's reading of the phrase, he contended, lacked support in reason or precedent.[62] Recent decisions had not specifically overruled the Civil Rights Cases, which still controlled.[63] He also denied that the commerce power would support this legislation but conceded that counsel who defended the bill could find cases on the other side. He deplored the invoking of both powers for "As a matter of policy, we are engaging in stretching the Constitution to the point where like a fiddle's string it is going to pop loose after a while."[64]

In the end, the Rules Committee, voting 11 to 4, reported the bill to the House with an open rule providing an airing of the constitutional issues in debate. Its hearings furnished members with the only published give-and-take on the bill in the form in which it came to the floor.

House Floor Debate. January 31 marked the first of ten days of House floor debate, and Representative Celler documented the constitutionality of Title II in detail. He placed in the record a long statement, the evident work of the Justice Department. For the first time in House discussions, the commerce-power argument received systematic treatment.[65] As for the Fourteenth-Amendment argument, the document asserted that although the present Court might conceivably overrule the Civil Rights Cases, Title II relied not on such a dubious eventuality but on the Court-expanded concept of state action.[66]

Representative Willis then rose to attack the constitutionality of Title II. "Custom or usage," he maintained, "was equivalent to affirmative action by a state" and such a conception, like the asserted scope of the commerce clause, constituted a "novel and dangerous experiment in political theory."[67]

An effort toward mediation and clarification along lines more clearly constitutional was launched by a member from Minnesota. The Republican Clark MacGregor faced the problem posed by the phrase "custom and usage." In the present bill, the phrase had a scope determined solely by the breadth with which one chose to read it. It could mean anything from officially-sanctioned discrimination of the sort set out in Lombard to distinctly private discrimination unsupported by prior state authorization, formal or informal. The Minnesotan now asserted that

the "custom and usage" to which the chairman [Celler] and I have been referring is not constituted merely by a practice in a neighborhood or by popular attitudes in a particular community. The cases clearly hold that this "custom and usage" consists of a practice which, although not embodied in law, receives notice and sanction to the extent that it is enforced by the officialdom of the State or the locality . . .[68]

In the light of this statement, the committee chairman saw fit to moderate his own position. He and Representative McCulloch were soon endorsing an effort to narrow the scope of the Title. On February 5, when the Title was up for amendment under the five-minute rule, Representative Charles E. Goodell, New York Republican, submitted an amendment, further amended by Representative Willis, to bring the meaning of "custom or usage" into line with MacGregor's interpretation.[69] The custom or usage necessary to support a finding of state action now read, "Custom or usage required or enforced by officials of the state or political subdivision thereof." Little debate ensued. Supported as it was by proponents and opponents of the legislation, the Goodell-Willis amendment passed handily.

In this respect Title II cleared the House without further change. The alteration which the Executive had intervened to initiate was completed, amid bipartisan negotiations, on the House floor. On February 10, the House passed the bill by a vote of 290 to 130.

Thus the House had extended the Administration's original bill to public accommodations which lay outside the sphere of the commerce power. It had also succeeded under executive pressures and with party negotiations in producing a bill more clearly constitutional than that precipitated by its own civil rights forces.

Senate Commerce Hearings. With the House subcommittee already at work, the Senate Commerce Committee began month-long hearings of its own on July 1, 1963. Its focus was on an Administration bill confined wholly to public accommodations. The seventeen members included twelve Democrats and five Republicans. The West here achieved fair representation with five members drawn from the mountain and Pacific states, including Chairman Warren Magnuson, Washington Democrat; only two were Southerners, and only one of these, Senator Strom Thurmond of South Carolina, carried his opposition into the filibuster.[70] The testimony of the forty-nine witnesses and the ninety-five other statements that fill three volumes illuminated the constitutional problem in many ways and from many vantage points. Local and state officials, members of Congress, executive officers, spokesmen for interest groups, law professors, and private individuals submitted views which ranged from that of Roy Wilkins of the National Association for the Advancement of Colored People to that of Governor Ross Barnett of Mississippi.

Although much testimony dealt with the international, social, and economic implications of the bill, some eighteen of the witnesses helped elucidate the constitutional questions. Once again, the Attorney General was a prominent witness. Although he repeated the opinion that the present Court might overturn the Civil Rights Cases, he preferred to play down the Fourteenth Amendment in favor of the commerce power.[71]

This committee, like that in the House, was deeply split on this question. Eight of the seventeen Senators remained uncommitted on the Fourteenth-Amendment approach, five of them from the Midwest and Far West.[72] The remaining nine included: Senators Frank J. Lausche of Ohio and Norris Cotton of New Hampshire, who were lukewarm to either basis; Philip A. Hart of Michigan and Mike Monroney of Oklahoma, who preferred the commerce clause; Strom Thurmond of South Carolina, who opposed any bill at all; and four, John O. Pastore of Rhode Island, Clair Engel of California, Thruston B. Morton of Kentucky, and Winston L. Prouty of Vermont, who preferred a strong Fourteenth-Amendment basis. Arguing with ingenuity and persistence, these last four relied, not on reversal of the Civil Rights Cases, but on the expanded state-action concept.[73]

The commerce power received far more consideration here than in the House. Senator Morton expressed a view common to many congressional Republicans, wary of federal intrusions into local economies, to the effect that use of that power would presage even more severe regulation of business activity. Senator Thurmond saw a threat to property rights, deeming it neither "right" nor constitutional "to force a man to use his private property in any way."[74]

Backers of the bill also detailed the arguments supporting use of the commerce power. They frequently cited Wickard v. Filburn with its rule upholding regulation of local activities which cumulatively affect interstate commerce. They pointed out that thirty states had public accommodations laws, and that the courts had upheld these laws against assertions of property rights.[75] The commerce power appeared to have the better of the doctrinal argument.

The most important single achievement of these hearings, however, lay in the testimony concerning the actual connection between racial discrimination in public accommodations and interstate commerce. Up to this point demonstration of that connection had rested mainly on general assertion, as in the original Administration bill, or personal experience, as occasionally related by witnesses. But the important factual evidence was the testimony of Under Secretary of Commerce Franklin D. Roosevelt, Jr. Confronting the committee with charts and graphs, he offered statistics in support of six contentions: 1. Discrimination was an obstacle to interstate travel. Thus, a Negro driving from

Washington to New Orleans would find that adequate hotel or motel accommodations for him were separated on the average by intervals of 174 miles.[76] 2. Discrimination distorted the pattern of expenditures by Negroes because of limited access to places of public accommodations. 3. Discrimination placed limitations on the ability of organizations to hold national and regional conventions in convenient places. 4. Discrimination had adverse effects in the entertainment field. 5. Discrimination caused disruptions of trade resulting from demonstrations protesting that discrimination. 6. Discrimination entailed many and various difficulties in the normal conduct of business particularly in the recruiting of professional and skilled personnel and in the selection of plant locations. Roosevelt's testimony later proved of crucial importance when the Supreme Court tested the constitutionality of Title II.

The twenty-third and final day of hearings came on August 2, and the committee report, based on the many-sided testimony and on discussions in executive session, appeared on February 10. The report, which was accompanied by several individual statements, discussed the bill and committee amendments concisely and judiciously.[77] Despite its fourteen-to-three lineup, this committee supplied the Senate with both background material and informed judgments concerning Title II.

Senate Judiciary Committee. On July 16, 1963, the summer's third set of simultaneous hearings opened before the Senate Judiciary Committee. For eleven days, spread over the next two months, the fifteen members heard argument on the Administration's omnibus bill. In the past, this committee, chaired since 1954 by Senator James O. Eastland, Mississippi Democrat, had bottled up almost every effort at civil rights legislation. Eight replacements since the Jenner-Butler discussions in 1958 had improved its geographical representativeness. Five of the ten Democrats and three of the five Republicans were new, and spokesmen for New England and the Middle Atlantic states had risen from zero to four; Senator Hiram L. Fong, Hawaii Democrat, was the sole member from the Far West. Senator Estes Kefauver's death midway in the proceedings left the South with four and the Midwest with five members.[78] Although the Senate leadership found it expedient later to circumvent the committee, that body had so evolved in recent years that it was now able to offer a remarkably focused and even learned argument on the applicable constitutional doctrine.

The first two days of hearings the committee devoted to testimony from its own members.[79] Most notable was a statement by Senator Sam J. Ervin, Jr., North Carolina Democrat, who by this time was widely recognized as the Senate's leading constitutional expert. In a twenty-page analysis of Title II he attacked both bases offered in support of the legislation. The commerce power, he insisted, ceased when persons or goods actually stopped moving in the channels of commerce. On stepping out of his car to seek a meal or lodgings, a traveler entered a phase of activity beyond the reach of that power.[80] As for the Fourteenth Amendment, the Civil Rights Cases remained the law of the land, and Congress possessed no power to deal with purely private discriminatory acts.[81] The suggestion that state licensing constituted state action he repudiated: That argument "wouldn't even have the stability of legal quicksand,"[82] since the official licensing had no connection with the act of discrimination. The Senator applied to both the asserted constitutional powers a detailed incisive probing of the many pertinent arguments.

A single outside witness appeared—the Attorney General. Although he did not enlarge on arguments he was pressing in other committees, his appearance from July 18 to the end of the hearings was a high point of the year-long discussions. A long, fruitful dialogue took place between the Administration's most effective spokesman and the Senator from North Carolina.

The Kennedy-Ervin confrontation yielded no new arguments. What it did yield was a coherent, focused, logical exposition, in an adversary setting, of the strengths and weaknesses of all the relevant constitutional arguments, arguments which heretofore had appeared only sporadically and at random. Out of this interchange gradually emerged the weakness of the Fourteenth-Amendment approach and the strength of the commerce-clause approach.

Senator Ervin directed his attack chiefly at the Fourteenth Amendment, keeping the Attorney General on the defensive. In pressing his attack, he insisted on taking up that amendment sentence by sentence, requesting the Attorney General to explain how each sentence could furnish support for the bill.[83] For each of Kennedy's arguments, Ervin cited case after case in opposition to it. Under such pressure, Kennedy replied repeatedly that the legislation would be valid under the commerce clause, although he continued to maintain that Fourteenth-Amendment arguments could be found for presentation before the Supreme Court.[84]

If Ervin held Kennedy on the defensive on the Fourteenth Amendment, their roles were reversed when the discussion turned to the commerce clause. On July 31, Ervin presented a long statement opposing the commerce-power basis. He warned repeatedly of the danger of stretching federal power to the most intimate aspects of private life and concluded: "Mr. Attorney General, unless you wish to make some comments on what I have had to say, I will ask a few questions with reference to the meaning of the public accommodations provisions and then try to pass on to other aspects of the bill."[85] This apparent effort to sidestep further discussion of the commerce clause failed; Kennedy insisted that discrimination had an adverse effect on interstate commerce and offered a series of modern cases, including Wickard, holding that the commerce power reached local activities if their cumulative effect on interstate commerce was disruptive. The Jones and Laughlin case, he showed, held immaterial the source of the impediment to commerce.[86] If Senator Ervin relied on Supreme Court precedents in opposing the Fourteenth-Amendment approach, Kennedy did the same in asserting the commerce power.

The hearings ended September 11 and were published five months later, on February 28. Thus the nine days of high-level adversary argument reached the Senate as a whole early in floor debate. Yet the absence of a committee report furnished civil rights backers with an argument for bypassing the committee later. It also prevented the Senate from benefiting by the committee's collective judgment.

Senate Floor Debate. Although two of its committees had labored over Title II, it was to the bill which the House had passed on February 10 that the Senate applied itself for nearly four months. Senators Humphrey and Kuchel, the party whips, captained the bipartisan coalition for the bill and Senator Russell, the opposition. The target of both forces was a small nucleus of the uncommitted.

Three distinct phases are discernible in the long Senate debate which ensued. The first of these, the preliminary debate from February 26 to March 26, was largely devoted to consideration of whether the bill should follow normal procedures and go to the Judiciary Committee or follow the precedent of the 1957 Act and be brought directly to the floor. As in 1957, Senators weighed the desirability of advance probing in committee against the likelihood that the committee would either bury the bill or alter it beyond repair. In the end they voted 67 to 17 to bypass Judiciary, but in spite of the absence of committee consideration, Title II received extensive constitutional examination on the floor during these preliminaries. On March 9, Senator Lister Hill, Alabama Democrat, launched the attack on the bill for the opposition,[87] and on three succeeding days other Southern Senators continued the assault.[88] Although these speakers offered little that was new, their statements, like most throughout the Senate debate, were clear and well-documented and spoke to the heart of the constitutional issues. The March 26 vote to take up the bill marked the end of the preliminaries. "In the battle for constitutional government," cried Senator Russell, "we have lost a skirmish . . . We shall now begin to fight the war."[89]

Senate debate now moved into the second phase, the filibuster, which was to last until June 10. The fact that Southern monopoly of the floor could be broken only if proponents of the bill mustered sixty-seven

309

votes, the two-thirds majority needed to invoke cloture, presented the bipartisan coalition with a problem in strategy and mathematics. They could anticipate some sixty-one votes for, and some thirty votes against cloture. This left a nine-man "swing" group which would decide the issue; besides two Democrats from Ohio and Oklahoma, these included seven Republicans from Delaware, Idaho, Iowa, Nebraska (2), New Hampshire, and South Dakota.[90] In addition to the traditional qualms over the use of cloture, these men had grave doubts over Titles II and VII, both of which encroached on age-old prerogatives of the business-man. Thus coalition leaders faced a twofold task: they had to produce a compromise bill acceptable not only to their own liberal supporters, but also to these conservative Republicans, and to the House coalition as well; second, they had to persuade Senator Dirksen, spokesman for these conservatives, to support the legislation and work for cloture among the uncommitted. Success in meeting these challenges ultimately brought success in achieving cloture.[91]

The extensive off-the-floor maneuvering which this cloture strategy necessitated significantly shifted the focus from the constitutional debate on the floor to the Senate's antechambers. But if the importance of the constitutional debate was limited, it was nevertheless of high quality. During this period five proponents directed their attention to the constitutional issues. Of these, the statement delivered on April 9 by Senator Magnuson, floor captain for Title II, was one of the ablest of the entire Senate debate. Drawing heavily on the findings of his own Commerce Committee, he elaborated both the commerce-power and Fourteenth-Amendment bases.[92] These five speeches of proponents were matched by five from the opponents, and although no new constitutional arguments were made, those Senators still attending debates heard statements from both sides which were pertinent and well prepared.

The end of the filibuster became a probability when the coalition leaders announced that compromise meetings off the floor had produced an acceptable bill.[93] Senator Dirksen had advanced some seventy amendments to moderate the bill, especially in its enforcement procedures. These formed the basis for a settlement among Senators from both sides of the aisle and the Attorney General, and on May 26 this second great substitute bill, the Mansfield-Dirksen compromise, was introduced. The three main changes in Title II affected its remedial or enforcement provisions: the Attorney General could now initiate court action only where a "pattern or practice" of discrimination, rather than a single such act, could be shown; precedence was to be given state public-accommodations laws for up to thirty days instead of merely a "reasonable time" before federal regulations would take effect; and judges would be able to delay court action for up to 120 days by calling in the Community Relations Service, which House debate had restored following House Committee elimination, as a means of promoting voluntary compliance.[94] A further adjustment of the bill was made on June 9, when the Southern bloc permitted a vote on the jury trial amendment; the Senator from Kentucky, Thruston Morton, moved a guarantee of jury trial in all cases of criminal contempt under the act, Title I excepted, and the amendment carried 51 to 48. These adjustments in the enforcement provisions won over the undecided. On June 10, the Senate, for the sixth time in its history and for the first time in civil rights legislation, adopted cloture by 71 to 29.[95]

The third and final phase of floor debate, from cloture to final passage, was devoted chiefly to amendments. The South had lost control of the floor and now altered its tactics, submitting most of the 560 amendments which reportedly awaited action. Yet the one-hour cloture limit on any one Senator meant that some, the first being Senator Ervin, soon exhausted their allotment of time; consequently between June 11 and 17 only 106 amendments received roll call votes.[96] Of thirty-one amendments to Title II, only two, of minor importance, were adopted—one further defining the circumstances in which the Attorney General could intervene in private suits and the other further assuring that private clubs would be exempted.[97] The final two days were devoted to general debate. Senator Barry Goldwater declared himself against the bill because he found Titles II and VII unconstitutional. On the nineteenth, the eighty-first day of debate, the Senate passed the Civil Rights Act by a vote of 73 to 27.

Title II emerged from the long Senate debate much as it had entered it. Executive pressure and bipartisan negotiations had led the House to define the scope of Title II along lines that met the constitutional scruples of most Senators. The Senate discussed that point, but its major contribution was not to scope but to enforcement procedures. In a sense, most of the floor talk was preliminary and contributory to the off-the-floor agreements resulting in the second substitute bill.

Final House Action. Back in the House, supporters of the bill moved adoption with all Senate amendments. Impetus for passage was now so great that opponents contented themselves with a single day of Rules Committee hearings.[98] Their chief complaint was procedural—the failure to send the bill to a joint conference committee for reconciliation of differences. After one hour of debate, the House passed the bill on July 2 by a vote of 289 to 126. President Johnson signed it the same evening.

311

Discussion Evaluated. Taken as a whole, the handling of constitutional questions associated with Title II was thorough and effective. The time lavished on committee and floor consideration and the availability of varied sources of constitutional advice helped assure that all pertinent questions should be raised and all pertinent arguments canvassed.

If discussion was exhaustive, the sledgehammer effect of executive, party, group, and public pressure for action made the achievement of genuine detachment difficult. If members brought constitutional questions into focus for deliberation, they did so only spasmodically in the several forums through which Title II made its way.

The relative scope of the Fourteenth Amendment and commerce power received its most satisfactory probing in the Senate Judiciary Committee and to a lesser extent in House Rules and on the House floor. Senate Commerce developed the factual link between discrimination and commerce, and Senate debate proliferated measures for enforcement. This time the Justice Department remained a directing and clarifying force.

Discussion of the central doctrinal questions fell short of the mark in the House subcommittee and the Senate Commerce Committee. Although argument was often pertinent, there was little evidence of logical development or direct rebuttal. Both forums showed a preference for the Fourteenth Amendment, interpreted broadly. Hence proponents of that position pressed grounds that a careful reading of court precedents would hardly justify and gave the Fourteenth-Amendment basis an excessive and distorted exposure at the expense of the commerce clause. Most participants simply presupposed the existence of the commerce power without probing the matter. In Senate Judiciary, however, members seemed open-minded as to the correct basis and the two protagonists, Senator Ervin and the Attorney General, conducted a dialogue that was pertinent, informed, searching, and illuminating. House Rules and House floor debate also helped to clarify the constitutional issues, the former through the statements of the opposed positions, and the latter through general debate and discussion of clarifying amendments. Note that in forums leaning heavily toward the Fourteenth Amendment, only the intervention of the Executive brought a measure of moderation and perspective.

Furthermore, members of both houses distinguished constitutional questions from policy and politics. The exploration of Title II went on with remarkably little partisan vituperation. Despite fundamental cleavages, members seemed to acknowledge the seriousness and complexity of the business before them.

It seems likely that the constitutional discussions contributed to the final results. House Committee and floor discussions helped prepare the ground for the clarifying Goodell-Willis amendment. Senate debate, fed by committee hearings, pointed the way toward such changes in implementation as the priority of state laws, the narrowing of intervention powers of the Attorney General, resort to the Community Relations Service, and the requirement of jury trial. The presence of uncommitted members, of course, made adjustment possible, but the discussion was an indispensable element in the process.

A study of voting figures, especially in the Senate, where roll calls were numerous, shows only limited freedom of action for most members. Table 10 presents an analysis by region of seven roll calls, two in the

TABLE 10. Regional Voting in Roll Calls on Civil Rights Act of 1964, Expressed in Percentages[a]

	House		Senate				
	1. For passage	2. For passage	3. For passage	4. For narrowing Title II	5. For requiring jury trial	6. For bypassing Judiciary Committee	7. For cloture
Region	Feb. 10	July 2	June 19	June 15	June 9	March 26	June 10
Middle Atlantic	99–1	100–0	100–0	13–87	20–80	100–0	100–0
New England	96–4	96–4	92–8	8–92	8–92	100–0	100–0
Midwest	89–11	89–11	95–5	19–81	41–59	100–0	95–5
Border	58–42	58–42	88–12	14–86	75–25	100–0	88–12
Far West	86–14	88–12	88–12	21–79	44–56	100–0	77–23
South	7–93	8–92	5–95	95–5	100–0	15–85	5–95
Total in Per Cent	69–31	70–30	73–27	33–67	52–48	80–20	71–29
Numerical Total	290–130	289–126	73–27	30–61	51–48	67–17	71–29

SOURCE: 22 CQWR, pp. 334, 1414, 1323, 1259, 1194, 638, and 1195.
[a] No account has been taken of nonvoting.

House and five in the Senate. Each vote is expressed in percentages of the total vote on that roll call. Columns 1 and 2 present the two House roll calls, in February and July, and reveal how slight was the change in spite of the intervening Senate phase; here the Far West showed the greatest flexibility in position—2 per cent. Column 3 gives the final Senate vote on the bill and shows Border State Senators voting for the bill in numbers 30 per cent higher than Border State Representatives. The remaining four columns represent earlier Senate roll calls. Column 4 presents an unsuccessful effort to narrow the coverage of Title II by excluding motels and restaurants which received substantial portions of their food and goods from interstate commerce. Here constitutional scruples may have entered in, and the results showed

313

Midwestern members departing from policy positions by 14 per cent, Middle Atlantic by 13 per cent, and Far Western by 9 per cent. Column 5 gives the successful vote to require jury trial. This time the Border States made the widest shift from policy goals—from 88 per cent for the bill to 75 per cent for jury trial, a shift of 63 per cent; the Midwest departed by 36 per cent and the Far West by 32 per cent; New Englanders refused to budge this time, showing the least interest in requiring juries. Columns 6 and 7 involve Senate procedure, 6 analyzing the heavy vote to bypass the Judiciary Committee, and 7 the vote for cloture. Even the South broke ranks on committee referral, while the Far West responded most strongly—11 per cent—to the argument for unlimited debate.

Note that whereas the Middle Atlantic and Midwestern States cast the heaviest majorities for the bill, it was New England that held most rigidly to its policy position. Inclusion of Maryland and Delaware explains the flexibility in the vote of the Middle Atlantic States. Here, again, the Border States and the Far West sustained the greatest flexibility.

The cohesion of the Southern Democratic bloc makes comparison of party voting less meaningful than comparison of regional. While the slight increase in majorities for the bill in the House is attributable to Democrats, Republicans showed greater flexibility than Democrats in nearly every Senate vote.[99] One may conclude that while tides of pressure were dominant in producing swings, committee and floor discussion had some effect on voting patterns.

One of the few Southerners to break with his region to support the bill testified to the value of the long discussion. In reversing his February vote against the bill, Democratic Representative Charles L. Weltner of Atlanta, Georgia, summoned the South to face the demands of change. After the "most thorough and sifting examination in legislative history," he was prepared to acknowledge the bill as "the law of the land," and "the verdict of the Nation."[100] "I will add my voice," he declared, "to those who seek reasoned and conciliatory adjustment to a new reality."[101]

PARTICIPANTS

In working toward settlement of the urgent constitutional questions associated with Title II, Congress showed more than ever its own lack of constitutional expertise. Here, the doctrinal issues depended upon court precedents, numerous and complex, and the related issues upon lessons of long experience and reflection. Yet lawyers were still abundant in both houses; the percentages were 57 in the House and 66 in the

Senate. The proportions from the regions varied from 91 per cent for the South to 43 per cent for the Border States, with the Middle Atlantic States represented by lawyers in the proportion of 80 per cent.[102] Besides monopolizing the seats on both Judiciary Committees, lawyers made up majorities on both the other committees concerned with Title II,[103] and, as usual, dominated floor debate.[104]

What Congress did contribute was not so much specialized legal knowledge as the skill in applying constitutional principles to broad constitutional questions and questions of implementation which long experience alone can supply. On the House side, the major impetus to detached and effective consideration came from Judge Smith of Virginia, Chairman of the Rules Committee, veteran of eight years on the state bench and of thirty-three years in the House. Representatives Celler with forty, McCulloch with sixteen, and Willis with fifteen years of service took leading parts in debate. It was the relative newcomer, Representative Lindsay, who, with evident support from Celler, pressed for the strong Fourteenth-Amendment position.

Leading Senators, too, spoke from experience. The filibusterers averaged sixteen years of senatorial experience and two years of House experience, while proponents averaged nine years in the Senate and four years in the House. Chairman Magnuson of the Commerce Committee, however, could now boast twenty years as Senator which, coupled with a base in the Northwest helped fit him here for a constructive constitutional role. The leader of the opposition, in the area of constitutional argument, was Senator Ervin of North Carolina. He had held public office twenty-eight years, three of them in his state legislature, thirteen as a judge, two in the House, and ten in the Senate. By 1964, Senators Hennings, Kefauver and O'Mahoney had all died, leaving to Senator Ervin the major burden of supplying Congress with its constitutional learning.

The story of the passage of the 1964 Act is the story of a search for the constitutional erudition which the members of Congress could no longer supply. In its extremity, Congress made extensive use of its own expert staff. In the House Judiciary Committee, for example, staff counsel William R. Foley for the majority and William H. Copenhaver for the minority gave valuable service. In addition, the two Offices of the Legislative Counsel, with their combined staff of twenty-two lawyers, drafted amendments running into the hundreds.[105] For quick answers and longer memoranda on constitutional points, as well as bill analyses, members called on the Legislative Reference Service. During the long course of discussion, the Service prepared several dozen lengthy and carefully documented studies, many relating to constitutional issues.[106] In a year in which the Service received 97,444 congressional inquiries, civil rights

315

was the topic of greatest concern to members. The Librarian of Congress categorized subjects of inquiry as "the right of petition and assembly," "constitutional history and the legislative histories of prior civil rights statutes," "comparisons of the pending Federal bill with the civil rights statutes of . . . States," "the right of jury trial, contempt powers of the courts . . . , Federal aid programs which might be affected by the proposed bill, filibusters and cloture, the scope of the Federal commerce power, and . . . pro and con arguments on many issues."[107] Members also turned for advice to the legal profession outside the government, gathering testimony from deans and professors from leading law schools throughout the country and soliciting the opinions of distinguished members of the bar.[108]

But the most remarkable departure from past practice was the dependence of Congress on the Executive, notably the Attorney General and the Department of Justice. It was not merely that officials from the Commerce and Labor Departments furnished the Commerce Committee with facts demonstrating the links between discrimination in public accommodations and interstate commerce; nor was it unorthodox that the Attorney General should respond to the bids of committees to testify and exert an influence to produce a bill more conformable to the Administration's views on constitutional and policy issues. All this was in line with normal legislative-executive relations. What was both novel and disturbing was evidence that Congress could no longer obtain from its own resources—its members, its staff, and its auxiliary agencies —the knowledge essential for settlement of constitutional controversies. That Congress had now turned to the Executive for that knowledge is seen in the character and volume of memoranda supplied it by Justice Department officials and likewise in the intense and seemingly uninterrupted negotiations which officials from the Justice Department, headed by the Attorney General, held initially with leading Representatives, subsequently with leading Senators. Had Congress, in its extremity, capitulated to the Executive not only for policy leadership and direction but also for constitutional advice?

This issue came to a head on May 26 when Senator Dirksen formally introduced the substitute bill on which he, Senator Humphrey, and the Attorney General had agreed. At this point Senator Russell rose to challenge the conduct of the Justice Department. Likening the Attorney General to the center horse of a "Troika" which also included Senators Humphrey and Dirksen, he quoted a letter he had dispatched to Kennedy on May 7, requesting a statement concerning the policies of furnishing legal opinions to individual members of Congress and of conferring with selected Senators.[109]

The Senator then inserted Kennedy's reply. It opened with a state-

316

ment of Attorney General Mitchell in 1932, distinguishing between "formal legal opinions," which statutes permitted him to render only to the President or to department heads, and answers to congressional requests for comment or suggestions concerning pending legislation affecting the Department. It was practice, said Mitchell, ". . . . to suggest such legal points as are pertinent and which ought to receive consideration by committees." Under that interpretation Kennedy thought it clearly permissible for the department at the request of Senators to transmit "legal discussions"[110] concerning provisions of the bill.

For support of the conferences in which Kennedy said he and his subordinates had participated at the suggestion of the majority and minority leaders, he relied on the powers of the President in relation to legislation. The President must inform the Congress on the state of the Union and recommend measures for adoption. The President could achieve this formally or informally and must necessarily depend on his department heads and their principal assistants. He cited a Hoover Commission task force to the effect that a department head as part of the executive branch ". . . has a constitutional obligation both to consult with and to inform the legislature."[111]

After placing most of this letter in the record, Senator Russell supplied several insertions of his own, all to show that the conduct of the Justice Department had violated the principle of the separation of powers. One statement quoted twelve declarations from Attorneys General between 1820 and 1939 declining to give legal opinions to either house, its committees, or its members. For example, Attorney General Edward Bates asserted in 1861 that for him to render official opinions to the legislature in the absence of statutory authority would violate his oath of office and be a "dangerous example." Attorney General Roger B. Taney, in 1832, had doubted that the Attorney General could legitimately "attempt to mark out the limitations of the legislative power." The Senator continued:

> Attorney General George H. Williams, in 1873, in a letter to the Congress, said: "I fully recognize the right of the head of any of the departments to call upon me for an official opinion in respect to any question of law pending before the department by whose head the call is made; and I consider it my duty promptly to respond to such a call; but I cannot recognize the right of any committee of Congress to call for such an opinion for their use in matters of legislation; and if given for that purpose, it would be entitled to no more consideration in Congress than the opinion of any other individual presumed to have a knowledge of legal matters."

That was the position of the Attorney General back in the days

317

when the Senate still entertained a rather high opinion of itself and thought that some of the lawyers in the Senate were fairly well qualified to pass upon constitutional questions.[112]

Further, the Senator reproduced a compilation of references to the recent *Congressional Record* "in which material was inserted by various Senators giving opinions, memorandums, and speech assistance, from the Attorney General or his staff." Eleven such cases were enumerated, involving communications from the Justice Department to backers of the pending bill, and using terms like "memorandum," "rebuttal," "opinion," "information," and "explanation". These the Senator regarded as legal opinions.[113] Deploring all these occurrences and Kennedy's personal role in creating the substitute bill, he concluded: "We have gotten so far away from the principle of the separation of powers as to give veto power in advance to the executive branch of the Government, not to the President himself, but to the Attorney General of the United States."[114]

The issue is a real one. Senators Ervin and Magnuson, it is true, helped in different ways to elucidate constitutional issues affecting Title II, and Senators from the West and Border States[115] promoted viable settlements of broad questions related to enforcement. Yet it required the firm, sustained intervention of the Attorney General and his aides to guide the House toward a satisfactory settlement of the doctrinal issue. And the volumes of hearings and debates teem with memoranda from the Department concerning constitutional interpretation.

Clearly, the Attorney General brought ability, energy, zeal, training, and experience to his task, and his leading aides likewise exhibited constitutional erudition and insight. Nevertheless, one may justifiably ask whether Congress should rely on the selfsame officials for strong executive leadership in policy matters and detached, deliberated judgments concerning constitutionality. The Attorney General had offered to assist Senator Russell in relation to the bill.[116] Yet could one reasonably expect a member's request for constitutional advice to receive from the Justice Department officials assigned to the task an opinion free from the influence and pressure of the White House? Since Justice Department lawyers must conform to Administration policy, would opponents of Administration bills receive the same abundant constitutional advice as supporters?

MODE

The handling of Title II departed at four points from normal congressional procedure. Most of these irregularities stemmed chiefly from inadequacies of the two Judiciary Committees. Questions of civil rights lay clearly within their jurisdiction, for the Legislative Reorganization Act of 1946 had assigned to them all legislation concerning "judicial proceedings" and "civil liberties."[117] Although regional representation had improved since 1958, the leadership of both committees ill-fitted them for impartial and representative decisions on civil rights bills. Chairmen Celler and Eastland were strongly biased respectively for and against such legislation and tended wherever possible to use their committees and subcommittees to further their goals. Senate Judiciary never referred the bill to its Subcommittee on Constitutional Rights, chaired since 1961 by Senator Ervin, and the otherwise promising Commerce Committee lacked familiarity with the subject. Nowhere in either house was there a standing committee which combined all the elements of legal and constitutional expertise, a reputation for impartiality, and representation of major sections and interests.

In 1957 committee inadequacies had forced the jury-trial issue to the Senate floor. This time the complexity of the bill and the imminence of a filibuster heightened the need for executive intervention in behalf of a viable bill. The year 1957 had also produced the United States Commission on Civil Rights, an independent high-level forum which supplied Congress with much of the data and thinking which the Judiciary Committees could not, or would not, provide.[118] Yet the subject of public accommodations had received only scant attention from the commission.

The first notable procedural vagary was the drafting and reporting of the midnight bill. The full House Judiciary Committee had met privately on October 22 to weigh the Attorney General's arguments against the strong subcommittee bill. Despite a pending motion to report that bill, Chairman Celler had recessed the committee to free members for secret conferences with the Administration and with Justice Department officials. After the weekend negotiations, the committee reconvened on the twenty-ninth. The stronger bill was voted down and Chairman Celler moved as an "amendment" the fifty-six-page substitute bill. One member of the committee later complained that the chairman had ruled ". . . that we would not be permitted to have an explanation of the substitute, that it would be read as a whole, and as an amendment, that we would not be permitted to debate it nor discuss it nor offer amendments to it nor to ask questions about it."[119]

Celler and McCulloch each spoke one minute for the bill, and a member then moved the previous question. The roll was called, and the committee voted to report by 23 to 11.[120]

Chairman Celler later attempted to justify these unorthodox proceedings, which admittedly had cemented a bipartisan coalition and produced a winning bill for the House floor. The subcommittee bill, he contended, had "practically contained every single subject" that appeared in the

319

midnight bill.[121] He argued that he had made no move in this extremely complex matter "without conferring almost momentarily throughout with the parliamentarian of the House," and securing his approval.[122]

Yet the new bill embodied important changes from the subcommittee bill, and one must view the proceedings from the standpoint of those committee members who opposed the bill. None of these had attended the crucial secret meetings. One later asserted, "We understood there had been some secret meetings going on about a proposal for a bill but none of us had seen it."[123] They first glimpsed the bill when Justice Department messengers handed them copies in Justice Department envelopes late on the eve of summary disposition.[124]

This first irregularity helped incur a second, the decision of the Rules Committee to hold nine days of hearings on the bill. While that committee normally serves as a sort of traffic director for House bills, on this occasion its hearings not only threw light on issues implicit in the bill, but exposed the aberration involved in the October conferences.

The third irregularity took place when the House bill reached the Senate. Ordinarily, under the Legislative Reorganization Act and Senate Rule 25, the presiding officer would have sent the bill to the Judiciary Committee. Yet the Senate had set up a contrary precedent in 1957 when, under Rule 14, the majority leader, Senator Lyndon B. Johnson, had objected to referring the pending civil rights bill to committee. Rule 14 provides that under some circumstances House bills can go directly to the Senate calendar for floor debate.[125] Accordingly, on February 26, Senator Mansfield objected to referral, upon which Senator Russell raised a point of order, the presiding officer ruled against him, and the Senate began a debate on the issue that lasted with interruptions a full month.

At the onset of debate the Senate voted against referral by 54 to 37. An attempt at referral for a limited period failed when Senators Javits and Eastland by objecting prevented unanimous consent.[126] Senator Gore of Tennessee said it would be almost tragic "if this issue, which is the most emotion-laden issue the Congress has dealt with for a hundred years, and which was the cause, in part, of the Civil War 100 years ago, should come before this body without the text of the bill having been the subject of hearings by any committee."[127] Southerners, reinforced by Senator Morse, persisted in their efforts at referral. The Oregonian urged adherence to established rules and contended that hearings, even for a limited time, would provide the courts with a legislative history and evidence of legislative intent.[128] The Southerners maintained that the irregular proceedings of the House Judiciary Committee made it obligatory on the Senate to give the bill a thorough reconsideration especially in view of important changes in the bill since

Senate committee hearings the previous summer.[129] Opponents argued that such action would be a waste of time and that the Judiciary Committee would not accord fair hearings.[130]

The Senate tabled Morse's proposal for limited referral by 50 to 34,[131] and called the bill up for floor debate. The month the Senate had spent in debating committee referral could have afforded a properly constituted judiciary committee or subcommittee time for the preliminary searching the parent body needed.

The fourth and final irregularity lay in the procedures under which the Senate conducted debate, combining as they did the two stages of filibuster and cloture. For ten weeks after March 30 and particularly after April 13, when the Southerners gained the floor permanently, Senator Russell exploited the traditional right of Senators individually or in groups to engage in unlimited debate. Lavish with time, Senators offered constitutional arguments in a haphazard manner and often talked to the nucleus of uncommitted members; yet many seemed distracted by events outside the chamber and preoccupied by the need either to protract or terminate the debate. The result was irrelevancies, lack of direct give-and-take, difficulty of amendment, and a public increasingly restless over governmental inaction in a time of disorder.

Cloture set in on June 10, after introduction of the Mansfield-Dirksen substitute bill had paved the way for the necessary two-thirds vote.[132] Cloture was, in a sense, the reverse of the filibuster. Now no member could speak more than one hour in all. An ice jam of amendments that had been gathering during previous weeks now broke in such volume as to overwhelm the Senators. In a single week, some 106 amendments were subjected to roll calls. Senators offering amendments had to allot their sixty minutes with care, even down to seconds, to make the best use of available time. The Vermont Republican, Senator George D. Aiken, accordingly, made it a rule to oppose any amendment whose supporter spoke on it no more than thirty seconds.[133] Republican Senator Mundt of South Dakota said cloture was making a "shambles" of the legislative process; no one, he asserted, seriously believed the Senate was giving careful consideration to any of the amendments.[134] By their conduct in the filibuster, especially their resistance to amendments, the Southerners had invited a rule so strict that many changes they themselves sought and might have obtained in regular debate were lost.[135]

How did the handling of Title II, under the operation of all these irregularities, compare with accepted standards of fairness?

First, in general members agreed in advance on procedure. Exceptions were the framing of the midnight bill and possibly also the conduct of Senate Judiciary hearings. Notable was the House floor debate, for which an open rule for equal time for majority and minority leaders was buttressed by informal agreement between supporters and opponents of the bill.

Second, the months of committee, chamber, and public discussion made clear to all the existence and even the precise formulation of constitutional questions. A departure from the rule, of course, occurred with the midnight bill, of which opponents on the committee had no prior knowledge other than rumor.

Third, the year of discussion, taken as a whole, afforded all parties and interests a fair hearing with respect to Title II. Notable were the House subcommittee hearings and likewise the Senate Commerce hearings, where Chairman Magnuson gave Senator Thurmond a free hand to invite his own opposition witnesses. The Senate Judiciary hearings, with the Ervin-Kennedy dialogue, the House Rules hearings, and the Senate filibuster gave opponents ample opportunity to offer constitutional arguments against Title II. Clearly, the opposition received equal and abundant time.

What was almost entirely lacking was a forum in which proponents and opponents met in direct, focused, and creative interchange, and from which amendments might issue. Both Judiciary Committees were deficient in this respect; that of the Senate produced no report, and that of the House produced a subcommittee bill of doubtful validity and acceptability, the substitute for which came as the fruit of secret ex parte consultations. Representative Madden, Indiana Democrat, opened floor debate by commending the "experienced and high-grade lawyers" on the Judiciary Committee and the opportunity the members now had to learn from those men about constitutionality.[136] Yet, as we have seen, a quarter of the committee members had confronted the midnight bill without attending the subcommittee hearings or possessing transcripts, without discussing Title II in committee sessions, without seeing the bill till the night before, and without a chance to put questions, advance objections, or propose amendments. Southern resentment was understandable.

The filibuster produced a somewhat comparable, though reverse result in the Senate. The intransigeance of the minority made a genuine face-to-face confrontation, with opportunity to amend, difficult if not impossible. It finally drove the moderate Republicans to accept Justice Department mediation in the achievement of a compromise bill.

This time it was on the House floor that Congress discussed, framed, and adopted its principal Title II amendments. Here in Committee of the Whole, members debated under an agreement between the bipartisan leaders and opponents which stated that no effort would be made to end discussion "until and unless every Member of the House who may desire to do so will have the full opportunity to offer and to discuss any amendment that he may wish to submit for consideration."[137] The result was fruitful discussion of constitutionality and action on nineteen amendments to Title II, including the Goodell-Willis amendment.[138] Before casting votes against the bill, two Southern Representatives lauded the just completed debate; one called the conduct of proceedings by Representatives Celler and Eugene J. Keogh, New York Democrat and chairman of the Committee of the Whole, "splendid and fair," and the other thought the discussion "good" and "sincere."[139]

Fourth, as indicated, intensive deliberation took place only in certain forums. Closed sessions of the Senate Commerce and House Judiciary Committees were evidently fruitful, but most influential in shaping legislation were the secret conferences of congressional and Justice Department officials.

Fifth, the record which Congress gave itself and the public of its deliberations and decisions excelled more in quantity than in quality. Most of the hearings were open, and all were subsequently published. In fact, the vast bulk of hearings (see Table 11) gave civil rights

TABLE 11. Calendar and Volume of Hearings and Reports Concerned with Title II, Civil Rights Act of 1964, 1963—1964[a]

Committee	Calendar				Volume in pages	
	Hearings held	Hearings published	Reports published	Debate begins	Hearings	Reports
House Judiciary	May 8–Aug. 2 (subcom'te); Oct. 15–16, 1963	Feb. 2, 1964	Nov. 20, 1963 (pt. 1); Dec. 2, 1963 (pt. 2)	Jan. 31, 1964	2,779	153
House Rules[b]	Jan. 9–29, 1964	Jan. 18 (pt. 1); Jan. 31 (pt. 2)	Jan. 30	Jan. 31	606	1
Senate Commerce	July 1–Aug. 2, 1963	Aug. 20, 1963 (pts. 1, 2); Feb. 10, 1964 (pt. 3)	Feb. 10, 1964	Feb. 26	1,575	348
Senate Judiciary	July 16–Sept. 11, 1963	Feb. 28, 1964	None	Feb. 26	483	None
Total					5,443	502

a Hearings exclusively on other titles, e.g. Title VII, have been omitted.
b House Rules hearings held in June 1964 have been omitted.

proponents a debating point against further hearings. Two aspects of committee output were censurable. One was the timing of hearing publication. As Table 11 shows, House Rules and Senate Commerce were reasonably punctual, but Senate Judiciary took five and one half months, and House Judiciary four months to publish their hearings, in each case after floor debate had begun. The other aspect was a general neglect of reports as a medium for analyzing evidence and conveying results of committee deliberations. The Commerce Committee was the exception, for its report contained not only the views of certain individuals, but a concise committee analysis of the bill with amendments and a reasoned defense of constitutionality. Senate Judiciary remained silent, and its House counterpart, instead of spelling out the constitutional position of the majority, reported only that of seven Republican members. In view of the great bulk of Senate hearings and floor debate, and notwithstanding elaborate coverage by the press, the Judiciary Committees failed to provide responsible reporting for the houses, the Court, and the country.

Similarly, voting records, especially in the House, did little to document individual responsibility. Innumerable House amendments came up in Committee of the Whole, where no roll calls are taken. This absence of roll calls combined with use of the "buddy" system with its strict supervision of voting by a pro-civil rights bloc, guaranteed that the public and constituents would remain in the dark, while a pressure group would possess accurate, minute-by-minute intelligence of the performance of members.[140] Only at its passage did the bill receive a House roll call.

On the other hand, most Senate amendments went through with little else but roll calls. Cloture afforded a maximum of voting, with a minimum of reasoned discussion.

If Senate committee documentation was more searching than House, House debate gave the courts and country a better example of focused deliberation than the Senate. For all its procedural vagaries, congressional discussion in its totality was searching and many-sided.

ATTITUDES

In their handling of the Civil Rights Act members occasionally voiced but seldom applied judicial monopoly ideas. The theory which had rationalized summary disposal of the Communist Control Act proved misleading, now as fully as with Jenner-Butler. The situation was comparable to that three decades earlier, when President Roosevelt offered his famous advice concerning the coal bill. The country again faced a grave domestic problem, this time less economic than social and moral. Public opinion and a powerful majority bloc pressed for action. But this time, both Southern members and the Executive reminded Congress of its responsibility.

Among those who, despite adverse precedents, favored judicial monopolism was Governor Carl Rolvaag, Minnesota Democrat; said he: "Senator, I would be perfectly willing—as a matter of fact I would be delighted if the Congress of the United States would pass the legislation and let the Supreme Court decide the issues."[141] On the Senate floor, Senator Russell deplored the way clergymen were flocking in relays to

Washington, demanding that Senators "resolve all constitutional doubts, however genuine they may be by voting in favor of the bill."[142] Senator Paul Douglas of Illinois offered one of the most forthright instances of the entire year: "Why not pass this law and let the Supreme Court make the decision as to whether or not it is constitutional? We are not constitutional lawyers . . . We are not overruling the Court. We are giving the Court the opportunity to reverse itself in accordance with changing views of the very meaning of the 14th amendment and of the commerce clause."[143] Asserted Senator Magnuson, "We can't stretch the Constitution and we can't condense it. The Constitution is there. It is as solid as that granite. It depends on how the Court interprets it."[144]

Thus the Constitution was a fixed and rigid quantity, which the judges alone could measure. Impatience with delays prompted Senator Magnuson to insist, "If we believe this should be done, we ought to use the legal means that exist,"[145] and Senator Keating, "the constitutionality of the bill . . . has to be ultimately decided by the Supreme Court anyway, and . . . we ought to get on with our work here."[146]

Such views, however, were not allowed to prevail. The Attorney General in 1964 agreed that before voting, Congress should discuss constitutionality—"an important question for every Member of Congress to consider."[147] As for himself, he deemed the legislation valid under the Thirteenth and Fourteenth Amendments, but conceded that a contrary argument was possible; he went on, "We are primarily relying on the commerce clause where there cannot be any constitutional question."[148]

Hints of judicial monopolism now provoked strong retorts from Southern Senators. When the Nebraskan, Senator Hruska, observed that the constitutional basis of such a bill was "primarily a legal question," and asked upon whom the responsibility of deciding constitutionality devolved, Senator Ervin replied that everybody associated with the federal government and who had taken the oath was ". . . under the obligation to refrain from supporting in any way a bill which he honestly believes to be unconstitutional."[149] When Senator Thurmond complained on the floor that some members, in their pursuit of a desired goal, were urging that Congress pass the bill and let the Court decide validity, Senator McClellan of Arkansas observed that such an exclusive reliance on the courts was an abdication of responsibility. "We are," he insisted, "failing to do our duty if we do not ascertain in our own minds and out of our convictions whether proposed legislation is constitutional according to our lights . . ."[150] Senator Monroney, from the Border State of Oklahoma, thought a member's duty also extended to ascertainment of constitutional facts, here the connection between discrimination and commerce.[151] On the other hand, Roy Wilkins, spokesman of the NAACP, warned of too great a congressional preoccupation with constitutionality. Congress, he said, had passed the NRA in spite of doubts about validity; to exaggerate constitutional issues would mean "asking the proponents of civil rights, and, incidentally, millions of people who suffer by reason of deprivation, to have a clear, uncontestable case before even presenting it for consideration."[152]

Once again, members revealed a regional divergence on responsibility. This divergence stemmed from disagreement concerning the nature of constitutional limitations. One side deemed the Constitution exclusively legal, with the corollary that all other issues were matters of policy; the other saw the Constitution as embracing not only legal rules but also what I have termed broad questions of spirit, convention, custom, practice, or tradition. For example, the Senate Commerce Committee report, after arguing that Congress possessed constitutional power to pass Title II, went on:

> As broad and as deep as are the powers of Congress, there is presented the more difficult problem of how those powers should be utilized. Gov. Farris Bryant of Florida, speaking in opposition to the bill said: "My position is purely and simply that while I believe that the Federal Government has the *power* to do, I do not believe it has the *right* to do what it is suggesting be done here." The chairman of the committee, Senator Magnuson, in the initial stages of the public hearings, stated the issue in another way. He observed:
>
> "This is a question of public policy and how far Congress wants to go under the authority of the commerce provision of the Constitution."[153]

To the Southerners, the issue, legality aside, was still partially constitutional. Senator Russell epitomized that view when on June 10, he said the bill went to "the very heart of our constitutional system," was "contrary to the spirit of the Constitution" as well as the letter and threatened, in its "broad aspects," "vast changes, not only in our social order, but in our very form of government."[154] The problem here was whether issues of "public policy" have the same fundamentality as issues of constitutionalism, broadly defined.

Near the close of the Senate debate, the prospective Republican candidate for President, Senator Goldwater of Arizona, rose to declare his opposition to the bill. He grounded his position on his conviction that Titles II and VII were unconstitutional, as abridgments of private property rights.[155] Implicit in his brief statement was the notion that in conscience, Senators are bound to oppose bills they deem against the Constitution. Coming, as it did, during the final weeks of the campaign for nomination, the statement brought quick retorts. The *New York*

326

Times referred editorially to the Senator as "acting as if he were himself the Supreme Court . . ."[156] A year earlier, Arthur Krock had likewise broached judicial monopoly ideas, for in advising two leading Southerners, Ralph McGill and Senator Stennis, to advance their constitutional readings with less confidence, he had asserted that the Constitution was "what the Supreme Court says it is, reversing interpretations from time to time."[157]

Doubtless, others among press and public viewed the Goldwater statement in similar terms, yet the long debate over the 1964 Act must have reawakened many to the obligation of the Legislature to give sustained thought to serious constitutional issues in passing laws. In spite of procedural vagaries and its dependence on outside experts, Congress, in the end, took note of constitutional issues and achieved meaningful settlements.

CONCLUSIONS

In passing Title II of the 1964 Civil Rights Act, Congress met a deeply felt need. For a century the American Negro had aspired with mounting earnestness to the full enjoyment of the rights of all Americans. Demonstrations and violence provided the catalyst, and Congress discovered, in words which Senator Dirksen took from Hugo, that "Stronger than all the armies is an idea whose time has come."[158] In defining and assuring these rights Congress caught up with the Supreme Court and gave the Negro a legislative bill of rights.

This time Congress conducted a genuine canvass of constitutional questions, both narrow and broad. For substantive power it relied less on the Fourteenth Amendment, a provision intended primarily as a shield for Negro rights, than on the commerce power as reinterpreted after 1936. Precedents from Depression crisis served the needs of racial crisis, revealing the sweep of court-construed grants of federal power. The debates, it is true, disclosed aspects of local commerce beyond federal and Title II control, yet the continuing growth of the national market could in time bring almost all economic transactions within the commerce clause. Early and unanimous Court confirmation gave witness to the success of congressional inquiries into both doctrine and the factual link between discrimination and commerce. As on other occasions, a minority of justices followed the lead of a minority of legislators, here in supporting a broad Fourteenth-Amendment position.[159] But the consensus in both branches relied on the commerce power.

The House achieved something like final settlement of these narrow questions of delegated power, so that the Senate could move on to the other issues. In delineating remedies and enforcement procedures—the

327

priority for state laws, the occasions for intervention by the Attorney General, and machinery for fostering voluntary compliance—Congress concerned itself with broad questions—the precise manner in which delegated powers should be exercised in the interest of constitutional principles and values. State and local autonomy, circumscription of administrative authority, and the freedom of the businessman served special purposes which, though relative to other considerations, were nonetheless real. In extending jury trial to those charged with disobeying court orders under the act, Congress was actually implementing constitutional provisions in the interest of an important procedural right. The long discussions of property rights and procedural rights in juxtaposition to rights to equal access to accommodations gave fresh proof that Congress, like the courts, engages in balancing competing rights and the values they serve.

The appeal to leave constitutional questions to the courts had slight influence on Congress in 1964. Court review of narrow questions was imminent, but the foremost Fourteenth Amendment precedent actually discouraged simple assertion of judicial monopolism. Civil rights lobbyists and members from North and West occasionally voiced it, almost in the words of FDR. Yet the reminders of congressional duty and the skillful constitutional arguments which opponents of the bill and the Attorney General reiterated forced members to plumb constitutional questions.

In shouldering its responsibility, Congress used its available machinery in a spirit of pragmatism. Senate Judiciary explored doctrinal questions through adversary argument; House Rules and House floor shaped the bill along doctrinal lines, Senate Commerce explored constitutional fact, and Senate floor elaborated measures of enforcement. Abundant time and pressures of public concern over against Southern and executive insistence made such a result possible.

Defects in the machinery, however, brought serious results. In the House a chairman and his largely hand-picked subcommittee committed to strong legislation produced a bill so dubious, constitutionally as well as politically, that the best efforts of the Executive, bipartisan leaders, the Rules Committee, and floor managers were required to restore balance. A Senate Judiciary Committee more representative of the nation than earlier, but still under a chairman dedicated to resisting legislation left the Senate without the guidance of a report. Moreover, the Senate lost a month in discussing further referral and ended by rebuffing the committee. The most informative report issued from the Commerce Committee, whose specialty, however, was remote from civil rights matters. House Rules, with a balanced makeup and a chairman who exposed procedural improprieties, produced hearings both

328

searching and well-timed. The thousands of pages of hearings, while helpful to the courts, to which they sometimes seemed directed, were of limited use to floor debaters. Concise and thoughtful reports might have reduced the evidence to a form more useful to harried members. Paradoxically, it was committees other than Judiciary that furnished Congress with some of the most fruitful discussion.

This time the House surpassed the Senate in the focus, genuineness, and fruitfulness of its debate, at least on the narrow question. Executive, bipartisan, and Rules Committee leadership corrected the distortion created by Judiciary, so that the ten days of debate, mostly in Committee of the Whole, elucidated issues and produced amendments defining Title II in essentially its final form. Senate debate, in spite of improvements in enforcement procedures and the public enlightenment afforded by saturation, seemed diffuse and misdirected. Filibuster and cloture were a parody on freedom of debate and made deliberated amendments almost unobtainable on the floor. Senator Ervin, it is true, expounded narrow questions, Southerners generally clarified broad questions, and Border and Far Western members furthered compromise and accommodation. Yet for the spelling out of substantive power, Congress now turned to nonmembers. Even though congressional staff, auxiliary agencies, and the legal profession rendered valuable help, the Executive was all-important. In 1963 President Kennedy intervened with the House Committee to obtain, not a doubtful bill as with President Roosevelt in 1935, but one clearly constitutional. Having corrected the vagaries of House civil rights enthusiasts in the autumn, the Attorney General went on the following spring to work for a bipartisan compromise bill in the Senate, with the moderating amendments which the filibuster prevented on the floor. Its own inattention to organs and procedures for constitutional settlements forced Congress to turn to the Executive not merely for policy but also for constitutional direction.

This link which bipartisan Senate leaders forged with the Justice Department showed signs of durability. Two months after the close of the civil rights debate, the Senate was debating the Dirksen-Mansfield rider. Its purpose was to stay execution of Supreme Court decisions concerning state legislative reapportionment,[160] and Senator Dirksen apologized for haste. Besides looking for guidance to "great lawyers" like Senators Ervin, Russell, Hruska, and Kuchel, he mentioned night sessions at which Justice Department officials had helped draft his proposal. He found comfort not only in the prospect of early court review, but in the express constitutional endorsement of the Deputy Attorney General, Nicholas Katzenbach.[161] Next spring Senator Mansfield was defending the Mansfield-Dirksen version of the Voting Rights bill against another advanced by Senator Edward M. Kennedy of Massachusetts. Constitutionality was a key factor, and he cried, "Where else is a majority leader, who is not a lawyer, but only a Senator, to turn for advice, if not to his colleagues who are lawyers, to disinterested legal aids of the Senate and to the relevant Department—the Department of Justice—of the Executive branch . . . ?"[162] Rumors that his opponents were claiming the support of the Justice Department prompted Senator Mansfield to place in the *Record* a letter proving that the now Attorney General Katzenbach preferred his version, chiefly on constitutional grounds.

What was questionable in all this was the continuing dependence of Congress on the Justice Department for direction essential to fundamental constitutional settlements. If individual rights now furnish the most significant legal limitations on federal power, and if Congress looks primarily to the Executive for guidance in interpreting those rights, Congress runs the risk of surrendering its own basic and independent responsibility to the Executive. Executive leadership in policy formulation is one thing, executive tutelage in constitutional settlements is quite another matter.

In fashioning Title II Congress performed valuable functions. It demonstrated that constitutional questions are no less matters of national interest than are policy goals. It facilitated expression of special and sectional interests, but confronted spokesmen of those interests with wider and more general concerns and purposes. Interest groups, party leaders, and the public at large discovered both the compelling need to secure to Negroes rights enjoyed by their white fellow-citizens and the need to preserve constitutional values. Congress thus accommodated interests and educated the public. This time the public also rediscovered the responsibility of Congress for constitutional questions. In placing the authority of the national Legislature behind the efforts of the Judiciary, Congress enhanced the legitimacy of the drive for equal rights.

If the result was a new step toward federal centralization, and partial relinquishment of legislative responsibility to the Executive, at least Congress brought the public with it in attacking a century-old problem.

I5   *Congress and the Constitution*

The problem of Congress today is the problem of the American nation. The country is like a space vehicle, thrust forward by unparalleled power at unimagined speed, toward a destination calculated with infinite care. What is missing is forethought concerning the survival and safety of the passengers both in flight and at the destination.

Congress faces just such a perplexity. The political system has moved into a new age without citizen awareness of change and the need for fresh insights and new modes of action. Men of science and technology have thrust it at a rising momentum into a climate of life of unprecedented complexity, interdependence, speed, and power. Crisis urgency and demands for new policies and programs have intensified the concentration of power at the center, in the Executive and in specialized experts. That concentration of power calls for bold new thought about the preservation of human values, especially those safeguarded by constitutional principles. The Constitution itself resulted from insight and innovation, from the application of principles and the values they embodied to a new and in part unprecedented situation. Another new age cries out for a parallel display of insight and innovation.

Yet at precisely this moment many would subordinate that task, postpone it, and consign it to an organ of government distinct from those concerned with current policy, whose mode is ponderous, tied to precedent, and restricted in its reach. The drying up of constitutional knowledge and wisdom, the decline of debate and procedures for discussion, the self-deprecation voiced by many members of Congress conform with judicial monopolism precisely at the time when actual legal power and public need make Congress something like a parliament. For three decades the Supreme Court has affirmed the broadest reading of federal power, left to Congress many aspects of its relations to the Executive, and often read congressional intent in a manner like that employed by British courts, that is, narrowly, so as to avoid confrontation with constitutional principle. In legal power Congress moves toward

331

Parliament; in self-identification and overt conduct, it moves away, looking for final decision either from the Executive or from the Judiciary.

All this makes it important to recapitulate the rise of the contending theories of responsibility, reassess that responsibility today, and explore possible reforms in the manner of its discharge.

THE THREE THEORIES

Each of the three theories of congressional responsibility that have contended for dominance has had its conceptual framework and its institutional background. Thomas Jefferson crystallized the view that legislatures have a strong responsibility for the independent decision of constitutional questions. In this he voiced Virginian notions of the capacity of the electorate, the representative function, the deliberative process in the legislature, and the separation of powers. The theory conformed to the character and practices of Southern and Border State legislatures, which long sustained something of the aristocratic and even judicial tone of the British Parliament.

For seven decades Congress acted on this theory at least in its handling of constitutional questions. Many of its decisions were effectively final. With the aid of executive studies and recommendations and limited assistance from small committees, the earliest Congresses threshed out settlements in the Committee of the Whole, balancing and applying constitutional principles as these best fitted the case. They reached decisions on narrow constitutional questions, including those which, though called "political," were nonetheless constitutional in character, settled broad questions, implemented and supplemented the original document, and prepared constitutional amendments. In only two pre-Civil War cases did the Supreme Court declare acts of Congress invalid, once innocuously, once disastrously. The never-absent threat of the state veto may have spurred Congress to responsible action. One may doubt whether judicial review could have made a start during those decades but for the prior debates and votes in Congress. These promoted education and the accommodation of interests, within and outside Congress, so that when court decisions came, they were essentially confirmations of what had already happened in Congress. Press coverage of Congress was evidently such that the public gained awareness of issues and arguments long before the Court took its stand.

The Civil War ended the hegemony of the Jeffersonian system and prepared the way for the Marshallian. Southerners, with their zeal for Jeffersonian views and practices, began their long absence. Border State men, with their moderating function and their appreciation of both Jeffersonian and Marshallian conceptions, fought a rear guard action.

War emergency reinforced the constitutional views and legislative methods of Northern Republicans, who once and for all made the standing committee the initial and dominant organ of legislative action and began looking to the courts, Marshall-wise, for chief guidance on constitutional issues.

By the last quarter of the century, conditions had stabilized. Lawyers were nationally professionalized and were very nearly shouldering all others from the halls of Congress. Those lawyers were talking of constitutionality as exclusively legal and referring at least some important constitutional disputes to the lawyer-manned Judiciary Committees for what in effect were advisory opinions.

Marshall's position accepted the theory of legislative responsibility while doubting its universal practice and put its principal trust in the Judiciary. It stressed individual liberty, the rule of law, and the independent Judiciary as leading defender of that rule. Although its exaltation of the judicial function could easily induce members of Congress to lean on the courts and neglect an independent inquiry by Congress, that result appeared only slowly. As the Sherman Act debate demonstrated, Congress continued to consider constitutional questions and to consider them effectively. Perhaps the return of Southerners like Senator James George to reinforce Border State men like Senator George Vest, thwarted tendencies toward complete dependence on court action. Debates, especially in the Senate, continued to explore constitutional questions in focus, informed and corrected as those debates often were by Judiciary Committee reports. The Court was now passing more frequently than earlier on acts of Congress, but doing so within a system which prepared parties, interest groups, sections, and citizens for its decisions by preliminary discussion and accommodation in the Legislature. If the Court was legitimatizing government action, that process had already been launched by the deliberations of the representative body.

In Senate oratory, even in 1890, one could detect faint murmurings of judicial monopolism. From newer Midwestern members, in this case Republicans, came assertions that legislation was necessarily imperfect and that only the Supreme Court could reach valid and binding constitutional settlements. In 1913 when members debated a prohibition measure, such comments were still rare, and most members continued to speak and act as though the representative legislature had not only the duty but also the capacity and essential function to give thought to constitutional objections.

By the late 1920's, however, the judicial monopoly theory had gained numerous advocates. Economic distress on the nation's farms was prompting backers of measures for agricultural relief to assert that constitutional questions were for the courts alone to decide. By the early

1930's paralysis had spread to the whole economy. The debates on the 1935 coal bill showed that judicial monopoly ideas had spread beyond the Midwest and won recruits from most sections.

Science, technology, urbanism, mass production, and national markets created a situation in which economic maladjustment caused economic paralysis. The effect: the imperious necessity of government action. President Roosevelt's dramatic opening call for "direct, vigorous action" recognized that necessity. Such action alone could deal with the crisis. Policy set the course for action by describing its objectives and character. Government was no longer a necessary evil, but a critically necessary good. Furthermore, a pragmatic cast of mind applied without the framers' knowledge and insight concerning constitutional principles and values could convert those principles into policies to be tried and judged in the same fashion as other policies. Under such conditions it was easy to see government action as comprising two essential phases, policy and administration.

The effects of all this were twofold. The great preoccupation with public policy, as a matter of sheer survival carried with it disputes over who should determine that policy. In general, power moved toward the center in Washington, and toward the Executive within the federal structure. Furthermore, matters were complex and technical and called for a host of permanent administrators and experts. During the long contention over the appropriate policy-making functions of Congress and the President, it was easy to conclude as the Supreme Court did in 1941, that the legislative function could receive adequate definition solely in relation to policy; thus, "The essentials of the legislative function are the determination of the legislative policy and its formulation as a rule of conduct."[1]

Crisis followed crisis, each with its fresh demand for government action. Policies for relief, recovery, reform soon had competition from policies for stopping Hitler, for maintaining neutrality, for waging total war; in place of these came other policies for planning the peace, for guaranteeing full employment, for halting Communist aggression, for maintaining a preponderance of world power, for controlling subversive activities in and out of government, for economic growth, for closing the missile gap, for winning the race in space, for assuring racial equality, and so on. Policy defines action, and action requires abundant power. Small wonder that the leisurely committee discussions and floor debates which lawyers had once conducted on constitutional restraints now appeared irrelevant or even obstructive. There was persuasiveness in Roosevelt's advice to the Representatives to swallow even reasonable constitutional doubts, pass the coal bill, and leave the constitutional

334

question to the courts. Then when the Court turned down this and other New Deal acts, that tribunal, and even the Constitution itself, took on the appearance of bars to progress, inappropriate for the new age.

Coming from a President this advice was radical, and the theory it embodied was equally radical. The early strong Presidents, from Jefferson to Lincoln, most of them coming from areas where Virginian ideas prevailed, had met judicial invalidations with appeals to the tripartite theory, in one form or another. But the New Yorker broke with tradition and minimized congressional responsibility. The effect was to invite court decisions barren of the traditional prior discussions in Congress.

The theory was not without roots in the past. A few at the beginning, like Elbridge Gerry and William L. Smith, had broached it vaguely, and when state denunciations of federal action began to threaten the Union, New Englanders like Daniel Webster offered the "exclusive" determination of constitutional questions by courts as the only alternative to anarchy. The theory must have got initial strength from ideas and practices of early Massachusetts and other Northeastern states and evidently flourished in the Midwest, where settlers from the East may have used it to curb the pretensions of their own new legislatures. It depended on a smoldering distrust of elected legislators and executives, and a corresponding exaltation of judges as infallible and incorruptible oracles. Story's and other commentaries and the case method of teaching the Constitution may by inference have fostered the impression that courts alone are reliable sources of constitutional wisdom. Yet expressions of fullblown judicial monopolism evidently remained somewhat sporadic and localized until the President's pronouncement in 1935.

The effects have been serious. Emergence of judicial monopolism has opened a running argument in the halls of Congress as to the function of that body in relation to the Constitution and constitutional matters. It has deterred needed reforms in organs and procedures for handling constitutional questions and improvements in reservoirs of expert advice. It has fostered the notion that the Constitution itself with its restraints on government power is essentially subordinate, technical, and too abstruse for any but lawyers in the courtroom and judges on the bench to discuss with sense. It has encouraged the belief that a law is not a law, but only a tentative, pressure-wrought statement of policy until judges in court subject it to judicial process and render formal judgment. In another forum, it has even induced so distinguished a statesman and lawyer as the late Adlai Stevenson to tell the United Nations General Assembly that it is bound by an advisory opinion of the Permanent Court of Justice, because: "The Court has ruled on the law; it remains to this Assembly to manifest at once its respect and its compliance by converting the law into policy."[2] This exaltation of the Permanent Court as expounder of the Charter calls to mind the early New Englander's exaltation of the Supreme Court as expounder of the Constitution.

How generally do members of Congress espouse this theory? No clear index is available, yet returns from a questionnaire suggest the extent to which they supported it in 1959. As shown in chapter 1, three of every eight members responded and of those having an opinion on the question whether Congress generally should "pass constitutional questions along to the court rather than form its own considered judgment on them," 31 per cent responded "yes." Non-lawyers were more apt than lawyers to hold this view; only 7 per cent of responding Senators took this stand in comparison with 36 per cent of Representatives.

But most significant were the regional divergences. Chapter 1 indicated the range as extending from 53 per cent of those from the Middle Atlantic States to 14 per cent of those from the South and Southwest. But the distribution becomes sharper and more distinct when based only on those questionnaires which members signed. As Table 12 indicates,

TABLE 12. Regional Support for Court Referral, as Shown by Signed Questionnaires, 1959; by Number and Per Cent

	Number		Per Cent	
Region	Yes	No	Yes	No
Middle Atlantic	6	6	50	50
Midwest	12	14	47	53
Border	2	5	29	71
Far West	5	15	25	75
New England	2	8	20	80
South	2	31	6	94
Total	29	79	27	73

SOURCE: Questionnaire to the Members of the 86th Congress, January 15, 1959.

not only does the over-all quota of those favoring judicial monopolism here decline from 31 to 27 per cent—a hint that members deem that theory somewhat unconventional—but its standing within each of the six regions employed in this book becomes clearer. Thus, half of the members from the Middle Atlantic States and approximately half from the Midwest (47 per cent) favored court referral, whereas only 6 per cent of Southerners favored it. The Border, Far Western, and New England States varied from 29 to 20 per cent.[3]

Furthermore, service in Congress evidently tends to weaken a member's commitment to judicial monopolism. Freshman members returning questionnaires favored monopolism at the rate of 47 per cent, those with up to ten years of experience at the rate of 26 per cent, and those with more than ten years 24 per cent. Although Southerners made up a heavy contingent of the experienced respondents, these quotas reflected general attitudes. In other words, the typical devotee of judicial monopolism is the new Middle Atlantic or Midwestern Representative lacking legal training; the typical opponent, the experienced Southern Senator who is also a lawyer.

These figures corroborate earlier findings. Judicial monopolism evidently remains the position of the minority, albeit a strong minority. At times, however, as when its supporters hold such command posts as committee chairmanships, its influence could be serious.

Admittedly, the doctrine may come to prevail. The identification of the Supreme Court with the Constitution may cease to be a literary flourish and acquire the force of a dogma. So radical a change would require equally radical reforms if a semblance of integrity in constitutional principles is to be maintained. It would require, for example, some form of the Butler-Javits amendment for total judicial surveillance of constitutional issues. It would call for complete abandonment by the Court of the traditional category of political questions where those questions are constitutional in purport. It would argue the wisdom of letting Congress, and presumably the Executive also, obtain advisory opinions from the Court. Finally, it would demand that those forms of constitutional settlement other than interpretation—implementation, supplementation, and amendment of the document—be divided between the Court and constitutional conventions. Thus, the judges would assume functions other than interpretation.

The Court itself should be kept scrupulously representative of regions, minorities, and interest groups; the practice of accepting *amici curiae* should be greatly extended; and the arguments of counsel as well as ensuing opinions given thorough and nationwide publicity. No longer should the Court presume acts of Congress constitutional. It should practice activism, not only in its one remaining significant constitutional area —individual rights—but in all areas of interpretation. That would complete the divorce between policy and constitutionality and carry judicial monopolism to its logical extreme.

To such a course there are serious objections. Whatever its plausibility in theory, judicial monopolism breaks down in practice. It invites public ignorance of constitutional issues (Communist Control Act), congressional neglect of broad questions (wiretapping bill) and questions of implementation of constitutional provisions (Reorganization Act and Middle East Resolution), and early Supreme Court invalidation (Guffey-Snyder Act) or Supreme Court self-restraint (Communist Control Act).

In the end it may succeed in returning the issue to Congress in a form more acute than before and more threatening to the constitutional order (Jenner-Butler bill).

Judicial monopolism is unhistorical, departing from the experience and practices of the past. It is illogical when based on the analogy to judicial review of state laws. In dealing with Congress, the Court is dealing with another national organ, applying national standards with important claims to national representation. The theory would make the Court more than a court: on the one hand, a kind of collective attorney general, rendering on-the-spot advice, without the benefit of prior deliberation in legislature or lower court; on the other, a kind of constitutional commission, improvising remedies for new and often unprecedented crises.

Judicial monopolism would make for inflexibility in adapting the Constitution to new, strange, and complex conditions. Judges depend heavily on precedent, the accumulated decisions of the past, and accordingly may lack the knowledge, experience, and techniques of thought essential to devising responses to the new. Witness the challenge of wire-tapping.

More important, in the end, that theory tends to weaken the standing of the Court and thereby of the Constitution and democracy itself. It postpones to the Judiciary the whole task of achieving accommodation of interests as these concern constitutional power. That would politicize the Court, giving its constitutional decrees the appearance of the impositions of the stronger group, reached without the full, free objections and counter-arguments of elected representatives. By removing constitutional discussion from the legislature and electoral campaigns, and by propagating the notion that constitutional issues are wholly legal, hence wholly technical, hence totally beyond the ken of the layman, it could foster a popular immaturity about the Constitution. At that point the Constitution becomes not a way of political life in a democracy, but a rote-learned traffic code, to be evaded wherever expert opinion discovers loopholes. When the investigation and maintenance of constitutional standards cease to bear on the conscience of legislator and voter, both will put their whole effort into getting what they can from the national arsenal and treasury. Under such conditions appeals to moderation, to a public interest, to compromise, to traditional constitutional principles sound to them like the selfish complaints of a disreputable minority. Numbers alone decide without the moderating influence of confrontation with enduring values and principles of the constitutional order, and accordingly, it is hard for those majorities to tolerate a subsequent frustration by the judges. In the end democratic election, involving to some degree a conscientious judgment by the citizen, becomes the dictatorial plebiscite, the managed response of the masses. At that stage the task of bar and bench is merely to adjust the symbols of the constitutional order to maintain the appearance of traditional legality. Judicial monopolism in practice would end by undermining both democracy and the Constitution.

THE RESPONSIBILITY OF CONGRESS

The review of congressional practice which the foregoing chapter brought to a close suggests the weaknesses of judicial monopoly and the existence of an important responsibility in Congress. The record demonstrates that constitutional questions involve fundamentals, not subordinates, and the consideration by Congress as well as the Court. The Constitution turns out to be neither subordinate to policy nor an instrument of policy. Instead, by channeling and regulating power it prevents political demands from disrupting the political system they are intended to serve and actually helps ensure the effective discharge of policy itself. Far from being a bar to progress, the Constitution actually ensures genuine progress and prevents retrogression. Unrestricted wiretapping or an overmuscular enforcement of civil rights might appear to guarantee progress, but the effects might frustrate achievement of the ends sought and return society to a state of arbitrary action and repression.

Nor is the Constitution exclusively technical. Embodying the spirit of a free and orderly community, it rests at many points on popular understanding, acceptance, and conviction. Its maintenance and adaptation to a strange new society is a matter of general public interest not of special interests. The legal profession could no more achieve that maintenance and adaptation singlehanded than a corps of experts on public health, acting without community comprehension and cooperation, could prevent epidemics.

Mention of the constitutional consensus calls up the concept of constitutional settlement developed in chapter 2. Experience suggests that instead of viewing the Constitution as a complex of Supreme Court decisions—what the judges say it is—it is more accurate and more precise to regard it as a congeries of rules, principles, and values, some embodied in law and some not, for limiting government power, which over time has been worked out in detachment from political demands, yet to some extent in the presence, direct or indirect, of both political forces and the public at large. Far from being the unison chant of the nine justices or fractions of that number, it represents the blending of many voices and many choruses, most of all an antiphony in which Congress and the Court sing the principal parts.

339

Within the walls of the concept of constitutional settlements, there is room for both the Jeffersonian and the Marshallian theories. Not that the tension between them is relaxed, it is rather that those points which the two conceptions have in common become manifest, and those points each emphasizes find their appropriate places. The political tripartite version exploits the special advantages of the representative legislature —its broad representativeness, its varied instruments for discussion and publicity, the political experience and skill in compromise of its members, its flexibility in devising special organs for special tasks—and emphasizes the representational, educational, accommodational, and creative aspects of the task of constitutional inquiry. The juristic version assures that a multitude of constitutional issues will receive final determination in a forum insulated from pressures of the immediate, firm in its adherence to fair process, peculiarly fitted to view the issue in the concrete setting of application to individuals, manned exclusively by lawyers, and subjected to the unremitting and usually judicious criticism of the legal profession. The very success of the tribunal Marshall helped to perfect has itself fostered the notion of judicial monopoly. Yet Marshall himself trusted far more in the intellectual persuasiveness and moral reputation of the Court than in any legal compulsion on Congress.

What is needed is delineation of congressional responsibility, both in scope and in degree. Thus, questions vary in form from interpretation to amendment of the document. This book has paid relatively little heed to the hundreds of questions which members dispose of through application of clear, pertinent Court precedents. The long-forming corpus of constitutional law which the courts have created furnishes answers to most questions. Here the member can safely lean on the Court; if a thorough perusal of precedents furnishes an acceptable answer, he may "let the Court decide."

Misgivings arise where precedents disclose a Court sharply divided with cogent arguments on both sides (Olmstead), or where age may suggest obsolescence of the precedent (McCardle and the Civil Rights Cases), or where the precedent is peripheral to the immediate question (cases cited in Reorganization Act debates), or where strong segments in Congress advance considerations creating doubts about the precise direction or even cogency of precedents (wiretapping bill). Experience suggests that in this difficult zone it were better for members to conduct an exploration of principles and values than relegate the issue to the Court. The effort of President Kennedy in pressing for a thorough inquiry and preliminary settlement in 1963 stood up while that of President Roosevelt in 1935 suggesting the shelving of the constitutional question met with early Court rebuff. The situations, of course, were different in many respects, but the contrast is suggestive.

340

This zone of narrow questions also includes those not yet brought to the Court, and those unlikely ever to reach it. The record here presented suggests that where Congress conducts a genuine search of principles, as in the 1789 removal power episode and in the Anderson dispute, the Court subsequently confirms it, often relying on congressional arguments. Where Congress fails to conduct such a search, as in the Sedition Act and Oath of Office Act debates, the result may be public rebuff, as in 1801, congressional embarrassment, and repeal (Oath of Office Act) or Court rejection in a parallel situation (Oath of Office Act). The zone of "political questions" may involve, as in the Middle East Resolution, genuine constitutional questions, and here the need of independent congressional inquiry is obviously mandatory. Whether the recent practice of Congress in expediting and facilitating the reference of doubtful questions to the courts is wise remains to be seen.

Then there are all those other questions not embraced by the term "narrow," which modern parlance lumps within the term public policy. Court reinterpretation of clauses granting federal powers to Congress, and to some degree of those concerning executive-legislative relations, has eliminated many questions of literal interpretation and converted them into broad questions. Notwithstanding the 1964 experience, substantive federal powers are so comprehensive, that the principal issue concerns manner and extent of exercise rather than interpretation of power. Congressional discretion in conferring power on the Executive presents a similar problem.

Other zones of special responsibility are those of implementation and amendment. In shaping the legislative veto, Congress was actually creating a new form of restraint on executive power, fashioned to meet the requirements of the new age. In proposing the Twenty-Second Amendment, it was constructing another such restraint with less genuine deliberation. Both forms of constitutional inquiry will and, one may add, should come increasingly before the legislators, and their obligation to give them focused thought is evident.

As one moves from narrow legal questions to broad questions and to questions of implementation and amendment, one leaves behind court precedents. The Legislature here faces the task of independently searching constitutional principles, and this is the fact of the matter. Legislators and scholars might well replace the term "policy" with the older term "principle" in epitomizing such questions. The term "constitutional policy" while inadequate at least has the merit of suggesting the special character of these questions. To term President Truman's dismissal of a commanding general publicly committed to a military policy opposed by the President a matter of policy fails to underscore its relationship with the free constitutional order.

In this realm beyond narrow questions and court precedents lie many of the challenges which today confront constitutional government: among them, the political leverage which control of vast welfare programs gives the President, the growth of a federal police force, the existence of a "military-industrial complex," the secrecy surrounding defense production and installations, and the expansion of intelligence and counter-intelligence programs. Court referral of such questions is an invitation to disaster but so also is branding them as policy.

Questions differ not only in form but in subject matter. Here, too, classification aids the assessment of responsibility. Four general categories are discernible.

First, individual rights have become the chief concern of the courts. This court preoccupation with individual rights has furnished a basis for the appeal to judicial monopoly. Yet that appeal turns out in practice to be chimerical. The Supreme Court has withheld its veto over acts of Congress in all but procedural matters, and Congress on its part finds issues such as wiretapping, regulation of subversive expression, and civil rights constantly recurring. While specific decisions on issues of individual rights pour from the courts, novel situations, interest-accommodation, and public understanding necessitate parallel settlements in Congress.

Second, from McCulloch to the 1937 decisions, the Court has umpired the federal division of powers, so productive of disputes in and out of the courts. The expanded interpretations of 1937 and subsequent years, however, have lessened the relevance of court precedents in this area and left it to Congress and the President to assure some measure of local autonomy and decentralization in the actual exercise of government power. The Court, it is true, has increasingly borne down on state powers in applying both constitutional provisions and congressional statutes but Congress exercises a parallel control of state powers in such matters as pre-emption. Here is an area of increasing congressional responsibility.

Third, ever since 1789 when Congress decided to let the President remove his chief subordinates, it has faced serious issues of the separation of powers. Such questions have gained accretions of court precedents, in some areas, but the evidence of the foregoing pages demonstrates that many congressional decisions here are effectively final. Since negative decisions in this area tend to qualify rather than block government action, political pressures tend to be more moderate than in other areas and the achievement of detachment in Congress less difficult.

Fourth, the control of its own organs and proceedings, as Jefferson made explicit, lies primarily with Congress. The Anderson affair lay partially in this area, and so has the recent problem of investigative committee procedures. The duty to search principles here is great.

These four areas are neither exhaustive nor watertight. Controversies from the Sedition Act to the Civil Rights Act present individual rights in collision with conceptions of federalism; the Anderson affair and many successors have juxtaposed individual rights with congressional control of internal proceedings. And some crucially important matters, such as civilian control of the military, fall neatly into none of the four areas.

Responsibility is a matter of extent as well as of classification. Is a member obliged to follow the example of those early members who sought personally to dispel all doubts about validity and even offered public demonstration of their convictions? Or should he adopt the Rooseveltian formula, so frequently repeated since 1935, and shelve all doubts "however reasonable" where measures seem to him necessary. An agreement on the matter in Congress is important, since the Court presumes measures to be constitutional on the hypothesis that Congress has settled all reasonable doubts of constitutionality. Furthermore, many decisions left clouded with doubt may prove to be final decisions.

This problem was epitomized in 1957 by Representative Walter H. Judd, Minnesota Republican. The House was considering an amendment to the pending civil rights bill which would require jury trial for those whom the courts found in criminal contempt. Grave constitutional questions, narrow and broad, were at stake, yet pressures against jury trial ran strong. This was the "acid test" of members' votes declared Representative Adam Clayton Powell, New York Democrat, for "the eyes of America are upon you, and American citizens . . . will know that you voted hypocrisy if you vote for trial by jury and then turn around and vote in favor of civil rights."[4] Said Judd,

It is very difficult for a person who is not a lawyer to be sure of just what is right when making up his mind on an issue like this . . .

I have listened long and hard during this debate. I certainly have no desire or disposition to deprive any person of any right that he has under our Constitution, and certainly not the right of trial by jury. So, at the outset, my general leaning was to vote for this trial-by-jury amendment. But the more I have listened, the more I changed to the decision to vote against it.

When there are complicated legal and technical arguments, and equally able men of both parties, men who are real legal experts . . . and these experts come to exactly opposite conclusions, 180 degrees

343

apart, then an ordinary person like myself has got to try to reduce the technicalities to simpler terms . . . and make up his own mind on them.[5]

Judd's quandary was real. Perhaps the most satisfactory formula would ask that members clear up all *substantial* doubts about constitutionality before supporting a measure they deem politically desirable or necessary. Such a formula, if extended to the responsibility for all the various kinds of questions confronting Congress, would call for organs and procedures for assuring detachment and also expert advice cast in terms the layman can comprehend.

MEASURES TO HELP EFFECTUATE RESPONSIBILITY

The quandary of Congress can be simply put: A. Congress must consider constitutional questions effectively; B. It can not. There are two alternative courses of action for meeting this quandary: A. Guarantee judicial monopoly by removing constitutional questions from Congress to the courts; or B. Improve the means for the discharge of congressional responsibility. The choice is difficult. I would choose the second.

It is important to avoid blanket assertions of congressional competence or incompetence, and examine all of the conditions which make for success or failure. Each of the elements of responsibility is significant here. The stability and flexibility of the constitutional order depend on the vigorous operation of moral and political sanctions as well as legal sanctions. The conscience of the legislator and such devices as election, division of powers, and checks and balances, continue now as earlier to enhance responsibility. Of equal importance are the objects of responsibility—applicable principles and values—and the factors which make for effective discharge of responsibility—qualified participants and expert advisers, effective organs and procedures, and appropriate attitudes. To the extent that these can be brought into play, the probability that congressional responsibility will operate is enhanced.

Numerous are the conditions that promote successful discharge. I shall comment on twelve, identifying each, suggesting possible reforms, and explaining its place in the developed system. The first four lie primarily outside the control of Congress, the remaining eight lie primarily within the control of a Congress organized and motivated to retool itself to serve one of its most critical functions for a new age.

A Public Informed and Moderate. Most fundamental of the conditions and most difficult to assure is a public informed, aware of its own constitutional responsibilities, and dedicated to a course of moderation and rational adjustment in constitutional controversies. Neither Congress, nor the Court, nor both in concert, can effectively resolve constitutional issues without an educated public—Jefferson's "bar of the public reason."

This requires, for one thing, publicity. Public comprehension of Court decisions has improved through the informed and interpretative coverage of such correspondents as Anthony Lewis of the *New York Times*. Press coverage and especially the televised press conference give the President abundant channels for bringing the views of the Executive on constitutional issues before the public. But full résumés of debates in Congress, balancing the pros and cons of constitutional issues, are rare. Committee hearings, especially when telecast live, have stolen the show, and while potentially informative, are more likely to entertain, shock, or bias than illuminate the viewers. What is needed is something to parallel the early press digests of debates which revealed diverse points of view on issues, not spasmodically and in isolation from one another, but systematically and serially, thus exposing the reasons which led to the legislative decisions. Magazines, the cinema, radio, and television are all potential channels for reaching the public with biographies of constitutional settlements.

Congress, itself, could do much to improve public awareness, by publishing a record of debates, not only honest in reporting actual discussion, but also accompanied by neutral summaries; the same goes for committee hearings, which like the *Record,* are subject to minute editing by participants before publication, often at the expense of both clarity and reliability.

Another means of continually realerting the public to the Constitution as the matrix of a free and orderly society is symbolism. Chief Justice Warren's appeal for informed public attachment to the Bill of Rights and his warning concerning the 1963 "State-rights" amendments suggest the influence which the presiding judge can wield. The outpouring of publicity from parties and interest groups, and the access of the chief policy-maker, the President, to the media may in time call for a vigorous counter-symbol. The Chief Justice may occupy the most strategic post for personifying the rule of law, for reminding citizens, interest groups, parties, and officials of the national interests and purposes served by the Constitution, and the need for intelligence, moderation, and detachment in achieving constitutional settlements.

Finally, there is need of citizen education on the nature and function of the Constitution designed for the age of crisis. Marshall pointed out that the generality of the Constitution helped ensure that it would be "understood by the public,"[6] showing the importance he attached to public awareness. Only a public which comprehends the meaning and worth of civil liberties, due process of law, division of powers, and other fundamentals can provide the foundation on which to rest settlements of recurrent constitutional crises. Here is a collective enterprise for lawyers, political scientists, and historians, working with schoolmen and experts in the new media and teaching aids.

A Responsible Judiciary. Another condition external to Congress which shapes the action of Congress is the conduct of the justices. By their statements, demeanor, and public activities the judges may mold both public understanding of constitutional principles and settlements and the attitudes of members of Congress. By taking stands on policies they may weaken the judicial reputation of the Court as a judicial body; by resting decisions on authority, rather than on reasoned argument, they may foster ignorance and immaturity on constitutional issues; by reiterating the function of the Court as ultimate arbiter of *all* constitutional questions, they may create misapprehensions about the real state of things. Statements of the reasons for and against decisions, cast in the language of the people, and circumspection about the true function of the Court in the process of constitutional settlements can promote education, accommodation, and awareness of the responsibility of Congress and public.

A Responsible Executive. Even more than the courts, the Executive has an immediate influence on what happens in Congress. From John Adams in the Sedition Act affair, to Dwight Eisenhower in that of the Jenner-Butler bill, Presidents have demonstrated that inaction may have worse consequences than action. Yet the crisis-born actions of FDR—in minimizing legislative responsibility in the soft coal case and in pressing a narrow, legalistic view of the legislative veto in the Reorganization Act episode—show the danger of action inadequately conceived. Of recent Presidents prior to President Kennedy, Harry S. Truman may in retrospect deserve the highest praise for his combination of firm presidential leadership in policy matters with a Missourian's alertness to constitutional realities and necessities. His silence in relation to the Twenty-Second Amendment was, of course, predetermined ethically and constitutionally. The effect, however, was to give the majority Republicans of the Eightieth Congress clear sailing with little resistance by their leaderless opponents.

Even though the President is the leading policy-maker of the government, the Constitution obliges him to take care that laws, not policies, be faithfully executed, and also shoulder important tasks affecting legislation. Experience suggests that in both areas—in directing the vast operations of the executive branch, and in pushing his policies through Congress—the President bears an increasingly heavy load of responsibility for the Constitution. While the Justice Department is and should be primarily a servant of the President rather than of Congress, it functions in both capacities under a heavy constitutional obligation. In enforcing the laws, in advising the President and department heads on the constitutional implications of policy, and in responding to requests by committee chairmen for legal advice about pending measures, the Attorney General is a spokesman, albeit provisional, of the Constitution. Accordingly, those in the Justice Department who prepare constitutional opinions should have the same sensitivity to constitutional principles, the same representativeness of party, regions, interests, and ingredients of experience, moderation, and wisdom, the same resort to a thoughtful, many-minded deliberative process, and the same acceptance of obligation one asks of legislators. Jefferson's insistence on "due proportion" for parties, and on fidelity to the Constitution in selecting his subordinates has a peculiar aptness for these officials. The fruit of such executive deliberations could be advice of value and persuasiveness both to President and Congress.

Yet recent experience has revealed pitfalls in too great a congressional dependence on the Justice Department. Attorneys General Kennedy and Katzenbach reversed the practice of some of their predecessors by putting the resources of that Department at the disposal of members of the bipartisan civil rights coalition. Whether the beneficiary of such a practice be a coalition or only the President's party, the effect may be to place the opposition in Congress at a distinct disadvantage. Two recourses suggest themselves. One is to insist that as executive leadership in policy matters continues to mount, Congress maintain an independent stance in the settlement of constitutional issues, broadly defined. The other is to provide the opposition party or bloc with resources of constitutional advice which equal those of the Justice Department. The parties provide important machinery for planning and managing high level constitutional debate, and the President's party has great advantages over the opposition in staff resources and publicity. There is much to be said, accordingly, for furnishing the opposition party with an institution and staff for developing and defending its position and presenting it forcefully to the public. One means would be the oft-mooted plan to assure the runner-up in the presidential election a four-year seat in the Senate.

Thus, in discharging its responsibility, Congress takes its cue from both the other branches.

Responsible Action by Private Groups. Private groups and their representatives also influence the discharge of responsibility by Congress. For a generation members of Congress have increasingly sprinkled hearings

347

and debates with letters and memoranda from lawyers, law professors and deans, and political scientists. Of even greater influence have been the recommendations or resolutions of groups such as the American Bar Association and the American Civil Liberties Union and the testimony of special interest groups.

Civil liberties, political science, and bar groups are peculiarly fitted to contribute constitutional knowledge and concern. Yet the confusion which the use of seemingly inconsistent statements by the American Bar Association injected into the handling of the Jenner-Butler bill shows the dangers in the misuse of group labels.[7] It suggests that before a group formally attaches its name to recommendations, it should make certain that those recommendations are the fruit of genuine deliberation, not of a small and sometimes unrepresentative committee, but of a properly constituted committee, or even better, of the group's governing body.

Another device that might bring valuable expert judgment to bear on many constitutional questions would be a joint committee of lawyers and political scientists. If formed by national associations for law and political science, such a committee might review and report on both pending measures and long-run problems. Both professions might well devote more attention to legislative organs and procedures for constitutional inquiry.

Special interest groups present a somewhat different problem. While they too may help in developing constitutional arguments, their dominance of particular legislative committees not only gives a distorted impulse to particular policies thus necessitating strong executive intervention, but tends to hamper due deliberation of constitutional issues. Perhaps like the administrative expert, the lobbyist should remain "on tap and not on top," and receive reminders, for example the constitutional oath, of the duty of his obligation to the general interest.

Acceptance of Responsibility by Members. That members of Congress ought to accept their responsibility is a truism. To vitalize that acceptance is another matter. Perhaps if the measures proposed in this chapter became a reality, the individual member could resume his traditional obligation with greater conviction and realism. Most recent constitutional debates have produced urgent appeals to minimize the member's obligation, with effects that have sometimes seemed important. Most noteworthy are the Communist Control Act and the Twenty-Second Amendment, when appeals to leave the task to others were loudest and came from the most authoritative sources.

Perhaps a return to a simpler, more pointed oath to support the Constitution would influence some, especially if national loyalty were made a separate article. Perhaps publicity for statements belittling responsibility would have a deterrent effect. In any event, members should be alerted to cues for a weakened obligation. Among such cues are the following: "The Court has spoken, the whole issue is foreclosed." "The Supreme Court is the mouthpiece of the Constitution." "Constitutionality is lawyers' business and only lawyers' business." "Constitutionality is clear, hence the only issue before us is one of policy." "Legislation is necessarily imperfect; the courts will correct constitutional vagaries." "Since the Court changes its interpretation from time to time, Congress should pass the bill and let the Court reconsider earlier holdings." This book has shown to what extent such appeals embody half-truths or less and their deleterious effects.

The responsibility of members is neither routine nor legalistic. It is manifold, embracing all the elements set forth in this book.

Identification and Definition of Constitutional Questions. As the Bradley case and its successors have demonstrated, members are wont to "spring" measures of dubious constitutionality and to stumble into constitutional discussions without advance definition or preparation. The constitutional issue was long hidden in Jenner-Butler, was precipitated tardily in Communist Control, and emerged only gradually in the Reorganization Act controversy. Members invite neglect of grave issues by misclassification, as when citation of court precedents in the Reorganization and Middle East episodes obscured the need to devise provisions supplementing the constitutional document. For proper handling, questions need to be flagged early, defined with precision, and classified.

Conceivably a small bipartisan committee or group of constitutional experts could serve this watchdog function and employ the systems of classification set out above. From the standpoint of form, narrow questions could be categorized as justiciable-precedential, justiciable-non-precedential, and nonjusticiable; and others as broad questions, questions of implementation, and questions of amendment. In subject matter, they may fall into the categories of A. individual rights; B. federalism; C. the separation of powers; and D. machinery and proceedings of Congress. This book suggests that questions under categories A and B are most likely to have direct impact on individual and group interests and to be weighted with court precedents. Here legal counsel, and public hearings for affected groups, may have special importance. Categories C and D concern the federal government itself, with somewhat indirect consequences for the public and interest groups. Here Congress must place heavy reliance on its own experience and on the advice of experts from fields such as comparative government. Timely advice from a student of Parliamentary practice, for example, might have expedited settlement of the legislative veto issue.

349

Committees and subcommittees in 1965 were already specializing in some of the above categories. Except for the Senate Judiciary Subcommittee on Constitutional Amendments, most of these units followed the second classification.[8]

Due notice, definition, and categorization of questions would contribute to their meaningful handling.

The Effect of Bicameralism. A further condition is the effect of bicameralism or, to put it differently, the problem of the lower house. Of the nine episodes from the modern Congress, only three, the pre-war soft-coal and wiretapping discussions and the 1964 Civil Rights Act debates, disclosed the House playing a constructive role. In contrast to the creative labors of the Representatives in the early decades, the Senate gradually assumed the role of constitutional guardian. In the past two decades the House has seemingly delegated the task of high constitutional inquiry to the Senate and busied itself with policy, borne down as it is under pressures of constituents, interest groups, parties, and the Executive. Since the House shares equally in the adoption of legislation and constitutional amendments, there is cause for concern in this record. Senate-House bargaining produced a rule-of-thumb compromise on jury trial in the 1957 Civil Rights Act discussions, and such bargains present a risk to the integrity of constitutional principle.

Recent and impending changes raise other possibilities. As the rapid redistricting of state legislatures brings in turn a more accurately representative House and as the two-party system extends across the South, the House is likely to become more assertive of a place equal to the Senate, less stable in membership, and more intensively the cockpit of party and other pressures. The arguments of Madison and others for a longer term for Representatives gain a new significance under such conditions, since length of tenure might enhance the acceptance of constitutional responsibility.

These developments suggest that Congress overtly accept the primacy of the Senate and let the Representatives presume the constitutional determinations of the Senate wise and valid. Conceivably a sort of modus vivendi could govern the matter by expediting constitutional questions to the upper house, with agreement that ordinarily bills raising such questions originate there. But this would entail some of the same objections as the judicial monopoly theory, and furthermore, recent experience suggests that the Senate is less able and willing than formerly to hold great debates.

Thus, it were better to fit the House to share in the discharge of responsibility. A four-year term would tend to heighten members' independence and accumulated experience, both so conducive to full and

350

focused inquiry into constitutional questions. Joint meetings of Senate and House committees concerned with constitutional questions might provide a greater representativeness, a sharing of experience, and a speedier transfer to the House of the insights and constitutional concern of the Senators.

The Quality of Floor Debate. Where the Senate has shone most brightly is in floor debate. In its "great debates" on the Middle East Resolution and the 1957 Civil Rights Act, the Senate continued to play the part which Jefferson cast for the Committee of the Whole. Thorough hearings in the Foreign Relations and Armed Services Committees set the stage for the Middle East discussion, while the 1957 debate on jury trial was somewhat impromptu. Jefferson's expectation that the Committee of the Whole would provide a talked-out decision on guiding principles conforming to the sense of the whole preliminary to committee inquiries and preparation of bills has a quaint ring in the modern Congress, even though it raises clear echoes in Parliament. Yet in practice the present inadequacies of the Judiciary Committee often invite bypassing and force the Senate to take up constitutional questions initially and exhaustively on the floor, in a manner reminiscent of Jefferson. Here is a task which the Senators, in spite of difficulties, must continue to discharge. Here, if anywhere in Congress, interests are brought to moderate their demands and accept a more inclusive interest, and the country is enlightened on constitutional controversies and settlements.

Yet senatorial time and energy have limits, and on many issues prior inquiries, often by committees other than Judiciary, have either obviated or lightened the burden of floor debate. The MacArthur hearings themselves resolved two acrid constitutional issues, one great, the other small; and in the Reorganization, Middle East, Civil Rights, and Jenner-Butler episodes, prior hearings gave a more or less satisfactory advance briefing to the debaters.

On the other hand, if 1964 is a fair test, then the filibuster and a decline in senatorial erudition may lower the quality of Senate debate. This calls for fresh thought on measures to plan and inform debates on critical issues and improvements in committees and other sources of expert advice.

Committees and Subcommittees: Organization and Procedure. Unlike those Elysian days when members of Congress could form their judgments from focused debates in Committee of the Whole, debates informed and given direction by the studies and reports of the Executive, members today depend on a variety of sources of advice. Some of these, as already shown, lie outside Congress, others within it. Three will receive treatment here: committees and subcommittees, auxiliary expert staffs, and national commissions.

Since that day long ago when standing committees elbowed the executive departments out of the preparatory role Hamilton and Jefferson had assigned to them, they have steadily risen in importance as constitutional advisers, mentors, and even leaders in Congress. When in January 1959 some 200 members filled out the author's questionnaire (see Appendix A), 178 of them took the trouble to mark an optional question concerning the sources of advice they used. The question was: "On whom do you ordinarily rely for advice when you encounter questions of constitutionality in committee or on the floor?" Members had eight options; they were asked to check all on whom they relied regularly and to indicate under a ninth any others not listed. Thirty-seven, all but two of them lawyers, wrote in "myself" as a ninth. The following are the options, listed in the order of preference:

Source	Per cent who checked
Committees and committee counsel	52
Other members	47
Legislative Reference Service	42
Office of the Legislative Counsel (Senate or House)	34
Members of own staff, including legal counsel	33
Myself	21
Department of Justice or other executive agencies	19
Non-governmental organizations	8
Private law firm	7

Both Senators and Representatives gave a high priority to committees, although Senators found their own personal staffs even more useful, and Representatives relied on other members almost as constantly as they did on committees. Several Representatives actually specified the House Judiciary Committee as a source, but no Senator followed this example. Clearly congressional responsibility is implemented primarily by standing committees.

But what committees serve most effectively? The Bradley and Middle East episodes show the caliber and usefulness of the combined Senate Foreign Relations and Armed Services Committees even on constitutional issues. It would be foolhardy, however, to place main reliance on committees charged with substantive problems of legislation, concerned as they are primarily with development and effectuation of specialized and often technical policies. A more promising alternative is the Judiciary Committee of each house. The Sherman Act discussions show how heavily the Senate and the House, too, one may presume, had come to depend on the constitutional deliberations and advice of that body, for all the jibes at this "grand mausoleum" of legislation. Even though the Finance Committee had worked out the policy aspects of the bill, the Senate referred it to Judiciary to deal with the constitutional objections which the debates had produced. The advice was sought and followed.

Yet this book has shown how for at least three decades the Senate has been dodging Judiciary or giving limited credence to its constitutional advice. The body to which the rules entrust a large quota of the Senate's constitutional questions, thus making it something of a Supreme Court for that house, has itself been directed and until very recently manned in a most unjudicious manner. Accordingly, unless the committee can be reorganized for effective discharge of these functions, the Senate should resort to a third alternative, a new special or standing committee on constitutional questions. Some of the same criticisms can be applied to the House Judiciary Committee. In 1963, the leadership and the composition of a subcommittee evidently largely handpicked by the chairman to reflect his own policy preferences contributed directly to executive intervention on the side of constitutional correctness.

Whatever committee assumes the task, theory and practice dictate several specifications for it. For one thing, it should be representative. A one-party committee initially drafted the Sedition Act of 1798 with disastrous results; since then, equity has evidently governed the allotment of committee seats between parties with the effect of thwarting efforts by one party to impose its constitutional readings on the other. But regions and interest groups have fared less well, both on committees concerned with policy and on the Judiciary Committees. This distortion in favor of particular regions and interests by lessening the possibility of many-sided deliberation and accommodation at a stage prior to the floor has vastly complicated the work of Congress, nowhere more than on constitutional issues. In departing from the representative principle the Judiciary Committees and subcommittees have jettisoned a leading advantage for Congress in this crucial function.

Committee selection can no longer be safely governed by personal preference and party loyalty. Region or interest domination of any committee tends to magnify the political-demand and veto potential of that region or interest and to invite presidential counterpressure. This tends to weaken the total influence of Congress. As 1963 demonstrated such conditions produce similar results in the handling of constitutional issues, except that here influence moves toward the courts as well as toward the Executive. If Congress is to retain its vital function in weighing constitutional questions, it must find some way to constitute the committees concerned in a manner representative not only of parties but of regions, of major interest groups, perhaps even of urban, suburban, and rural areas.

This would enable Congress to make its maximum contribution, as would another reform; since the presence of laymen can force lawyers to discuss technical points in everyday language and thus promote public understanding, the inclusion of non-lawyers in the Judiciary Committees or their alternatives should be sought.

Another problem is that of leadership. The great powers which time has concentrated in the chairman make his selection a matter of the utmost importance to the effective handling of committee business. Here is a post calling for the highest display of a judicious temperament, knowledge of constitutional law and constitutional principles, and relative freedom from the political demands of interested constituents. Chairmen Eastland and Celler illustrate at opposite ends of the political spectrum the difficulty some legislators face in trying to satisfy voters with extreme positions while simultaneously presiding as impartial moderators. Since chairmen now rise to their position solely by length of uninterrupted tenure in Congress, some change would have to be made in the selection process; election by the full committee, a limited term, or imposition of a qualification such as previous judicial experience might help assure chairmen suited to the special requirements of the position.

A Judiciary Committee or constitutional committee manned and led in a manner appropriate for its task could safely be trusted with important powers. Not only could bills having important constitutional implications be referred to it, but constitutional questions arising in other committees or on the floor could also be submitted to it for its judgment. It is likely that a large proportion of statutes which the Court in recent decades has voided never went to Judiciary. In the Lovett decision, for example, Judiciary Committee members in the House, and in the Covert decision, in the Senate, evidently had to await floor debate to press their constitutional objections to the legislation.[9] The case analyses of the modern Congress have disclosed the crucially important work of such Judiciary Committee members as Senators O'Mahoney, Kefauver, Hennings, Cooper, and Ervin. To enhance the influence of such men, Congress might well make sure, first, that in both houses each member of the Judiciary Committee or constitutional committee serve on other standing committees with as broad a distribution among those committees as possible, and second, that constitutional questions of substantial difficulty, wherever or whenever they arise in the legislative process, be referred at the petition of a prescribed quota of members to that committee.

Many of these strictures also apply to subcommittees. They, too, should embody the representative principle and be directed by a moderate, judicious chairman. Conceivably committees or subcommittees could exist for most of the major categories of constitutional questions. Such a development is already well under way. The question is not so much whether organs exist for each category, but how to lead, man, and coordinate those that do exist. For the Judiciary Committees to undertake the entire spectrum of constitutional questions might tax their members—in 1965, sixteen in the Senate, thirty-five in the House. The Senate committee in that year had ten standing and four special subcommittees; the House, five standing and two special subcommittees. Not all subcommittees, of course, need be large, and much of the work of organizing hearings and digesting results can be handled by permanent staffs.

Of importance equal to committee organization is committee procedure. One who contrasts the impartial and temperate probes which the Senate Commerce and House Ways and Means Committees conducted into the soft-coal bill in 1935 to the initial phase of the Jenner-Butler inquiry in 1957 would conclude that hearings have become less judicial in character and more biased and publicity-centered. Although such a trend would accord with presuppositions of the judicial monopoly theory, it tells only part of the story. A basic requirement here is agreement on the purpose of committee hearings in the handling of constitutional questions.

Comments which four Representatives made on the 1959 questionnaire bring out the importance both of committees and of committee procedure in the House. Wrote one experienced lawyer member from New England: "Constitutional questions are usually threshed out in committee rather than before the House, and if the committee goes ahead notwithstanding, although the argument can still be made in the House, it is not then too powerful." The actual process of committee discussion in the House was described by a non-lawyer from the Far West with more than a decade in the lower chamber: "All committees have lawyer members. In general the lawyer members argue the point of constitutional validity in the process of committee drafting of a law. The lay members usually follow the consensus of opinion of the lawyer members, or the legal counsel after study advises us of his opinion. Those who oppose the above are free to vote and argue in the Committee or on the Floor their viewpoint—the House decides by accepting or rejecting a dissenting amendment . . ."

Yet others hinted at laxity in the operations of committees when constitutional questions were at stake. Said another Far Western Representative, himself a lawyer:

I would say that Congress does not seriously enough consider questions of constitutionality and that there is no source of information on the subject readily available to ALL members of Congress. Further-more by reason of the tortuous course of legislation through two equal bodies with the result often determined by a handful of members in a conference it is most often difficult to establish the intent of the Congress as a whole outside the literal language of a statute. I would say that statements made in debate were of minimal significance in determining legislative intent. Reports accompanying bills to the floor are a more official expression of opinion but they are most generally written by some committee employee and are not approved by individual members.

Finally, a lawyer from a Border State confessed his dissatisfaction at the attitude of many fellow-committee members: "Constitutional issues are seldom raised except by Congressmen who feel as I do about the matter. Usually when the issue is raised in . . . the committee on which I serve, I am the one who raises it. There are very few Congressmen who seem to be willing to raise the question."[10]

Of course, committee action is somewhat less crucial in the Senate, but the tenor of these comments is pertinent to both houses. The fore-going chapters suggest three leading purposes for committee procedure where constitutional issues are involved: first, to gather pertinent evi-dence and arguments with maximum fairness, thoroughness, and de-tachment; second, to provide a searching deliberation on the question by a body knowledgeable and representative; and third, to incorporate the resulting decision in a report designed to convey light rather than confusion.

This book maintains that for constitutional questions of many sorts adequate procedure entails a series of common stages. For committees one could state these as follows:

First, advance agreement on procedure. General committee accep-tance and enforcement of canons of fairness could help avert such measures as the original Jenner bill and the kind of one-man hearing that produced it.

Second, adequate preparation. Those conducting committee or sub-committee inquiries need to state the questions in controversy clearly in advance, give full open notice to interested parties, interest groups, mem-bers of Congress, pertinent executive departments, and the public, and adhere to the stated purpose till completion of the inquiry. Committee staff could be supplemented by appropriate outside experts, drawn from a permanent roster. Important here are clear advance notice and solici-tation of testimony both representative and informed.

Third, fair hearings. A firm, fair, and courteous treatment of all wit-nesses and correspondents elicits the fullest testimony. To be effective, hearings will be more than a perfunctory recording of ill-digested opinions, but rather a means by which Congress conducts a two-way conversation with the public. Through this channel, Congress informs itself of the opinions and preferences of interest groups, localities, parties, and the public and simultaneously conveys to those with passionately held convictions and special interests the complexity and many-sidedness of constitutional questions. With floor debate becoming increasingly per-functory and committee-managed, hearings also offer members of Congress a more fruitful opportunity to present and defend their views. Where hearings have failed to elicit full and balanced presentations, re-sumption can serve the interests of the house and actually conserve its time. Such a resumption might have expedited a decision on the legisla-tive veto; such action, thanks to Senator Hennings, led to moderation of the original Jenner bill.

Fourth, publication of hearings and synopses. Because of the great volume and varying quality of hearings, there would be merit in full publication not only of honest transcripts, but also of digests and sum-mary statements prepared in as impartial and professional a manner as possible.

Fifth, general deliberation by the full committee. In closed committee sessions, Congress on many issues reaches some of its most significant determinations. Important, therefore, are full perusal of the record by all committee members, thorough and searching discussion, and clear pre-cise voting. Here is a counterpart of the early Committee of the Whole and of the modern Court conference. Publicity at this stage is unneces-sary, provided the other procedural requirements are met.

Sixth, an informative report. While some reports have been addressed to floor debaters with a view to affording focus and background to de-bate, others are pointed to constituents and special interest groups or to the Supreme Court. Committees exist primarily to serve the parent house. Only reports which define questions precisely, state reasons pro and con cogently, and identify the authors and those supporting the majority and minority positions clearly can prepare the chamber for intelligent judgments on constitutional issues.

Such are the objectives and methods which experience would seem to prescribe for committee and subcommittee work. Employment of pro-cedures such as these by committees constituted in the manner described would do as much as any single reform to equip Congress to cope effec-tively with constitutional questions.

Availability of Auxiliary Expert Staff. But committees can meet only part of the need for adequate sources of advice. Members today feel keenly the need of abundant and readily accessible expert advice. Some

357

continue, it is true, to rely in part on their own best judgment for direction. More than a fifth of those returning the 1959 questionnaire so indicated while acknowledging the value of other sources. One experienced Southern Senator with legal training recorded at the foot of the list of possible sources his reliance on "my own judgment plus combinations of above," and a colleague from the South wrote, "My personal opinion coupled with that of legal counsel of my own staff as well as that of the committee; and all others. I try to get the best composite opinion possible." A Southern lawyer-Representative: "My own library, and research, and also the legal opinions of qualified constitutional lawyers." A Western Representative: "I check the Constitution myself and listen carefully to the debate—and try to do my own thinking," and a New Englander: "I consult a great deal on complex questions, but always make up my own mind."

But most members seemed less self-reliant. Members need expert advice. Nearly three-fourths of Senators responding to the questionnaire put down their own staffs as a leading source, while only a quarter of Representatives, lacking funds for such luxuries, followed suit. Instead, Representatives to the extent of 48 per cent noted "other members" as a regular source. Note also that high on the list of reservoirs of expert advice for both houses were the Legislative Reference Service of the Library of Congress (42 per cent) and the Offices of the Legislative Counsel, one for each house (34 per cent). Sources more remote from Congress were checked with diminishing frequency on the questionnaires: Justice and other departments—19 per cent (a quota which by 1964 would doubtless have been higher), non-governmental organizations—8 per cent, and private law firms—7 per cent.

Members need, at their right hand, the best in expert knowledge. The case analyses suggest that that knowledge must include legal rules and precedents, notably the constitutional law of the Supreme Court. In addition, for many constitutional issues, there is need of authoritative knowledge of American government, American constitutional history, the history and theory of American democracy, public administration, and comparative government. Men versed both in law and in political science, with some knowledge of history as well, would seem best fitted to advise on the whole range of constitutional issues.

The twenty-two members of the combined Offices of the Legislative Counsel and the more numerous experts in the Legislative Reference Service continue to supplement congressional office and committee staffs. Legislative Counsel, however, shy away from all but strictly legal questions in their work of bill-drafting. The more flexible and many-sided LRS would seem to offer members their most promising reservoir,

358

apart from committees, for advice on the whole range of constitutional questions confronting them. Congress might well consider greatly expanding the present hard-pressed staff of the Service and encouraging it to experiment with group consultations by varied specialists on difficult constitutional issues.[11] Even on narrow constitutional issues such consultation could prove fruitful, and on broad questions and those of implementation, supplementation, and amendment the widest range of the best expert advice is essential.

In addition, since members of Congress constantly seek advice from distinguished authorities on constitutional law and other specialties, in the law and graduate schools, might not Congress bring such scholars to Washington for assignments of a year or more? Congress, the scholars, and future students would all benefit from such an association. Other means for checking the constitutionality of legislation before rather than after passage suggest themselves, among them the appointment in each house of a "constitutionalist" to render the same sort of prompt, informed advice on technical constitutional questions that the parliamentarian provides on procedural. Another would be the appointment of a diversified and experienced committee of former federal judges, enjoying judicial perquisites and tenure, to render constitutional advice at the instance of Congress.

A menace lurks, of course, in treating constitutional law as exclusively the monopoly of a few highly specialized experts. Of all fields of knowledge, this one should as far as possible be the possession of all who contribute to constitutional settlements, whether members of Congress or not. Yet the above changes could go far toward equipping the houses with the ubiquitous and proficient help they need.

Resort to National Commissions of Inquiry. Finally, some controversies bring out constitutional issues for which even ideal committees employing exemplary procedures working in the framework of the best expert advice could prove inadequate. High political tension and the burden of legislative work conspire to thwart the thorough investigation and searching deliberation which such questions demand if an explosion is to be averted. For these Congress may with value resort to that compromise between the standing committee and the constitutional convention—the national commission of inquiry. President Truman's Committee on Civil Rights of 1946 was an effort to achieve common ground before a problem of grave and nationwide proportions came to a head. Eleven years later, Congress itself finally took action after the problem had deepened by setting up the United States Commission on Civil Rights. The United States Commission on Government Security, 1955–

1957, might have proved of incalculable value in averting the hysteria and excesses of the early 1950's had Congress authorized it in the late 1940's. As late as August 1954, Congress might have lightened the pressure for the precipitate Communist Control Act had members accepted Senator Magnuson's proposal for an investigative commission. The commission device deserves further study and a more receptive congressional mind.

Several requirements for such commissions suggest themselves. First, representativeness—not merely of parties, but of regions or groups which the issue places in competition, and of the public in general. Second, participation of distinguished citizens and political leaders and possibly of experts with a common touch and broad practical experience. Such participants would furnish political experience, read public needs into technical issues, and translate technical concepts into everyday English. Third, expertise, either as a constituent element of membership or within the working staff; knowledge of law may, for many issues, need to be supplemented by knowledge of other disciplines. Fourth, adequate funds, compensation, time, facilities, subpoena powers, and means of publicity. Commissions of this sort may prove serviceable not only for issues involving interpretation of constitutional provisions in novel and controversial policy situations, for example, governmental security, but for implementation, supplementation, and even amendment of the document.

Avoidance of Last-Minute Action. From 1798 to 1958, recurrent crises have demonstrated that public excitement and party contentiousness may force measures of dubious constitutionality or wisdom onto the floor in the last hectic days of a pre-election session. At such times those seeking immediate political advantage may overleap all the hurdles which reason, experience, and tradition have put up to assure deliberation. At such times, too, members may secure passage of measures which later prove highly questionable, without full awareness of their true character.[12]

To depend on the courts alone to counteract such excesses is neither wise nor safe. In 1798, Congress set a termination date to the operation of the Sedition Act, a valuable model since reconsideration would occur in a nonelection year. There, in fact, the electorate rejected the legislation by returning the opposition party to power. The Communist Control Act is a modern instance of precipitate action. Conceivably it might have been averted had the Executive taken a firm line at an early stage, had the Senate possessed a Judiciary Committee on the 1890 pattern, or had the whole matter of Communists in government been referred earlier to a national commission. In fact, for avoidance of hasty or ill-advised action, all conditions affecting responsibility have significance.

CONCLUSIONS

In the path of all these proposed reforms is one stubborn fact: millions of Americans, including many in high places, identify the Constitution with the Supreme Court and consequently expect and demand little of their representatives. Under such conditions, is reform possible? Perhaps one should rather ask, in view of the dependence of constitutional government on a pervasive constitutional responsibility, is change necessary? Some of the best of the founding minds and a century and three-quarters of experience demonstrate a continuing and inescapable congressional encounter with constitutional issues.

For change to come about, it is important to identify and refute two attitudes which help sustain the judicial monopoly theory. On the one hand, lawyers, in their zeal to safeguard the fundamental law from the meddlesome and blundering hands of politicians, tend to thrust on the judges the task not only of interpreting most of the Constitution's provisions but of preserving the Constitution as a whole. That burden the Court never has carried, never could carry. To make the Court sole guardian of the Constitution would produce the total tyranny of policy and convert the political process into a no-holds-barred battle of giants, with the Court as the first casualty. Judicial review can function only where discussion of constitutional issues, accommodation of interests, special and general, and disclosure of constitutional principles begin elsewhere, in quarters closer to the sources of public opinion. "What a situation," cried Abraham Baldwin, in asking members of the First Congress to imagine themselves in the role of justices forced to decide *de novo* the validity of a presidential dismissal of a cabinet secretary, "almost too great for human nature to bear. They would feel great relief at having had the question decided by the representatives of the people." One may add that the people would feel a like relief at having a host of other issues, not subject to court review, resolved in a responsible manner by their representatives.

On the other hand political scientists tend to arrive at the same conclusion about the judicial function from other premises. In a rapidly shrinking world, with new nations by the score struggling to form governments efficient in the making and effectuation of policy, men inevitably search for common elements in all political systems. It is plausible to conclude that all systems reveal a common political process, with forces of individual and group pressures producing what every system aspires to, efficient policy. The search for similarities, however, may overlook essential differences; it runs the risk of minimizing the distinction between those systems in which the struggle of forces takes place in a framework of divided power and the rule of law and those in which it does not. The effect is to becloud the influence of shared values and supporting principles in tempering the political process and to ignore the long course of history that has taught men those values and principles. The brakes and canals that today control and direct the political process in fully constitutional governments were purchased by a millenium of history in the West. The price of these defenses of civilized values was pain, anguish, and blood. For full efficacy, these safeguards require the comprehension, acceptance, and support of all those who participate in the political process, not of judges alone. Any other view invites a weakening of the constitutional order.

Madison's advice to the First Congress has relevance. Jefferson viewed a congressional involvement with constitutional inquiries as essential to an informed electorate, the "safest depository of ultimate power." Madison saw it as essential to the integrity of the Legislature itself: "It is incontrovertibly of as much importance to this branch of the government as to any other that the Constitution should be preserved entire . . . the breach of the Constitution in one point, will facilitate the breach in another; a breach in this point may destroy that equilibrium by which the House retains its consequence and share of power . . ."

With the military assuming power in more and more emerging nations, and with the Executive assuming a mounting dominance at home, Americans might well heed this advice. They might with profit couple their efforts toward efficient policy-making with a simultaneous effort to renew and adapt constitutional government for themselves and to exemplify it for the world they would lead.

Appendix A   Appendix B   Notes

Table of Court Cases   Index

Appendix A. Questionnaire to the Members of the Eighty-Sixth Congress: Analysis of Returns

On January 16, 1959, a questionnaire headed "The Role of Congress in Constitutional Interpretation" was mailed from Cambridge, Massachusetts, to every member of the new Eighty-Sixth Congress. The questions, be it noted, were cast almost exclusively in narrow constitutional terms. Three kinds of information were sought and obtained: first, statistics on the amount of support given various attitudes toward the responsibility of Congress for the consideration of constitutional questions; second, explanatory comments disclosing elements of the problem and the grounds on which members based their attitudes; and third, information on means for overcoming obstacles which confront members in the discharge of responsibility.

This questionnaire had not only to present meaningful questions, but to present them in a form that would elicit a maximum number of responses. "I am sorry," replied a Senator from a large Northeastern state, "that with mail pouring in at a rate of approximately 1,000 letters a day that I cannot afford the luxury of devoting the time I would like to this interesting problem." Accordingly, the questionnaire was confined to both sides of a single page, was accompanied by a brief, four paragraph explanatory letter, and was sent out at a time when the burden of legislative work was lightest. Replies were sought with or without identifying signatures. To obtain light on factors affecting attitudes, however, each was asked to check his house, whether or not he was a lawyer, whether he was newly elected, had served up to ten years, or had served more than ten years, and from which of five regions he came. At that early stage of this project, no separate provision was made for the Border States; West Virginia and Oklahoma, together with Arizona and New Mexico, were assigned to the "South and Southwest" and Kentucky and Missouri to the Midwest. Otherwise the regions were similar to those employed throughout this book.

Six questions appeared on the face of the questionnaire, each answerable with a check mark. They related to the frequency of constitutional questions in Congress, the character of responsibility, the genuineness of

365

issues, the value of congressional discussions, the weight which courts should accord to congressional determinations, and the relative importance of various types of issues. On the reverse side appeared an optional seventh question concerning sources of advice and a space for general comments.

Of 534 members, 203 filled out and returned the questionnaire by mid-February. Thus, roughly 38 per cent of members supplied returns in time to be included in computations at the Harvard Statistical Laboratory. Ninety-three were returned unsigned. Besides the 203 a number replied by letter, and eight others returned the questionnaire too late to be included in the computations. This response was doubtless evidence of widespread concern about the problem, whetted, no doubt, by the recent Jenner-Butler and related debates.

One could question the reliability of a 38 per cent return since the sample was limited to those members having sufficient time and interest to respond. Yet the 38 per cent quota holds up with reasonable dependability when returns are examined by categories. Thus, Senators responded at the rate of 36 per cent, Representatives 38 per cent; the range by region ran from 31 per cent from the Midwest to 47 per cent from the Far West; new members made returns at the rate of 43 per cent, experienced members at the rate of 37 per cent; lawyers at the rate of 38 per cent and non-lawyers, 35 per cent. Furthermore, comparisons within each house between the size of groups, such as lawyers, within the sample and the actual totals of corresponding groups produce roughly similar results. Thus lawyers comprised 56 per cent of the Representatives who responded as against 56 per cent of the House as a whole. The corresponding figures for the Senate were 71 per cent and 62 per cent. At the least, the returns clearly provide evidence of leading attitudes and concepts and of the extent to which each commands support. In addition, the numerous comments suggest the rationale behind each position.

FREQUENCY OF OCCURRENCE OF CONSTITUTIONAL QUESTIONS

A vast majority of members who responded found constitutional questions a common occurrence. The first question read:

1. How often do questions of constitutionality arise in the course of your legislative work? (Check one.)
   _____ Very rarely or never   _____ Occasionally
                    _____ Frequently

Of 193 who answered the question, 14 per cent marked "Very rarely or never," 60 per cent "Occasionally," and 26 per cent "Frequently." Only 6 per cent of responding Senators marked "Rarely," as compared with 15 per cent of Representatives. Regions showed a range in favor of "Rarely" from 23 per cent from Middle Atlantic States to 3 per cent from the South and Southwest. Regions preferred "Frequently" as follows: South and Southwest—41 per cent, Middle Atlantic—31 per cent, New England—18 per cent, Midwest—15 per cent, Far West—13 per cent. Not only do most members evidently find constitutional issues a regular occurrence, but the legislators also differ in their notion of what they comprise.

CHARACTER OF RESPONSIBILITY

The second question sought members' conceptions of the Constitution-interpreting function of Congress in relation to the Judiciary:

2. Generally speaking, should Congress pass constitutional questions along to the courts rather than form its own considered judgment on them?
    _____ Yes   _____ No   _____ No Opinion

Of 187 members who marked either "Yes" or "No," 58, or 31 per cent, marked "Yes." This percentage, however, was not repeated among the categories. Only 7 per cent of Senators indicated "Yes," as against 36 per cent of Representatives. Of lawyers, 26 per cent chose "Yes" as compared with 38 per cent of non-lawyers. The five regions showed the following ratios and percentages for "Yes" and "No":

Middle Atlantic	17–15	53–47 per cent
Midwest	18–27	40–60 per cent
New England	5–12	29–71 per cent
Far West	9–23	28–72 per cent
South and Southwest	8–51	14–86 per cent
Undesignated	1–1	
Total	58–129	31–69 per cent

New members tended to favor "Yes" at a rate (45 per cent) somewhat higher than the average (31 per cent), but note that most of the new members who responded (20 of 31) came from the Midwest and Middle Atlantic States.

A number of respondents added comments which help to explain their

367

answers. Three who failed to mark the question added: "Both," "Confusing question," and "It depends on the problem."

Several of those who marked "Yes," thus preferring court-referral, qualified this response. One declared, "Congress should not pass laws obviously unconstitutional." Another observed that Congress, in passing legislation, should be aware of constitutional questions and added that when the courts failed to follow congressional intent, Congress should pass corrective legislation. Constitutional questions could be discussed, observed a Far Western lawyer-member, "but we know we can't settle them." A Border State member failed to mark the options and observed that, while Congress should form its own judgment, "personally I put much more weight in Supreme Court's judgment"; he explained, in answering the next question, that in Congress constitutional objections are commonly political maneuvers. A new member from the Far West, with state legislative experience, said that when Congress finds itself in conflict with the courts, Congress should amend the Constitution to prevent "misconstruction." "Our judicial system," he explained, "has vested in it a tremendous responsibility . . . The Federal judiciary has well followed (basically) the tradition of being above partisanship. Congress has a solemn obligation to preserve the judiciary's integrity."

Members who, in marking "No," supported independent congressional judgment also made explanations. A New England lawyer reported a "definite tendency" to follow a contrary course; a Middle Atlantic member said recent court decisions had influenced his choice; a Midwestern lawyer thought a contrary course impractical, for there was "no reason to waste our time passing void legislation." A Senator stressed the responsibility of Congress in "initial consideration," and a Representative assumed "legislative Counsel could point out pro's and con's on tight questions." One new Representative from the South stated "No, not if the answer is quite clear to the member," and a Border State representative maintained that while Congress should not act if legislation is "clearly unconstitutional," it should act "if legislation appears to definitely be good, and constitutionality only questioned." A Middle Atlantic Representative assumed a responsibility in all three branches, but stated that since members of Congress were less "learned in the law" than the Court, and since constitutional questions before Congress were unlikely to be as "clearly defined as those confronting the President, . . . the performance of the Congress in the constitutional area should not be of the same 'high' standard." A Southern Senator did not believe that Congress should feel itself "absolutely bound on constitutional questions" but thought it should "exercise care not to enact legislation which is patently unconstitutional." A Representative wrote that "If a proposal seems pretty clearly unconstitutional," that would strongly influence most members in voting against it; "if there were merely a doubt, I think most members would decide their vote on the merits of the legislation and leave the constitutional question to the courts." A Senator clearly identifiable as Midwestern found the yes or no option insufficient and said:

I feel quite sincerely that Congress must of necessity be concerned with the Constitutionality of the measures which it enacts so that our statute books are not encumbered with a multitude of provisions that are eventually going to be a subject of "test actions" in the courts. There are, however, issues which do come before Congress where the Constitutional question is extremely close and both the pros and cons can be debated very plausibly; in these instances I do not feel that the paramount consideration of Congress should be the Constitutional issue and I feel that Congress should then concern itself primarily with the substantive aspects of the proposal and leave the Constitutional question in the hands of the Court.

Others who marked "No," however, stressed the oath-bound duty of all officials to heed constitutional issues. "No officer," asserted a Midwestern Senator, "can escape deciding what he has a constitutional right to do . . . or not to do." A lawyer-Senator from the Far West observed: "While primary and final responsibility for constitutional interpretation rest with the courts, this certainly does not relieve the executive and legislative branches from important responsibilities in this regard, and the whole system would break down promptly if any of the three branches were to ignore their duties under the constitution." A Border State Senator disliked the simple yes-no option and reasoned: "The Congress, in the course of its own legislative activity, must form its own decisions and opinions on constitutional questions wherever its work touches upon constitutional problems. It cannot abdicate its own responsibility in the matter by passing it on to the courts."

Thus, the simple two-to-one majority by which members favored a positive role for Congress requires qualification. The majority was itself divided, some favoring a restricted, some a thorough-going responsibility. Some seemed to deny a responsibility for doubtful questions, some to confine it to the clarification of legislative intent.

MOTIVATION FOR THE RAISING OF CONSTITUTIONAL QUESTIONS

The two-to-one cleavage on responsibility is illuminated by answers to the next two questions. Question 3 read:

369

3. In your experience when constitutional questions are raised in your house are they more likely to be bona fide issues or political maneuvers? (Check one.)

____ Bona fide issues   ____ Political maneuvers
____ No Opinion

This effort to measure impressions of congressional motives got a mixed response. Eleven members failed to mark it and fourteen others checked "No Opinion." Of the remaining 178, 16 per cent showed their dissatisfaction with the given options by designating both "Bona fide" and "Political maneuvers"; 54 per cent checked "Bona fide" and 30 per cent, "Political maneuvers." Senators marked "Bona fide" at the rate of 72 per cent and Representatives 51 per cent; lawyers, 59 per cent and non-lawyers, 47 per cent. Members from the South and Southwest favored it by 71 per cent and, at the other extreme, Middle Atlantic members, by 42 per cent. The same regions favored "Political maneuvers" by 16 per cent and 42 per cent, respectively. New Englanders showed the heaviest preference for both (31 per cent). Moreover, a clear correlation appeared between responses to question 2 and question 3. Half of all those favoring referral to the courts deemed issues in Congress primarily political maneuvers; while 19 per cent of those supporting a role for Congress held this same view. A quarter of those favoring court referral thought questions bona fide, while 59 per cent of those highlighting congressional responsibility held the same view. More than a score commented on the question. Nearly all implied that motives were mixed. The comments ranged all the way from "Bona fide most of the time" to political maneuvers "too often" and "I'm afraid it may often be true." A non-lawyer Representative from the Far West wrote "Both, . . . in terms of the Members who raise them," and a Far Western Senator, "Bona fide issues if I am opposed to the bill, maneuvers if I favor passage." "There are times," wrote a Far Western Representative, "when serious arguments are made, but in a great majority of cases the first attack on any new legislative approach is that it is unconstitutional. (It usually isn't.)" A Midwestern Senator observed that while constitutional questions were often bona fide, they were also a traditional resort of the "professional politician when he wanted a bill defeated." He bracketed constitutional objections along with arguments that bills are "poorly drawn, unsound, etc." as "the usual stereotype basis of objection."

To some, constitutional objections had a subjective ring, and several said motives were beyond detection. A Border State Senator explained that when Senators from the deep South raise constitutional issues, they do it both from personal conviction about constitutional principle and in conformity with the political views of their constituents. He wrote, "The motives of political behavior are too rich, too varied, and too complex to be analyzed in terms of such a rigid and arbitrary classification of values." Yet the members of Congress, wrote a veteran Representative from New England, are "experienced and wise enough" to distinguish between the genuine and the political and to make allowance for the latter. A lawyer-Representative, although new to Congress, asserted that bona fide character may depend on the type of issue; thus, questions concerning relations among the three branches of the government, prerogatives and problems of the legislative branch, and many matters relating to foreign affairs are predominantly bona fide; questions relating to "social and economic powers," "federalism," and "federal government policy" often involve political maneuvers. This observation corroborates tendencies revealed in the course of this book.

Thus, while many found motives hard to assess, a majority having opinions on the point, especially those affirming responsibility, tended to regard constitutional objections to legislation as genuine.

INFLUENCE OF DISCUSSION ON CONGRESSIONAL ACTION

Question 4 dealt with the actual effect of congressional discussion on congressional action. It read:

4. Do you think that debates or committee discussions on constitutional questions have significant influence on the voting on those questions?
_____ Yes _____ No _____ No Opinion

Fourteen respondents bypassed the question, and 13 checked "No Opinion." Of the remaining 176, 118 or 67 per cent marked "Yes," and 58 or 33 per cent marked "No." Senators marked "Yes," at the rate of 81 per cent and Representatives, 64 per cent, but this time lawyers differed little from non-lawyers. Members from Middle Atlantic States showed the lowest quota (56 per cent) for "Yes," and paradoxically, Midwestern members the highest (77 per cent). New members appeared to expect discussion to affect results at a rate (76 per cent) somewhat higher than the average.

This two-to-one congressional endorsement of constitutional discussions showed a distinct relationship to responses to questions 2 and 3. Of those members who on question 2 acknowledged a significant responsibility for the consideration of constitutional issues, 69 per cent saw value in congressional discussion. Furthermore, of those who on question 3 deemed questions bona fide, 77 per cent thought discussion had a significant influence on the outcome. On the other hand, of those who thought questions should ordinarily be referred to the courts, 47 per cent doubted the utility of discussion. Those who thought issues primarily political maneuvers negated influence at the rate of 64 per cent.

In comments, many sought to put the question into proper focus. Three thought discussion should wield a greater influence than at present, one stipulating "when a real constitutional question is raised." Two acknowledged that discussion had an influence sometimes, three thought discussion had some but not significant influence, others thought influence was conjectural or infrequent. Three qualified the situations in which discussion was influential, thus, "where there is a bona fide objection," "Yes, except where there is a deep-seated prejudice or feeling and politics is apparent," and "in some areas debate and discussion can be very helpful;" and a fourth thought that committee discussions as embodied in committee reports had a major influence. A Middle Atlantic member distinguished "consideration" of constitutional questions, which he thought proper for Congress at the time of committee and floor discussion, and "determination," which he said was generally left to the Court.

Thus, a strong majority of respondents attributed value to constitutional discussions in Congress and thought that votes are affected by prior discussion. Yet these members differed among themselves on the degree of influence which discussions exert and the precise occasions when this happens. A strong minority was skeptical, apathetic, or dissatisfied about the question.

WEIGHT WHICH COURTS SHOULD ATTACH TO CONGRESSIONAL DETERMINATIONS

Since, under the influence of the tripartite theory, federal judges have long accorded respect to congressional determinations of constitutional import, it seemed advisable to sound out congressional attitudes on the matter. Question 5 sought responses along a graduated scale:

5. When the courts are called on to decide a constitutional question, how much weight do you think they should attach to an earlier determination of the same question by Congress? (Check one.)
   _____ No weight at all   _____ Limited weight
   _____ A great deal of weight   _____ Controlling weight

All but 12 of the 203 respondents answered the question. The results were "No weight at all"—16 per cent, "Limited weight"—40 per cent,

"A great deal of weight"—40 per cent, and "Controlling weight"— 4 per cent. Thus, while approximately five-sixths of members having an opinion thought the courts should accord some weight to congressional determinations, one-sixth were evidently prepared to abandon the traditional presumption of validity. Only slight differences appeared between the two houses, but lawyers, perhaps out of respect for the Judiciary, showed a greater readiness to mark "No weight" (23 per cent) than non-lawyers (10 per cent). A rather striking variation appeared among members according to experience in Congress. The longer a member has served in Congress, the greater the deference he would appear to expect the courts to pay to congressional findings of constitutionality. Table 13 presents the evidence.

TABLE 13. Attitudes Toward Judicial Deference According to Length of Congressional Service, in Percentages, 1959

Length of service	Number responding	No weight	Limited weight	Great deal of weight	Controlling weight
No previous service	36	28	50	22	0
Up to 10 years	91	19	40	37	4
Over 10 years	59	7	32	54	7
Undesignated	5	0	60	40	0
Over-all	191	16	40	40	4

SOURCE: Question 5, Questionnaire to the Members of the 86th Congress, 1959.

Region, too, appeared to affect responses. At one extreme was the South and Southwest; 6 of the 8 Representatives who checked "Controlling weight" were from that region, while 11 of the 31 who checked "No weight at all" were from the Midwest. Regional variations come out strikingly when responses are grouped in two categories: minimum weight (including "No weight" and "Limited weight") and maximum weight (including "A great deal of weight" and "Controlling weight"). The regions voted as follows for minimum and maximum weight, respectively:

South and Southwest	39 per cent	61 per cent
New England	47 per cent	53 per cent
Middle Atlantic	50 per cent	50 per cent
Far West	66 per cent	34 per cent
Midwest	78 per cent	22 per cent

Again, the South and Midwest appeared at opposite extremes. All this would appear to confirm the conclusion that the strongest champions of judicial monopolism come from the Midwest, and that new members arrive with a preference for that doctrine exceeding that of their more experienced associates.

One might have supposed that those who on question 2 had favored shunting constitutional questions to the courts would expect the courts to assign little weight to congressional determinations and that those who favored independent congressional consideration would pretty unanimously have ascribed weight to them. The results do not bear out this supposition. Of the 58 who supported court referral on question 2, 56 checked question 5 as follows: "No weight at all"—8, "Limited weight"—29, "A great deal of weight"—18, and "Controlling weight" —1. Thus, 19 or 33 per cent of the 58 would accord heavy or complete weight to constitutional decisions of Congress. Of the 129 who supported congressional determinations on question 2, 123 marked question 5 as follows: "No weight at all"—21, "Limited weight"—41, "A great deal of weight"—54, "Controlling weight"—7. Thus, 16 per cent of these would deny all weight to congressional determinations in the courts, and 32 per cent would accord them only limited weight. Comparisons of questions 3 and 4 with question 5 yield similar results. Of 62 who responded favorably to congressional action on questions 2, 3, and 4, no fewer than 10 checked "No weight at all," and 17, "Limited weight." Of 17 who downgraded congressional action on these three questions, only 3 favored "No weight at all," while 9 favored "Limited weight," and 5 "A great deal of weight."

These apparent inconsistencies receive partial explanation from written comments. Several who stressed the duty of Congress to probe questions found in this a ground for judicial deference. Among those checking "A great deal of weight" were a Far Western Senator, "Congress on legislative issues has an obligation to determine that the bills it enacts are in conformity with the Constitution; subject of course to judicial review," and a Middle Atlantic Representative, "In floor debate constitutional objections, sincere or otherwise, are generally raised to defeat a bill. But when Congress has actually voted on a constitutional issue that action should be seriously considered." A Midwest Senator, who bypassed the question, stated that the enactment of a law should *"prima facie* stamp it as constitutional . . . The court should then . . . determine" through its own inquiries "whether the presumption of constitutionality had been removed." A Southern Representative, who checked none of the alternatives, said simply "Congress does not have the power to determine the constitutionality of a matter." And another, who checked "No weight," "Assuming a 100 per cent honest court which does not let itself be influenced by political implications . . ." "It is not possible to force Congress," wrote a new Representative from the Middle Atlantic States, "to pass upon the constitutional question and very rarely has a bill . . . become law in which the Congress has specifically attempted to make a constitutional determination." Congressional decision-making differs from court decision-making, a Border State Senator wrote, for "The kind of determination arrived at by the Congress is not at all the same as that arrived at by the Court, nor was it so intended." Two Representatives thought the Court should pay heed to its own prior decisions, and a Border State Representative, favoring "A great deal of weight," explained, "since it must be presumed that Congress acted with knowledge of prior decisions." Here were markedly contrasting views of the function of Congress and the deference to which its decisions are entitled.

Further analysis reveals some of the considerations which led members to assign weight. For several, the intent of Congress in passing legislation had importance. A Far West Representative favored finality for court decisions, but thought the courts should "give a great deal of weight to the purpose and meaning of Congress." Five other members commented in a similar vein, and a Border State Senator observed that in a situation like the Alien and Sedition Acts, in which Congress had "intended to subvert the Constitution," the courts should give little weight to its action. Others favored a selective assignment of weight; courts should extend weight "if the debate on the issue is serious," pay heed to the "reasons underlying such determinations," and give special deference to a long-standing law. A Middle Atlantic Senator and a Far Western Representative were agreed in attaching weight to committee discussion as reflected in committee reports. A New England Representative would attribute little influence to congressional determinations, except "insofar as social need might affect the answer to the constitutional question." A Southern Senator favored a great deal of weight, since "The constitution must live and grow with the times." Clearly members qualified the weight appropriate for congressional findings not only in degree but in accordance with a variety of factors, many of them under the control of Congress itself.

To summarize, members supported the traditional presumption of validity for acts of Congress by a heavy majority, with greatest support drawn from those with longest service and those from the South and New England. Again, conceptions of weight appropriate for congressional determinations were only partially correlated with conceptions of congressional responsibility. Finally, for some, weight should depend

375

on specific aspects of congressional action, including legislative intent, the quality of congressional discussion, and congressional findings of social need.

RANGE AND RELATIVE IMPORTANCE OF ISSUES

The purpose of the next question was to sound out attitudes toward the extent of responsibility relative to particular types of issues. The question omitted clear alternative choices, but suggested broad categories of issues in order to spur members to develop their own views of the problem. It read:

6. Are there any types of constitutional questions to which Congress should pay particular attention? (For example: conduct of foreign relations, federal-state relations, separation of powers, individual rights, non-justiciable questions, etc.)

Only 125 answered this question by check marks or comments, or by both. Many respondents simply underlined one or more of the types suggested in parentheses. The five categories were marked as follows: federal-state relations—38 per cent, separation of powers—32 per cent, individual rights—32 per cent, conduct of foreign relations—10 per cent, non-justiciable questions—8 per cent.

In comments, a few showed they thought the question either irrelevant or gratuitous. One new lawyer-Representative from the Midwest simply wrote "None—matter for judicial branch," and another Midwestern lawyer thought that ultimate decision was for the courts to make and not for Congress. As might be expected, the bloc of members checking "federal-state relations" included many Southerners; one Southern Senator wrote, "The field of Federal-State relations will continue chaotic until we return to constitutional principles." A Southern Representative wrote "Yes, the constitutional limitations on federal powers, including particular reserved powers of the states," and another Representative mentioned the problem of pre-emption. Yet members from all regions marked this category.

Of the one-third marking separation of powers, three Representatives furnished examples. A Middle Atlantic member mentioned "budget structure and procedure" and the limitations on the right of the Executive to sequester appropriated funds; a Far Westerner stressed the control of information from the executive branch, since assertions of executive privilege, "if unchallenged would make the Congress but a creature of the executive, entirely dependent on him for all information regarding the activities of the departments and agencies of government which it

376

might require in the course of its legislative activities." Congress, he continued, must remember its constitutional responsibilities and "resist any efforts of the executive to expand into an area of judicial or legislative responsibility." A Southern Representative asserted, "Congress ought to find a way to keep the courts from usurping legislative prerogatives." Those who marked individual rights also made comments. One member thought the major problem was to keep a balance between the branches of government that would ensure "maximum protection for the individual in a world that moves in the direction of more and more centralization and state control."

The low ratings of foreign relations and "non-justiciable questions" were surprising. Eight members, including six who failed to mark the item, made comments hinting at the significance of non-justiciable questions. A Far Western Senator called for special attention to "constitutional questions which, because of non-justiciability, or for other reasons, are not in practice susceptible to court determination"; and a Midwestern lawyer to "legislation dealing with non-justiciable questions"; and a Middle Atlantic member to "the execution of constitutional principles when they are little disputed or announced by the courts." A Southern Senator specified the validity of appropriations under the power to tax and spend for the general welfare; two Middle Atlantic Senators, Senate rules of procedure; and a Representative, "political questions." One Border State member, new to Congress however, exempted from congressional concern "purely political questions that do not in fact involve a constitutional question," and another called for special heed to "economic questions."

If two Midwesterners had suggested that Congress need attend to no area, others called for attention to all the areas. Among them were several Border State men, including a Senator who added, "assuming that constitutional questions are questions of fundamental principle," a non-lawyer Representative who stated that "fuller understanding tends to minimize conflict and encroachment," and a new lawyer-Representative who said, "I do not believe that we can pick and choose among parts of the Constitution." One New England Representative said all types of questions merited "careful study and consideration by those sworn to uphold the Constitution," and another, constitutionality of any pending legislation was "always important." Similar observations came from a Southern, a Far Western, a Midwestern, and two Middle Atlantic members.

The weak response to question 6 makes generalization difficult. Perhaps the phrasing of the question deterred some from answering it, especially those who viewed the courts as exclusive constitutional mouthpiece and those who favored congressional concern with all types of questions. Note, however, that those who signified preferences gave approximately equal stress to the three major areas employed in this book. Were it not for comments, the returns might well prompt misgivings about members' awareness of the finality of congressional decisions concerning foreign relations and non-justiciable questions generally.

SOURCES OF ADVICE

Question 7 sought to elicit information on the sources to which members habitually resorted for the necessary constitutional advice. The following presents the question and the options, with the per cent of respondents who marked each given in brackets:

7. *Optional question:* On whom do you ordinarily rely for advice when you encounter questions of constitutionality in committee or on the floor? (Check those you rely on regularly.)
Other members of your house [47 per cent]
Members of your own staff, including legal counsel [33 per cent]
A committee and its legal counsel [52 per cent]
Office of Legislative Counsel (of your house) [34 per cent]
Legislative Reference Service (Library of Congress) [42 per cent]
Department of Justice or other executive agencies [19 per cent]
Legal counsel for a non-governmental organization [8 per cent]
Private law firm [7 per cent]
Other (Please specify) [26 per cent]

Although the results appear at some length in chapter 15, several points may be stressed here.

First, the question elicited 178 replies, or 88 per cent of all respondents, a remarkable proportion considering that it was optional and appeared on the reverse side of the questionnaire. This result and the numerous comments reflect a strong concern with the problem of securing readily accessible and competent advice.

Second, members indicated a great variety of sources for advice. The above figures show this as do members' annotations. Among those named were the American Bar Association, the American Civil Liberties Union, "my own [law] firm," "Friends whom I trust and respect," "Noted lawyers in whom I have confidence," "Harvard and Columbia law professors," "Law school faculty" (these last two from New England), "Individual lawyers," "People in private life whom I trust," "The best opinions available, all sought and considered," and "the person or persons I think best qualified to answer. It may be any one of those you have named."

Third, both legal training and experience wielded influence on members' preferences. All but two of the members who wrote down "myself" or the equivalent as a leading source were lawyers. The 70 non-lawyers checked "other members" at the rate of 61 per cent, as against 37 per cent of the lawyers. Note the way non-lawyers and lawyers rated other sources, respectively: committees and committee counsel—49 per cent and 55 per cent; LRS—46 per cent and 39 per cent; OLC—41 per cent and 28 per cent; own staff—34 per cent and 32 per cent; Justice and other departments—24 per cent and 14 per cent; non-governmental organizations—13 per cent and 6 per cent; private law firm—9 per cent and 5 per cent; "myself"—3 per cent and 34 per cent. Experience seemed to enhance reliance on other members, for new members marked it at the rate of 34 per cent and those with more than ten years in Congress, 56 per cent; the same groups favored committees at the rate of 50 per cent and 64 per cent, respectively, but downgraded the Legislative Counsel from 53 per cent to 33 per cent. Three Representatives, all lawyers with congressional experience, disclosed what they meant by "other members": thus, "some very able constitutional lawyers," "those who show knowledge of the Constitution," and members "learned in the law."

Fourth, members craved sources as accessible as possible. All five listed congressional sources were rated ahead of the Executive and that in turn ahead of private organizations. Note that 72 per cent of Senators consulted members of their own office staffs as against 25 per cent of Representatives, whose budgets were less ample and who accordingly had to depend more heavily on "other members." All categories strongly rated the LRS which, although situated in the Library of Congress, maintains flexible service including quick answers to telephone requests. One Border State Representative, although experienced and legally trained, wanted a one volume book "setting out the Constitution . . . wherein each line or clause is annotated showing at least in brief the reason and history behind it as well as Supreme Court decisions construing or authoritatively referring to it."

Fifth, the members depended most heavily on committees: Senators by 69 per cent, Representatives by 49 per cent. Those units, one may conclude, are expected to possess specialized knowledge not only on policy matters but also on constitutional questions.

GENERAL COMMENTS

About a quarter of those responding added comments either in the space provided or in accompanying letters. Many expressed considered views on the general problem of congressional responsibility, and a few dealt with matters not specifically raised by the seven questions.

379

Recent Supreme Court Decisions. A dozen members, chiefly Southern, reflected a critical attitude toward the Supreme Court for its recent holdings. Some thought the Court had confused the law through its decisions, some that it was indulging in law-making, and some that it was actually amending the Constitution. Thus a Southern lawyer-Representative, "One of the grave dangers facing our Country today is the present 'law making' attitude of our Supreme Court and its utter disregard for 'stare decisis' on matters involving constitutional issues. Proper procedures for amending the Constitution are available and should be strictly followed . . ." Others, however, objected strongly to efforts to discipline the Court by statute.

Need of Clear Definitions. Several mentioned the difficulty of assessing the responsibility of Congress in the absence of a clear definition of "constitutional questions." Would a matter concerning rules of debate, for example, asked one member, be understood as such a question?

Grounds for Congressional Responsibility. Several members who asserted an independent responsibility in Congress set out the supporting grounds for that position. First and foremost of these was the separation of powers. A Far Western Senator thought each branch had important responsibilities, for "the whole system would break down promptly if any of the three branches were to ignore their duties . . ." A New England Representative, objecting to judicial legislation, thought that generally "each branch should perform its own function without intruding on the function of other branches." A Southern Representative offered a five-step analysis of the tripartite theory, blending Jeffersonian with Marshallian concepts. (1) Since all actions by Congress must accord with the Constitution, Congress is responsible for determining whether a specific proposed action is constitutional and "all enactments of the Congress imply—if there is no actual statement to this effect—that in the opinion of the Congress the action is in conformance with the Constitution." (2) Congress, in deciding whether its contemplated action is constitutional, refers to Supreme Court opinions and precedents, but there is no "absolute necessity" for Congress to accept such opinions or precedents as "determining." It may express its own opinions regardless of court precedents and indeed it has done so. The Court, on its part, has actually reversed itself in upholding acts of Congress as in the late 1930's. (3) The executive branch has a similar responsibility to determine the constitutionality of its own actions and in doing so may reach results contrary to judicial precedent. (4) But the Supreme Court is made the final judge of constitutionality. It resolves conflicts in interpretation and on any specific issue the judgment of the Court is "the law— at least until such a time as the Supreme Court changes its mind or modifies its opinion." (5) Both Congress and the Executive have the responsibility for making their own decisions on the constitutionality of their actions. "Otherwise, if both the Legislative and Executive branches had to accept previous decisions or opinions of the Court without question, the Supreme Court would be placed in the position not only of determining the constitutionality of actions or enactments already made, but also of predetermining future actions and enactments. It would thus be in a position of becoming the most powerful and dominant branch of our government because, in effect, it alone could determine the general trend of governmental policy." This distinction between the future and general and the past and specific is suggestive. In how broad a zone does the decision of the specific bind Congress in determining the general?

A second ground was the oath of office. The growing tendency of members to "Waive any doubts" about constitutionality and leave it to the courts was not, said a Southern Representative, in line with the oath, "which places a burden upon the individual to reach a conclusion for himself." A Middle Atlantic Representative said "concern about constitutionality is a prime task of both Houses," since new members swore to uphold only the Constitution. A Southern Representative referred critically to President Franklin D. Roosevelt's advice that Congress pass legislation "irrespective of its constitutionality."

A new Far Western Representative suggested a third ground: the desire of Congress to pass legislation that would pass the test of the Court and hence prove useful rather than unsettling to the country. A Senator suggested a fourth reason, also practical in nature. Neglect of congressional responsibility might result in crowding court dockets and render the present number of district courts insufficient.

Grounds for Exclusive Judicial Cognizance. Those who tended to minimize the responsibility of Congress also advanced supporting grounds. First, the separation of powers and its corollary, checks and balances, were cited by several. Thus a Far Western Representative thought congressional concern with constitutionality should not become a "fetish"; that was one of the "principal purposes" of the Judiciary—to check Congress; "Let them do the job."

A second, and related, ground was the notion of the Constitution as exclusively a body of law appropriate only for court interpretation. A non-lawyer Representative from the Far West observed simply that questions of constitutionality are reserved to the federal courts and that Congress should conform to decisions embodying interpretations of the Constitution. A new Representative from the Far West with legal training invoked the Marbury case in favoring court referral; he did not wish to

381

"disturb the traditional 'separation of powers' approach to such matters."

Third, decisions of Congress are only provisional in any case. Said a Midwestern non-lawyer Senator, Congress did not always accept arguments of unconstitutionality, "since it is established that the final appeal on this question is the Supreme Court."

Fourth, Congress was ill-fitted to determine constitutional questions. One new Representative said Congress lacked expertise and the "time and consideration" which such questions require. Others cited the partisan political atmosphere of Congress. By the same token, the Court appealed to several, because of its nonpolitical, nonpartisan atmosphere and its special procedures.

Procedure in the House. The matter of procedures for constitutional inquiries evoked comments from experienced Representatives, drawn from several regions. The great dependence of members on committees received emphasis here. From these comments, treated at length in chapter 15, emerges the idea that in the House, at least, constitutional issues ordinarily receive consideration, if anywhere, in committee. Yet the dependence on experts and the tendency of members to pass over constitutional objections unless they are clearly established manifest themselves even at the committee stage.

CONCLUSIONS

The findings of the questionnaire tend to corroborate those of the case analyses. They demonstrate that while most members of Congress seem to find constitutional questions a common occurrence, they differ among themselves on important aspects of the problem. The question of scope drew the weakest and most widely varying response. Statistics and annotations both implied that agreement on precise definitions of the term "constitutional questions" is essential.

The outlines of distinct theories of responsibility emerge from the returns. The approximate one-third of respondents who favored court referral of questions tended to associate this view with doubts as to the bona fide character of most constitutional objections and as to the effectiveness of discussion. The large contingent who affirmed independent congressional judgment tended to see objections as genuine or at least mixed in character and to expect discussion to influence action. Only in comments did distinctions between Jeffersonian and Marshallian theories make their appearance. Senators and lawyers reflected a greater confidence in Congress than did Representatives and non-lawyers. Yet many departed from the foregoing patterns, and others qualified their positions in comments.

The five-sixths of respondents who thought the courts should give weight to constitutional judgments of Congress evidently held this view with little relation to their attitudes toward congressional responsibility. The principal factor which correlated with support for judicial deference to Congress was length of congressional service. That Midwesterners predominated among the one-sixth who denied such deference conforms to the foregoing chapters.

The comments brought out two aspects of the problem not treated in questions. Many members asserted that doubtful questions could safely be left to the courts, while others seemed worried by this practice and insisted on a full individual obligation to oppose doubtful measures. Many observed that Congress should specify its intent in passing laws and that courts should respect such intent.

Comments also elucidated ingredients of the rationale for each theory. Both the advocates of court referral and those of congressional inquiry invoked the separation of powers, but they then parted company. Those minimizing congressional responsibility took literally Marshall's conception of the Constitution as law which judges interpret and laid heavy stress on the shortcomings of Congress—its lack of expertise, its monumental work load, its partisan and political spirit, its apparent inability to focus its deliberations on precise constitutional questions. Supporters of Congress cited the oath, questioned the infallibility and objectivity of the judges, and feared that passage of unconstitutional laws would clog the courts and embitter congressional-judicial relations.

On question 7 and in comments, members also reflected practical difficulties in the discharge of responsibility. They, and particularly the non-lawyers, revealed a profound need for competent constitutional advice constantly accessible. While Senators relied heavily on their personal staffs, members in general leaned primarily on committees, on other members, and on the Legislative Reference Service. If the evidence of 1964, as reflected in chapter 14, is a fair guide, then members will increasingly have to turn to nonmembers for guidance—principally expert staff, auxiliary agencies, and committees.

The great prominence given committees and committee counsel suggests their importance in congressional deliberations. Under suitable reforms, committees might serve as forums for considering numerous questions with thoroughness, flexibility, expertise, and freedom from obstructionism.

Appendix B.   List of Washington, D.C., Interviews

Barth, Alan, Editorial Department, *Washington Post,* March 3, 1965.

Boots, Charles F. (and Pinion, Dwight J.), Assistant Counsel, Senate Office of the Legislative Counsel, December 18, 1958.

Brant, Irving, biographer of James Madison, Library of Congress, December 19, 1958.

Clayton, James, Assistant Managing Editor, *Washington Post,* March 3, 1965.

Coffin, Frank M., Representative from Maine, December 17, 1958.

Craft, Edward O., Legislative Counsel, House Office of the Legislative Counsel, March 2, 1965.

Creech, William A., Chief Counsel and Staff Director, Subcommittee on Constitutional Rights, Senate Judiciary Committee, March 1, 1965.

Curtis, Thomas B., Representative from Missouri, March 4, 1965.

Cushman, Dr. Robert E., National Historical Publications Commission, March 3, 1965.

Deschler, Lewis, House Parliamentarian, December 17, 1958.

Dick, Mrs. Bess E., Staff Director, Judiciary Committee, March 3, 1965.

Dolan, Joseph, Administrative Assistant to Senator Robert F. Kennedy of New York, March 1, 1965.

Ervin, Sam J., Jr., Senator from North Carolina, March 4, 1965.

Filvaroff, David, Special Assistant to the Deputy Attorney General, Department of Justice, March 3, 1965.

Fosdic, Dr. Dorothy, Consultant to Senator Henry Jackson of Washington, December 19, 1958.

Galloway, Dr. George B., Senior Specialist, American Government and Public Administration, Legislative Reference Service, Library of Congress, December 16, 1958, March 2, 1965.

Greene, Harold H., Chief, Appeals and Research Section, Civil Rights Division, Department of Justice, March 2, 1965.

Hilsman, Roger, Jr., Deputy Director, Legislative Reference Service, December 19, 1958.

Horwitz, Solis, Administrative Assistant, Democratic Policy Committee, Senate, December 18, 1958.

Hughes, Thomas L., Legislative Assistant to Senator Hubert H. Humphrey of Minnesota, December 18, 1958.

Keating, Kenneth B., Representative from New York, December 19, 1958.

Lindsay, John V., Representative from New York, March 3, 1965.

Perley, Allan H., Legislative Counsel, House Office of the Legislative Counsel, December 17, 1958.

Reuss, Henry S., Representative from Wisconsin, March 3 or 4, 1965.

Riddick, Floyd M., Assistant Senate Parliamentarian, December 15, 1958.

Schlei, Norbert A., Assistant Attorney General, Office of Legal Counsel, Department of Justice, March 2, 1965.

Shuman, Howard E., Administrative Assistant to Senator Paul Douglas of Illinois, December 16, 1958.

Simms, John H., Legislative Counsel, Senate Office of the Legislative Counsel, March 1, 1965.

Slayman, Charles H., Jr., Chief Counsel and Staff Director, Subcommittee on Constitutional Rights, Senate Judiciary Committee, December 16, 1958.

Small, Dr. Norman J., Legislative Attorney, American Law Division, Legislative Reference Service, March 4, 1965.

Stein, Harry N., Chief, American Law Division, Legislative Reference Service, March 4, 1965.

Watkins, Charles L., Senate Parliamentarian, December 15, 1958.

Welsh, William B., Research Director, Democratic National Committee, December 17, 1958.

Notes

CHAPTER 1. INTRODUCTION: CRISIS AND DISCORD

1. Coyle v. Smith, 221 U.S. 559 (1911).
2. Remarks of Senator James O. Eastland (Miss.), Chairman of the Senate Judiciary Committee. 104 *Cong. Rec.*, pt. 10, p. 12468 (1958).
3. *Ibid.*, p. 12457.
4. *Ibid.*, p. 12469.
5. *Alaska Statehood*, Hearings before the Senate Committee on Interior and Insular Affairs on S. 49, 85th Cong., 1st sess. (1957), pp. 104–133. S. Rept. 1163, 85th Cong., 1st sess. (1957), pp. 5–6, 24–25. Senator George W. Malone (Nev.) filed a brief minority report.
6. 104 *Cong. Rec.*, pt. 10, pp. 12471–12472, 12650. Senator Malone voted to sustain the point of order. At the final vote, Senators Malone and Joseph C. O'Mahoney (Wyo.) were absent.
7. Remarks of Senator John Sherman Cooper (Ky.), *ibid.*, p. 12456.
8. *Ibid.*, pp. 12458–12459.
9. *Ibid.*, p. 12468.
10. *Ibid.*
11. *Ibid.*, p. 12471. The vote on the point of order was 28–53. The bill passed the Senate June 30 and was approved by the President July 7, 1958.
12. For a fuller discussion, see below, chapter 13.
13. *Limitation of Appellate Jurisdiction of the United States Supreme Court*, Hearings before Internal Security Subcommittee of the Senate Committee on the Judiciary on S. 2646, 85th Cong., 2nd sess. (1958), p. 39.
14. He added that it was "also the only check that Congress has against the improper invasion of the rights reserved to the states." S. Rept. 1586, 85th Cong., 2nd sess. (1958), p. 4. Senator Butler drafted the committee's majority report favoring the bill.
15. 104 *Cong. Rec.*, pt. 14, p. 18680.
16. A year later the state of Michigan demonstrated what could happen when members of a legislature fail to come to grips with a major constitutional issue, and, swallowing doubts, refer the matter to the courts. In desperation because the two parties were deadlocked while the state was sinking into financial indebtedness, amounting in June to $110,000,000, the legislature adopted a use-tax which members had repeatedly assailed as violating the state constitution. Later, by a 5–3 vote, the State Supreme Court held that the tax was invalid. In a concurring opinion, Judge Eugene Black declared, "A rather manifest question of constitutional law was . . .

387

left for judicial consideration." Lockwood *v.* Nims, 357 Mich. 517, 98 N.W. 2d 753, 762 (1959).

The contending parties in the legislature had never succeeded in putting aside politics and giving serious thought to the constitutional issue. Delays produced by court litigation only served to deepen the crisis in which the state wallowed. (Note that the state House of Representatives was evenly divided, with 55 members from each party; the Senate had 19 Republicans and 12 Democrats, but the Governor, G. Mennen Williams, was a Democrat. For data see *New York Times,* Jan. 1–Oct. 23, 1959, especially July 19, Aug. 30, and Oct. 23.)

17. Remarks of Senator Javits on S. J. Res. 57, introduced Feb. 26, 1959, 105 *Cong. Rec.,* pt. 3, p. 2997 (1959).

18. S. Res. 165, 102 *Cong. Rec.,* pt. 3, p. 3005 (1956).

19. 101 *Cong. Rec.,* pt. 5, p. 6088 (1955).

20. 102 *Cong. Rec.,* pt. 3, p. 3006 (1956).

21. In supporting the Dirksen-Mansfield rider to a foreign aid bill, Senator John Stennis (Miss.) declared, "There is nothing sacred and untouchable about judicial decisions." Congress, he insisted, had the power and the duty "to bring into this forest of confusion, this trouble area, order out of chaos, and . . . to make a bold, clear-cut assertion of the legislative authority . . ." 110 *Cong. Rec.,* Aug. 15, 1964, p. 19127, and Sept. 15, 1964, p. 21428. Senator Frank Church of Idaho, however, while acknowledging widespread opposition to the decisions of the Court, could not forsake his "allegiance to the Constitution" nor his oath to uphold it. *Ibid.,* Sept. 10, 1964, p. 21226. The Constitution gave the Court the task of "identifying constitutional rights," declared Senator Philip A. Hart (Mich.), and "we are not the reviewing authority of the Supreme Court, and we are not supposed to put the Supreme Court out of business." *Ibid.,* Sept. 16, 1964, p. 21581 and Sept. 15, 1964, p. 21428.

22. Letter to Congressman Samuel B. Hill, July 5, 1935, in Franklin D. Roosevelt, *Public Papers and Addresses,* comp. Samuel I. Rosenman, 13 vols., vol. IV (New York: Random House, 1938–1950), pp. 297–298. Also found in 79 *Cong. Rec.,* pt. 12, p. 13449 (1935). See below, chapter 8.

23. Merlo J. Pusey, *Charles Evans Hughes,* 2 vols., vol. I (New York: Macmillan, 1951), p. 204.

24. "Fireside Chat", Mar. 9, 1937, *Public Papers,* vol. VI (New York: Macmillan, 1941), pp. 122–133. Note that the Senate Judiciary Committee, in adversely reporting out the bill, stated that the President was undermining the constitutional role of the Court by making the Constitution what "the executive or legislative branches of the government choose to say it is . . ." S. Rept. 711, 75th Cong., 1st sess. (1937), p. 23.

25. Remarks of Representative John A. Martin (Colo.), 77 *Cong. Rec.,* pt. 1, p. 2750 (May 2, 1933).

26. *Public Papers,* vol. II (Random House), p. 15.

27. The questionnaire was sent on Jan. 15, 1959, to the members of the Eighty-Sixth Congress, and most replies were received by early February. An accompanying letter described the purpose of the questionnaire and sought to enlist the interest of the members. Anonymity was offered those who preferred it, but all were asked to indicate their house, region, and length of service and to state whether or not they were lawyers. Simple

responses were requested to seven questions and space was provided for comments. For a fuller discussion of the questionnaire and the returns, see Appendix A.

28. The questionnaire also showed that Representatives favored court referral in numbers greater than Senators and non-lawyers, than lawyers. One question probed conceptions of the weight that the courts should accord to constitutional determinations by Congress. A small proportion of members favored no weight with Midwesterners leading the regions in advocating this position.

29. Separate opinion in Ogden v. Saunders, 12 Wheat. 213, 270 (1827).

30. President Franklin D. Roosevelt, himself, in an editorial note to the 1935 letter quoted above, deduced a legislative presumption of validity from the judicial presumption of validity. *Public Papers*, vol. IV, p. 298.

31. *E.g.*, see concurring opinion of Justice Frankfurter in Dennis v. United States, 341 U.S. 494, 525 (1951) and dissenting opinion of Justice Black, *ibid.*, 580–581. Compare Chief Justice Warren's assertion of reviewing power in Watkins v. United States, 354 U.S. 178, 181 (1957), with Justice Harlan's defense of congressional responsibility in Barenblatt v. United States, 360 U.S. 109, 111 (1959).

32. Cooper v. Aaron, 358 U.S. 1, 18.

33. *Ibid.*, 24.

34. See: Patricia C. Acheson, *The Supreme Court* (New York: Dodd, Mead, 1961); Alexander M. Bickel, *The Least Dangerous Branch: The Supreme Court at the Bar of Politics* (Indianapolis: Bobbs-Merrill, 1962); Charles L. Black, Jr., *The People and the Court: Judicial Review and Democracy* (New York: Macmillan, 1960); Edmond Cahn, *Supreme Court and Supreme Law* (Bloomington, Ind.: Indiana University Press, 1954); Charles P. Curtis, *Law as Large as Life: A Natural Law for Today and the Supreme Court as Its Prophet* (New York: Simon and Schuster, 1959); John P. Frank, *Marble Palace: The Supreme Court in American Life* (New York: Knopf, 1958); Paul A. Freund, *The Supreme Court of the United States: Its Business, Purposes and Performance* (Cleveland: World Publishing, 1961); Charles S. Hyneman, *The Supreme Court on Trial* (New York: Atherton Press, 1963); Robert G. McCloskey, *The American Supreme Court* (Chicago: University of Chicago Press, 1960); Alpheus T. Mason, *The Supreme Court: Palladium of Freedom* (Ann Arbor: University of Michigan Press, 1962); Alpheus T. Mason and William M. Beaney, *The Supreme Court in a Free Society* (Englewood Cliffs, N.J.: Prentice-Hall, 1959); Wallace Mendelson, *Justices Black and Frankfurter: Conflict in the Court* (Chicago: University of Chicago Press, 1961); Leo Pfeffer, *This Honorable Court: A History of the United States Supreme Court* (Boston: Beacon Press, 1965); Fred Rodell, *Nine Men: A Political History of the Supreme Court from 1790 to 1955* (New York: Random House, 1955); Eugene Victor Rostow, *The Sovereign Prerogative: The Supreme Court and the Quest for Law* (New Haven: Yale, 1962); Glendon Austin Schubert, *Constitutional Politics: The Political Behavior of Supreme Court Justices and the Constitutional Policies that They Make* (New York: Holt, Rinehart and Winston, 1960); Bernard Schwartz, *The Supreme Court: Constitutional Revolution in Retrospect* (New York: Ronald Press, 1957); Martin Shapiro, *Law and Politics in the Supreme Court: New Approaches to Political Juris-*

prudence (New York: Free Press of Glencoe, 1964); Carl Brent Swisher, *The Supreme Court in Modern Role* (New York: New York University Press, 1958).

35. Thus, the Court's action in invalidating many New Deal laws prompted such critical commentaries as: Robert K. Carr, *Democracy and the Supreme Court* (Norman, Okla.: University of Oklahoma Press, 1936); Edward S. Corwin, *Twilight of the Supreme Court: A History of Our Constitutional Theory* (New Haven: Yale, 1934) and *Court over Constitution: A Study of Judicial Review as an Instrument of Popular Government* (Princeton: Princeton University Press, 1938); Irving Brant, *Storm over the Constitution* (Indianapolis: Bobbs-Merrill, 1936); John M. Henry, *Nine Above the Law: Our Supreme Court* (Pittsburgh: R. T. Lewis Co., 1936); Robert H. Jackson, *The Struggle for Judicial Supremacy: A Study of a Crisis in American Power Politics* (New York: Knopf, 1941); Drew Pearson and Robert S. Allen, *The Nine Old Men* (New York: Doubleday, Doran, 1937). A conservative defense of the Court was David Lawrence, *Nine Honest Men* (New York: Appleton-Century, 1936).

36. See Rosalie Gordon, *Nine Men against America: The Supreme Court and Its Attack on American Liberties* (New York: Devin-Adair, 1958, pamphlet); and A. M. Scott, *The Supreme Court vs. the Constitution: An Essay on How Judges Become Dictators* (New York: Exposition Press, 1963, paperback).

37. See Mason and Beaney, *Supreme Court in a Free Society*, p. 1.

38. Arthur F. Bentley, *The Process of Government: A Study of Social Pressures* (Chicago: University of Chicago Press, 1908).

39. *Ibid.,* pp. 220, 422.

40. Bentley defined "group" in a way which tended to identify interest with group and group with organized group or "mass activity." *Ibid.,* p. 211. "Pressure," says Bentley, "is broad enough to include all forms of the group influence upon group, from battle and riot to abstract reasoning and sensitive morality." *Ibid.,* p. 259. Elsewhere he says, "the power of the underlying interests . . . pump all the logic into theory that theory ever obtains." *Ibid.,* p. 390.

41. One analyst of congressional processes objects to the traditional notion of a legislature as a group of men who "deliberate upon and adopt laws." Instead he employs the parlance of military conflict. Strategy and tactics play a crucial part and "the rules and procedures are the codes of battle." "A statute is merely one of the things that can happen as a result of the struggle . . ." Bertram M. Gross, *The Legislative Struggle: A Study in Social Combat* (New York: McGraw-Hill, 1953), p. 4.

42. See: Robert Bendiner, *Obstacle Course on Capitol Hill* (New York: McGraw-Hill, 1964); Daniel M. Berman, *In Congress Assembled: The Legislative Process in the National Government* (New York: Macmillan, 1964); Richard Bolling, *House Out of Order* (New York: Dutton, 1965); James Burnham, *Congress and the American Tradition* (Chicago: H. Regnery, 1959); Charles L. Clapp, *The Congressman* (Washington: Brookings, 1963); Joseph S. Clark, *Congress: The Sapless Branch* (New York: Harper & Row, 1964) and *The Senate Establishment* (New York: Hill and Wang, 1963); George B. Galloway, *History of the House of Representatives* (New York: Crowell, 1961); Kenneth B. Keating, *Government of the People* (Cleveland: World Publishing, 1965); Neil MacNeil, *Forge of Democracy:*

The House of Representatives (New York: David McKay, 1963); Donald R. Matthews, *U.S. Senators and Their World* (Chapel Hill: University of North Carolina Press, 1960); Clem Miller, *Member of the House,* ed. John W. Baker (New York: Scribner, 1962); Robert L. Peabody and Nelson W. Polsby, *New Perspectives on the House of Representatives* (Chicago: Rand McNally, 1963); Norman C. Thomas and Karl A. Lamb, *Congress: Politics & Practice* (New York: Random House, 1964); David B. Truman, *The Congress and America's Future* (Englewood Cliffs, N.J.: Prentice-Hall, 1965) and *The Congressional Party* (New York: Wiley, 1959); William S. White, *Home Place: The Story of the U.S. House of Representatives* (Boston: Houghton Mifflin, 1965); Roland A. Young, *The American Congress* (New York: Harper, 1958). Omitted here are books on special aspects of congressional work or machinery.

43. S. Con. Res. 2, 111 *Cong. Rec.,* Mar. 9, 1965, p. 4429 and Mar. 11, 1965, p. 4649.

44. This seems to be the implication in passages from Professor Charles L. Black, Jr. See his *The People and the Court* (New York: Macmillan, 1960), pp. 47–55.

45. Thus in 1958 he called for "a declaratory act of Congress assertive of the correct reading of the Constitution" on points presented by two internal security cases. See his letter to the editor, *New York Times,* Mar. 16, 1958, pt. IV, p. 10E.

46. Learned Hand, *The Bill of Rights* (Cambridge, Mass.: Harvard, 1958), p. 29.

47. *Ibid.,* p. 38, cf. p. 73ff.

48. Herbert Wechsler, "Toward Neutral Principles of Constitutional Law," 73 *Harvard Law Review* (1959), pp. 1, 3–9, reprinted in Wechsler, *Principles, Politics, and Fundamental Law* (Cambridge, Mass.: Harvard, 1961).

49. *Ibid.,* p. 17, citing Passenger Cases, 8 How. 283, 470 (1849).

50. Henry M. Hart, Jr., "The Time Chart of the Justices," 73 *Harvard Law Review* (1959), pp. 84, 124.

51. *Ibid.,* pp. 99–101.

CHAPTER 2. CONSTITUTIONAL SETTLEMENTS

1. *Military Situation in the Far East,* Hearings before the Committee on Armed Services and the Committee on Foreign Relations, United States Senate, 82nd Cong., 1st sess. (1951), in 5 parts, pt. 5, p. 3179 (App. D); hereafter cited as Hearings.

2. William S. White, *Citadel: The Story of the U.S. Senate* (New York: Harper, 1956), pp. 241–242; for a general account, see John W. Spanier, *The Truman-MacArthur Controversy and the Korean War* (Cambridge, Mass.: Harvard, 1959).

3. *New York Times,* May 20, 1951, pt. IV, p. 1.

4. The members were: (from the Armed Services Committee) Senators Russell (Ga.), chairman, Harry F. Byrd (Va.), Lyndon B. Johnson (Tex.), Estes Kefauver (Tenn.), Lester C. Hunt (Wyo.), John C. Stennis (Miss.), Russell B. Long (La.), Democrats; and Styles Bridges (N.H.), Leverett Saltonstall (Mass.), Wayne Morse (Ore.), William F. Knowland (Calif.), Harry P. Cain (Wash.), and Ralph E. Flanders (Vt.), Republicans; (from the Foreign Relations Committee) Senators Tom Connally (Tex.), chair-

man, Walter F. George (Ga.), Theodore Francis Green (R.I.), Brien McMahon (Conn.), J. W. Fulbright (Ark.), John J. Sparkman (Ala.), and Guy M. Gillette (Iowa), Democrats; and Alexander Wiley (Wis.), H. Alexander Smith (N.J.), Bourke B. Hickenlooper (Iowa), Henry Cabot Lodge, Jr. (Mass.), Charles W. Tobey (N.H.), and Owen Brewster (Me.), Republicans.

5. Hearings, pt. 1, p. 2.

6. *Ibid.*, pt. 2, p. 763.

7. *Ibid.*, p. 765.

8. *New York Times,* May 16, 1951, p. 25. The seven Republicans were: Senators Bridges, Smith, Hickenlooper, Knowland, Cain, Brewster, and Flanders. Senator Homer Ferguson, Republican of Michigan, also attended the meeting, and he became director of the legal inquiry. *Ibid.*

9. *Hearings,* pt. 2, pp. 912–913; *New York Times,* May 19, 1951, p. 2. The term "whitewash" had gained currency the previous year. As early as February 1950, Senator Joseph R. McCarthy, Wisconsin Republican, warned that a proposed Senate inquiry into his charges of disloyalty in the State Department might develop into a "whitewash." A subcommittee headed by Senator Millard E. Tydings, Maryland Democrat, and including Senators Green and McMahon, Democrats, and Hickenlooper and Lodge, Republicans, conducted the inquiry. In spite of this inquiry and President Truman's disclosure of certain confidential government files to its members, the charge was reiterated by Republicans and became an important feature of the 1950 congressional elections. Senator Tydings was defeated in this election.

10. Arthur Krock, *New York Times,* May 18, 1951, p. 26.

11. Hearings, pt. 2, p. 785.

12. *Ibid.*, pp. 803–804. See his remarks in 97 *Cong. Rec.,* pt. 5, p. 5777 (1951).

13. They were Senators Russell, Connally, Fulbright, George, Green, Kefauver, Long, McMahon, Sparkman, and Stennis.

14. They were Senators Bridges, Cain, Knowland, and Wiley; Senator Cain, although not clearly declaring himself on the ruling, appeared generally to endorse Senator Bridges' position, *ibid.*, p. 803. They now favored discussing the appeal the next day, when General Bradley would be absent for other commitments. Some may have preferred to shelve the issue until the appearance of Secretary Acheson, their principal target.

15. Senator Saltonstall to the last wished to avoid the issue by a withdrawal of the original question to General Bradley. *Ibid.*, p. 822. Senator Lodge strongly opposed a prompt settlement because it introduced a legalistic element into the proceedings; he wished, however, to retain the possibility of citations at the close of the hearings. *Ibid.*, pp. 804–805, 825. Senator Brewster admitted that he was uncertain about the proper decision. *Ibid.*, p. 823. The eight were Senators Byrd, Gillette, Hunt, and Johnson (Democrats) and Senators Flanders, Hickenlooper, Smith, and Tobey (Republicans). Senator Hickenlooper, although pressing for clarification of the attitude of the President and of the effect of the chair's ruling on a compliant witness, left his own position unclear. Hearings, pt. 1, p. 719; pt. 2, p. 799.

16. *Ibid.*, pt. 2, p. 764, 766.

17. *Ibid.*, pp. 798, 800, 801.

18. *Ibid.*, p. 768.

19. See the publications of the Hennings Subcommittee, especially *Free-*

dom of Information and Secrecy in Government, Hearings before the Subcommittee on Constitutional Rights of the Senate Judiciary Committee on S. 921, 85th Cong., 2nd sess. (1958–1959), pt. 1, p. 29. For several thorough studies of the general problem, *ibid.,* appendix, and *Power of the President to Withhold Information from the Congress, Memorandums of the Attorney General,* compiled by the Subcommittee on Constitutional Rights of the Senate Judiciary Committee, 85th Cong., 2nd sess. (1958), pt. 2 (committee print); Edward S. Corwin, *The President: Office and Powers, 1787– 1957,* 4th rev. ed. (New York: New York University Press, 1957), p. 113.

20. Said he: "Could we not make a unanimous-consent agreement that when the committee meets tomorrow morning at 10 o'clock, . . . that the time be equally divided between the time when we meet and when we recess at 1 o'clock, time be equally divided one-half to be under the control of the chairman of the committee, one-half to be under the control of the Senator from Wisconsin, to allocate for the proper presentation of the views of the two contending points of view. That gives this committee, as we do in the Senate, the right to pass on it . . . It does give us a reasonable limitation of time where we can all see this thing being brought to a head and where we can proceed with our business." Hearings, pt. 2, pp. 828–829.

21. Through the press, the President had twice indicated his belief that the sought-for testimony was privileged. Senator Wiley, however, contended that even were the President to deny the committee access to the coveted information, Congress would still have a legal right to it. *Ibid.,* p. 846.

22. *Ibid.,* pp. 766, 794.

23. *Ibid.,* p. 852.

24. *Ibid.,* p. 862.

25. *Ibid.,* p. 805. Senator George had previously ascribed the privilege to the witness himself, irrespective of a presidential declaration. *Ibid.,* p. 787.

26. *Ibid.,* p. 827.

27. Before release each day, the transcript of the hearings was censored for matters affecting military security by military experts under the supervision of Vice Admiral Arthur C. Davis. The record as thus censored received wide publication.

28. Hearings, pt. 2, p. 860.

29. *Ibid.,* p. 839.

30. *Ibid.,* pt. 4, p. 3124.

31. *Ibid.,* pt. 2, p. 872.

32. *Ibid.,* pp. 840, 845.

33. *Ibid.,* p. 842.

34. His 30 years as a trial lawyer, he told the committee, had exposed him to "some of the tactics, the psychological tactics that go on, and go on in Government, too." *Ibid.,* p. 915. The Senator's argument the third day lacked something in accuracy. In citing Marbury v. Madison (1 Cranch 137, 1803), as authority for holding the President subject to subpoena, he asserted that Jefferson had complied with that decision. *Ibid.,* p. 842. He may have had in mind the Burr case, although in neither did Jefferson obey a subpoena. (United States v. Burr, 25 Fed. Cas. 1 [nos. 14629a, 14693], 1806, 1807). Despite innumerable congressional precedents, a House committee staff study in 1956 asserted that in the absence of judicial precedents executive refusals of information requested by Congress were not "constitutional law," but rested on a "naked claim of privilege." "The Right of the Congress to

Obtain Information from the Executive and from other Agencies of the Federal Government," a Government Operations Committee staff study, in *Availability of Information from Federal Departments and Agencies,* Hearings of a Subcommittee of House Government Operations Committee (committee print), 84th Cong., 2nd sess. (1956), p. 3027.

35. From the famous secret speech to the Twentieth Congress of the Communist Party, text released by the State Department, *New York Times,* June 5, 1956, p. 14.

36. Herbert J. Spiro, *Government by Constitution: The Political Systems of Democracy* (New York: Random House, 1959), p. 212. I have gained many valuable insights from this book.

37. Federalist No. 51, Hamilton, Madison, and Jay, *The Federalist,* ed. Jacob E. Cooke (Cleveland: World, 1961), p. 349.

38. Carl J. Friedrich, *The Philosophy of Law in Historical Perspective* (Chicago: University of Chicago Press, 1958), p. 220. See also his *Constitutional Government and Democracy: Theory and Practice in Europe and America,* rev. ed. (Boston: Ginn, 1950), p. 131. I have relied heavily on both these works.

39. Hearings, pt. 5, p. 3602. This report was signed by the same eight Republican members who attended strategy meetings during the Bradley episode.

40. *Ibid.,* pt. 2, p. 855.

41. Sir Raymond Evershed, "Government under Law in Post-war England," in Arthur E. Sutherland, ed., *Government under Law* (Cambridge, Mass.: Harvard, 1956), pp. 149–168, 161. I am indebted to Professor V. H. Galbraith for several suggestions concerning my handling of British constitutional practice.

42. Reports, XII, 64–65, quoted in Friedrich, *Philosophy of Law,* p. 79.

43. Ralph V. Harlow, *The History of Legislative Methods in the Period before 1825* (New Haven: Yale, 1917), pp. 92–103.

44. W. Ivor Jennings, *Parliament,* 2nd ed. (Cambridge, Eng.: Cambridge University Press, 1957), pp. 270–272. According to Jennings, the British have made increasing use of large standing committees, but this trend has met steady resistance. The Labour Government sent its nationalization bills to standing committees, but the Conservatives on regaining power recurred to having all major bills, those of constitutional as well as social importance, sent first to the Committee of the Whole House. The Speaker in 1945 opposed specialized committees: "We want," he declared, "to consult experts and then bring our common sense to bear . . ." *Ibid.,* p. 272.

45. 105 *Cong. Rec.,* pt. 3, p. 2997 (1959).

46. Senator Byrd opposed the Truman policy, *New York Times,* April 12, 1951, p. 19. The *Times* report showed that Senator Smith supported MacArthur's policies. *Ibid.,* April 29, 1951, p. 37. Senators Smith and Flanders were among the eight Republicans who signed the minority statement criticizing the President. See above, note 39.

47. The Democrats who opposed the ruling were Senators Fulbright and Gillette. The Republicans who supported it were Senators Smith, Lodge, Tobey, Saltonstall, Morse, and Flanders.

48. Even though the regions are shown in the map, their states are listed here for added convenience.

New England: Connecticut, Maine, Massachusetts, New Hampshire, Rhode Island, and Vermont.

Middle Atlantic: Delaware, Maryland, New Jersey, New York, and Pennsylvania.

South: Alabama, Arkansas, Florida, Georgia, Louisiana, Mississippi, North Carolina, South Carolina, Tennessee, Texas, and Virginia.

Border: Kentucky, Missouri, Oklahoma, West Virginia.

Midwest: Illinois, Indiana, Iowa, Kansas, Michigan, Minnesota, Nebraska, North Dakota, Ohio, South Dakota, and Wisconsin.

Far West: Alaska, Arizona, California, Colorado, Hawaii, Idaho, Montana, Nevada, New Mexico, Oregon, Utah, Washington, and Wyoming.

Unless otherwise noted, Maryland and Delaware will be treated as Middle Atlantic states.

49. The following are among the tests applied in subsequent case analyses in judging effectiveness of consideration:

a. Are the arguments pertinent to the question?

b. Does the argument follow a logical or sequential order?

c. Are there clear, pertinent rebuttals?

d. Is the argument free from political charge and counter-charge?

e. Does discussion at later stages evince reliance on earlier discussion?

f. Is there evidence of a change of votes following discussion?

g. Do positions of uncommitted members become crystallized following discussion?

h. Does voting appear to depart from commitments to the policy question or from normal party or regional commitments?

50. Hearings, pt. 3, p. 2064.

51. Comment of Senator Clair Engel, California Democrat, in *Civil Rights—Public Accommodations,* Hearings before the Committee on Commerce, United States Senate, 88th Cong., 1st sess. (1963), pt. 1, p. 248.

52. Part I, Art. 30.

53. *London Times,* June 1, 1953, Supplement no. 52,636.

54. Max Farrand, *Records of the Federal Convention of 1787,* 4 vols. (New Haven: Yale, 1911–1937), II, 87, July 23, 1787.

55. Oliver Wolcott said in the Connecticut ratifying convention, that the oath requirement was "a direct appeal to that God who is the avenger of perjury." Jonathan Elliot, ed., *Debates in the Several State Conventions on the Adoption of the Federal Constitution* . . . , 2nd ed., 5 vols. (Philadelphia, 1876), II, 202. Justice William Johnson later observed that the Founding Fathers had prescribed oaths in order to bind the conscience because they believed in a "Searcher of Hearts." Letter to Thomas Cooper, March 26, 1823, quoted in Donald G. Morgan, *Justice William Johnson* (Charleston, S.C.: University of South Carolina Press, 1954), p. 145.

56. Charles A. Beard, *An Economic Interpretation of the Constitution* (New York: Macmillan, 1918).

57. Washington to David Stuart, Philadelphia, July 1, 1787, in Farrand, *Records,* III, 51.

58. Federalist No. 1, *The Federalist,* ed. Cooke, p. 3.

59. Jefferson to Adamantios Coray, Oct. 31, 1823, in *Writings,* ed. Andrew Lipscomb and Albert Bergh, 20 vols. (Washington, D.C., 1903), XV, 480.

60. Farrand, *Records,* II, 11, July 14.

61. Compiled from Max Farrand, *The Framing of the Constitution of the United States* (New Haven: Yale, 1913), chapter 2; and Winton U. Solberg, ed., *The Federal Convention and the Formation of the Union of the American States* (New York: Liberal Arts Press, 1958), appendix I, pp. 387–406.

62. Sept. 14, 1786, in Henry Steele Commager, *Documents of American History,* 6th ed. (New York: Appleton-Century-Crofts, 1958), p. 133. Madison later explained that his purpose in keeping a record of the proceedings was to inform posterity on the origins of the Union—he, himself, having met frustration in his researches into the "process" as well as "the principles—the reasons, & the anticipations" which had prevailed in the formation of earlier confederations. Farrand, *Records,* III, 550.

63. Farrand, *Records,* I, 132, June 6; 101, June 4 and 339, June 20; 291, June 18; and 321, June 19.

64. Jefferson to Wythe, Jan. 22, 1797, in *Writings,* ed. Paul L. Ford, 10 vols. (New York, 1892–1899), VII, 110.

65. Farrand, *Records,* III, 112.

66. Farrand, *Records,* I, 16, May 29. Later, the delegates, under the pressure of time, voted against resuming the Committee of the Whole, over the opposition of Delaware, Maryland, and Virginia. *Ibid.,* II, 196, Aug. 7.

67. *Ibid.,* 115, July 25.

68. Thus, the committee which engineered the Great Compromise between the large and small states consisted of 11 members, one from each participating state. The Committee on Detail consisted of Rutledge (S.C.), Randolph (Va.), Gorham (Mass.), Ellsworth (Conn.), and Wilson (Pa.). The Committee on Style consisted of Dr. Johnson (Conn.), Hamilton (N.Y.), Morris (Pa.), Madison (Va.), and King (Mass.). This last committee contained only convinced supporters of the Constitution, a condition made acceptable by the nature of their task.

69. Farrand, *Records,* III, 109, May 28.

70. Madison recorded the explanation of Rufus King of Massachusetts and that of George Mason as follows: "As the acts of the Convention were not to bind the Constituents it was unnecessary to exhibit this evidence of the votes; and improper as changes of opinion would be frequent in the course of the business and would fill the minutes with contradictions. Col. Mason seconded the objection; adding that such a record of the opinions of members would be an obstacle to a change of them on conviction; and in case of its being hereafter promulged [sic] must furnish handles to the adversaries of the Result of the Meeting." Farrand, *Records,* I, 10, May 28.

71. For this rule as recommended by the Committee on Rules at the suggestion of Butler of South Carolina see *ibid.,* 15–16, May 29.

72. *Ibid.,* II, 89, July 23.

73. Both the Virginia and New Jersey Plans called for federal action on the states as under the Articles of Confederation, but after six weeks of discussion, Madison could call that proposal an "exploded" idea. *Ibid.,* 9, July 14.

74. Gouverneur Morris, "An Oration upon the Death of General Washington," New York, Dec. 31, 1799, *ibid.,* III, 381–382. Charles Pinckney made a similar appeal. *Ibid.,* 108, May 28.

75. *Ibid.,* I, 214–215, June 12.

CHAPTER 3. TRIAL AND ERROR, 1789–1801

1. Chisholm v. Georgia, 2 Dallas 419 (1793).

2. Speech delivered April 30, 1789, 1 Richardson, *Messages and Papers,* pp. 52–53.

3. Edward S. Corwin, *Court over Constitution: A Study of Judicial Review as an Instrument for Popular Government* (Princeton: Princeton University Press, 1938), chapters 1–2.

4. *Ibid.;* William Winslow Crosskey, *Politics and the Constitution in the History of the United States,* 2 vols. (Chicago: University of Chicago Press, 1953), II, 1002–1007.

5. Act of June 1, 1789, 1 *Stat.* 23.

6. Act of Aug. 6, 1861, 12 *Stat.* 326 c. 64. The oath continues: "and that I will bear true faith, allegiance, and loyalty to the same, any ordinance, resolution, or law of any State Convention or Legislature to the contrary notwithstanding; and, further, that I do this with a full determination, pledge, and purpose, without any mental reservation or evasion whatsoever; and, further, that I will well and faithfully perform all the duties which may be required of me by law. So help me God."

7. Act of May 13, 1884, 23 *Stat.* 22. 5 U.S.C. 16. The prolixity of this oath has caused difficulties. My tape recordings of recent inaugural ceremonies reveal that two Vice Presidents, Richard Nixon (1956) and Lyndon Johnson (1960) through confusion and omissions failed to take the oath in its complete statutory form.

8. The Civil War left untouched the oath for state officeholders. Congress, by oversight, or more likely because disloyalty in state governments was not a practical issue, simply let the 1789 oath stand. 4 U.S.C. 101.

9. Federalist No. 10, *The Federalist,* ed. Jacob E. Cooke (Cleveland: World, 1961), p. 62.

10. *Ibid.,* p. 64.

11. *Ibid.,* p. 65.

12. *Ibid.,* p. 528.

13. Article II, sec. 2, reads in part, "He [the President] . . . shall nominate, and by and with the advice and consent of the Senate, shall appoint ambassadors, other public ministers and consuls, judges of the Supreme Court, and all other officers of the United States, whose appointments are not herein otherwise provided for, and which shall be established by law: but the Congress may by law vest the appointment of such inferior officers, as they think proper, in the President alone, in the courts of law, or in the heads of departments."

14. See Myers v. United States, 272 U.S. 52 (1926).

15. Remarks of James Jackson, 1 *Annals of Congress,* pp. 529–530 (1789). He saw a design to create a precedent as to foreign affairs that could be applied to the more controversial matter of the Treasury.

16. Remarks of Alexander White, *ibid.,* p. 518.

17. William Maclay, *Journal,* ed. Edgar S. Maclay (New York: D. Appleton, 1890), p. 114.

18. *Ibid.,* p. 115.

19. See Chief Justice William Howard Taft's opinion in the Myers decision cited above, note 14. For a full discussion of the debate on the substantive issues, see James Hart, *The American Presidency in Action 1789* (New York:

Macmillan, 1948), pp. 155–197, esp. 155–156. See also Leonard D. White, *The Federalists: A Study in Administrative History* (New York: Macmillan, 1948), pp. 20–25; and Edward S. Corwin, *The President: Office and Powers, 1787–1957,* 4th ed. (New York: New York University Press, 1957), pp. 86–88.

20. Sixty-seven per cent of New England Senators were lawyers, 63 per cent of others were lawyers; 56 per cent of New England Representatives were lawyers, 42 per cent of others were lawyers. Of the 12 Southerners who spoke in the debates, 6 were evidently non-lawyers; of these 4 received part of their education abroad. Three of the 6 were planters, Carroll, Sumter, and Page; 2 were doctors, Bland and Tucker, and 1 was a professional officeholder and Revolutionary leader—Jackson. Note that Maryland will be considered as a Southern state throughout this chapter. Figures compiled principally from the *Biographical Directory of the American Congress 1774–1949,* 81st Cong., 2nd sess., H. Doc. 607 (1950). I have relied heavily on this and on the 1961 edition.

21. Eight of the 59 Representatives, and 10 of the 22 Senators had been delegates to the Philadelphia Convention. Of the 27 who spoke in the House debate, 18 were lawyers, 17 had served in state legislatures, 5 in state courts, 15 in the Continental Congress, 5 in state constitutional conventions, 6 in the Philadelphia Convention, and 8 in state conventions to ratify the Constitution; 4 had held state or federal executive posts and 3 had signed the Declaration of Independence.

22. 1 *Annals of Congress,* p. 486.

23. White says Washington kept on close personal terms with Madison, but never made him, as he later made Hamilton, the spokesman of the Administration. *The Federalists.* 58–59.

24. Speaking for the bill were Madison, Abraham Baldwin (Ga.), John Vining (Dela.), Elias Boudinot (N.J.), and Egbert Benson (N.Y.); against it were James Jackson (Ga.), William L. Smith (S.C.), and Elbridge Gerry (Mass.).

25. 1 *Annals of Congress,* p. 383.

26. *Ibid.,* p. 524. Madison urged the need of "cautious deliberation."

27. *Ibid.,* p. 537.

28. When the House voted 30–18 to amend the bill so as to confirm presidential removal power, only two states out of those having more than one delegate, Maryland and Pennsylvania, cast unanimous votes. *Ibid.,* p. 580. On one crucial vote, when the House passed the bill by 29–22, only three states, Georgia, New Jersey, and Pennsylvania, cast unanimous votes. *Ibid.,* p. 590. Oddly the Middle States endorsed the bill by 14–2, while the South opposed it by 10–11, and New England by 5–9. *Ibid.,* p. 590.

29. On May 19, Boudinot, in Committee of the Whole, brought up the question of establishing executive departments. Madison moved a resolution for the establishment of a Department of Foreign Affairs which included an assertion of presidential removal. The House debated this and related principles that day and the 20th, whereupon the committee rose and reported the resolution. On the 21st, the House concurred in the resolution and appointed a select committee of 11 to bring in a bill. One June 2, Baldwin, for the committee, reported a bill which thereupon received its first reading. On the 16th, the House returned to Committee of the Whole for debate on the bill and amendments, debate which continued through the 19th. On the

22nd, the House took up the bill as reported from the committee, debated, and amended it. On third reading the bill was passed June 24. It got its first reading in the Senate June 25 and was debated there from July 14 to 18. On the 18th the bill at third reading was amended and passed. It was returned to the House on the 20th and passed with the Senate amendments. The President signed on July 27.

30. Note that supporters of the bill moved on June 22 to alter the bill so as to give it the appearance of confirming rather than conferring presidential power, and the motion was carried by 30–18. 1 *Annals of Congress*, p. 580.

31. 1 *Annals of Congress*, p. 101. The pertinent rule provided that customary limits on the time members could speak would not apply here. Boudinot headed a committee of 11 which spent five days drafting the House rules; a corresponding Senate committee, under Ellsworth, spent nine days in framing rules. In both houses the subject occupied much time.

32. 1 *Annals of Congress*, p. 374.

33. *Ibid.*, p. 370.

34. *Ibid.*

35. Maryland was the only state not represented and two members came from New Jersey. Seven of the 11 later supported presidential removal: Jeremiah Wadsworth (Conn.), Vining (Dela.), Baldwin (Ga.), Benson (N.Y.), Thomas Fitzsimons (Pa.), Aedanus Burke (S.C.), and Madison (Va.). Three opposed removal: Gerry (Mass.), Samuel Livermore (N.H.), and Lambert Cadwalader (N.J.). Boudinot (N.J.) did not vote on the constitutional point, but voted for the final bill.

36. 1 *Annals of Congress*, p. 578.

37. *Ibid.*, pp. 470, 509.

38. *Ibid.*, p. 472.

39. *Ibid.*, p. 473.

40. *Ibid.*, p. 505.

41. *Ibid.*, pp. 534–537; cf. *ibid.*, p. 580.

42. The following appear to have indicated their acceptance of judicial review: Fisher Ames and Theodore Sedgwick of Massachusetts (*ibid.*, pp. 477, 523), Peter Silvester and John Laurance of New York (*ibid.*, pp. 562, 486), Madison and Alexander White of Virginia (*ibid.*, pp. 501, 518), Abraham Baldwin of Georgia (*ibid.*, p. 560), and, by implication, John Page of Virginia (*ibid.*, p. 550).

43. See remarks of Boudinot (*ibid.*, p. 470), Madison (*ibid.*, p. 501), Sedgwick (*ibid.*, p. 523), and Baldwin (*ibid.*, p. 560).

44. *Ibid.*, p. 560.

45. Among them were Ames and Sedgwick of Massachusetts (*ibid.*, pp. 477, 523), Sherman of Connecticut (*ibid.*, p. 576), Benson, Silvester, and Laurance of New York (*ibid.*, pp. 505, 561, and 486), Boudinot of New Jersey (*ibid.*, p. 468), Hartley of Pennsylvania (*ibid.*, p. 480), Vining of Delaware (*ibid.*, p. 464), Stone of Maryland (*ibid.*, p. 492), Madison and Lee of Virginia (*ibid.*, pp. 461 and 524), and Baldwin of Georgia (*ibid.*, p. 560), and, by implication, Jackson of Georgia (*ibid.*, p. 530).

46. Of the Philadelphia delegates, Baldwin, Madison, and Sherman supported House action; Daniel Carroll of Maryland and George Clymer of Pennsylvania were silent on the point; Gerry, as shown, was ambiguous. State convention delegates included Benson, Ames, Madison, Sedgwick, Stone, and Hartley who avowed support for congressional determination and

Thomas Scott of Pennsylvania and Sumter who took no position. Three lawyers, Theodorick Bland of Virginia, Benjamin Huntington of Connecticut, and Samuel Livermore of New Hampshire took no position on congressional responsibility.

47. *Ibid.*, p. 459. Among those professing genuine doubt and insisting on House consideration were Madison (*ibid.*, p. 461), Boudinot (*ibid.*, pp. 470, 528), Stone (*ibid.*, p. 492), and Silvester (*ibid.*, p. 561).

48. *Ibid.*, p. 492.

49. *Ibid.*, p. 501.

50. *Ibid.*, p. 547.

51. *Ibid.*, p. 500.

52. *Ibid.*

53. *Ibid.*, p. 501.

54. *Ibid.*, pp. 546–547.

55. See Manning J. Dauer, *The Adams Federalists* (Baltimore: Johns Hopkins, 1953), pp. 122, 170.

56. James Morton Smith, *Freedom's Fetters: The Alien and Sedition Laws and American Civil Liberties* (Ithaca: Cornell, 1956), p. 182. I have relied heavily on this valuable study and also on Dauer, *Adams Federalists,* cited above.

57. Smith, *Freedom's Fetters,* p. 182.

58. The Naturalization Act was approved June 18, 1798, 1 *Stat.* 566; the Alien Friends Act, June 25, 1798, *ibid.,* p. 570; and the Alien Enemies Act, July 6, 1798, *ibid.,* p. 577.

59. Section 1 dealt with unlawful conspiracies or combinations; section 3 made truth a defense in prosecutions for libel under the act and gave the jury the right to judge the law and fact under the direction of the Court; section 4 set the expiration date for the act at March 3, 1801. *Ibid.,* p. 596.

60. See Smith, *Freedom's Fetters,* pp. 176–187; see also Frank M. Anderson, "The Enforcement of the Alien and Sedition Laws," *Annual Report of the American Historical Association,* 1912 (Washington, 1913), pp. 113–117.

61. Joseph Story, *Commentaries on the Constitution of the United States,* ed. Melville M. Bigelow, 5th ed., 2 vols. (Boston, 1891), II, sec. 1892.

62. Leonard W. Levy, *Legacy of Suppression: Freedom of Speech and Press in Early American History* (Cambridge, Mass.: Harvard, 1960), chapter 6.

63. Marshall returned from the XYZ mission on June 18, and during his campaign for Congress in the fall, declared he would not have voted for the Sedition Act. Letter to "Freeholder" in the *Times and Virginia Advertiser* (Alexandria), Oct. 11, 1798, reprinted in Albert J. Beveridge, *Life of John Marshall,* 4 vols. (Boston: Houghton Mifflin, 1916–1919), II, 575–577.

64. Stevens Thomson Mason to Jefferson, July 6, 1798, Jefferson Papers, Library of Congress, Washington, D.C. (copy by courtesy of Dr. Julien Boyd). The margin in the House was especially small at this time, for of the 106 Representatives, 55 were Federalists, and 51 were Republicans. Dauer, *Adams Federalists,* p. 171.

65. 8 *Annals of Congress,* p. 1962 (1798).

66. *Ibid.,* p. 1966.

67. *Ibid.,* p. 2161.

68. *Ibid.,* pp. 2164–2165.

69. *Ibid.*, p. 2151.

70. For a summary of the substantive constitutional arguments, especially those of the Republicans, see Levy, *Legacy of Suppression,* pp. 258–266.

71. 8 *Annals of Congress,* p. 2151.

72. *Ibid.*, pp. 2154, 2144.

73. *Ibid.*, p. 2110.

74. See Smith, *Freedom's Fetters,* pp. 150–151.

75. Article by J. G. deR. Hamilton in *D.A.B.*, VIII, p. 285.

76. Voting for the bill were 28 lawyers and 16 non-lawyers; against it were 15 lawyers and 26 non-lawyers. The 9 Federalist speakers were William Craik (Md.), James A. Bayard (Dela.), John W. Kittera and Samuel Sitgreaves (Pa.), Samuel Dana and John Allen (Conn.), Samuel Sewall (Mass.), Harper, and Otis; the 8 Republicans were Albert Gallatin (Pa.), Edward Livingston (N.Y.), John Nicholas and Thomas Claiborne (Va.), Nathaniel Macon, Robert Williams, and Joseph McDowell (N.C.), and Abraham Baldwin (Ga.). Note the regional distribution.

77. Quotas of lawyers by regions were: in the Senate, New England 80 per cent, Middle Atlantic 63 per cent, South 60 per cent, West (Kentucky and Tennessee) 100 per cent; in the House, New England 62 per cent, Middle Atlantic 41 per cent, South 47 per cent, West 67 per cent.

78. 8 *Annals of Congress,* p. 2151.

79. *Ibid.*, pp. 2147–2151.

80. Macon continued: "The people of this country, almost to a man, understand the nature both of the State and Federal Governments, which could not be said of the great bulk of the people in Europe, who do not trouble themselves about the concerns of Government." *Ibid.*, p. 2106.

81. Harper and Otis were both 33 and John Allen of Connecticut 35; of the Republicans, Albert Gallatin was 37, John Nicholas 41, Livingston 34, and Nathaniel Macon 41.

82. Dauer finds that at this session only 12 Representatives could be classed as "moderates," whereas at the first session of the Fifth Congress there had been 23 and in the Fourth Congress, 29. *Adams Federalists,* pp. 170–171.

83. 8 *Annals of Congress,* p. 1997.

84. *Ibid.*

85. Hamilton to Wolcott June 29, 1798, in Hamilton's *Works,* ed. J. C. Hamilton, 7 vols. (New York, 1850–1851), VI, 307, quoted in Smith, *Freedom's Fetters,* p. 109.

86. 7 *Annals of Congress,* p. 599 (1798). John E. Howard, a Maryland Federalist, voted against the bill. Alexander Martin, North Carolina Republican, voted for it, although previously he had supported efforts to obstruct or weaken it. Smith, *Freedom's Fetters,* p. 111.

87. Mason to Jefferson, July 6, 1798, Jefferson Papers, CIV, 17825, Library of Congress, as quoted in Smith, *Freedom's Fetters,* p. 111.

88. In the House, Sewall requested permission May 16 and obtained it May 18 for his committee (Commerce and Defense) to bring in an omnibus alien and sedition bill; he reported the bill June 4, and the House debated it in Committee of the Whole June 16; the House took up the Senate alien friends bill on June 18 and 19 in Committee of the Whole, passed it on June 21 and recommitted Sewall's omnibus bill. After giving notice on June 23,

Senator Lloyd sought and obtained permission June 26 to bring in a sedition bill. The first reading took place the same day. On June 27, it was given a second reading and was referred to a special committee under Lloyd's chairmanship. The bill was reported July 2 and was debated and passed July 4; the House took up the Senate bill and debated and defeated a motion to reject it July 5, defeated an effort to refer it to a select committee, and received Harper's proposals on July 6; the House debated the bill in Committee of the Whole, July 9, and debated, amended, and passed it on third reading July 10; the Senate took up the House amendments July 11 and passed the amended bill July 12; President Adams signed it July 14.

89. Letters to Madison May 3 and June 21, 1798 in Jefferson, *Writings,* ed. Andrew Lipscomb and Albert E. Bergh, 20 vols. (Washington, 1903), X, 40, 49 and *Writings,* ed. P. L. Ford, 10 vols. (New York, 1892–1899), VII, 246, 272.

90. The motion lost 36–47. Smith, *Freedom's Fetters,* called it a straight party vote, p. 125; but Dauer terms Tillinghast, who voted with the majority, a Republican, pp. 306–309.

91. See motion of Joseph McDowell of North Carolina. 8 *Annals of Congress,* p. 2114.

92. This select committee consisted of Senators Lloyd, chairman, Uriah Tracy (Conn.), Richard Stockton (N.J.), Nathaniel Chipman (Vt.), and Jacob Read (S.C.). 7 *Annals of Congress,* p. 591. All supported the bill in the end. In fact, this committee chosen on July 27 was drawn from those who had already favored stiff legislation on three previous roll call votes. See 7 *Annals of Congress,* pp. 590, 591, 596, 599.

93. Mason to Jefferson, July 6, 1798. See above note 64.

94. Remarks of Samuel Sewall, July 6, 8 *Annals of Congress,* p. 2114.

95. 7 *Annals of Congress,* p. 698.

96. *Ibid.,* for other remarks of Gallatin, *ibid.,* pp. 694, 695; likewise of Nicholas, *ibid.,* pp. 693–694.

97. See Lauros G. McConachie, *Congressional Committees: A Study of the Origins and Development of Our National and Local Legislative Methods* (New York: Crowell, 1898), pp. 94, 95.

98. *Works,* ed. Seth Ames, 2 vols. (Boston, 1854), I, 64. Cited in Ralph V. Harlow, *The History of Legislative Methods in the Period Before 1825* (New Haven: Yale, 1917), p. 128.

99. 7 *Annals of Congress,* p. 696.

100. *Ibid.,* p. 700.

101. McConachie, *Congressional Committees,* pp. 95–97.

102. Dauer, *Adams Federalists,* p. 150. The Sewall Committee was appointed Nov. 29, 1797; its members were Samuel Sewall (Mass.), Samuel Dana (Conn.), James H. Imlay (N.J.), Josiah Parker (Va.), and Thomas Pinckney (S.C.), Federalists; and Edward Livingston (N.Y.) and Samuel Smith (Md.), Republicans. H. Journal, 5th Cong., 2nd sess. (1797), p. 36.

103. De Alva Stanwood Alexander, *History and Procedure of the House of Representatives* (Boston: Houghton Mifflin, 1916), pp. 66–71.

104. 8 *Annals of Congress,* p. 2171. Voting with the Federalists was Tillinghast of Rhode Island, a notorious fence sitter. Voting with the Republicans were George Dent and William Matthews of Maryland and Stephen Bullock of Massachusetts. Dauer, *Adams Federalists,* pp. 303–309.

105. See above, note 104.

106. Remarks of Baldwin, June 21, 8 *Annals of Congress,* p. 2004.

107. *Ibid.,* p. 2156.

108. Remarks of John Nicholas of Virginia, *ibid.,* p. 2144.

109. Remarks of Robert Williams of North Carolina, *ibid.,* p. 1963.

110. *Ibid.,* p. 2105.

111. *Ibid.,* p. 2013.

112. See remarks of Robert Williams, *ibid.,* p. 1965; Edward Livingston, *ibid.,* pp. 2007 and 2154; and Samuel Smith of Maryland, *ibid.,* p. 2133.

113. Mason to Jefferson, July 6, 1798, see above, note 64. To judge from the Senate vote, "M" could only have been Martin (N.C.).

114. 8 *Annals of Congress,* p. 2014.

115. *Ibid.,* p. 2104.

116. *Ibid.,* p. 2111.

117. *Ibid.,* p. 2152.

118. *Ibid.,* p. 2096. Bayard of Delaware objected to permitting juries to determine questions of law, on the ground that such might empower juries to declare the law unconstitutional instead of leaving this to the Judiciary, which ought to determine it. *Ibid.,* p. 2136.

119. *Ibid.,* p. 2111.

120. *Ibid.,* p. 2152.

121. *Ibid.,* p. 2105.

122. Otis at one point cited Commonwealth v. Oswald, referring no doubt to Republic v. Oswald, 1 Dallas 319 (1788). The pertinence of the case is questionable.

123. Letter to James Madison, Feb. 26, 1799, in *Writings,* ed. Ford, VII, 369, 371.

124. John C. Miller, *The Federalist Era* (New York: Harper, 1960), p. 242.

125. Beveridge, *Life of John Marshall,* II, 455.

126. Resolution adopted June 15, 1799, in Herman V. Ames, *State Documents on Federal Relations* (Philadelphia: University of Pennsylvania Press, 1906), pp. 24–25. The Rhode Island legislature resolved that in its opinion Article III vested "in the Federal Courts, exclusively, and in the Supreme Court of the United States, ultimately, the authority of deciding on the constitutionality of any act or law of the Congress of the United States." Adopted Feb. 1799. *Ibid.,* p. 17.

CHAPTER 4. THE EMERGING THEORIES

1. The statement was contained in a paragraph omitted from the final draft of Jefferson's first annual message to Congress, Dec. 8, 1801. It read in part, "Our country has thought proper to distribute the powers of it's government among three equal & independent authorities, constituting each a check on one or both of the others, in all attempts to impair it's constitution. To make each an effectual check, it must have a right in cases which arise within the line of it's proper functions, where, equally with the others, it acts in the last resort & without appeal, to decide on the validity of an act according to its own judgment, & uncontrouled by the opinion of any other department." Albert J. Beveridge, *Life of John Marshall,* 4 vols. (Boston: Houghton Mifflin, 1916–1919), III, 605, Appendix A. For a discussion of the roots of the theory and the question of Jefferson's consistency, see

Wallace Mendelson and Samuel Krislov, "Jefferson on Judicial Review," 10 *Journal of Public Law* (1961), pp. 113–124. I am indebted to Dumas Malone for the opportunity to read portions of the manuscript of the fourth volume of his biography of Jefferson. Dr. Malone thinks Jefferson's position was not inconsistent with earlier stands, but different from them in emphasis. It is well known that Jefferson had earlier viewed judicial review as an important safeguard against legislative oppression.

2. Speech delivered March 4, 1801, 1 Richardson, *Messages and Papers,* pp. 321–322.

3. *Ibid.,* pp. 323–324.

4. *Ibid.,* p. 324.

5. Speech delivered Dec. 8, 1801, 1 Richardson, *Messages and Papers,* pp. 326, 332.

6. Thus to Abigail Adams he defended his presidential pardons for Sedition Act violators on the ground of unconstitutionality, notwithstanding judicial enforcement. See Abigail Adams to Jefferson, May 20, July 1, Aug. 18, and Oct. 25, 1804 and Jefferson to Abigail Adams, June 13, July 22, and Sept. 11, 1804, in the *Adams-Jefferson Letters,* ed. Lester J. Cappon, 2 vols. (Chapel Hill: University of North Carolina Press, 1959), I, 268–282.

He directed his District Attorney, George Hay, during the Burr trial, to ignore an allusion made by Marshall to the Marbury case. Letter dated June 2, 1807, in Jefferson, *Writings,* ed. Andrew Lipscomb and Albert E. Bergh, 20 vols. (Washington, 1903), XI, 213.

He rebutted a proposition of a correspondent, holding that judges have exclusive authority to decide on the constitutionality of laws. Letter to William H. Torrance, June 11, 1815, *ibid.,* XIV, 302. He advised Judge Spencer Roane to the same effect in a letter dated Sept. 6, 1819, *ibid.,* XV, 212, and took a somewhat similar stand in a letter to William C. Jarvis, Sept. 28, 1820, *ibid.,* p. 276.

7. Abigail Adams to Jefferson, Aug. 18, 1804, in *Adams-Jefferson Letters,* ed. Cappon, I, 276–278.

8. Letter to Torrance, June 11, 1815, in *Writings,* ed. Lipscomb and Bergh, XIV, 303.

9. *Ibid.,* p. 304. (Italics are Jefferson's.)

10. *Ibid.,* pp. 304–305.

11. William C. Jarvis, *The Republican; or a Series of Essays on the Principles and Policies of Free States* (Pittsfield: Phinehas Allen, 1820).

12. *Ibid.,* p. 84.

13. *Ibid.,* p. 149.

14. Jefferson to Jarvis, September 28, 1820, in *Writings,* ed. Lipscomb and Bergh, XV, 277.

15. *Ibid.,* p. 277.

16. *Ibid.,* p. 278.

17. *Ibid.*

18. *Ibid.*

19. The tests he applied in selecting executive personnel were "Is he honest? Is he capable? Is he faithful to the Constitution?" Quoted in Leonard D. White, *The Jeffersonians* (New York: Macmillan, 1956), p. 352.

20. 2 *Stat.* pp. 157–158. The Judiciary Act of 1789 had constituted three circuits, in each of which the court should consist of any two justices of the Supreme Court and the District Judge. 1 *Stat.* pp. 74–75.

21. Donald G. Morgan, *Justice William Johnson* (Columbia, S.C.: University of South Carolina Press 1954), p. 52.

22. "Yet even in that department [the Judiciary]," he wrote, "we call in a jury of the people to decide all controverted matters of fact, because to that investigation they are entirely competent, leaving thus as little as possible, merely the law of the case, to the decision of the judges. And true it is that the people, especially when moderately instructed, are the only safe, because the only honest, depositories of the public rights, and should therefore be introduced into the administration of them in every function to which they are sufficient . . ." Jefferson to Adamantios Coray, Oct. 31, 1823, in *Writings,* ed. Lipscomb and Bergh, XV, 482–483.

23. Jefferson to Wythe, Feb. 28, 1800, *ibid.,* II, 335–336. Jefferson said here that the rules of the House of Representatives had been similar to those of the Continental Congress, i.e., "unparliamentary," and "so awkward and inconvenient that it was impossible sometimes to get at the true sense of the majority." He hoped that Senate presidents, by using his *Manual,* would institute a better system there, and by this example bring about improvement in the House, as well.

24. Jefferson to Edmund Pendleton, April 19, 1800, *ibid.,* XVIII, 221.

25. The *Manual,* he wrote, "was a mere compilation, into which nothing entered of my own but the arrangement, and a few observations necessary to explain that and some of the cases." Jefferson to John Campbell, Sept. 3, 1809, *ibid.,* XII, 308.

26. *Manual of Parliamentary Practice for the Use of the Senate of the United States* (Washington: Davis and Force, 1820 printing), preface.

27. By a strict adherence to sound rules, he continued, "the weaker party can only be protected from those irregularities and abuses, which these forms were intended to check, and which the wantonness of power is but too often apt to suggest to large and successful majorities." *Manual,* sec. 1.

28. Three regular editions, 1801, 1812, and 1813 followed the initial private printing. Twelve later printings appeared in the United States, prior to the Civil War. During the same period, the *Manual* appeared in Europe in French, Spanish, and German. *Writings,* ed. Lipscomb and Bergh, XX, 15–16. (See bibliography in rear of vol. XX.)

29. See Herbert J. Spiro, *Government by Constitution* (New York: Random House, 1959), pp. 240–256; and Carl J. Friedrich, *Constitutional Government and Democracy,* rev. ed. (Boston: Ginn, 1950), pp. 306–309, 321–322.

30. See above, chapter 2.

31. *Manual,* sec. 12.

32. Joseph Cooper, "Congress and Its Committees: A Historical and Theoretical Approach to the Proper Role of Committees in the Legislative Process" (unpublished Ph.D. dissertation, Department of Government, Harvard University, 1960), pp. 1–49.

33. William Johnson, *Eulogy on Thomas Jefferson* (Charleston, S.C.: C. C. Sebring, 1826), pamphlet, p. 21.

34. Lewis Deschler, *Rules of the House of Representatives,* H. Doc. No. 766, 81st Cong., 1st sess. (1949), pp. v–vi.

35. On state practice, see Robert Luce, *Legislative Procedure* (Boston: Houghton Mifflin, 1922), pp. 91, 102–104.

36. De Alva Stanwood Alexander, *History and Procedure of the House of Representatives* (Boston: Houghton Mifflin, 1916), pp. 182–183.

37. Remarks of James Sloan, 15 *Annals of Congress,* pp. 1114–1115 (1806). Quoted in Cooper, "Congress and Its Committees," p. 38.

38. See my "Marshall, the Marshall Court, and the Constitution," a chapter in W. Melville Jones, ed., *Chief Justice John Marshall, A Reappraisal* (Ithaca, N.Y.: Cornell, 1956), pp. 174–177.

39. In reply to my questionnaire in 1959, one Representative who minimized congressional responsibility declared that he accepted "the spirit, the letter and all the implications of Marbury v. Madison."

40. 1 Cranch 137, 163 (1803).

41. *Ibid.,* p. 158.

42. *Ibid.,* p. 163.

43. *Ibid.,* p. 167.

44. *Ibid.,* p. 177.

45. *Ibid.,* pp. 165–166.

46. *Ibid.,* p. 166.

47. Marshall defined political questions as those "which are, by the constitution and laws, submitted to the executive." 1 Cranch 170. Presumably he would have defined congressional political questions in somewhat similar terms, embracing matters such as those identified by Jefferson. Obviously, though, he reserved to the Court a right to judge the scope of the substantive powers of Congress.

Jefferson, too, had cited moral and political sanctions in justifying the pardoning of the Sedition Act victims. Note this passage from the paragraph deleted before delivery from his First Annual Message: "Called on by the position in which the nation had placed me, to exercise in their behalf my free & independent judgment, I took the act into consideration, compared it with the constitution, viewed it under every aspect of which I thought it susceptible, and gave to it all the attention which the magnitude of the case demanded. On mature deliberation, in the presence of the nation and under the tie of the solemn oath which binds me to them & to my duty, I do declare that I hold that act to be in palpable & unqualified contradiction to the constitution." Beveridge, *Marshall,* III, 605–606.

48. 1 Cranch, p. 179.

49. 4 Wheaton 316, 401 (1819).

50. Thus: "Is it so improbable that they [the framers] should confer on the judicial department the power of construing the constitution and laws of the Union in every case, in the last resort, and of preserving them from all violation from every quarter, *so far as judicial decisions can preserve them* . . . ?" Cohens v. Virginia, 6 Wheaton 264, 388 (1821); and an important object of the Judicial Department "was the preservation of the constitution and laws of the United States, *so far as they can be preserved by judicial authority* . . ." ibid., p. 391. (Italics supplied.)

51. *Ibid.,* p. 405. From this statement a later Court concluded that the exercise of this, its most important duty, "was not given to it [the Court] as a body with revisory power over the action of Congress." Justice Day, in Muskrat v. United States, 219 U.S. 346, 361 (1911).

52. Veto of the Bank bill, July 10, 1832, 2 Richardson, *Messages and Papers,* p. 582.

53. Said he in reference to the Dred Scott decision, "At the same time, the candid citizen must confess that if the policy of the Government upon vital questions affecting the whole people is to be irrevocably fixed by deci-

sions of the Supreme Court, the instant they are made in ordinary litigation between parties in personal actions the people will have ceased to be their own rulers, having to that extent practically resigned their Government into the hands of that eminent tribunal." First Inaugural, March 4, 1861, 6 *ibid.,* p. 9.

54. 4 Wheaton 400–401 (1819).

55. William W. Story, *Life and Letters of Joseph Story,* 2 vols. (Boston, 1851), I, 215.

56. Beveridge, *Marshall,* IV, 87.

57. Story, *Life and Letters,* I, 215–216.

58. Beveridge, *Marshall,* IV, 310; Charles Warren, *The Supreme Court in United States History,* rev. ed., 2 vols. (Boston: Little, Brown, 1926), I, 288.

59. Jefferson to William Johnson, Oct. 27, 1822, in Jefferson, *Writings,* ed. P. L. Ford, 10 vols. (New York, 1892–1899), X, 225.

60. *Niles Weekly Register,* XVI (March 20, 1819), p. 65.

61. *Ibid.,* XXXIII (Jan. 19, 1828), p. 329.

62. Robert B. Luce, *Legislative Problems* (Boston: Houghton Mifflin, 1935), pp. 91–92.

63. Johnson to Jefferson, Dec. 10, 1822, Jefferson Papers, vol. 223, Library of Congress.

64. Concurring opinion in Martin *v.* Hunter's Lessee, 1 Wheaton 304, 373–374 (1816).

65. Warren, *Supreme Court,* I, 337.

66. Anderson *v.* Dunn, 6 Wheaton 204, 228–229 (1821). See below, chapter 5.

67. Thus, in 1820 he included in a draft bankruptcy bill a section providing that, "nothing herein contained shall be construed to impair the right of the states to legislate and adjudicate on subjects of insolvency or bankruptcy, so far as no provision is made for such cases by this act, except only so far as relates to persons declared involuntary bankrupts in pursuance of this act." *A Bill to Establish an Uniform System of Bankruptcy in the United States* (Washington: privately printed, 1820), p. 15; quoted in Morgan, *Johnson,* p. 118. For further discussion of Johnson's handling of the problem of pre-emption, see *ibid.,* pp. 239–249, 253.

68. Taylor to Johnson, Sept. 11, 1830, in *Niles Weekly Register,* XXXIX (Oct. 2, 1830), p. 99.

69. Johnson to Taylor, Sept. 22, 1830, in *Niles Weekly Register,* XXXIX (Oct. 9, 1830), p. 119. See Morgan, *Johnson,* p. 265.

70. "Hamilton" (pseud.), *Review of a Late Pamphlet under the Signature of "Brutus"* (Charleston, S.C.: James S. Burgess, 1828), p. 24. Discussed in Morgan, *Johnson,* pp. 260–261.

71. *Review of a Late Pamphlet,* p. 22.

72. *Ibid.,* p. 15. (Italics are Johnson's.)

73. *Ibid.,* p. 16.

74. Undated letter to Monroe, Monroe Papers, XX, fol. 2568, Library of Congress, quoted in Morgan, *Johnson,* pp. 123–124.

75. Johnson to Jefferson, Dec. 10, 1822, Jefferson Papers, vol. 223, Library of Congress, quoted in Morgan, *Johnson,* p. 184.

76. On this whole subject, see Morgan, *Johnson,* chapter 10, also published as an article entitled "The Origin of Supreme Court Dissent," *William*

and Mary Quarterly, 3d Ser., X (1953), pp. 353–377.

77. 9 Wheaton 1, 223 (1824).

78. Note that in the Little Rock Case in 1959, the Court issued its opinion over the signature of all nine justices, an action dictated, no doubt, by public criticism of the more anonymous unanimous opinions in the earlier desegregation decisions. Cooper *v.* Aaron, 358 U.S. 1, 4 (1958).

79. Joseph Story, *Commentaries on the Constitution of the United States,* 5th ed. (Boston: Little, Brown, 1891), preface, p. x.

80. *Ibid.* "It is not, then, by artificial reasoning founded upon theory, but upon a careful survey of the language of the Constitution itself, that we are to interpret its powers and its obligations." *Ibid.,* sec. 372.

81. *Ibid.,* sec. 339, citing "1 Black. Comm. 45."

82. *Ibid.,* sec. 374. Yet see his fulminations on the power of legislatures and the unreliability of legislative majorities. Secs. 534, 535.

83. *Ibid.,* sec. 375.

84. *Ibid.,* sec. 1294, note 2. (Italics are Story's.)

85. *Ibid.*

86. *Ibid.*

87. *Ibid.,* sec. 375, note 1.

88. *Ibid.,* sec. 377.

89. See George Edward Woodbine, "Joseph Story," *D.A.B.,* XVIII, 106–107.

90. Learned Hand, *The Bill of Rights* (Cambridge, Mass.: Harvard, 1958), p. 4.

91. On Jan. 27, 1830, Webster declared that the people had sought security from unconstitutional laws not in the state veto but in the moral responsibility of officials, in political accountability at elections, in judicial review, and finally in their own power to amend. 6 *Register of Debates,* 21st Cong., 1st sess., pt. 1, p. 79 (1830). In the same speech, however, he asserted that New Englanders had entrusted decision on the constitutionality of the Embargo laws to the courts: "Who," he asked, "is to judge between the people and the Government?" It was plain, he replied, that "the constitution . . . confers on the Government itself, to be exercised by its appropriate department, and under its own responsibility to the people, this power of deciding ultimately and conclusively upon the just extent of its own authority." *Ibid.,* p. 76. He maintained that under the supreme law clause and Article III, Congress had established in the Judiciary Act of 1789 "a mode . . . for bringing *all* questions of constitutional power to the final decision of the Supreme Court." (Italics supplied.) *Ibid.,* p. 78.

CHAPTER 5. THE JEFFERSONIAN SYSTEM

1. Anderson *v.* Dunn, 6 Wheaton 204 (1821).

2. 31 *Annals of Congress,* p. 594 (1818). Those who measure the validity of congressional determinations by consulting motivation should study the reply of Joseph Hopkinson, Pennsylvania Federalist. In denying that party principle had governed the earlier House, he asked how the gentleman from New Hampshire could "know the motives of the members of that Congress"; how did he acquire "the power to enter their hearts and see that they did not decide this question on our own laws, but on those of a foreign country?" *Ibid.,* p. 596.

3. *Niles Weekly Register,* XIII (vol. I n.s.) (Dec. 20, 1817), p. 257.

4. 4 Wheaton 316 (1819).

5. 31 *Annals of Congress,* p. 581.

6. Ernest J. Eberling, *Congressional Investigations* (New York: Columbia, 1928), pp. 302–303.

7. Carl Beck, *Contempt of Congress* (New Orleans: Houser Press, 1959), p. 7.

8. McGrain *v.* Daugherty, 273 U.S. 168–169 (1927).

9. Eberling, *Congressional Investigations,* p. 15.

10. Telford Taylor, *Grand Inquest* (New York: Simon & Schuster, 1955), p. 10. The colonial and early state history of legislative investigations and contempts is set forth in an article by Charles S. Potts, "The Power of Legislative Bodies to Punish for Contempt," 74 *University of Pennsylvania Law Review* (1926), p. 691.

11. Eberling, *Congressional Investigations,* pp. 15, 24.

12. Taylor, *Grand Inquest,* p. 12.

13. 5 *Annals of Congress,* pp. 166–244 (1795).

14. 10 *Annals of Congress,* pp. 68–184 (1800).

15. 31 *Annals of Congress,* pp. 580–581.

16. *Ibid.,* p. 583.

17. *Ibid.,* p. 600.

18. *Ibid.,* p. 602.

19. *Ibid.,* p. 606.

20. *Ibid.,* pp. 606–607.

21. *Ibid.,* p. 607.

22. *Ibid.,* pp. 611–612.

23. *Ibid.,* p. 616.

24. *Ibid.,* p. 623.

25. *Ibid.,* pp. 621–622.

26. *Ibid.,* p. 635.

27. *Ibid.,* p. 668. (Italics are Holmes'.)

28. *Ibid.,* pp. 672–673.

29. *Ibid.,* pp. 700–701.

30. *Ibid.,* p. 735. He also cited *inter alia* United States *v.* Hudson and Goodwin, 7 Cranch 32 (1812) and *Ex parte* Bollman and Swartwout, 4 Cranch 75 (1807). 31 *Annals of Congress,* p. 716.

31. *Ibid.,* p. 773.

32. On Monday, John Rhea, Tennessee Republican, moved to strike the reference to "great doubts" contained in the preamble to Spencer's resolution. Next day, Spencer withdrew the preamble, and Rhea then moved to strike all but the opening phrase and to substitute a declaration that the House had competent power to punish Anderson and an order for the appearance of the prisoner. The next day (Wednesday), he modified his amendment to make it a definite assertion of the general power of contempt. The following day Pitkin moved to postpone the main question indefinitely; this was passed 117–42. Tallmadge then moved that Anderson be brought to the bar and Rich moved an amendment denying the power of the House to judge or punish any individuals "its own members excepted." This was voted down by a large majority. *Ibid.,* p. 776. Culbreth then made his motion; this was defeated as described in the text. *Ibid.* The vote on Tallmadge's amendment was 118–45. Next day, after Anderson's hearing,

Poindexter moved to weaken the force of the original resolution. He was defeated 108–54. *Ibid.,* p. 789.

33. For what they are worth in this time of shifting party allegiances, the figures are: Republicans, 66–30 for the contempt power; Federalists, 25–1 for the power; undesignated, 28–15 for the power.

34. The states were Ohio, Kentucky, Tennessee, Mississippi, and Louisiana. Votes from other states included *inter alia:* Massachusetts, 13 for and 5 against; New York, 17–7; Pennsylvania, 19–2; Virginia, 13–5; South Carolina, 4–3; Georgia, 6–0.

35. This vote on internal improvements was one of several which the House took at this session. It occurred on March 14 and, as shown, favored the power 89–75. 32 *Annals of Congress,* p. 1385 (1819). About half, 59, of the 119 who had supported the contempt power here endorsed a limited power over improvements, while 47 of the remainder opposed such a power. Of the 47 who had opposed the contempt power, 22, including 11 Westerners, favored power over improvements, and 21 opposed that power.

36. Eleven came from the South, 6 came from New England, 6 from the Middle Atlantic States, and 6 from the West. New York contributed 4, Pennsylvania 3, and Massachusetts, Kentucky, and New Hampshire 2 each.

37. Ball and Pindall of Virginia were evidently the only non-lawyers. The leaders were: for the contempt power—Forsyth, Hopkinson, Sergeant, and Rhea; against the power—Beecher, Barbour, and Spencer.

38. 31 *Annals of Congress,* p. 622.

39. Thus, 52 per cent of the Southerners and 57 per cent of Middle Atlantic Representatives were lawyers.

40. 31 *Annals of Congress,* p. 684.

41. For Virginia and Maryland the corresponding figure was 47 per cent.

42. Of the 29, 18 had served in state legislatures, 6 in state or local courts, 9 as law officers, one (Hopkinson) as counsel in such leading controversies as the Chase impeachment trial, 2 in state constitutional conventions, and one in a state convention that ratified the federal Constitution.

43. All four of the leading proponents of power and one of the three leading opponents (Barbour) had served previously in Congress.

44. Thus Spencer, newcomer from New York, called precedent the "eternal refuge and expedient of a cause that shrinks from inspection, and would hide itself in the obscurity of example." He was almost sure the Anderson case would never be "mingled with the common rubbish of precedent." 31 *Annals of Congress,* p. 616. The Pennsylvania Federalist, Hopkinson, in contrast spoke of adherence to precedents "as the certainty of the law; as the great safety of every right to the citizen." *Ibid.,* p. 726.

45. *Ibid.,* p. 658.

46. *Ibid.,* p. 740. Yet Charles Mercer of Virginia also admired the common law: "Had I the tongue of Henry, I would portray to you its excellence." *Ibid.,* p. 638.

47. Joseph Story, *Commentaries on the Constitution of the United States,* 5th ed. (Boston, 1891), sec. 846. For Johnson's position see 6 Wheaton 224–235, and Donald G. Morgan, *Justice William Johnson* (Columbia, S.C.: University of South Carolina Press, 1954), pp. 119–122.

48. 31 *Annals of Congress,* pp. 400–401.

49. Ralph V. Harlow, *History of Legislative Methods in the Period Before 1825* (New Haven: Yale, 1917), p. 216. The corresponding Senate com-

mittee was set up in 1816. George B. Galloway, *The Legislative Process in Congress* (New York: Crowell, 1953), p. 274.

50. 31 *Annals of Congress,* pp. 404–405.

51. *Ibid.,* p. 401.

52. For much of this material see Joseph Cooper, "Congress and Its Committees" (cited in chapter 4, note 32), pp. 50–65.

53. In spite of President Monroe's adverse comments on the power in his message, some House leaders evidently wanted a vote on power to precede the drafting of bills. Accordingly, the House, led by William Lowndes of South Carolina, from March 6–14 weighed the power in Committee of the Whole and then approved one of four resolutions variously defining the power. 31 *Annals of Congress,* pp. 1114, 1281. The debate was thorough and informed and, incidentally, anticipated much of Marshall's reasoning in the McCulloch case the following year. Note, however, that a committee had prepared the way in a detailed report with recommendations and that the committee had acted on its own initiative in developing the principles to be applied in the subsequent resolutions (rather than act on principled instructions of the whole House). The prior consideration by the House was perfunctory in the extreme. *Ibid.,* p. 401. The committee report, however, was positive and comprehensive. *Ibid.,* p. 451. On this issue, at least, the power of the committee was beginning to be felt.

This select Committee on Roads, Canals, and Seminaries of Learning was itself divided on the final vote. Voting for the only resolution that passed were Tucker (Va.), chairman, Tallmadge (N.Y.), and George Robertson (Ky.). Against the resolution was Clagett (N.H.). Absent were Storrs (N.Y.), William Lewis (Va.), and Samuel Ingham (Pa.). This committee contained two non-lawyers, Lewis and Ingham.

54. See Cooper, "Congress and Its Committees," pp. 57–58.

55. See Harlow, *History of Legislative Methods,* especially chapter 10.

56. *Ibid.,* pp. 210ff.

57. Leonard D. White, *The Jeffersonians: A Study in Administrative History* (New York: Macmillan, 1956), pp. 55–56.

58. 31 *Annals of Congress,* p. 613.

59. *Ibid.,* p. 624.

60. *Ibid.,* p. 684. Whitman felt moved to speak since no gentleman "in the course of his remarks" had "embraced my view of it." *Ibid.,* p. 740. Settle would not presume to change the decided views of others, yet he would not for that reason "decline submitting the reasons which would determine his vote on this question." *Ibid.,* p. 700. Others, as might be expected, cited the oath of office as additional ground: see remarks by Ball, *ibid.,* p. 603, and Ervin, *ibid.,* pp. 645–646.

61. *Ibid.,* p. 612.

62. See Quarles's assertion that the House was seeking a "full and ample discussion of the subject, by every member who chose to exercise that right . . ." *Ibid.,* p. 678.

63. Note Henry Tucker's early appeal for reference to a select committee: "No matter how light the subject might be that was proposed to the consideration of the House, he should not choose to act on it, without calling on some committee of the House to take it into their particular consideration, and to produce a clear and connected view of it." *Ibid.,* p. 595.

64. When the House took up the resolutions on internal improvements,

411

William Lowndes of South Carolina at one point asked (and later got) the House to separate the constitutional question from what he called "the question of expediency . . . or from any embarrassments of detail." *Ibid.*, p. 1135. After a favorable vote on one of the resolutions, he announced jubilantly that "after the decision of this House to-day, there could be no doubt that a large majority of the House entertain the conviction of the power of Congress to appropriate money for the purpose of constructing roads and canals. The sense of the House being thus ascertained . . ." 32 *Annals of Congress,* p. 1389.

65. See Rich's (Vt.) statement, quoted above, p. 110. Smyth (Va.) called constitutional questions when governed by legislative precedents "legal questions." "When frequently decided the same way," he said, they "should be regarded as settled, as the law should become certain." 31 *Annals of Congress,* p. 699. Of course, Jefferson himself intimated that legislative decisions on some matters affecting its proceedings became matters of "law." See his *Manual of Parliamentary Practice,* sec. 3.

66. *Niles Weekly Register* for the 12 months in which this session fell gives graphic proof of the esteem in which many must have held Congress. Four columns of small print in the index for the volumes of that year are required to itemize all the references to "Congress," from Sept. 1817 to Sept. 1818, while the "Supreme Court" receives mention twice, once for the opening, once for the recess! Of the 16 "Law Cases" referred to, 15 are concerned with business in courts other than the Supreme Court. The exception was United States *v.* Bevans, 3 Wheaton 336 (1818).

67. In his annual message, President Monroe said he wished to dispel any uncertainty concerning the power. Said he, "I have bestowed upon the subject all the deliberation which its great importance and a just sense of my duty required, and the result is a settled conviction in my mind that Congress do not possess the right." The Constitution, he said, did not contain it expressly or impliedly and he felt obligated to suggest a constitutional amendment. It was proper and indeed it supported our institutions in "cases of doubtful construction, especially of such vital interest," to follow that course. He was confident that if the power was needed it would be granted. 2 Richardson, *Messages and Papers,* p. 587.

The House committee that reported out resolutions supporting internal improvements applied the same theory with different results. It denied that the threat of a presidential veto on a bill for reasons of unconstitutionality should deter it from reaching its own determination of the issue. Congress might make its own inquiry and register a constitutional majority (two-thirds) in favor of the power and thus override the veto; to hold back through fear of such a veto would be a "dereliction of their privileges." 31 *Annals of Congress,* p. 452. Later, Tucker, committee chairman, denied that a pending constitutional amendment in the Senate should inhibit the House from reaching its own decision on the power. He would not be bound by the "deliberations of one branch of the Government or the declarations of another." *Ibid.,* p. 1115.

68. Veto of Cumberland Road Bill, May 4, 1822, 2 Richardson, *Messages and Papers,* p. 142.

69. *Congressional Globe,* 28th Cong., 1st sess. (1843), pt. 1, p. 278. The previous year President Tyler had signed the Reapportionment Act, but submitted his reasons for doing so. He "yielded . . . to the opinion of the

Legislature" and left "questions which may arise hereafter, if unhappily such should arise, to be settled by full consideration of the several provisions of the Constitution and the laws and the authority of each House to judge of the elections, returns, and qualifications of its own members." 4 Richardson, *Messages and Papers,* pp. 159–160, treated in Laurence F. Schmeckebier, *Congressional Apportionment* (Washington: Brookings, 1941), p. 133. (Adapted in part from a student paper by Nancy J. FitzGerald.)

70. De Alva Stanwood Alexander, *History and Procedure of the House of Representatives* (Boston: Houghton Mifflin, 1916), p. 233.

CHAPTER 6. STRESS OF WAR

1. Letter to Erastius Corning and Others, [June 12,] 1863, in *Collected Works,* ed. Roy P. Basler, 8 vols. (New Brunswick, N.J.: Rutgers, 1953), VI, 260, 263.

2. *Congressional Globe,* 37th Cong., 1st sess. (1861), pt. 1, p. 26.

3. H. Rept. 16, 37th Cong., 2nd sess. (1862).

4. *Cong. Globe,* 37th Cong., 1st sess. (1861), pt 1, p. 456. See above, chapter 3.

5. 12 *Stat.* 376; *ibid.,* p. 430.

6. *Ibid.,* p. 502.

7. *Cong. Globe,* 37th Cong., 3rd sess. (1863), pt. 2, pp. 1553–1554.

8. *Ibid.,* pp. 1554, 1555–1562.

9. *Cong. Globe,* 38th Cong., 1st sess. (1863), pt. 1, p. 56.

10. *Ibid.,* p. 331.

11. *Ex parte* Garland, 4 Wallace 333 (1867).

12. Harold M. Hyman, *Era of the Oath* (Philadelphia: University of Pennsylvania Press, 1954), p. 115.

13. *Ibid.,* pp. 48–134.

14. For example, R. R. Butler, elected to the House from Tennessee, was a member of Tennessee's secessionist legislature in 1861, and although no one doubted his statement that he had remained in the legislature to work for the Union, the oath nonetheless excluded him from office. H. Rept. 18, 40th Cong., 2nd sess. (1868).

15. 15 *Stat.* 85.

16. *Cong. Globe,* 41st Cong., 1st sess. (1869), p. 886.

17. The President allowed the measure to become law without his signature; he would approve a repeal of the oath of past loyalty, but he would, he said, never endorse a measure which relieved Confederate soldiers, for whom the test had been designed, of that obligation, while leaving the past loyalty oath in effect for the Union soldier "who [had] fought and bled for his country . . ." 7 Richardson, *Messages and Papers,* pp. 122–123.

18. 15 *Cong. Rec.,* pt. 4, p. 4174 (1884).

19. The House Judiciary Committee had the bill, H. R. 371, from March 24 to June 4.

20. The past loyalty oath read: "I, A.B., do solemnly swear (or affirm) that I have never voluntarily borne arms against the United States since I have been a citizen thereof; that I have voluntarily given no aid, countenance, counsel, or encouragement to persons engaged in armed hostility thereto; that I have neither sought nor accepted nor attempted to exercise the functions of any office whatever, under any authority or pretended

authority in hostility to the United States; that I have not yielded a voluntary support to any pretended government, authority, power or constitution within the United States hostile or inimical thereto . . ." There follows the future loyalty oath.

21. 12 *Stat.* 502. *Cong. Globe,* 37th Cong., 2nd sess. (1862), pt. 3, p. 2861.

22. *Ibid.,* p. 2564.

23. *Ibid.*

24. *Ibid.*

25. *Ibid.,* p. 2565.

26. The Senate Judiciary Committee had the bill from June 4 to June 10.

27. *Ibid.,* p. 2693.

28. *Ibid.,* p. 2862.

29. *Ibid.,* p. 2694.

30. *Ibid.,* p. 2695.

31. *Ibid.,* p. 2862.

32. The members of the House Judiciary Committee were Republicans John Bingham (Ohio), William Kellogg (Ill.), Albert Porter (Ind.), Alexander Diven (N.Y.), and James Wilson (Iowa); Democrats George Pendleton (Ohio) and Henry May (Md.); and Benjamin Thomas (Mass.), who called himself a Conservative Unionist.

33. The members of the Senate Judiciary Committee were Republicans Lyman Trumbull (Ill.), chairman, Lafayette Foster (Conn.), John Ten Eyck (N.J.), Edgar Cowan (Pa.), and Ira Harris (N.Y.); and Democrats James Bayard (Dela.) and Lazarus Powell (Ky.).

34. The conferees were Senators Trumbull, Preston King, New York Republican, and Garrett Davis, Kentucky Democrat; and Representatives Wilson, Bingham, and John Phelps, Missouri Democrat.

35. Before the war, in the 36th Congress (1859–1861), the Judiciary Committee contained members from Delaware, Missouri, Kentucky, and Louisiana and also Ohio, Democrats; and from Illinois and Connecticut, Republicans. The wartime committee was firmly in the hands of Northern Republicans. See above, note 33. It contained four holdovers, Trumbull, Foster, Bayard, and Powell and three new members, Cowan, Harris, and Ten Eyck, in place of members from Louisiana, Missouri, and Ohio. The pre-war committee averaged seven years previous experience in Congress, and the three new members, one year. The House committee reflected similar changes.

36. See above, notes 32, 33, and 35.

37. *Cong. Globe,* 37th Cong., 2nd sess., pt. 3, p. 2564.

38. The House took up the currency bill of 1863 for debate at the evening session on Feb. 19, 1863. The bill had been passed by the Senate on Feb. 12 and referred to the House Ways and Means Committee. In the debate which followed committee action, Representative Elbridge Gerry Spaulding soon raised the constitutional issue—whether or not Congress was empowered to issue a national paper currency. Representative John William Noell, Missouri Democrat, then offered an amendment requesting that the bill be referred to the Committee on the Judiciary, "with instructions to inquire and report: 1. How far the bill interferes with the rights of the States to regulate their own internal financial concerns. 2. How far the bill interferes with vested rights under existing valid State laws. 3. Whether or not the effect of the bill is to charter within the limits of the States local banks having no national charac-

ter and whether or not, in this, the bill is unconstitutional. 4. . . ." *Cong. Globe,* 37th Cong., 3rd sess. (1863), p. 1117. In explaining his amendment on the following day, Noell stated:

> There are involved in it [the bill] not only measures of policy, but measures of constitutional law. It has appeared to me, and it still appears to me, that we ought not to consider these questions of constitutional law if it can possibly be avoided, without having them referred to the committee of the House organized for the purpose of investigating such questions . . .
>
> I, for one, am not prepared at this time, if I can avoid the responsibility, to determine that [the constitutional] question. I desire earnestly that it may be sent to the Committee on the Judiciary, to be there considered and fully investigated, and the result of their labors reported for the information and action of the House. *Ibid.,* p. 1145.

Noell's amendment was ignored. The bill passed the House the same day, after less than two full days of debate.

My discussion of the National Currency Act is based in part on a student paper by Jane R. Wiedlea.

39. *Cong. Globe,* 37th Cong., 2nd sess., pt. 3, p. 2693.

40. *Ibid.,* p. 2861.

41. *Ibid.,* pt. 4, p. 3012.

42. *Ibid.,* pt. 3, pp. 2694–2695.

43. On April 27, 1864, the Senate was debating the National Bank Act of that year and considering whether Congress had power, after converting state banks into federal banks, to consent to state taxation of national bank securities. Note an interchange between Senator Zachariah Chandler, Michigan Republican, who had no doubt about the power but thought the bill would pass only if the banks were exempted from state taxation and Senator Reverdy Johnson, Maryland Democrat, who thought Congress could not grant such an exemption. Mr. Chandler said:

> Sir, I have not got the "Constitution on the brain." I believe that this great Government has got the power of salvation within it. I believe that it is constitutional to do whatever is requisite to save the Constitution and the Government. Some men who have the "Constitution on the brain" cannot do anything to save the Government. I have not that, thank God.

Johnson replied to Chandler thus:

> The honorable Senator from Michigan talks about his never having the disease which he has so well characterized as "Constitution on the brain." So far from that being a disease, it is what we have sworn to have, if it be a disease at all . . . If the honorable member means—and he can mean nothing else—that he is for giving a liberal construction to the Constitution for carrying out all its powers as it is necessary to do so for the benefit of the country at large, he and I entertain in that respect the same opinion; and if, by the Constitution as it is, looking to its history and looking to its words, it be clear, as I submit it is in my judgment, that every species of property was supposed to be left to State taxation as well as to the taxation of the United States, with the single exception [of taxes on imports], then he who takes from the States the right to tax what the Constitution leaves them the right to tax, wars against the Constitution, sins against it. *Cong. Globe,* 38th Cong., 1st sess. (1864), pt. 2, p. 1892.

After this defense of state power, Senator Charles Sumner, Radical Republican from Massachusetts, stated his positon. Explicitly avowing that he raised no constitutional objection, he presented a detailed analysis of Marshall's opinion in McCulloch v. Maryland, which he thought was unsurpassed as an example of "that 'pure reason' which belonged to this magistrate." He also drew on Weston v. Charleston, 2 Peters 449 (1829), holding that states lacked authority to tax the income from federal securities; citing Story's *Commentaries* he contended that the reason of the law, if not its words, argued against congressional concession of power to tax the banks. He said he was arguing not that Congress could not grant the power to the states, but that Congress should not grant it, a matter he deemed solely one of policy. *Cong. Globe,* 38th Cong. 1st sess., pt. 2, pp. 1893–1894.

Sumner's approach to the 1864 question as one of policy was shared by others in Congress, a fact which militated against examining the broad aspects of the dispute. Senator Jacob M. Howard, Michigan Republican, raised the issue of legal power, affirming that the states alone had power to levy the tax, and hence congressional action was ruled out. *Ibid.,* p. 1898. Others tended to assume the power to control the matter in Congress and to view the adjustment of federal and state taxes as solely one of expediency.

In discussing the currency bill of 1863, members seemed agreed that Congress should give serious thought to constitutional questions; none advised leaving them to the courts. Some, like Senator John Sherman, Ohio Republican, had no doubts as to the constitutionality of the bill and spelled out the appropriate constitutional grounds. Others had serious doubts and tried in speeches to point them out. Some, like James Doolittle, Wisconsin Republican doubted constitutional power but saw the bill as necessary to success in the war effort. *Cong. Globe,* 37th Cong., 3rd sess. (1863), pt. 1, pp. 881–882. Jacob Collamer, Vermont Republican, shared this view but opposed the bill as probably inoperative before the return of peace. *Ibid.,* p. 869. Senator Henry Wilson, Massachusetts Republican, said that in view of the existence of greenbacks in circulation, the "judges will pause long before declaring them illegal." *Ibid.,* p. 881. Representative John B. Alley, Massachusetts Republican, said Congress should give preference to the "great questions" of finance over "abstract theories." *Ibid.,* pt. 2, p. 1147.

44. The National Currency Act (12 *Stat.* 665), became law Feb. 25, 1863, and the National Bank Act (13 *Stat.* 99), June 30, 1864. Both bills went to the House Ways and Means Committee and the Senate Finance Committee. According to Thaddeus Stevens (*Cong. Globe,* 38th Cong., 1st sess. (1864), pt. 2, p. 1287) the House committee held hearings on the 1864 bill. The Senate debated the 1863 bill three days and the House two days. The House debated the 1864 bill eleven days and the Senate three days, after which it went to a conference committee. Senate debate in both cases was more thorough and effective.

45. Scott v. Sanford, 19 Howard 393 (1857). Benjamin F. Wright points out that the Court held ten acts of Congress unconstitutional during the tenure of Chief Justice Salmon P. Chase, 1865–1873, and twelve during the next quarter century, 1874–1898. See Wright, *Growth of American Constitutional Law* (Boston: Houghton Mifflin, 1942), pp. 82, 86. The Court, of course, invalidated only two acts of Congress between 1789 and 1861.

46. *The Constitution of the United States: Analysis and Interpretation,* prepared by the Legislative Reference Service, Library of Congress, ed.

416

Norman Small and Lester S. Jayson (1964 ed.). Fifteen of the twenty-two laws were passed after the Civil War and several were unrelated to war or Reconstruction.

CHAPTER 7. THE MARSHALLIAN SYSTEM

1. United States *v*. E. C. Knight Co., 156 U.S. 1 (1895).

2. Eliot Jones, *The Trust Problem in the United States* (New York: Macmillan, 1921), pp. 19–25.

3. See Samuel P. Hays, *The Response to Industrialism, 1885–1914* (Chicago: University of Chicago Press, 1957), pp. 137–138, 188–190.

4. See Oswald W. Knauth, *The Policy of the United States Towards Industrial Monopoly* (New York: Columbia, 1914), pp. 13–19, for a fuller discussion of the rise of concern in the 1880's. The New York case against the sugar trust referred to is The People of the State of New York *v*. The North River Sugar Refining Co., 121 N.Y. 582 (1890). The report of the Senate select committee is S. Rept. 829, 51st Cong., 1st sess. (1890). The reports of the House Committee on Manufactures are H. Rept. 3112, 50th Cong., 1st sess. (1888) and H. Rept. 4165, 50th Cong., 2nd sess. (1889).

5. Matthew Josephson, *The Politicos, 1865–96* (New York: Harcourt Brace, 1938), pp. 61–315.

6. Hays, *Response to Industrialism*, p. 143.

7. Jones, *Trust Problem*, pp. 318–319. The Republican platform read: "We declare our opposition to all combinations of capital, organized in trusts or otherwise, to control arbitrarily the condition of trade among our citizens; and we recommend to Congress and the state legislatures, in their respective jurisdictions, such legislation as will prevent the execution of all schemes to oppress the people by undue charges on their supplies, or by unjust rates for the transportation of their products to market." The Democratic platform read: ". . . the interests of the people are betrayed when by unnecessary taxation, trusts and combinations are permitted to exist, which, while unduly enriching the few that combine, rob the body of our citizens by depriving them of the benefits of natural competition."

8. 20 *Cong. Rec.*, pt. 2, pp. 1120–1121, 1167–1169, 1457–1462 (1889).

9. 9 Richardson, *Messages and Papers*, p. 43.

10. Albert H. Walker, *History of the Sherman Law of the United States of America* (New York: Equity Press, 1910), pp. 162–178.

11. Addyston Pipe and Steel Co. *v*. United States, 175 U.S. 211 (1899).

12. United States *v*. Joint Traffic Association, 171 U.S. 505 (1898).

13. Note also that this decision resulted in part from inept prosecution. The Attorney General had furnished evidence only on the sugar trust's purchase of sugar refineries in Philadelphia. Had the government introduced evidence on the extent to which the trust controlled the transportation and sale of sugar throughout the country a different decision might have resulted. Four years after this the Court, on similar evidence, supported the government in its suit against the cast-iron pipe trust. Addyston Pipe and Steel Co. *v*. United States. See Walker, *History of the Sherman Law*, pp. 90–98.

14. 156 U.S. 1, 12, 13 (1895).

15. S. 3445. 19 *Cong. Rec.*, pt. 8, p. 7513 (1888). The bill was introduced on Aug. 14, 1888.

16. 20 *Cong. Rec.*, pt. 2, p. 1167.

17. *Ibid.,* p. 1457.
18. *Ibid.,* p. 1167.
19. *Ibid.,* p. 1169.
20. *Ibid.,* p. 1460.
21. He had been reporter of the Supreme Court of Mississippi between 1855 and 1863. In 1872 he had prepared a Digest of the Mississippi Reports which covered all of the decisions of the Mississippi high court through 1870. In 1879 he was appointed to the Mississippi Supreme Court and was immediately chosen Chief Justice by his associates on the bench. Article by Charles S. Sydnor, *Dictionary of American Biography,* VII, 216–217.
22. 20 *Cong. Rec.* pt. 2, p. 1460. He quoted Justice McLean in the License Cases 5 Howard 504, 588 (1847) and cited Railroad Co. *v.* Husen, 95 U.S. 465 (1878).
23. 20 *Cong. Rec.,* pt. 2, p. 1460.
24. The major part of the constitutional debate was on the Sherman bill and the Finance Committee substitute. The key section of the Sherman bill read as follows: "That all arrangements, contracts, agreements, trusts, or combinations between persons or corporations made with a view or which tend to prevent full and free competition in the importation, transportation or sale of articles imported into the United States, or in the production, manufacture, or sale of articles of domestic growth of production, or domestic raw material that competes with any similar article upon which a duty is levied by the United States, or which shall be transported from one State or Territory to another, and all arrangements, contracts, agreements, trusts or combinations between persons or corporations, designed or which tend to advance the cost to the consumer of any such articles, are hereby declared to be against public policy, unlawful and void." Walker, *History of the Sherman Law,* p. 3. The important section of the Finance Committee substitute, introduced on March 21 after George's objections of Feb. 27, read as follows: "That all arrangements, contracts, agreements, trusts, or combinations between two or more citizens or corporations, or both, of different States, or between two or more citizens or corporations, or both, of the United States and foreign states, or citizens or corporations thereof, made with a view or which tend to prevent full and free competition in the importation, transportation, or sale of articles imported into the United States, or with a view or which tend to prevent full and free competition in articles of growth, production or manufacture of any State or Territory of the United States with similar articles of the growth, production, or manufacture of any other State or Territory, or in the transportation or sale of like articles, the production of any State or Territory of the United States, into or within any other State or Territory of the United States; and all arrangements, trusts, or combinations between such citizens or corporations, made with a view or which tend to advance the cost to the consumer of any such articles, are hereby declared to be against public policy, unlawful and void." *Ibid.,* pp. 8–9.
25. 21 *Cong. Rec.,* pt. 2, p. 1768 (1890). Said George: "Mr. President, I now proceed to show that the bill is utterly unconstitutional. The task is an easy one, since the principles applicable to this examination have again and again been settled by the Supreme Court. I warn Senators now that no attempt will be made to show the bill unconstitutional upon that narrow and strict theory of State rights which they may suppose is entertained by the

Southern people and by them only. In all I shall say on this subject I shall plant my arguments on an exposition of the Constitution made by the tribunal which the Constitution itself appoints to perform that duty."

26. Brown *v.* Maryland, 12 Wheaton 419 (1827).

27. 21 *Cong. Rec.,* pt. 2, pp. 1765–1772 (1890).

28. *Ibid.,* pt. 3, p. 2465.

29. *Ibid.,* pp. 2607, 2730. This distinction was adopted by the Supreme Court in the cases of Standard Oil *v.* United States, 221 U.S. 1 (1911); and United States *v.* American Tobacco Co., 221 U.S. 106 (1911).

30. *Ibid.,* pp. 2467–2468.

31. *Ibid.,* p. 2460.

32. *Ibid.,* p. 2461.

33. *Ibid.,* pp. 2461–2462.

34. *Ibid.,* p. 2462.

35. *Ibid.,* p. 2558.

36. *Ibid.,* p. 2600.

37. *Ibid.,* p. 2607.

38. *Ibid.,* p. 2731. For comments on the rise of the Judiciary Committees, particularly in the House, see Lauros G. McConachie, *Congressional Committees* (New York, 1898), pp. 200, 213, and 254.

39. 21 *Cong. Rec.,* pt. 3, p. 2602.

40. *Ibid.,* p. 2606.

41. *Ibid.,* p. 2610.

42. *Ibid.,* p. 2604.

43. The committee members were: Republicans George Edmunds (Vt.), John Ingalls (Kans.), George Hoar (Mass.), James Wilson (Iowa), and William Evarts (N.Y.); and Democrats James Pugh (Ala.), Richard Coke (Texas), George Vest (Mo.), and James George (Miss.).

44. According to the best evidence available the new bill was written by several members of the Judiciary Committee. Albert H. Walker claims that Edmunds wrote all of sections 1, 2, 3, 5, and 6, except for seven words in sec. 1, which were authored by Evarts. Sec. 4 was the work of Senator George, sec. 7 of Senator Hoar, and sec. 8 of Senator Ingalls. See Joseph B. Foraker, *Notes of a Busy Life,* 2 vols. (Cincinnati: Stewart & Kidd, 1916), II, 164.

45. Walker, *History of the Sherman Law,* p. 35.

46. The principal section of the final bill read as follows: "Every contract, combination in the form of trust or otherwise, or conspiracy, in restraint of trade or commerce among the several States, or with foreign nations, is hereby declared to be illegal." *Ibid.,* p. 29.

47. 21 *Cong. Rec.,* pt. 4, p. 3148.

48. *Ibid.,* p. 3147.

49. *Ibid.,* pt. 5, p. 4101.

50. *Ibid.*

51. Thus, the Republicans voted 6–19 on the first motion and 10–22 on the second, a minimal increase for referral. Democrats, however, changed from a 9–9 tie on the first motion to a 21–6 lineup on the second.

52. The 19 Midwest Republicans voted 0–11 the first time and 2–13 the second. The 21 Southern Democrats, on the contrary, voted 4–5 the first time and 14–3 the second. Three of them shifted from "nay" to "yea" votes, the only Senators to reverse their positions.

419

53. There is substantial evidence that the constitutional question about the scope of the commerce power was treated as a bona fide question by Congress in this debate. Senator George's role is particularly convincing. For example, his arguments were so well thought of that they even had an effect on Senator Sherman, who said that George's questions about the bill had prompted him to make a full defense of the bill, both as to its effectiveness and as to its constitutionality. See 21 *Cong. Rec.,* pt. 3, p. 2456. Also, after 1890 George tried unsuccessfully to exempt agreements among workingmen from the operation of the antitrust law. Therefore, it is hard to believe that he offered his constitutional views merely as an apologist for the trusts. In addition, many other Senators acted as if the debate were genuinely constitutional.

Other evidence, however, suggests that the constitutional gambit of some Senators was only a shrewd political maneuver designed to produce a law more to their liking. The statements of Senators Pugh and Vance about the nature of the Judiciary Committee, cited above, are revealing. Furthermore, the Judiciary Committee, once it was awarded custody of the bill, made sweeping changes which were greater than those needed to meet the bulk of the constitutional objections. Dual federalism was stated by Southern Democrats as one general argument to link the destruction of trusts with low tariffs. Northern Republicans adopted this argument in order to make the bill less punitive. The later careers of the "high constitutionalists," Edmunds and George Hoar, Republican of Massachusetts, were noteworthy. Both spent a substantial amount of time after 1890 advising trusts on how to evade the provisions of the law which they, in large part, wrote. (See Josephson, *The Politicos,* p. 459; see also Foraker, *Notes of a Busy Life,* II, 345.) Finally, there is the unsettling fact that the Judiciary Committee had had the Reagan trust bill before it since August of 1888 and done nothing about it. See Winfield S. Kerr, *John Sherman,* 2 vols. (Boston: Sherman, French, 1908), II, 206. The committee acted only when it was in the political interests of its members to do so.

54. Of the 330 members of the House, 69 per cent had had legal training. Sixty-seven of the 82 Senators were lawyers. Of those 67 Senators, 40 were variously described by the *Biographical Directory* as having studied law, been admitted to the bar, been lawyers by profession, and so on; in other words, their legal education is obscure. Nine others had studied with specified individuals or, in two cases, law firms. Eighteen Senators had either attended or been graduated from law schools: thus, Vest had attended the law department of Transylvania University; Platt, the Litchfield Law School (later Yale); and Hoar the "Dane" Law School, Harvard. The dominance by lawyers in this debate may also have been a reflection of the growing power and influence of lawyers in the society in general. The formation of the American Bar Association in 1878 apparently was related to this improved status. See Benjamin Twiss, *Lawyers and the Constitution* (Princeton: Princeton University Press, 1942), chapter 7. Also see Edward S. Corwin, *Liberty against Government* (Baton Rouge: Louisiana State Press, 1948), pp. 137–138.

55. The ten were: Republicans Sherman (Ohio), Edmunds (Vt.), Platt (Conn.), Hoar (Mass.), and Hiscock (N.Y.); and Democrats George (Miss.), Vest (Mo.), Reagan (Texas), Pugh (Ala.), and David Turpie (Ind.).

56. The seven were: Republicans Sherman (Ohio), William Allison (Iowa), and Hiscock (N.Y.); and Democrats Daniel Voorhees (Ind.), James Beck (Ky.), Isham Harris (Tenn.), and Vance (N.C.). The non-lawyers were Republicans Justin Morrill (Vt.), chairman, John Jones (Nev.), and Nelson Aldrich (R.I.); and Democrat John McPherson (N.J.).

57. 21 *Cong. Rec.*, pt. 3, p. 2570. See also p. 2465.

58. *Ibid.*, p. 2604.

59. *Ibid.*, p. 2606.

60. *Ibid.*, p. 2608.

61. Thus, Sherman had spent 6 years in the House, 25 in the Senate, and 4 as Secretary of the Treasury. Edmunds had been in the Vermont legislature for 7 years and had served as Speaker there for 3. He had been in the Senate for 24 years. Platt had been the Speaker of the Connecticut House and had been in the Senate for 11 years. Hoar had spent 8 years in the House and 13 in the Senate. Hiscock had spent 12 years in the House and had come to the Senate in 1889. George had been a state supreme court justice and a Senator for 9 years. Vest had served in the Confederate Congress and had been in the Senate for 11 years. Reagan had spent 16 years in the House and had been Postmaster General of the Confederacy; he came to the Senate in 1887. Pugh had been in the House before the Civil War, spent 4 years in the Confederate Congress, and had been in the Senate for 10 years. Turpie had been a judge and Speaker of the Indiana House and had come to the Senate in 1887 after having served there briefly in 1863.

62. McConachie stated that at the second session of the 53rd Congress, the House committee presented more than 80 reports. McConachie, *Congressional Committees*, pp. 213-214.

63. 21 *Cong. Rec.*, pt. 4, pp. 3145-3153.

64. The income tax was included in the Wilson-Gorman Tariff Act adopted Aug. 27, 1894. 28 *Stat.* 509, 553. While the House Ways and Means Committee was framing a reduction in the tariff, a subcommittee under a chairman partial to the income tax, Benton McMillen, Tennessee Democrat, began work on a bill to levy such a tax and offset expected losses in customs receipts. The full committee reported out the tax bill as a rider to the tariff, and the House debated it for three days, beginning Jan. 29, 1894, and both rider and bill passed Feb. 1. It then went to the Senate Finance Committee which reported the rider intact. The Senate debated the income tax for six days, beginning June 21, and passed the rider June 28 and the entire bill July 3. It devoted most of the first two days to the constitutional question, whether the income tax was a direct tax, hence requiring apportionment by population among the states by the terms of Article I, sec. 9. Both houses held separate votes on the rider itself, the House passing it by 182-48 (122 absent) and the Senate by 40-24 (21 absent). Within a year the Supreme Court held the income tax unconstitutional. Pollock v. Farmers' Loan & Trust Company, 157 U.S. 429 and 158 U.S. 601 (1895).

All but one of the 22 leading speakers in the congressional debates were lawyers and the exception, Senator James Smith, Jr., New Jersey Democrat, deprecated his own inability to discuss constitutionality. 26 *Cong. Rec.*, pt. 4, p. 3783, (1894). Nine of the 11 members of Senate Judiciary were among the 17 Senators who led in discussion. Senate Finance and Senate Judiciary now had 11 members each; every region had representation on each, none more than 3 members. House committee representation was less fair, the South having 6 out of 17 members on the Judiciary and the Midwest 6 out of 17 on Ways and Means. Senate debate was more ample, more deliberate, better focused and informed, and less tinged with party rancor than House debate.

65. 21 *Cong. Rec.*, pt. 3, p. 2557.

66. *Ibid.*, p. 2608.

67. *Ibid.*, p. 2570.

68. *Ibid.*, p. 2608.

69. *Ibid.*, p. 2463.

70. *Ibid.*, p. 2600.

71. *Ibid.*, p. 2606.

72. In Springer *v.* United States, 102 U.S. 586 (1880), the Court upheld the Civil War income tax in consonance with earlier precedents. In general the Senators took the Springer precedent seriously but also went behind it to explore the principles involved. On June 26, Senator William Lindsay, Kentucky Democrat, opposed the explicit exemption of interest from state and local bonds from the coverage of the act. The courts, he said, would construe the act, minus such a list, as evincing an intent in Congress to tax only such incomes as could be constitutionally reached under the federal tax power. It was better to let the courts settle the question than, by attempting to enumerate, to fail to include the whole scope of the constitutional limitation and "put ourselves in the attitude of intending to do that which we have no constitutional power to do." 26 *Cong. Rec.*, pt. 7, p. 6814 (1894). Lindsay's confidence in the Court as final arbiter here was Marshallian. Senator George Gray, Delaware Democrat, had asserted that, in spite of the Springer case, it was the duty of federal legislators to respect the autonomy of the states; he doubted that congressional intent would have any effect on the Court if it came to pass on constitutionality. *Ibid.*, pp. 6815, 6817. Senator Donelson Caffery, Louisiana Democrat, agreed that the Senate was the place to settle this constitutional question: "Why embarrass the Supreme Court with a question which the Senate . . . can as well decide for itself here and now?" *Ibid.*, p. 6817. Senator George Hoar, Massachusetts Republican, was even more Jeffersonian. Failure by Congress to settle constitutional uncertainties by enumerating exemptions would leave it to individual tax collectors in the first instance, and the Supreme Court in the last, to decide on applications of the law. Congress, he said, would be "derelict in its duty" to "make a general phrase, and leave it to the courts hereafter to settle." Even though the Court on its part might affirm constitutionality, Congress was "bound to write in . . . all such constitutional limitations as may seem in our judgment, as constitutional lawyers, to be sound and to be requisite." The state of Kentucky, he said, was the "last place in this country" from which he expected to hear the suggestion that a Senator was bound to yield his opinion to the Court. *Ibid.*, p. 6817.

House advocates, on the contrary, tended to expect an unquestioning adherence to the Springer and other precedents. Representative Andrew J. Hunter, Illinois Democrat, said vaguely that the constitutionality of the income tax was so well settled by the courts that members could "with perfect security dismiss it from further consideration." 26 *Cong. Rec.*, pt. 9, appendix 1, p. 182. Omer M. Kem, Nebraska Populist, impatiently insisted that the Court had determined the issue unanimously in the Springer case, and he treated further discussion as pointless. *Ibid.*, p. 298. These Midwesterners, in expecting mechanical adherence to precedents, were hinting at judicial monopoly.

73. In 1888, the Court had upheld a state prohibition law and distinguished in its opinion between the manufacture of intoxicants, a matter subject to state police-power regulation, and interstate commerce, a matter subject to federal. Kidd v. Pearson, 128 U.S. 1, 20 (1888).

74. This was "An act divesting intoxicating liquors of their interstate character in certain cases"; it permitted states with prohibition laws to intercept shipments of liquor. In 1890, Congress, following the decision in Leisy v. Hardin, 135 U.S. 100 (1890), had passed the Wilson Act, permitting state control of liquor that came from outside the state and was sold within. That act was upheld in In re Rahrer, 140 U.S. 545 (1891), but was interpreted so as to prevent the state from exercising any control over the liquor until it had come to rest. The Webb-Kenyon Act, backed by dry forces, was designed to eliminate this final qualification on state power. Two narrow questions, both justiciable, were involved: 1. Could Congress divest liquor of its interstate character? and 2. Had Congress here made a constitutionally forbidden delegation of its power to the states?

75. Both houses sent the bill to their Judiciary Committees, composed in the Senate of 16 lawyers and in the House of 21 lawyers. Ten of the 11 most active participants in the constitutional floor debate in the Senate were lawyers, as were 13 of the 14 in the House. The 11 leading participants in the Senate debate had held public office for an average of 18 years (8 years in Congress and 10 years in state office); the 14 in the House debate, an average of 15 years (11 years in Congress and 4 years in state office).

76. See remarks of Senator William Kenyon, Iowa Republican. 49 *Cong. Rec.*, pt. 1, p. 707 (1912), Senator John Kern, Indiana Democrat, *ibid.*, pt. 5, p. 4298 (1913), and Representatives Henry Clayton, Alabama Democrat, *ibid.*, p. 4434, Richard Bartholdt, Missouri Republican, *ibid.*, p. 4444, Byron Harrison, Mississippi Democrat, *ibid.*, pt. 3, 2838 and Hubert Stephens, Mississippi Democrat, *ibid.*, pt. 5, 4443.

77. 49 *Cong. Rec.*, pt. 5, p. 4292 (1913).

78. *Ibid.*, p. 4442.

79. *Ibid.*, p. 4446. Note, however, that Lenroot himself believed the act constitutional. He warned that too great a preoccupation with constitutional doubts would have prevented approval of the Interstate Commerce Commission, the Sherman Act, and other necessary reforms, and in the future would prevent adaptation to "changing conditions in economic development." *Ibid.*, pp. 4445–4446.

80. Remarks of Senators George Sutherland, Utah Republican, 49 *Cong. Rec.*, pt. 3, p. 2911, John Thornton, Louisiana Democrat, *Ibid.*, p. 2912, and John Williams, Mississippi Democrat, *ibid.*, pt. 5, p. 4298; and Representatives Richard Bartholdt, Missouri Republican, *ibid.*, p. 4444, Swagar Sherley, Kentucky Democrat, *ibid.*, pt. 3, p. 2840, Augustus Stanley, Kentucky Democrat, *ibid.*, pt. 5, p. 4442, John Small, North Carolina Democrat, *ibid.*, pt. 3, p. 2833, and Byron Harrison, Mississippi Democrat, *ibid.*, p. 2838.

81. *Ibid.*, pt. 5, p. 4444.

82. *Ibid.*, p. 4442.

83. *Ibid.*, pt. 3, p. 2914.

84. Clark Distilling Company *v.* Western Maryland Railway Company, 242 U.S. 311, 325 (1917).

85. See Noel T. Dowling and F. Morse Hubbard, "Divesting an Article of Its Interstate Character," 5 *Minnesota Law Review* (1921), pp. 100, 130, 268.

CHAPTER 8. FEDERALISM IN CRISIS

1. Schechter Poultry Corp. *v.* United States, 295 U.S. 495 (1935).

2. Franklin D. Roosevelt, *Public Papers and Addresses,* comp. Samuel I. Rosenman, IV (New York: Random House, 1938), pp. 297–298. This letter also appears in 79 *Cong. Rec.,* pt. 12, p. 13499 (1935). The full text of the Roosevelt letter is as follows:

My dear Mr. Hill:

Your sub-committee of the Ways and Means has pending before it H.R. 8479, "A Bill to stabilize the bituminous coal mining industry and promote its interstate commerce," etc., and I understand that questions of the constitutionality of some of its provisions have arisen in the sub-committee.

This industry, from the standpoint of the operators and the miners, has had many years of difficulty. The product is a great natural resource entitled to the consideration of the Congress both as to the conditions under which it is produced and distributed and as to measures which may be taken for its conservation. The deposits are limited to a few States, the consumption is nation-wide. Competition and over expansion have brought destructive price reductions, which have inevitably reacted upon labor standards with a resulting dislocation, restriction and obstruction of interstate commerce and a recurring danger of industrial strife. Circumstances such as these present the strongest possible illustration of how conditions of production directly affect commerce among the States.

Admitting that mining coal, considered separately and apart from its distribution in the flow of interstate commerce, is an intra-state transaction, the constitutionality of the provisions based on the commerce clause of the Constitution depends upon the final conclusion as to whether production conditions directly affect, promote or obstruct interstate commerce in the commodity.

Manifestly, no one is in a position to give assurance that the proposed act will withstand constitutional tests, for the simple fact that you can get not ten but a thousand differing legal opinions on the subject. But the situation is so urgent and the benefits of the legislation so evident that all doubts should be resolved in favor of the bill, leaving to the courts, in an orderly fashion, the ultimate question of constitutionality. A decision by the Supreme Court relative to this measure would be helpful as indicating, with increasing clarity, the constitutional limits within which this Government must operate. The proposed bill has been carefully drafted by employers and employees working cooperatively. An opportunity should be given to the industry to attempt to work out some of its major problems. I hope your committee will not permit doubts as to constitutionality, however reasonable, to block the suggested legislation.

Very sincerely yours,
Franklin D. Roosevelt

The President's advice was somewhat unprecedented. Hitherto Presidents had asserted both their own constitutional responsibility and that of Congress. One of the strongest statements of the traditional position was President Taft's, quoted in part in the foregoing chapter.

3. Carter v. Carter Coal Co., 298 U.S. 238 (1936).

4. See generally: Record, vols. 1, 2, 3, Carter v. Carter Coal Co., 298 U.S. 238 (1936), and particularly the trial judge's findings at vol. 1, pp. 111–212; *Stabilization of the Bituminous Coal Mining Industry,* Hearings before Subcommittee of the Senate Committee on Interstate Commerce on H.R. 8479, 74th Cong., 1st sess. (1935), hereafter cited as Senate Hearings; *Stabilization of Bituminous Coal Mining Industry,* Hearings before Subcommittee of the House Committee on Ways and Means on H.R. 8479, 74th Cong., 1st sess. (1935), hereafter cited as House Hearings; S. Rept. 470, 74th Cong., 1st sess. (1935); H. Rept. 1800, 74th Cong., 1st sess. (1935); and Arthur M. Schlesinger, Jr., *The Coming of the New Deal* (Boston: Houghton Mifflin, 1959), p. 89.

5. House Hearings, p. 158.

6. Schlesinger, *Coming of the New Deal,* p. 118.

7. Record, vol. 3, p. 1003, Carter v. Carter Coal Co., 298 U.S. 238 (1936).

8. Schlesinger, *Coming of the New Deal,* p. 365.

9. *Ibid.,* p. 89.

10. Separate opinion of Chief Justice Hughes in Carter v. Carter Coal Co., 298 U.S. 238, 331.

11. Schlesinger, *Coming of the New Deal,* p. 140.

12. See Merle Fainsod, Lincoln Gordon, and Joseph C. Palamountain, *Government and the American Economy* (New York: Norton, 1959), pp. 621–638. See Arthur M. Schlesinger, Jr., *The Politics of Upheaval* (Boston: Houghton Mifflin, 1960), pp. 334–336.

13. See S. Rept. 470.

14. H. Rept. 1800.

15. Captive coal is coal produced by those who consume it. Steel companies and railroads, for example, were large producers of captive coal.

16. 49 *Stat.* 991, ch. 824 (1935).

17. 50 *Stat.* 72, ch. 127 (1937).

18. Sunshine Anthracite Coal Co. v. Adkins, 310 U.S. 381 (1940).

19. The Justice declared: "If the strategic character of this industry in our economy and the chaotic conditions which have prevailed in it do not justify legislation, it is difficult to imagine what would." *Ibid.,* p. 395.

20. Suits for injunction were entered in the two courts on Aug. 31 and Sept. 10, respectively. In the District of Columbia Court, 20 witnesses were heard, including producer and labor spokesmen, experts, and government officials. This testimony and the 200 exhibits ran to over 1,200 pages of record. The trial judge found 181 findings of facts, exceeding in detail those found by Congress. He found that prices, wages, rates, and other conditions of local production directly burdened or substantially affected interstate commerce. He declared the labor provisions invalid according to precedents. But the tax and other provisions were separable and these he upheld. He thus reviewed *de novo* the facts previously found by Congress. Record, vol. 3, pp. 1179–1199, Carter v. Carter Coal Co., 298 U.S. 238 (1936). The trial judge in Kentucky differed. Although he received much the same evi-

dence, he denied that it was the function of the Judiciary to go into the "factual field" to determine constitutionality in a proceeding directly attacking an act of Congress. This, he said, would amount to "a collateral attack upon the legislative inquiry, judgment, and declaration" in an area where Congress has superior avenues of information; such findings cannot be "impeached by the testimony of opinion witnesses." He declared: "Judges are usually occupied with matters specifically brought to their attention, and it could hardly be said they have the current knowledge of the movement of the commerce stream that the Congress of the United States has, and certainly the Courts have no power to make a widespread investigation of things that affect interstate commerce." He defined the judge's function thus: "The facts of which the Court may take judicial notice, and the ultimate facts as shown in the hearings before the Congress are some evidence of its declaration that the Bituminous Coal Industry as now conducted affects interstate commerce, and this being true, the Court is without power to substitute a judgment for that of Congress regardless of its opinion as to the wisdom of the legislation." Record, pp. 55–56, 70–71, R. C. Tway Coal Co. *v.* Glenn, 298 U.S. 238 (1936), considered as a companion case in Carter. These views of the Kentucky judge were similar to those expressed in Congress during discussion of the bill, see remarks of Representative Fred M. Vinson, House Hearings, p. 33.

21. Members of the subcommittee were Democrats Matthew M. Neely (W.Va.), chairman, Sherman Minton (Ind.), later a Supreme Court Justice, and A. Harry Moore (N.J.); and Republican James J. Davis (Pa.).

22. S. Rept. 470.

23. *Ibid.,* p. 1.

24. *Ibid.,* pp. 3–4.

25. Domestic coal is coal consumed in the same state in which it is mined.

26. Members of the subcommittee were Democrats Hill (Wash.), Thomas H. Cullen (N.Y.), Fred M. Vinson (Ky.), and Jere Cooper (Tenn.); and Republicans Allen T. Treadway (Mass.), Frank Crowther (N.Y.), and Roy O. Woodruff (Mich.). The full House Committee, unlike its Senate counterpart, gave extended consideration to the bill, and this consideration is reflected in the committee report. Other members of the full committee were Democrats Robert L. Doughton (N.C.), chairman, Christopher D. Sullivan (N.Y.), Morgan G. Sanders (Texas), John W. McCormack (Mass.), David J. Lewis (Md.), John W. Boehne, Jr. (Ind.), Claude A. Fuller (Ark.), Wesley E. Disney (Okla.), Arthur P. Lamneck (Ohio), Frank H. Buck (Cal.), Richard Duncan (Mo.), Chester Thompson (Ill.), J. Twing Brooks (Pa.), and John Dingell (Mich.); and Republicans Isaac Bacharach (N.J.), Harold Knutson (Minn.), Daniel Reed (N.Y.), and Thomas Jenkins (Ohio).

27. Of 40 witnesses, 21 represented coal operators and shippers, 3 represented related businesses, 6 were from the miners' unions, and 2 were from another union. The remainder were Representatives or private citizens.

28. H. Rept. 1800. This is a 61-page report and represents a whole range of views on the major issue. The majority report devotes 10 of its 19 pages to the "constitutional basis of legislation." Representative Lewis adds a 24-page statement broadly interpreting the general welfare clause of the Constitution. A three-page minority report, signed by Republicans Treadway, Bacharach, Crowther, Knutson, Reed, and Woodruff, argues against constitutionality. A larger minority report, filed by Democrat Cooper and con-

curred in by Democrats Sanders, Fuller, Lamneck, and Thompson, maintains that this bill is in direct conflict with the Schechter holding. Finally, Republican Knutson gives his own brief case for unconstitutionality.

29. They relied on the authority of Schechter, Heisler v. Thomas Colliery Co., 260 U.S. 245 (1922) and Oliver Iron Co. v. Lord, 262 U.S. 172 (1923). In Heisler the Court upheld a recent state tax on anthracite coal, applied when the coal was ready for market, on the ground that, even though the coal was shipped in interstate commerce, it was not yet in interstate commerce when the tax was applied. In Oliver Iron the Court upheld a state tax on the business of mining iron ore, although most of the ore was shipped in interstate commerce, on the grounds that mining was not interstate commerce but like manufacturing was a local business subject to local regulation and taxation, and that the tax affected interstate commerce only indirectly.

30. H. Rept. 1800, pp. 6, 8. The case of Norman v. Baltimore and Ohio Railroad Co., 294 U.S. 240 (1935), was frequently cited in Congress. Particularly applicable was the Court's statement: "The point is whether the gold clauses do constitute an actual interference with the monetary policy of Congress in the light of its broad power to determine that policy. Whether they may be deemed to be such an interference depends upon an appraisement of economic conditions and upon determination of questions of fact. With respect to those conditions and determinations, the Congress is entitled to its own judgment. We may inquire whether its action is arbitrary or capricious, that is, whether it has reasonable relation to a legitimate end. If it is an appropriate means to such an end, the decisions of the Congress as to the degree of necessity of the adoption of that means is final." *Ibid.*, p. 311.

31. H. Rept. 1800, pp. 1–3.

32. Chicago Board of Trade v. Olsen, 262 U.S. 1 (1923). A similar regulation was struck down in Hill v. Wallace, 259 U.S. 44 (1922). The Court in Olsen upheld regulation where it was clearly based on the commerce clause whereas in Hill it voided a regulation based on the taxing power.

33. Tagg Bros. v. United States, 280 U.S. 420 (1930); Stafford v. Wallace, 258 U.S. 495 (1922). See also Swift & Co. v. United States, 196 U.S. 375 (1905).

34. Coronado Co. v. United Mine Workers, 268 U.S. 295 (1925) reversed the decision in United Mine Workers v. Coronado Coal Co., 259 U.S. 345 (1922).

35. Bailey v. Drexel Furniture Co., 259 U.S. 20 (1922), in which the Court struck down a federal tax on production which made use of child labor. Hill v. Wallace, 259 U.S. 44 (1922).

36. Only the courts made the distinction between the power of Congress to regulate prices, on the one hand, and wages and hours, on the other. This distinction was mentioned in a general way in the House Hearings both in Warrum's testimony and in some of the briefs which were submitted. The committee reports and the floor debate indicate, however, that this distinction was little used as a basis for developing the constitutional arguments. Similarly, only the courts considered the constitutionality of the provision which made contractual agreements between two-thirds of the producers and half of the miners binding on all.

37. In this House vote of 194–168, 172 Democrats voted for the bill and 92, half of them Southerners, voted against it. Only 15 Republicans voted for the bill while 74 voted against it. Minor parties provided the remaining

votes: three Farmer-Laborites and four Progressives voting for the bill and two Progressives voting against it. The Senate vote of 45–37 for passage showed a similar pattern. The Democrats split, with 39 voting yea and 24, again half of them Southerners, voting nay. Only five Republicans voted for it while 12 voted against it. One Progressive was for the bill and the lone Farmer-Laborite voted nay.

38. Thus, New England voted nearly 4–1 against the bill and the South almost 4–3 against; the Midwest voted 6–5 for the bill, the Middle Atlantic States 5–3, the Border States and Far West 2–1. Kentucky split almost evenly in the final vote.

At least one member of the Ways and Means Committee evidently voted against the bill after having concurred in the majority report favoring passage. Since 11 of the 25 committee members signed minority reports, at least 12 of the remaining 14 must have approved the unsigned majority report. The 14 included 3 who voted against final passage, Democrats John W. McCormack (Mass.), Wesley E. Disney (Okla.), and Frank H. Buck (Calif.), at least one of whom thus reversed his position.

39. Lawyers numbered 68 of the 96 Senators; 14 of the 20 members of the full committee, 3 of the 4 of the subcommittee, and 8 of the 11 most active participants in the constitutional debate. Those last 11 were Democrats Matthew M. Neely (W. Va.), Burton K. Wheeler (Mont.), William H. Dieterich (Ill.), Alben W. Barkley (Ky.), Joseph F. Guffey (Pa.), Marvel M. Logan (Ky.), Millard E. Tydings (Md.), Royal S. Copeland (N.Y.), David I. Walsh (Mass.), and William H. King (Utah); and Republican James J. Davis (Pa.). Five of the 11 served on the Commerce Committee.

40. Lawyers numbered 257 of the 435 House members, 12 of the 25 members of the full committee, and 3 of the 7 members of the subcommittee. Fourteen of the 16 most active participants in the constitutional debate were lawyers. These 16 were Democrats Vinson (Ky.), Hill (Wash.), Cooper (Tenn.), Lewis (Md.), Adolph J. Sabath (Ill.), Mell G. Underwood (Ohio), D. J. Driscoll (Pa.), Maury Maverick (Texas), John R. Mitchell (Tenn.), and Walter M. Pierce (Ore.); and Republicans Treadway (Mass.), Knutson (Minn.), Reed (N.Y.), Carl E. Mapes (Mich.), Ralph E. Church (Ill.), and Charles A. Wolverton (N.J.). Treadway and Knutson were non-lawyers. Seven of the 16 were members of the Ways and Means Committee.

41. 79 *Cong. Rec.*, pt. 12, p. 13450 (1935). In his own minority statement filed with the committee report, he was happy to state that "eminent Counsel declare most confidently that it is unconstitutional . . ." (H. Rept. 1800, p. 59.) Treadway spoke of the measure being "recognized as unconstitutional by the great majority of able lawyers who have expressed themselves upon it." (79 *Cong. Rec.*, pt. 12, p. 13435.) He later challenged two of his opponents in these words: "The gentleman now interrupting me [Hill] and the other gentleman [Vinson] are able lawyers. They are trying to feed it to the House that this bill is constitutional. We know better and all lawyers know better." (*Ibid.*, p. 13546.)

42. 79 *Cong. Rec.*, pt. 12, p. 13433.

43. *Ibid.*, p. 13450.

44. *Ibid.*, p. 13490.

45. *Ibid.*, pt. 13, p. 13970.

46. The 16 leading House participants had served in Congress an average of 10 ½ years; 13 had held office in their states.

47. For details about hearings and other aspects of House committee work, see George Galloway, *History of the United States House of Representatives*, H. Doc. 246, 87th Cong., 1st sess. (1962), pp. 76–84.

48. House Hearings, pp. 49–50.

49. 79 *Cong. Rec.*, pt. 12, pp. 13458–13459.

50. 79 *Cong. Rec.*, pt. 5, p. 5647 (1935). After Guffey had introduced his bill in January it was given to the Committee on Interstate Commerce. This committee reported the bill favorably in April. Four days later, Marvel Logan, Kentucky Democrat and chairman of the Committee on Mines and Mining, moved to send the bill to his own committee. The Senate actually agreed to this motion and was ready to go on to other business when Burton Wheeler, Montana Democrat and chairman of the Interstate Commerce Committee, objected and pointed out that neither Guffey nor Matthew Neely, West Virginia Democrat and chairman of the subcommittee which had considered the bill, was present. Logan retorted that the bill should have been given to his committee in the first place. But the Senate reversed its decision and followed regular procedure thereafter until final passage of the bill.

51. Had the soft-coal bill gone to the 22-man House Mines Committee, it would have received consideration from members distributed as follows: Midwest—7, Middle Atlantic—5, Border—3, Far West—3, South—2, and New England—0. One seat was vacant and Alaska had a nonvoting seat.

52. In 1924, the Republican party had pledged measures to restore agriculture to equal standing with other industries. Senator Charles L. McNary of Oregon and Representative Gilbert N. Haugen of Iowa, Republican chairmen respectively of the Senate and House Agriculture Committees took the lead in pressing for action. Both committees held hearings and reported the bill; both houses conducted somewhat limited debates leading to early passage and veto. Although the process was repeated in 1928, at no time was a clear and searching confrontation made between the constitutional position of the farmer-oriented committees and those of the Administration. Note the makeup of the committees in the 69th Congress (1925–1927): Senate Agriculture and Forestry Committee (total 16): South—5, Midwest—5, Far West—3, Border—2, New England—1, Middle Atlantic—0; House Agriculture Committee (total 21): Midwest—12, South—3, Middle Atlantic—3, Border—3, New England—0, Far West—0.

The McNary-Haugen bill would have dealt with the surpluses of farm commodities through a Farm Board, with power to stabilize prices through contracts to control and dispose of those surpluses. The bill authorized the board to impose an "equalization fee" on production, transportation, or processing of the commodity to assist in fixing prices. The key constitutional question was whether Congress could enact such a fee under the commerce and other powers.

53. 79 *Cong. Rec.*, pt. 13, p. 13772.

54. *Ibid.*, p. 14080.

55. *Ibid.*, p. 14363, citing 49 *Cong. Rec.*, pt. 5, p. 4291 (1913).

56. 79 *Cong. Rec.*, pt. 12, p. 13435.

57. H. Rept. 1800, pp. 47–48.

58. The four spokesmen for the tripartite theory averaged 18 years of previous congressional experience ranging from Tydings' 12 years to Treadway's and King's 22 years. Average experience of the second group was 8

years; 2 Midwesterners averaged 20 years, Vinson from Kentucky had 8 years, Guffey and Wolverton from the Middle Atlantic averaged 4 years, Pierce of Oregon had 2 years, and Maverick was a new member.

59. 79 *Cong. Rec.*, pt. 10, p. 10818.

60. *Ibid.*, pt. 12, p. 13449.

61. *Ibid.*, p. 13475.

62. *Ibid.*, p. 13438.

63. *Ibid.*, p. 13545.

64. *Ibid.*, p. 13490.

65. *Ibid.*, p. 13516.

66. *Ibid.*, p. 13472.

67. Remarks of W. H. Sproul, 69 *Cong. Rec.*, pt. 7, p. 7463 (1928). See also remarks of Republican Representatives Thomas Hall (N.D.), 68 *Cong. Rec.*, pt. 2, p. 3389 (1927); Fred S. Purnell (Ind.), 69 *Cong. Rec.*, pt. 7, p. 7463; L. J. Dickinson (Iowa), *ibid.*, pt. 7, p. 7656, and the Missouri Democrat, Ralph F. Lozier, *ibid.*, pt. 7, p. 7583.

68. Remarks of C. G. Selvig, *ibid.*, pt. 7, p. 7291; see also remarks of Olger B. Burtness, North Dakota Republican, *ibid.*, pt. 7, pp. 7664–7665, and Senator Smith W. Brookhart, Iowa Republican, *ibid.*, pt. 8, p. 9875.

69. *Ibid.*, pt. 7, p. 7490.

70. Said he, "There is no question that is firmer in the minds of all lawyers than this, laid down by Judge Cooley and Judge Marshall, and all of them, that no man should vote for any bill in this House unless he believes beyond a reasonable doubt that it is a constitutional law . . . When we pass a law here and it goes to the Supreme Court, that court will not declare it unconstitutional unless beyond a reasonable doubt they believe it to be so. Why? Because they have the right, or used to have that right, to rely upon the fact that every Member of Congress who votes for a bill here has determined in his own mind after examination and study that beyond a doubt in his mind it is constitutional. Therefore, the court not only has the reliance of its own examination, but it can say, 'Here are 435 men in whom we have confidence, who, when they took the oath of office swore practically to the fact that they would vote for no law to pass this body until they had determined that it was a constitutional law . . .' This is a great body, but it is a great body because we are expected to discharge our duties . . ." *Ibid.*, pt. 7, p. 7586. See also remarks of Representative Percy E. Quin, Mississippi Democrat, 68 *Cong. Rec.*, pt. 4, p. 3701; and Charles H. Brand, Georgia Democrat, 69 *Cong. Rec.*, pt. 7, p. 7572. Representative Carl R. Chindblom, Illinois Republican, deplored the new attitude, saying the House and Senate were once "great forums for the discussion of constitutional questions" and regretted the absence of a serious discussion of constitutional issues on this occasion. Now, he said, "Members hesitate to discuss constitutional issues in the House because such debate is frowned upon and ridiculed by many of their colleagues." 68 *Cong. Rec.*, pt. 4, p. 3862. See also remarks of Senator Simeon D. Fess, Ohio Republican, 69 *Cong. Rec.*, pt. 6, p. 6091 (1928).

71. This opinion was expressed to me by a leading nonmember official of Congress who has served there for several decades. A similar observation appears in Roland Young, *The American Congress* (New York: Harper Bros., 1958), p. 97.

72. Nebbia *v.* New York, 291 U.S. 502 (1934); Norman *v.* Baltimore and Ohio Railroad Co., 294 U.S. 240 (1935); and Home Building and Loan

Association *v.* Blaisdell, 290 U.S. 398 (1934) comforted advocates. Opponents put forward Panama Refining Co. *v.* Ryan, 293 U.S. 388 (1935); Railroad Retirement Board *v.* Alton Railroad Co., 295 U.S. 330 (1935); and Schechter Poultry Corp. *v.* United States, 295 U.S. 495 (1935).

73. See for example National Labor Relations Board *v.* Jones & Laughlin Steel Corporation, 301 U.S. 1 (1937), Mulford *v.* Smith, 307 U.S. 38 (1939), United States *v.* Darby, 312 U.S. 100 (1941), and Wickard *v.* Filburn, 317 U.S. 111 (1942); Helvering *v.* Davis, 301 U.S. 619 (1937), and Steward Machine Co. *v.* Davis, 301 U.S. 548 (1937); Ashwander *v.* Tennessee Valley Authority, 297 U.S. 288 (1936), Korematsu *v.* United States, 323 U.S. 214 (1944).

74. An example of the problem of federal pre-emption of power—a problem of increasing concern in the 1950's—is represented by section 14C of the Taft-Hartley Act of 1947. 61 *Stat.* 160.

CHAPTER 9. SEPARATION OF POWERS IN THE ADMINISTRATIVE STATE

1. President's Committee on Administrative Management, *Report with Special Studies* (Washington: G. P. O., 1937).
2. 40 *Stat.* 556–557.
3. John D. Millett and Lindsay Rogers, "The Legislative Veto and the Reorganization Act of 1939," 1 *Public Administration Review* (1941), pp. 176, 178.
4. 47 *Stat.* 382.
5. Millett and Rogers, "The Legislative Veto," p. 178.
6. 37 Ops. Atty. Gen. 63–64 (1933).
7. 47 *Stat.* 1489.
8. Robert W. Ginnane, "The Control of Federal Administration by Congressional Resolutions and Committees," 66 *Harvard Law Review* (1953), pp. 569, 577.
9. 81 *Cong. Rec.,* pt. 1, p. 188 (1937).
10. 59 *Stat.* 613 (1945); 63 *Stat.* 205 (1949).
11. 54 *Stat.* 4 (1940); 54 *Stat.* 672 (1940); 55 *Stat.* 32 (1941); 55 *Stat.* 841 (1941); 56 *Stat.* 187 (1942); 56 *Stat.* 24 (1942).
12. See 91 *Cong. Rec.,* pt. 7, p. 9345 (1945). For a discussion of remaining constitutional issues see Joseph and Ann Cooper, "The Legislative Veto and the Constitution," 30 *George Washington Law Review* (March 1962), pp. 467–516.
13. S. Rept. 232, 81st Cong., 1st sess. (1949), pp. 19–20.
14. See Ginnane, "Control of Federal Administration," pp. 605–608; Joseph Cooper, "The Legislative Veto: Its Promise and Its Perils," 7 *Public Policy* (1956), pp. 128, 132–138; Arthur Krock, in *New York Times,* July 15, 1955, p. 20.
15. There were three other constitutional questions of lesser importance. These were: 1. Does the congressional power to appropriate funds include the power to control the expenditure by means of a pre-audit? 2. Does the removal power of the President extend to the proposed Civil Service Administrator? 3. May one Congress make laws controlling the procedure and rules of later Congresses? These questions will not be treated here.
16. This practice was defended by the Senate Committee on the Judiciary in a special report on the subject in 1897: ". . . we hold that the clause in

the Constitution which declares that every order, resolution, or vote must be presented to the President, to 'which the concurrence of the Senate and House of Representatives may be necessary,' refers to the necessity occasioned by the requirement of the other provisions of the Constitution, whereby every exercise of 'legislative powers' involves the concurrence of the two Houses; and every resolution not so requiring such concurrent action, to wit, not involving the exercise of legislative powers need not be presented to the President. In brief, the nature or substance of the resolution, and not its form, controls the question of its disposition." S. Rept. 1335, 54th Cong., 2nd sess. (1897), p. 8.

17. See W. Ivor Jennings, *Parliament* (Cambridge, Eng.: Cambridge University Press, 1957), pp. 479–516. As early as 1932, the Donoughmore Committee recommended a uniform pattern for Parliamentary control of this nature. Such uniform control was finally established by law in 1945 and 1946. I am indebted to Professor Gerhard Loewenberg for calling the British experience to my attention.

18. Panama Refining Co. *v.* Ryan, 293 U.S. 388 (1935); Schechter Poultry Corp. *v.* United States, 295 U.S. 495 (1935); Carter *v.* Carter Coal Co., 298 U.S. 238 (1936).

19. Isbrandtsen-Moller Co. *v.* United States, 14 F. Supp. 495 (S.D.N.Y., 1936); Swayne and Hoyt, Ltd. *v.* United States, 10 Am. Mar. Cas. 1790 (S. Ct. D. C., 1936). (The Shipping Board cases.)

20. See, for example, the statement of Senator Abe Murdock, Utah Democrat, during debate on the Reorganization Act of 1945. Murdock said: "One of the most important questions the committee had to decide was whether to require the approval of both Houses of the Congress in order to permit a reorganization plan to go into effect. This decision involved consideration of a constitutional question, and the committee felt its responsibility most keenly. The responsibility was particularly great because of the expectation that the Supreme Court probably would refuse to pass upon the constitutionality of any reorganization act approved by the Congress, on grounds that it is a political question and not properly subject to court review." 91 *Cong. Rec.,* pt. 8, p. 10269 (1945).

21. The members of this Joint Committee were the members of the Select Committees of the two houses. The members of the original Senate Select Committee were Democrats Joseph Robinson (Ark.), chairman, James Byrnes (S.C.), Harry Byrd (Va.), Joseph O'Mahoney (Wyo.), Alben Barkley (Ky.), and Pat Harrison (Miss.); Republicans Charles McNary (Ore.) and John Townsend (Dela.); and Robert LaFollette, Jr. (Wis.), Progressive. When Robinson died in July 1937, Byrnes became chairman and Fred Brown, New Hampshire Democrat, was added to the committee. Brown was defeated in the 1938 elections and Scott Lucas, Illinois Democrat, took his place on the committee in 1939.

The members of the original House Select Committee were Democrats James Buchanan (Texas), chairman, John Cochran (Mo.), Lindsay Warren (N.C.), Fred Vinson (Ky.), J. W. Robinson (Utah), James Mead (N.Y.), and Frank Kniffin (Ohio); and Republicans John Taber (N.Y.) and Charles Gifford (Mass.). When Buchanan died in February of 1937, Cochran assumed the chairmanship and the vacancy was filled by Harry Beam, Illinois Democrat. After the 1938 elections, Vinson, Mead, and Kniffin did not return to Congress. They were replaced by E. E. Cox, Georgia

Democrat, William Schulte, Indiana Democrat, and Everett Dirksen, Illinois Republican.

22. See *Reorganization of the Executive Departments,* Hearings before the Joint Committee on Government Organization, 75th Cong., 1st sess. (1937); hereafter cited as Joint Hearings. The witnesses were Louis Brownlow, Luther Gulick, and Charles Merriam, committee members; A. E. Buck and C. M. Hester, committee consultants; and Lewis Meriam and Daniel Selko of the Brookings Institution.

23. Gulick relied on Isbrandtsen-Moller *v.* United States because in that case the District Court held that by appropriating money for the work of the Shipping Board in the Department of Commerce after the transfer of that board by executive order the Congress had, in effect, approved the transfer.

24. Joint Hearings, p. 94.

25. *Ibid.,* p. 171.

26. *Reorganization of the Government Agencies,* Hearings before Select Committee on Government Organization, U. S. Senate, on S. 2700, 75th Cong., 1st sess. (1937); hereafter cited as Senate Hearings. The range of witnesses at these hearings was wider than at the Joint Hearings, but this did not provide a broader discussion of the constitutional issues. In addition to 20 members of the Administration and affected governmental agencies and the experts from the Brownlow Committee and the Brookings Institution, the committee took testimony from outsiders interested in the bill, including four representatives of the lumbering industry, an official of the Grange, two representatives of the American Medical Association, and seven representatives of various transportation interests.

27. Senate Hearings, p. 8.

28. 81 *Cong. Rec.,* pt. 8, p. 8855 (1937), evidently quoted from a 1932 report by President Hoover.

29. 82 *Cong. Rec.,* pt. 1, p. 35 (1937).

30. Field *v.* Clark, 143 U.S. 649 (1892); Buttfield *v.* Stranahan, 192 U.S. 470 (1904); United States *v.* Grimaud, 220 U.S. 506 (1911); Hampton and Co. *v.* United States, 276 U.S. 394 (1928); Radio Commission *v.* Nelson Bros. Co., 289 U.S. 266 (1933); Panama Refining Co. *v.* Ryan, 293 U.S. 388 (1935); Schechter Poultry Corp. *v.* United States, 295 U.S. 495 (1935).

31. 83 *Cong. Rec.,* pt. 3, p. 2746 (1938).

32. *Ibid.,* p. 2748.

33. *Ibid.,* p. 3025. Wheeler was a lawyer and had served as a federal district attorney for five years.

34. *Ibid.,* pp. 2740–2741.

35. *Ibid.,* p. 3034.

36. *Ibid.,* pp. 3248–3250.

37. *Ibid.,* pt. 4, p. 4487.

38. This was a nation-wide Sunday afternoon broadcast, and next day members of the House received thousands of protest telegrams. *New York Times,* April 4, 1938, pp. 1, 8. By the end of the week, the *Times* reported that an unprecedented number of telegrams had been sent to Congress. *Ibid.,* April 10, 1938, p. 2.

39. 83 *Cong. Rec.,* pt. 5, p. 5005.

40. Humphrey's Executor (Rathbun) *v.* United States, 295 U.S. 602 (1935); Morgan *v.* United States, 298 U.S. 468 (1936).

41. 83 *Cong. Rec.*, pt. 5, p. 5006.

42. *Ibid.*, pp. 5006–5007.

43. *Ibid.*, pp. 5118–5119.

44. 84 *Cong. Rec.*, pt. 2, p. 2305 (1939).

45. *Ibid.*, pt. 3, p. 2377.

46. Currin *v.* Wallace, 306 U.S. 1 (1939).

47. 84 *Cong. Rec.*, pt. 3, p. 2961.

48. *Ibid.*, p. 3087.

49. For example, certain arguments were raised, seemingly forgotten, and then resurrected to be treated as if fresh material. As late as the 1939 Senate debate, Senator Wheeler declared that the opinion of Attorney General Mitchell on the legislative veto "was called to my attention only today . . ." (84 *Cong. Rec.*, pt. 3, p. 2964.) He then proceeded to explain that opinion as if it had never appeared in debate.

50. Party loyalty was particularly strong among the Republicans. With insignificant exceptions, the Republicans voted as a unit in opposing the bill in all phases. In the 1937 Senate vote on the bill, 14 Republicans voted against it and none for it. In the vote on the Wheeler amendment, 22 Republicans were for it and none against. In the vote on final passage in 1939, 19 Republicans were against it and only 2, Robert A. Taft of Ohio and Clyde Reed of Kansas, both newcomers to Congress, were for it. The Democrats tended to break into opposing groups. Most of those Senators and Representatives who defied FDR's wishes were not Southern conservatives but on most issues enthusiastic New Dealers. Indeed, it was Southerners like Byrnes and Cox who were the strongest Administration supporters during this struggle. When the Senate passed the bill in 1937, 26 Democrats out of the 74 Democrats voting opposed it. Twenty Democrats supported the Wheeler amendment. In the final vote on the bill, 58 Democrats voted for it and only 3 (King of Utah, Millard Tydings of Maryland, and Peter Gerry of Rhode Island) voted against it. In the House, even on the initial passage of the bill in 1937, 28 Democrats broke with the Administration. On the 1938 motion to recommit the bill, the Democrats split 108 for recommittal and 193 against. By the time the Sumners amendment was rejected only 35 Democratic Representatives voted against the Administration position and only 6 House Democrats voted against the final version of the bill in 1939.

51. Forty-one of the 47 Representatives were Democrats, 5 were Republicans, and 1 was a Progressive. Altogether 85 Representatives (63 Democrats, 17 Republicans, 4 Progressives, and 1 Farmer-Laborite) voted for the first bill and then voted for recommittal in the spring of 1938. Seventy-four Representatives (65 Democrats, 7 Republicans, and 2 Progressives) voted for recommittal and then voted for the 1939 bill. Fifteen of the 16 Senators were Democrats and the other a Farmer-Laborite. Only 4 of the Senators were Southerners and this group which initially opposed the President's requests included such staunch New Dealers as Wagner (N.Y.), Homer Bone (Wash.), Francis Maloney (Conn.), and Prentiss Brown (Mich.).

52. In the 75th Congress, 84 per cent of the 25 leading Senate participants were lawyers. 78 per cent (7 of 9) of the members of the Senate Select Committee were lawyers. In the House, 80 per cent of the 25 leading participants and 78 per cent (7 of 9) of the Select Committee members were lawyers.

53. 83 *Cong. Rec.*, pt. 5, p. 5010 (1938); *ibid.*, p. 5009; 84 *Cong. Rec.*, pt. 3, p. 3034 (1939).

54. George B. Galloway, *The Legislative Process in Congress* (New York: Thomas Y. Crowell, 1953), pp. 407–409.

55. From information contained in a letter from Dr. Hugh L. Elsbree, Director, Legislative Reference Service, dated April 21, 1959. Dr. Elsbree noted that, at the time of appointment, most of these attorneys were recent law school graduates; many had backgrounds in political science and several in economics and other social sciences.

56. See Frederic P. Lee, "The Office of the Legislative Counsel," 29 *Columbia Law Review* (1929), p. 381; Harry W. Jones, "Bill-drafting Services in Congress and the State Legislatures," 65 *Harvard Law Review* (1952), p. 441. In 1958, each branch employed 11 counsel. Interviews with Allan H. Perley, House OLC, and Charles F. Boots and Dwight J. Pinion, Senate OLC, Dec. 17, 18, 1958.

57. Thus, the members of the House Select Committee as originally appointed had each served an average of 15 years in Congress. The members of the original Senate Committee had served in the Senate an average of 11½ years.

58. Each house established its own Select Committee by resolution. Each house also passed a Joint Resolution providing for the two Select Committees to meet jointly. The Joint Committee itself could only investigate, since it could not introduce legislation into either house. Furthermore, votes in a joint committee are taken with the delegation of each house having one vote, instead of each member having one vote. But each house looked to its own Select Committee to draft legislation, and, in the House, any such legislation would have privileged status and would automatically bypass the Rules Committee.

59. Representative John O'Conner, New York Democrat and chairman of the Rules Committee, made this point but was challenged by minority leader, Bertrand Snell, New York Republican, who said that the Committee on Expenditures in the Executive Departments should have the bill. The chairman and ranking minority member of this committee were picked for duty on the Select Committee.

60. H. Rept. 1487, 75th Cong., 1st sess. (Aug. 10, 1937); H. Rept. 2033, 75th Cong., 3rd sess. (March 30, 1938); H. Rept. 120, 76th Cong., 1st sess. (March 3, 1939); S. Rept. 169, 76th Cong., 1st sess. (March 14, 1939).

61. The committee minority in both houses in both 1938 and 1939 complained about the lack of hearings in those years. See, for example, H. Rept. 120, 76th Cong., 1st sess. (March 3, 1939), p. 9.

62. 83 *Cong. Rec.*, pt. 4, p. 4576 (1938).

63. *Ibid.*, pt. 3, p. 2741.

64. 84 *Cong. Rec.*, pt. 3, p. 3043 (1939). Senator Brown's reference to Evans v. Gore, 253 U.S. 245 (1920), was not quite accurate. But the majority in that case, speaking through Mr. Justice Van Devanter, did have something to say which seemed to verge on the judicial monopoly theory. The case dealt with the application of federal income taxes to the salaries of federal judges. Van Devanter said in the course of his opinion, "Moreover, it appears that, when this taxing provision was adopted, Congress regarded it as of uncertain constitutionality and both contemplated and intended that the question should be settled by us in a case like this." He then approvingly quoted, in a footnote, a statement made by the chairman of the House committee which had reported the income tax bill without an exemption for judicial salaries. This Representative said: "I wish to say, Mr. Chair-

man, that while there is considerable doubt as to the constitutionality of taxing . . . federal judges' or the President's salaries, . . . we cannot settle it; we have not the power to settle it. No power in the world can settle it except the Supreme Court of the United States. Let us raise it, as we have done, and let it be tested, and it can only be done by some one protesting his tax and taking an appeal to the Supreme Court." 253 U.S. 245, 248. Note that the Court too labored under doubts which were finally resolved in 1939. O'Malley v. Woodrough, 307 U.S. 277 (1939).

65. 83 *Cong. Rec.,* pt. 4, pp. 4190–4191.

66. Note that Congress long remained ignorant of the British experience. After 1939 the forms of the legislative veto proliferated: there were one-house, two-house, and committee vetoes exercised both positively and negatively. The British, on the other hand, adopted a uniform procedure in the Acts of 1945 and 1946. Jennings, *Parliament,* pp. 504, 516.

67. See Cooper and Cooper, "The Legislative Veto and the Constitution," p. 470, n. 11.

CHAPTER 10. SEPARATION OF POWERS IN THE COLD WAR

1. See above, chapter 2.

2. For the text of the Eisenhower speech asking for this power, see 103 *Cong. Rec.,* pt. 1, pp. 224–227 (1957).

3. *Ibid.,* pt. 2, p. 2232. (Italics supplied.)

4. See, for example, the remarks of Senator Wayne Morse, Oregon Democrat, 104 *Cong. Rec.,* pt. 15, pp. 19563–19564 (1958).

5. The economic provisions also raised questions—for example: Was it constitutional for Congress to give the President a $200 million appropriation for economic aid to be used at his discretion? What limits should Congress place on the exercise of this discretion?

6. *The Constitution of the United States of America: Analysis and Interpretation,* prepared by the Legislative Reference Service, Library of Congress, ed. Edward S. Corwin (1953), p. 547. United States v. Curtiss-Wright Export Corp., 299 U.S. 304 (1936). In 1948 the Court declared: "The President, both as Commander-in-Chief and as the Nation's organ for foreign affairs, has available intelligence services whose reports are not and ought not to be published to the world . . . Even if courts could require full disclosure, the very nature of executive decisions as to foreign policy is political, not judicial. Such decisions are wholly confided by our Constitution to the political departments of the government, Executive and Legislative. They are delicate, complex, and involve large elements of prophecy. They are and should be undertaken only by those directly responsible to the people whose welfare they advance or imperil." Justice Jackson, for the Court, in Chicago & Southern Airlines v. Waterman Steamship Corp., 333 U.S. 103, 111 (1948).

7. *Economic and Military Cooperation with Nations in the General Area of the Middle East,* Hearings before Committee on Foreign Affairs, House of Representatives, on H. J. Res. 117, 85th Cong., 1st sess. (1957); hereafter cited as House Hearings.

8. The 32 members of this committee were Democrats Thomas S. Gordon (Ill.), chairman, Thomas E. Morgan (Pa.), A. S. J. Carnahan (Mo.), Clement J. Zablocki (Wis.), Omar Burleson (Texas), Brooks Hays (Ark.),

Edna F. Kelly (N.Y.), Wayne L. Hays (Ohio), Robert C. Byrd (W. Va.), Armistead I. Selden (Ala.), John L. Pilcher (Ga.), Barratt O'Hara (Ill.), L. H. Fountain (N.C.), Dante Fascell (Fla.), Frank Coffin (Me.), Leonard Farbstein (N.Y.), and D. S. Saund (Calif.); and Republicans Robert B. Chiperfield (Ill.), John M. Vorys (Ohio), Frances P. Bolton (Ohio), Lawrence H. Smith (Wis.), Chester E. Merrow (N.H.), Walter H. Judd (Minn.), James C. Fulton (Pa.), Donald L. Jackson (Calif.), Karl M. LeCompte (Iowa), Edmund P. Radwan (N.Y.), Albert P. Morano (Conn.), Marguerite S. Church (Ill.), E. Ross Adair (Ind.), Winston L. Prouty (Vt.), and Alvin M. Bentley (Mich.).

9. House Hearings, pp. 5–6.

10. *Ibid.*, p. 291.

11. *Ibid.*, p. 148.

12. *Ibid.*, p. 308.

13. *Ibid.*, p. 47.

14. *Ibid.*, p. 323.

15. *Ibid.*, p. 25

16. *Ibid.*, p. 51.

17. H. Rept. 2, 85th Cong., 1st sess. (1957), p. 7.

18. 103 *Cong. Rec.*, pt. 1, p. 1190 (1957).

19. *Ibid.*, p. 1202.

20. *Ibid.*, p. 1319. The reference was to the unsuccessful proposal of Senator John W. Bricker, Ohio Republican.

21. *Ibid.*, p. 1214.

22. *Ibid.*, p. 1152.

23. *Ibid.*, pp. 1192–1193.

24. *Ibid.*, p. 1150.

25. *The President's Proposal on the Middle East,* Hearings before the Committee on Foreign Relations and the Committee on Armed Services, United States Senate, on S. J. Res. 19 and H. J. Res. 117, 85th Cong., 1st sess. (1957); hereafter cited as Senate Hearings.

26. The 15 members of the Foreign Relations Committee were Democrats Theodore F. Green (R.I.), chairman, J. W. Fulbright (Ark.), John S. Sparkman (Ala.), Hubert H. Humphrey (Minn.), Mike Mansfield (Mont.), Wayne Morse (Ore.), Russell Long (La.), and John F. Kennedy (Mass.); and Republicans Alexander Wiley (Wis.), H. Alexander Smith (N.J.), Bourke B. Hickenlooper (Iowa), William Langer (N.D.), William F. Knowland (Calif.), George D. Aiken (Vt.), and Homer E. Capehart (Ind.). The 15 members of the Armed Services Committee were Democrats Richard B. Russell (Ga.), chairman, Harry F. Byrd (Va.), Lyndon B. Johnson (Texas), Estes Kefauver (Tenn.), John Stennis (Miss.), Stuart Symington (Mo.), Henry M. Jackson (Wash.), and Sam J. Ervin, Jr. (N.C.); and Republicans Leverett Saltonstall (Mass.), Styles Bridges (N.H.), Ralph E. Flanders (Vt.), Margaret Chase Smith (Me.), Francis Case (S.D.), Prescott Bush (Conn.), and Frank Barrett (Wyo.).

27. Senate Hearings, pt. 1, p. 234.

28. *Ibid.*, p. 27.

29. *Ibid.*, p. 251.

30. *Ibid.*, pt. 2, pp. 861, 867.

31. *Ibid.*, pt. 1, p. 326.

32. *Ibid.*, pt. 2, p. 722.

33. S. Rept. 70, 85th Cong., 1st sess. (1957), p. 9.

34. 103 *Cong. Rec.*, pt. 2, p. 2314 (1957).

35. *Ibid.*, p. 2232.

36. *Ibid.*, pt. 3, p. 2990.

37. *Ibid.*, pt. 2, p. 2693.

38. *Ibid.*, p. 2530.

39. *Ibid.*, p. 2400.

40. *Ibid.*, p. 2232.

41. The House roll calls revealed splits in both parties. In the vote on January 30 to pass the resolution, the Democrats favored the resolution by 188–35, and the Republicans by 167–26. In the final vote on March 7, Democrats supported it by 186–33, and Republicans by 164–27. The one roll call in the House showing any substantial divergence by party was on the adoption of a closed rule for debate, January 29; Republicans supported the rule by 144–51, but the Democrats, expressing their resentment, supported it by only 118–95. House Committee votes were almost unanimous. For example, in the vote to report the resolution, only two dissented, Mrs. Marguerite Church of Illinois and Lawrence Smith of Wisconsin, both Republicans.

From the outset, party was more important in the Senate. The Humphrey-Mansfield amendment was adopted in committee by a straight party-line vote of 15 Democrats against 13 Republicans. When the committee voted to report the resolution favorably, 8 Democrats were the only dissenters. On the floor, only two roll calls produced a bipartisan vote. One was the unanimous adoption of Senator O'Mahoney's amendment; the other, a rejection of Curtis' amendment to have the resolution expire almost simultaneously with the end of Eisenhower's term. Democrats voted against this by 30–13, and Republicans by 28–17. The other roll calls showed strong party unity, especially among Republicans. On the roll call approving an amendment calling on the President to support the United Nations Emergency Force in the Middle East, all 46 voting Democrats cast favorable votes; only two Republicans joined them, while 43 other Republicans voted Nay. In rejecting Senator Morse's restrictive amendment, Democrats voted 24 in favor, and 23 against; Republicans, 4 in favor, 41 against. In the March 5 roll call on final passage, Democrats favored it by 30–16, Republicans by 42–3.

42. *Ibid.*, p. 2492.

43. In the House, only 44 per cent of the members of the Foreign Affairs Committee (14 of 32) were lawyers, and only 60 per cent of the leading participants in the debate (15 of 25) were lawyers. In the Senate only 53 per cent (16 of 30) of the combined Committees on Foreign Relations and Armed Services were lawyers and only 67 per cent (8 of 12) of the leading participants in the constitutional debate were lawyers.

44. See, for example, House Hearings, p. 51; remarks of Senators Mansfield and Capehart, Senate Hearings, pt. 2, pp. 881, 899.

45. 103 *Cong. Rec.*, pt. 1, p. 1166 (1957).

46. *Ibid.*, pt. 2, p. 2672.

47. In January 1959, members responding to the author's questionnaire commented on sources of constitutional advice regularly used; 72 per cent of the 32 Senators responding checked "members of own staff, including legal counsel" as such a source, the highest percentage for any of the sources listed. Of responding Representatives, 25 per cent checked it.

48. *Ibid.*, pt. 3, p. 2883; *ibid.*, pt. 2, p. 2544.

49. It was not until the close of the second day of hearings that all the new members were selected. The last chosen, D. S. Saund, California Democrat, did not report until near the close of the fourth session of the committee.

50. George B. Galloway, *The Legislative Process in Congress* (New York: Thomas Y. Crowell, 1953), p. 594.

51. Foreign relations is an area in which the Senate has specific functions not accorded the House and in which the Senators think of themselves as especially competent and responsible. The Senate Foreign Relations Committee has always had the highest prestige in the Senate whereas the House Foreign Affairs Committee, according to one expert, is "far down the line in prestige and popularity on the floor . . ." Appropriations, Ways and Means, Agriculture, and Armed Services rank well above Foreign Affairs. Even Banking and Currency, Judiciary, and Interstate and Foreign Commerce have been ranked higher. Holbert N. Carroll, *The House of Representatives and Foreign Affairs* (Pittsburgh: University of Pittsburgh Press, 1958), pp. 274–275.

52. Senate Hearings, pt. 1, p. 102.

53. House Hearings, p. 200.

54. 103 *Cong. Rec.*, pt. 2, p. 2233 (1957).

55. Representative Wayne Hays, Ohio Democrat and House Committee member, left a meeting of his committee declaring, ". . . I am not going to be here, because I do not believe in hiding this thing behind closed doors." House Hearings, p. 55.

56. For example, see the statements of Representative Ross Bass, Tennessee Democrat, 103 *Cong. Rec.*, pt. 1, p. 1313, and Senator William Jenner, Indiana Republican, *ibid.*, pt. 2, p. 2528.

57. These two were Mrs. Church, 103 *Cong. Rec.*, pt. 1, p. 1183, and Bruce Alger, Texas Republican, *ibid.*, p. 1314.

58. Senate Hearings, pt. 1, p. 192. For similar statements, see the comments of Senators Morse, *ibid.*, pp. 300–301, Fulbright, *ibid.*, pt. 2, p. 787, and Jenner, 103 *Cong. Rec.*, pt. 2, p. 2528.

59. *Ibid.*, pp. 2232–2233.

60. *Ibid.*, pt. 3, p. 2927.

61. Senate Hearings, pt. 2, p. 887.

62. 103 *Cong. Rec.*, pt. 1, p. 1204. See also the statement of Representative Carnahan (Mo.), *ibid.*, p. 1205.

63. *Ibid.*, pt. 2, p. 2683.

64. Senate Hearings, pt. 2, pp. 884–885. For the full dialogue, see pp. 884–898.

CHAPTER 11. AMENDMENT BY DEFAULT

1. See above, chapter 2.

2. The *Times* stated that this proposal stood at the top of the Republican program as announced by Speaker Joseph W. Martin, Massachusetts Republican. See *New York Times*, Feb. 5, 1947, p. 1.

3. The House defeated the Dirksen proposal for a single six-year term, this time submitted by Representative Emanuel Celler of New York; Representative William Colmer, Mississippi Democrat, proposed convention ratification, but a division vote of 134–74 defeated it. The Senate, on March 10, defeated the proposal for convention ratification by a vote of 63–20. It killed Senator Magnuson's proposal by 50–34, another proposal, providing for two

terms, coupled with direct nomination and election, and still another for single six-year terms for all elected federal officials.

4. *New York Times,* April 1, 1947, p. 23.

5. *Ibid.,* Jan. 27, 1951, p. 9.

6. *Ibid.,* Feb. 27, 1951, pp. 1, 25. According to *Life* magazine, five states were "Jockeying to see which would be the 36th." The Nevada Legislature "cleared decks" for action by having the Assembly ratify "early in the day"; on learning by telephone that Utah had ratified shortly before 4:00 p.m., Pacific time, the Senate "rushed into session" and ratified at 4:30 p.m. See *Life,* March 12, 1951, p. 46.

7. *New York Times,* Oct. 6, 1956, p. 10.

8. *Ibid.,* p. 1.

9. *New York Times,* May 5, 1959, pp. 1, 3.

10. *Ibid.,* Feb. 20, 1959, p. 16.

11. See Richard Strout, "The 22nd Amendment: A Second Look," *New York Times Magazine,* July 28, 1957, pp. 26–27.

12. *Ibid.,* p. 27.

13. The members of the subcommittee were Democrats Edward Burke (Neb.), chairman, Frederick Van Nuys (Ind.), and Tom Connally (Texas); and Republicans Warren Austin (Vt.) and Alexander Wiley (Wis.).

14. *Third Term for President of the United States,* Hearings before a Subcommittee of the Committee on the Judiciary, United States Senate, 76th Cong., 3rd sess. (1940); hereafter cited as 1940 Hearings.

15. The members of this subcommittee were Democrats Carl Hatch (N.M.), chairman, Joseph O'Mahoney (Wyo.), and Burton Wheeler (Mont.); and Republicans Kenneth Wherry (Neb.) and E. H. Moore (Okla.).

16. *Term of President of the United States,* Hearings before a Subcommittee of the Committee on the Judiciary, United States Senate, 79th Cong., 1st sess. (1945); hereafter cited as 1945 Hearings.

17. Appearing in person were Senators Lee O'Daniel, Texas Democrat, Arthur Capper, Kansas Republican, and Wayne Morse, Oregon Republican. Another Republican Senator, Hugh Butler of Nebraska, sent the statement.

18. 1945 Hearings, p. 6.

19. Members of the House Committee were Republicans Earl Michener (Mich.), chairman, John Robsion (Ky.), Chauncey Reed (Ill.), John Gwynne (Iowa), Louis Graham (Pa.), Raymond Springer (Ind.), Frank Fellows (Me.), Earl Lewis (Ohio), John Jennings (Tenn.), Angier Goodwin (Mass.), Clifford Case (N.J.), E. Wallace Chadwick (Pa.), Albert Reeves (Mo.), Kenneth Keating (N.Y.), and Edward Devitt (Minn.); and Democrats Emanuel Celler (N.Y.), Francis Walter (Pa.), Sam Hobbs (Ala.), William Byrne (N.Y.), Estes Kefauver (Tenn.), Joseph Bryson (S.C.), Fadjo Cravens (Ark.), Thomas Lane (Mass.), Martin Gorski (Ill.), Michael Feighan (Ohio), Frank Chelf (Ky.), and Ed Gossett (Texas). As usual, the West was underrepresented.

20. Representative Raymond Springer, Indiana Republican and chairman of the subcommittee, later stated that 16 or 18 persons had submitted their views. 93 *Cong. Rec.,* pt. 1, p. 864 (1947). The *Times* listed four of these witnesses, all Representatives. They were John W. McCormack, Democrat of Massachusetts, and Republicans Ellsworth Buck of New York, Everett M. Dirksen of Illinois, and William Lemke of North Dakota. *New York*

Times, Feb. 4, 1947, p. 18. Representative Michener stated the day before the hearings that he would appear. *Ibid.,* Feb. 2, 1947, p. 1. Representative Karl Mundt, South Dakota Republican, declared on the House floor that he also testified. 93 *Cong. Rec.,* pt. 1, p. 857.

21. H. Rept. 17, 80th Cong., 1st sess. (1947); hereafter cited as H. Rept.
22. *Ibid.,* p. 2.
23. These were Cravens (Ark.), Kefauver (Tenn.), Chelf (Ky.), Lane (Mass.), Bryson (S.C.), and Gorski (Ill.).
24. H. Rept., p. 9.
25. See remarks of Republican Representatives Leo Allen (Ill.), Robsion (Ky.), Mundt (S.D.), and Raymond Burke (Ohio). 93 *Cong. Rec.,* pt. 1, pp. 841, 849, 858 (1947).
26. *Ibid.,* p. 863.
27. H. Rept., pp. 1–2.
28. The members of the Senate Judiciary Committee were Republicans Alexander Wiley (Wis.), William Langer (N.D.), Homer Ferguson (Mich.), Chapman Revercomb (W.Va.), E. H. Moore (Okla.), Forrest Donnell (Mo.), and John Sherman Cooper (Ky.); and Democrats Pat McCarran (Nev.), Harley Kilgore (W.Va.), James Eastland (Miss.), Warren Magnuson (Wash.), J. William Fulbright (Ark.), and J. Howard McGrath (R.I.).
29. S. Rept. 34, 80th Cong., 1st sess. (1947).
30. *Ibid.,* p. 1.
31. *Ibid.,* p. 2.
32. 93 *Cong. Rec.,* pt. 2, pp. 1771–1773 (1947).
33. *Ibid.,* pp. 1773–1774.
34. *Ibid.,* p. 1949.
35. *Ibid.,* p. 1964.
36. *Ibid.,* p. 1804.
37. *Ibid.,* p. 1863.
38. *Ibid.,* p. 1866.
39. *Ibid.*
40. *Ibid.*
41. *Ibid.,* p. 1938.
42. *Ibid.,* p. 1941.
43. *Ibid.,* p. 1939.
44. *Ibid.,* p. 1955.
45. Of the 47 House Democrats voting for the amendment, 37 came from the South; of the 13 Senate Democrats voting for it, 9 came from the South. Among Democratic Senators supporting the amendment were John McClellan (Ark.), Walter George (Ga.), Herbert O'Connor (Md.), Millard Tydings (Md.), James Eastland (Miss.), Kenneth McKellar (Tenn.), Harry F. Byrd (Va.), and Willis Robertson (Va.). On the roll call defeating Senator Magnuson's "perfected" amendment, 34 Democrats supported it, but 5 Democrats and 45 Republicans opposed it; the 5 Democrats opposing it were Senators Edwin Johnson (Colo.), Allen Ellender (La.), Eastland (Miss.), McKellar (Tenn.), and W. Lee O'Daniel (Texas).
46. Thus, Senator J. Howard McGrath, Rhode Island Democrat, was given credit for having convinced several Republicans in committee of the wisdom of convention ratification. Senator Wiley indicated that floor debate had convinced him of the desirability of the convention method. In the Senate vote on the method of ratification, the Democrats split 15 for con-

441

ventions and 24 for legislatures; the Republicans split 5 for conventions and 39 for legislatures. The 5 Republicans voting for convention ratification were Cooper (Ky.), Donnell (Mo.), Henry Cabot Lodge (Mass.), Langer (N.D.), and Wiley (Wis.).

47. In the Senate, where 65 per cent of members were lawyers, 92 per cent of those speaking in the debate were lawyers. The only non-lawyers to speak were Senators "Pappy" O'Daniel (Texas) and singer Glen Taylor (Idaho), both Democrats. In the House, where 55 per cent of the members were lawyers, 78 per cent of the speakers were lawyers.

48. The deleterious results of this excessive speed were indicated in an exchange that took place on the House floor among members of the Judiciary Committee. The committee had amended the original Michener resolution. This change was slight, involving only a reworded sentence and a phrase which was dropped. It did not affect the substance of the Michener resolution. Yet on the floor Michener said he thought that if the members of the committee could vote again they would vote against the reworded version. He said the amendment had been "offered by a member of the committee who wrote it out with a pencil during a reading of the resolution . . ." Representative John Jennings, Tennessee Republican, disagreed with Michener.

Mr. Jennings . . . . We carefully, deliberately, thoughtfully considered the language that we adopted by a majority vote . . . It is crystal clear . . .
Mr. Michener. I do not want to be misunderstood. We considered the amendment for about 5 minutes . . . It was a penciled memorandum, such as an amendment that is offered on the floor. No attention was given at all to the language, and that is what I meant . . . I am confident that this language as now written in the amendment will not go into the Constitution after some of the people who did support it give it further consideration.

93 *Cong. Rec.,* pt. 1, p. 870.

49. 93 *Cong. Rec.,* pt. 2, p. 1867 (1947).

50. For Senator Wiley's explanation of this compromise, see *ibid.*

51. *Ibid.,* p. 1964.

52. *Ibid.,* pt. 1, pp. 841–842.

53. *New York Times,* Feb. 2, 1947, p. 39.

54. See the protest of Senator Pat McCarran, Nevada Democrat, against a prepared list of speakers. His protest was of doubtful merit since on getting the floor, he himself spoke on an entirely unrelated subject. 93 *Cong. Rec.,* pt. 2, p. 1781.

55. *Ibid.,* pt. 1, p. 845. See also *ibid.,* p. 870.

56. 1945 Hearings, p. 13.

57. *Ibid.,* pp. 16–18.

58. 93 *Cong. Rec.,* pt. 2, p. 1940.

59. *Ibid.,* pp. 1954–1955. Senator Wiley also gave weight to prior House passage of the measure.

60. *Ibid.,* p. 1866.

61. *Ibid.,* pt. 1, p. 856.

62. *Ibid.,* pt. 2, p. 1681.

63. *Ibid.,* pt. 1, pp. 853, 845, 854.

64. *Ibid.,* p. 861.

65. *Ibid.,* p. 855.

66. *Ibid.,* pt. 2, p. 2392.

67. *Ibid.*, p. 1773.

68. McCulloch *v.* Maryland, 4 Wheaton 316, 407 (1819).

69. The states ratified this amendment in 286 days, the second fastest ratification in history. The amendment was approved by the state legislatures almost unnoticed by the general public. A contest developed at the end to see which state would be the 38th, and Kansas eventually triumphed over Ohio, thus adding luster to its centennial celebrations. See *New York Times,* March 30, p. 1 and March 31, 1960, p. 13.

70. It began as a proposal to allow state governors to make appointments to vacant seats in the House of Representatives. The Senate Judiciary Committee reported this to the Senate in July 1959. In September, the Subcommittee on Constitutional Amendments of this committee held one day of hearings on a proposal to give D.C. residents the vote in presidential elections, but Chairman Eastland of the full committee prevented further action on this proposal. Accordingly, Senator Keating, a Judiciary Committee member, bypassed the committee and on February 2, 1960, presented the proposal on the floor where the eight speeches favoring it, none being opposed, filled only five *Record* pages. Finally the Senate passed a package of three proposals for amendment—that reported by the committee, that for a D.C. vote, and a third to outlaw the poll tax. In May, the House Judiciary Committee, after subcommittee hearings, pared these three down to the D.C. proposal, and on June 14 the House debated this amendment for two hours, passing it by a voice vote. When this amendment returned to the Senate floor, only four Senators spoke on the merits of the proposal even though the House version differed markedly from the package which the Senate had originally sent to the House. The Senate passed it the same day by a voice vote.

71. Representative George Meader, Michigan Republican, said: "We should also remember that only five . . . resolutions have been presented by the Congress to the States and have failed of ratification. Thus, we realize that when we are proposing to add a 23d amendment to the Constitution we are taking a very serious step." Meader further pointed out that Congress had given no thorough consideration to problems closely related to the pending question: namely, full home rule for the Capital District and the status of American territories such as Puerto Rico and the Virgin Islands. "The resolution before us is piecemeal legislation and it is also compromised legislation." 106 *Cong. Rec.*, pt. 10, p. 12559 (1960).

72. *New York Times,* May 23, 1963, p. 23. Between January and May, states had voted to ask Congress to call a convention for proposal of amendments as follows: 12 states had favored an amendment to end all constitutional restraints on state apportionment of state legislatures; 11 states, an amendment to permit amendment of the Constitution by state legislatures without the participation of any national forum; and 3 states, an amendment to create a "Court of the Union," composed of the 50 state chief justices, to review Supreme Court decisions. The movement was checked only when the Chief Justice, President Kennedy, and others called national attention to it. Article by Anthony Lewis, *ibid.*, May 19, 1963, pp. 1, 81.

73. Since the foregoing pages were drafted, Congress has proposed two additional amendments under circumstances which confirm some of my strictures. Congress completed passage August 27, 1962, and the states completed ratification in 1963 of the 24th Amendment, outlawing the poll tax in

federal elections. Said Representative Emanuel Celler, New York Democrat and chairman of the House Judiciary Committee, which reported the amendment, "I am a pragmatist. I want results, not debate. I want a law, not a filibuster. I crave an end to the poll tax, not unlimited, crippling amendments." 108 *Cong. Rec.,* pt. 13, p. 1765 (1962). Congress evidently deemed an amendment necessary to abolish the poll tax in federal elections. Yet in 1965, the Senate came within four votes of passing Senator Edward M. Kennedy's proposal to outlaw the poll tax in state elections by simple legislation! 111 *Cong. Rec.,* May 11, 1965, p. 9733. On April 13, 1965, Congress completed action on the 25th Amendment, to regularize procedure in case of presidential inability. For an account of some of the hazards this amendment overcame in the Senate, see an article by Fred Graham, *New York Times,* July 4, 1965, pt. IV, p. 4E.

Chapter 12. Individual Rights and National Insecurity

1. Tot *v.* United States, 319 U.S. 463 (1943), United States *v.* Lovett, 328 U.S. 303 (1946), United States *v.* Cardiff, 344 U.S. 174 (1952), Toth *v.* Quarles, 350 U.S. 11 (1955), Reid *v.* Covert, 354 U.S. 1 (1957), Trop *v.* Dulles, 356 U.S. 86 (1958), Kennedy *v.* Mendoza-Martinez, 372 U.S. 144 (1963), Schneider *v.* Rusk, 377 U.S. 163 (1964), Aptheker *v.* Secretary of State, 378 U.S. 500 (1964), Lamont *v.* Postmaster General, 381 U.S. 301 (1965), United States *v.* Brown, 381 U.S. 437 (1965), and United States *v.* Romano, 382 U.S. 136 (1965).

2. See, for example, Glendon A. Schubert, *Constitutional Politics* (New York: Holt, Rinehart and Winston, 1960), pp. 192–206.

3. In all but six Congresses from the 65th to the 86th, bills relating to wiretapping were introduced. See *Wiretapping, Eavesdropping and the Bill of Rights,* Hearings before the Subcommittee on Constitutional Rights of the Committee on the Judiciary, United States Senate, 86th Cong., 1st sess. (1959), pt. 4, pp. 781–1031. These hearings appeared in six parts during the 2nd session of the 85th and 1st session of the 86th Congresses.

4. The 4th Amendment reads: "The right of the people to be secure in their persons, houses, papers, and effects, against unreasonable searches and seizures, shall not be violated, and no warrants shall issue, but upon probable cause, supported by oath or affirmation, and particularly describing the place to be searched, and the persons or things to be seized." The 5th Amendment reads in part, "No person . . . shall be compelled in any criminal case to be a witness against himself . . ."

5. Olmstead *v.* United States, 277 U.S. 438 (1928). There seemed at that date to be a prevalent public attitude that enforcement of the law by wiretapping was unethical and unfair. In 1924 a popular protest against wiretapping by agents of the Federal Bureau of Investigation and the Prohibition Bureau led Attorney General Harlan Fiske Stone to ban wiretapping under the "Unethical Tactics Code." This ban, however, reached only the F.B.I., and so Prohibition agents continued to perfect their technique of tapping telephones. See W. S. Fairfield and C. Clift, "The Wiretappers," *Reporter,* December 23, 1952, p. 10.

6. 277 U.S. 464.

7. *Ibid.,* p. 485. Two other justices took similar positions, while Justice Holmes thought the evidence inadmissible because secured in violation of state law.

8. See sec. 605, 48 *Stat.* 1103.

9. In 1937 the Court again reviewed convictions for bootlegging based on wiretap evidence, but this time the defendant argued that the evidence ought to be excluded not because of the Constitution, but because of congressional intent. The Court was persuaded that in section 605 Congress had altered the common-law rule admitting illegally obtained evidence insofar as wiretap evidence was concerned, and so it reversed these convictions. Nardone *v.* United States, 302 U.S. 379 (1937). In the second Nardone case in 1939, the Court extended the ruling in the first to embrace intrastate as well as interstate communications and to evidence only indirectly obtained from wiretapping. Nardone *v.* United States, 308 U.S. 338 (1939); Weiss *v.* United States, 308 U.S. 321 (1939).

10. A major effort to legalize wiretapping came during the Red scare of the early 1950's. After the Court had ordered the release of Judith Coplon, a known Soviet spy, because of wiretap evidence, the House, in 1954, again considered the problem. This time it passed a bill to authorize wiretapping for national defense purposes, but the Senate balked. The Supreme Court declined to overrule Olmstead, but this was offset by the two Nardone cases, which in practice somewhat neutralized its effects. The problem was to become complicated by state laws on wiretapping and the question how far section 605 restrained state law enforcement officers. See Schwartz *v.* Texas, 344 U.S. 199 (1952), Benanti *v.* United States, 355 U.S. 96 (1957), and Mapp *v.* Ohio, 367 U.S. 643 (1961).

On the other hand, wiretapping has long been employed by federal agents in practice. Such activities are *sub rosa* and hard to document, yet they do take place. For data on the numbers of wiretaps maintained by the F.B.I. in 1958 and 1959, see *Wiretapping and Eavesdropping: Summary Report of Hearings, 1958–1961,* by the Subcommittee on Constitutional Rights of the Committee on the Judiciary, United States Senate, 87th Cong., 2nd sess. (1962), p. 18.

11. *To Authorize Wire Tapping,* Hearings before Subcommittee No. 1 of the Committee on the Judiciary, United States House of Representatives, 77th Cong., 1st sess. (1941), p. 200; hereafter cited as House Wiretapping Hearings.

12. Louis F. McCabe, Vice President of the National Lawyers' Guild, urged study of recent as well as earlier Court reasoning. Said he, "There yet lingers some doubt as to the constitutionality of wire tapping; and in recent years, the decisions of the Supreme Court [in other wiretapping cases], the stiffened position of the Court on all questions involving civil rights, and the public revulsion against wire tapping, all tend to strengthen those doubts as to the constitutionality of wire tapping. In short, as lawyers we cannot candidly say that the pending bills are unquestionably constitutional." *Ibid.,* p. 55.

13. 87 *Cong. Rec.,* pt. 5, p. 5772 (1941).

14. House Wiretapping Hearings, pp. 99, 154, and 172.

15. *New York Times,* Feb. 7, 1954, p. 42; Feb. 6, 1954, p. 6. Senator William E. Jenner, Indiana Republican, alluded to the "Fair Dealers and their Communist brain trust," *ibid.,* Feb. 13, 1954, p. 1.

16. *Internal Security Legislation,* Hearings before Subcommittee No. 1 of the Committee on the Judiciary, United States House of Representatives, 83rd Cong., 2nd sess. (1954), p. 10; hereafter cited as Hearings.

17. Hearings, p. 136.

18. 100 *Cong. Rec.,* pt. 11, p. 14210 (1954).

19. See, for example, the *New York Times,* August 13, 1954, p. 1; and August 14, 1954, p. 1.

20. It forms Title I of the latter act, 64 *Stat.* 987.

21. 68 *Stat.* 775.

22. Arthur Krock, "The Rescue Squad Saves Due Process," *New York Times,* August 20, 1954, p. 18.

23. See *Annual Reports of the Attorney General* for the years 1955–1964.

24. Two state courts have considered the act and held it constitutional. In Salwen v. Rees, 108 A. 2d 265 (N.J., 1954), a New Jersey court denied that a candidate for office could appear on the ballot under the Communist party label. *In re* Albertson's Claim, 168 N.E. 2d 242 (N.Y., 1960), the New York Court of Appeals took up the claim of a party employee for state unemployment compensation. This court upon limited investigation followed the congressional finding that the Communist party was a conspiracy. It upheld the act against arguments that it was a bill of attainder, an ex post facto law, and a violation of due process of law.

25. Communist Party v. Catherwood, 367 U.S. 389 (1961).

26. 100 *Cong. Rec.,* pt. 12, p. 15115 (1954).

27. 367 U.S. 392. Justice Black concurred without opinion. In United Electrical, Radio & Machine Workers v. Brownell, 232 F. 2d 687 (1956), a suit brought by the union to have sections 5–11 of the act declared unconstitutional and to enjoin defendant, the Court made summary judgment for defendant on the grounds that a court will not interfere with administrative proceedings not on their face incapable of affording due process before final administrative action.

28. Statement by J. Edgar Hoover concerning the 17th National Convention, Communist Party of the United States, December 10–13, 1959, before Senate Judiciary Committee, 86th Cong., 2nd sess. (1960). 106 *Cong. Rec.,* pt. 1, pp. 599–602 (1960).

29. 100 *Cong. Rec.,* pt. 11, p. 14610.

30. *Ibid.,* p. 14647.

31. Sixteen of the 35 who gave testimony were Representatives and one was a Senator. The rest included 2 members of the Administration, one state judge, 6 union officials, 2 representatives of civil liberties groups, 4 of veterans' groups, 2 of the National Lawyers Guild, and 1 of the Communist party.

32. Hearings, p. 10.

33. *Ibid.,* p. 9.

34. *Ibid.,* p. 20.

35. *Ibid.,* p. 104, citing Dennis v. United States, 341 U.S. 494, 501 (1951), affirming convictions of 11 top Communist party leaders under the Smith Act of 1940.

36. Wieman v. Updegraff, 344 U.S. 183 (1952). This decision struck down an Oklahoma statute because it failed specifically to specify "knowing" membership in the outlawed group.

37. Hearings, p. 140.

38. The 6 members of the subcommittee were Republicans Louis E. Graham (Pa.), chairman, Ruth Thompson (Mich.), and DeWitt S. Hyde (Md.); and Democrats Emanuel Celler (N.Y.), Francis E. Walter (Pa.), and Michael A. Feighan (Ohio) (temp.).

39. Hearings, pp. 161–162.
40. The co-sponsoring Senators were Democrats Paul H. Douglas (Ill.), John F. Kennedy (Mass.), Mike Mansfield (Mont.), George A. Smathers (Fla.), John O. Pastore (R.I.), James E. Murray (Mont.), Olin D. Johnston (S.C.), Burnet R. Maybank (S.C.), Clinton P. Anderson (N.M.), Stuart Symington (Mo.), Henry M. Jackson (Wash.), Warren G. Magnuson (Wash.), John Stennis (Miss.), Herbert H. Lehman (N.Y.), Edwin C. Johnson (Col.), A. S. Mike Monroney (Okla.), Lister Hill (Ala.), Robert S. Kerr (Okla.), and Price Daniel (Texas); and Independent Wayne Morse (Ore.).
41. 100 *Cong. Rec.*, pt. 11, p. 14209 (1954).
42. *Ibid.*, p. 14210.
43. *Ibid.*, p. 14211.
44. *Ibid.*, p. 14212.
45. *Ibid.*, p. 14215.
46. *Ibid.*, p. 14219.
47. *Ibid.*, p. 14233.
48. *Ibid.*, p. 14714.
49. *Ibid.*, pt. 12, p. 15107.
50. *Ibid.*, p. 15102.
51. American Communications Association *v.* Douds, 339 U.S. 382, 433 (1950).
52. 100 *Cong. Rec.*, pt. 11, p. 14720.
53. *Ibid.*, pt. 12, p. 15115.
54. *Ibid.*
55. *Ibid.*, pt. 11, p. 14643.
56. *Ibid.*, pp. 14651–14652.
57. *Ibid.*, p. 14643.
58. *Ibid.*, pp. 14644, 15085.
59. *Ibid.*, pt. 12, p. 15321.
60. *Ibid.*, pt. 11, p. 14647.
61. *Ibid.*, p. 14658.
62. A traditional liberal-conservative split over labor issues occurred on the vote on Butler's amendments tightening up the provisions respecting unions. Seventeen liberal Democrats were joined by the Independent Morse and Republican Langer in opposing these amendments. But 41 Republicans and 21 Democrats supported the amendments. Another liberal-conservative split occurred on the vote on Magnuson's proposal that Congress establish a commission to investigate the whole problem. The vote on this took place immediately before debate began on Humphrey's substitute and significantly Humphrey and 17 others of the 21 sponsors of the Humphrey amendment were willing to vote for this postponement. They were joined by other Democrats and by Republicans Ives of New York and Cooper to make up the 31 who favored this proposal. But 13 Democrats joined 44 Republicans to defeat it.

Two Senate votes show a strict party division. Both in effect concerned the question of retaining criminal penalties for membership in the party. Republicans opposed these penalties because the Administration had assured them that such a provision would hamper Administration efforts to enforce existing security laws. The Senate, however, favored the criminal provision by votes of 41–39 and 43–39. In those votes Republicans supplied 38 of the losing votes and 3 on the winning side. In the first vote, Democrats were split 37 for to 1 against, and in the second vote, 39–1. Senator Morse voted with the Democrats. In the first of these votes the pressure for party unity was so strong that the Democratic leadership was able to persuade Kefauver and Alton A. Lennen, North Carolina Democrat, to pair their negative votes, thus preventing a tie vote which would have defeated the measure.

The only House vote in which party was a factor was that on Dies's motion to instruct the House conferees to accept the Senate amendments, that is, to accept the criminal provisions. On this vote Democrats voted 151–1 for Dies's proposal while 56 of the 155 Republicans voting broke with the Administration and voted with the Democrats.

63. Of the 12 most active participants in the Senate's constitutional debate, only three were non-lawyers. The 12 included Democrats Humphrey, Daniel, Magnuson, Pat McCarran (Nev.), Mansfield, Smathers, Hennings, and Kefauver; and Republicans Butler, Cooper, William Knowland (Calif.), and Homer Ferguson (Mich.). The non-lawyers were Humphrey (political scientist), Mansfield (historian), and Knowland (publisher).

In the House all 12 leading participants in the debate were lawyers. The 12 included Democrats Multer, Celler, John B. Williams (Miss.), O'Hara, Dies, Walter, and Dodd; and Republicans Chauncey W. Reed (Ill.), Burdick, DeWitt S. Hyde (Md.), Javits, and Halleck.

The ten conferees who produced the final bill were all members of the Judiciary Committees and hence lawyers. The 10 were Senate Republicans Langer, Arthur V. Watkins (Utah), and Butler; Senate Democrats McCarran, and Harley M. Kilgore (W.Va.); House Republicans Chauncey Reed, Graham, and Hyde; and House Democrats Celler and Walter.

Thirteen of the 16 Representatives who had testified in the earlier House hearings were lawyers.

64. 100 *Cong. Rec.*, pt. 11, pp. 14645–14646.

65. *Ibid.*, p. 14226.

66. *Ibid.*, p. 14647.

67. The one-third figure was the estimate of Representative O'Hara. *Ibid.*, p. 14651.

68. *Ibid.*, p. 14641.

69. *Ibid.*, pp. 14608–14609.

70. *Ibid.*, p. 14653.

71. *Ibid.*, p. 14658.

72. *Ibid.*

73. *Ibid.*, p. 14643.

74. See, for example, the statement of Cooper, *ibid.*, pt. 11, p. 14233 and that of Kefauver, *ibid.*, pt. 12, p. 15108.

75. As shown earlier, Representative Celler called part of the bill unconstitutional but also indicated that since he liked another part of the bill he would vote for the whole thing. Representative O'Hara took the same position.

76. Senator Daniel's equation of his separability clause with a calming of all fears about constitutional questions is certainly based on this attitude. Knowland adopted the same view. At another place in the debate Daniel made it clear that the Humphrey-Butler bill which he was advocating was a constitutional catch-all:

"I believe that if it is constitutionally possible ever to single out an organization and say that membership therein is a violation of the law, the language of the bill properly does that very thing.

"However, suppose we are wrong about that. Suppose the Court should say it is unconstitutional to single out a certain organization by name; and that we ought to single out certain actions of the members of the organization, and the purposes and designs of the organization in general, so that any organization violating these prescribed actions might come under the law. That is in the Humphrey substitute just as clearly as it could be placed in it." *Ibid.*, pt. 11, p. 14225.

77. *Ibid.*, p. 14216.

78. *Ibid.*, p. 14221.

79. *Ibid.*, p. 14648.

80. *Ibid.*, p. 14652.

81. *Ibid.*, p. 14645.

82. *Ibid.*, p. 14653.

83. *Ibid.*, pt. 12, p. 15116.

84. Senator Hennings was referring to the Bill of Rights Day speech of the Chief Justice, delivered Dec. 15, 1954. *Security and Constitutional Rights,* Hearings before the Subcommittee on Constitutional Rights of the Committee on the Judiciary, United States Senate, 84th Cong., 2nd sess., pt. 1, p. 1 (1955). Part 2 contains two additional days of hearings in June 1956, at the next session.

85. *Ibid.*, pt. 1, p. 3. In 1959 the subcommittee, having been expanded to nine members, resumed hearings on the problem with emphasis on procedural rights; see *Security and Constitutional Rights,* Hearings before the Subcommittee on Constitutional Rights of the Committee on the Judiciary, United States Senate, 86th Cong., 1st sess., pt. 3 (1959).

86. See above, note 10.

87. See above, note 1.

88. A cursory study of the enactment of three of the provisions voided by the Court since 1945 suggests the prominence of such factors as complex technicalities of policy, undue reliance on executive recommendations or those of standing committees concerned with specialized policy areas, and the absence of, or failure to employ, facilities for focusing informed attention on constitutional issues.

Section 401 of the Nationality Act of 1940, as amended in 1944, which was voided in Trop *v.* Dulles, 356 U.S. 86 (1958), came to Congress as part of a comprehensive code prepared and backed by three executive departments. Evidently neither executive experts nor congressional committees succeeded in isolating and deliberating on constitutional issues involved in depriving certain wartime deserters of citizenship, nor in distinguishing the more traditional deprivation of the *rights* of citizenship, for which there was precedent, from deprivation of citizenship itself. Wartime pressures enhanced the difficulty, of course. In the brief 1943 House debate, Republican Representative Hamilton Fish of New York, asking for constitutional clarification, found a "very important issue." He wished "some Constitutional lawyer in the House" would explain the extent of servicemen's constitutional rights and under what power Congress could deprive native-born Americans not convicted of treason of citizenship. 89 *Cong. Rec.*, pt. 3, p. 3238 (1943).

In 1943, Congress adopted a rider to an urgent deficiency appropriations bill, denying salaries to three named officials whom the House Unamerican Activities Committee and a five-man House Appropriations subcommittee had deemed subversive. The Court held the provision void three years later. United States *v.* Lovett, 328 U.S. 303 (1946). Despite constitutional objections by Representatives Coffee, Hobbs, Burdick, Kefauver, and Celler, three of whom served on the Judiciary Committee, and the later protests of the Senate and the President, the House persevered in accepting the decision of the subcommittee, stood by the rider, and when the Executive declined to defend it in the Supreme Court, got Congress to hire its own counsel. Speaking for the Court, Justice Black brought out inadequacies of the congressional handling of the question. *Ibid.*, 308–312.

In Reid *v.* Covert, 354 U.S. 1 (1957), the Court struck down a section of the Uniform Code of Military Justice of 1950. The section provided for military trials of civilian dependents abroad accused of capital crimes. A committee of lawyers chiefly from the military services and headed by a law professor had drafted this elaborate code. Armed Services Committees in both houses studied it and reported it with little change. The Senate defeated 43 to 33 an effort to refer it to the Judiciary Committee for study of constitutional questions. Senator Pat McCarran, Nevada Democrat and committee chairman, had pressed this effort, insisting that the basic question was "the limit to which we have permitted or will expand the jurisdiction of military courts over the lives and fortunes of our ordinary citizens and nationals." 96 *Cong. Rec.*, pt. 1, p. 1368 (1950). Senator Morse, although a member of the Armed Services Committee, had backed McCarran. *Ibid.*, p. 1369. The Senate supported the claim of the Armed Services Committee over matters of military justice and rejected that of the Judiciary Committee even though the latter was entrusted by the Legislative Reorganization Act of 1946 with matters concerning "judicial proceedings, civil and criminal, generally," and "civil liberties." Remarks of McCarran, *ibid.*, p. 1368.

The foregoing discussion is based in part on papers by Jane R. Wiedlea, Pamela M. Gold, and Marion A. Fitch, all members of an advanced class in constitutional law.

89. Missouri, Kansas & Texas Railway Company *v.* May, 194 U.S. 267, 270 (1903).

CHAPTER 13. CONGRESS IN DILEMMA

1. S. Rept. 711, 75th Cong., 1st sess. (1937), p. 23.
2. Cole *v.* Young, 351 U.S. 536 (1956).
3. Pennsylvania *v.* Nelson, 350 U.S. 497 (1956).
4. Slochower *v.* Board of Education, 350 U.S. 551 (1956).
5. Konigsberg *v.* State Bar of California, 353 U.S. 252 (1957); a somewhat similar decision was reached in Schware *v.* Board of Bar Examiners of New Mexico, 353 U.S. 232 (1957).
6. Watkins *v.* United States, 354 U.S. 178 (1957).
7. Yates *v.* United States, 354 U.S. 298 (1957).
8. Brown *v.* Board of Education of Topeka, 347 U.S. 483 (1954), and Brown *v.* Board of Education of Topeka, 349 U.S. 294 (1955).
9. For an informed and perceptive account of this whole struggle in Congress by one who was on the scene, see Walter F. Murphy, *Congress and the Court: A Case Study in the American Political Process* (Chicago: University of Chicago Press, 1962), especially chapters 7–10.
10. This bill passed the House by a vote of 241–155 on July 17, 1958. A corresponding measure was offered the Senate as an amendment to S. 654, and motion to table was rejected by 39–46 on August 20, 1958. When this amendment and its parent bill came up on August 21, the Senate voted to recommit by 41–40.

11. *Limitation of the Appellate Jurisdiction of the United States Supreme Court,* Hearings before the Subcommittee to Investigate the Administration of the Internal Security Act of the Senate Judiciary Committee, 85th Cong., 1st sess. (1957), pp. 2, 13; pt. 2, 85th Cong., 2nd sess. (1958); hereafter cited as Hearings.

12. Hearings, pt. 1, pp. 1–2.

13. S. Rept. 1586, 85th Cong., 2nd sess. (1958). This report is entitled: *Limitation of Supreme Court Jurisdiction and Strengthening of Antisubversive Laws.*

14. This was a House bill dealing with appeals of rulings of federal administrative agencies. 104 *Cong. Rec.,* pt. 14, pp. 18521–18523 (1958).

15. *Ibid.,* pp. 18634–18687.

16. See H.R. 486, 634, 659, and 1133, 86th Cong., 1st sess.; H.R. 1939 would have made exceptions to the appellate jurisdiction of the Courts of Appeals and the Supreme Court and to the jurisdiction of the District Courts in actions relating to public schools; note, however, that Senator Jenner had retired from the Senate and hence was not present in the 86th Congress to press his proposals. In April and May, the Senate Judiciary Committee considered bills to counter decisions of the Court in the field of internal security, but the method employed was that advanced by Senator Butler—amending statutes to clarify the congressional intent. These bills, sponsored in the main by Senator Eastland, dealt with the problems raised by Yates, Nelson, and Cole decisions; other bills dealt with decisions concerning passports and immigration. See S. 1299–1304, 86th Cong., 1st sess. (1959).

17. See S. J. Res. 57, introduced Feb. 26, 1959, 105 *Cong. Rec.,* pt. 3, pp. 2996–2997 (1959). The hearing was held by the Subcommittee on Constitutional Amendments May 28, *New York Times,* May 29, 1959, p. 8. Senator Javits had introduced a similar proposal (S. J. Res. 169) the previous May, 104 *Cong. Rec.,* pt. 6, pp. 7807, 7843–7851 (1958).

18. See, for example, Uphaus v. Wyman, 306 U.S. 72 (1959) *re* Nelson; Beilan v. Board of Education, 357 U.S. 399, decided June 30, 1958 and Lerner v. Casey, 357 U.S. 468 (1958) decided June 30, 1958 *re* Slochower; Konigsberg v. State Bar of California, 266 U.S. 26 (1961), *re* Konigsberg; Barenblatt v. United States, 360 U.S. 109 (1959) *re* Watkins. See Murphy, *Congress and the Court,* chapter 10.

19. *Ex parte* McCardle, 6 Wallace 318 (1868). There the Court affirmed a power in Congress to remove a portion of its appellate jurisdiction, in this instance concerned with denials of the writ of habeas corpus.

20. Murphy, *Congress and the Court,* pp. 199–222.

21. Remarks on S. J. Res. 169, 104 *Cong. Rec.,* pt. 6, p. 7845 (1958).

22. Hearings, pt. 1 passim. An appendix included the texts of nine pertinent Supreme Court decisions.

23. 104 *Cong. Rec.,* pt. 17, p. D47. Senator John A. Carroll, Colorado Democrat and member of the committee, asserted in the debate that a motion to table Hennings' request had lost by only one vote. 104 *Cong. Rec.,* pt. 14, pp. 18683–18684. But Senator Butler stated that the committee had resolved unanimously to hold further hearings. Probably two separate motions were involved. *Ibid.,* p. 18647. Senator Carroll may have been the first to raise the issue of further hearings, see Murphy, *Congress and the Court,* p. 157.

24. Hearings, pt. 2, p. 97.

25. Testimony of Andrew W. Green, *ibid.,* p. 313.

26. Testimony of Mrs. Enid Griswold of the Women's Patriotic Conference, *ibid.*, p. 531.

27. The 11 expert witnesses included: opposing the bill—Ernest Angell, American Civil Liberties Union; Leonard Boudin, Emergency Civil Liberties Union; Dean Jefferson Fordham, University of Pennsylvania Law School; Arthur Freund, attorney of St. Louis; Thomas Harris, AFL-CIO; Senator Hennings; Joseph Rauh, Americans for Democratic Action; Benjamin Smith, National Lawyers Guild; for the bill—former Dean Clarence Manion, Notre Dame University Law School; Frank Ober, attorney of Baltimore City, Md.; Robert Morris, former congressional committee counsel.

28. Hearings, pt. 2, pp. 351, 548.

29. *Ibid.*, p. 573.

30. *Ibid.*, p. 691.

31. *Ibid.*, p. 243. See also arguments of Joseph Rauh, Americans for Democratic Action, pp. 49–50, and of Attorney General Thomas D. McBride of Pennsylvania, *ibid.*, p. 617.

32. *Ibid.*, p. 380. See arguments of Thomas Harris, *ibid.*, p. 341.

33. *Ibid.*, p. 357.

34. *Ibid.*, p. 280.

35. *Ibid.*, p. 688.

36. *Ibid.*, p. 573.

37. Letter from W. J. Wagner, Associate Professor of Law, Notre Dame University Law School. *Ibid.*, p. 445.

38. 104 *Cong. Rec.*, pt. 17, pp. D127, D167, D216, D238, D246 (1958).

39. *New York Times,* March 27, 1958, p. 17. The nominee would be asked, "Do you, in contemplation of the necessity of taking an oath to support and defend the Constitution of the United States, understand that such oath will demand that you support and defend the provisions of Article I, Section I, of the Constitution, that 'all legislative powers herein granted shall be vested in a Congress of the United States, which shall consist of a Senate and a House of Representatives' and that therefore you will be bound by such oath not to participate knowingly in any decision to alter the meaning of the Constitution itself or of any law as passed by the Congress and adopted under the Constitution?" This pledge was actually administered to a nominee for a district judgeship on March 26. *Ibid.*

40. 104 *Cong. Rec.*, pt. 5, p. 6096.

41. See remarks of Senator Butler, on April 16, 104 *Cong. Rec.*, pt. 5, p. 6497, replying to Senator Hennings' press release and "Memorandum Setting Forth Objections to Senator Butler's Proposed Amendment to S 2646, the So-Called Jenner Bill . . . ," issued April 6 by Senator Hennings, *ibid.*, p. 6503.

42. *New York Times,* April 2, 1958, p. 20.

43. *Ibid.*, April 24, 1958, pp. 18, 21.

44. S. Rept. 1586, p. 4.

45. Senator Wiley concurred with the minority report, and also expressed additional views; Senator Dirksen also expressed individual views, although supporting all of the bill except section 1. Senator Kefauver had reservations concerning sections 3 and 4.

46. *Ibid.*, p. 12.

47. *Ibid.*, p. 13.

48. 104 *Cong. Rec.*, pt. 11, p. 14090.

49. *Ibid.*, pt. 14, p. 18520.
50. *Ibid.*, p. 18643.
51. *Ibid.*, p. 18680.
52. *Ibid.*, p. 18686.
53. *Ibid.*, p. 18645.
54. *Ibid.*, p. 18646.
55. *Ibid.*, pp. 18680–18683 and 18686–18687.
56. *Ibid.*, p. 18651.
57. *Ibid.*, p. 18680.
58. *Ibid.*, p. 18681.
59. *Ibid.*, p. 18682.
60. *Ibid.*, p. 18683.
61. *Ibid.*, p. 18679.
62. *Ibid.*, pp. 18682–18683. On his part, Senator Hennings appealed for action "in a responsible manner." *Ibid.*, p. 18685.
63. *Ibid.*, pp. 18651–18652. The two stages referred to by Senator Javits were first, definition of legislative intent, as employed in sections 3 and 4, and second, assuming a subsequent holding of unconstitutionality, withdrawal of appellate jurisdiction as in section 1.
64. *Ibid.*, p. 18687.
65. Party strongly influenced the vote of Middle Atlantic and Midwest Senators: Republicans: for tabling—9, against—15; Democrats: for—6, against—0. The 8 Border State Senators were equally divided between parties.
66. 14 *Congressional Quarterly Almanac,* 1958, p. 34. Note that the number of lawyers in the Senate has varied from 63 per cent in 1950 to 54 per cent in 1952 and 59 per cent in 1958, and up to 66 per cent in 1964. The number in the House has varied from 56 per cent in 1950 to 54 per cent in 1958, and up to 57 per cent in 1964.
67. In 1958 Southern Senators included the same quota of lawyers as New York City Representatives—86 per cent. Other regions fell far short of the South in both houses; Senate figures ranged from 33 per cent for New England to 60 per cent for the Middle Atlantic and Western states.
The quota of Southern Representatives who were lawyers was 74 per cent. Other regions ranged from 42 per cent for the Far West to 55 per cent for the Border States.
68. 105 *Cong. Rec.*, pt. 3, pp. 2996–2997 (1959). Observe that on Feb. 16, 1953, Senator Butler had introduced S. J. Res. 44 to freeze the appellate jurisdiction of the Supreme Court as it then stood and to freeze the number of justices at nine. 99 *Cong. Rec.*, pt. 1, pp. 1106–1107.
69. 105 *Cong. Rec.*, pt. 3, p. 2997.
70. See the comment of Murphy, *Congress and the Court,* p. 172, concerning the part of J. G. Sourwine in preparing this report, published April 28, 1958: *Internal Security Annual Report for 1957.* S. Rept. 1477, Committee on the Judiciary, United States Senate, 85th Cong., 2nd sess. (1958).
71. Hearings, pt. 2, p. 389.
72. Remarks of Senator Eastland, Feb. 3, 104 *Cong. Rec.*, pt. 2, p. 1481, and comment of Chief Counsel J. G. Sourwine, Feb. 26, Hearings, pt. 2, pp. 161–162.
73. Senator Hennings evidently had a better response from expert witnesses than did the committee counsel. On February 26, counsel Sourwine reported that Senators had submitted 34 names of invitees, that of these,

4 had accepted and 7 had made submissions for the record; the rest had declined. After screening out unsolicited communications which were seemingly "inspired" or in the form of "straw votes," 103, as shown earlier, remained for inclusion in the record. *Ibid.,* p. 162. Senator Hennings submitted for the record both his form letter soliciting pro and con opinions from law school deans and professors and practicing lawyers and the full replies received to that date. *Ibid.,* pp. 391–453.

74. Senators Hennings and Watkins launched a probe to determine who had authorized and who had financed its printing and circulation as a subcommittee publication. *New York Times,* April 10, 1958, p. 13. A *Times* editorial denounced the publication as "a fantastic document," saying that, "even for the hearings of a Subcommittee of which Senator James O. Eastland of Mississippi is chairman, this kind of nonsense is a new high." *Ibid.,* p. 28. As late as May 15, Senator Hennings reported the episode as still a mystery. S. Rept. 1586, p. 13.

75. 104 *Cong. Rec.,* pt. 5, p. 6498.

76. S. Rept. 1586, p. 14.

77. Said Senator Hennings, "If the motion to table should fail, we can anticipate full, lengthy, virile debate and discussion on all phases of this question . . ." 104 *Cong. Rec.,* pt. 14, p. 18684.

CHAPTER 14. ENTER THE EXECUTIVE

1. In 1875 Congress enacted a broad statute providing civil and criminal sanctions against racial discrimination in public accommodations, 18 *Stat.,* pt. 3, 335, held unconstitutional as violating the 14th Amendment in the Civil Rights Cases, 109 U.S. 3 (1883).

2. 78 *Stat.* 241. Section 201(a) provides that the particular establishments enumerated in 201(b) fall within the coverage of the act if their "operations affect commerce or if discrimination or segregation . . . is supported by state action"; 201(c) and 201(d) further define "affect commerce" and "state action" respectively.

3. Constitution, 13th Amendment, sec. 2; 14th Amendment, sec. 5; 15th Amendment, sec. 2.

4. Missouri *ex rel.* Gaines *v.* Canada, 305 U.S. 337 (1938); Nixon *v.* Hernden, 273 U.S. 536 (1927), Nixon *v.* Condon, 286 U.S. 73 (1932), Grovey *v.* Townsend, 295 U.S. 45 (1935), Smith *v.* Allwright, 321 U.S. 1 (1948); and Shelley *v.* Kraemer, 334 U.S. 1 (1948).

5. Although bills began to appear in numbers, and although President Truman named a committee of distinguished citizens to study the problem and laid a ten-point program before Congress, nothing resulted. President Eisenhower in 1956 endorsed a four-point program which Attorney General Herbert Brownell brought forward and which the House passed but which died in the Senate Judiciary Committee. This bill would have fortified the right to vote, authorized enforcement of existing laws by civil action as well as by criminal prosecution, and created a special commission to investigate civil rights and a new division of the Justice Department to enforce them.

6. In the 1956 elections Negroes had gained dramatically in Negro neighborhoods. See 13 *Congressional Quarterly Almanac* (1957), pp. 554–555, 808–809; hereafter cited as *CQA.*

7. 71 *Stat.* 634. Bipartisan support and the absence of a concerted fili-

buster produced the 1957 Act. The act empowered the Attorney General to sue for injunctions when individuals were threatened with infringement on their right to vote. Those convicted of contempt could incur penalties of up to $1,000 fine or six months imprisonment. An Assistant Attorney General was provided to head up the Civil Rights Division.

This act was, in effect, a rehearsal for 1964. In the House, Chairman Celler's Judiciary Subcommittee No. 5 gave civil rights forces a preferred position from which to launch a strong bill. The House Rules Committee and even more the Senate Judiciary Committee gave Southerners potential roadblocks. In the end, House pressure overcame Rules after nine days of hearings, and the Senate by-passed Judiciary by bringing the House bill directly to the floor.

It was on the Senate floor that Congress came to grips with the question of jury trial. Civil rights backers saw the effort to assure jury trial as an effort to block enforcement by referring decisions to unsympathetic Southern juries. Opponents insisted that a fundamental procedural right was at stake and further that jury trial would furnish a necessary cushion to federal enforcement by assuring a degree of local participation in the process. In the Senate, jury trial prevailed, but before the bill reached the White House Congress had engaged in one of those rule-of-thumb compromises typical of the legislative branch. Federal judges could dispense with jury trial except when the penalty exceeded 45 days imprisonment or $300 fine. This congressional guarantee of jury trial was retained in the 1960 Act and, for voting cases, in the 1964 Act. Significantly the Supreme Court was moving in a parallel course in its decisions of 1958 and 1964. See Green v. United States, 356 U.S. 165 (1958) and United States v. Barnett, 376 U.S. 681 (1964), especially 694, note 12. Initiation of jury trial evidently lay with Senator Ervin of North Carolina with assistance from Senator Johnston of South Carolina, who, as members of the Hennings Subcommittee on Constitutional Rights, filed a minority report favoring jury trial and other safeguards. *Civil Rights,* Minority Report (to accompany S. 83), Subcommittee on Constitutional Rights of the Committee on the Judiciary, United States Senate, 85th Cong., 1st sess. (1957) (subcommittee print). It was promoted on the floor by Senator Kefauver of Tennessee and Senator O'Mahoney of Wyoming with the assistance of Senator Frank Church of Idaho.

Finally, the 1957 Act assured a thorough airing of problems of civil rights by establishing a bipartisan Commission on Civil Rights. The hearings and reports of this independent body illuminated the nature and extent of discrimination and furnished impetus to the drive for additional legislation.

8. 74 *Stat.* 86.

9. See 16 *CQA* (1960), pp. 788, 801. Both platforms stressed voting rights, schools, employment, public housing, public facilities, and Senate rules as areas of reform to be considered. Neither platform mentioned discrimination in privately-owned public accommodations.

10. In 1961, he secured extension of the United States Civil Rights Commission for two years. 75 *Stat.* 545. In 1962, he backed a bill to restrict discriminatory use of literacy tests in registration which died in a filibuster. See 108 *Cong. Rec.,* pt. 6, pp. 8410–8411 (1962). He also supported a constitutional amendment to outlaw the poll tax in federal elections which came into force in 1964. His major advances were achieved largely under his executive powers; see Executive Order No. 10925, March 6, 1961, barring

discrimination in employment practices of government agencies and government contractors. Executive Order No. 11063, November 24, 1962, barred discrimination in housing financed with federal assistance.

11. See issues of the *New York Times*, April–August 1963, passim.

12. 22 *Congressional Quarterly Weekly Report*, Feb. 21, 1964, p. 364; hereafter cited as *CQWR*.

13. 110 *Cong. Rec.*, March 26, 1964, p. 6244. See *ibid.*, March 13, 1964, p. 491.

14. 22 *CQWR*, Feb. 21, 1964, p. 364.

15. The eleven titles of the bill dealt with the following: I—protection of voting rights; II—prohibition of discrimination in places of public accommodation; III—prohibition of discrimination in publicly-owned facilities; IV—desegregation of school facilities; V—extension of the Civil Rights Commission for four years; VI—termination of federal funds for programs where discrimination is practiced; VII—prohibition of discrimination in the employment practices of businesses and unions; VIII—accumulation of registration and voting statistics; IX—authorization of removal of civil rights cases to federal courts and of intervention by the Attorney General in suits involving a denial of equal protection of the law; X—establishment of a Community Relations Service; XI—provision for jury trials in criminal contempt cases arising from violation of court orders, etc.

16. See President Johnson's remarks upon signing the bill, *New York Times*, July 3, 1964, p. 9, and his State of the Union Message, Jan. 4, 1965, *ibid.*, Jan. 5, 1965, p. 16. Department of Justice, Press Release, June 14, 1965 (furnished the author by officials of the department).

17. Heart of Atlanta Motel *v.* United States, 85 S. Ct. 1, 2 (1964).

18. Heart of Atlanta Motel *v.* United States, 379 U.S. 241 (1964); Katzenbach *v.* McClung, 379 U.S. 294 (1964); the majority in both cases rested decision on the commerce power exclusively.

19. Heart of Atlanta Motel *v.* United States, 379 U.S. 241, 252 (1964).

20. *New York Times*, July 12, 1964, sec. 4, p. 1.

21. See *ibid.*, July 2, p. 1; July 4, p. 5; July 12, 1964, sec. 4, p. 1. The Department of Justice attributed the widespread compliance largely to "responsible leadership by businessmen throughout the country seeking to prevent disorder and to foster respect for law." Department of Justice, "A Review of the Activities of the Department of Justice in Civil Rights in 1964," p. 1 (copy furnished the author by the department). The department had received 650 complaints concerning individual incidents of apparent racial discrimination by restaurants, motels, and theaters. *Ibid.*

22. *New York Times*, Jan. 24, 1965, p. 39.

23. The suggestion arose during committee consideration in both houses that the 13th Amendment provided a basis for the legislation. *Civil Rights— Public Accommodations*, Hearings before the Committee on Commerce, United States Senate, 88th Cong., 1st sess. (1963), in three parts, pt. 2, p. 776; hereafter cited as Senate Commerce Hearings. It was even suggested at one point that the postal power afforded an adequate ground for the bill. Testimony of Joseph L. Rauh, Vice Chairman, Americans for Democratic Action, *Civil Rights*, Hearings before Subcommittee No. 5 of the Committee on the Judiciary, United States House of Representatives, 88th Cong., 1st sess. (1963), in four parts, pt. 3, p. 1872. (Parts 1–3 comprise the hearings of the subcommittee. Part 4 consists of the full-committee hearings. All four parts are hereafter cited as House Judiciary Hearings.)

24. Civil Rights Cases, 109 U.S. 3 (1883).

25. 18 *Stat*. pt. 3, 335, 336.

26. 109 U.S. 11.

27. Peterson *v*. City of Greenville, 373 U.S. 244 (1963).

28. Burton *v*. Wilmington Parking Authority, 365 U.S. 715 (1961).

29. Lombard *v*. Louisiana, 373 U.S. 267 (1963).

30. Shelley *v*. Kraemer, 334 U.S. 1 (1948).

31. Lombard *v*. Louisiana, 373 U.S. 267, 282–283 (1963).

32. See above, chapter 7.

33. See above, chapter 8.

34. National Labor Relations Board *v*. Jones & Laughlin Steel Corp., 301 U.S. 1 (1937).

35. Wickard *v*. Filburn, 317 U.S. 111 (1942).

36. The members of the subcommittee were Democrats Celler, Peter W. Rodino (N.J.), Byron G. Rogers (Colo.), Harold D. Donohue (Mass.), Jack B. Brooks (Texas), Herman Toll (Pa.), and Robert W. Kastenmeier (Wis.); and Republicans William M. McCulloch (Ohio), William E. Miller (N.Y.) (soon to be the 1964 Republican vice-presidential candidate), George Meader (Mich.), and William C. Cramer (Fla). Only Meader and Cramer voted against the bill on February 10, 1964. For comments to the effect that the subcommittee had been stacked by Celler, see the exchange between Representative Edwin E. Willis, Louisiana Democrat, Chairman, and Howard Smith of the House Rules Committee, *Civil Rights*, Hearings before the Committee on Rules, United States House of Representatives, on H. R. 7152, 88th Cong., 2nd sess. (1964), in two parts, pt. 1, p. 295; hereafter cited as House Rules Hearings.

37. House Judiciary Hearings, pt. 2, p. 1247.

38. *Ibid.*, p. 1706.

39. Initially, the subcommittee stayed within the narrow compass of the President's message of February 28. On May 23, however, Edmund F. Rovner of the International Union of Electrical Workers, AFL-CIO, first hinted at the need of public-accommodations legislation, seeming to suggest both the commerce clause and the 14th Amendment as possible sources of power. *Ibid.*, pt. 2, p. 1144. His reference to the commerce clause had little effect on the subcommittee.

40. *Ibid.*, p. 1220.

41. *Ibid.*, p. 1213.

42. *Ibid.*, p. 1214. See also the exchange between Celler and Pemberton, *ibid.*, p. 1216.

43. Section 203, by implication, provided an alternative power basis under the 14th Amendment for enforcement of rights created under the commerce power. House Rules Hearings, pt. 1, pp. 14–17. For the text of the initial Administration bill, see *ibid.*, pp. 2–39.

44. House Judiciary Hearings, pt. 2, p. 1376.

45. *Ibid.*, pp. 1395–1396.

46. *Ibid.*, p. 1605.

47. *Ibid.*, pp. 1601, 1608.

48. *Ibid.*, pt. 3, pp. 2453–2459. The witness, Charles J. Bloch, an attorney from Macon, Georgia, later had a short discussion of the case inserted into the record of the hearings.

49. H. Rept. 914, 88th Cong., 1st sess. (1963), in 2 parts, pt. 1, p. 44.

50. *Ibid.*, p. 45.

51. House Judiciary Hearings, pt. 4, p. 2656.

52. The *Congressional Quarterly Weekly Report* provides a clue to what happened. This source mentions an agreement between Administration officials and McCulloch and Celler for a moderate version of Title II. It continues, "Almost immediately civil rights groups brought heavy pressure on Celler to reverse his position and press for a more sweeping bill. Celler agreed and refused to back modifications despite Administration requests. Within Judiciary Subcommittee No. 5, headed by Celler himself, a coalition of Republicans and Northern Democrats lined up behind stiff provisions of the type requested by civil rights organizations." 21 *CQWR* 1879 (1963). The author received a similar impression of subcommittee motivation from conversations in Washington in March 1965.

53. The 21 Democrats on the committee were Celler (N.Y.), Michael Feighan (Ohio), Frank Chelf (Ky.), Edwin Willis (La.), Peter Rodino (N.J.), E. L. Forrester (Ga.), Byron Rogers (Colo.), Harold Donohue (Mass.), Jack Brooks (Texas), William Tuck (Va.), Robert Ashmore (S.C.), John Dowdy (Texas), Basil Whitener (N.C.), Roland Libonati (Ill.), Herman Toll (Pa.), Robert Kastenmeier (Wis.), Jacob Gilbert (N.Y.), James Corman (Calif.), William St. Onge (Conn.), George Senner (Ariz.), and Don Edwards (Calif.). The 14 Republicans were William McCulloch (Ohio), William Miller (N.Y.), Richard Poff (Va.), William Cramer (Fla.), Arch Moore (W.Va.), George Meader (Mich.), John Lindsay (N.Y.), William Cahill (N.J.), Garner Shriver (Kan.), Clark MacGregor (Minn.), Charles Mathias (Md.), James Bromwell (Iowa), Carleton King (N.Y.), and Patrick Martin (Calif.).

54. House Judiciary Hearings, pt. 4, p. 2656.

55. *Ibid.*, p. 2700.

56. 21 *CQWR*, Nov. 1, 1963, p. 1879.

57. Text of committee bill, House Rules Hearings, pt. 1, pp. 45–46.

58. The members of the committee were Democrats Smith, William Colmer (Miss.), Ray Madden (Ind.), James Delaney (N.Y.), James Trimble (Ark.), Richard Bolling (Mo.), Thomas O'Neill (Mass.), Carl Elliott (Ala.), B. F. Sisk (Calif.), and John Young (Texas); and Republicans Clarence Brown (Ohio), Katharine St. George (N.Y.), H. Allen Smith (Calif.), Elmer Hofman (Ill.), and William Avery (Kan.).

59. *Ibid.*, p. 114.

60. *Ibid.*, p. 115.

61. *Ibid.*, p. 114. The reference is to Simkins *v.* Moses Cone Memorial Hospital (C.A. 4, Nov. 1, 1963).

62. House Rules Hearings, pt. 1, p. 271.

63. *Ibid.*, pp. 273–274.

64. *Ibid.*, p. 276.

65. 110 *Cong. Rec.*, Jan. 31, 1964, pp. 1460–1462.

66. *Ibid.*, pp. 1462–1463.

67. *Ibid.*, p. 1472.

68. *Ibid.*, pp. 1460–1462.

69. *Ibid.*, Feb. 5, 1964, pp. 1879, 1884.

70. The members of the committee were Democrats Magnuson (Wash.), John O. Pastore (R.I.), A. S. Mike Monroney (Okla.), Strom Thurmond (S.C.), Frank J. Lausche (Ohio), Ralph Yarborough (Texas), Clair Engle (Calif.), E. L. Bartlett (Alaska), Vance Hartke (Ind.), Gale W. McGee

(Wyo.), Philip A. Hart (Mich.), and Howard W. Cannon (Nev.); and Republicans Norris Cotton (N.H.), Thruston B. Morton (Ky.), Hugh Scott (Pa.), Winston L. Prouty (Vt.), and J. Glenn Beall (Md.).

71. Senate Commerce Hearings, pt. 1, p. 166.

72. The 8 were Democratic Senators Magnuson (Wash.), Yarborough (Texas), Bartlett (Alaska), Hartke (Ind.), McGee (Wyo.), and Cannon (Nev.); and Republicans Scott (Pa.) and Beall (Md.).

73. Senator Morton favored the position written into the pending Cooper-Dodd bill, namely, that state licensing constituted state action. Senate Commerce Hearings, pt. 1, pp. 188–189. Others invoked the recent sit-in decision, which implied that even a limited degree of official sanction brought private discrimination within the coverage of the Amendment. *Ibid.*, p. 192. Senator Pastore even assumed that the proposed legislation gave protection to a constitutional right—the right to be free from discrimination in privately-owned establishments held out to the public, an argument never accepted by a majority of the Court. *Ibid.*, pp. 145–149. For comments by Senators Hart and Monroney on the commerce power, see *ibid.*, pp. 180–188 and p. 68.

74. *Ibid.*, p. 425.

75. *Ibid.*, pp. 106, 19–21.

76. *Ibid.*, pt. 2, p. 694. See Senator Humphrey's floor speech, 110 *Cong. Rec.*, March 30, 1964, p. 6311. See, also, 379 U.S. 252–253. The treatment of this general subject has benefited from insights contained in a paper furnished the author by Mr. Michael B. Keating, a student at the Harvard Law School.

77. S. Rept. 848, 88th Cong., 2nd sess. (1964), in 2 parts. Pt. 1 contains committee report and individual views; pt. 2 contains individual views of Senator Prouty.

78. The members were Democrats James O. Eastland (Miss.), Olin D. Johnston (S.C.), John L. McClellan (Ark.), Sam J. Ervin, Jr. (N.C.), Thomas J. Dodd (Conn.), Philip A. Hart (Mich.), Edward V. Long (Mo.), Edward M. Kennedy (Mass.), Birch Bayh (Ind.), and Quentin N. Burdick (N.D.) (Burdick replaced Estes Kefauver, a Tennessee Democrat, who died on August 10, 1963); and Republicans Everett M. Dirksen (Ill.), Roman L. Hruska (Neb.), Kenneth B. Keating (N.Y.), Hiram L. Fong (Hawaii), and Hugh Scott (Pa.).

79. The committee received statements from Senators Long, Ervin, Hart, Keating, Hruska, and Dodd.

80. *Civil Rights—The President's Program, 1963,* Hearings before the Committee on the Judiciary, United States Senate, 88th Cong., 1st sess. (1963), p. 36; hereafter cited as Senate Judiciary Hearings.

81. *Ibid.*, p. 180.

82. *Ibid.*, p. 35.

83. *Ibid.*, pp. 175–189.

84. Kennedy had earlier insisted that to attribute to the states discriminatory acts of private individuals solely because of a license would load the legislation with "very heavy burdens which it need not carry." *Ibid.*, p. 96. Yet he conjectured that the Civil Rights Cases might now be overruled, since the Jim Crow laws had come after that decision and had fostered the attitude which had brought about racial discrimination. Hence the discrimination had its ultimate origin in state action. *Ibid.*, pp. 184–186; 151–152.

85. *Ibid.*, p. 215.

86. National Labor Relations Board *v.* Jones & Laughlin Steel Corp., 301 U.S. 1 (1937); Senate Judiciary Hearings, p. 217.

87. 110 *Cong. Rec.,* March 9, 1964, pp. 4593–4599.

88. See remarks of Senators John Stennis (Miss.), *ibid.,* March 10, 1964, pp. 4645–4648; John J. Sparkman (Ala.), *ibid.,* March 10, 1964, pp. 4680–4681; Allen J. Ellender (La.), *ibid.,* March 11, 1964, pp. 4833–4835; and A. Willis Robertson (Va.), *ibid.,* March 12, 1964, pp. 4906–4908.

89. *Ibid.,* March 26, 1964, p. 6244.

90. The nine were Senators Lausche (Ohio) and J. Howard Edmondson (Okla.), Democrats, and Bourke B. Hickenlooper (Iowa), John J. Williams (Dela.), Len B. Jordan (Idaho), Carl T. Curtis (Neb.), Hruska (Neb.), Karl E. Mundt (S.D.), and Cotton (N.H.), Republicans.

91. All nine of the "swing" group voted for cloture, although Senators Hickenlooper and Cotton opposed the bill on the final vote.

92. 110 *Cong. Rec.,* April 9, 1964, pp. 7169–7185.

93. *New York Times,* May 14, 1964, p. 1.

94. 110 *Cong. Rec.,* May 26, 1964, pp. 11539, 11546.

95. Twenty-three Democrats and six Republicans opposed cloture. The Republicans were Senators Wallace F. Bennett (Utah), Barry Goldwater (Ariz.), Edwin L. Mechem (N.M.), Milward L. Simpson (Wyo.), John Tower (Texas), and Milton R. Young (N.D.), while the Democrats included Senators Alan Bible (Nev.), Carl Hayden (Ariz.), Robert C. Byrd (W.Va.), and every Southern Senator except Yarborough of Texas (and, of course, Tower).

96. 22 *CQWR,* June 19, 1964, p. 1199.

97. 110 *Cong. Rec.,* June 11, 1964, pp. 12994, 13219.

98. *Civil Rights,* Hearing before the Committee on Rules, House of Representatives, on H. Res. 789, 88th Cong., 2nd sess. (1964).

99. The support of House Democrats increased from 61 per cent in February to 63 per cent in July, while the Republicans held steady at 80 per cent. In the Senate, where Democrats supported the bill by 69 per cent and Republicans by 82 per cent, Republicans showed a greater willingness to narrow the coverage of Title II (40 per cent) than Democrats (30 per cent). Moreover 60 per cent of Republicans, as compared with 47 per cent of Democrats, backed the requirement of jury trial. Every Republican vote on bypassing Judiciary was affirmative, and Republicans backed cloture by 82 per cent, as compared with 66 per cent of Democrats. Northern Democrats held more firmly to their policy position than did Republicans.

100. 110 *Cong. Rec.,* July 2, 1964, p. 15362.

101. *Ibid.,* p. 15363.

102. Figures adapted from 19 *CQA* (1963), p. 34. The regional percentages were: South, 91 per cent; Middle Atlantic, 80 per cent; New England, 67 per cent; Far West, 62 per cent; Midwest, 59 per cent; and Border, 43 per cent. The six Senators from New York, Pennsylvania, and New Jersey were all lawyers. In the House, the Representatives from the South numbered 72 per cent lawyers, and those from New York City, seat of greatest civil rights support, 74 per cent.

103. Eight of the 15 members of the House Rules Committee were lawyers, including Representatives Smith, Colmer, Madden, Delaney, Trimble, Elliott, and Young, Democrats; and Smith (Calif.), Republican. Eleven of the 17 members of the Senate Commerce Committee were lawyers, including

Magnuson, Pastore, Thurmond, Lausche, Yarborough, Engle, Hartke, Hart, and Cannon, Democrats; and Cotton and Scott, Republicans.

104. All 18 leading participants in House debate were lawyers, all but 5 from the Judiciary Committee. All but 3 [Senators Jordan (N.C.), Byrd (Va.), and Tower (Texas)] of the 19 filibustering Senators were lawyers. Twelve of the 14 proponents who led in constitutional discussions were lawyers, the exceptions being the two Democratic leaders, Senators Mansfield and Humphrey.

105. Interviews with John H. Simms, Legislative Counsel, Senate Office of the Legislative Counsel, March 1, and Edward O. Craft, Legislative Counsel, House Office of the Legislative Counsel, March 2, 1965.

106. Interviews with Harry N. Stein, Chief, and Norman J. Small, Legislative Attorney, American Law Division, and George B. Galloway, Senior Specialist in American Government and Public Administration, Legislative Reference Service, March 2, 1965.

107. *Annual Report of the Librarian of Congress for the Fiscal Year 1964* (Washington: Library of Congress, 1965), pp. 20, 21.

108. The Senate Commerce Committee based its report in part on an 11-page brief elicited from Professor Paul A. Freund of the Harvard Law School. S. Rept. 872, pp. 12–13, 82. During floor debate, Senators Humphrey and Kuchel obtained a memorandum from Harrison Tweed of New York City and Bernard G. Segal of Philadelphia supporting the constitutionality of Titles II and VII. The memorandum bore 22 signatures, including those of three former Attorneys General, four law school deans, and four former presidents of the American Bar Association. 110 *Cong. Rec.*, April 7, 1964, pp. 6831–6832. The statement soon provoked an attack on the group's impartiality from Senator Russell and a constitutional rebuttal from Senator Ervin. 110 *Cong. Rec.*, April 11, 1964, pp. 7462–7472. Many of the signatories were known proponents of civil rights legislation, and Tweed and Segal were co-chairmen of the Lawyers' Committee for Civil Rights under Law.

109. 110 *Cong. Rec.*, May 26, 1964, p. 11549.

110. *Ibid.*

111. *Ibid.*

112. *Ibid.*, p. 11550.

113. *Ibid.*, p. 11551.

114. *Ibid.*

115. Senator Morton of Kentucky, for example, was instrumental in moving jury trial in the Senate. Note that Senators Mansfield, Kuchel, and Humphrey all came from states where civil rights problems are less aggravated than in the South or Northeast.

116. The Attorney General ended his reply by saying: "We desire to be as helpful as possible to the Congress in its consideration of this important legislation, and if there is any way that we can be of service to you in that regard, we shall be most pleased to do so." From a copy furnished the author by Mr. Norbert Schlei, Head, Office of Legal Counsel, Department of Justice. The Senator omitted the statement from the *Record*.

117. 60 *Stat.* 812, 818 and 827.

118. The commission was authorized to investigate charges of interferences with the right to vote, to study legal developments violating equal protection of the laws, and to appraise federal laws and policies affecting equal protection. Here was a body of six members which was bipartisan,

included lawyers, gave representation to both South and North, and included a Negro. Its members in 1965 included two university presidents, a newspaper editor, a political scientist, a law-school dean, and a state assistant attorney general. The commission no longer included political leaders, as it had originally. A professional staff partially atoned for its paucity of numbers and its part-time character. Its reports, based on fair and comprehensive hearings, illumined important aspects of the problem.

119. Testimony of Representative Dowdy, House Rules Hearings, pt. 2, p. 521. See also comments of opponents in H. Rept. 914, 88th Cong., 1st sess. (1963), pt. 1, pp. 45–46, 63.

120. Testimony of Chairman Celler, House Rules Hearings, pt. 1, p. 149.

121. *Ibid.*, p. 98.

122. *Ibid.*, p. 99.

123. Testimony of Representative Dowdy, House Rules Hearings, pt. 2, p. 521.

124. See H. Rept. 914, pt. 1, p. 117.

125. Rule 14 provides, ". . . every bill . . . of the House of Representatives which shall have received a first and second reading without being referred to a committee, shall, if objection be made to further proceeding thereon, be placed on the Calendar." Rule 7 provides that the Senate can move directly to consideration of a bill on the calendar without the motion being debatable, if the motion is made during the morning hour. Here, however, Senator Russell objected to the customary motion to dispense with the reading of the journal and extended his discussion on the journal until the morning hour had passed. Accordingly, Mansfield's motion to consider now became debatable.

126. 110 *Cong. Rec.*, Feb. 26, 1964, p. 3583, and Feb. 27, 1964, p. 3688.

127. *Ibid.*, Feb. 26, 1964, p. 3582.

128. *Ibid.*, March 12, 1964, p. 4881.

129. *Ibid.*, March 20, 1964, p. 5603.

130. *Ibid.*, March 23, 1964, p. 5786. They also now feared that extensive Senate amending of the House bill would produce House dissent and the necessity of a conference committee, with the likelihood of a filibuster against the conference committee report.

131. *Ibid.*, March 26, 1964, p. 6244.

132. On June 1, Senator Mansfield announced that a cloture petition would be filed on June 6, with voting to follow on June 9, later postponed to the 10th. The Senate adopted it by 71–29. Under Rule 22, a two-thirds vote of Senators present and voting was required for adoption of cloture. Under cloture each Senator might speak no more than one hour, during which time he might speak on pending business or on any amendments offered prior to cloture. No new amendments could be made without unanimous consent, a courtesy liberally extended on this occasion.

133. 22 *CQWR,* June 19, 1964, p. 1199.

134. *Ibid.*

135. *Ibid.*, p. 1206.

136. 110 *Cong. Rec.*, Jan. 31, 1964, p. 1448.

137. *Ibid.*, p. 1452.

138. The House defeated an amendment to strike Title II by a vote of 63–144. *Ibid.*, Feb. 5, 1964, p. 1913.

139. Remarks of Democratic Representatives Basil L. Whitener, North

Carolina, and Joe D. Waggonner, Jr., Louisiana. *Ibid.*, Feb. 10, 1964, p. 2699.

140. 22 *CQWR*, Feb. 21, 1964, p. 365. As late as June 10, Senator Harry Byrd was protesting the conduct of House voting. He asserted that of 146 amendments offered, 79 were subjected to voice votes, and that of the rest, 58 were decided by division or teller vote. He maintained that a majority of members was present at only 21 of the 58. 110 *Cong. Rec.*, June 10, 1964, p. 12768. Of course, in Committee of the Whole, 100 constitutes a quorum.

141. Senate Commerce Hearings, pt. 2, p. 1126.

142. 110 *Cong. Rec.*, March 26, 1964, p. 6244.

143. *Ibid.*, June 16, 1964, p. 13434.

144. Senate Commerce Hearings, pt. 1, p. 430.

145. *Ibid.*, p. 254.

146. Senate Judiciary Hearings, p. 204.

147. Senate Commerce Hearings, pt. 1, p. 84.

148. Senate Judiciary Hearings, p. 167.

149. *Ibid.*, p. 39.

150. 110 *Cong. Rec.*, May 7, 1964, p. 10047; for similar comments by Senator Thurmond, see Senate Commerce Hearings, pt. 2, pp. 848–849 and 1126.

151. Senate Commerce Hearings, pt. 1, p. 154.

152. *Ibid.*, pt. 2, pp. 848–849.

153. S. Rept. 872, p. 13. (Italics supplied.)

154. 110 *Cong. Rec.*, June 10, 1964, pp. 12855–12857; cf. similar comments, *ibid.*, March 26, 1964, pp. 6244–6245.

155. *Ibid.*, June 18, 1964, pp. 13825–13826.

156. *New York Times,* June 20, 1964, p. 24.

157. *Ibid.*, June 13, 1963, p. 32. The *Times* spoke of the argument concerning the commerce and 14th Amendment powers as they emerged in hearings as "not important" and observed that what counted was a "strong law" that recognized the Negro in "every American way"; it viewed the long floor debates as more successful in "befogging than in clarifying" the bill, said constitutional arguments against Title II "hardly rise to the level of serious discussion." *Ibid.*, June 27, 1963, p. 16, May 4, 1964, p. 28, and May 5, 1964, p. 42. Except in the quoted passage, Krock took a different position. He envisaged from the outset serious constitutional questions for congressional examination, reported House debates as serving the national interest by providing a high-level discussion of constitutional issues, and declared that the filibuster had made it possible to add jury trial and other modifications, thus exposing and limiting "some of the sumptuary powers granted to the Federal Government." *Ibid.*, June 20, 1963, p. 32, Feb. 6, 1964, p. 28, April 28, 1964, p. 36, and June 11, 1964, p. 32.

158. 110 *Cong. Rec.*, June 10, 1964, p. 12866.

159. See concurring opinions of Justices Douglas and Goldberg, construing the act as based in part on a broad reading of state action under the 14th Amendment. Heart of Atlanta Motel *v.* United States, 379 U.S. 241, 280–281, 291–292 (1964).

160. Reynolds *v.* Sims, 377 U.S. 533 (1964) and related cases.

161. 110 *Cong. Rec.*, Aug. 12, 1964, p. 18567, Aug. 13, 1964, p. 18845. This rider to a foreign aid bill would have declared a stay of execution to give time for Congress to propose a corrective constitutional amendment.

The version finally passed by the Senate embodied a more moderate sense resolution. 110 *Cong. Rec.*, Sept. 24, 1964, p. 22078.

162. 111 *Cong. Rec.*, May 7, 1965, p. 9587. The outcome of the long effort in Congress to do away with poll taxes is a partial commentary on the strength of judicial monopoly ideas. After having outlawed the state poll taxes for voters in federal elections by constitutional amendment, Congress here weighed the Kennedy Amendment, with its general declaration that state poll taxes for state elections were unconstitutional, against the Mansfield-Dirksen bill for expediting test cases challenging such poll taxes to the courts. The latter finally secured passage.

CHAPTER 15. CONGRESS AND THE CONSTITUTION

1. Opp Cotton Mills, Inc. *v.* Administrator, 312 U.S. 126, 145 (1941).

2. *New York Times,* Sept. 21, 1962, p. 10.

3. Pertinent also may be a Senate vote in 1961 on the Keating amendment to a bill authorizing certain federal appropriations for aid to church schools. Notwithstanding adverse legal precedents, this amendment was intended to provide for judicial review of the question whether such appropriations violated the 1st Amendment. Senator Keating, New York Republican, urged, "This is the time to express to the full our support for the judiciary by permitting this coequal branch of our Republic to exercise its scrutiny over the constitutionality of enactments and disbursements." 107 *Cong. Rec.*, pt. 7, p. 8628. The vote—32–62—which killed the amendment was a partial reflection of opinion on the policy question and likewise on the problem of civil rights. Yet the lineup gives a further hint of regional variations in the willingness of members to shift responsibility to the Court. Thus, the several regions registered the following quotas in favor of the Keating amendment: Middle Atlantic—80 per cent; Midwest—56 per cent; New England —42 per cent; Border States—25 per cent; Far West—20 per cent; South— 0 per cent. *Ibid.,* p. 8640.

4. 103 *Cong. Rec.*, pt. 7, p. 9193 (1957).

5. *Ibid.,* pp. 9212–9213.

6. McCulloch *v.* Maryland, 4 Wheaton 316, 407 (1819).

7. See Walter F. Murphy, *Congress and the Court: A Case Study in the American Political Process* (Chicago: University of Chicago Press, 1962), p. 255 and note. See above, chapter 13.

8. The following is a rough categorization of the standing committees, subcommittees, and joint committees, in 1965, grouped according to the subject matter of constitutional issues. In the case of subcommittees, the parent standing committee is given in parentheses. Omitted are the five numbered subcommittees of the House Judiciary Committee, since no clear indication of jurisdiction is available.

A. Senate: Freedom of Communications (Commerce); Immigration and Naturalization (Judiciary); Constitutional Rights (Judiciary); Internal Security (Judiciary). House: Unamerican Activities. Joint: Security (Atomic Energy).

B. Senate: Intergovernmental Relations (Government Operations). House: Intergovernmental Relations (Government Operations); State Taxation of Interstate Commerce (Judiciary).

C. Senate: Central Intelligence (Armed Services); Federal Power Commission Procedures (Commerce); State Department Organization and Public Affairs (Foreign Relations); Reorganization and International Organizations (Government Operations); National Security Staffing and Operations (Government Operations); Improvements in Judicial Machinery (Judiciary); Administrative Practice and Procedure (Judiciary). House: Departmental Oversight and Consumer Relations (Agriculture); Central Intelligence Agency (Armed Services); Executive and Legislative Reorganization (Government Operations); Government Activities (Government Operations); Foreign Operations and Government Information (Government Operations).

D. Senate: Standing Senate Rules (Rules and Administration); Privileges and Elections (Rules and Administration). House: Elections (Administration); House Rules. Joint: Organization of Congress; Security (Atomic Energy). Adapted from 23 *Congressional Quarterly Weekly Report,* April 30, 1965, pp. 790–813.

9. United States *v.* Lovett, 328 U.S. 303 (1946), and Reid *v.* Covert, 354 U.S. 1 (1957). See chapter 12, note 88.

10. See below, Appendix A.

11. In 1959 the Director of the LRS reported that consultations in the preparation of reports and review of reports took place. Within the limits of deadlines, consultation was greater and review more elaborate in connection with difficult reports than with others. Letter to the author from Dr. Hugh L. Elsbree, April 21, 1959.

12. It could well have been inadvertence that brought the disclaimer affidavit provision of the National Defense Education Act to the Senate floor on August 13, 1958, a week before the Jenner-Butler debate and 11 days before adjournment. Once it was out on the floor, few presumably would have opposed it even had notice of a constitutional question been given and time for discussion arranged. It took Congress four years to moderate its terms.

Table of Court Cases

Index

Members of Congress are identified by state and, where known, by party. The following abbreviations are used for certain political parties: D., Democrat; Dem.-Rep., Democratic-Republican (Jeffersonian); Fed., Federalist; R., Republican.

471